WORKSHOPS IN COMPUTING

Series edited by C. J. van Rijsbergen

Also in this series

Object Orientation in Z
Susan Stepney, Rosalind Barden and
David Cooper (Eds.)

Code Generation – Concepts, Tools, Techniques
Proceedings of the International Workshop on Code Generation, Dagstuhl, Germany, 20–24 May 1991
Robert Giegerich and Susan L. Graham (Eds.)

Z User Workshop, York 1991, Proceedings of the Sixth Annual Z User Meeting, York, 16–17 December 1991
J.E. Nicholls (Ed.)

Formal Aspects of Measurement
Proceedings of the BCS-FACS Workshop on Formal Aspects of Measurement, South Bank University, London, 5 May 1991
Tim Denvir, Ros Herman and R.W. Whitty (Eds.)

AI and Cognitive Science '91
University College, Cork, 19–20 September 1991
Humphrey Sorensen (Ed.)

5th Refinement Workshop, Proceedings of the 5th Refinement Workshop, organised by BCS-FACS, London, 8–10 January 1992
Cliff B. Jones, Roger C. Shaw and
Tim Denvir (Eds.)

Algebraic Methodology and Software Technology (AMAST'91)
Proceedings of the Second International Conference on Algebraic Methodology and Software Technology, Iowa City, USA, 22–25 May 1991
M. Nivat, C. Rattray, T. Rus and G. Scollo (Eds.)

ALPUK92, Proceedings of the 4th UK Conference on Logic Programming, London, 30 March – 1 April 1992
Krysia Broda (Ed.)

Logic Program Synthesis and Transformation
Proceedings of LOPSTR 92, International Workshop on Logic Program Synthesis and Transformation, University of Manchester, 2–3 July 1992
Kung-Kiu Lau and Tim Clement (Eds.)

NAPAW 92, Proceedings of the First North American Process Algebra Workshop, Stony Brook, New York, USA, 28 August 1992
S. Purushothaman and Amy Zwarico (Eds.)

First International Workshop on Larch
Proceedings of the First International Workshop on Larch, Dedham, Massachusetts, USA, 13–15 July1992
Ursula Martin and Jeannette M. Wing (Eds.)

Persistent Object Systems
Proceedings of the Fifth International Workshop on Persistent Object Systems, San Miniato (Pisa), Italy, 1–4 September 1992
Antonio Albano and Ron Morrison (Eds.)

Formal Methods in Databases and Software Engineering, Proceedings of the Workshop on Formal Methods in Databases and Software Engineering, Montreal, Canada, 15–16 May 1992
V.S. Alagar, Laks V.S. Lakshmanan and
F. Sadri (Eds.)

Modelling Database Dynamics
Selected Papers from the Fourth International Workshop on Foundations of Models and Languages for Data and Objects, Volkse, Germany, 19–22 October 1992
Udo W. Lipeck and Bernhard Thalheim (Eds.)

14th Information Retrieval Colloquium
Proceedings of the BCS 14th Information Retrieval Colloquium, University of Lancaster, 13–14 April 1992
Tony McEnery and Chris Paice (Eds.)

Functional Programming, Glasgow 1992
Proceedings of the 1992 Glasgow Workshop on Functional Programming, Ayr, Scotland, 6–8 July 1992
John Launchbury and Patrick Sansom (Eds.)

Z User Workshop, London 1992
Proceedings of the Seventh Annual Z User Meeting, London, 14–15 December 1992
J.P. Bowen and J.E. Nicholls (Eds.)

Interfaces to Database Systems (IDS92)
Proceedings of the First International Workshop on Interfaces to Database Systems, Glasgow, 1–3 July 1992
Richard Cooper (Ed.)

AI and Cognitive Science '92
University of Limerick, 10–11 September 1992
Kevin Ryan and Richard F.E. Sutcliffe (Eds.)

Theory and Formal Methods 1993
Proceedings of the First Imperial College Department of Computing Workshop on Theory and Formal Methods, Isle of Thorns Conference Centre, Chelwood Gate, Sussex, UK, 29–31 March 1993
Geoffrey Burn, Simon Gay and Mark Ryan (Eds.)

continued on back page...

M. Nivat, C. Rattray, T. Rus and G. Scollo (Eds.)

Algebraic Methodology and Software Technology (AMAST'93)

Proceedings of the Third International Conference on Algebraic Methodology and Software Technology, University of Twente, Enschede, The Netherlands
21–25 June 1993

Published in collaboration with the
British Computer Society

BCS
FACS

Springer-Verlag
London Berlin Heidelberg New York
Paris Tokyo Hong Kong
Barcelona Budapest

Maurice Nivat
LITP, Université Paris VII, 2 Place Jussieu
75251 Paris-Cedex 05, France

Charles Rattray, BSc, MSc, FIMA, FBCS, C.Eng., C.Math.
Department of Computing Science
University of Stirling, Stirling, FK9 4LA, Scotland, UK

Teodor Rus, PhD
Department of Computer Science
University of Iowa, Iowa City, IA 52242, USA

Giuseppe Scollo, PhD
Fac. Informatica, University of Twente
PO Box 217, NL-7500 AE Enschede, The Netherlands

ISBN-13: 978-3-540-19852-9 e-ISBN-13: 978-1-4471-3227-1
DOI: 10.1007/978-1-4471-3227-1

British Library Cataloguing in Publication Data
Algebraic Methodology and Software Technology (AMAST '93) : Proceedings of the Third International Conference on Algebraic Methodology and Software Technology, University of Twente, The Netherlands, 21–25 June 1993. –
(Workshops in Computing Series)
I. Nivat, Maurice II. Series
005.101512

Library of Congress Cataloging-in-Publication Data
International Conference on Algebraic Methodology and Software
Technology (3rd : 1993 : University of Twente)
Algebraic methodology and software technology (AMAST'91) : proceedings of the Third International Conference on Algebraic Methodology and Software Technology, University of Twente, The Netherlands, 21–25 June 1993 / M. Nivat ... [et al.] (eds.).
p. cm. – (Workshops in computing)
"Published in collaboration with the British Computer Society." Includes bibliographical references and index.

1. Software engineering–Congresses. 2. Abstract data types (Computer science)–Congresses. I. Nivat, M. II. British Computer Society. III. Title. IV. Series.
QA76.758.I5713 1993 93–38672
005.1'01'512–dc20 CIP

Softcover reprint of the hardcover 1st edition 1994

Typesetting: Camera ready by authors
Printed by Antony Rowe Ltd., Chippenham, Wiltshire
34/3830-543210 Printed on acid-free paper

Preface

The goal of the AMAST conferences is to foster algebraic methodology as a foundation for software technology, and to show that this can lead to practical mathematical alternatives to the ad-hoc approaches commonly used in software engineering and development. The first two AMAST conferences, held in May 1989 and May 1991 at the University of Iowa, were well received and encouraged the regular organization of further AMAST conferences on a biennial schedule. The third Conference on Algebraic Methodology and Software Technology was held in the campus of the University of Twente, The Netherlands, during the first week of Summer 1993. Nearly a hundred people from all continents attended the conference.

The largest interest received by the AMAST conference among the professionals extended to include the administration organizations as well. AMAST'93 was opened by the Rector of the University of Twente, followed by the Local Chairman. Their opening addresses open this proceedings, too.

The proceedings contains 8 invited papers and 32 selected communications. The selection was very strict, for 121 submissions were received. The topics of the invited papers and selected communications cover both theory and practice, and span a wide variety of algebraic and software development issues, including: algebraic metamathematics, functional programming, relation algebra, order-sorted algebra, category theory in software engineering, modular system design, real-time system specification, testing theory and applications, algebraic semantics of concurrency, process algebra, modal logics and reactive systems, design and refinement principles, object-oriented design and programming, equational and logic programming, algebraic specification in software engineering.

The AMAST goal motivates interest in showcasing software systems that have been developed, or help development, by algebraic methods, techniques and tools. This was materialized in the AMAST'93 programme by seven demonstrations of such systems. One of them relates to the communication by Eric Wagner; short descriptions of the other six systems form the closing part of this proceedings.

In addition to the proceedings, a special issue of the journal *Theoretical Computer Science* is dedicated to AMAST'93, where some of the selected communications appear in extended form.

With AMAST'93, besides research, education has taken a distinguished place within the scope of AMAST, and the first conference day, referred to as the Education Day, was devoted to the topic of mathematical education of software developers. Hans-Jörg Kreowski opened the Education Day with an invited talk on *Some tentative thoughts on teaching computer science*. A lively discussion ensued immediately after his talk. Two sessions then followed, each with an invited talk and an open, informal discussion; conclusions were drawn by Hans-Jörg Kreowski. Yuri Gurevich moderated the morning session on education in which Teodor Rus presented his interpretation of the invited talk *Mathematics of computation for (software and other) engineers* of David Parnas, prevented from attending the conference by a medical emergency. The conference expressed sympathy and best wishes for a complete recovery to David Parnas. István Németi moderated the afternoon session on education in which Jacques Printz gave an invited talk on *Mathematical training for the software developers: a practical experience*, based on his extensive professional experience in applying formalism to large software development projects. Space constraints prevent the inclusion of contributions to the Education Day in this proceedings, but the Organizing Committee is exploring avenues to make these available, possibly in refined form to a wide audience.

In continuity with the tradition of the AMAST conferences, very low registration fees were made possible by generous support from the sponsors. The main financial resources were granted by the Commission of the European Communities, within the ESPRIT Basic Research Programme, and by the US Office of Naval Research. Additional financial and organizational support was provided by the universities and institutions represented in the Organizing Committee, and by the British Department of Trade and Industry. The AMAST'93 conference was held under the auspices and with the cooperation of EATCS, ACM SIGACT and SIGSOFT, ASL, BCS FACS, and by the ESPRIT Basic Research working groups ASMICS and COMPASS.

The numerous and well-qualified offers to host future AMAST meetings testify to the interest in the AMAST goals. The fourth AMAST conference will be held at Concordia University, Montréal, Canada, on July 3–7 1995, and will be organized by V.S. Alagar. Then AMAST'96 will follow, at München University, Germany, and will be organized by Martin Wirsing. As can be inferred from this, and in view of the growing number of submissions, the AMAST conference series will become an annual event after AMAST'95. Holding these conferences more frequently will allow a wider recognition of original contributions to the AMAST goals and will give greater opportunities for success in the effort to capture the attention of the entire spread of those working in software engineering.

August 1993

M. Nivat
C. Rattray
T. Rus
G. Scollo

Organizing Committee

General chairman:
Maurice Nivat, Université de Paris VII, France

Program chairman:
Giuseppe Scollo, University of Twente, Enschede, The Netherlands

Publicity chairmen:
Charles Rattray, University of Stirling, Scotland
Teodor Rus, University of Iowa, Iowa City, Iowa, USA
V.S. Alagar, Concordia University, Montréal, Quebec, Canada

Education Day chairman:
Hans-Jörg Kreowski, Universität, Bremen, Germany

Local chairman:
Ed Brinksma, University of Twente, Enschede, The Netherlands

Finance chairman:
Frans van der Avert, University of Twente, Enschede, The Netherlands

International Committee:
Mohammed Bettaz, University of Constantine, Algeria
Christine Choppy, Université de Paris-Sud, Orsay, France
Pierre Deransart, INRIA, Rocquencourt, France
Arthur Fleck, University of Iowa, Iowa City, Iowa, USA
Luigi Logrippo, University of Ottawa, Ontario, Canada
Michael O'Donnell, University of Chicago, Illinois, USA
Juan Quemada, University of Madrid, Spain
Ralph Wachter, Office of Naval Research, Arlington, Virginia, USA

Local Committee (University of Twente, Enschede, The Netherlands):
Herman Balsters
Han Bäumer
Pim van den Broek
Rolf de By
Maarten Fokkinga
Pim Kars
Mark van der Voort
Job Zwiers

Secretariat (University of Twente, Enschede, The Netherlands):
Charlotte Bijron, Alice Hoogvliet-Haverkate, Joke Lammerink, Yvonne Rokker

Program Committee

Referees

Besides the members of the Organizing and Program Committees:

H. Alblas	V. Ambriola	H. Andréka
R. Bagnara	R.I. Becker	M. Bellia
L. Bergmans	J.A. Bergstra	C. Bettini
A. Blass	T. Bolognesi	E. Börger
S. Bruell	M. Caneve	F. Cardone
M. Cerioli	P. Ciancarini	E. Ciapessoni
H. Comon	A. Corradini	P. Degano
R. De Nicola	J. Desharnais	H. Eertink
A. Fantechi	G. Ferrari	L. Fribourg
H. Garavel	R.v. Glabbeek	G. Ghelli
S. Gnesi	N. Halbwachs	M. Johnson
S.M. Kahrs	J.-P. Katoen	H. Kirchner
R. Langerak	R.D. Maddux	A. Maggiolo-Schettini
M.J. Maher	V. Manca	M. Maouche
R. Marciano	S. Martini	E. Moggi
P. Oude Luttighuis	C. Palamidessi	J. Palsberg
F. Parisi-Presicce	L.C. Paulson	A. Poigné
V. Pratt	J. Printz	G. Reggio
H. Reichel	A. Rensink	D. Rosenzweig
F. Rossi	I. Sain	A. Salibra
V. Sassone	S.A. Schneider	A. Skou
S. Tschantz	D.A.Wolfram	H. Zhang

Contents

System Demonstrations

Opening Address by the Rector of the University of Twente

Ladies and Gentlemen,

It is a pleasure and honour for me to welcome you at the third international conference on Algebraic Methodology and Software Technology. We, at the University of Twente are proud that so many scientists from all over the world are gathered at our campus in order, as we understand, to consolidate a firm base of algebraic methodology to software engineering.

When going through the few lines of text of the conference program, forwarded to me by the organizing committee my thoughts went back to discussions we had almost 25 yeards ago when I was employed at the Thomas Watson research center in Yorktown Heights.

In experimental physics we sometimes faced complicated algebraic problems that hopefully could be solved using APL. Functions suggested by algorithms did, however, not always lead to solutions that were acceptable for physical intuition, For the 1970 user of APL it became clear that no total overlap existed of algebra and the software available at that time. And, as a consequence we dreamed of a direct translation of physical phenomena in a programming language. A hierarchic relation between mathematics and programming was thus turned into an analogy between the two. The argument was the empirical origin of mathematics and the fact that attention given to a schema instead of the object schematized can lead as well to a mathematical description as to a description by a programming language. And in both cases evidence could be based on intuitional, logical or numerical arguments.

After those years I more and more trusted the outcome of computer programmes and my doubt based on principle discussions has disappeared with the years. But today I'm asking myself again, is it a hierarchical or only an analogous relation between the two.

From your program I get the impression that hierarchy should be obvious and I'm sure that the thoughts of a Rector on your program are not the most important ones. I hope, however, I gave you the impression that even an experimental physicist appreciates your effort.

I hope that your stay here will be fruitful and enjoyable and I herewith open this conference and thank you for your attention.

Prof.dr. Th.J.A. Popma, Rector Magnificus, 21 June 1993

Welcoming Address AMAST'93

Ladies and Gentlemen,

It is a pleasure and a privilege to welcome you on behalf of the local organizers to this third edition of the international conference on Algebraic Methodology and Software Technology here at the University of Twente. We are proud that our university has been selected to host the first European edition of AMAST when it was decided to cross the Atlantic after the successful previous conferences held at the University of Iowa in 1989 and 1991.

The University of Twente is one of the three Technical Universities in The Netherlands (the other two being at Delft and Eindhoven), and has as such a strong commitment to, and tradition of, combining fundamental research with an application-oriented attitude. Computer science at Twente in particular has a strong tradition in research and education that build on a strong interaction between theory and practice. Organizationally, Twente is unique in this country for having an independent Faculty of Computer Science with an excellent technical infrastructure. Educationally, it is the second largest computer science institute of the country in terms of numbers of students. In a study that was recently published in the Communications of the ACM concerning the curricula of a number of major European computer science institutes our programme compared favourably with the others, and was particularly cited for its broad orientation. In research the faculty has distinguished itself by its very strong participation in international research projects, most notably those in the framework of the ESPRIT and RACE programmes of the CEC.

It is only natural that we here at Twente should feel very attracted towards the goals of AMAST. After all, there is nothing more practical than a good theory! The search for good theories, however, is not an easy one, and one must be always careful to resist the temptation to confuse a model with the reality it tries to account for. To quote no one less than Albert Einstein on this issue:

As far as the laws of mathematics refer to reality, they are not certain; and as far as they are certain, they do not refer to reality.

It is my sincere hope that the programme of this third AMAST conference will help to further clarify and improve the application of formal methods to software technology, and thus extend the success of the first two editions. In particular, I trust that the programme of today, the Education Day, which focusses on the role of formal methods in the education of software engineers, will be a source of contemplation and inspiration for all.

Ladies and gentlemen, many here at Twente have worked very hard to make the organization of this conference a success. Except for the weather, we have things pretty much under control and I wish you a both intellectually and socially stimulating week here with us.

Thank you for your attention.

Prof.dr. Ed Brinksma, Local Chairman, 21 June 1993

Invited Papers

Applying Algebraic Logic to Logic

Hajnal Andréka, István Németi and Ildikó Sain
Mathematical Institute of the Hungarian Academy of Sciences
Budapest, P.O.B. 127, H-1364, Hungary
h2644and@ella.hu, h1469nem@ella.hu, h1468sai@ella.hu

1 Introduction

The idea of solving problems in logic by first translating them to algebra, then using the powerful methodology of algebra for solving them, and then translating the solution back to logic, goes back to Leibnitz and Pascal. Papers on the history of Logic (e.g. Anellis–Houser [4], Maddux [14]) point out that this method was fruitfully applied in the 19th century not only to propositional logics but also to quantifier logics (De Morgan, Peirce etc. applied it to quantifier logics too). The number of applications grew ever since. (Though some of these remained unnoticed, e.g. the celebrated Kripke–Lemmon completeness theorem for modal logic w.r.t. Kripke models was first proved by Jónsson and Tarski in 1948 using algebraic logic.)

For brevity, we will refer to the above method or procedure as "applying Algebraic Logic (AL) to Logic". This expression might be somewhat misleading since AL itself happens to be a part of logic, and we do not intend to deny this. We will use the expression all the same, and hope, the reader will not misunderstand our intention.

In items (i) and (ii) below we describe two of the main motivations for applying AL to Logic.

(i) This is the more obvious one. When working with a relatively new kind of problem, it is often proved to be useful to "transform" the problem into a well understood and streamlined area of mathematics, solve the problem there and translate the result back. Examples include the method of Laplace Transform in solving differential equations (a central tool in Electrical Engineering).

At this point we should dispell a misunderstanding. In certain circles of logicians there seems to be a belief that AL applies only to syntactical problems of logic and that semantical and model–theoretic problems are not treated by AL or at least not in their original model theoretic form. Nothing can be as far from the truth as this belief, as e.g. looking into the present paper should reveal. A variant of this belief is that the main bulk of AL is about offering a cheap pseudo semantics to Logics as a substitute for intuitive, model theoretic semantics. Again, this is very far from being true. (This is a particularly harmful piece of misinformation, because this "slander" is easy to believe if one looks only superficially into a few AL papers.) To illustrate how far this

* Research supported by Hungarian National Foundation for Scientific Research grant No 1911.

belief is from truth, the semantical–model theoretic parts of the present paper emphasize that they start out from a logical system $\mathcal{L}$ whose semantics is as intuitive and as non–algebraic as it wants to be, and then we transform $\mathcal{L}$ into algebra, paying special attention to not distorting its semantics in the process; and anyway, finally we translate the solutions back to the very original non–algebraic framework (including model theoretical semantics).

In the present paper we define the algebraic counterpart $\mathsf{Alg}_f(\mathcal{L})$ of a logic $\mathcal{L}$ together with the algebraic counterpart $\mathsf{Alg}_m(\mathcal{L})$ of the semantical–model theoretical ingredients of $\mathcal{L}$. Then we formulate some equivalence theorems, which to essential logical properties of $\mathcal{L}$ associate natural and well investigated properties of $\mathsf{Alg}_f(\mathcal{L})$ such that if we want to decide whether $\mathcal{L}$ has a certain property, we will know what to ask from our algebraician colleague about $\mathsf{Alg}_f(\mathcal{L})$. The same devices are suitable for finding out what one has to change in $\mathcal{L}$ if we want to have a variant of $\mathcal{L}$ having a desirable property (which $\mathcal{L}$ lacks). For all this, first we have to define what we understand by a logic $\mathcal{L}$ in general (because otherwise it is impossible to define e.g. the function Alg_f associating a class $\mathsf{Alg}_f(\mathcal{L})$ of algebras to each logic $\mathcal{L}$).

(ii) With the rapidly growing variety of applications of logic (in diverse areas like computer science, linguistics, AI, law etc.) there is a growing number of new logics to be investigated. In this situation AL offers us a tool for economy and a tool for unification in various ways. One of these is that $\mathsf{Alg}_f(\mathcal{L})$ is always a class of algebras, therefore we can apply the same machinery namely Universal Algebra to study all the new logics. In other words we bring all the various logics to a kind of "normal form" where they can be studied by uniform methods. Moreover, for most choices of $\mathcal{L}$, $\mathsf{Alg}_f(\mathcal{L})$ (and $\mathsf{Alg}_m(\mathcal{L})$) tend to appear in the same "area" of Universal Algebra, hence specialized powerful methods lend themselves to studying $\mathcal{L}$. There is a fairly well understood "map" available for the landscape of Universal Algebra. By using our algebraization process and equivalence theorems we can project this "map" back to the (far less understood) landscape of possible logics.

The full version of this paper, containing all the full proofs, many examples and exercises, is [3]. The approach reported here is strongly related to works of Blok and Pigozzi, cf. e.g. [7], their papers in Andréka–Monk–Németi [1], Czelakowski [9], Font–Jansana [10]. A more ambitious version of the present approach is in Andréka–Németi–Sain [2] (cf. also Henkin–Monk–Tarski [12] section 5.6).

Acknowledgement: The authors are very grateful to Ágnes Kurucz for substantial contribution to both the contents and the form of the full version [3] of this paper. The authors are grateful to Wim Blok, Josep M. Font, Ramon Jansana and Don Pigozzi for most valuable suggestions. Special thanks are due to Font and Jansana for carefully reading the full version of this paper, suggesting improvements, and writing a paper ([11]) on the connection between the presently reported approach and the Blok–Pigozzi approach. Thanks are due to Ágoston Eiben, Johan van Benthem and Yde Venema for carefully reading the full version, and for helpful remarks. Also thanks are due to the following students of Logic Graduate School Budapest for helpful remarks, suggestions, working out exercises of the full version: Viktor Gyuris, Ben Hansen, Maarten Marx, Szabolcs Mikulás and András Simon.

2 General framework for studying logics

Defining a logic is an experience similar to defining a language. (This is no coincidence if you think about the applications of logic in e.g. theoretical linguistics.) So how do we define a language, say a programming language like PASCAL. First one defines the *syntax* of PASCAL. This amounts to defining the set of all PASCAL programs. This definition tells us which strings of symbols count as PASCAL programs and which do not. But this information in itself is not very useful, because having only this information enables the user to write programs but the user will have no idea what his programs will do. (This is more sensible if instead of PASCAL we take a more esoteric language like ALGOL 68.) Indeed, the second, and more important step in defining PASCAL amounts to describing what the various PASCAL programs will do when executed. In other words we have to define the meaning, or *semantics* of the language, e.g. of PASCAL. Defining semantics can be done in two steps: (i) we define the class M of *possible machines* that understand PASCAL, and then (ii) to each machine $\mathfrak{M}$ and each string φ of symbols that counts as a PASCAL program we tell what $\mathfrak{M}$ will do if we "ask" it to execute φ. In other words we define the *meaning* $mng(\varphi, \mathfrak{M})$ of program φ in machine $\mathfrak{M}$.

The procedure remains basically the same if the language in question is not a programming language but something like a natural language or a simple declarative language like first–order logic. When teaching a foreign language, e.g. German, then one has to explain which strings of symbols are German sentences and which are not (e.g. "Der Tisch ist rot" is a German sentence while "Das Tisch ist rot" is not). This is called explaining the syntax of German. Besides this, one has to explain what the German sentences mean. This amounts to defining the semantics of German. If we want to formalize the definition of semantics (for, say, a fragment of German) then one again defines a class M of possible situations or with other words, "possible worlds" in which our German sentences are interpreted, and then to each situation $\mathfrak{M}$ and each sentence φ we define the meaning or denotation $mng(\varphi, \mathfrak{M})$ of φ in situation (or possible world) $\mathfrak{M}$.

At this point we could discuss the difference between a language and a logic, but we do not do that. For our present purposes it is enough to say that the two things are very–very similar.[1]

Soon (in Definition 2.2 below) we will define what we mean by a logic. (The carefully chosen word would be "logical system".) Roughly speaking, a *logic* $\mathcal{L}$

[1] The philosophical minded reader might enjoy looking into the book [15], cf. e.g. B.Partee's paper therein.

is a five–tuple

$$\mathcal{L} = \langle F_{\mathcal{L}}, \vdash_{\mathcal{L}}, M_{\mathcal{L}}, mng_{\mathcal{L}}, \models_{\mathcal{L}} \rangle ,$$

where

- $F_{\mathcal{L}}$ is a set, called the set of all *formulas* of $\mathcal{L}$;
- $\vdash_{\mathcal{L}}$ is a binary relation between sets of formulas and individual formulas, that is, $\vdash_{\mathcal{L}} \subseteq \mathcal{P}(F_{\mathcal{L}}) \times F_{\mathcal{L}}$ (for any set X, $\mathcal{P}(X)$ denotes the powerset of X); $\vdash_{\mathcal{L}}$ is called the ***provability relation*** of $\mathcal{L}$;
- $M_{\mathcal{L}}$ is a class, called the class of all ***models*** (or ***possible worlds***) of $\mathcal{L}$;
- $mng_{\mathcal{L}}$ is a function with domain $F_{\mathcal{L}} \times M_{\mathcal{L}}$, called the ***meaning function*** of $\mathcal{L}$;
- $\models_{\mathcal{L}}$ is a binary relation, $\models_{\mathcal{L}} \subseteq M_{\mathcal{L}} \times F_{\mathcal{L}}$, called the ***validity relation*** of $\mathcal{L}$.

Intuitively, $F_{\mathcal{L}}$ is the collection of "texts" or "sentences" or "formulas" that can be "said" in the language $\mathcal{L}$. For $\Gamma \subseteq F_{\mathcal{L}}$ and $\varphi \in F_{\mathcal{L}}$, the intuitive meaning of $\Gamma \vdash_{\mathcal{L}} \varphi$ is that φ is provable (or derivable) from Γ with the syntactic inference system (or deductive mechanism) of $\mathcal{L}$. In all important cases, $\vdash_{\mathcal{L}}$ is subject to certain (well–known) conditions like $\Gamma \vdash_{\mathcal{L}} \varphi$ and $\Gamma \cup \{\varphi\} \vdash_{\mathcal{L}} \psi$ imply $\Gamma \vdash_{\mathcal{L}} \psi$ for any $\Gamma \subseteq F_{\mathcal{L}}$ and $\varphi, \psi \in F_{\mathcal{L}}$. The meaning function tells us what the texts belonging to $F_{\mathcal{L}}$ mean in the possible worlds from $M_{\mathcal{L}}$. The validity relation tells us which texts are "true" in which possible worlds (or models) under what conditions. In all the interesting cases the relation $\models_{\mathcal{L}}$ is definable from $mng_{\mathcal{L}}$. A typical possible definition of $\models_{\mathcal{L}}$ from $mng_{\mathcal{L}}$ is the following.

$$\mathfrak{M} \models_{\mathcal{L}} \varphi \quad \text{iff} \quad (\forall \psi \in F_{\mathcal{L}})\big[mng_{\mathcal{L}}(\psi, \mathfrak{M}) \subseteq mng_{\mathcal{L}}(\varphi, \mathfrak{M})\big],$$

for all $\varphi \in F_{\mathcal{L}}$, $\mathfrak{M} \in M_{\mathcal{L}}$. However, in general there is *no* explicit connection required between $mng_{\mathcal{L}}$ and $\models_{\mathcal{L}}$.

When no confusion is likely, we omit the subscripts $\mathcal{L}$ from $F_{\mathcal{L}}$, $\vdash_{\mathcal{L}}$ etc.

Usually $F_{\mathcal{L}}$ and $\vdash_{\mathcal{L}}$ are defined by what is called grammars in mathematical linguistics. $\langle F_{\mathcal{L}}, \vdash_{\mathcal{L}} \rangle$ together with the grammar defining them is called the ***syntactical part*** of $\mathcal{L}$, while $\langle M_{\mathcal{L}}, mng_{\mathcal{L}}, \models_{\mathcal{L}} \rangle$ is the ***semantical part*** of $\mathcal{L}$.

When defining a logic, a typical definition of F has the following recursive form. Two sets, P and $Cn(\mathcal{L})$ are given; P is called the set of primitive or ***atomic formulas*** and $Cn(\mathcal{L})$ is called the set of ***logical connectives*** of $\mathcal{L}$ (these are operation symbols with finite or infinite ranks). Then we require F to be the smallest set H satisfying items (1) and (2) below.

(1) $P \subseteq H$
(2) for every $\varphi_1, \ldots, \varphi_n \in H$ and $c \in Cn(\mathcal{L})$ of rank n, $c(\varphi_1, \ldots, \varphi_n) \in H$.

For example, in propositional logic, if p_1, p_2 are propositional variables (atomic formulas according to the terminology of this paper), then $(p_1 \wedge p_2)$ is defined to be a formula (where $\wedge$ is a logical connective of rank 2).

For formulas $\varphi \in F$ and models $\mathfrak{M} \in M$, $mng(\varphi, \mathfrak{M})$ and $\mathfrak{M} \models \varphi$ are defined in uniform ways (by some finite "schemas").

Given a logic $\mathcal{L}$, for $\varphi \in F_{\mathcal{L}}$ we say that φ is *valid* (in $\mathcal{L}$), in symbols $\models_{\mathcal{L}} \varphi$, iff $(\forall \mathfrak{M} \in M_{\mathcal{L}})\ \mathfrak{M} \models \varphi$. For φ as above and $\Gamma \subseteq F_{\mathcal{L}}$ we say that φ is a *semantical consequence* of Γ, in symbols $\Gamma \models^{c}_{\mathcal{L}} \varphi$, iff

$$(\forall \mathfrak{M} \in M_{\mathcal{L}})\ [(\forall \psi \in \Gamma)\ \mathfrak{M} \models \psi \implies \mathfrak{M} \models \varphi].$$

One of the important topics of Logic is the study of the connection between semantical consequence $\Gamma \models^{c}_{\mathcal{L}} \varphi$ and the syntactical consequence $\Gamma \vdash_{\mathcal{L}} \varphi$. If the two coincide then $\vdash_{\mathcal{L}}$ is said to be strongly complete and sound (for $\mathcal{L}$).

Instead of the general conception of a logic outlined above, in many cases we will consider only four of its five components: $F_{\mathcal{L}}$, $M_{\mathcal{L}}$, $mng_{\mathcal{L}}$ and $\models_{\mathcal{L}}$. Namely, we found that we can simplify the theory *without loss of generality* by not dragging $\vdash_{\mathcal{L}}$ along with us for the following reason. The validity relation $\models_{\mathcal{L}}$ (or the function $mng_{\mathcal{L}}$ if you like) induces the *semantical consequence relation* $\models^{c}_{\mathcal{L}} \subseteq \mathcal{P}(F_{\mathcal{L}}) \times F_{\mathcal{L}}$ as given above. There is a natural temptation to try to replace $\vdash_{\mathcal{L}}$ with $\models^{c}_{\mathcal{L}}$ in the theory, though at several places (e.g. at completeness theorems) this would be a grave over–simplification. Surprisingly enough, we found that all the theorems we prove for $\models^{c}_{\mathcal{L}}$ carry over to $\vdash_{\mathcal{L}}$, whenever the theorems are not about connections between $\models^{c}_{\mathcal{L}}$ and $\vdash_{\mathcal{L}}$ (see explanation below). Therefore we decided to drop $\vdash_{\mathcal{L}}$ for the time being and introduce it only where we must say something about $\vdash_{\mathcal{L}}$ which cannot be said about $\models^{c}_{\mathcal{L}}$ in itself.[2]

The reader interested in logics in the purely syntactical sense $\langle F_{\mathcal{L}}, \vdash_{\mathcal{L}}\rangle$ is invited to read our paper in the way described as follows.

Let $\mathcal{L}_s = \langle F, \vdash\rangle$ be a logic in the syntactical sense. To simplify the arguments below, we assume that $\mathcal{L}_s$ has a derived logical connective "$\leftrightarrow$" just as classical logics do. Intuitively, $(\varphi \leftrightarrow \psi)$ expresses that φ and ψ are equivalent. Of course, we assume the usual properties of "$\leftrightarrow$", e.g. $\{\varphi, (\varphi \leftrightarrow \psi)\} \vdash \psi$ etc. In Remark 2.1 below the present discussion, we will show how to eliminate the assumption of the expressibility of "$\leftrightarrow$". (However, the reader may safely skip Remark 2.1, since we will not rely on it later.)

Assume we want to study the "syntactical logic" $\mathcal{L}_s = \langle F, \vdash\rangle$. To be able to apply the theorems of the present paper, we will associate a class $M_{\vdash}$ of models, a $mng_{\vdash}$ etc. to $\mathcal{L}_s$. The class of models we use is

$$M_{\vdash} \stackrel{\text{def}}{=} \{T \subseteq F \ :\ T \text{ is closed under } \vdash\}.$$

For any model $T \in M_{\vdash}$ and formula $\varphi \in F$,

$$mng_{\vdash}(\varphi, T) \stackrel{\text{def}}{=} \{\psi \in F : T \vdash (\varphi \leftrightarrow \psi)\}.$$

[2]These considerations, together with the ones which follow them, grew out from discussions with Wim Blok, Joseph M. Font, Ramon Jansana and Don Pigozzi. In particular, Remark 2.1 is due to Font and Jansana; for more information on this line see [11].

Further, validity in models $T \in M_\vdash$ is defined as

$$T \models_\vdash \varphi \iff \varphi \in T .$$

Now, if we want to investigate the "syntactical logic" $\langle F, \vdash \rangle$, we apply our theorems to the logic

$$\mathcal{L}_\vdash \stackrel{\text{def}}{=} \langle F, M_\vdash, mng_\vdash, \models_\vdash \rangle .$$

The semantical consequence relation $\models^c_\vdash$ induced by $\models_\vdash$ coincides with the original syntactical one $\vdash$. (This is easy to check.) Hence, applying the theorems to the logic $\mathcal{L}_\vdash$ yields results about $\langle F, \vdash \rangle$ as was desired. In other words, $\mathcal{L}_\vdash$ is an equivalent reformulation of the "syntactic logic" $\langle F, \vdash \rangle$, hence studying $\mathcal{L}_\vdash$ is the same as studying $\langle F, \vdash \rangle$.

REMARK 2.1 (Eliminating the assumption of the expressibility of "$\leftrightarrow$" in $\mathcal{L}$): Here we show that in the above argument showing that our results can be applied to any syntactical logic $\mathcal{L}_s = \langle F, \vdash \rangle$, the assumption of expressibility of "$\leftrightarrow$" in $\mathcal{L}_s$ is not needed. It will turn out in Definition 3.1.1 in section 3 that for any logic $\mathcal{L}$, the set of formulas $F_\mathcal{L}$ has an algebraic structure, that is, $F_\mathcal{L}$ is the universe of an algebra $\underset{\sim}{F}$. (The operations of $\underset{\sim}{F}$ are the logical connectives of $\mathcal{L}$ collected in $Cn(\mathcal{L})$.) Let $T \in M_\vdash$ be given. Recall e.g. from [7] that the Leibniz congruence $\Omega(T) \subseteq F \times F$ associated to T is the biggest congruence relation of $\underset{\sim}{F}$ with the property $(\forall \varphi \in T)(\forall \psi \in F \setminus T)\langle \varphi, \psi \rangle \notin \Omega(T)$. Now we can define $mng_\vdash$ without using "$\leftrightarrow$":

$$mng_\vdash \stackrel{\text{def}}{=} \{\psi \in F : \varphi \, \Omega(T) \, \psi\} .$$

The rest of the definitions of $M_\vdash$, $\models_\vdash$ and the argumentation based on them remains the same. Since "$\leftrightarrow$" was not used anywhere except in the definition of $mng_\vdash$, this shows that no assumption (like the existence of "$\leftrightarrow$") is needed in our argument showing how to apply the present theory of "semantical logics" $\langle F, M, mng, \models \rangle$ to the study of syntactical logics $\langle F, \vdash \rangle$. ◀

Summing up, for a while we will concentrate our attention on the simplified form $\mathcal{L} = \langle F_\mathcal{L}, M_\mathcal{L}, mng_\mathcal{L}, \models_\mathcal{L} \rangle$ of a logic. For the reasons outlined above, this temporary restriction of attention will not result in any loss of generality.

Now we turn to nailing down our definitions formally in the form we will use them. For any set X, X^* denotes the set of all finite sequences ("words") over X.

DEFINITION 2.2 (logic): By a *logic* $\mathcal{L}$ we mean an ordered quadruple

$$\mathcal{L} \stackrel{\text{def}}{=} \langle F_\mathcal{L}, M_\mathcal{L}, mng_\mathcal{L}, \models_\mathcal{L} \rangle,$$

where (i)–(v) below hold.

(i) $F_{\mathcal{L}}$ (called the set of *formulas*) is a subset of finite sequences (called *words*) over some set X (called the *alphabet* of $\mathcal{L}$) that is, $F_{\mathcal{L}} \subseteq X^*$;
(ii) $M_{\mathcal{L}}$ is a class (called the class of *models*);
(iii) $mng_{\mathcal{L}}$ is a function with domain $F_{\mathcal{L}} \times M_{\mathcal{L}}$ (called the *meaning function*);
(iv) $\models_{\mathcal{L}}$ (called the *validity relation*) is a relation between $M_{\mathcal{L}}$ and $F_{\mathcal{L}}$ that is, $\models_{\mathcal{L}} \subseteq M_{\mathcal{L}} \times F_{\mathcal{L}}$. (According to the tradition, instead of "$\langle \mathfrak{M}, \varphi \rangle \in \models_{\mathcal{L}}$" we write "$\mathfrak{M} \models_{\mathcal{L}} \varphi$".)
(v) $\models_{\mathcal{L}}$ is determined by $mng_{\mathcal{L}}$, that is, for all $\varphi, \psi \in F_{\mathcal{L}}$ and $\mathfrak{M} \in M_{\mathcal{L}}$ we have $[mng_{\mathcal{L}}(\varphi, \mathfrak{M}) = mng_{\mathcal{L}}(\psi, \mathfrak{M})$ and $\mathfrak{M} \models_{\mathcal{L}} \varphi] \Longrightarrow \mathfrak{M} \models_{\mathcal{L}} \psi$. ◄

In the above definition, we nailed down the expression "model of $\mathcal{L}$" instead of the more suggestive one "possible world of $\mathcal{L}$" only for purely technical reasons, namely, to avoid a danger of potential ambiguity with the literature.

DEFINITION 2.3 (semantical consequence, valid formulas):
Let $\mathcal{L} = \langle F_{\mathcal{L}}, M_{\mathcal{L}}, mng_{\mathcal{L}}, \models_{\mathcal{L}} \rangle$ be a logic. For every $\mathfrak{M} \in M_{\mathcal{L}}$ and $\Sigma \subseteq F_{\mathcal{L}}$,

$$\mathfrak{M} \models^c_{\mathcal{L}} \Sigma \overset{\text{def}}{\Longleftrightarrow} (\forall \varphi \in \Sigma)\, \mathfrak{M} \models_{\mathcal{L}} \varphi,$$
$$Mod_{\mathcal{L}}(\Sigma) \overset{\text{def}}{=} \{\mathfrak{M} \in M_{\mathcal{L}} \ : \ \mathfrak{M} \models_{\mathcal{L}} \Sigma\}.$$

$Mod_{\mathcal{L}}(\Sigma)$ is called the *class of models of* Σ.

A formula φ is said to be *valid*, in symbols $\models_{\mathcal{L}} \varphi$, iff $Mod_{\mathcal{L}}(\{\varphi\}) = M_{\mathcal{L}}$.

For any $\Sigma \cup \{\varphi\} \subseteq F_{\mathcal{L}}$,

$$\Sigma \models^c_{\mathcal{L}} \varphi \overset{\text{def}}{\Longleftrightarrow} Mod_{\mathcal{L}}(\Sigma) \subseteq Mod_{\mathcal{L}}(\{\varphi\}),$$
$$Csq_{\mathcal{L}}(\Sigma) \overset{\text{def}}{=} \{\varphi \in F_{\mathcal{L}} \ : \ \Sigma \models_{\mathcal{L}} \varphi\}.$$

If $\varphi \in Csq_{\mathcal{L}}(\Sigma)$ then we say that φ is a *semantical consequence of* Σ (in logic $\mathcal{L}$). Csq abbreviates "consequence". ◄

For simplicity, most often we omit the superscript c from $\models^c_{\mathcal{L}}$.

DEFINITION 2.4 (theory, set of validities):
Let $\mathcal{L} = \langle F_{\mathcal{L}}, M_{\mathcal{L}}, mng_{\mathcal{L}}, \models_{\mathcal{L}} \rangle$ be any logic. For any $K \subseteq M_{\mathcal{L}}$ let the *theory of* K be defined as

$$Th_{\mathcal{L}}(K) \overset{\text{def}}{=} \{\varphi \in F_{\mathcal{L}} \ : \ (\forall \mathfrak{M} \in K)\, \mathfrak{M} \models_{\mathcal{L}} \varphi\}.$$

$Th_{\mathcal{L}}(K)$ is called the theory of K in $\mathcal{L}$. If $K = \{\mathfrak{M}\}$ for some $\mathfrak{M} \in M_{\mathcal{L}}$ then instead of $Th_{\mathcal{L}}(\{\mathfrak{M}\})$ we write $Th_{\mathcal{L}}(\mathfrak{M})$.

The set $Th_{\mathcal{L}}(M_{\mathcal{L}})$ is called the *set of validities* of $\mathcal{L}$. ◄

It the rest of this section we give examples for logics in the sense of Definition 2.2 above. Some of them are well-known, but we recall their definitions for illustrating that they are special cases of the concept defined in Definition 2.2.

EXAMPLE 2.5 (propositional or sentential logic $\mathcal{L}_S$):
Let P be a set, called the set of *atomic formulas* of $\mathcal{L}_S$. Let $\{\wedge, \neg\}$ be a set disjoint from P, called the set of *logical connectives* of $\mathcal{L}_S$ (usually called *Boolean connectives*).

Propositional (or *sentential*) *logic* (corresponding to P) is defined to be a quadruple $\mathcal{L}_S \stackrel{\text{def}}{=} \langle F_S, M_S, mng_S, \models_S \rangle$, for which conditions (i)–(iii) below hold.

(i) The set F_S of formulas is the smallest set H satisfying

- $P \subseteq H$
- $\varphi, \psi \in H \Longrightarrow (\varphi \wedge \psi),\ \neg\varphi \in H$.
  (That is, the alphabet of this logic is $\{\wedge, \neg\} \cup P$.)

(ii) The class M_S of *models* of $\mathcal{L}_S$ is defined by

$$M_S \stackrel{\text{def}}{=} \{\langle W, v\rangle : W \text{ is a non-empty set and } v : P \to \mathcal{P}(W)\}.$$

If $\mathfrak{M} = \langle W, v\rangle \in M_S$ then W is called the set of *possible states* (or *worlds*[3] or *situations*) of $\mathfrak{M}$.

(iii) Let $\langle W, v\rangle \in M_S$, $w \in W$ and $\varphi \in F_S$. We define the binary relation $w \Vdash_v \varphi$ by recursion on the complexity of the formulas:

- if $p \in P$ then $\quad (w \Vdash_v P \stackrel{\text{def}}{\Longleftrightarrow} w \in v(p))$
- if $\psi_1, \psi_2 \in F_S$, then

$$w \Vdash_v \neg\psi_1 \stackrel{\text{def}}{\Longleftrightarrow} w \nVdash_v \psi_1$$
$$w \Vdash_v (\psi_1 \wedge \psi_2) \stackrel{\text{def}}{\Longleftrightarrow} w \Vdash_v \psi_1 \text{ and } w \Vdash_v \psi_2.$$

If $w \Vdash_v \varphi$ then we say that φ is *true in* w, or w *forces* φ.

Now $mng_S(\varphi, \langle W, v\rangle) \stackrel{\text{def}}{=} \{w \in W : w \Vdash_v \varphi\}$. $\langle W, v\rangle \models_S \varphi$ (φ is *valid in* $\langle W, v\rangle$), iff for every $w \in W$, $w \Vdash_v \varphi$. ◄

It is important to note that the set P of atomic formulas is a *parameter* in the definition of $\mathcal{L}_S$. Namely, in the definition above, P is a fixed but *arbitrary* set. So in a sense $\mathcal{L}_S$ is a function of P, and we could write $\mathcal{L}_S(P)$ to make this explicit. However, the choice of P has only limited influence on the behaviour of $\mathcal{L}_S$, therefore, following the literature we write simply $\mathcal{L}_S$ instead of $\mathcal{L}_S(P)$. From time to time, however, we will have to remember that P is a freely chosen parameter because in certain investigations the choice of P does influence the behaviour of $\mathcal{L}_S = \mathcal{L}_S(P)$.

---

[3]It is *important* to keep the two senses in which "possible world" can be used separate. The elements $\langle W, v\rangle$ of M_S can be called possible worlds since we inherit this usage from the general concept of a logic. At the same time, the elements $w \in W$ can be called "possible states or worlds" as a technical expression of modal logic. So there is a potential confusion here, which has to be kept in mind.

EXAMPLE 2.6 (modal logic $S5$):
The set of connectives of *modal logic* $S5$ is $\{\wedge, \neg, \Diamond\}$. The set of formulas (denoted as F_{S5}) of $S5$ is defined as that of propositional logic $\mathcal{L}_S$ together with the following clause:

$$\varphi \in F_{S5} \implies \Diamond\varphi \in F_{S5}.$$

Let $M_{S5} \stackrel{\text{def}}{=} M_S$. The definition of $w \Vdash_v \varphi$ is the same as in the propositional case but we also have the case of $\Diamond$:

$$w \Vdash_v \Diamond\varphi \stackrel{\text{def}}{\iff} (\exists w' \in W)\ w' \Vdash_v \varphi.$$

Then $mng_{S5}(\varphi, \langle W, v\rangle) \stackrel{\text{def}}{=} \{w \in W : w \Vdash_v \varphi\}$, and the validity relation $\models_{S5}$ is defined as follows.

$$\langle W, v\rangle \models_{S5} \varphi \quad \stackrel{\text{def}}{\iff} \quad (\forall w \in W)\ w \Vdash_v \varphi.$$

Now, modal logic $S5$ is $S5 \stackrel{\text{def}}{=} \langle F_{S5}, M_{S5}, mng_{S5}, \models_{S5}\rangle$. ◄

REMARK 2.7: According to a rather respectable (and useful) tradition, an extra–Boolean connective is called a *modality* iff it distributes over disjuction. (E.g. $\Diamond$ in $S5$ is a modality.) This will not be true for all of our extra-Boolean connectives that we will call modalities here (it is left to the reader to check for which ones is it true). Thus, regrettably, we sometimes ignore this useful tradition. For this tradition cf. e.g. Venema [20, Appendix A (pp. 143–152)]. ◄

The following logic, called *difference logic* or *some–other–time logic*, is discussed e.g. in Sain [18], Venema [20], Roorda [16]. K. Segerberg traces back this logic to von Wright. It might be interesting to note that difference logic is stronger than the Intermittent Assertions Method, for proving invariance properties.

EXAMPLE 2.8 (difference logic $\mathcal{L}_D$):
The set of connectives of *difference logic* $\mathcal{L}_D$ is $\{\wedge, \neg, D\}$. The set of formulas (denoted as F_D) of $\mathcal{L}_D$ is defined as that of propositional logic $\mathcal{L}_S$ together with the following clause:

$$\varphi \in F_D \implies D\varphi \in F_D.$$

Let $M_D \stackrel{\text{def}}{=} M_{S5} (= M_S)$. The definition of $w \Vdash_v \varphi$ is the same as in the propositional case but we also have the case of D:

$$w \Vdash_v D\varphi \stackrel{\text{def}}{\iff} (\exists w' \in W \setminus \{w\})\ w' \Vdash_v \varphi.$$

Then $mng_D(\varphi, \langle W, v\rangle) \stackrel{\text{def}}{=} \{w \in W : w \Vdash_v \varphi\}$, and the validity relation $\models_D$ is defined as follows.

$$\langle W, v\rangle \models_D \varphi \quad \stackrel{\text{def}}{\Longleftrightarrow} \quad (\forall w \in W)\ w \Vdash_v \varphi.$$

Now, difference logic $\mathcal{L}_D$ is $\mathcal{L}_D \stackrel{\text{def}}{=} \langle F_D, M_D, mng_D, \models_D\rangle$. ◀

The logics $\mathcal{L}_{\kappa\text{-times}}$ to be introduced next play quite an essential rôle in Artificial Intelligence in the theory what is called there "*stratified logic*", cf. e.g. works of H.J.Ohlbach, see e.g. [8].

EXAMPLE 2.9 (κ–times logic $\mathcal{L}_{\kappa\text{-times}}$, twice logic Tw):
Let κ be any cardinal. The set of connectives of *κ–times logic* $\mathcal{L}_{\kappa\text{-times}}$ is $\{\wedge, \neg, \Diamond_\kappa\}$. The set of formulas (denoted as $F_{\Diamond_\kappa}$) of $\mathcal{L}_{\kappa\text{-times}}$ is defined as that of propositional logic $\mathcal{L}_S$ together with the following clause:

$$\varphi \in F_{\Diamond_\kappa} \implies \Diamond_\kappa\varphi \in F_{\Diamond_\kappa}.$$

Let $M_{\Diamond_\kappa} \stackrel{\text{def}}{=} M_{S5} (= M_S)$. The definition of $w \Vdash_v \varphi$ is the same as in the propositional case but we also have the case of $\Diamond_\kappa$:

$$w \Vdash_v \Diamond_\kappa\varphi \quad \stackrel{\text{def}}{\Longleftrightarrow} \quad (\exists H \subseteq W)(|H| = \kappa \text{ and } (\forall w' \in H)\ w' \Vdash_v \varphi)\,.$$

Then $mng_{\Diamond_\kappa}(\varphi, \langle W, v\rangle) \stackrel{\text{def}}{=} \{w \in W : w \Vdash_v \varphi\}$, and the validity relation $\models_{\Diamond_\kappa}$ is defined as follows.

$$\langle W, v\rangle \models_{\Diamond_\kappa} \varphi \quad \stackrel{\text{def}}{\Longleftrightarrow} \quad (\forall w \in W)\ w \Vdash_v \varphi.$$

Now, κ–times logic $\mathcal{L}_{\kappa\text{-times}}$ is $\mathcal{L}_{\kappa\text{-times}} \stackrel{\text{def}}{=} \langle F_{\Diamond_\kappa}, M_{\Diamond_\kappa}, mng_{\Diamond_\kappa}, \models_{\Diamond_\kappa}\rangle$. We note that if $\kappa = 2$ then logic $\mathcal{L}_{2\text{-times}}$ is also called *Twice logic* and denoted as Tw. ◀

The following examples are some *arrow logics*. The field of arrow logics grew out of application areas in Logic, Language and Computation, and plays an important rôle there, cf. e.g. van Benthem [5, 6], and the proceedings of the Arrow Logic day at the conference "Logic at Work" (December 1992, Amsterdam [CCSOM of Univ. of Amsterdam]).

So far the *extra–Boolean connectives* ($\Diamond$, D, $\Diamond_\kappa$) were all unary modalities. In the following examples some of the extra–Booleans are binary modalities.

EXAMPLE 2.10 (arrow logics $\mathcal{L}_{\text{ARWO}}$, $\mathcal{L}_{\text{ARROW}}$, $\mathcal{L}_{\text{RA}}$): The set of connectives of *arrow logics* $\mathcal{L}_{\text{ARWO}}$, $\mathcal{L}_{\text{ARROW}}$ and $\mathcal{L}_{\text{RA}}$ is $\{\wedge, \neg, \circ, \smile, Id\}$, where $\circ$ is a binary, $\smile$ is a unary, and Id is a zero–ary modality.

- The set of formulas (denoted as F_{ARWO}) of $\mathcal{L}_{\text{ARWO}}$ is defined as that of propositional logic $\mathcal{L}_S$ together with the following clauses:

$$\varphi, \psi \in F_{\text{ARWO}} \implies (\varphi \circ \psi),\ \varphi^{\smile} \in F_{\text{ARWO}}$$
$$Id \in F_{\text{ARWO}}$$

The models are those of propositional logic $\mathcal{L}_S$ enriched with three relations, called *accessibility relations*. That is,

$$M_{\text{ARWO}} \stackrel{\text{def}}{=} \{\langle\langle W, v\rangle, C_1, C_2, C_3\rangle \;:\; \langle W, v\rangle \in M_S,\; C_1 \subseteq W \times W \times W, C_2 \subseteq W \times W,\; C_3 \subseteq W\}.$$

For propositional connectives $\neg$ and $\wedge$ the definition of $w \Vdash_v \varphi$ is the same as in the propositional case. For the new connectives we have:

$$\begin{aligned}
w \Vdash_v (\varphi \circ \psi) &\stackrel{\text{def}}{\iff} (\exists w_1, w_2 \in W) \\
&\qquad (C_1(w, w_1, w_2) \text{ and } w_1 \Vdash_v \varphi \text{ and } w_2 \Vdash_v \psi) \\
w \Vdash_v \varphi^{\smile} &\stackrel{\text{def}}{\iff} (\exists w' \in W)(C_2(w, w') \text{ and } w' \Vdash_v \varphi) \\
w \Vdash_v Id &\stackrel{\text{def}}{\iff} C_3(w).
\end{aligned}$$

Now, $mng_{\text{ARWO}}(\varphi, \langle W, v\rangle) \stackrel{\text{def}}{=} \{w \in W : w \Vdash_v \varphi\}$, and the validity relation $\models_{\text{ARWO}}$ is defined as follows.

$$\langle W, v\rangle \models_{\text{ARWO}} \varphi \quad \stackrel{\text{def}}{\iff} \quad (\forall w \in W)\; w \Vdash_v \varphi.$$

Now arrow logic $\mathcal{L}_{\text{ARWO}}$ is defined to be

$$\mathcal{L}_{\text{ARWO}} \stackrel{\text{def}}{=} \langle F_{\text{ARWO}}, M_{\text{ARWO}}, mng_{\text{ARWO}}, \models_{\text{ARWO}}\rangle.$$

- $F_{\text{ARROW}} \stackrel{\text{def}}{=} F_{\text{ARWO}}$. $M_{\text{ARROW}} \stackrel{\text{def}}{=} M_{\text{PAIR}}$.
  For connectives $\neg$, $\wedge$ and $\circ$ the definition of $w \Vdash_v \varphi$ is the same as in the case of $\mathcal{L}_{\text{PAIR}}$. For the new connectives we have:

$$\begin{aligned}
\langle a, b\rangle \Vdash_v \varphi^{\smile} &\stackrel{\text{def}}{\iff} [\langle b, a\rangle \in W \text{ and } \langle b, a\rangle \Vdash_v \varphi] \\
\langle a, b\rangle \Vdash_v Id &\stackrel{\text{def}}{\iff} a = b.
\end{aligned}$$

  As usual, $mng_{\text{ARROW}}(\varphi, \langle W, v\rangle) \stackrel{\text{def}}{=} \{w \in W : w \Vdash_v \varphi\}$, and the validity relation $\models_{\text{ARROW}}$ is defined by

$$\langle W, v\rangle \models_{\text{ARROW}} \varphi \quad \stackrel{\text{def}}{\iff} \quad (\forall w \in W)\; w \Vdash_v \varphi.$$

  Arrow logic $\mathcal{L}_{\text{ARROW}}$ is defined by

$$\mathcal{L}_{\text{ARROW}} \stackrel{\text{def}}{=} \langle F_{\text{ARROW}}, M_{\text{ARROW}}, mng_{\text{ARROW}}, \models_{\text{ARROW}}\rangle.$$

- $F_{\text{RA}} \stackrel{\text{def}}{=} F_{\text{ARROW}}$. $M_{\text{RA}} \stackrel{\text{def}}{=} M_{\text{REL}}$. The definitions of $w \Vdash_v \varphi$, mng_{RA} and $\models_{\text{RA}}$ are the same as in the case of $\mathcal{L}_{\text{ARROW}}$.
  Arrow logic $\mathcal{L}_{\text{RA}}$ is $\mathcal{L}_{\text{RA}} \stackrel{\text{def}}{=} \langle F_{\text{RA}}, M_{\text{RA}}, mng_{\text{RA}}, \models_{\text{RA}}\rangle$. $\mathcal{L}_{\text{RA}}$ is also called as the *logic of relation algebras*. ◀

Next we define first-order logic (in a slightly non-traditional form). ω denotes the set of all natural numbers.

EXAMPLE 2.11 (first-order logic $\mathcal{L}_{\mathrm{FOL}}$, rank-free formulation): Let $V \stackrel{\mathrm{def}}{=} \{v_i : i \in \omega\}$ be a set, called the set of *variables* of $\mathcal{L}_{\mathrm{FOL}}$. As before, let P be an arbitrary set, called the set of *atomic formulas* of $\mathcal{L}_{\mathrm{FOL}}$. (Now, we will think of atomic formulas as relation symbols, hence we write $R \in P$ instead of $p \in P$ as in case of $\mathcal{L}_S$.)

(i) The set F_{FOL} is the smallest set H satisfying

- $P \subseteq H$
- $(v_i = v_j) \in H \quad$ for each $i, j \in \omega$
- $\varphi, \psi \in H,\ i \in \omega \implies (\varphi \wedge \psi),\ \neg\varphi,\ \exists v_i\varphi \in H.$

(ii) The class M_{FOL} of *models* of $\mathcal{L}_{\mathrm{FOL}}$ is

$$M_{\mathrm{FOL}} \stackrel{\mathrm{def}}{=} \{\mathfrak{M} : \mathfrak{M} = \langle M, R^{\mathfrak{M}}\rangle_{R\in P},\ M \text{ is a non-empty set and } R^{\mathfrak{M}} \subseteq {}^nM \text{ for some } n \in \omega\ (R \in P)\}.$$

If $\mathfrak{M} \in M_{FOL}$ then M and $R^{\mathfrak{M}}$ denote parts of $\mathfrak{M}$ determined by the convention $\langle M, R^{\mathfrak{M}}\rangle = \mathfrak{M}$. (That is, if $\mathfrak{M}$ is given, then M denotes the universe of $\mathfrak{M}$. Further, for $R \in P$, $R^{\mathfrak{M}}$ denotes the meaning of R in $\mathfrak{M}$.)

(iii) Validity relation $\models_{FOL}$.

In $\mathcal{L}_{S5}$ the "basic semantical units" were the possible situations $w \in W$. In $\mathcal{L}_{\mathrm{FOL}}$ the basic semantical units are the evaluations of individual variables into models $\mathfrak{M}$, where $q \in {}^{\omega}M$ and q evaluates variables v_i as element $q_i \in M$ in the model $\mathfrak{M}$. To follow model theoretic tradition, instead of $\mathfrak{M}, q \Vdash \varphi$ we will write $\mathfrak{M} \models \varphi[q]$ (though the former would be more in the line with our definitions of $\mathcal{L}_{S5}$ etc.).

Let $\mathfrak{M} = \langle M, R^{\mathfrak{M}}\rangle_{R\in P} \in M_{\mathrm{FOL}}$, $q \in {}^{\omega}M$ and $\varphi \in F_{\mathrm{FOL}}$. We define the ternary relation "$\mathfrak{M} \models \varphi[q]$" by recursion on the complexity of φ as follows:

- $\mathfrak{M} \models R[q] \stackrel{\mathrm{def}}{\iff} \langle q_0, \ldots, q_{n-1}\rangle \in R^{\mathfrak{M}}$ for some $n \in \omega \quad (R \in P)$
- $\mathfrak{M} \models (v_i = v_j)[q] \stackrel{\mathrm{def}}{\iff} q_i = q_j \quad (i, j \in \omega)$
- if $\psi_1, \psi_2 \in F_{\mathrm{FOL}}$, then

$$\begin{aligned}
\mathfrak{M} \models \neg\psi_1[q] &\stackrel{\mathrm{def}}{\iff} \text{not } \mathfrak{M} \models \psi_1[q] \\
\mathfrak{M} \models (\psi_1 \wedge \psi_2)[q] &\stackrel{\mathrm{def}}{\iff} \mathfrak{M} \models \psi_1[q] \text{ and } \mathfrak{M} \models \psi_2[q] \\
\mathfrak{M} \models \exists v_i\psi_1[q] &\stackrel{\mathrm{def}}{\iff} (\exists q' \in {}^{\omega}M)(\forall j \in \omega) \\
&\qquad [j \neq i \Rightarrow (q'_j = q_j \ \&\ \mathfrak{M} \models \psi_1[q'])].
\end{aligned}$$

If $\mathfrak{M} \models \varphi[q]$ holds then we say that q *satisfies* φ in $\mathfrak{M}$.

Now we define mng_{FOL} as follows.

$$mng_{\mathrm{FOL}}(\varphi, \mathfrak{M}) \stackrel{\mathrm{def}}{=} \{q \in {}^{\omega}M : \mathfrak{M} \models \varphi[q]\}.$$

(iv) Validity is defined by $\mathfrak{M} \models_{\mathrm{FOL}} \varphi \overset{\mathrm{def}}{\iff} (\forall q \in {}^{\omega}M)\ \mathfrak{M} \models \varphi[q]$.
(v) *First-order logic* (in rank-free form) is

$$\mathcal{L}_{\mathrm{FOL}} \overset{\mathrm{def}}{=} \langle F_{\mathrm{FOL}}, M_{\mathrm{FOL}}, mng_{\mathrm{FOL}}, \models_{\mathrm{FOL}} \rangle . \qquad \blacktriangleleft$$

For more on $\mathcal{L}_{\mathrm{FOL}}$ see e.g. Henkin–Tarski [13], Simon [19], Venema [20], Henkin–Monk–Tarski [12, section 4.3]. Intuitive explanations about $\mathcal{L}_{\mathrm{FOL}}$ can also be found in [3].

3 Bridge between the world of logics and the world of algebras

The algebraic counterpart of classical sentential logic $\mathcal{L}_S$ is the variety BA of Boolean algebras. Why is this so important? The answer lies in the general experience that it is usually much easier to solve a problem concerning $\mathcal{L}_S$ by translating it to BA, solving the algebraic problem, and then translating the result back to $\mathcal{L}_S$ (than solving it directly in $\mathcal{L}_S$).

In this section we extend applicability of BA to $\mathcal{L}_S$ to applicability of algebra in general to logics in general. We will introduce a standard translation method from logic to algebra, which to each logic $\mathcal{L}$ associates a class of algebras $\mathsf{Alg}(\mathcal{L})$. (Of course, $\mathsf{Alg}(\mathcal{L}_S)$ will be a BA.) Further, this translation method will suggest us how to find the algebraic question corresponding to a logical question. If the logical question is about $\mathcal{L}$ then its algebraic equivalent will be about $\mathsf{Alg}(\mathcal{L})$. For example, if we want to decide whether $\mathcal{L}$ has the proof theoretic property called Craig's interpolation property, then it is sufficient to decide whether $\mathsf{Alg}(\mathcal{L})$ has the so called amalgamation property (for which there are powerful methods in the literature of algebra). If the logical question concerns connections between several logics, say between $\mathcal{L}_1$ and $\mathcal{L}_2$, then the algebraic question will be about connections between $\mathsf{Alg}(\mathcal{L}_1)$ and $\mathsf{Alg}(\mathcal{L}_2)$. (The latter are quite often simpler, hence easier to investigate.)

3.1. Fine–tuning the framework

The definition of a logic in section 2 is very wide. Actually, it is too wide for proving interesting theorems about logics. Now we will define a subclass of logics which we will call *nice logics*. Our notion of a nice logic is wide enough to cover the logics mentioned in the previous section, moreover, it is broad enough to cover almost all logics investigated in the literature. (Certain quantifier logics might need a little reformulation for this, but that reformulation does not effect the essential aspects of the logic in question as we will see.) On the other hand, the class of nice logics is narrow enough for proving interesting theorems about them, that is, we will be able to establish typical logical facts that hold for most logics studied in the literature.

Before reading Def.3.1.1 below, it might be useful to contemplate the common features of the logics we defined in section 2 ($\mathcal{L}_S$, $S5$, $\mathcal{L}_D$, $\mathcal{L}_{\kappa\text{-times}}$, arrow logics, $\mathcal{L}_{\mathrm{FOL}}$). In all these logics, the biconditional "$\leftrightarrow$" is available as a derived connective. In condition (3) of Def.3.1.1 a new symbol "∇" will occur, denoting a derived connective of the logic in question. At first reading it is a good idea to identify "∇" with our old biconditional "$\leftrightarrow$". Certainly, if we replaced condition (3) with the simpler assumption that "$\leftrightarrow$" is expressible in our logic $\mathcal{L}$ then all theorems would remain true. However, at a second reading of the definition it might be useful to observe that our condition (3) is a weaker assumption than expressibility of "$\leftrightarrow$" (and that this makes the class of nice logics broader).

We also note that the theorems of section 3.2 below (based on the next definition) can be proved in a more general setting (cf. [2]). Here we do restrictions in order to make the methodology more transparent. The reader who would find the definition below too restrictive is asked to consult section 4 ("Generalizations") of [3], where several conditions are either eliminated or it is explained how to eliminate them, and references are given where the elimination is done.

DEFINITION 3.1.1 (nice logic, strongly nice logic):
Let $\langle F, M, mng, \models\rangle$ be a logic in the sense of Definition 2.2 (i.e. F is a set, M is a class, mng is a function with domain $F \times M$, and $\models \subseteq M \times F$).

We say that $\mathcal{L}$ is a *nice logic* if conditions (1–4) below hold for $\mathcal{L}$.

(1) A set $Cn(\mathcal{L})$, called the set of *logical connectives* of $\mathcal{L}$, is fixed. Every $c \in Cn(\mathcal{L})$ has some rank $rank(c) \in \omega$. The set of all logical connectives of rank k is denoted by $Cn_k(\mathcal{L})$.
There is a set P, called the set of *atomic formulas* (or *parameters* or *propositional variables*), such that F is the smallest set satisfying conditions (a–b) below.
   (a) $P \subseteq F$
   (b) if $c \in Cn_k(\mathcal{L})$ and $\varphi_1, \ldots, \varphi_k \in F$ then $c(\varphi_1, \ldots, \varphi_k) \in F$.
The word–algebra generated by P using the logical connectives from $Cn(\mathcal{L})$ as algebraic operations is denoted by $\underset{\sim}{F}$, that is,
$\underset{\sim}{F} = \langle F, c\rangle_{c \in Cn(\mathcal{L})}$. $\underset{\sim}{F}$ is called the *formula algebra* of $\mathcal{L}$.

(2) We assume that the function $mng_{\mathfrak{M}} \stackrel{\text{def}}{=} \langle mng(\varphi, \mathfrak{M}) : \varphi \in F\rangle$ is a homomorphism from $\underset{\sim}{F}$ for every $\mathfrak{M} \in M$.

(3) We assume that there are *"derived" connectives* "ε" and "δ" (unary) and "∇" (binary) of $\mathcal{L}$ with the following properties:
   (i) $(\forall \mathfrak{M} \in M)(\forall \varphi, \psi \in F)\big[\mathfrak{M} \models (\varphi \nabla \psi) \iff mng_{\mathfrak{M}}(\varphi) = mng_{\mathfrak{M}}(\psi)\big]$.
   (ii) $(\forall \mathfrak{M} \in M)(\forall \varphi \in F)\big[\mathfrak{M} \models \varepsilon(\varphi)\nabla\delta(\varphi) \iff \mathfrak{M} \models \varphi\big]$.
(By "derived" we mean that "ε, δ" and "∇" are not necessarily members of $Cn(\mathcal{L})$. They are only "built up" from elements of $Cn(\mathcal{L})$. But we do not know from which elements of $Cn(\mathcal{L})$ "ε", "δ", or "∇" are built up, or how. We do not care!)

(4) $(\forall \psi, \varphi_0, \ldots, \varphi_n \in F)(\forall p_0, \ldots, p_n \in P)\big[\models \psi(\overline{p}) \implies \models \psi(\overline{p}/\overline{\varphi})\big]$, where $\overline{p} = \langle p_0, \ldots, p_n\rangle$, $\overline{\varphi} = \langle \varphi_0, \ldots, \varphi_n\rangle$, and $\psi(\overline{p}/\overline{\varphi})$ denotes the formula that we get from ψ after simultaneously substituting φ_i for every occur-

rence of p_i $(0 \leqslant i \leqslant n)$ in ψ. We refer to this condition as '*$\mathcal{L}$ has the substitution property*'.

$\mathcal{L}$ is called ***strongly nice*** iff it is nice and satisfies condition (5) below.

(5) $(\forall s \in {}^P F)(\forall \mathfrak{M} \in M)(\exists \mathfrak{N} \in M)(\forall \varphi(p_{i_0}, \ldots, p_{i_n}) \in F)$

$$(+) \qquad mng_{\mathfrak{N}}(\varphi) = mng_{\mathfrak{M}}(\varphi(p_{i_0}/s(p_{i_0}), \ldots, p_{i_n}/s(p_{i_n}))) .$$

Let $\hat{s} \in {}^F F$ be the natural extension of s to $\underset{\sim}{F}$. Then (+) says

$$mng_{\mathfrak{N}}(\varphi) = mng_{\mathfrak{M}}(\hat{s}(\varphi)) .$$

If this property holds, then we say that the logic '*$\mathcal{L}$ has the semantical substitution property*' (the model $\mathfrak{N}$ is the substituted version of $\mathfrak{M}$ along substitution s).

Logics satisfying conditions (1), (2) and (5) above are called ***structural*** ones. ◀

Structural logics nicely match the most general logics studied in the general theory of propositional logics, cf. Font–Jansana [11].

To simplify the rest of this material, when dealing with nice logics, we will usually assume that $\varepsilon(\varphi) = True$ and $\delta(\varphi) = \varphi$. That is, we asume that ε is a *zero–ary* connective, and for helping intuition, we denote it by "*True*" instead of ε.[4] We will prove our theorems for this simplified form of a nice logic. It is left to the reader as an exercise to check that the proofs go through for the original definition, too.

If $\mathfrak{A}$ and $\mathfrak{B}$ are two similar algebras, then $Hom(\mathfrak{A}, \mathfrak{B})$ denotes the set of all homomorphisms from $\mathfrak{A}$ into $\mathfrak{B}$.

REMARKS 3.1.2:

(i) An equivalent form of (+) above is the very natural condition

$$\left(\forall h \in Hom(\underset{\sim}{F}, \underset{\sim}{F})\right) (\forall \mathfrak{M} \in M)(\exists \mathfrak{N} \in M)\ mng_{\mathfrak{N}} = mng_{\mathfrak{M}} \circ h .$$

Since h is just a substitution, this form makes it explicit that $\mathfrak{N}$ is the h–substituted version of $\mathfrak{M}$.

(ii) Item (2) of Definition 3.1.1 above is a purely logical criterion. Namely, it is Frége's principle of compositionality.

(iii) The simplification introduced right after Definition 3.1.1 saying that $\varepsilon(\varphi) = True$ and $\delta(\varphi) = \varphi$ implies the following connection between $\models$ and *mng*:

$$(\forall \varphi \in F)\left[\models \varphi \implies (\forall \mathfrak{M} \in M)\ mng_{\mathfrak{M}}(\varphi) = mng_{\mathfrak{M}}(True)\right].$$

[4] This simplification somewhat restricts generality, e.g. it excludes Relavance Logic.

This does not follow from the original definition. ◄

REMARK 3.1.3 (Connections with the Blok–Pigozzi approach):
Here we mention only a small part of these connections.

Let $\mathcal{L} = \langle F_\mathcal{L}, M_\mathcal{L}, mng_\mathcal{L}, \models_\mathcal{L}\rangle$ be a logic. Recall that $\models^c_\mathcal{L}$ denotes the semantical consequence relation $\models^c_\mathcal{L} \subseteq \mathcal{P}(F) \times F$ induced by $\models_\mathcal{L}$. Recall from the discussion of the connection between logics with $\vdash_\mathcal{L}$ and without $\vdash_\mathcal{L}$ preceding Definition 2.2 that the pair $\langle F_\mathcal{L}, \models^c_\mathcal{L}\rangle$ can be considered to be a logic in the purely syntactical sense. The $\langle F_\mathcal{L}, \models^c_\mathcal{L}\rangle$ part of a strongly nice logic $\mathcal{L}$ is always algebraizable in the sense of Blok and Pigozzi. Actually, their definition is more general.

A small sample of references is Blok–Pigozzi [7], their papers in [1], Czelakowski [9], Font–Jansana [10]. ◄

* * *

Next we turn to ***inference systems***. Inference systems (usually denoted as $\vdash$) are syntactical devices serving to recapture (or at least to approximate) the semantical consequence relation of the logic $\mathcal{L}$. The idea is the following. Suppose $\Sigma \models^c_\mathcal{L} \varphi$. This means that, in the logic $\mathcal{L}$, the assumptions collected in Σ semantically imply the conclusion φ. (In any possible world $\mathfrak{M}$ of $\mathcal{L}$, that is, in any $\mathfrak{M} \in M_\mathcal{L}$, whenever Σ is valid in $\mathfrak{M}$, then also φ is valid in $\mathfrak{M}$.) Then we would like to be able to reproduce this relationship between Σ and φ by purely syntactical, "finitistic" means. That is, by applying some formal rules of inference (and some axioms of the logic $\mathcal{L}$) we would like to be able to derive φ from Σ by using "paper and pencil" only. In particular, such a derivation will always be a finite string of symbols. If we can do this, that will be denoted by $\Sigma \vdash \varphi$.

DEFINITION 3.1.4 (formula scheme):
Let $\mathcal{L}$ be a nice logic with the finite set $Cn(\mathcal{L})$ of logical connectives (cf. (1) of Def.3.1.1). Fix a countable set $A = \{A_i : i < \omega\}$, called the set of *formula variables*. The set $Fms_\mathcal{L}$ of *formula schemes* of $\mathcal{L}$ is the smallest set satisfying conditions (a–b) below.

(a) $A \subseteq Fms_\mathcal{L}$,

(b) if $c \in Cn_k(\mathcal{L})$ and $\Phi_1, \ldots, \Phi_k \in Fms_\mathcal{L}$ then $c(\Phi_1, \ldots, \Phi_k) \in Fms_\mathcal{L}$.

An *instance of a formula scheme* is given by substituting formulas for the formula variables in it. ◄

DEFINITION 3.1.5 (Hilbert–style inference system):
Let $\mathcal{L}$ be a nice logic. An *inference rule* of $\mathcal{L}$ is a pair $\langle\langle B_1, \ldots, B_n\rangle, B_0\rangle$, where every B_i $(i \leqslant n)$ is a formula scheme. This inference rule will be denoted by

$$\frac{B_1, \ldots, B_n}{B_0}.$$

An *instance of an inference rule* is given by substituting formulas for the formula variables in the formula schemes occurring in the rule.

A *Hilbert–style inference system* (or *calculus*) for $\mathcal{L}$ is a finite set of formula schemes (called *axiom schemes*) together with a finite set of inference rules. ◀

DEFINITION 3.1.6 (derivability):
Let $\mathcal{L}$ be a nice logic and let $\vdash$ be a Hilbert–style inference system for $\mathcal{L}$. Assume $\Sigma \cup \{\varphi\} \subseteq F_{\mathcal{L}}$. We say that φ is $\vdash$*–derivable* (or *–provable*) from Σ iff there is a finite sequence $\langle \varphi_1, \ldots, \varphi_n \rangle$ of formulas (an $\vdash$*–proof of* φ *from* Σ) such that φ_n is φ and for every $1 \leqslant i \leqslant n$

- $\varphi_i \in \Sigma$ or
- φ_i is an instance of an axiom scheme (an *axiom* for short) of $\vdash$ or
- there are $j_1, ..., j_k < i$, and there is an inference rule of $\vdash$ such that $\frac{\varphi_{j_1}, \ldots, \varphi_{j_k}}{\varphi_i}$ is an instance of this rule.

We write $\Sigma \vdash \varphi$ if φ is $\vdash$–provable from Σ. (We will often identify an inference system $\vdash$ with the corresponding derivability relation.) ◀

DEFINITION 3.1.7 (complete and sound Hilbert–type inference system): Let $\mathcal{L}$ be a nice logic and let $\vdash$ be a Hilbert–type inference system for $\mathcal{L}$. Then

$\vdash$ is *weakly complete* for $\mathcal{L}$ iff $(\forall \varphi \in F_{\mathcal{L}})(\models_{\mathcal{L}} \varphi \implies \vdash \varphi)$;

$\vdash$ is *finitely complete* for $\mathcal{L}$ iff $(\forall \Sigma \subseteq_{\omega} F_{\mathcal{L}})(\forall \varphi \in F_{\mathcal{L}})(\Sigma \models_{\mathcal{L}} \varphi \implies \Sigma \vdash \varphi)$; that is, we consider only finite Σ's;

$\vdash$ is *strongly complete* for $\mathcal{L}$ iff $(\forall \Sigma \subseteq F_{\mathcal{L}})(\forall \varphi \in F_{\mathcal{L}})(\Sigma \models_{\mathcal{L}} \varphi \implies \Sigma \vdash \varphi)$;

$\vdash$ is *weakly sound* for $\mathcal{L}$ iff $(\forall \varphi \in F_{\mathcal{L}})(\vdash \varphi \implies \models_{\mathcal{L}} \varphi)$;

$\vdash$ is *strongly sound* for $\mathcal{L}$ iff

$$(\forall \Sigma \subseteq F_{\mathcal{L}})(\forall \varphi \in F_{\mathcal{L}})(\Sigma \vdash \varphi \implies \Sigma \models_{\mathcal{L}} \varphi). \quad ◀$$

3.2. Algebraic characterizations of completeness and compactness properties via Alg_m and Alg_f

In Definition 3.2.1 below, we associate two classes of algebras to any logic $\mathcal{L}$ in the sense of Definition 2.2.

For any class K of similar models, $\mathbf{I}K \stackrel{\text{def}}{=} \{\mathfrak{M} : (\exists \mathfrak{N} \in K)\ \mathfrak{M} \cong \mathfrak{N}\}$.

DEFINITION 3.2.1: (algebraic counterpart of a logic)
Let $\mathcal{L} = \langle F, M, mng, \models \rangle$ be a logic satisfying conditions (1),(2) of Definition 3.1.1 above.

(i) Let $K \subseteq M$. Then for every $\varphi, \psi \in F$

$$\varphi \sim_K \psi \stackrel{\text{def}}{\iff} (\forall \mathfrak{M} \in K)\ mng_{\mathfrak{M}}(\varphi) = mng_{\mathfrak{M}}(\psi).$$

$$\mathsf{Alg}_f(\mathcal{L}) \stackrel{\text{def}}{=} \mathbf{I}\left\{\underset{\sim}{F}/{\sim_K} \,:\, K \subseteq M\right\}.$$

(Alg$_f$ is often called the class of Lindenbaum–Tarski algebras.)

(ii) $$\mathsf{Alg}_m(\mathcal{L}) \stackrel{\text{def}}{=} \mathbf{I}\left\{ mng_{\mathfrak{M}}(\underset{\sim}{F}) \ : \ \mathfrak{M} \in M \right\},$$

where $mng_{\mathfrak{M}}$ was defined in item (2) of Definition 3.1.1, and for any homomorphism $h : \mathfrak{A} \longrightarrow \mathfrak{B}$, $h(\mathfrak{A})$ is the homomorphic image of $\mathfrak{A}$ along h i.e., $h(\mathfrak{A})$ is the smallest subalgebra of $\mathfrak{B}$ such that $h : \mathfrak{A} \longrightarrow h(\mathfrak{A})$. ◀

FACT 3.2.2: For nice logics $\mathsf{Alg}_f(\mathcal{L}) = \mathbf{I}\left\{\underset{\sim}{F}/{\sim_\Gamma} : \Gamma \subseteq F\right\}$, where $\varphi \sim_\Gamma \psi \stackrel{\text{def}}{\Longleftrightarrow} (\forall \mathfrak{M} \in M)\left[\mathfrak{M} \models \Gamma \Longrightarrow mng_{\mathfrak{M}}(\varphi) = mng_{\mathfrak{M}}(\psi)\right]$.
Proof: For every $K \subseteq M$, $\underset{\sim}{F}/{\sim_K} = \underset{\sim}{F}/{\sim_{Th(K)}}$; and for every $\Gamma \subseteq F$, ${\sim_\Gamma} = \underset{\sim}{F}/{\sim_{Mod(\Gamma)}}$ hold (cf. Defs.2.3 and 2.4). ∎

In Theorem 3.2.3 below, we will give a sufficent and necessary condition for a strongly nice logic to have a finitely complete Hilbert–style inference system.

By a quasi–variety we mean a class of algebras axiomatizable by ***quasi–equations***, that is, implications of the form $(e_1 \wedge e_2 \wedge \cdots \wedge e_k) \rightarrow e_0$, where $e_0, e_1, \ldots, e_k$ are equations.

THEOREM 3.2.3. *Assume $\mathcal{L}$ is strongly nice. Then*

$\mathsf{Alg}_m(\mathcal{L})$ generates a finitely axiomatizable quasi–variety

$$\Longleftrightarrow$$

($\exists$ Hilbert–style $\vdash$)($\vdash$ is finitely complete and strongly sound for $\mathcal{L}$).

Proof: See in [3]. ∎

Having found the algebraic counterpart of "finitely complete", let us try to characterize "weakly complete". Since weak completeness is slightly weaker than finite completeness, we have to weaken the algebraic counterpart of finite completeness for characterizing weak completeness. This way we obtain condition (∗) below, where $Eq_{\mathcal{L}}$ and $Qeq_{\mathcal{L}}$ denote the set of all equations and the set of all quasi–equations, respectively, of the language of $\mathsf{Alg}_m(\mathcal{L})$.

(∗) $(\exists \text{ finite } Ax \subseteq Qeq_{\mathcal{L}})$
$$\left[(\forall e \in Eq_{\mathcal{L}})(\mathsf{Alg}_m(\mathcal{L}) \models e \Longrightarrow Ax \models e) \ \& \ \mathsf{Alg}_m(\mathcal{L}) \models Ax\right].$$

That is, the equational theory of $\mathsf{Alg}_m(\mathcal{L})$ is finitely axiomatizable by quasi–equations valid in $\mathsf{Alg}_m(\mathcal{L})$.

THEOREM 3.2.4. *Assume that $\mathcal{L}$ is nice. Then*

$$(*) \iff (\exists \textit{ Hilbert-style } \vdash)(\vdash \textit{ is weakly complete and strongly sound for } \mathcal{L}).$$

In particular, if the equational theory of $\mathsf{Alg}_m(\mathcal{L})$ is finitely axiomatizable, then $\mathcal{L}$ admits a weakly complete Hilbert–style inference system.

Proof: See in [3]. ∎

DEFINITION 3.2.5 (deduction term):
Let $\mathcal{L} = \langle F, M, mng, \models\rangle$ be a nice logic. We say that $\mathcal{L}$ *has a deduction theorem*, iff

$$(\exists(\Phi_1\Delta\Phi_2) \in Fms_{\mathcal{L}}))\,(\forall\Sigma \subseteq F)(\forall\varphi,\psi \in F)\,(\Sigma \cup \{\varphi\} \models \psi \iff \Sigma \models \varphi\Delta\psi)\ ,$$

where "$\varphi\Delta\psi$" denotes an instance of scheme "$\Phi_1\Delta\Phi_2$". Such a "$\Phi_1\Delta\Phi_2$" is called a *deduction term* for $\mathcal{L}$. ◀

PROPOSITION 3.2.6. *$\mathcal{L}_S$ and $S5$ have deduction terms.*

Proof: It is not hard to show that "$\Phi_1 \to \Phi_2$" and "$\Box\Phi_1 \to \Box\Phi_2$" (where $\Box$ is the abbreviation of $\neg\Diamond\neg$) are suitable deduction terms for propositional logic and $S5$, respectively. ∎

The following theorem states that for any nice logic the existence of a deduction term and that of a weakly complete Hilbert–style calculus provides a finitely complete inference system.

THEOREM 3.2.7. *Assume $\mathcal{L}$ has a deduction theorem, and (∃ Hilbert–style ⊢) (⊢ is weakly complete and strongly sound for $\mathcal{L}$). Then*

$$(\exists \textit{ Hilbert-style } \vdash)(\vdash \textit{ is finitely complete and strongly sound for } \mathcal{L}).$$

Proof: See in [3]. ∎

* * *

Recall that in Definition 3.1.1 above (and also in the logics studied so far), in each case, there was a parameter P, which was the set of atomic formulas. The choice of P influenced what the set F of formulas would be. Thus in fact, our old definition of a logic yields a family

$$\langle\langle F^P, M^P, mng^P, \models^P\rangle : \ P \text{ is a set}\rangle$$

of logics. The members of this family do not differ significantly except that the cardinality of P matters sometimes.

DEFINITION 3.2.8 (general logic):
A *general logic* is defined to be a function

$$\mathbf{L} \stackrel{\text{def}}{=} \langle \mathcal{L}^\kappa \ : \ \kappa \text{ is a cardinal} \rangle ,$$

where for each cardinal κ, $\mathcal{L}^\kappa = \langle F^\kappa, M^\kappa, mng^\kappa, \models^\kappa \rangle$ is a logic in the sense of Definition 2.2, that is, F^κ is a set, M^κ is a class, mng^κ is a function with domain $F^\kappa \times M^\kappa$, and $\models^\kappa \subseteq M^\kappa \times F^\kappa$.

$\mathbf{L}$ is called a *(strongly) nice general logic* iff conditions (1–3) below hold for $\mathbf{L}$.

(1) $\mathcal{L}^\kappa$ is a (strongly) nice logic in the sense of Def.3.1.1 for each cardinal κ.
(2) For each cardinal κ, the set P^κ of atomic formulas of the logic $\mathcal{L}^\kappa$ is of cardinality κ. If κ and λ are cardinals with $\lambda \leqslant \kappa$ then $P^\lambda \subseteq P^\kappa$ (which implies that $F^\lambda \subseteq F^\kappa$).
(3) For all cardinals $\lambda \leqslant \kappa$

$$\{ mng^\lambda_{\mathfrak{M}} \ : \ \mathfrak{M} \in M^\lambda \} = \{ (mng^\kappa_{\mathfrak{M}}) \restriction F^\lambda \ : \ \mathfrak{M} \in M^\kappa \} .$$

Intuitively, this requirement says that $\mathcal{L}^\lambda$ is the "natural" restriction of $\mathcal{L}^\kappa$. ◄

REMARK 3.2.9: As a corollary of item (3) of Definiton 3.2.8 above we note that for all cardinals κ and λ, if $\Gamma \cup \{\varphi\} \subseteq F^\kappa \cap F^\lambda$ then

$$\Gamma \models^\kappa \varphi \iff \Gamma \models^\lambda \varphi. \qquad ◄$$

DEFINITION 3.2.10 (algebraic counterpart of a general logic):
Let $\mathbf{L} = \langle \mathcal{L}^\kappa : \kappa \text{ is a cardinal} \rangle$ be a nice general logic. Then

$$\mathsf{Alg}_f(\mathbf{L}) \stackrel{\text{def}}{=} \bigcup \{ \mathsf{Alg}_f(\mathcal{L}^\kappa) \ : \ \kappa \text{ is a cardinal} \} ,$$

$$\mathsf{Alg}_m(\mathbf{L}) \stackrel{\text{def}}{=} \bigcup \{ \mathsf{Alg}_m(\mathcal{L}^\kappa) \ : \ \kappa \text{ is a cardinal} \}$$

(cf. Def.3.2.1). ◄

THEOREM 3.2.11. *For strongly nice general logics*

$$\mathsf{Alg}_f(\mathbf{L}) = \mathbf{SP}\mathsf{Alg}_m(\mathbf{L}).$$

Proof: See in [3]. ∎

DEFINITION 3.2.12 (compactness of a logic, compactness of a general logic): Let $\mathcal{L} = \langle F, M, mng, \models \rangle$ be a logic. We say that

(i) $\mathcal{L}$ is *satisfiability compact* if

$$(\forall \Gamma \subseteq F) \left[(\forall \text{ finite } \Sigma \subseteq \Gamma)(\Sigma \text{ has a model}) \Longrightarrow (\Gamma \text{ has a model}) \right] , \text{ and}$$

(ii) $\mathcal{L}$ is *consequence compact* if

$$\Gamma \models \varphi \Longrightarrow (\exists \text{ finite } \Sigma \subseteq \Gamma) \ \Sigma \models \varphi, \quad \text{for every } \Gamma \cup \{\varphi\} \subseteq F.$$

A general logic $\mathbf{L} = \langle \mathcal{L}^\kappa : \kappa \text{ is a cardinal} \rangle$ is called ***satisfiability (consequence) compact*** if for each cardinal κ, the logic $\mathcal{L}^\kappa$ is satisfiability (consequence) compact. ◀

For an arbitrary class K of algebras,

$$\mathsf{UpK} \stackrel{\text{def}}{=} \mathbf{I}\{\mathbf{P}_{i \in I}\mathfrak{A}_i/\mathcal{F} : \; I \text{ is a set}, \mathcal{F} \text{ is an ultrafilter over } I \text{ and } (\forall i \in I)\mathfrak{A}_i \in \mathsf{K}\} .$$

We say that K is **Up**-*closed* if $\mathsf{UpK} \subseteq \mathsf{K}$.

Our next theorem gives a sufficent condition for satisfiability compactness of a general logic.

THEOREM 3.2.13. *Assume* $\mathbf{L}$ *is a strongly nice general logic. Then*

$$(\mathsf{Alg}_f(\mathbf{L}) \textit{ is } \mathbf{Up}\textit{–closed}) \Longrightarrow (\mathbf{L} \textit{ is satisfiability compact}) .$$

Proof: See in [3]. ∎

Our next theorem states that the condition of Theorem 3.2.13 above is sufficient and also necessary for consequence compactness, and so for strong completeness (cf. Theorem 3.2.15 below).

THEOREM 3.2.14. *(cf. [2, Thm.2.8]) Assume* $\mathbf{L}$ *is a strongly nice general logic. Then* $(\mathsf{Alg}_f(\mathbf{L})$ *is* $\mathbf{Up}$*–closed)* $\Longleftrightarrow$ *(*$\mathbf{L}$ *is consequence compact).*

Proof: See in [3]. ∎

THEOREM 3.2.15. *Assume* $\mathbf{L} = \langle \mathcal{L}^\kappa : \kappa \text{ is a cardinal} \rangle$ *is a strongly nice general logic. Then*

$$\mathsf{Alg}_f(\mathbf{L}) \textit{ is a finitely axiomatizable quasi–variety}$$

$$\Longleftrightarrow$$

$$(\exists \textit{ Hilbert–style } \vdash)(\forall \textit{ cardinal } \kappa)$$
$$(\vdash \textit{ is strongly complete and strongly sound for } \mathcal{L}^\kappa).$$

Proof: See in [3]. ∎

References

1. Andréka,H. Monk,J.D. and Németi,I. (ed.s) Algebraic Logic. Proc. Conf. Budapest 1988, Colloq. Math. Soc. J. Bolyai vol. 54, North–Holland, Amsterdam, 1991; v+746 pp.
2. Andréka,H., Németi,I. and Sain,I. Abstract model theoretic approach to algebraic logic. Preprint (1984), updated in 1988, 1992; 70 pp.
3. Andréka,H., Németi,I., Sain,I. and Kurucz,Á. Methodology for Applying Algebraic Logic to Logic. Lecture Notes, based on the 1991 Spring Semester of Logic Graduate School, Budapest 1993.

4. Anellis,I.H. and Houser,N. The nineteenth century roots of universal algebra and algebraic logic: A critical–bibliographical guide for the contemporary logician. In: Algebraic Logic (Proc. Conf. Budapest 1988), Colloq. Math. Soc. J. Bolyai vol. 54, North–Holland, Amsterdam, 1991; 1–36.
5. van Benthem,J. Language in Action (Categories, Lambdas and Dynamic Logic). North–Holland, Amsterdam, 1991.
6. van Benthem,J. Dynamic Arrow Logic. Institute of Logic, Language and Computation, University of Amsterdam, preprint, 1992; To appear in Jan van Eick, Albert Visser (eds.) "Logic and Information Flow", Kluwer, Dortrecht.
7. Blok,W.J. and Pigozzi,D. Algebraizable logics. Memoirs Amer. Math. Soc. vol. 77,396, 1989; vi+78 pp.
8. del Cerro,L.F., Gabbay,D., Herzig,A. and Ohlbach,H.J. Overview on the Current State of Translation Methods for Non–classical Logics. Preprint, Imperial College, 1993; 4 pp.
9. Czelakowski,J. Logic, algebras and consequence operators., Preprint, 1993; 79 pp.
10. Font,J.M. and Jansana,R. A general algebraic semantics for deductive systems. Preprint, Univ. of Barcelona, 1993.
11. Font,J.M. and Jansana,R. On the identity of the notions of strongly nice general logic and regularly algebraizable deductive system. Preprint, Univ. of Barcelona, 1993.
12. Henkin,L. Monk,J.D. and Tarski,A. Cylindric Algebras Part I and Part II. North–Holland, Amsterdam, 1985.
13. Henkin,L. and Tarski,A. Cylindric Algebras. Lattice Theory, Proc. of symposia in pure mathematics vol. 2, ed. R.P. Dilworth, Americal Mathematical Society, Providence 1961; 83–113.
14. Maddux,R. The origin of the calculus of relations. Studia Logica, 1991; vol. L, No 3/4: 421–456 pp.
15. "Possible worlds in Humanities, Arts and Sciences. W.de Gruyer, Berlin–New York, 1989; 450 pp."
16. Roorda,D. Resource Logics. Proof-Theoretical Investigations. Ph.D. Dissertation, Institute for Logic, Language and Computation, Univ. of Amsterdam, 1991.
18. Sain,I. Is "Some–Other–Time" sometimes better than "Sometime" in proving partial correctness of programs? Studia Logica, 1988; vol. XLVII, No 3: 279–301.
19. Simon,A. Finite Schema Completeness for Typeless Logic and Representable Cylindric Algebras. Algebraic Logic (Proc. Conf. Budapest 1988) Colloq. Math. Soc. J. Bolyai vol 54, North–Holland, Amsterdam, 1991; 665–670.
20. Venema, Y. Many–Dimensional Modal Logic. Ph.D. Dissertation, Institute for Logic, Language and Computation, Univ. of Amsterdam, 1992.

Relation Algebras for Reasoning about Time and Space

Roger D. Maddux

Department of Mathematics, Iowa State University

Ames, Iowa U.S.A.

Abstract

This paper presents a brief introduction to relation algebras, including some examples motivated by work in computer science, namely, the 'interval algebras', relation algebras that arose from James Allen's work on temporal reasoning, and by 'compass algebras', which are designed for similar reasoning about space. One kind of reasoning problem, called a 'constraint satisfaction problem', can be defined for arbitrary relation algebras. It will be shown here that the constraint satisfiability problem is NP-complete for almost all compass and interval algebras.

1. Relation Algebras

Composition of binary relations was introduced to logic by Augustus De Morgan [28] [29] (see [30, pp. 55–57, 208, 221, *etc.*]). De Morgan observed that the syllogism "every A is a B, every B is a C, so every A is a C" remains valid if the copula "is" is replaced by any transitive relation L. De Morgan went further, noting that if LM is the composition of the relation L with the relation M, that is, A is an LM of B just in case A is an L of an M of B, then the following syllogism is valid: "if every A is an L of a B, and every B is an M of a C, then every A is an LM of a C." De Morgan [29] (see [30, p. 222]) denoted the converse of the relation L by L^{-1} and its contrary by not-L, and observed that these operations commute: the converse of the contrary of L is the contrary of the converse of L. Around the same time, George Boole [7] [6] created algebra from the logic of classes. Starting with [31] in 1870, Charles Sanders Peirce applied Boole's ideas to create algebra from De Morgan's logic of relations, "and after many attempts produced a good general algebra of logic, together with another algebra specially adapted to dyadic relations (*Studies in Logic*, by members of the Johns Hopkins University, 1883, Note B, 187–203). Schröder developed the last in a systematic manner" in [35] (quotation from [26]). Peirce [32] laid out his calculus in 17 pages. F. W. K. Ernst Schröder's investigation [35] extended this to 649 pages. His book remains today the only exhaustive treatise on the calculus of relations. For additional survey and historical material on relation algebras see [8], [11], [12], [13], [14], [20], [21], [22], [23], [24], [37], and [38].

Consider an arbitrary classs, called the 'universe of discourse' or simply the 'universe'. The universe could, depending on the situation and purposes, contain all possible mathematical objects, or all states of a machine, or all real numbers, or just a finite set of letters. The fundamental operations of the calculus of relations are natural set-theoretical operations on binary relations over the universe. In addition to the Boolean operations of union, intersection, and complementation, there are the 'relative' (as Peirce calls them), or 'Peircean' (as Tarski calls them) operations, namely the binary operation of 'relative addition' (Peirce's name), the binary operation of 'relative multiplication' (Peirce's name) or 'composition' (De Morgan's name) and the unary operation of conversion. There are also four distinguished relations, namely the universal relation, the empty relation, the identity relation, and the diversity relation. The definitions of these operations and distinguished relations are listed below. In these definitions, x and y are arbitrary binary relations on the universe. By a ***binary relation*** we simply mean a class of ordered pairs. The ordered pair whose first element is p and whose second element is q is denoted $\langle p, q\rangle$. Thus p is an x of q if and only if $\langle p, q\rangle \in x$.

$$
\begin{aligned}
x + y &= \textit{union of } x \text{ and } y = \{\langle p, q\rangle : \langle p, q\rangle \in x \text{ or } \langle p, q\rangle \in y\} \\
x \cdot y &= \textit{intersection of } x \text{ and } y = \{\langle p, q\rangle : \langle p, q\rangle \in x \text{ and } \langle p, q\rangle \in y\} \\
\overline{x} &= \textit{complement of } x \\
&= \{\langle p, q\rangle : p, q \text{ are in the universe, but } \langle p, q\rangle \notin x\} \\
x \dagger y &= \textit{relative sum of } x \text{ and } y \\
&= \{\langle p, r\rangle : \text{for every } q \text{ in the universe, } \langle p, q\rangle \in x \text{ or } \langle q, r\rangle \in y\} \\
x ; y &= \textit{relative product of } x \text{ and } y \\
&= \{\langle p, r\rangle : \text{ for some } q,\ \langle p, q\rangle \in x \text{ and } \langle q, r\rangle \in y\} \\
\breve{x} &= \textit{converse of } x = \{\langle q, p\rangle : \langle p, q\rangle \in x\} \\
1 &= \textit{universal relation} = \{\langle p, q\rangle : p, q \text{ are in the universe}\} \\
0 &= \textit{empty relation} = \emptyset \\
1' &= \textit{identity relation} = \{\langle p, p\rangle : p \text{ is in the universe}\} \\
0' &= \textit{diversity relation} = \{\langle p, q\rangle : p, q \text{ are in the universe, } p \neq q\}
\end{aligned}
$$

Both De Morgan and Peirce denoted the composition of x and y simply by "xy", but Schröder [35] used "$x;y$", as is done here. The notation "$x|y$" was used by Whitehead and Russell [45] and adopted by Tarski and his school [10]. Peirce introduced the notation "$\breve{x}$" for the converse of x. Schröder introduced "1'" and "0'" for the identity and diversity relations. Here are some laws in the calculus of relations. These laws hold for every possible universe, and all possible binary relations x, y, and z.

(i) $(x + y) + z = x + (y + z)$

(ii) $x + y = y + x$

(iii) $x = \overline{\overline{x} + y} + \overline{\overline{x} + \overline{y}}$

(iv) $x \cdot y = \overline{\overline{x} + \overline{y}}$

(v) $1 = x + \overline{x}$

(vi) $0 = \overline{1}$

(vii) $x;(y;z) = (x;y);z$

(viii) $x;1' = x$

(ix) $(x + y);z = x;z + y;z$

(x) $\breve{\breve{x}} = x$

(xi) $(x+y)^{\smile} = \breve{x} + \breve{y}$

(xii) $(x;y)^{\smile} = \breve{y};\breve{x}$

(xiii) $\breve{x};\overline{x;y} + \overline{y} = \overline{y}$

(xiv) $0' = \overline{1'}$

(xv) $x \dagger y = \overline{\overline{x};\overline{y}}$

A *relation algebra* is an algebra of the form $\mathfrak{A} = \langle A, +, \cdot, ^-, 0, 1, \dagger, ;, ^{\smile}, 0', 1'\rangle$ that satisfies the identities (i)-(xv) above. Identities (i)–(vi) say that $\langle A, +, \cdot, ^-, 0, 1\rangle$ is a Boolean algebra (called the *Boolean part* or *Boolean reduct* of $\mathfrak{A}$). One of the most significant laws of the calculus of relations is De Morgan's "Theorem K" (see [30, pp. 186–7, 224] or [24, p. 434–5]), which asserts that the following statements are equivalent: $x;y \leq z$, $\breve{x};\overline{z} \leq \overline{y}$, $\overline{z};\breve{y} \leq \overline{x}$. After minor Boolean transformations Theorem K becomes the *cycle law*, that the following statements are equivalent: $x;y \cdot z = 0$, $\breve{x};z \cdot y = 0$, $z;\breve{y} \cdot x = 0$. The cycle law and De Morgan's Theorem K hold in every relation algebra because they can be proved from axioms (i)–(xv). There are many other equivalent axiomatizations for relation algebras. For example, equations (ix)–(xiii) can be replaced with the cycle law or with Theorem K. Also, equations (i)–(vi) can be replaced with some other set of equations that define Boolean algebras.

The algebra containing all binary relations on the universe U is denoted $\mathfrak{Re}(U)$. Identities (i)–(xv) hold in $\mathfrak{Re}(U)$, so $\mathfrak{Re}(U)$ is a relation algebra. Relation algebras are defined by equations, so it follows that subalgebras, homomorphic images, and direct products of relation algebras are again relation algebras. The algebras that can be obtained from algebras of the form $\mathfrak{Re}(U)$ by forming subalgebras, homomorphic images, and direct products are called *representable* relation algebras. Roger Lyndon [18] showed that not all relation algebras are representable. It follows that the axioms (i)–(xv) are incomplete, in the sense that there are equations which hold in every algebra of the form $\mathfrak{Re}(U)$ but cannot be derived from (i)–(xv). J. Donald Monk [27] proved that the equations that hold in every algebra of the form $\mathfrak{Re}(U)$ does not have a finite axiomatization.

Let $\mathfrak{A}$ be a relation algebra. An element x of $\mathfrak{A}$ is an *atom* if x is not 0 and there is no other element between x and 0, that is, either $x \cdot y = x$ or $x \cdot y = 0$ for every y in $\mathfrak{A}$. Let $At\mathfrak{A}$ be the set of atoms of $\mathfrak{A}$. It is easy to prove that the converse of an atom is an atom, *i.e.*, , if $x \in At\mathfrak{A}$ then $\breve{x} \in At\mathfrak{A}$. The relation algebra $\mathfrak{A}$ is said to be *atomic* if there is an atom below every nonzero element, that is, if $y \neq 0$ then there is some $x \in At\mathfrak{A}$ such that $x \leq y$. $\mathfrak{A}$ is said to be *complete* if every subset X of $\mathfrak{A}$ has a least upper bound $\sum X$ and greatest lower bound $\prod X$.

It turns out that if $\mathfrak{A}$ is both complete and atomic, then the structure of $\mathfrak{A}$ is entirely determined by its atoms and the action of the relative operations on the atoms. For a precise statement of this fact, let $C(\mathfrak{A}) = \{\langle a, b, c\rangle : a, b, c \in At\mathfrak{A}$ and $a;b \geq c\}$ and $I(\mathfrak{A}) = \{a : a \in At\mathfrak{A}$ and $a \leq 1'\}$. $C(\mathfrak{A})$ is the set of *cycles* of $\mathfrak{A}$ and $I(\mathfrak{A})$ is the set of *identity atoms* of $\mathfrak{A}$. Define the *atom structure* of $\mathfrak{A}$ to be $\mathfrak{At}\mathfrak{A} = \langle At\mathfrak{A}, C(\mathfrak{A}), ^{\smile}, I(\mathfrak{A})\rangle$. Any two complete atomic relation algebras with the isomorphic atom structures are isomorphic. For any $a, b, c \in At\mathfrak{A}$, let $[a, b, c] = \{\langle a, b, c\rangle, \langle\breve{a}, c, b\rangle, \langle b, \breve{c}, \breve{a}\rangle, \langle\breve{b}, \breve{a}, \breve{c}\rangle, \langle\breve{c}, a, \breve{b}\rangle, \langle c, \breve{b}, a\rangle\}$. By the cycle law, the set $C(\mathfrak{A})$ of cycles of $\mathfrak{A}$ is a union of sets of the form $[a, b, c]$.

We refer to such sets as *cyclesets*. The identity element, the converse of x, and the relative product of x and y can be computed from the atom structure as follows: $1' = \sum I(\mathfrak{A})$, $\breve{x} = \sum\{\breve{a} : x \geq a \in At\mathfrak{A}\}$, and $x;y = \sum\{c :$ there are $a, b \in At\mathfrak{A}$ with $a \leq x$, $b \leq y$, and $\langle a, b, c\rangle \in C(\mathfrak{A})\}$. Hence to specify a complete atomic relation algebra it suffices to list its atoms, to list its identity atoms, to indicate the converse of each atom, and, finally, to list the cyclesets $[a, b, c]$. This is especially convenient when $\mathfrak{A}$ is finite. We present several examples of relation algebras using this method.

2. Interval Algebras

To define the interval algebra IA [1] [2] take the universe U to be the set of all 'events', where an event is simply a pair of real numbers, the second of which is larger than the first. The first number in an event is its 'starting time', the second its 'ending time'. (Our model for time here is just the real numbers.) Seven binary relations on events are defined in the list below, where x, x', y, y' are real numbers and $\langle x, x'\rangle$, $\langle y, y'\rangle$ are events.

$$\begin{aligned}
&\text{identity:} && 1' = \{\langle\langle x, x'\rangle, \langle y, y'\rangle\rangle : x = y < x' = y'\}\\
&\text{precedes:} && p = \{\langle\langle x, x'\rangle, \langle y, y'\rangle\rangle : x < x' < y < y'\}\\
&\text{during:} && d = \{\langle\langle x, x'\rangle, \langle y, y'\rangle\rangle : y < x < x' < y'\}\\
&\text{overlaps:} && o = \{\langle\langle x, x'\rangle, \langle y, y'\rangle\rangle : x < y < x' < y'\}\\
&\text{meets:} && m = \{\langle\langle x, x'\rangle, \langle y, y'\rangle\rangle : x < x' = y < y'\}\\
&\text{starts:} && s = \{\langle\langle x, x'\rangle, \langle y, y'\rangle\rangle : x = y < x' < y'\}\\
&\text{finishes:} && f = \{\langle\langle x, x'\rangle, \langle y, y'\rangle\rangle : y < x < x' = y'\}
\end{aligned}$$

These seven relations are studied in [42] and are used in some computer programs [5] [25] [36]. They generate a finite subalgebra of $\mathfrak{Re}(U)$, called the *interval algebra*, or simply the IA. The IA has 13 atoms, namely 1', p, $\breve{p}$, d, $\breve{d}$, o, $\breve{o}$, m, $\breve{m}$, s, $\breve{s}$, f, and $\breve{f}$. (It turns out that p alone will generate the IA, and so will each of the elements $\breve{p}$, m, $\breve{m}$, o, and $\breve{o}$ [17] [16, Theorem 4.4].) If we start with the rational numbers instead of the reals, or, in fact, any dense linear ordering without endpoints, then the resulting algebra is isomorphic to the IA. But if we use some other infinite linear ordering, then the relation algebra generated by 1', p, d, o, m, s, and f may be infinite. This happens, for example, when we use the integers. If we start with a finite linear ordering on U, then the subalgebra generated by 1', p, d, o, m, s, and f will be $\mathfrak{Re}(U)$. Any relation algebra obtained in this way will be called *an* interval algebra (while *the* IA is the one obtained from the reals or rationals). The IA has 75 cyclesets: $[1', 1', 1']$, $[1', s, s]$, $[1', m, m]$, $[1', p, p]$, $[1', o, o]$, $[1', f, f]$, $[1', d, d]$, $[s, 1', s]$, $[s, s, s]$, $[s, m, p]$, $[s, p, p]$, $[s, o, m]$, $[s, o, p]$, $[s, o, o]$, $[s, f, d]$, $[s, d, d]$, $[m, 1', m]$, $[m, s, m]$, $[m, m, p]$, $[m, p, p]$, $[m, o, p]$, $[m, f, s]$, $[m, f, o]$, $[m, f, d]$, $[m, d, s]$, $[m, d, o]$, $[m, d, d]$, $[p, 1', p]$, $[p, s, p]$, $[p, m, p]$, $[p, p, p]$, $[p, o, p]$, $[p, f, s]$, $[p, f, m]$, $[p, f, p]$, $[p, f, o]$, $[p, f, d]$, $[p, d, s]$, $[p, d, m]$, $[p, d, p]$, $[p, d, o]$, $[p, d, d]$, $[o, 1', o]$, $[o, s, o]$, $[o, m, p]$, $[o, p, p]$, $[o, o, m]$, $[o, o, p]$, $[o, o, o]$, $[o, f, s]$, $[o, f, o]$, $[o, f, d]$, $[o, d, s]$, $[o, d, o]$, $[o, d, d]$, $[f, 1', f]$, $[f, s, d]$, $[f, m, m]$, $[f, p, p]$, $[f, o, s]$, $[f, o, o]$, $[f, o, d]$, $[f, f, f]$, $[f, d, d]$, $[d, 1', d]$, $[d, s, d]$, $[d, m, p]$, $[d, p, p]$, $[d, o, s]$,

	$1'$	p	$\breve{p}$	d	$\breve{d}$	o	$\breve{o}$
$1'$	$1'$	p	$\breve{p}$	d	$\breve{d}$	o	$\breve{o}$
p	p	p	1	$pdoms$	p	p	$pdoms$
$\breve{p}$	$\breve{p}$	1	$\breve{p}$	$\breve{p}d\breve{o}\breve{m}f$	$\breve{p}$	$\breve{p}d\breve{o}\breve{m}f$	$\breve{p}$
d	d	p	$\breve{p}$	d	1	$pdoms$	$\breve{p}d\breve{o}\breve{m}f$
$\breve{d}$	$\breve{d}$	$p\breve{d}om\breve{f}$	$\breve{p}\breve{d}\breve{o}\breve{m}\breve{s}$	$1'd\breve{d}o\breve{o}s\breve{s}f\breve{f}$	$\breve{d}$	$\breve{d}o\breve{f}$	$\breve{d}\breve{o}\breve{s}$
o	o	p	$\breve{p}\breve{d}\breve{o}\breve{m}\breve{s}$	dos	$p\breve{d}om\breve{f}$	pom	$1'd\breve{d}o\breve{o}s\breve{s}f\breve{f}$
$\breve{o}$	$\breve{o}$	$p\breve{d}om\breve{f}$	$\breve{p}$	$d\breve{o}f$	$\breve{p}\breve{d}\breve{o}\breve{m}\breve{s}$	$1'd\breve{d}o\breve{o}s\breve{s}f\breve{f}$	$\breve{p}\breve{o}\breve{m}$
m	m	p	$\breve{p}\breve{d}\breve{o}\breve{m}\breve{s}$	dos	p	p	dos
$\breve{m}$	$\breve{m}$	$p\breve{d}om\breve{f}$	$\breve{p}$	$d\breve{o}f$	$\breve{p}$	$d\breve{o}f$	$\breve{p}$
s	s	p	$\breve{p}$	d	$p\breve{d}om\breve{f}$	pom	$d\breve{o}f$
$\breve{s}$	$\breve{s}$	$p\breve{d}om\breve{f}$	$\breve{p}$	$d\breve{o}f$	$\breve{d}$	$\breve{d}o\breve{f}$	$\breve{o}$
f	f	p	$\breve{p}$	d	$\breve{p}\breve{d}\breve{o}\breve{m}\breve{s}$	dos	$\breve{p}\breve{o}\breve{m}$
$\breve{f}$	$\breve{f}$	p	$\breve{p}\breve{d}\breve{o}\breve{m}\breve{s}$	dos	$\breve{d}$	o	$\breve{d}\breve{o}\breve{s}$

FIGURE 1. Products for the interval algebra, first part.

$[d, o, m]$, $[d, o, p]$, $[d, o, o]$, $[d, o, d]$, $[d, f, d]$, $[d, d, d]$. Although all relative products in the IA can be computed from the cycles, it is convenient to also have the products in a table. The table of relative products of atoms of the IA is given in Figs. 1 and 2. To save space the + signs are omitted, so, for example, $pdoms = p + d + o + m + s$. The table appeared first in [2]. It not only shows relative products of atoms in the IA, but also shows containments for the Allen-Hayes algebra [3] [4]. By the *Allen-Hayes algebra* we mean the direct product of 'all' interval algebras, *i.e.*, the direct product of an indexed system of algebras containing one algebra from each isomorphism type of interval algebras. The Allen-Hayes algebra contains the elements $1'$, p, $\breve{p}$, d, $\breve{d}$, o, $\breve{o}$, m, $\breve{m}$, s, $\breve{s}$, f, and $\breve{f}$. They form a partition, *i.e.*, they are pairwise disjoint and $1 = 1' + p + \breve{p} + d + \breve{d} + o + \breve{o} + m + \breve{m} + s + \breve{s} + f + \breve{f}$. Finally, the relative product of any two of them is contained in (and not necessarily equal to) the corresponding entry in the table.

3. Compass Algebras

Let the universe be the set of all points in the n-dimensional Euclidean space $\mathbb{R}^n$, where $\mathbb{R}$ is the set of real numbers. Let $\mathbb{R}^+$ be the set of positive real numbers. For every vector $\mathbf{v}$ in $\mathbb{R}^n$ define two binary relations on $\mathbb{R}^n$ as follows:

$$D_{\mathbf{v}} = \{\langle \mathbf{x}, \mathbf{y} \rangle : \mathbf{x}, \mathbf{y} \in \mathbb{R}^n \text{ and for some } r \text{ in } \mathbb{R}^+, \mathbf{x} + r\mathbf{v} = \mathbf{y}\},$$
$$E_{\mathbf{v}} = \{\langle \mathbf{x}, \mathbf{y} \rangle : \mathbf{x}, \mathbf{y} \in \mathbb{R}^n \text{ and for some } r \text{ in } \mathbb{R}, \mathbf{x} + r\mathbf{v} = \mathbf{y}\}.$$

Here are some easily proved properties of these relations.

	m	$\breve{m}$	s	$\breve{s}$	f	$\breve{f}$
1'	m	$\breve{m}$	s	$\breve{s}$	f	$\breve{f}$
p	p	$pdoms$	p	p	$pdoms$	p
$\breve{p}$	$\breve{p}d\breve{o}\breve{m}f$	$\breve{p}$	$\breve{p}d\breve{o}\breve{m}f$	$\breve{p}$	$\breve{p}$	$\breve{p}$
d	p	$\breve{p}$	d	$\breve{p}d\breve{o}\breve{m}f$	d	$pdoms$
$\breve{d}$	$\breve{d}o\breve{f}$	$\breve{d}\breve{o}\breve{s}$	$\breve{d}o\breve{f}$	$\breve{d}$	$\breve{d}\breve{o}\breve{s}$	$\breve{d}$
o	p	$\breve{d}\breve{o}\breve{s}$	o	$\breve{d}o\breve{f}$	dos	pom
$\breve{o}$	$\breve{d}o\breve{f}$	$\breve{p}$	$d\breve{o}f$	$\breve{p}\breve{o}\breve{m}$	$\breve{o}$	$\breve{d}\breve{o}\breve{s}$
m	p	$1'f\breve{f}$	m	m	dos	p
$\breve{m}$	$1's\breve{s}$	$\breve{p}$	$d\breve{o}f$	$\breve{p}$	$\breve{m}$	$\breve{m}$
s	p	$\breve{m}$	s	$1's\breve{s}$	d	pom
$\breve{s}$	$\breve{d}o\breve{f}$	$\breve{m}$	$1's\breve{s}$	$\breve{s}$	$\breve{o}$	$\breve{d}$
f	m	$\breve{p}$	d	$\breve{p}\breve{o}\breve{m}$	f	$1'f\breve{f}$
$\breve{f}$	m	$\breve{d}\breve{o}\breve{s}$	o	$\breve{d}$	$1'f\breve{f}$	$\breve{f}$

FIGURE 2. Products for interval algebra, second part.

Theorem 1. (i) $D_0 = E_0 = 1' = \{ \langle \mathbf{x}, \mathbf{x} \rangle : \mathbf{x} \in \mathbb{R}^n \}$,

(ii) $\breve{D}_{\mathbf{v}} = D_{-\mathbf{v}} = \{ \langle \mathbf{x}, \mathbf{y} \rangle :$ *for some* r *in* $\mathbb{R}^+$, $\mathbf{x} - r\mathbf{v} = \mathbf{y} \}$,

(iii) $D_{\mathbf{v}} ; D_{\mathbf{v}} = D_{\mathbf{v}}$,

(iv) $D_{\mathbf{v}} = D_{r\mathbf{v}}$ and $E_{\mathbf{v}} = E_{r\mathbf{v}}$ whenever $r \in \mathbb{R}^+$,

(v) $E_{\mathbf{v}} = \breve{E}_{\mathbf{v}} = E_{\mathbf{v}} ; E_{\mathbf{v}} = D_{\mathbf{v}} ; \breve{D}_{\mathbf{v}} = \breve{D}_{\mathbf{v}} ; D_{\mathbf{v}} = D_{\mathbf{v}} + \breve{D}_{\mathbf{v}} + D_0$,

(vi) $E_{\mathbf{v}}$ *is an equivalence relation on* $\mathbb{R}^n$,

(vii) $D_{\mathbf{v}} ; D_{\mathbf{w}} = D_{\mathbf{w}} ; D_{\mathbf{v}} = \{ \langle \mathbf{x}, \mathbf{y} \rangle :$ *for some* r, s *in* $\mathbb{R}^+$, $\mathbf{x} + r\mathbf{v} + s\mathbf{w} = \mathbf{y} \}$,

(viii) $E_{\mathbf{v}} ; E_{\mathbf{w}} = E_{\mathbf{w}} ; E_{\mathbf{v}} = \{ \langle \mathbf{x}, \mathbf{y} \rangle :$ *for some* r, s *in* $\mathbb{R}$, $\mathbf{x} + r\mathbf{v} + s\mathbf{w} = \mathbf{y} \}$,

(ix) $\langle \mathbf{x}, \mathbf{y} \rangle \in E_{\mathbf{v}}$ *if and only if* $\mathbf{y} - \mathbf{x}$ *is in the subspace spanned by* $\mathbf{v}$,

(x) $\langle \mathbf{x}, \mathbf{y} \rangle \in E_{\mathbf{v}} ; E_{\mathbf{w}}$ *if and only if* $\mathbf{y} - \mathbf{x}$ *is in the subspace spanned by* $\mathbf{v}$ *and* $\mathbf{w}$,

(xi) $\langle \mathbf{x}, \mathbf{y} \rangle \in E_{\mathbf{v}_1} ; \ldots ; E_{\mathbf{v}_m}$ *if and only if* $\mathbf{y} - \mathbf{x}$ *is in the subspace spanned by* $\mathbf{v}_1, \ldots, \mathbf{v}_m$.

For any m vectors $\mathbf{v}_1, \ldots, \mathbf{v}_m \in \mathbb{R}^n$, let $\mathfrak{C}_n[\mathbf{v}_1, \ldots, \mathbf{v}_m]$ be the subalgebra of $\mathfrak{Re}(\mathbb{R}^n)$ generated by the relations $D_{\mathbf{v}_1}, \ldots, D_{\mathbf{v}_m}$. $\mathfrak{C}_n[\mathbf{v}_1, \ldots, \mathbf{v}_m]$ is called the *n-dimensional compass algebra determined by* $\mathbf{v}_1, \ldots, \mathbf{v}_m$. If $\mathbf{v}$ and $\mathbf{w}$ are a linearly dependent pair of nonzero vectors, then either $D_{\mathbf{v}} = D_{\mathbf{w}}$ or $D_{\mathbf{v}} = \breve{D}_{\mathbf{w}}$. If $\mathbf{v}$ and $\mathbf{w}$ both appear in a list of vectors generating a compass algebra, then $\mathbf{v}$ can be deleted from the list, and the same compass algebra will still be obtained from the remaining vectors. Even if the vectors are pairwise linearly independent, deleting one of them may not result in a strictly smaller compass algebra. The structure of $\mathfrak{C}_n[\mathbf{v}_1, \ldots, \mathbf{v}_m]$ depends heavily on the choice of

	1'	a	$\breve{a}$
1'	1'	a	$\breve{a}$
a	a	a	1
$\breve{a}$	$\breve{a}$	1	a

FIGURE 3. Products for $\mathfrak{C}_1[\langle 1\rangle]$

	1'	0'
1'	1'	0'
0'	0'	1

FIGURE 4. Products for $\mathfrak{C}_1[\langle 0\rangle]$

vectors. But if $\mathbf{v}_1, \ldots, \mathbf{v}_m$ is a linear independent set of vectors, then the structure of $\mathfrak{C}_n[\mathbf{v}_1, \ldots, \mathbf{v}_m]$ is completely determined by m. More exactly, if $\mathbf{v}_1, \ldots, \mathbf{v}_m$ and $\mathbf{v}'_1, \ldots, \mathbf{v}'_m$ are two linearly independent sets of vectors in $\mathbb{R}^n$ (hence $m \leq n$), then $\mathfrak{C}_n[\mathbf{v}_1, \ldots, \mathbf{v}_m]$ is isomorphic to $\mathfrak{C}_n[\mathbf{v}'_1, \ldots, \mathbf{v}'_m]$.

The 1-dimensional compass algebra $\mathfrak{C}_1[\langle 1\rangle]$ generated by the 1-dimensional vector $\langle 1\rangle$ has three atoms, namely $D_{\langle 1\rangle}$, $D_{\langle -1\rangle}$, and $D_{\langle 0\rangle}$. $\mathfrak{C}_1[\langle 1\rangle]$ is known as the 'Point Algebra' [15] [17] [16] [39] [40] [41] [43] [44]. For a description of the structure of $\mathfrak{C}_1[\langle 1\rangle]$ in terms of atoms and cycles, let $1' = D_{\langle 0\rangle}$, $a = D_{\langle 1\rangle}$, and $\breve{a} = D_{\langle -1\rangle}$. Then the cyclesets of $\mathfrak{A}$ are $[1', 1', 1']$, $[1', a, a]$, $[a, 1', a]$, and $[a, a, a]$. The table of relative products of atoms is in Fig. 3. Every 1-dimensional vector in 1-space must determine one of the relations $D_{\langle 1\rangle}$, $D_{\langle -1\rangle}$, or $D_{\langle 0\rangle}$, so no new 1-dimensional compass algebras are obtained by considering two or more vectors in 1-dimensional space. However, there is one other 1-dimensional compass algebra, namely $\mathfrak{C}_1[\langle 0\rangle]$. This algebra has two atoms, namely $D_{\langle 0\rangle} = 1'$ and $D_{\langle 1\rangle} + D_{\langle -1\rangle} = 0'$. The cyclesets of $\mathfrak{A}$ are $[1', 1', 1']$, $[1', 0', 0']$, and $[0', 0', 0']$, and the table of relative products of atoms is in Fig. 4. By comparing this and the previous table it can be seen that $\mathfrak{C}_1[\langle 0\rangle]$ is isomorphic to a subalgebra of $\mathfrak{C}_1[\langle 1\rangle]$, the one with atoms 1' and $a + \breve{a}$. Also, $\mathfrak{C}_1[\langle 0\rangle]$ is isomorphic to $\mathfrak{C}_n[\langle 0\rangle]$ for every integer n.

Now we consider 2-dimensional compass algebras. Among these are particular algebras which inspired the name "compass algebra". We start with the compass algebra $\mathfrak{C}_2[\langle 1, 0\rangle, \langle 0, 1\rangle]$. We would get the same algebra with any two linearly independent vectors in $\mathbb{R}^2$, but these two allow us to dub $E_{\langle 1,0\rangle}$ the 'east-west' direction, while $E_{\langle 0,1\rangle}$ is the 'north-south' direction. Thus $C_2[\langle 0, 1\rangle, \langle 1, 0\rangle]$ is a '2-directional' algebra of relations. 'East', 'west', 'north', and 'south' are the relations $D_{\langle 1,0\rangle}$, $D_{\langle -1,0\rangle}$, $D_{\langle 0,1\rangle}$, and $D_{\langle 0,-1\rangle}$, respectively. In the standard Euclidean plane of analytic geometry, the points 'east' of the origin are all the points on the positive part of the x-axis, and so on. $\mathfrak{C}_2[\langle 1, 0\rangle, \langle 0, 1\rangle]$ has nine atoms, namely $D_{\langle 0,0\rangle}$, $D_{\langle 1,0\rangle}$, $D_{\langle -1,0\rangle}$, $D_{\langle 0,1\rangle}$, $D_{\langle 0,-1\rangle}$, $D_{\langle 0,1\rangle};D_{\langle 1,0\rangle}$,

	1'	a	$\breve{a}$	b	$\breve{b}$	c	$\breve{c}$	d	$\breve{d}$
1'	1'	a	$\breve{a}$	b	$\breve{b}$	c	$\breve{c}$	d	$\breve{d}$
a	a	a	$1'a\breve{a}$	b	$\breve{b}\breve{c}\breve{d}$	b	$\breve{d}$	bcd	$\breve{d}$
b	b	b	bcd	b	1	b	$ab\breve{d}$	bcd	$ab\breve{d}$
c	c	b	d	b	$d\breve{a}\breve{b}$	c	$1'c\breve{c}$	d	$ab\breve{d}$
d	d	bcd	d	bcd	$d\breve{a}\breve{b}$	d	$d\breve{a}\breve{b}$	d	1
$\breve{a}$	$\breve{a}$	$1'a\breve{a}$	$\breve{a}$	bcd	$\breve{b}$	d	$\breve{b}$	d	$\breve{b}\breve{c}\breve{d}$
$\breve{b}$	$\breve{b}$	$\breve{b}\breve{c}\breve{d}$	$\breve{b}$	1	$\breve{b}$	$d\breve{a}\breve{b}$	$\breve{b}$	$d\breve{a}\breve{b}$	$\breve{b}\breve{c}\breve{d}$
$\breve{c}$	$\breve{c}$	$\breve{d}$	$\breve{b}$	$ab\breve{d}$	$\breve{b}$	$1'c\breve{c}$	$\breve{c}$	$d\breve{a}\breve{b}$	$\breve{d}$
$\breve{d}$	$\breve{d}$	$\breve{d}$	$\breve{b}\breve{c}\breve{d}$	$ab\breve{d}$	$\breve{b}\breve{c}\breve{d}$	$ab\breve{d}$	$\breve{d}$	1	$\breve{d}$

FIGURE 5. Products for $\mathfrak{C}_2[\langle 1,0\rangle, \langle 0,1\rangle]$

$D_{\langle 0,1\rangle};D_{\langle -1,0\rangle}$, $D_{\langle 0,-1\rangle};D_{\langle 1,0\rangle}$, and $D_{\langle 0,-1\rangle};D_{\langle 0,-1\rangle}$. The last four atoms could be called 'northeasterly', 'northwesterly', 'southeasterly', and 'southwesterly', respectively, since they do not correspond exactly with directions of the compass. The points in the Euclidean plane which can be reached by going northeasterly from the origin are exactly those in the first quadrant. Let

$$
\begin{array}{ll}
1' = D_{\langle 0,0\rangle} = \text{identity} & \\
a = D_{\langle 1,0\rangle} = \text{east} & b = a;c = c;a = \text{northeasterly} \\
\breve{a} = D_{\langle -1,0\rangle} = \text{west} & \breve{b} = \breve{c};\breve{a} = \breve{a};\breve{c} = \text{southwesterly} \\
c = D_{\langle 0,1\rangle} = \text{north} & d = \breve{a};c = c;\breve{a} = \text{northwesterly} \\
\breve{c} = D_{\langle 0,-1\rangle} = \text{south} & \breve{d} = \breve{c};a = a;\breve{c} = \text{southeasterly}
\end{array}
$$

Then the 33 cyclesets of $\mathfrak{C}_2[\langle 1,0\rangle, \langle 0,1\rangle]$ are $[1',1',1']$, $[1',a,a]$, $[a,1',a]$, $[1',b,b]$, $[b,1',b]$, $[1',c,c]$, $[c,1',c]$, $[1',d,d]$, $[d,1',d]$, $[a,a,a]$, $[a,b,b]$, $[a,c,b]$, $[a,d,b]$, $[a,d,c]$, $[a,d,d]$, $[b,a,b]$, $[b,b,b]$, $[b,c,b]$, $[b,d,b]$, $[b,d,c]$, $[b,d,d]$, $[c,a,b]$, $[c,b,b]$, $[c,c,c]$, $[c,d,d]$, $[d,a,b]$, $[d,a,c]$, $[d,a,d]$, $[d,b,b]$, $[d,b,c]$, $[d,b,d]$, $[d,c,d]$, $[d,d,d]$. The relative products of atoms are given in Fig. 5. The compass algebra $\mathfrak{C}_2[\langle 1,0\rangle, \langle 1,1\rangle, \langle 0,1\rangle]$ has 13 atoms, namely 1', a, b, c, d, e, f, $\breve{a}$, $\breve{b}$, $\breve{c}$, $\breve{d}$, $\breve{e}$, and $\breve{f}$, where $1' = D_{\langle 0,0\rangle}$, $a = D_{\langle 1,0\rangle}$, $b = D_{\langle 1,0\rangle};D_{\langle 1,1\rangle}$, $c = D_{\langle 1,1\rangle}$, $d = D_{\langle 1,1\rangle};D_{\langle 0,1\rangle}$, $e = D_{\langle 0,1\rangle}$, and $f = D_{\langle 0,1\rangle};D_{\langle -1,0\rangle}$. There are 89 cyclesets, each having the form $[x,y,z]$ with x,y,z in $\{1',a,b,c,d,e,f\}$. The cyclesets are not listed, but they can be read from the tables of relative products in Figs. 6, 7.

Set $\hat{x} = x + \breve{x}$ for every x in $\mathfrak{C}_2[\langle 1,0\rangle, \langle 1,1\rangle, \langle 0,1\rangle]$. Then $1' + \hat{a} = E_{\langle 1,0\rangle}$, $1' + \hat{c} = E_{\langle 1,1\rangle}$, $1' + \hat{e} = E_{\langle 0,1\rangle}$, *etc.* and 1', $\hat{a}$, $\hat{b}$, $\hat{c}$, $\hat{d}$, $\hat{e}$, and $\hat{f}$ are the atoms of a subalgebra called the 'symmetric subalgebra' of $\mathfrak{C}_2[\langle 1,0\rangle, \langle 1,1\rangle, \langle 0,1\rangle]$. The table of products for this subalgebra is in Fig. 8. Consider the 2-dimensional compass algebra $\mathfrak{C}_2[\langle 1,0\rangle, \langle 1,1\rangle, \langle 0,1\rangle, \langle -1,1\rangle]$. Besides the directions 'east-west' $E_{\langle 1,0\rangle}$ and 'north-south' $E_{\langle 0,1\rangle}$, this algebra has directions 'northeast-southwest' $E_{\langle 1,1\rangle}$ and 'southeast-northwest' $E_{\langle -1,1\rangle}$. There are 17 atoms, namely $D_{\langle 0,0\rangle}$

	1'	a	ă	b	b̌	c	c̆
1'	1'	a	ă	b	b̌	c	c̆
a	a	a	1'aă	b	b̌c̆ďĕf̌	b	ďĕf̌
ă	ă	1'aă	ă	bcdef	b̌	def	b̌
b	b	b	bcdef	b	1	b	abďĕf̌
b̌	b̌	b̌c̆ďĕf̌	b̌	1	b̌	defăb̌	b̌
c	c	b	def	b	defăb̌	c	1'cc̆
c̆	c̆	ďĕf̌	b̌	abďĕf̌	b̌	1'cc̆	c̆
d	d	bcd	def	bcd	defăb̌	d	defăb̌
ď	ď	ďĕf̌	b̌c̆ď	abďĕf̌	b̌c̆ď	abďĕf̌	ď
e	e	bcd	f	bcd	făb̌	d	făb̌
ĕ	ĕ	f̌	b̌c̆ď	abf̌	b̌c̆ď	abf̌	ď
f	f	bcdef	f	bcdef	făb̌	def	făb̌
f̌	f̌	f̌	b̌c̆ďĕf̌	abf̌	b̌c̆ďĕf̌	abf̌	ďĕf̌

FIGURE 6. Products for $\mathfrak{C}_2[\langle 1,0\rangle, \langle 1,1\rangle, \langle 0,1\rangle]$, first part

	d	ď	e	ĕ	f	f̌
1'	d	ď	e	ĕ	f	f̌
a	bcd	ďĕf̌	bcd	f̌	bcdef	f̌
ă	def	b̌c̆ď	f	b̌c̆ď	f	b̌c̆ďĕf̌
b	bcd	abďĕf̌	bcd	abf̌	bcdef	abf̌
b̌	defăb̌	b̌c̆ď	făb̌	b̌c̆ď	făb̌	b̌c̆ďĕf̌
c	d	abďĕf̌	d	abf̌	def	abf̌
c̆	defăb̌	ď	făb̌	ď	făb̌	ďĕf̌
d	d	1	d	abcdf̌	def	abcdf̌
ď	1	ď	făb̌c̆ď	ď	făb̌c̆ď	ďĕf̌
e	d	făb̌c̆ď	e	1'eĕ	f	abcdf̌
ĕ	abcdf̌	ď	1'eĕ	ĕ	făb̌c̆ď	f̌
f	def	făb̌c̆ď	f	făb̌c̆ď	f	1
f̌	abcdf̌	ďĕf̌	abcdf̌	f̌	1	f̌

FIGURE 7. Products for $\mathfrak{C}_2[\langle 1,0\rangle, \langle 1,1\rangle, \langle 0,1\rangle]$, second part

	1'	$\hat{a}$	$\hat{b}$	$\hat{c}$	$\hat{d}$	$\hat{e}$	$\hat{f}$
1'	1'	$\hat{a}$	$\hat{b}$	$\hat{c}$	$\hat{d}$	$\hat{e}$	$\hat{f}$
$\hat{a}$	$\hat{a}$	1'$\hat{a}$	$\hat{b}\hat{c}\hat{d}\hat{e}\hat{f}$	$\hat{b}\hat{d}\hat{e}\hat{f}$	$\hat{b}\hat{c}\hat{d}\hat{e}\hat{f}$	$\hat{b}\hat{c}\hat{d}\hat{f}$	$\hat{b}\hat{c}\hat{d}\hat{e}\hat{f}$
$\hat{b}$	$\hat{b}$	$\hat{b}\hat{c}\hat{d}\hat{e}\hat{f}$	1	$\hat{a}\hat{b}\hat{d}\hat{e}\hat{f}$	$\hat{a}\hat{b}\hat{c}\hat{d}\hat{e}\hat{f}$	$\hat{a}\hat{b}\hat{c}\hat{d}\hat{f}$	$\hat{a}\hat{b}\hat{c}\hat{d}\hat{e}\hat{f}$
$\hat{c}$	$\hat{c}$	$\hat{b}\hat{d}\hat{e}\hat{f}$	$\hat{a}\hat{b}\hat{d}\hat{e}\hat{f}$	1'$\hat{c}$	$\hat{a}\hat{b}\hat{d}\hat{e}\hat{f}$	$\hat{a}\hat{b}\hat{d}\hat{f}$	$\hat{a}\hat{b}\hat{d}\hat{e}\hat{f}$
$\hat{d}$	$\hat{d}$	$\hat{b}\hat{c}\hat{d}\hat{e}\hat{f}$	$\hat{a}\hat{b}\hat{c}\hat{d}\hat{e}\hat{f}$	$\hat{a}\hat{b}\hat{d}\hat{e}\hat{f}$	1	$\hat{a}\hat{b}\hat{c}\hat{d}\hat{f}$	$\hat{a}\hat{b}\hat{c}\hat{d}\hat{e}\hat{f}$
$\hat{e}$	$\hat{e}$	$\hat{b}\hat{c}\hat{d}\hat{f}$	$\hat{a}\hat{b}\hat{c}\hat{d}\hat{f}$	$\hat{a}\hat{b}\hat{d}\hat{f}$	$\hat{a}\hat{b}\hat{c}\hat{d}\hat{f}$	1'$\hat{e}$	$\hat{a}\hat{b}\hat{c}\hat{d}\hat{f}$
$\hat{f}$	$\hat{f}$	$\hat{b}\hat{c}\hat{d}\hat{e}\hat{f}$	$\hat{a}\hat{b}\hat{c}\hat{d}\hat{e}\hat{f}$	$\hat{a}\hat{b}\hat{d}\hat{e}\hat{f}$	$\hat{a}\hat{b}\hat{c}\hat{d}\hat{e}\hat{f}$	$\hat{a}\hat{b}\hat{c}\hat{d}\hat{f}$	1

FIGURE 8. Products for the symmetric subalgebra of $\mathfrak{C}_2[\langle 1,0\rangle, \langle 1,1\rangle, \langle 0,1\rangle]$

	1'	a	$\breve{a}$	b
1'	1'	a	$\breve{a}$	b
a	a	a	1'$a\breve{a}$	b
$\breve{a}$	$\breve{a}$	1'$a\breve{a}$	$\breve{a}$	b
b	b	b	b	1

FIGURE 9. Products for $\mathfrak{C}_2[\langle 1,0\rangle]$

and 16 others, listed counterclockwise from the x-axis: $D_{\langle 1,0\rangle}$, $D_{\langle 1,0\rangle};D_{\langle 1,1\rangle}$, $D_{\langle 1,1\rangle}$, $D_{\langle 1,1\rangle};D_{\langle 0,1\rangle}$, $D_{\langle 0,1\rangle}$, $D_{\langle 0,1\rangle};D_{\langle -1,1\rangle}$, $D_{\langle -1,1\rangle}$, $D_{\langle -1,1\rangle};D_{\langle -1,0\rangle}$, $D_{\langle -1,0\rangle}$, $D_{\langle -1,0\rangle};D_{\langle -1,-1\rangle}$, $D_{\langle -1,-1\rangle}$, $D_{\langle -1,-1\rangle};D_{\langle 0,-1\rangle}$, $D_{\langle 0,-1\rangle}$, $D_{\langle 0,-1\rangle};D_{\langle 1,-1\rangle}$, $D_{\langle 1,-1\rangle}$, $D_{\langle 1,-1\rangle};D_{\langle 1,0\rangle}$.

The 2-dimensional compass algebra $\mathfrak{C}_2[\langle 1,0\rangle]$ has just four atoms, namely $D_{\langle 0,0\rangle}$, $D_{\langle 1,0\rangle}$, $D_{\langle -1,0\rangle}$, and $F = (\mathbb{R}^2 \times \mathbb{R}^2) \cdot \overline{D_{\langle 0,0\rangle} + D_{\langle 1,0\rangle} + D_{\langle -1,0\rangle}}$. Note that F is a symmetric relation, *i.e.*, $\breve{F} = F$, unlike $D_{\langle 1,0\rangle}$ or $D_{\langle -1,0\rangle}$. The points of the plane which are in the relation F to the origin are all those which lie in the upper half plane or lower half plane (*i.e.*, not on the x-axis). Let $1' = D_{\langle 0,0\rangle}$, $a = D_{\langle 1,0\rangle}$, $\breve{a} = D_{\langle -1,0\rangle}$, and $b = \overline{1' + a + \breve{a}}$. Then the cyclesets of $\mathfrak{C}_2[\langle 1,0\rangle]$ are $[1',1',1']$, $[1',a,a]$, $[a,1',a]$, $[1',b,b]$, $[a,a,a]$, $[a,b,b]$, $[b,b,b]$, and the relative products of atoms are given in Fig.9. This algebra illustrates a general phenomenon. If $\mathbf{v}_1,\ldots,\mathbf{v}_m \in \mathbb{R}^n$ are pairwise linearly independent but do not span $\mathbb{R}^n$, then $\mathfrak{C}_n[\mathbf{v}_1,\ldots,\mathbf{v}_m]$ will have only one atom for the subspace orthogonal to the subspace spanned by $\mathbf{v}_1,\ldots,\mathbf{v}_m$. Notice that this situation must arise whenever the number of directions is less than the number of dimensions, *i.e.*, whenever $m < n$.

Now we consider 3-dimensional compass algebras. Let $\mathbf{u} = \langle 1,0,0\rangle$, $\mathbf{v} = \langle 0,1,0\rangle$, $\mathbf{w} = \langle 1,1,0\rangle$, $\mathbf{x} = \langle -1,1,0\rangle$ and $\mathbf{y} = \langle 0,0,1\rangle$. The 3-dimensional compass algebra generated by a single vector in $\{\mathbf{u},\mathbf{v},\mathbf{w},\mathbf{x},\mathbf{y}\}$ has 4 atoms. The algebra generated by any two vectors in $\{\mathbf{u},\mathbf{v},\mathbf{w},\mathbf{x},\mathbf{y}\}$ has 10 atoms. Note that

$\mathbf{u}, \mathbf{v}, \mathbf{w}, \mathbf{x}$ all lie in the same 2-dimensional subspace. Hence any three vectors in $\{\mathbf{u}, \mathbf{v}, \mathbf{w}, \mathbf{x}\}$ generate a 3-dimensional compass algebra with 14 atoms, while $\mathfrak{C}_3[\mathbf{u}, \mathbf{v}, \mathbf{w}, \mathbf{x}]$ has 18 atoms. The vector $\mathbf{y}$ and any two vectors in $\{\mathbf{u}, \mathbf{v}, \mathbf{w}, \mathbf{x}\}$ form a linearly independent set, and generate a compass algebra with 27 atoms. The vector $\mathbf{y}$ and any three vectors in $\{\mathbf{u}, \mathbf{v}, \mathbf{w}, \mathbf{x}\}$ generate a compass algebra with 39 atoms. Finally, $\mathfrak{C}_3[\mathbf{u}, \mathbf{v}, \mathbf{w}, \mathbf{x}, \mathbf{y}]$ has 51 atoms.

Not every compass algebra determined by a finite set of vectors is finite. Let $\mathbf{z} = \langle 1,1,1\rangle$. Then $\mathfrak{C}_3[\mathbf{u}, \mathbf{v}, \mathbf{y}, \mathbf{z}] = \mathfrak{C}_3[\langle 1,0,0\rangle, \langle 0,1,0\rangle, \langle 0,0,1\rangle, \langle 1,1,1\rangle]$ is infinite. To see this, let $X_0 = E_{\mathbf{u}}$, $Y_0 = E_{\mathbf{v}}$, $Z_0 = E_{\mathbf{y}}$, and, for every integer n, $X_{n+1} = X_n ; E_{\mathbf{z}} \cdot Y_n ; Z_n$, $Y_{n+1} = Y_n ; E_{\mathbf{z}} \cdot X_n ; Z_n$, and $Z_{n+1} = Z_n ; E_{\mathbf{z}} \cdot X_n ; Y_n$. Then X_n, Y_n, and Z_n are all distinct equivalence relations for every n. In particular,

$$
\begin{array}{lll}
X_0 = E_{\langle 1,0,0\rangle} & Y_0 = E_{\langle 0,1,0\rangle} & Z_0 = E_{\langle 0,0,1\rangle} \\
X_1 = E_{\langle 0,1,1\rangle} & Y_1 = E_{\langle 1,0,1\rangle} & Z_1 = E_{\langle 1,1,0\rangle} \\
X_2 = E_{\langle 2,1,1\rangle} & Y_2 = E_{\langle 1,2,1\rangle} & Z_2 = E_{\langle 1,1,2\rangle} \\
X_3 = E_{\langle 2,3,3\rangle} & Y_3 = E_{\langle 3,2,3\rangle} & Z_3 = E_{\langle 3,3,2\rangle} \\
X_4 = E_{\langle 6,5,5\rangle} & Y_4 = E_{\langle 5,6,5\rangle} & Z_4 = E_{\langle 5,5,6\rangle} \\
\vdots & \vdots & \vdots
\end{array}
$$

4. Some NP-complete Constraint Satisfiability Problems

Let $\mathfrak{A}$ be a relation algebra. An *$\mathfrak{A}$-matrix* is a matrix of elements of $\mathfrak{A}$. Suppose M is an n-by-n $\mathfrak{A}$-matrix. We say M is *zeroless* if no entry in M is 0, and M is *closed* if $M_{ii} \leq 1'$, $(M_{ij})^{\smile} = M_{ji}$, and $M_{ij} \leq M_{ik} ; M_{kj}$ whenever $1 \leq i, j, k \leq n$. If N is another n-by-n matrix, we say N is a *reduction* of M, in symbols, $N \leq M$, if $N_{ij} \leq M_{ij}$ whenever $1 \leq i, j \leq n$. If X is a set of elements of $\mathfrak{A}$, we say M is *bounded by* X if every entry of M is included in some element of X.

A *binary constraint matrix* is a matrix of binary relations. An n-by-n binary constraint matrix M determines an n-ary relation $R(M) = \{\langle p_1, \ldots, p_n\rangle : \langle p_i, p_j\rangle \in M_{ij}$ whenever $1 \leq i, j \leq n\}$. The matrix M specifies a *binary constraint problem*. The *solutions* to this problem are the n-tuples in $R(M)$, and the problem is *solvable* if it has a solution. Let U be the set of elements that appear in any pair in any relation in M. Each n-tuple $\langle p_1, \ldots, p_n\rangle$ of elements of U corresponds naturally to an n-by-n matrix N of atoms of $\mathfrak{Re}(U)$, where $N_{ij} = \{\langle p_i, p_j\rangle\}$ whenever $1 \leq i, j \leq n$. Note that $\langle p_1, \ldots, p_n\rangle$ is a solution to M if and only if its corresponding matrix N is a reduction of M. Furthermore, as a binary constraint problem, M has a solution just in case there is a closed zeroless reduction of M bounded by the set of atoms of $\mathfrak{Re}(U)$.

This last observation permits us to generalize the concept of constraint satisfaction to arbitrary atomic relation algebras. Let $\mathfrak{A}$ be an atomic relation algebra and let M be an $\mathfrak{A}$-matrix. We say that M is *proto-solvable over* $\mathfrak{A}$ if there is a closed zeroless reduction of M which is bounded by the set of atoms of $\mathfrak{A}$. Note that if N is a closed zeroless $\mathfrak{A}$-matrix bounded by the atoms of $\mathfrak{A}$, then all the entries in N must actually be atoms of $\mathfrak{A}$. Such a matrix, whose entries are all atoms of $\mathfrak{A}$, is called *atomic*. So the $\mathfrak{A}$-matrix M is proto-solvable if it has a closed atomic reduction N. Such an N is called a ***proto-solution***. The ***constraint satisfiability problem*** for an atomic relation algebra $\mathfrak{A}$ is this: given an $\mathfrak{A}$-matrix, determine whether it has a proto-solution.

For an $\mathfrak{Re}(U)$-matrix M, the solutions and proto-solutions (over $\mathfrak{Re}(U)$) are in a one-to-one correspondence, as observed above. But for matrices over atomic subalgebras of $\mathfrak{Re}(U)$, such a correspondence may not exist. Indeed, it is easy to find a set U, a finite subalgebra $\mathfrak{A}$ of $\mathfrak{Re}(U)$, and an $\mathfrak{A}$-matrix M such that M has a proto-solution but no solution. For example, let $U = \{1, 2, 3\}$, let $\mathfrak{A}$ be the subalgebra of $\mathfrak{Re}(U)$ with atoms 1' and 0' ($\mathfrak{A}$ is isomorphic to $\mathfrak{C}_1[\langle 0\rangle]$), and let $M = \begin{pmatrix} 1' & 0' & 0' & 0' \\ 0' & 1' & 0' & 0' \\ 0' & 0' & 1' & 0' \\ 0' & 0' & 0' & 1' \end{pmatrix}$. Then M is a proto-solution of itself, but it has no solution, since any solution of M must be a quadruple $\langle p_1, p_2, p_3, p_4\rangle$ with distinct entries, but there are only three elements in U. On the other hand, M can be considered as a $\mathfrak{C}_1[\langle 0\rangle]$-matrix, in which case it does have solutions, namely all quadruples of distinct real numbers.

We have seen that proto-solutions can exist when solutions do not. It is also possible for solutions to exist when proto-solutions do not: an infinite atomic subalgebra $\mathfrak{A}$ of $\mathfrak{Re}(U)$, where U is a countable infinite set, and an $\mathfrak{A}$-matrix M with a solution but no proto-solution over $\mathfrak{A}$. Examples of this are more difficult to construct, but can be found in [18] and [19]. For such an example, however, it is necessary that $\mathfrak{A}$ be infinite [16, Theorem 5.7].

For the IA, the situation is quite nice. An IA-matrix has a solution if and only if it has a proto-solution [17] [16] and this is true for all isomorphic copies of the IA which are embedded in algebras $\mathfrak{Re}(U)$ where U is not necessarily the set of events based on real numbers. Constraint satisfiability for the IA is NP-complete. A sketch of a proof of this was given in [43]. The idea of that proof is to reduce the 3-clause satisfiability problem (for propositional calculus) to constraint satisfiability for the IA. (Additional details for that proof are given in [44].) Another proof is sketched in [40], where graph-colorability is reduced to constraint satisfiability for the IA. Both of these proofs deal with solutions, not proto-solutions, but, in view of the remarks made above, this makes no difference to the IA.

The NP-completeness of the constraint satisfiability problem for the IA follows from Theorem 2 below. This theorem is not restricted to the IA and indeed applies some compass algebras. It also applies to infinite algebras, such as the Allen-Hayes algebra, and to nonrepresentable algebras.

Theorem 2. *Assume $\mathfrak{A}$ is a relation algebra with elements $x, y, z \neq 0$, such that*

(i) $1', x, \breve{x}, y, \breve{y}, z, \breve{z}$ *are pairwise disjoint,*

(ii) $z \cdot z ; y = 0$,

(iii) $y \cdot x ; y = 0$,

(iv) $x \cdot x ; y = 0$,

(v) $z \cdot x ; z = 0$,

(vi) $y \cdot y ; z = 0$,

(vii) $x \cdot z;x = 0$,

(viii) $z \leq x;y$, $x \leq z;\breve{y}$, $y \leq \breve{x};z$,

(ix) $1' \leq x;\breve{x} \cdot \breve{x};x \cdot y;\breve{y} \cdot \breve{y};y \cdot z;\breve{z} \cdot \breve{z};z$.

Then following problem is NP-complete: **(R)** *Determine whether a matrix M over $\mathfrak{A}$ has a closed zeroless reduction bounded by* $\{1', x, \breve{x}, y, \breve{y}, z, \breve{z}\}$.

Proof. It suffices to show that Graph 3-Colorability [9] is reducible to **(R)**. Let $G = \langle V, E\rangle$ be a graph (*i.e.*, E is a symmetric binary relation on V that is disjoint from the identity relation on V). We may assume without loss of generality that the set V of vertices of G is $\{4, \ldots, |V| + 3\}$, where $|V|$ is the cardinality of V. Let $n = |V| + 3$. Let M be the n-by-n $\mathfrak{A}$-matrix determined by the following stipulations:

(i) $M_{ii} = 1'$ for $1 \leq i \leq n$,

(ii) $M_{12} = x$, $M_{21} = \breve{x}$, $M_{23} = y$, $M_{32} = \breve{y}$, $M_{13} = z$, $M_{31} = \breve{z}$,

(iii) $M_{i1} = 1' + \breve{x} + \breve{z}$, $M_{1i} = 1' + x + z$, $M_{i2} = 1' + x + \breve{y}$, $M_{2i} = 1' + \breve{x} + y$, $M_{i3} = 1' + y + z$, and $M_{3i} = 1' + \breve{y} + \breve{z}$ whenever $i \in V$ (*i.e.*, $4 \leq i \leq n$),

(iv) $M_{ij} = M_{ji} = x + \breve{x} + y + \breve{y} + z + \breve{z}$ whenever $i, j \in V$ and $\langle i, j\rangle \in E$,

(v) in all other cases, $M_{ij} = 1$.

We will show that there is a natural one-to-one correspondence between 3-colorings of the graph G and closed zeroless reductions of M which are bounded by $\{1', x, \breve{x}, y, \breve{y}, z, \breve{z}\}$. It follows that M has a closed zeroless reduction bounded by $\{1', x, \breve{x}, y, \breve{y}, z, \breve{z}\}$ just in case the graph G is 3-colorable.

Suppose that N is a closed zeroless reduction of M which is bounded by $\{1', x, \breve{x}, y, \breve{y}, z, \breve{z}\}$. We will show that N determines a 3-coloring $\gamma : V \to \{1, 2, 3\}$ of G. First, since $1', x, \breve{x}, y, \breve{y}, z, \breve{z}$ are pairwise disjoint, N is zeroless, and N is bounded by $\{1', x, \breve{x}, y, \breve{y}, z, \breve{x}\}$, we concluded that if $1 \leq i, j \leq n$, then exactly one of the following seven statements holds: $N_{ij} \leq 1'$, $N_{ij} \leq x$, $N_{ij} \leq \breve{x}$, $N_{ij} \leq y$, $N_{ij} \leq \breve{y}$, $N_{ij} \leq z$, $N_{ij} \leq \breve{z}$. Now we look at the possible values of N_{i1}, N_{i2}, and N_{i3} for an arbitrary $i \in V$, *i.e.*, for $4 \leq i \leq n$. Since $N \leq M$, we have $N_{12} \leq x$, $N_{23} \leq y$, $N_{13} \leq z$, $N_{i1} \leq 1' + \breve{x} + \breve{z}$, $N_{i2} \leq 1' + x + \breve{y}$, and $N_{i3} \leq 1' + y + z$. If $N_{i1} \leq 1'$, then $N_{i2} \leq N_{i1};N_{12} \leq 1';x = x$ and $N_{i3} \leq N_{i1};N_{13} \leq 1';z = z$. Similarly, if $N_{i2} \leq 1'$, then $N_{i1} \leq N_{i2};N_{21} \leq 1';\breve{x} = \breve{x}$ and $N_{i3} \leq N_{i2};N_{23} \leq 1';y = y$. Finally, if $N_{i3} \leq 1'$, then $N_{i1} \leq N_{i3};N_{31} \leq 1';\breve{z} = \breve{z}$ and $N_{i2} \leq N_{i3};N_{32} \leq 1';\breve{y} = \breve{y}$. From these observations it follows that $N_{ik} \leq 1'$ for at most one $k \in \{1, 2, 3\}$. To show $N_{ik} \leq 1'$ for at least one $k \in \{1, 2, 3\}$, we assume $N_{i1} \leq \breve{x} + \breve{z}$, $N_{i2} \leq x + \breve{y}$, and $N_{i3} \leq y + z$, and derive a contradiction. There are two cases. First, if $N_{i3} \leq y$, then $N_{i1} \leq (\breve{x} + \breve{z}) \cdot N_{i3};N_{31} \leq (\breve{x} + \breve{z}) \cdot y;\breve{z} \leq \breve{x}$ and $N_{i2} \leq (x + \breve{y}) \cdot N_{i3};N_{32} \leq (x + \breve{y}) \cdot y;\breve{y} \leq \breve{y}$ by (ii) and (iii), respectively. From these last two equations we get $N_{i2} \leq \breve{y} \cdot N_{i1};N_{12} \leq \breve{y} \cdot \breve{x};x = 0$ by (iv), contradicting the assumption that N is zeroless. Second, if $N_{i3} \leq z$, then $N_{i1} \leq (\breve{x} + \breve{z}) \cdot N_{i3};N_{31} \leq (\breve{x} + \breve{z}) \cdot z;\breve{z} \leq \breve{z}$ and $N_{i2} \leq (x + \breve{y}) \cdot N_{i3};N_{32} \leq (x + \breve{y}) \cdot z;\breve{y} \leq x$ by (v) and (vi), respectively. From these last two equations we get $N_{i2} \leq x \cdot N_{i1};N_{12} \leq x \cdot \breve{z};x = 0$ by (vii), again contradicting the assumption that N is zeroless. This exhausts the possibilities. Thus we have $N_{ik} \leq 1'$ for exactly one $k \in \{1, 2, 3\}$. This allows us to define $\gamma : V \to \{1, 2, 3\}$ by $\gamma(i) = k$ if and only if f $N_{ik} \leq 1'$, for every $i \in V$. Now if $\langle i, j\rangle \in E$, then we must have $\gamma(i) \neq \gamma(j)$, for if $\gamma(i) = \gamma(j) = k$, then we have $N_{ik} \leq 1'$ and $N_{jk} \leq 1'$, from which we obtain

$x + \breve{x} + y + \breve{y} + z + \breve{z} = N_{ij} \leq N_{ik};N_{kj} \leq 1';\breve{1}' = 1'$, contradicting (i). Thus γ is a 3-coloring of G.

For the other direction, if we have a 3-coloring $\gamma : V \to \{1, 2, 3\}$ of G, we can get a closed zeroless reduction $N \leq M$ which is bounded by $\{1', x, \breve{x}, y, \breve{y}, z, \breve{z}\}$ as follows. Set $N_{12} = x$, $N_{21} = \breve{x}$, $N_{23} = y$, $N_{32} = \breve{y}$, $N_{13} = z$, $N_{31} = \breve{z}$, and $N_{ii} = 1'$ whenever $1 \leq i \leq n$. For all $i, j \in V$, and every $k \in \{1, 2, 3\}$, set $N_{ik} = N_{\gamma(i)k}$, $N_{ki} = N_{k\gamma(i)}$, and $N_{ij} = N_{\gamma(i)\gamma(j)}$. It follows from (viii) and (ix) that this definition gives a closed zeroless matrix N. Obviously, N is bounded by $\{1', x, \breve{x}, y, \breve{y}, z, \breve{z}\}$. The fact that γ is a 3-coloring of G is used to show that $N \leq M$. □

Corollary 3. *Constraint satisfiability is NP-complete for both the algebra* $C_2[\langle 1, 0\rangle, \langle 1, 1\rangle, \langle 0, 1\rangle]$ *and its symmetric subalgebra.*

Proof. Use Theorem 2 with $x = \hat{a}$, $y = \hat{c}$, and $z = \hat{e}$. □

Corollary 4. *Constraint satisfiability is NP-complete for both the interval algebra and the Allen-Hayes algebra.*

Proof. Use Theorem 2 with $x = m$, $y = f$, and $z = s$. □

Theorem 2 applies to a 3-directional compass algebra. For 2-directional compass algebras we need another theorem.

Theorem 5. *Let* $\mathfrak{A}$ *be a relation algebra with nonzero elements* x, y, z *such that*

(i) $1', x, \breve{x}, y, \breve{y}, z, \breve{z}$ *are pairwise disjoint,*
(ii) $y \cdot x;x = 0$,
(iii) $y \cdot x;y = 0$,
(iv) $y \cdot y;x = 0$,
(v) $y \cdot y;z = 0$,
(vi) $y \cdot z;y = 0$,
(vii) $y \cdot z;z = 0$,
(viii) $x \cdot z;x = 0$,
(ix) $x \cdot x;z = 0$,
(x) $z \leq z;z$, $z \leq z;\breve{z}$, $z \leq \breve{z};z$,
(xi) $y \leq y;y$, $y \leq y;\breve{y}$, $y \leq \breve{y};y$,
(xii) $y \leq x;z$, $x \leq y;\breve{z}$, $z \leq \breve{x};y$,
(xiii) $y \leq z;x$, $z \leq y;\breve{x}$, $x \leq \breve{z};y$,
(xiv) $z \leq z;y$, $z \leq z;\breve{y}$, $y \leq \breve{z};z$,
(xv) $z \leq y;z$, $y \leq z;\breve{z}$, $z \leq \breve{y};z$,
(xvi) $z \leq z;x$, $z \leq z;\breve{x}$, $x \leq \breve{z};z$,
(xvii) $z \leq x;z$, $x \leq z;\breve{z}$, $z \leq \breve{x};z$,
(xviii) $1' \leq x;\breve{x} \cdot \breve{x};x \cdot y;\breve{y} \cdot \breve{y};y \cdot z;\breve{z} \cdot \breve{z};z$.

Then the following problem is NP-complete: **(R)** *Determine whether a network* N *over* $\mathfrak{A}$ *with labels in* $\{y, x + y + z, z + \breve{z}\}$ *has a closed zeroless reduction bounded by* $\{1', x, \breve{x}, y, \breve{y}, z, \breve{z}\}$.

Proof. As in the previous proof, we show that Graph 3-Colorability [9] is reducible to (**R**). Let $G = \langle V, E\rangle$ be a graph with vertex set $V = \{3, \ldots, |V|+2\}$, Let $n = |V| + 2$. Let M be the n-by-n $\mathfrak{A}$-matrix determined by the following stipulations: $M_{12} = y$, $M_{21} = \breve{y}$, $M_{1i} = M_{i2} = x + y + z$ for every $i \in V$, $M_{ij} = z + \breve{z}$ whenever $i, j \in V$ and $\langle i, j\rangle \in E$, The 3-colorings of G correspond to closed zeroless reductions of M which are bounded by $\{1', x, \breve{x}, y, \breve{y}, z, \breve{z}\}$.

Suppose that N is a closed zeroless reduction of M which is bounded by $\{1', x, \breve{x}, y, \breve{y}, z, \breve{z}\}$. We show that N determines a 3-coloring $\gamma : V \to \{1, 2, 3\}$. First, if $1 \leq i, j \leq n$, then exactly one of the following seven statements holds: $N_{ij} \leq 1'$, $N_{ij} \leq x$, $N_{ij} \leq \breve{x}$, $N_{ij} \leq y$, $N_{ij} \leq \breve{y}$, $N_{ij} \leq z$, and $N_{ij} \leq \breve{z}$. Now we look at the possible values of N_{1i} and N_{i2} for an arbitrary $i \in V$. We have $N_{12} \leq y$, $N_{1i} \leq x+y+z$, $N_{i2} \leq x+y+z$. Hence there are nine cases, six of which are ruled out because they contradict one of the hypotheses. For example, if $N_{1i} \leq x$ and $N_{i2} \leq y$, then by (iii) we have $N_{12} \leq y \cdot N_{1i};N_{i2} \leq y \cdot x;y = 0$, contradicting the assumption that N is zeroless. The following table shows which cases are ruled out by hypotheses (ii)–(vii).

	$N_{i2} \leq x$	$N_{i2} \leq y$	$N_{i2} \leq z$
$N_{1i} \leq x$	No, by (ii).	No, by (iii).	
$N_{1i} \leq y$	No, by (iv).		No, by (v).
$N_{1i} \leq z$		No, by (vi).	No, by (vii).

The remaining three cases are used to define $\gamma : V \to \{1, 2, 3\}$. For every $i \in V$,

$$\gamma(i) = \begin{cases} 1 & \text{if } N_{1i} \leq z \text{ and } N_{i2} \leq x \\ 2 & \text{if } N_{1i} \leq y \text{ and } N_{i2} \leq y \,. \\ 3 & \text{if } N_{1i} \leq x \text{ and } N_{i2} \leq z \end{cases}$$

Now we must show $\gamma(i) \neq \gamma(j)$ whenever $\langle i, j\rangle \in E$. Since N is closed and $N \leq M$, we have $N_{ij} \leq z + \breve{z}$ and $N_{ji} \leq z + \breve{z}$. If $\gamma(i) = 1$ then $N_{i2} \leq x$, so by (ix) we get $N_{j2} \leq (x + y + z) \cdot N_{ji};N_{i2} \leq (x + y + z) \cdot (z + \breve{z});x \leq (x + y + z) \cdot (z;x + \breve{z};x) \leq y + z$. Therefore, either $N_{j2} \leq y$ and $\gamma(j) = 2$, or else $N_{j2} \leq z$ and $\gamma(j) = 3$. Thus $\gamma(i) \neq \gamma(j)$. If $\gamma(i) = 2$ then $N_{i2} \leq y$, so $N_{j2} \leq (x+y+z)\cdot N_{ji};N_{i2} \leq (x+y+z)\cdot(z+\breve{z});y \leq (x+y+z)\cdot(z;y+\breve{z};y) \leq x+z$. by (vi). Thus either $N_{j2} \leq x$ and $\gamma(j) = 1$, or else $N_{j2} \leq z$ and $\gamma(j) = 3$. Again, $\gamma(i) \neq z(j)$. Finally, if $\gamma(i) = 3$ then $N_{1i} \leq x$, so $N_{1j} \leq (x + y + z) \cdot N_{1i};N_{ij} \leq (x + y + z) \cdot x;(z + \breve{z}) \leq (x + y + z) \cdot (x;z + x;\breve{z}) \leq y + z$ by (viii). Either $N_{j2} \leq x$ and $\gamma(j) = 2$, or else $N_{j2} \leq z$ and $\gamma(j) = 1$. Hence $\gamma(i) \neq \gamma(j)$. This completes the proof that $\gamma(i) \neq \gamma(j)$ whenever $\langle i, j\rangle \in E$, and shows that γ is a 3-coloring of G.

For the other direction, if we have a 3-coloring $\gamma : V \to \{1, 2, 3\}$, we can get a closed zeroless reduction $N \leq M$ which is bounded by $\{1', x, \breve{x}, y, \breve{y}, z, \breve{z}\}$. Set

$N_{12} = y$, $N_{21} = \breve{y}$, and $N_{ii} = 1'$ whenever $1 \leq i \leq n$. For all $i, j \in V$, set

$$N_{ij} = \begin{cases} 1' & \text{if } \gamma(i) = \gamma(j) \\ z & \text{if } \gamma(i) > \gamma(j) \\ \breve{z} & \text{if } \gamma(i) < \gamma(j) \end{cases},$$

$$N_{1i} = \begin{cases} z & \text{if } \gamma(i) = 1 \\ y & \text{if } \gamma(i) = 2 \\ x & \text{if } \gamma(i) = 3 \end{cases}, \quad N_{i2} = \begin{cases} x & \text{if } \gamma(i) = 1 \\ y & \text{if } \gamma(i) = 2 \\ z & \text{if } \gamma(i) = 3 \end{cases},$$

$$N_{i1} = \begin{cases} \breve{z} & \text{if } \gamma(i) = 1 \\ \breve{y} & \text{if } \gamma(i) = 2 \\ \breve{x} & \text{if } \gamma(i) = 3 \end{cases}, \quad N_{2i} = \begin{cases} \breve{x} & \text{if } \gamma(i) = 1 \\ \breve{y} & \text{if } \gamma(i) = 2 \\ \breve{z} & \text{if } \gamma(i) = 3 \end{cases}.$$

It follows from (x)–(xviii) that N is closed and zeroless. Obviously, N is bounded by $\{1', x, \breve{x}, y, \breve{y}, z, \breve{z}\}$. The fact that γ is a 3-coloring of G is used to show that $N \leq M$. □

To see the necessity of (x)–(xviii), consider the following example. Let $G = \langle V, E \rangle$ where $V = \{3, 4, 5\}$ and $E = \emptyset$. Let $\gamma : V \to \{1, 2, 3\}$ be the 3-coloring of G defined by $\gamma(i) = i - 2$ for every $i \in V$. The resulting N is shown below. The matrix N is closed if and only if (x)–(xviii) hold.

$$N = \begin{pmatrix} 1' & y & z & y & x \\ \breve{y} & 1' & \breve{x} & \breve{y} & \breve{z} \\ \breve{z} & x & 1' & \breve{z} & \breve{z} \\ \breve{y} & y & z & 1' & \breve{z} \\ \breve{x} & z & z & z & 1' \end{pmatrix}$$

Corollary 6. *Constraint satisfiability for $C_2[\langle 1, 0 \rangle, \langle 0, 1 \rangle]$ is NP-complete. The same is true for any compass algebra with at least two directions.*

Proof. By Theorem 5, with $x = a$, $y = c$, and $z = d$. □

These theorems can be extended to show that essentially all but the most trivial compass and interval algebras have NP-hard constraint satisfaction problems.

References

[1] James F. Allen, *An interval-based representation of temporal knowledge*, Proceedings of the Seventh International Joint Conference on Artificial Intelligence, (IJCAI), 1981, pp. 221–226.

[2] James F. Allen, *Maintaining knowledge about temporal intervals*, Communications of the Association for Computing Machinery **26(11)** (November 1983), 832–842.

[3] James F. Allen and Patrick J. Hayes, *A commonsense theory of time*, Proceedings of the International Joint Conference on Artificial Intelligence (IJCAI), 1985, pp. 528–531.

[4] James F. Allen and Patrick J. Hayes, *Moments and points in an interval-based temporal logic*, Tech. Report TR 180, Department of Computer Science, University of Rochester, December 1987.

[5] James F. Allen and Johannes A. Koomen, *Planning using a temporal world model*, Proceedings of the Eighth International Joint Conference on Artificial Intelligence, Karlsruhe, W. Germany, August 1983 (IJCAI), 1983, pp. 741–747.

[6] George Boole, *An investigation of the laws of thought on which are founded the mathematical theories of logic and probabilities*, Walton and Maberley, London, 1854.

[7] George Boole, *The mathematical analysis of logic; being an essay towards a calculus of deductive reasoning*, B. Blackwell, Oxford, 1948, first published in London and Cambridge, 1847.

[8] Louise H. Chin and Alfred Tarski, *Distributive and modular laws in the arithmetic of relation algebras*, University of California Publications in Mathematics, New Series **1** (1951), 341–384.

[9] Michael R. Garey and David S. Johnson, *Computers and Intractibility, A Guide to the Theory of NP-Completeness*, W. H. Freeman, New York, 1979.

[10] Leon Henkin, J. Donald Monk, and Alfred Tarski, *Cylindric Algebras, Part I*, North--Holland, Amsterdam, 1971.

[11] Leon Henkin, J. Donald Monk, and Alfred Tarski, *Cylindric Algebras, Part II*, North--Holland, Amsterdam, 1985.

[12] Bjarni Jónsson, *Varieties of relation algebras*, Algebra Universalis **15** (1982), 273–298.

[13] Bjarni Jónsson, *The theory of binary relations*, Algebraic Logic (Proc. Conf. Budapest 1988) (Amsterdam) (H. Andréka, J. D. Monk, , and I. Németi, eds.), Colloq. Math. Soc. J. Bolyai, vol. 54, North-Holland, 1991, pp. 245–292.

[14] Bjarni Jónsson and Alfred Tarski, *Boolean algebras with operators, Part II*, American Journal of Mathematics **74** (1952), 127–162.

[15] Peter B. Ladkin and Roger D. Maddux, *Representation and reasoning with convex time intervals*, Tech. Report KES.U.88.2, Kestrel Institute, April 1988.

[16] Peter B. Ladkin and Roger D. Maddux, *On binary constraint problems*, Tech. Report TR 102, Department of Computing Science and Mathematics, University of Stirling, April 1992, revised February 1993, to appear in the Journal of the Association for Computing Machinery.

[17] Peter B. Ladkin and Roger D. Maddux, *On binary constraint networks*, Tech. Report KES.U.88.8, Kestrel Institute, November 1988.

[18] Roger C. Lyndon, *The representation of relational algebras*, Annals of Mathematics (series 2) **51** (1950), 707–729.

[19] Roger D. Maddux, *Topics in Relation Algebras*, Ph.D. thesis, University of California, Berkeley, 1978, pp. iii+241.

[20] Roger D. Maddux, *Some varieties containing relation algebras*, Transactions of the American Mathematical Society **272** (1982), 501–526.

[21] Roger D. Maddux, *Finite integral relation algebras*, Universal Algebra and Lattice Theory, Springer-Verlag, 1985, Proceedings of the Southeastern Conference in Universal Algebra and Lattice Theory, Charleston, S.C., July 11-14, 1984, Lecture Notes in Mathematics **1149**, pp. 175–197.

[22] Roger D. Maddux, *Introductory course on relation algebras, finite-dimensional cylindric algebras, and their interconnections*, Algebraic Logic (Proc. Conf. Budapest 1988) (Amsterdam) (H. Andréka, J. D. Monk, and I. Németi, eds.), Colloq. Math. Soc. J. Bolyai, vol. 54, North-Holland, 1991, pp. 361–392.

[23] Roger D. Maddux, *Pair-dense relation algebras*, Transactions of the American Mathematical Society **328** (1991), 83–131.

[24] Roger D. Maddux, *The origin of relation algebras in the development and axiomatization of the calculus of relations*, Studia Logica **50 (3/4)** (1991), 421–455.

[25] J. Malik and T. O. Binford, *Reasoning in time and space*, Proceedings of the Eighth International Joint Conference on Artificial Intelligence, Karlsruhe, W. Germany, August 1983 (IJCAI), 1983, pp. 343–345.

[26] J. M. Martin, *Dictionary of Philosophy and Psychology*, Macmillan & Co., New York, 1911, second edition.

[27] J. Donald Monk, *On representable relation algebras*, Michigan Mathematical Journal 11 (1964), 207–210.

[28] Augustus De Morgan, *On the symbols of logic, the theory of the syllogism, and in particular of the copula, and the application of the theory of probabilities to some questions in the theory of evidence*, Transactions of the Cambridge Philosophical Society 9 (1856), 79–127, reprinted in [30].

[29] Augustus De Morgan, *On the syllogism, no. IV, and on the logic of relations*, Transactions of the Cambridge Philosophical Society 10 (1864), 331–358, reprinted in [30].

[30] Augustus De Morgan, *On the Syllogism, and Other Logical Writings*, Yale University Press, New Haven, 1966, edited, with an Introduction by, Peter Heath.

[31] Charles Sanders Peirce, *Description of a notation for the logic of relatives, resulting from an amplification of the conceptions of Boole's calculus of logic*, Memoirs of the American Academy of Sciences 9 (1870), 317–378, reprinted by Welch, Bigelow and Co., Cambridge, Mass., 1870, pp. 1–62; also reprinted in [33] and [34].

[32] Charles Sanders Peirce, *Note B: the logic of relatives*, Studies in Logic by Members of the Johns Hopkins University (Boston) (C. S. Peirce, ed.), Little, Brown, and Co., 1883, book reprinted, with an Introduction by Max H. Fisch and a Preface by Achim Eschbach, by John Benjamins Publishing Co., Amsterdam and Philadelphia, 1983, pp. lviii, vi+203; paper reprinted in [33], pp. 187–203.

[33] Charles Sanders Peirce, *Collected Papers, Volume III*, Harvard University Press, Cambridge, 1933, edited by Charles Hartshorne and Paul Weiss.

[34] Charles Sanders Peirce, *Writings of Charles S. Peirce, A Chronological Edition* , Indiana University Press, Bloomington, 1984, edited by Edward C. Moore, Max H. Fisch, Christian J. W. Kloesel, Don D. Roberts, and Lynn A. Ziegler.

[35] F. W. K. Ernst Schröder, *Vorlesungen über die Algebra der Logik (exacte Logik), Volume 3, Algebra und Logik der Relative, part I*, second ed., Chelsea, Bronx, New York, 1966, first published in Leipzig, 1895.

[36] R G. Simmons, *The use of quantitative and qualitative simulations*, Proceedings of Third National Conference on Artificial Intelligence (AAAI-83) Washington, D. C., August 1983, 1983.

[37] Alfred Tarski, *On the calculus of relations*, The Journal of Symbolic Logic 6 (1941), 73–89.

[38] Alfred Tarski and Steven R. Givant, *A Formalization of Set Theory without Variables*, Colloquium Publications, vol. 41, American Mathematical Society, 1987.

[39] P. G. van Beek, *Reasoning about qualitative temporal information*, Proceedings of AAAI-90, the Eighth National Conference on Artificial Intelligence, AAAI Press, 1990, pp. 728–734.

[40] P. G. van Beek and R. Cohen, *Approximation algorithms for temporal reasoning*, Proceedings of IJCAI89, the 11th Joint Conference on Artifical Intelligence, Morgan Kaufmann, 1989, short version of [41], pp. 1291–1296.

[41] P. G. van Beek and R. Cohen, *Exact and approximate reasoning about temporal relations*, Computational Intelligence 6 (1990), 132–144, long version of [40].

[42] J. F. A. K. van Benthem, *The Logic of Time*, Reidel, 1983.

[43] M. Vilain and H. Kautz, *Constraint propagation algorithms for temporal reasoning*, Proceedings of AAAI-86, Morgan Kaufmann, 1986, pp. 377–382.

[44] M. Vilain, H. Kautz, and P. G. van Beek, *Constraint propagation algorithms for temporal reasoning*, Readings in Qualititative Reasoning About Physical Systems (Weld and de Kleer, eds.), Morgan Kaufmann, 1989, revised version of [43].

[45] Alfred North Whitehead and Bertrand Russell, *Principia Mathematica, Volume I*, Cambridge University Press, Cambridge, England, 1910, Second edition, 1925.

On the value of commutative diagrams in information modelling

Michael Johnson and C.N.G. Dampney
School of Mathematics and Computing, Macquarie University
Sydney, AUSTRALIA

Abstract

Category theory has been widely used in computer science, but usually in a very sophisticated manner. This paper argues that elementary category theoretic notions can have important value in the "real world" of software engineering. Perhaps the most elementary categorical notion is that of commutative diagram. Drawing on experience from several applications of category theory to information modelling in major business enterprises we show how commutative diagrams have been used to develop new methodologies in ER-modelling, constraint specification and process modelling. They also suggest new but as yet untested techniques for information model partitioning and information system architecture. The methodologies described here have a firm theoretical basis using the recently isolated theory of lextensive categories and this basis is briefly outlined.

1 Introduction

Category theory is an algebraic methodology that has had extensive use in computer science. It has been particularly valuable in distinguishing syntax and semantics by the use of classifying categories and structure preserving functors into the category of sets (in a manner analogous to its use in universal algebra). This paper outlines a classifying category setting for information models based on entity-relationship (ER) diagrams and traces several of its consequences for information modelling methodology.

There have been several category theoretic treatments of information systems (see [5] [6] [8] [9]) but to the authors' knowledge none of them has influenced information modelling methodologies until now. The results reported here are predominantly empirical, and are based on consultancy work that we have undertaken for Telecom Australia, Caltex Oil Australia and several smaller enterprises.

The most remarkable feature of the work is that one of the simplest of categorical notions — commutative diagrams — played a central role in the discovery of the new methodologies.

The paper is organised as follows. Section 2 reviews the dominant information modelling methodology which is entity-relationship modelling. In Section 3 we review the definition of a category and indicate how an ER-model is essentially a category—the *classifying category* or *theory* for the information model. A brief analysis of this view shows that our classifying categories are at least boolean and lextensive [2] and that the category theoretic treatment yields immediately a query language. This is the main theoretical section of the paper. In Section 4 we note that the main difference between an ER-model and its classifying category is the specification of commutative diagrams which amount to integrity constraints upon data which can be stored in the information model. This has led to a change in the main methodologies by giving constraint specification a much greater role in the development of information models. We show how to treat both static constraints and dynamic constraints and we illustrate these using examples drawn from industry. Section 5 treats process modelling which is traditionally the next stage in the development of a system after information (ER) modelling and it shows how the categorical treatment greatly simplifies process modelling. Finally Section 6 records implications of the category theoretic framework for developing different user views of an information model and for the underlying architecture of information systems.

Overall our approach has become known as the Federated Information System (FIS) approach to information modelling and information system engineering.

Acknowledgments: The authors gratefully acknowledge the Australian Research Council (ARC) and Caltex Oil Australia for supporting this research.

2 Information Models

Information models are widely used in industry because they are usually the first step in the development of an information system, and because they can provide a corporate overview and are hence valuable in strategic planning. An information model is a formal description of those aspects of reality about which a business needs to maintain information. Thus information modelling is about abstracting from reality with a particular formalism in mind, and the choice of formalism can affect the resulting model.

There are several formalisms that are used as a basis for information models but by far the dominant technique is called *Entity-Relationship* (ER) *modelling* [3].

The ER approach is a graphical modelling technique. An *entity* is a class of something about which the business needs to store information. Examples might include CUSTOMER, EMPLOYEE, ORDER, INVOICE and PRODUCT. Each entity will correspond to a set of things at a particular point in time (for example the current set of employees). The information that we store about entities comes in two forms: there are *relationships* between entities (for example an order may be for several products and a product may appear on several orders so there is a many-to-many relationship between PRODUCT and ORDER) and entities have certain *attributes* (for example a product may have a product number and a price, an employee has a name, an address, a salary and so on). Often one attribute for each entity is treated as the *key attribute* so that for example a product may be always accessed via its product number. Entities are usually represented graphically as rectangular boxes, relations as lines joining the boxes (with "crows-feet" to indicate possibly multi-valued relations when necessary), and attributes as oval boxes. An example is shown in Figure 1.

A more detailed example appears in Figure 2 which is a strategic model of the Australian coal industry.

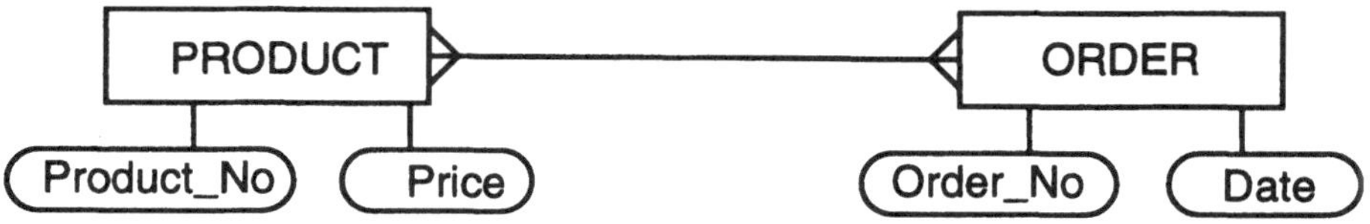

Figure 1: A simple ER model fragment

The graphical nature of ER-models is a very important aspect of their popularity. Other specification techniques such as Z are more powerful but harder to learn. The great value of a graphical model is that an analyst can show it to businesspeople and with only a brief explanation they can understand and if necessary correct the model.

There is an extensive methodology of ER-modelling including the reduction of models to various normal forms. The details need not concern us here except for one aspect: Many-to-many relationships can always be transformed into two many-to-one relationships by the introduction of a new entity. For example in the model above we can introduce an entity ORDER_LINE. One instance of this entity will be the order of a particular product on a particular order. Thus there will be many-to-one relations (functions) between ORDER_LINE and PRODUCT and between ORDER_LINE and ORDER. (This is just the usual "tabulation" of a relation.)

3 Category theory

A category consists of a collection of *objects* and a collection of *arrows*, with each arrow having a specified source and target among the objects (this much is just a directed graph) together with a *composition* of arrows, defined whenever the arrows have a common source and target, which is associative and has identities.

Thus a category may be thought of as a directed graph together with information about composition. This information may be expressed by giving a set of relations (eg f composed with g is equal to h composed with k) and those relations are often expressed as *commutative diagrams* (a diagram is said to commute if any two composable paths of arrows in the diagram with common start point and common end point have equal composites).

Examples of categories include the category **set** whose objects are sets and whose arrows are functions between sets; **grp** whose objects are groups and whose arrows are group homomorphisms; more generally T-**alg** whose objects are algebras from some theory T and whose arrows are T-homomorphisms; and numerous *small categories* which can be generated by drawing a directed graph, adding identities at each vertex, and specifying composites for composable pairs of arrows.

One of the great advantages of category theory is that it has provided a graphical framework for much of mathematics. Many properties that seem to be about the internal structure of objects such as being a one element set or being the cartesian product of two sets, can be characterised by universal properties of arrows and these permit graphical arguments to prove theorems.

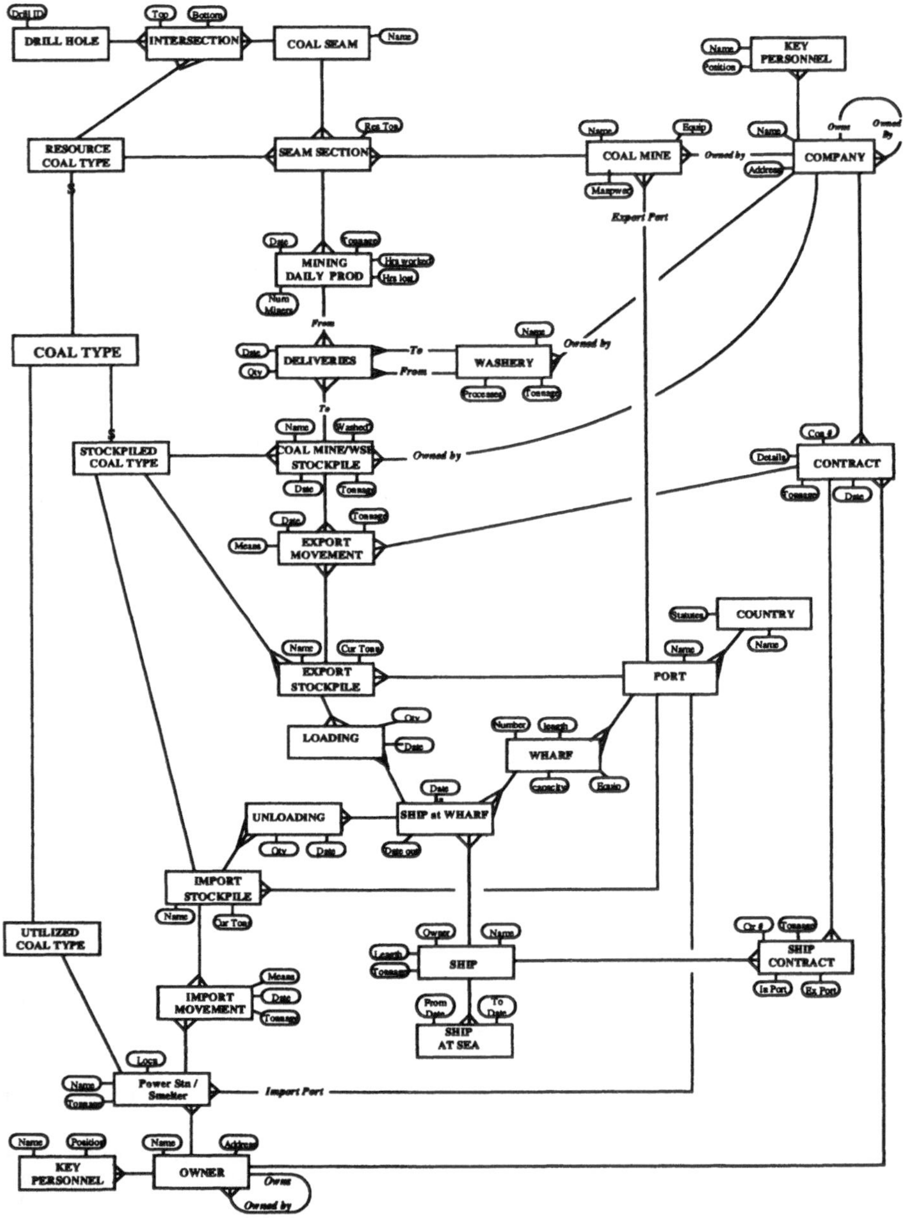

Figure 2: A strategic model of the Australian coal industry

Further examples and definitions of specific universal properties such as pullback, terminal object and coproduct can be found in any of the basic texts [7] [10] [1].

3.1 A category theoretic view of an ER-model

We aim now to show how an ER-model is essentially a category. This is motivated by the categorical treatment of universal algebra above (the T-**alg** example) and is treated in full in [5]. By analogy with universal algebra we will call the category the *theory* or *classifying category* of the ER-model.

Consider an ER-model, normalised as described at the end of the preceding section so that all relations are many-to-one. This model may be viewed as a directed graph whose vertices are the entities and attributes of the model and whose arrows are the relationships oriented from the many-valued entity to the one-valued entity together with arrows from each entity to each of its attributes. Notice that if the vertices of this graph are thought of as sets, and the arrows as functions, then the intended semantics of the ER-model is still well represented here (and this can be made formal via a functor to **set** in the usual way).

It remains to consider composition. Since the many-to-one relations in the model are intended to represent real world many-to-one relations (functions) there are real world compositions and we argue that these should be represented in the model. Many of the compositions are free in the sense that formal composites can just be added to the model (or indeed left out since such formality can be added later), but when there is a closed loop of arrows it is important to determine, by considering the real world semantics, whether the diagram commutes. Once this has been done for all possible composites we have constructed a classifying category for the ER-model.

It is remarkable that extant ER-modelling methodologies have ignored this question of commuting diagrams. Typically an analyst spends a great deal of time and effort developing a model and eventually passes it to a programmer to implement. Often it is important that the resultant program check the constraint implied by the commutativity of certain diagrams, but since the analyst has not recorded which diagrams commute it is up to the less experienced programmer to try to reconstruct the intended semantics and to decide whether a given diagram should commute!

In fact, in our experience, searching for commutative diagrams actually results in a better ER-model because it often clarifies the nature of relationships and because it provides a test of the model as it is being developed. A detailed example based on Figure 2 appears in Section 4.1.

The search for commutative diagrams has also found its way in disguise into some special rules in standard methodologies. The "double-vee" rule used in the British Standards methodology is one instance of a rule which helps to locate commutative diagrams (although it is not expressed that way).

In summary, we view the specification of which diagrams commute in an ER-model as an important part of the information modelling methodology. We are developing CASE tools which will provide assistance with this process.

3.2 Classifying categories and lextensive categories

Universal algebra suggests a better version of the classifying category discussed above. Often an algebraic theory can be presented in several different ways, but there is a single canonical classifying category (up to equivalence of categories) obtained by taking any one of the presentations and "closing it up" under certain basic operations like taking limits. Similarly we would expect the classifying category of an information system to satisfy certain basic exactness properties and the category described in Section 3.1 is just a presentation for the canonical classifying category.

So, what basic exactness properties are required? We need a terminal object I, and arrows $I \to A$ will be used to specify instances of the entity A. We need finite coproducts for two reasons. First, entities often have substructure which is best indicated by coproducts (so for example in a small retail business the entity EMPLOYEE might be the coproduct of the entities DRIVER, SALESPERSON, CLERICAL_STAFF and MANAGEMENT). Secondly, attributes are fixed sets (so for example PRODUCT_NO might be the set of all four digit numbers—of course most of these numbers won't be used at any particular point in time, but the relationship between PRODUCT and PRODUCT_NO allows us to see which ones are currently valid product numbers). Thus attributes are usually $\sum^n I$ for some n ($n = 10000$ in our product numbers example). This is technically very important since the injection $i_k : I \to \sum^n I$ allows us to pick out attribute number k from which, if the attribute is a key attribute, we can obtain information about a particular instance of the corresponding entity. Finally we need pullbacks, both to allow us to compose relations and to allow us to access the entity instances with particular attribute values.

Furthermore we expect the coproducts to behave well. They should be disjoint and universal. Thus in the presence of pullbacks and a terminal object we expect our classifying category to be a *lextensive category* [2].

Finally, we expect subobjects to be complemented with $I + I$ acting as a subobject classifier. An extensive category with this property is called a Boolean category and is necessarily lextensive.

3.3 The query language

For use in Section 4 it is worth noting that the internal logic of the lextensive classifying category of an information model forms a query language for that model. Thus the standard queries arise as objects of the classifying category.

The semantics of the information model will be given by lextensive functors from its classifying category to **set**. Such functors will necessarily carry the object representing a query to the set of records which satisfy the query.

4 Constraint specification

We show by example how to model the vast majority of the integrity constraints required in information systems by using ER-modelling with commutative diagrams. Some examples of the constraints which can be treated include the requirement that in a database of students, courses, classes and class times, it is required that no student have a clash between two timetabled classes; when an order is delivered it must be delivered to the proper customer's address; and when a contractor engages in some work involving a business resource there must be a contract that specifies that contractor's right to use that resource.

Some complicated constraints require the use of the query language outlined above (since a constraint may apply only to certain entities determined by a description that can be used as a query).

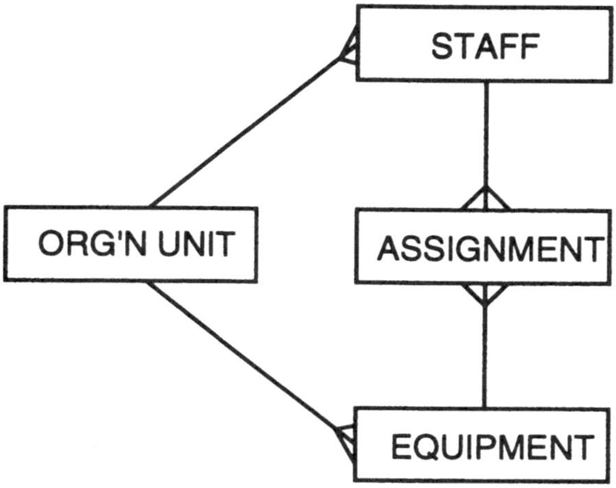

Figure 3: An information model with a single static constraint (the diagram is required to commute)

4.1 Static constraints

A static constraint is a constraint which must be satisfied throughout the life of the information system. Such constraints may be easily modelled using commutative diagrams and they are very common. As an illustrative example consider the model shown in Figure 3. The model involves members of staff and pieces of equipment, both of which belong to some organisational units within a business. Pieces of equipment may be assigned to the use of one or more members of staff. It may be a rule of the business that a piece of equipment can only be assigned to a member of staff if they are both part of the same organisational unit. This rule may be enforced simply by requiring the diagram to commute. Of course, if there is no such rule then the diagram may or may not commute depending on whether the assignments happen to "accidentally" only assign equipment to staff when the equipment and the staff belong to the same organisational unit.

Now that we have seen how static constraints are modelled by commutative diagrams, it is appropriate to return to Figure 2 and to see how the search for commutative diagrams can improve the resulting information model (as promised in Section 3.1).

The model shown in Figure 2 was completed before we had realised the importance of commutative diagrams. Nevertheless it contains many static constraints, one example being a four-sided commutative diagram that ensures that every export movement happens under a contract involving a company (as supplier) which must be the same company which owns the stockpile being moved for export. Furthermore the search for commutative diagrams reveals possible improvements of the model: It is surprising that the entity LOADING is not involved in a commutative diagram with some contractual entity. In fact there should be a many-to-one relation between LOADING and SHIP CONTRACT which says that each loading onto a ship occurs under a ship contract

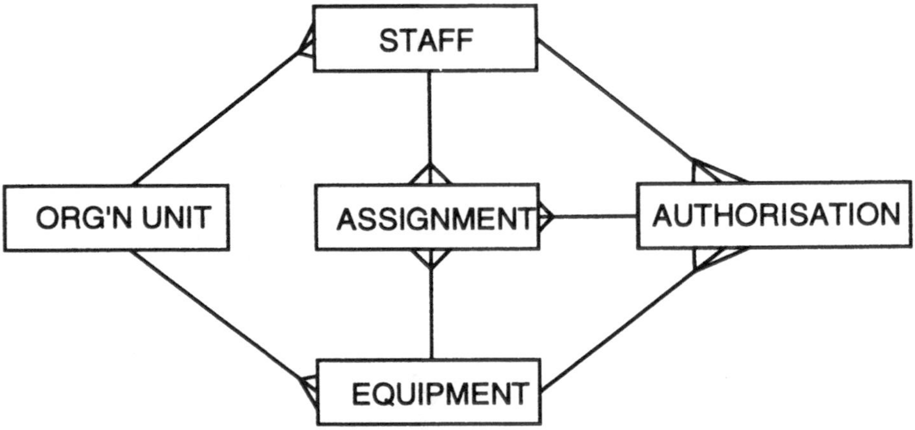

Figure 4: An ER fragment with a dynamic constraint (the two triangles on the right hand side are required to commute)

that involves that ship. In addition, that ship contract indicates under which (export) contract the export is to take place. However, in order to obtain the commutative diagram which will ensure that the (export) contract is the very contract which resulted in the export stockpile we must move the relation between EXPORT MOVEMENT and CONTRACT so that it goes between EXPORT STOCKPILE and CONTRACT. This results in no loss because the EXPORT MOVEMENT to CONTRACT relation can be recovered by composition, and it permits the important constraint (commutative diagram) that the composite from LOADING to EXPORT STOCKPILE to CONTRACT is equal to the composite LOADING to SHIP CONTRACT to CONTRACT.

4.2 Dynamic constraints

There are many examples of business rules and government regulations which provide constraints which are variable. For example there are work practices which have required that only a certain class of employee can engage in certain classes of work but which are now being liberalised with industrial relations reforms which are underway in a number of countries. To accommodate these *dynamic constraints* we must have an entity which embodies the constraint information, since only instances of entities can be created and destroyed in an information system.

An extension of the previous example which incorporates a dynamic constraint appears in Figure 4. Once again staff may be assigned the use of pieces of equipment, but if we require the two triangles to commute then there must have been a prior authorisation which said that that particular assignment was permitted. Thus, if staff are only allowed to use equipment that they have been trained to use then when a person attends a training session for a particular piece of equipment there will be an entry placed in AUTHORISATION recording that they are permitted to use that equipment. They may never be assigned that piece of equipment, but if they are then the relationship between

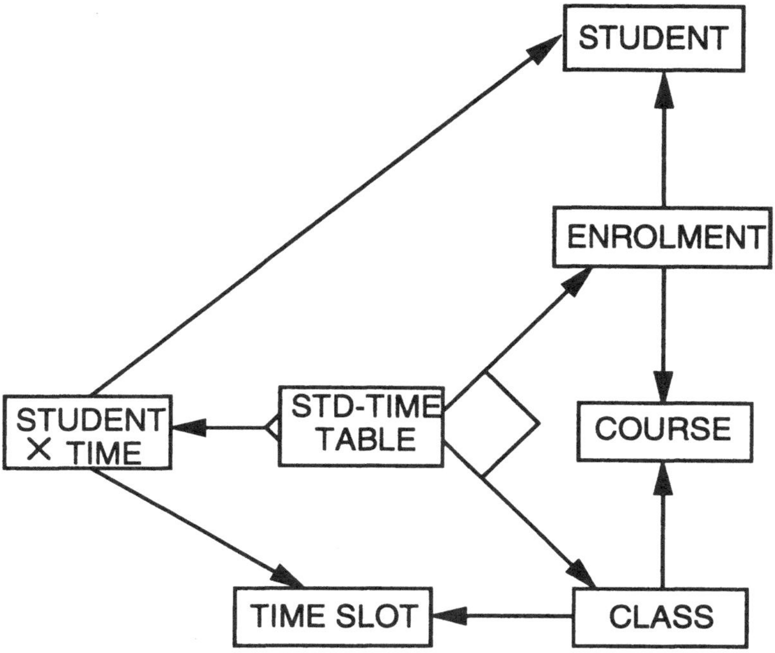

Figure 5: A student-class information model expressed in categorical (rather than ER) notation. The requirement that the central horizontal arrow be monic expresses the "no clashes" constraint.

ASSIGNMENT and AUTHORISATION will refer back to the entry made after their training.

Interestingly there may also be higher level constraints implied here. If the static constraint described in Section 4.1 still applies here, then since the left quadrilateral and the two triangles commute, the outside quadrilateral must commute too. But this constrains possible authorisations: A staff member may only be *authorised* to use a piece of equipment if that staff member and that piece of equipment belong to the same organisational unit.

4.3 Constraints and queries

Some constraints are so specific as to involve queries. For example the constraint that in a database of students, courses, classes and class times, it is required that no student have a clash between two timetabled classes, it is necessary to proceed as follows (Figure 5). First since the relationship between students and courses may be many-to-many we introduce a new entity called ENROLMENT. Each instance of ENROLMENT indicates that a particular student is enrolled in a particular course. We assume that each course has several classes each with a time slot. If we form the pullback of the arrows from ENROLMENT and CLASS into COURSE then what we obtain is essentially a time-table: Instances of the pullback may be thought of as triples (student, course, class) where the student is enrolled in the course which has as one of its classes the class. Of course there is a map from this TIME-TABLE entity to the product of STUDENT and TIME SLOT. To satisfy the constraint we simply require that this map be monic (which of course can be stated in a Boolean category).

5 Process modelling

Once a satisfactory ER-model has been developed it is common to work out a process model for the business which shows the important processes carried out by the business and how they trigger one another. The process model will be much less general than the ER-model since it will tell us about how the business is currently organised (and this may change despite the information needs of the business remaining the same).

Traditionally the process model is influenced by the ER-model, but our new methodology for ER-modelling makes the link explicit. Consider the diagrams in the ER-model which have been specified as commuting. Typically each of these loops represents an individual process and reconciliation cycle. This is because, in order to update the information system, it is usually necessary to update an instance at each vertex of the diagram and then finally to check that commutativity has been preserved (see Figure 6).

Thus to develop the process model one calculates a kind of graph dual of the ER-model in which specified commutative diagrams correspond to processes and common vertices between such commutative diagrams correspond to triggers between the processes.

Of course it is often the case that an analyst can further refine the process model, but it is useful to note that the greater part of the work of developing a process model has already been done if one has specified the commutative diagrams in the ER-model.

It should be noted that not all process and reconciliation cycles are as simple as those suggested by Figure 6. Figure 7 shows the processes cycle involved in preparing a loan in a bank process model.

6 Views and architectural implications

The methodology that we have been describing also has some as yet untested implications for other aspects of information system development.

One particularly difficult problem in dealing with large information systems is the presentation of different *views* of the system for different users. The problem is essentially one of how to partition the system so that users can see a relatively complete view related to the aspects that are of relevance to them without having to look at the whole system. The recognition of commuting diagrams as processes suggests that the best partitioning would be obtained by choosing a related group of commutative diagrams. This will be developed in work currently in progress. An early example is shown in Figure 8 where four views of an information model have been derived by selecting commuting diagrams from a much larger and more detailed model.

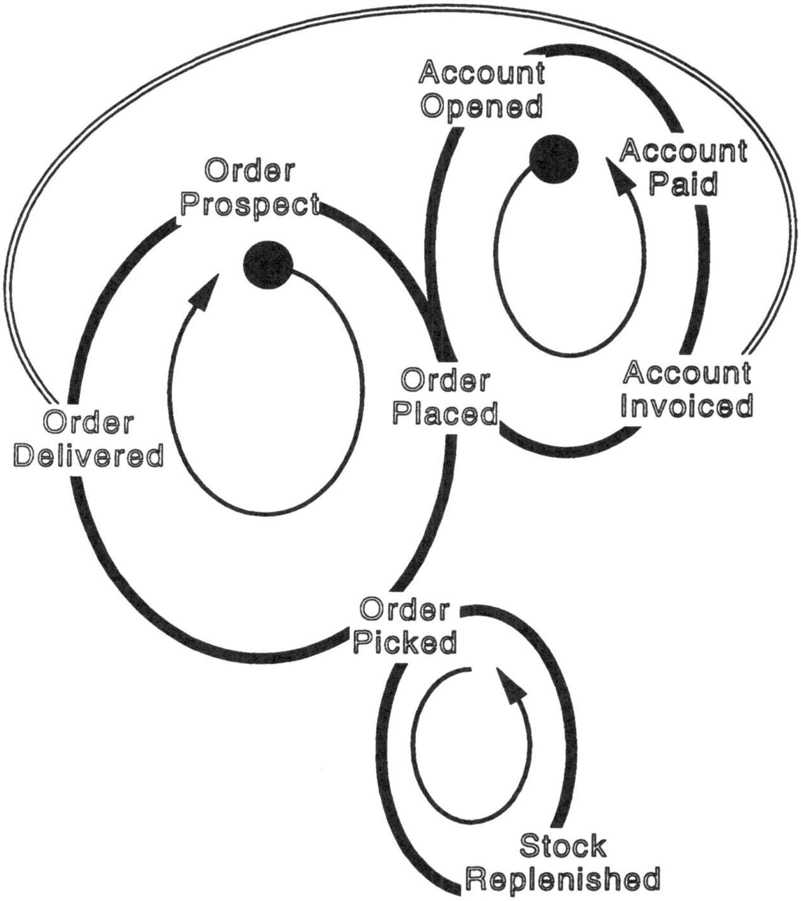

Figure 6: An example of interacting process and reconciliation cycles (the double lines from Order Delivered to Account Invoiced represent a trigger—we assume that an account is not to be invoiced until the corresponding order has been delivered)

This partitioning can be carried further. The growth of very large information systems has led to problems of complexity and context retention which might best be solved by allowing business units a certain autonomy with their information systems. However, integration of such systems is necessary and the complexity of the interaction between subsystems can be dangerous. We propose the development of a corporate information (ER) model which can be used to determine, via commutative diagrams how to partition the system into subsystems. This will require duplicating entities that happen to fall into two subsystems and providing a message passing mechanism to allow the two

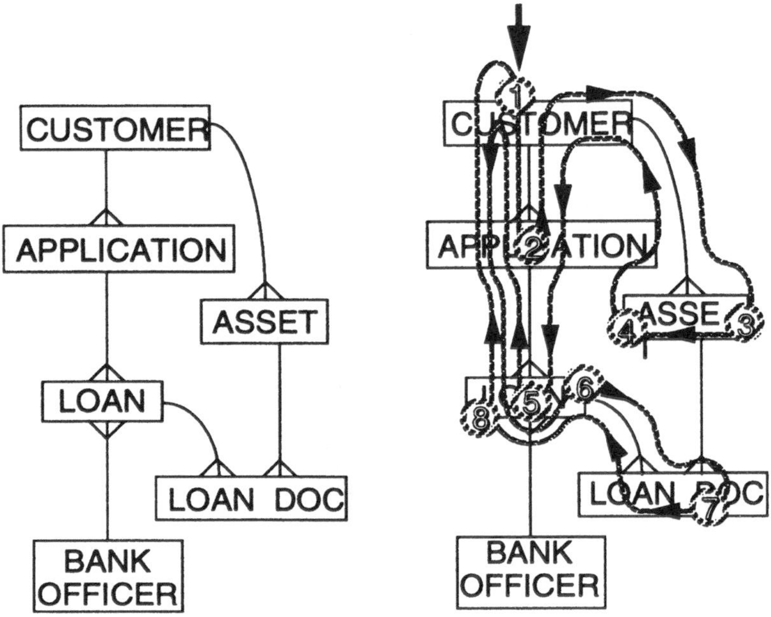

Figure 7: A fragment of a banking information model and its process cycle. The numbered processes are: (1) Check identification, (2) Initiate application, (3) Appraise assets, (4) Check title to assets, (5) Check previous loans (credit history), (6) Gain bank officer approval, (7) Finalise loan documents, (8) Complete loan.

copies to remain synchronised. However, if the partitioning is done well, and we believe an analysis based on commutative diagrams will do this, then it is likely that the interaction between subsystems will be quite manageable.

This proposed architecture for information systems is the source of the name Federated Information Systems.

An example of a federated information system appears in Figure 9.

References

[1] M. Barr and C. Wells, *Category theory and computer science*, Prentice Hall, 1990.

[2] A. Carboni, S. Lack and R.F.C. Walters, Introduction to extensive and distributive categories, *Pure Mathematics Report* 92-9, University of Sydney, 1992.

[3] P.P.S. Chen, The entity relationship model—towards a unified view of data, *ACM Transactions on Database Systems*, 1 (1976), 9–36.

[4] C.N.G. Dampney, M. Johnson and P. Deuble, Taming large complex information systems in D.G. Green and T. Bossomaier (eds) *Complex Systems* IOS Press, Amsterdam, (1993), 210–222.

[5] C.N.G. Dampney, M. Johnson and G.P. Monro, An illustrated mathematical foundation for ERA, in C.M.I. Rattray and R.G. Clarke (eds) *The unified computation laboratory*, Oxford University Press, Oxford, (1992), 77–84.

[6] C.A. Gunther, The mixed power domain, to appear in *Theoretical Computer Science.*

[7] Saunders Mac Lane, *Categories for the Working Mathematician*, Graduate Texts in Mathematics 5, Springer-Verlag, 1971.

[8] R. Rosebrugh and R.J. Wood, Relational databases and indexed categories, *Canadian Mathematical Society Conference Proceedings* 13 (1992), 391–407.

[9] S. Vickers, Geometric theories and databases, *London Mathematical Society Lecture Notes* 177 (1992), 288–314.

[10] R.F.C. Walters, *Categories and computer science*, Cambridge University Press, 1992.

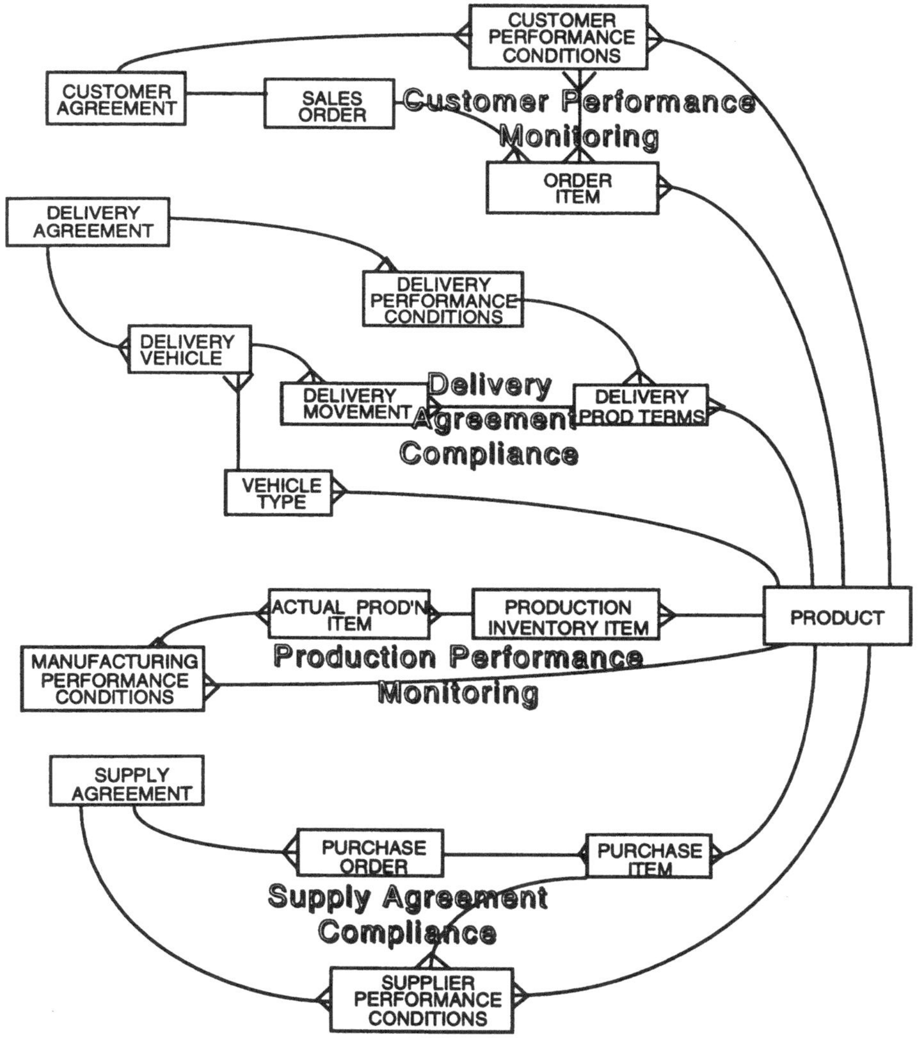

Figure 8: Four views extracted from a large information model by selecting commuting diagrams

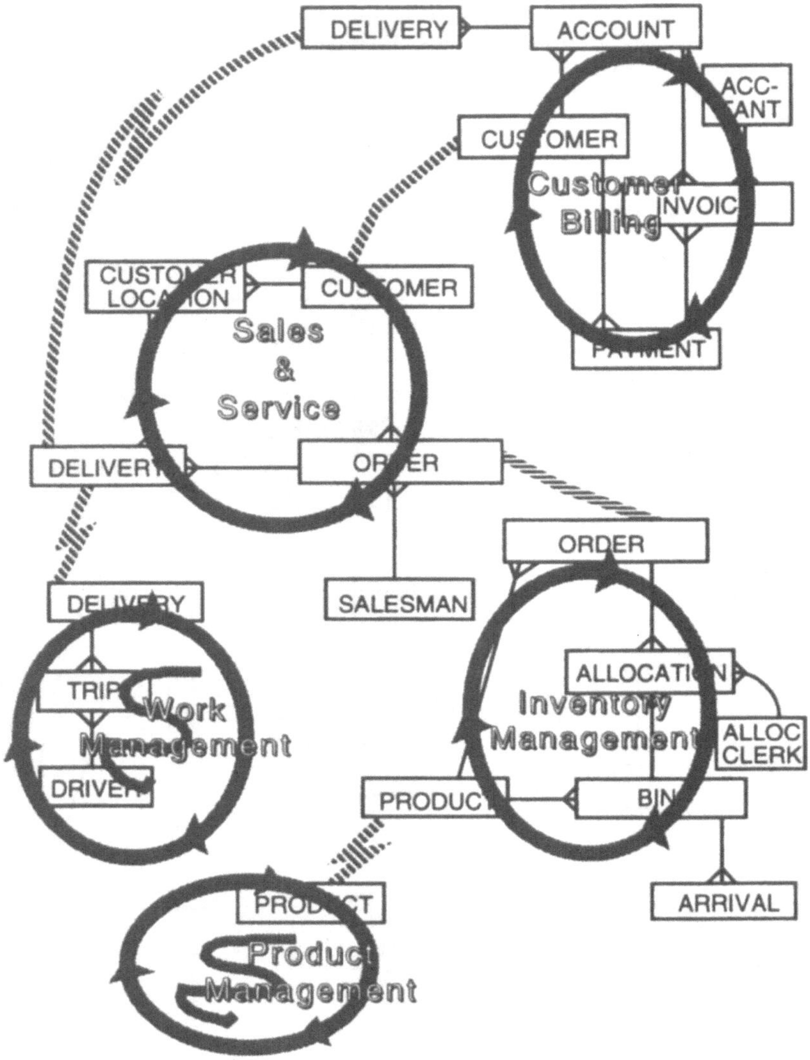

Figure 9: A fragment of a federated information system

Rigorous specification of real-time systems

Steve Schneider
Programming Research Group
Oxford University, U.K.

Abstract

This paper provides an introduction to the use of timed CSP in reasoning about real-time systems. The language of timed CSP and the denotational timed failures model are reviewed, and the underlying theory is discussed. The algebraic style of specification is discussed, followed by the behavioural requirement specification approach. A simple timed buffer example is treated using both methods.

1 Introduction

A real-time system is one whose correct operation relies upon some consideration of its quantitative timed behaviour; examples include traffic lights, gas burners, washing machines, and nuclear power plants. Many specifications on such systems are concerned with explicit timing properties such as response time or delay time. To reason rigorously about them, it is necessary to be able to capture real-time properties in a precise way, and to have some model of computation that incorporates time.

There are a number of approaches that have been taken to provide a rigorous foundation for reasoning about real-time systems. One approach is to focus attention on specifications, providing a language suitable for capturing and reasoning about real-time requirements independent of any particular formalism for describing systems. Metric temporal logic [15] and the duration calculus [27] are two examples. Such specification languages are generally supported mathematically by an underlying model, and may be used with a variety of system description formalisms.

The complementary approach is to begin with a way of describing processes. There are many ways timed systems may be described, including timed automata [2], timed graphs [16], timed petri nets (e.g. [6]), a multitude of timed process algebras [3, 12, 17, 5, 26, 22, 19], timed versions of LOTOS [20, 4]

Processes or abstract programs are often used as specifications in their own right, by treating them as descriptions of how a system is intended to behave. In this case, another essential part of the specification is how a proposed implementation should relate to the specifying process. It may be required to be equivalent with respect to a set of axioms (as is often the case when the underlying semantics is axiomatic), or bisimilar, or testing equivalent (both with respect to an operational semantics), or equal in some denotational model. Alternatively, some notion of refinement may be preferred: a set of axioms might define a notion of refinement, or perhaps some simulation relation should hold between specification and implementation, or the implementation should pass more tests, or else their meanings should be related by some refinement in a denotational model.

In addition, the specification-oriented and the process-oriented approaches are often combined. A programming language may be provided together with an independent way of talking about properties. For example, timed graphs may be related to temporal logic [1]; an occam-like language [14] may use metric temporal logic as a specification language, or a process algebra may be used in conjunction with a Hennessy-Milner style logic [10]. Furthermore, any language with a denotational semantics will support specifications expressed directly as properties on elements of the denotational model.

This paper describes two approaches that may be taken with the process algebra of timed Communicating Sequential Processes (CSP). It begins by reviewing the language, which is an extension of Hoare's CSP [13] which includes an explicit timing construct. Its denotational semantics is then given in terms of timed traces and timed refusals. The underlying theory is reviewed, as it is this theory which underpins all application of CSP. Finally, two approaches to specification are discussed. The language may be used as a specification language in the sense above, leading to processes as 'algebraic' specifications. The CSP approach to nondeterminism as underspecification leads naturally to a refinement relationship between a specification captured as a process, and a proposed implementation which should be at least as deterministic. The denotational semantics also makes it possible to capture requirements as properties on elements of the semantic model. This is done by specifying acceptable behaviour in a typical execution, and then requiring that all possible executions of a proposed implementation meet this specification.

2 Communicating Sequential Processes

In common with other process algebras, CSP is concerned purely with the communication patterns of processes, abstracting away internal state information which may be separated from communication behaviour. This abstraction remains appropriate for real-time systems since they are generally reactive, maintaining continual interaction with their environment.

Events

A process is modelled in terms of the possible interactions it can have with its environment. These interactions are described in terms of instantaneous atomic synchronisations, or *events*. This notion of synchronisation is considered to be primitive: both asynchronous communication and communication by means of shared memory may be modelled in terms of it. When a process will be cooperating with its environment for some length of time, this is modelled in terms of an event at the point where they agree to cooperate. For example, a couple involved in a wedding service will be interacting for some time, yet there is a precise instant at which they become married.

Computational model

A number of assumptions are made about the underlying model of computation.

- **Maximal progress** A synchronisation event occurs as soon as all participants are ready to perform it.
- **Maximal parallelism** Every process has a dedicated processor; processes do not compete for processor time.
- **Finite variability** No process may perform infinitely many events, or undergo infinitely many state changes, in a finite interval of time.
- **Real-time** The time domain is taken to be the non-negative real numbers. Thus it is possible for events to occur at any non-negative real time. Since the reals are dense, our maximal parallelism assumption above means that there is no positive lower bound on the time difference between two independent events occurring at different times.

The language of CSP

Let Σ be the set of all possible events. The terms of CSP are given by the following Backus-Naur form:

P	$::=$	$Stop \mid Skip \mid P\,;P \mid a \longrightarrow P \mid$	sequential
		$P \square P \mid P \sqcap P \mid P \overset{t}{\triangleright} P \mid$	choice
		$P\ {}_A\|_A\ P \mid P \parallel\!\mid P \mid$	parallel
		$P \setminus A \mid f(P) \mid f^{-1}(P) \mid$	abstraction
		$X \mid \mu X \bullet P$	recursion

where a is drawn from Σ, A is drawn from $\mathcal{P}(\Sigma)$, t from $[0, \infty)$, f is a function $\Sigma \rightarrow \Sigma$, and X is drawn from the set of process variables. CSP *processes* are terms with no free process variables (every process variable is bound by some μ expression), for which every recursive expression is time-guarded, in the sense that there is some $t > 0$ for which any execution must take at least t to reach a recursive invocation; for a full discussion of time-guardedness, see [8].

The process *Stop* represents the deadlocked process, unable to engage in any events or make any progress. The process *Skip* is the immediately terminating process. A sequential composition $P\ ;\ Q$ initially behaves as P, but once P terminates, control is immediately passed, and the subsequent behaviour is that of Q. Thus we would expect $Skip\,; P = P$ for any P, and $Stop\,; P = Stop$, and indeed the semantic model supports these equations.

The prefix process $a \longrightarrow P$ is ready initially to engage in event a. It will continue to wait until its environment is also ready to perform it, at which point it will synchronise on this event. Once the event is performed its subsequent behaviour will be that of process P. There is no delay between the occurrence of a and the beginning of P.

An external choice $P \square Q$ is initially ready to engage in events that either P or Q is ready to engage in. The first event performed resolves the choice in favour of the component that was able to perform it, and the subsequent behaviour is given by this component. If both components were able to perform the first event, then the choice is resolved nondeterministically.

An internal choice $P \sqcap Q$ behaves either as P or as Q, but unlike the external choice, the environment cannot influence the way the choice is resolved.

The timeout choice $P \overset{t}{\triangleright} Q$ initially behaves as process P. If an event is performed before time t, then the choice is resolved in favour of P which continues to execute, and Q is discarded. If no such event is performed, then the timeout occurs at time t, and the subsequent behaviour is that of Q.

The parallel combination $P \;{}_A\|_B\; Q$ allows P to engage in events from the set A (only), and Q to engage in events from the set B (only). The processes P and Q must synchronise on all events in the intersection $A \cap B$ of these two interfaces, but other events are performed independently. The asynchronous parallel combination $P \mid\mid\mid Q$ represents the independent concurrent execution of P and Q, with no synchronisation between them on any events.

The hiding operator $P \setminus A$ allows encapsulation of events in the set A; these events are made internal to the process, and are thus removed from the control of the environment. Since the cooperation of the environment is no longer required for these events, the only participants will be the components of P, and so the maximal progress assumption tells us that these internal events will occur as soon as P is ready to perform them. Hence internal events occur as soon as they are ready.

The interface renaming operators $f(P)$ and $f^{-1}(P)$ have the effect of changing the names of events through the alphabet mapping function f.

Recursion

A recursive term $\mu X \bullet P$ behaves as P, with every occurrence of X in P representing an immediate recursive invocation. Thus we will have the usual law

$$\mu X \bullet P = P[\mu X \bullet P/X]$$

As stated before, we require that any recursive term of the form $\mu X \bullet P$ has that P is t-guarded for X for some $t > 0$.

Generalised operators

A number of derived operators may be defined. The delay process *Wait* t, a timed form of *Skip*, which does nothing for t units of time and then terminates successfully, may be defined by the following equivalence:

$$\mathit{Wait}\ t \quad = \quad \mathit{Stop} \overset{t}{\triangleright} \mathit{Skip}$$

The timeout choice waits for t units of time, but the process *Stop* is unable to perform any event, and so the timeout will never be resolved in its favour. Thus at time t control is passed to *Skip*, which then terminates immediately.

A delayed form of prefixing may then be defined:

$$a \xrightarrow{t} P \quad = \quad a \longrightarrow (\mathit{Wait}\ t\ ; P)$$

After the performance of event a, there is a delay of t units of time before control reaches P. The original version of timed CSP [22, 21] treated prefixing as automatically delayed, with a constant delay δ. This would now be written as $a \xrightarrow{\delta} P$.

Generalising choice to allow infinite choices is often useful. The prefix choice $a : A \longrightarrow P_a$ is initially willing to perform any event from set A, and remains so willing until some event is chosen. Its subsequent behaviour, given by P_a, is dependent upon that event. Using this operator, an input construct can be defined, allowing the input on channel in of any item x in a set M:

$$in?x : M \longrightarrow Q(x) \quad = \quad a : in.M \longrightarrow P_a$$

where the set $in.M = \{in.m \mid m \in M\}$ and $P_{in.m} = Q(m)$ for every $m \in M$. The atomic synchronisation events here are of the form $in.m$.

Infinite nondeterministic choice may also be defined. The process $\sqcap_{j \in J} P_j$ for some indexing set J may behave as any of its arguments P_j. Thus for example a nondeterministic delay over some interval I may be defined:

$$Wait\ I \quad = \quad \sqcap_{t \in I} Wait\ t$$

This may delay for any time drawn from the interval I. If each of the P_i is t-guarded for X, then so is their infinite choice. Furthermore, if P is t-guarded for X, then $Wait\ I\ ; P$ is $(t + \inf I)$-guarded for X

Finally, it is straightforward to generalise recursion to mutual recursion (finite or infinite); for further details see [8].

A mathematical model

Notation

The variables t and u range over $\mathbf{R}^+$, the set of non-negative real numbers. Variable s ranges over $(\mathbf{R}^+ \times \Sigma)^*$, the finite sequences of timed events. We also use $\aleph \subseteq \mathbf{R}^+ \times \Sigma$.

We use the following operations on sequences: $\#s$ is the length of the sequence s; $s_1 \frown s_2$ denotes the concatenation of s_1 and s_2. We define the beginning and end of a sequence of timed events as follows: $begin(\langle(t, a)\rangle \frown s) = t$, $end(s \frown \langle(t, a)\rangle = t$, and for convenience $begin(\langle\rangle) = \infty$ and $end(\langle\rangle) = 0$. The notation $s_1 \preceq s_2$ means that s_1 is a subsequence of s_2, and $s_1 \leq s_2$ means that s_1 is a prefix of s_2. The following projections on sequences are defined by list comprehension, where $(u, a) \leftarrow s$ considers each timed event (u, a) in turn from s, analogous to a set comprehension $(u, a) \in s$:

$$
\begin{aligned}
s \lhd t &= \langle (u, a) \mid (u, a) \leftarrow s, u \leq t \rangle \\
s \blacktriangleleft t &= \langle (u, a) \mid (u, a) \leftarrow s, u < t \rangle \\
s \rhd t &= \langle (u, a) \mid (u, a) \leftarrow s, u \geq t \rangle \\
s \uparrow I &= \langle (u, a) \mid (u, a) \leftarrow s, u \in I \rangle \\
s \upharpoonright A &= \langle (u, a) \mid (u, a) \leftarrow s, a \in A \rangle \\
s \setminus A &= \langle (u, a) \mid (u, a) \leftarrow s, a \notin A \rangle \\
s - t &= \langle (u - t, a) \mid (u, a) \leftarrow s, u \geq t \rangle \\
s + t &= \langle (u + t, a) \mid (u, a) \leftarrow s \rangle \\
strip(s) &= \langle a \mid (u, a) \leftarrow s \rangle \\
\sigma(s) &= \{ a \mid s \upharpoonright \{a\} \neq \langle\rangle \}
\end{aligned}
$$

We also define a number of projections on sets of timed events:

$$\begin{aligned}
\aleph \lhd t &= \{(u,a) \mid (u,a) \in \aleph, u < t\} \\
\aleph \rhd t &= \{(u,a) \mid (u,a) \in \aleph, u \geq t\} \\
\aleph \upharpoonright A &= \{(u,a) \mid (u,a) \in \aleph, a \in A\} \\
\aleph - t &= \{(u-t,a) \mid (u,a) \in \aleph, u \geq t\} \\
\sigma(\aleph) &= \{a \mid (u,a) \in \aleph\} \\
end(\aleph) &= sup\{u \mid (u,a) \in \aleph\}
\end{aligned}$$

We will use $(s, \aleph, u) - t$ as an abbreviation for $(s - t, \aleph - t, max\{0, u - t\})$, and $end(s, \aleph)$ for $\max\{end(s), end(\aleph)\}$.

Observations

To provide a denotational semantics for the CSP operators, we construct a model of possible meanings for processes. This will be given in terms of observations that may be made of processes as they execute. We first define a set of possible observations OBS, and then associate with each process the set of observations that may be made. Processes are considered to be the same if the associated sets of observations are identical.

Any observation of an execution of a process must include a record of those events that were performed, and the times at which they occurred. A *timed trace* is a finite sequence of timed events, drawn from the set $[0, \infty) \times \Sigma$, such that the times associated with the events appear in non-decreasing order. Formally, we define the set TT of all possible timed traces as

$$TT = \{s \in ([0,\infty) \times \Sigma)^* \mid \langle (t_1, a_1), (t_2, a_2) \rangle \preceq s \Rightarrow t_1 \leq t_2\}$$

Timed traces provide much information concerning the possible executions of processes. But these systems are reactive, and so we are also interested in knowing when they will be able to interact with an environment which is ready to perform certain events, and when they will not be able to do so. Although this information may be deduced from the trace information in the case of deterministic systems, it is well known that trace information is not sufficient in the case of nondeterministic systems. For example, the traces of

$$a \longrightarrow Stop \quad \text{and} \quad Stop \sqcap a \longrightarrow Stop$$

are the same, yet the first must always respond in an environment in which a is ready, whereas the second may not.

We will therefore also record *timed refusal* information. A timed refusal is made up of those events (with times) which the process refused to engage in during an execution. Our assumption of finite variability allows us to simplify the treatment of such sets. Since a process will continue to refuse an event while it remains in the same state, and since only finitely many state changes are possible in a finite time, we may consider a timed refusal as a step function from times to sets of events, containing the information about which set of events may be refused at which times.

Refusal information at a time t is considered to be subsequent to the events recorded in the trace at that time. For example, in the process

$$a \longrightarrow Stop \,\Box\, b \longrightarrow Stop$$

the event b cannot be refused before any events have occurred. But at the instant a occurs, the possibility of b is withdrawn and so it may be refused from t onwards. Thus we consider the step function to be closed at the lower end of a step, and open at the upper end. Observe that once a single a has occurred, then it too may be refused from that instant onwards, since no further copies of a are possible for the process.

Refusal sets are formally defined as those sets of events which can be expressed as finite unions of refusal tokens; this captures the required step structure:

$$\begin{aligned} RTOK &= \{[b, e) \times A \mid 0 \leq b < e < \infty \wedge A \subseteq \Sigma\} \\ RSET &= \{\bigcup R \mid R \in \mathcal{P}_{fin}(RTOK)\} \end{aligned}$$

A single observation will consist of a *timed failure*, made up of a trace $s \in TT$, a refusal set $\aleph \in RSET$, and a time $t < \infty$ which is the duration of the observation, which is considered to begin at time 0. This time must therefore be greater than or equal to all times mentioned in s and $\aleph$. The trace and refusal are both recorded during the same execution. The information that $(s, \aleph, t)$ is an observation of P tells us that P has some execution up to time t during which the events in s were performed and the events in $\aleph$ were refused. In contrast to the untimed failures model for CSP, this refusal contains information concerning events that were refused before, during and after the performance of s, whereas an untimed refusal set contains only information after the end of the trace.

Our set of observations is thus given by

$$OBS = \{(s, \aleph, t) \mid end(s) \leq t \wedge end(\aleph) \leq t\}$$

and processes will be associated with subsets of OBS.

The model

We identify a number of healthiness conditions, or axioms of the model TM_F which we would expect any set of observations consistent with some process to meet. Thus the timed failures model TM_F is defined to be those subsets S of OBS satisfying the following conditions:

1. $(\langle\rangle, \{\}, 0) \in S$
2. $(s \frown s', \aleph, t) \in S \Rightarrow (s, \aleph \lhd begin(s'), t) \in S$
3. $(s, \aleph, t) \in S \wedge \aleph' \in RSET \wedge \aleph' \subseteq \aleph \Rightarrow (s, \aleph', t) \in S$
4. $(s, \aleph, t) \in S \Rightarrow$
$$\begin{aligned} \exists \aleph' \in RSET \bullet \; & \aleph \subseteq \aleph' \wedge (s, \aleph', t) \in S \\ & \wedge \forall (u, a) \in [0, t) \times \Sigma \bullet \\ & (u, a) \notin \aleph' \Rightarrow (s \lhd u \frown \langle (u, a) \rangle, \aleph' \lhd u, u) \in S \\ & \wedge \\ & (u > 0 \wedge \neg \exists \varepsilon > 0 \bullet ((u - \varepsilon, u) \times \{a\} \subseteq \aleph')) \\ & \qquad \Rightarrow (s \lhd u \frown \langle (u, a) \rangle, \aleph' \lhd u, u) \in S \end{aligned}$$
5. $\forall n, \exists u \bullet \forall s, \aleph \bullet (s, \aleph, u) \in S \Rightarrow \# s < n$
6. $(s, \aleph, t) \in S \Rightarrow \forall u \geq end(s, \aleph) \bullet (s, \aleph, u) \in S$

Axiom 1 states that the empty observation must be possible. Axioms 2 and 3 state that if a particular observation is possible, then observations containing less information must also be possible. Axiom 4 essentially states that any event must be possible or refusible: that there must be a 'complete' extension of the observed refusal set such that any timed event not in the complete refusal could have been performed. Axiom 5 enforces a speed limit on processes, which implies finite variability. Axiom 6 states that the same traces and refusals may be observed however long the process is watched. This last axiom implies that the duration information is redundant; the possible durations may be deduced from the trace and refusal information alone. However, we retain this information as an aid to specification.

The semantic function $\mathcal{F}_T$

We provide semantics only for the basic terms of the language without free variables; this may be lifted in the usual way [8] to the language containing free variables.

The semantic function

$$\mathcal{F}_T : TCSP \longrightarrow TM_F$$

is defined by the following set of equations:

$$\mathcal{F}_T[\![Stop]\!] \mathrel{\widehat{=}} \{(s, \aleph, t) \mid s = \langle\rangle\}$$

$$\mathcal{F}_T[\![Skip]\!] \mathrel{\widehat{=}} \{(\langle\rangle, \aleph, t) \mid \surd \notin \sigma(\aleph)\} \cup \{(\langle(u, \surd)\rangle, \aleph, t) \mid t \geq u \geq 0 \wedge \surd \notin \sigma(\aleph \lhd u)\}$$

$$\begin{aligned}\mathcal{F}_T[\![P\,;Q]\!] \mathrel{\widehat{=}} \{(s, \aleph, t) \mid\ & \surd \notin \sigma(s) \wedge (s, \aleph \cup ([0, t) \times \{\surd\})) \in \mathcal{F}_T[\![P]\!] \\ \vee\ & s = s_P{}^\frown s_Q \wedge \surd \notin \sigma(s_P) \\ & \wedge (s_Q, \aleph, t) - u \in \mathcal{F}_T[\![Q]\!] \wedge begin(s_Q) \geq u \wedge \\ & (s_P{}^\frown\langle(u, \surd)\rangle, \aleph \lhd u \cup ([0, u) \times \{\surd\}), u) \in \mathcal{F}_T[\![P]\!]\}\end{aligned}$$

$$\begin{aligned}\mathcal{F}_T[\![a \longrightarrow P]\!] \mathrel{\widehat{=}}\ & \{(\langle\rangle, \aleph, t) \mid a \notin \sigma(\aleph)\} \\ \cup\ & \{(\langle(u, a)\rangle^\frown s, \aleph, t) \mid a \notin \sigma(\aleph \lhd u) \wedge (s, \aleph, t) - u \in \mathcal{F}_T[\![P]\!]\}\end{aligned}$$

$$\begin{aligned}\mathcal{F}_T[\![P \mathbin{\Box} Q]\!] \mathrel{\widehat{=}}\ & \{(\langle\rangle, \aleph, t) \mid (\langle\rangle, \aleph, t) \in \mathcal{F}_T[\![P]\!] \cap \mathcal{F}_T[\![Q]\!]\} \\ \cup\ & \{(s, \aleph, t) \mid s \neq \langle\rangle \wedge (s, \aleph, t) \in \mathcal{F}_T[\![P]\!] \cup \mathcal{F}_T[\![Q]\!] \\ & \wedge (\langle\rangle, \aleph \lhd begin(s), begin(s)) \in \mathcal{F}_T[\![P]\!] \cap \mathcal{F}_T[\![Q]\!]\}\end{aligned}$$

$$\mathcal{F}_T[\![P \sqcap Q]\!] \mathrel{\widehat{=}} \mathcal{F}_T[\![P]\!] \cup \mathcal{F}_T[\![Q]\!]$$

$$\mathcal{F}_T[\![P \overset{u}{\rhd} Q]\!] \;\widehat{=}\; \{(s,\aleph,t) \mid begin(s) \le u \wedge (s,\aleph,t) \in \mathcal{F}_T[\![P]\!]\} \;\cup\; \{(s,\aleph,t) \mid begin(s) \ge u \wedge (\langle\rangle, \aleph \lhd u, u) \in \mathcal{F}_T[\![P]\!] \wedge (s,\aleph,t) - u \in \mathcal{F}_T[\![Q]\!]\}$$

$$\mathcal{F}_T[\![P \;{}_A\|_B\; Q]\!] \;\widehat{=}\; \{(s,\aleph,t) \mid \exists \aleph_P, \aleph_Q \bullet \aleph \upharpoonright (A \cup B) = (\aleph_P \upharpoonright A) \cup (\aleph_Q \upharpoonright B) \wedge s = s \upharpoonright (A \cup B) \wedge (s \upharpoonright A, \aleph_P, t) \in \mathcal{F}_T[\![P]\!] \wedge (s \upharpoonright B, \aleph_Q, t) \in \mathcal{F}_T[\![Q]\!]\}$$

$$\mathcal{F}_T[\![P \interleave Q]\!] \;\widehat{=}\; \{(s,\aleph,t) \mid \exists s_P, s_Q \bullet s \in s_P \interleave s_Q \wedge (s_P,\aleph,t) \in \mathcal{F}_T[\![P]\!] \wedge (s_Q,\aleph,t) \in \mathcal{F}_T[\![Q]\!]\}$$

where $s_P \interleave s_Q$ is the set of timed traces consisting of an interleaving of s_P and s_Q.

$$\mathcal{F}_T[\![P \setminus A]\!] \;\widehat{=}\; \{(s \setminus A, \aleph, t) \mid (s, \aleph \cup ([0,t) \times A), t) \in \mathcal{F}_T[\![P]\!]\}$$

$$\mathcal{F}_T[\![f(P)]\!] \;\widehat{=}\; \{(f(s), \aleph, t) \mid (s, f^{-1}(\aleph), t) \in \mathcal{F}_T[\![P]\!]\}$$

$$\mathcal{F}_T[\![f^{-1}(P)]\!] \;=\; \{(s, \aleph, t) \mid (f(s), f(\aleph), t) \in \mathcal{F}_T[\![P]\!]\}$$

The infinite choice constructs are not always well defined, since axiom 5 might be violated if there is no speed limit which applies to all of the arguments simultaneously. We say that a set of processes R is *uniformly bounded* if the union $\bigcup R \subseteq OBS$ meets axiom 5. In such cases, the following definitions apply:

$$\mathcal{F}_T[\![\textstyle\bigsqcap_{i \in I} P_i]\!] \;\widehat{=}\; \bigcup_{i \in I} \mathcal{F}_T[\![P_i]\!]$$

$$\mathcal{F}_T[\![a : A \longrightarrow P_a]\!] \;=\; \{(\langle\rangle, \aleph, t) \mid A \cap \sigma(\aleph) = \{\}\} \cup \{(\langle(u,a)\rangle^\frown s, \aleph, t) \mid a \in A \wedge A \cap \sigma(\aleph \lhd u) = \{\} \wedge (s,\aleph,u) - t \in \mathcal{F}_T[\![P(a)]\!]\}$$

A full treatment of these operators requires a more complex model [18, 23].

In order to give a meaning to recursive constructs, the intention is that the recursive process $\mu X \bullet P$ should be a solution of the equation $X = P$. Thus we also allow recursive equations as process definitions: the equation $P = F(P)$ defines P to be the process $\mu X \bullet F(X)$.

It is by no means necessary that such equations should have solutions at all, and we must impose some structure on the model in order to guarantee that they do. A distance function d between processes is defined:

$$S \lhd u \;=\; \{(s,\aleph,t) \in S \mid t < u\}$$

$$d(S_1, S_2) \;=\; \inf\{2^{-t} \mid S_1 \lhd t = S_2 \lhd t\}$$

Thus the longer S_1 and S_2 are indistinguishable, the closer together they are under d. In fact, the distance function is a metric, and the space (TM_F, d) is a complete metric space [21].

Now define a function $F(Y)$ to be t-constructive if

$$S_1 \lhd u = S_2 \lhd u \quad \Rightarrow \quad F(S_1) \lhd (u+t) = F(S_2) \lhd (u+t)$$

If a term P is t-guarded in X, it follows that the resulting function on X corresponds to a t-constructive function F on TM_F (for any instantiation of the other process variables). But this means that F is a contraction mapping: that is,

$$\exists \alpha < 1 \bullet \forall S_1, S_2 \bullet d(F(S_1), F(S_2)) \leq \alpha d(S_1, S_2)$$

where a suitable α is 2^{-t}. Thus we conclude from Banach's fixed point theorem [25] that the function F has a *unique* fixed point in the complete metric space (TM_F, d).

It is now possible to give a meaning to a recursive term of the form $\mu X \bullet P$ for P t-guarded in X with $t > 0$. If P contains no free variables other than X then we have

$$\mathcal{F}_T[\![\mu X \bullet P]\!] \quad = \quad \text{The unique fixed point of the function corresponding to } \lambda X \bullet P$$

This approach may be lifted to terms P containing other free variables in the usual way, by evaluating the recursion while the values of the other variables remain fixed (see [8]). It also extends easily to mutual recursion.

This semantic model corresponds in a natural way to an operational testing approach [11] to identifying and distinguishing processes. An operational semantics of the language in terms of a timed transition system, has been given [24]. A test is a CSP process T. A process P may pass a test T if there is some execution given by the operational semantics of $(P\ {}_{\Sigma}\|_{\Sigma}\ T) \setminus \Sigma$ for which T passes through a 'success' state. Two processes are equivalent under may testing if the set of tests they may pass are exactly the same. Then it turns out [24] that this notion of equivalence is the same as equivalence in the model TM_F: processes are equivalent under may testing precisely when they have exactly the same timed failures. Thus the denotational semantics is fully abstract with respect to the operational semantics; this result implies that both timed trace congruence and untimed trace congruence are the same as timed failures equivalence.

3 Specification

3.1 Process algebra specification

As observed earlier, a common approach to specification is to use processes themselves as descriptions of required behaviour. By considering nondeterminism as underspecification, we consider an implementation or refinement of P to be a process Q which behaves as P but which may be more deterministic; some of the nondeterminism in P may be resolved in Q. Thus P is refined by Q if Q has fewer behaviours than P. This is written $P \sqsubseteq Q$, and defined

$$P \sqsubseteq Q \quad \Leftrightarrow \quad \mathcal{F}_T[\![Q]\!] \subseteq \mathcal{F}_T[\![P]\!]$$

A process Q meets a specification P when $P \sqsubseteq Q$.

Consider for example a specification for a one-place buffer which takes between one second and eight seconds from inputting a message to enabling it for output. The next input may follow output immediately, and must be possible within five seconds of the last output.

$$B \quad = \quad in?x \longrightarrow Wait\,[1,8]\,;\, out!x \longrightarrow Wait\,[0,5)\,;\, B$$

Thus the process $Q = in?x \xrightarrow{3} out!x \xrightarrow{2} Q$ meets this specification, since it is a refinement of B; any possible behaviour of Q is also possible for B, and therefore acceptable.

As a larger example we will consider the following more complicated requirement, similar to a problem posed in [28]: we wish to specify a process modelling an n-place unordered buffer of type T, which has certain constraints on input, output, and throughput:

- There must be at least 2 seconds between consecutive inputs;
- It must be ready to accept input no more than 10 seconds since the last input (if not full).
- There must be at least 4 seconds between consecutive outputs;
- It should always be ready to output within 10 seconds of the last output (if not empty).
- Any particular item must be available for output exactly 5 seconds after it is input, subject to the other constraints.

The first two constraints impose lower and upper bounds on the times at which the process should enable input. These are simultaneously captured by the following process:

$$IN \quad = \quad in?x : T \longrightarrow Wait\,[2,10]\,;\, IN$$

Similarly, the bounds imposed by the next two constraints are captured by

$$OUT \quad = \quad out?x : T \longrightarrow Wait\,[4,10]\,;\, OUT$$

Observe that OUT is prepared to allow any event of the form $out.m$; it is not constraining the nature of the output in any way, it is only constraining the time at which output becomes possible.

Finally, the fifth constraint may be captured for a buffer of size one as follows:

$$1BUFF \quad = \quad in?x : T \xrightarrow{5} out!x \longrightarrow 1BUFF$$

An unordered buffer of size n may be considered as a combination of n buffers of size 1 operating independently.

$$nBUFF \quad = \quad |||_{i=1}^{n}\, 1BUFF$$

where $|||_{i=1}^{n} P_i = P_1 \parallel\!\mid P_2 \parallel\!\mid \ldots \parallel\!\mid P_n$. Since the interleaving operator $\parallel\!\mid$ is associative (i.e. $\mathcal{F}_T[\![(P \parallel\!\mid Q) \parallel\!\mid R]\!] = \mathcal{F}_T[\![P \parallel\!\mid (Q \parallel\!\mid R)]\!]$), this is well defined.

The full specification may then be given as the parallel combination of these three specifications:

$$SPEC \quad = \quad (IN \ {}_{in.T}\|_{out.T} \ OUT) \ {}_{in.T \cup out.T}\|_{in.T \cup out.T} \ nBUFF$$

The event set associated with each component specification consists of those events that the specification is concerned with. The process *IN* imposes no constraints upon the events in *out.T*, so these events do not appear in its interface set, indicating that they can occur without the involvement of *IN*. Observe also that it is the constraint imposed by *nBUFF* that prevents input when the buffer is full, and output when empty; the processes *IN* and *OUT* are not concerned with these aspects of the buffer's behaviour.

The compositional nature of the denotational semantics allows for a compositional treatment of refinement: if refinements of each of the specifications *IN*, *OUT*, and *nBUFF* are independently found, then their parallel composition will be a refinement of the entire specification *SPEC*. This compositionality is essential for large-scale verification.

3.2 Behavioural requirement specification

An alternative approach is to describe directly those observations that are acceptable, in terms of statements about traces and refusals. A specification in this style will be a predicate S on observations or behaviours, and a process P will meet a specification if the predicate holds for every observation in its semantics. In this case, we write P **sat** S, which is defined formally as follows:

$$P \textbf{ sat } S \quad = \quad \forall (s, \aleph, t) \in \mathcal{F}_T[\![P]\!] \bullet S$$

This approach allows for a variety of levels of abstraction, since the specification S may be concerned only with some aspects of behaviour, and may ignore others, for example the timing information. Timing properties are addressed by considering the times at which events occur.

$$S2 \quad = \quad \forall x, y, u_1, u_2 \bullet (\langle (u_1, in.x), (u_2, out.x) \rangle \preceq s) \Rightarrow u_1 + 1 \leq u_2$$

The specification *S2* states that there must be a delay of at least one second between any input and any subsequent output.

All specifications that simply consider the trace s component of the observation are safety specifications, in Lamport's sense that 'nothing bad will happen': a constraint is imposed on which events are permissible and at what times. A process can fail such a specification only by performing some undesirable event. In particular, the deadlock process *Stop* will meet any satisfiable specification concerned simply with traces.

To specify that a process should make some progress, it is necessary to consider the refusal information. To say that the process is initially willing to accept any input, we require that it is unable to refuse input events to begin with:

$$S3 \quad = \quad s = \langle\rangle \Rightarrow in.T \cap \sigma(\aleph) = \{\}$$

To say that output must be available within one second of input we write

$$\begin{aligned} S4 \quad = \quad & \forall u, x \bullet foot(s \upharpoonright in.T \cup out.T) = (u, in.x) \\ & \Rightarrow out.T \not\subseteq \sigma(\aleph \uparrow [u + 1, t)) \end{aligned}$$

For the purposes of comparison and contrast, we return to the five requirements on the n-place unordered buffer. These are respectively rendered as behavioural requirement specifications below. We must also make the n-place requirement explicit, in *B0*. Observe in *B1* and *B3* that the lower bound of the desired response time is captured by a trace specification stating that events cannot appear too close together; these are safety properties. The upper bound requirements given by *B2* and *B4* must be captured by an assertion about the readiness of the process to engage in further events by a particular time, expressed in terms of refusals. We do not insist that some event must be performed (unless we make an assumption about the environment), since a process does not have sole control over the performance of events.

B0. $\quad 0 \leq \#(s \upharpoonright in.T) - \#(s \upharpoonright out.T) \leq n$

B1. $\quad \forall u \bullet \#(s \upharpoonright in.T \uparrow (u, u+2)) \leq 1$

B2. $\quad (\#(s \upharpoonright in.T) - \#(s \upharpoonright out.T) < n) \Rightarrow$
$$in.T \cap \sigma(\aleph \rhd end(s \upharpoonright in.T) + 10) = \{\}$$

B3. $\quad \forall u \bullet \#(s \upharpoonright out.T \uparrow (u, u+4)) \leq 1$

B4. $\quad (\#(s \upharpoonright in.T) - \#(s \upharpoonright out.T) > 0) \Rightarrow$
$$out.T \cap \sigma(\aleph \rhd end(s \upharpoonright out.T) + 10) = \{\}$$

B5. $\quad ((s + 5) \upharpoonright in.T)\ before_{in,out}\ (s \upharpoonright out.T)$

where $s\ before_{in,out}\ s'$ holds if every output event $out.m$ in s' has some corresponding input event $in.m$ in s. It may be defined as follows:

$$s\ before_{in,out}\ s' \quad \Leftrightarrow \quad bag(s' \downarrow out) \subseteq bag(s \downarrow in)$$

where $(s \downarrow c)$ is the sequence of messages m that appear in s on channel c (i.e. when $c.m$ is in the trace); and $bag(s \downarrow c)$ is the corresponding bag of messages.

This last specification illustrates a feature of the model-based approach: that we always have the opportunity to provide new definitions appropriate for particular applications.

Thus we would expect our algebraic specification process *SPEC* to meet the conjunction of these requirements:

$$SPEC \quad \mathbf{sat} \quad B0 \wedge B1 \wedge B2 \wedge B3 \wedge B4 \wedge B5$$

Verification

The composition nature of the denotational semantics allows for a specification oriented proof system for establishing claims of the form P **sat** S. A proof obligation on a compound process P can be reduced or factored into proof obligations on its components.

For example, the following rule is given for lockstep parallel composition:

$$\frac{\begin{array}{l} P_1 \ \mathbf{sat}\ S_1 \\ P_2 \ \mathbf{sat}\ S_2 \\ \forall \aleph \bullet [(\exists \aleph_1, \aleph_2 \bullet \aleph = \aleph_1 \cup \aleph_2 \wedge S_1[\aleph_1/\aleph] \wedge S_2[\aleph_2/\aleph]) \Rightarrow S] \end{array}}{P_1 \ {}_{\Sigma}\|_{\Sigma}\ P_2 \ \mathbf{sat}\ S}$$

Thus to prove that a parallel combination meets S, it is sufficient to find S_1 and S_2 which the components meet and whose combination implies S.

The proof system, containing a rule for each operator, is given in [7]. The soundness of the rules follows from the semantic equations. The rules are also complete, in the sense that if the conclusion is true, then there are specifications S_i such that the antecedents are all simultaneously true. For example, for binary operators there are specifications S_1 and S_2 such that the antecedents are all simultaneously true.

The rule for recursion is also straightforward:

$$\frac{\begin{array}{l}\exists X \bullet X \textbf{ sat } S \\ \forall X \bullet (X \textbf{ sat } S \Rightarrow P \textbf{ sat } S)\end{array}}{(\mu X \bullet P) \textbf{ sat } S}$$

Its soundness follows from the fact that any predicate on processes of the form X **sat** S is closed in the metric space TM_F, for any specification S; and that any contraction which maps a non-empty closed set into itself has its unique fixed point in the closed set.

Current and future research

Although an operational and denotational semantics for timed CSP have been given and shown to be equivalent, there is not yet an equivalent axiomatic semantics. There are many laws for transforming process descriptions [21], but these laws do not form a complete set. An approach similar to that taken in [5] appears promising, and may complete the trinity of complementary semantic approaches. This would give more backup to the algebraic specification style, since the claim $P \sqsubseteq Q$ might then be established by equational reasoning, as it is equivalent to the claim $P = P \sqcap Q$. Different specification styles might be appropriate for different parts of a development, and could be used in tandem since they are unified by the underlying model.

Specification macros [9] are under investigation to make behavioural requirement specifications more palatable. Specification clichés are captured at a higher level to make requirements easier to read and understand. For example, the specification $S4$ stating that output should be available one second after input is rendered '*in* at $t \Rightarrow$ *out* from $t + 1$'.

Machine assisted verification is another area of great interest, both in terms of support for proofs that processes meet behavioural requirement specifications, and also in terms of the model-checking approach for algebraic specifications. The latter approach is based upon operational semantics, and the states of a proposed implementation are explored and checked against corresponding states in the specification.

Acknowledgements

This material draws on the work of many researchers involved with the timed CSP group in Oxford. In particular it is a pleasure to acknowledge the contributions made by Bill Roscoe, Mike Reed, Tony Hoare, Jim Davies, Dave Jackson, and Gavin Lowe. Thanks are also due to the anonymous referee for a number of suggestions which have improved the paper.

I am also grateful to the UK Science and Engineering Research Council for their support under research fellowship B91/RFH/312.

References

[1] R. Alur, C. Courcoubetis, and D. Dill, Model-checking in dense real-time, *Information and Computation* (1993).

[2] R. Alur and D. Dill, The theory of timed automata, LNCS 600 (1991).

[3] J.C.M Baeten and J.A. Bergstra, Real-time process algebra, *Formal Aspects of Computing* (1991).

[4] T. Bolognesi and F. Lucidi, Timed process algebras with urgent interactions and a unique powerful binary operator, LNCS 600 (1991).

[5] Liang Chen, Timed processes: models, axioms and decidability, PhD thesis, University of Edinburgh (1992).

[6] J.E. Coolahan and N. Roussopoulos, A timed Petri net methodology for specifying real-time system timing constraints, in *Proceedings, International Workshop on Timed Petri Nets*, Torino, Italy, 1985.

[7] J.W. Davies and S.A. Schneider, Factorising proofs in Timed CSP, LNCS 442 (1990).

[8] J.W. Davies and S.A. Schneider, Recursion induction for real-time processes, *Formal Aspects of Computing* to appear (1993).

[9] J.W. Davies, Specification and proof in real-time CSP, Cambridge University Press (1993).

[10] M. Hennessy and A.J.R.G. Milner, Algebraic laws for nondeterminism and concurrency, *Journal of ACM* (1985).

[11] M. Hennessy, An algebraic theory of processes, M.I.T press (1988).

[12] M. Hennessy and T. Regan, A process algebra for timed systems, report 5/91, University of Sussex (1991).

[13] C.A.R. Hoare, Communicating Sequential Processes, Prentice-Hall (1985).

[14] J Hooman, Specification and compositional verification of real-time systems, PhD thesis, Eindhoven University of Technology (1991).

[15] R.L.C. Koymans, Specifying message passing and time-critical systems with temporal logic, PhD thesis, Eindhoven University of Technology (1989).

[16] N. Lynch and F. Vaandrager, Forward and backward simulations for timing-based systems, LNCS 600 (1991).

[17] F. Moller and C. Tofts, A temporal calculus of communicating systems, LNCS 458 (1990).

[18] M.W. Mislove, A.W. Roscoe, and S.A. Schneider, Fixed points without completeness, submitted for publication (1992).

[19] X. Nicollin, X and J. Sifakis, The algebra of timed processes ATP: theory and application, RT-C26, Projet SPECTRE, Laboratoire de Génie Informatique de Grenoble (1990).

[20] J. Quemada and A. Fernandez, Introduction of quantitative relative time into LOTOS, in *Protocol Specification, Testing and Verification VII* North Holland (1987).

[21] G.M. Reed, A Uniform Mathematical Theory for Real-Time Distributed Computing, Oxford University DPhil thesis (1988).

[22] G.M. Reed and A. W. Roscoe, A Timed Model for Communicating Sequential Processes, *Theoretical Computer Science* (1988).

[23] S.A. Schneider, Unbounded nondeterminism for real-time processes, Oxford University Technical Report 13–92 (1992).

[24] S.A. Schneider, An operational semantics for timed CSP, *Information and Computation*, to appear.

[25] W.A. Sutherland, Introduction to metric and topological spaces, Oxford University Press (1975).

[26] Wang Yi, A calculus of real time systems, Ph.D. Thesis, Chalmers University of Technology, Sweden (1991).

[27] Zhou Chaochen, C.A.R. Hoare, and A.P. Ravn, A calculus of durations, in *Information Processing Letters* 40,5 (1991).

[28] J.J. Zic, A comparison of two real-time description techniques, University of New South Wales, SCS&E Report 9308 (1993).

Full Abstraction in Structural Operational Semantics
(extended abstract)

Rob van Glabbeek*
Computer Science Department, Stanford University
Stanford, CA 94305, USA
rvg@cs.stanford.edu

Abstract

This paper explores the connection between semantic equivalences for concrete sequential processes, represented by means of transition systems, and formats of transition system specifications using Plotkin's structural approach. For several equivalences in the linear time – branching time spectrum a format is given, as general as possible, such that this equivalence is a congruence for all operators specifiable in that format. And for several formats it is determined what is the coarsest congruence with respect to all operators in this format that is finer than partial or completed trace equivalence.

1 Preorders and equivalences on labelled transition systems

Definition 1 A *labelled transition system (LTS)* is a pair $(\mathbf{P}, \longrightarrow)$ with $\mathbf{P}$ a set (of *processes*) and $\longrightarrow \subseteq \mathbf{P} \times A \times \mathbf{P}$ for A a set (of *actions*).

Notation: Write $p \xrightarrow{a} q$ for $(p,a,q) \in \longrightarrow$ and $p \xrightarrow{a}$ for $\exists q \in \mathbf{P} : p \xrightarrow{a} q$.

The elements of $\mathbf{P}$ represent the processes we are interested in, and $p \xrightarrow{a} q$ means that process p can evolve into process q while performing the action a. By an action any activity is understood that is considered as a conceptual entity on a chosen level of abstraction. Different activities that are indistinguishable on the chosen level of abstraction are interpreted as occurrences of the same action $a \in A$. Actions may be instantaneous or durational and are not required to terminate, but in a finite time only finitely many actions can be carried out (i.e. only *discrete* systems are considered).

Below several semantic preorders and equivalences will be defined on processes represented by means of labelled transition systems. These preorders can be defined in terms of the *observations* that an experimentator could make during a session with a process.

*This work was supported by ONR under grant number N00014-92-J-1974.

Definition 2 The set $\mathbb{O}_A$ of *potential observations* over an action set A is defined inductively by:

$T \in \mathbb{O}_A$. The trivial observation, obtained by terminating the session.

$a\varphi \in \mathbb{O}_A$ if $\varphi \in \mathbb{O}_A$ and $a \in A$. The observation of an action a, followed by the observation φ.

$\widetilde{X} \in \mathbb{O}_A$ for $X \subseteq A$. The investigated system cannot perform further actions from the set X.

$X \in \mathbb{O}_A$ for $X \subseteq A$. The investigated system can now perform any action from the set X.

$\bigwedge_{i\in I} \varphi_i \in \mathbb{O}_A$ if $\varphi_i \in \mathbb{O}_A$ for all $i \in I$. The systems admits each of the observations φ_i.

$\neg\varphi \in \mathbb{O}_A$ if $\varphi \in \mathbb{O}_A$. (It can be observed that) φ cannot be observed.

Definition 3 Let $(\mathbb{P}, \rightarrow)$ be a LTS, labelled over A. The function $\mathcal{O}_A : \mathbb{P} \rightarrow \mathcal{P}(\mathbb{O}_A)$ of *observations* of a process is inductively defined by the clauses below.

$$
\begin{array}{ll}
T & \in \mathcal{O}_A(p) \\
a\varphi & \in \mathcal{O}_A(p) \text{ if } p \xrightarrow{a} q \wedge \varphi \in \mathcal{O}_A(q) \\
\widetilde{X} & \in \mathcal{O}_A(p) \text{ if } p \stackrel{a}{\not\rightarrow} \text{ for } a \in X \\
X & \in \mathcal{O}_A(p) \text{ if } p \xrightarrow{a} \text{ for } a \in X \\
\bigwedge_{i\in I} \varphi_i & \in \mathcal{O}_A(p) \text{ if } \varphi_i \in \mathcal{O}_A(p) \text{ for all } i \in I \\
\neg\varphi & \in \mathcal{O}_A(p) \text{ if } \varphi \notin \mathcal{O}_A(p)
\end{array}
$$

As the structure of the set A of actions will play no rôle of significance in this paper, the corresponding index will from here on be omitted. Below several sublanguages of observations are defined.

$\mathbb{O}_T$ $\quad \varphi ::= T \mid a\psi$ — the *(partial) trace* observations

$\mathbb{O}_{CT}$ $\quad \varphi ::= T \mid a\psi \mid \widetilde{A}$ — the *completed trace* observations

$\mathbb{O}_F$ $\quad \varphi ::= T \mid a\psi \mid \widetilde{X}$ — the *failure* observations

$\mathbb{O}_R$ $\quad \varphi ::= T \mid a\psi \mid \widetilde{X} \wedge Y$ — the *readiness* observations

$\mathbb{O}_{FT}$ $\quad \varphi ::= T \mid a\psi \mid \widetilde{X} \wedge \psi$ — the *failure trace* observations

$\mathbb{O}_{RT}$ $\quad \varphi ::= T \mid a\psi \mid \widetilde{X} \wedge \psi \mid X \wedge \psi$ — the *ready trace* observations

$\mathbb{O}_S$ $\quad \varphi ::= T \mid a\psi \mid \bigwedge_{i\in I} \varphi_i$ — the *simulation* observations

$\mathbb{O}_{FS}$ $\quad \varphi ::= T \mid a\psi \mid \widetilde{X} \mid \bigwedge_{i\in I} \varphi_i$ — the *failure simulation* observations

$\mathbb{O}_{RS}$ $\quad \varphi ::= T \mid a\psi \mid \widetilde{X} \mid X \mid \bigwedge_{i\in I} \varphi_i$ — the *ready simulation* observations

$\mathbb{O}_B$ $\quad \varphi ::= T \mid a\psi \mid \bigwedge_{i\in I} \varphi_i \mid \neg\psi$ — the *bisimulation* observations

$\mathbb{O}_{nS}$ $\quad \varphi ::= T \mid a\psi \mid \bigwedge_{i\in I} \varphi_i \mid \neg\psi$ ($\psi \in \mathbb{O}_{mS}$ for some $m < n$) — the *n-nested simulation* observations

For each of these notions N, $\mathcal{O}_N(p)$ is defined to be $\mathcal{O}(p) \cap \mathcal{P}(\mathbb{O}_N)$.

Definition 4 Two processes $p, q \in \mathbb{P}$ are *N-equivalent*, denoted $p =_N q$, if $\mathcal{O}_N(p) = \mathcal{O}_N(q)$.
p is *N-prequivalent* to q, denoted $p \sqsubseteq_N q$, if $\mathcal{O}_N(p) \subseteq \mathcal{O}_N(q)$.

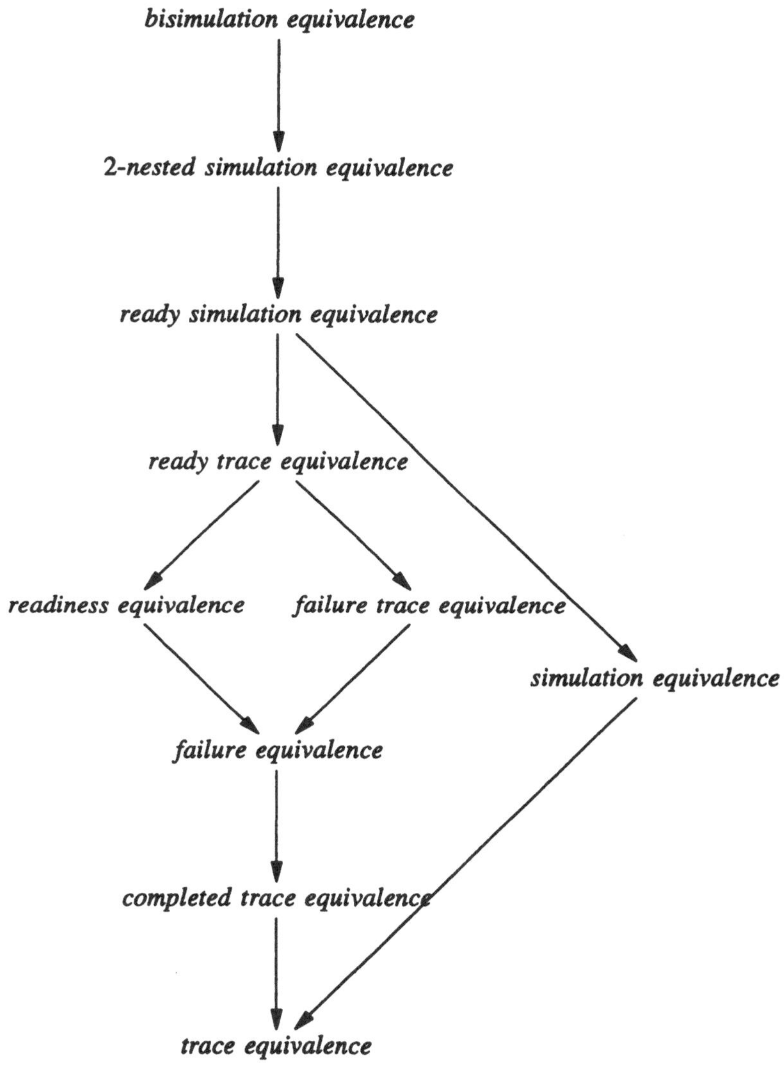

Figure 1: The linear time – branching time spectrum

On the left these equivalences are ordered w.r.t. inclusion. In VAN GLABBEEK [5] the observations above and the corresponding equivalences are motivated by means of testing scenarios, phrased in terms of 'button pushing experiments' on generative and reactive machines. There it is also observed that restricted to the domain of finitely branching, concrete, sequential processes, most semantic equivalences found in the literature 'that can be defined uniformly in terms of action relations' coincide with one of the equivalences defined above. The same can be said for preorders. Here *concrete* refers to the absence of internal actions (τ-moves) or internal choice. In order to facilitate the connections with other work it is worth remarking that on the mentioned domain readiness equivalence coincides with *acceptance-refusal* equivalence, failure equivalence coincides with Hennessy and De Nicola's *(must) testing equivalence*, failure trace equivalence coincides with Phillips *refusal (testing)*, and ready trace equivalence coincides with *barbed* equivalence and with *exhibited behaviour* equivalence. In order to clarify a few more relations, the following *relational characterizations* of certain equivalences may be helpful.

Definition 5 Let $(\mathbb{P}, \longrightarrow)$ be an LTS. A *ready simulation* is a relation $R \subseteq \mathbb{P} \times \mathbb{P}$ satisfying

- $pRq \wedge p \xrightarrow{a} p' \quad \Rightarrow \quad \exists q' : q \xrightarrow{a} q' \wedge p'Rq'$
- $pRq \wedge p \stackrel{a}{\not\longrightarrow} \quad \Rightarrow \quad q \stackrel{a}{\not\longrightarrow}$

Theorem 1 $p \sqsubseteq_{RS} q$ iff $p \sqsubseteq_{FS} q$ iff there is a ready simulation R with pRq.

Proof: "$p \sqsubseteq_{RS} q \Rightarrow p \sqsubseteq_{FS} q$" is trivial. For "$p \sqsubseteq_{FS} q \Rightarrow$ there is a ready simulation R with pRq" it suffices to establish that $\sqsubseteq_{FS}$ is a ready simulation.

- Suppose $\mathcal{O}_{FS}(p) \subseteq \mathcal{O}_{FS}(q)$ and $p \xrightarrow{a} p'$. I have to show that $\exists q' \in \mathbb{P}$ with $q \xrightarrow{a} q'$ and $\mathcal{O}_{FS}(p') \subseteq \mathcal{O}_{FS}(q')$. Let Q be $\{q' \in \mathbb{P} \mid q \xrightarrow{a} q' \wedge \exists \varphi_{q'} \in \mathcal{O}_{FS}(p') - \mathcal{O}_{FS}(q')\}$. Then $a \bigwedge_{q' \in Q} \varphi_{q'} \in \mathcal{O}_{FS}(p) \subseteq \mathcal{O}_{FS}(q)$, so there must be a $q' \in \mathbb{P}$ with $q \xrightarrow{a} q'$ and $q' \notin Q$.
- Let $\mathcal{O}(p) \subseteq \mathcal{O}(q)$ and $p \stackrel{a}{\not\longrightarrow}$. Then $\widetilde{\{a\}} \in \mathcal{O}_{FS}(p) \subseteq \mathcal{O}_{FS}(q)$ and hence $q \stackrel{a}{\not\longrightarrow}$.

Finally I have to prove that for R a ready simulation one has $pRq \Rightarrow (\varphi \in \mathcal{O}_{RS}(p) \Rightarrow \varphi \in \mathcal{O}_{RS}(q))$. I will do so with induction on φ.

- Suppose pRq and $a\varphi \in \mathcal{O}_{RS}(p)$. Then there is a $p' \in \mathbb{P}$ with $p \xrightarrow{a} p'$ and $\varphi \in \mathcal{O}_{RS}(p')$. As R is a ready simulation, there must be a $q' \in \mathbb{P}$ with $q \xrightarrow{a} q'$ and $p'Rq'$. So by induction $\varphi \in \mathcal{O}_{RS}(q')$, and hence $a\varphi \in \mathcal{O}_{RS}(q)$.

The cases that φ is T, $\widetilde{X}$, X or $\bigwedge_{i \in I} \varphi_i$ are straightforward. □

Definition 6 Let $(\mathbb{P}, \longrightarrow)$ be an LTS. A *simulation* is a relation $R \subseteq \mathbb{P} \times \mathbb{P}$ satisfying

- $pRq \wedge p \xrightarrow{a} p' \quad \Rightarrow \quad \exists q' : q \xrightarrow{a} q' \wedge p'Rq'$

A *bisimulation* is a symmetric simulation.

Theorem 2 $p \sqsubseteq_S q$ iff there is a simulation R with pRq.
$p \sqsubseteq_B q$ iff $p =_B q$ iff there is a bisimulation R with pRq.

2 Structural Operational Semantics

In this paper $\mathcal{V}$ and $\mathcal{N}$ are two disjoint countably infinite sets of *variables* and *names*. Many concepts that will appear are parameterized by the choice of $\mathcal{V}$ and $\mathcal{N}$, but as in this paper this choice is fixed, a corresponding index is suppressed.

Definition 7 *(Signatures).* A *function declaration* is a pair (f, n) of a *function symbol* $f \in \mathcal{N}$ and an *arity* $n \in \mathbb{N}$. A function declaration $(c, 0)$ is also called a *constant declaration*. A *signature* is a set of function declarations. The set $\mathbb{T}(\Sigma)$ of *terms* over a signature Σ is defined inductively by:

- $\mathcal{V} \subseteq \mathbb{T}(\Sigma)$,
- if $(f, n) \in \Sigma$ and $t_1, \ldots, t_n \in \mathbb{T}(\Sigma)$ then $f(t_1, \ldots, t_n) \in \mathbb{T}(\Sigma)$.

A term $c()$ is often abbreviated as c. For $t \in \mathbb{T}(\Sigma)$, $\mathcal{V}(t)$ denotes the set of variables that occur in t. $T(\Sigma)$ is the set of *closed* terms over Σ, i.e. the terms $t \in \mathbb{T}(\Sigma)$ with $\mathcal{V}(t) = \emptyset$. A *$\Sigma$-substitution* σ is a partial function from $\mathcal{V}$ to $\mathbb{T}(\Sigma)$. If σ is a substitution and S any syntactic object, then $S[\sigma]$ denotes the object obtained from S by replacing, for x in the domain of σ, every occurrence of x in S by $\sigma(x)$. In that case $S[\sigma]$ is called a *substitution instance* of S.

Definition 8 *(Transition system specifications).* Let Σ be a signature. A *positive Σ-literal* is an expression $t \xrightarrow{a} t'$ and a *negative Σ-literal* an expression $t \xrightarrow{a}\!\!\!\!\!/\;$ with $t, t' \in \mathbb{T}(\Sigma)$ and $a \in \mathcal{N}$. For $t, t' \in \mathbb{T}(\Sigma)$ the literals $t \xrightarrow{a} t'$ and $t \xrightarrow{a}\!\!\!\!\!/\;$ are said to *deny* each other. A *transition formula* over Σ is an expression of the form $\frac{H}{\alpha}$ with H a set of Σ-literals (the *antecedents* of the the rule) and α a Σ-literal (the *conclusion*). A formula $\frac{H}{\alpha}$ with $H = \emptyset$ is also written α. A literal or transition formula is *closed* if it contains no variables. An *action rule* is a transition formula with a positive conclusion. A *transition system specification (TSS)* is a pair (Σ, R) with Σ a signature and R a set of action rules over Σ. A TSS is *positive* if all literals in the antecedents of its rules are positive.

The concept of a TSS was introduced in GROOTE & VAANDRAGER [7]; the negative premisses were added in GROOTE [6]. The notion constitutes the first formalization of PLOTKIN's *Structural Operational Semantics (SOS)* [8] that is sufficiently general to cover most, if not all, of its applications.

Definition 9 *(Proof).* Let $P = (\Sigma, R)$ be a TSS. A *proof* of a transition formula $\frac{H}{\alpha}$ from P is a well-founded, upwardly branching tree of which the nodes are labelled by Σ-literals, such that:

- the root is labelled by α, and
- if β is the label of a node q and K is the set of labels of the nodes directly above q, then
  - either $K = \emptyset$ and $\beta \in H$,
  - or $\frac{K}{\beta}$ is a substitution instance of a rule from R,

If a proof of $\frac{H}{\alpha}$ from P exists, then $\frac{H}{\alpha}$ is *provable* from P, notation $P \vdash \frac{H}{\alpha}$.

Definition 10 *(Transition relation).* Let Σ be a signature. A ***transition relation*** over Σ is a relation $\longrightarrow \subseteq T(\Sigma) \times \mathcal{N} \times T(\Sigma)$. Elements (t, a, t') of a transition relation are written as $t \xrightarrow{a} t'$. Thus a transition relation over Σ can be regarded as a set of closed positive Σ-literals (***transitions***). A closed literal α ***holds*** in a transition relation T, notation $T \models \alpha$, if $\alpha \in T$ or $\alpha = (t \overset{a}{\not\longrightarrow})$ and $(t \xrightarrow{a} t') \in T$ for no $t' \in T(\Sigma)$. Write $T \models H$, for H a set of closed literals, if $T \models \alpha$ for all $\alpha \in H$.

A positive TSS specifies a transition relation in a straightforward way as the set of all derivable transitions. But as pointed out in GROOTE [6], it is much less trivial to associate a transition relation to a TSS with negative premisses. Several solutions are proposed in [6] and [3]. The most general of those is through the notion of ***stability***. It is not difficult to show that the concept of stability defined below is the same as that of Bol and Groote.

Definition 11 *(Stable transition relation).* Let $P = (\Sigma, R)$ be a TSS and let $\longrightarrow$ be a transition relation over Σ. $\longrightarrow$ is ***stable*** for P if:

$$\alpha \in \longrightarrow \quad \Leftrightarrow \quad \begin{array}{l}\text{there is a closed transition formula } \frac{H}{\alpha} \text{ without} \\ \text{positive antecedents with } P \vdash \frac{H}{\alpha} \text{ and } T \models H.\end{array}$$

According to BOL & GROOTE [3] the transition relation ***associated*** to a TSS is its unique stable transition relation if it exists. They argue that there is no satisfying way to accociate a tranition relation to a TSS that has no or multiple stable transition relations.

3 Formats and congruence theorems

Definition 12 *(ntyft/ntyxt-format).* An action rule $\frac{H}{t \xrightarrow{a} t'}$ over a signature Σ is in ***ntyft-format*** if t has the form $f(x_1, \ldots, x_n)$ for certain $(f, n) \in \Sigma$ and $x_1, \ldots, x_n \in \mathcal{V}$, and all its positive antecedents have the form $t \xrightarrow{a} y$ with $y \in \mathcal{V} - \mathcal{V}(t)$ and all y different. It is in ***ntxft-format*** if t has the form $x \in \mathcal{V}$ and all its positive antecedents have the form $t \xrightarrow{a} y$ with $x \neq y \in \mathcal{V}$ and all y different. A TSS is in ***ntyft/ntyxt-format*** if all its rules are in ***ntyft*** or ***ntyxt***-format.

Definition 13 The ***bound*** variables of an action rule $\frac{H}{t \xrightarrow{a} t'}$ over a signature Σ are inductively defined as the ones that occur in t or in the target s' of a positive antecedent $(s \xrightarrow{b} s') \in H$ where s contains bound variables only. The rule is ***pure*** if all variables that occur in it are bound, and a TSS is ***pure*** if it consists of pure rules only. A rule has ***no lookahead*** if all bound variables in the source of its antecedents also occur in the source of its conclusion. ***Connectedness*** is the smallest equivalence relation between the bound variables that appear in a rule such that x and y are connected if there is an antecedent $x \xrightarrow{a} y$.

Definition 14 A TSS is in ***bisimulation format*** if it is positive after reduction —as defined in [3]—and in ***ntyft/ntyxt***-format. A TSS is in ***nested simulation format*** or ***tyft/tyxt-format*** if it is positive and in ***ntyft/ntyxt***-format. A TSS is in *ready simulation format* if it is in bisimulation format and its rules have no lookahead. A TSS is in *ready trace format* if it is in ready simulation format and no two occurrences of variables in the target of a rule are connected in that rule. A TSS is in *failure format* if it is positive, in ready simulation format, and all occurrences of variables in the antecedents of a rule are different.

Definition 15 *(nxyft-format).* An action rule $\frac{H}{t \xrightarrow{a} t'}$ over a signature Σ is in *nxyft-format* if it is in *ntyft*-format and its positive antecedents have the form $x \xrightarrow{a} y$ with $x, y \in \mathcal{V}$. A TSS is in *nxyft-format* if all its rules are in *nxyft*-format.

Theorem 3 Every TSS in bisimulation format can be converted into an equivalent TSS in pure *nxyft*-format. Moreover the conversion preserves the formats of Definition 14.

The proof of this theorem will appear in the full version of this paper. Theorem 3 has independently been found by WILLEM JAN FOKKINK [4]. Using Theorem 3, the following theorem follows easily from the slightly less general results published in [3, 7, 2, 9], except for the congruence theorem for ready trace semantics, which is new. In BLOOM [1] a format for readiness congruence is presented, as well as evidence that the ready trace format can be further generalized.

Theorem 4 *(Congruence).* Bisimulation equivalence is a congruence for any TSS in bisimulation format. Similarly, n-nested simulation equivalence (for any $n \in \mathbb{N}$) is a congruence for any TSS in nested simulation format, ready simulation equivalence is a congruence for any TSS in ready simulation simulation format, ready trace equivalence is a congruence for any TSS in ready trace format and failure equivalence as well as trace equivalence are congruences for any TSS in failure format.

4 Full abstraction

Definition 16 An equivalence is said to be *fully abstract* with respect to a set of operators L and another equivalence $\sim_{obs}$ if it is the coarsest congruence with respect to the operators in L that is finer that $\sim_{obs}$. An equivalence on labelled transition systems is *fully abstract* with respect to a TSS-format and an equivalence $\sim_{obs}$ if it is the coarsest congruence with respect to all operators specifiable by a TSS in that format that is finer that $\sim_{obs}$.

The following theorem, stated a bit differently, has in a slightly less general form been proven in [3, 7, 2, 9], except for the case of ready trace semantics. A proof will appear in the full version of this paper.

Theorem 5 Bisimulation equivalence is fully abstract w.r.t. the bisimulation format and trace equivalence. 2-nested simulation equivalence is fully abstract for the n-nested simulation format and completed trace equivalence. Simulation equivalence (=1-nested simulation equivalence) is fully abstract for the n-nested simulation format and trace equivalence. Ready simulation equivalence is fully abstract for the ready simulation simulation format and trace equivalence, as well as for the positive ready simulation format and completed trace equivalence. Ready trace equivalence is fully abstract for the ready trace format and trace equivalence. And failure equivalence is fully abstract for the failure format and completed trace equivalence.

References

[1] B. Bloom. Ready, set, go: Structural operational semantics for linear-time process algebras. Technical Report TR 93-1372, Department of Computer Science, Cornell University, Ithaca, New York, August 1993.

[2] B. Bloom, S. Istrail, and A.R. Meyer. Bisimulation can't be traced: Preliminary report. In *Conference Record of the* 15th *ACM Symposium on Principles of Programming Languages,* San Diego, California, pages 229–239, 1988. Full version available as Technical Report 90-1150, Department of Computer Science, Cornell University, Ithaca, New York, August 1990. Accepted to appear in *Journal of the ACM.*

[3] R.N. Bol and J.F. Groote. The meaning of negative premises in transition system specifications (extended abstract). In J. Leach Albert, B. Monien, and M. Rodríguez, editors, *Proceedings* 18th *ICALP,* Madrid, volume 510 of LNCS, pages 481–494. Springer-Verlag, 1991. Full version appeared as Report CS-R9054, CWI, Amsterdam, 1990.

[4] W.J. Fokkink. The tyft/tyxt format reduces to tree rules, 1993. To appear as CWI Report, Amsterdam.

[5] R.J. van Glabbeek. The linear time – branching time spectrum. In J.C.M. Baeten and J.W. Klop, editors, *Proceedings CONCUR 90,* Amsterdam, volume 458 of LNCS, pages 278–297. Springer-Verlag, 1990.

[6] J.F. Groote. Transition system specifications with negative premises. Report CS-R8950, CWI, Amsterdam, 1989. An extended abstract appeared in J.C.M. Baeten and J.W. Klop, editors, *Proceedings CONCUR 90*, Amsterdam, LNCS 458, pages 332–341. Springer-Verlag, 1990.

[7] J.F. Groote and F.W. Vaandrager. Structured operational semantics and bisimulation as a congruence. *Information and Computation,* 100(2):202–260, October 1992.

[8] G.D. Plotkin. A structural approach to operational semantics. Report DAIMI FN-19, Computer Science Department, Aarhus University, 1981.

[9] R. de Simone. Higher-level synchronising devices in MEIJE–SCCS. *Theoretical Computer Science,* 37:245–267, 1985.

Synchronous Observers and the Verification of Reactive Systems

Nicolas Halbwachs
Verimag Laboratory* and Stanford University†

Fabienne Lagnier, Pascal Raymond
Verimag Laboratory*
Rue Lavoisier, 38330 - Montbonnot St.Martin, France

Introduction

Synchronous programming [20, 14] is a useful approach to design reactive systems. A synchronous program is supposed to *instantly* and *deterministically* react to events coming from its environment. The advantages of this approach have been pointed out elsewhere [20]. Synchronous languages are simple and clean, they have been given simple and precise formal semantics, they allow especially elegant programming style. They conciliate concurrency (at least at the description level) with determinism. They can be compiled into a very efficient sequential code, by means of a specific compiling technique: The control structure of the object code is a finite automaton which is synthesized by an exhaustive simulation of a finite abstraction of the program.

Concerning program verification, it has been argued [8, 16, 29] that the practical goal, for reactive programs, is generally to verify some simple logical safety properties: By a *safety* property, we mean, as usual, a property which expresses that something will never happen, and by a *simple logical* property, we mean a property which depends on logical dependences between events, rather than on complex relations between numerical values.

For the verification of such properties also, the synchronous approach has some advantages: Since the parallel composition is synchronous, the desired properties of a program can be easily and modularly expressed by means of an *observer*, i.e., another program which observes the behavior of the first one and decides whether it is correct. Thus, the same language is used to write the program and its desired properties. The verification then consists in checking that the parallel composition of the program and its observer never causes the observer to complain. This verification can often be performed by traversing the finite control automaton built by the compiler. This automaton is generally much smaller than in the asynchronous case, where non-deterministic interleaving of processes is likely to result in state explosion.

---

*Verimag is a joint laboratory of CNRS, Institut National Polytechnique de Grenoble, Université J. Fourier and Vérilog SA associated with IMAG.

†This work was performed while the first author was on leave in Stanford University, partially supported by the Department of the Navy, Office of the Chief of Naval Research under Grant N00014-91-J-1901, and by a grant from the Stanford Office of Technology Licensing. This publication does not necessarily reflect the position or the policy of the U.S. Government and no official endorsement of this work should be inferred.

An observer can also be used to express known properties of the program environment. As a reactive system is embedded into an environment with which it tightly interacts, the environment must be strongly taken into account in program design and verification. Generally, the critical properties of a reactive system are only required to hold provided the environment also behaves correctly, that is, under some assumptions about the environment. In [17], we verified a very simple railways control system, and the most important part was the description of the realistic behavior of the trains (they obey the signals, they do not jump from one track to another, etc.). In [16], we used this ability of taking the environment into account in the verification, to propose a modular verification technique: When two processes run in parallel, each of them is part of the other's environment; so any property which is proved about one of them, can be used as an assumption about the other's environment.

So, our verification approach can be summarized by three simple ideas: (1) restriction to safety properties; (2) expression of these properties by means of a synchronous, deterministic observer; (3) taking into account assumptions about the environment. This paper is a survey of our specification and verification techniques, in a very general, language independent, framework. Section 1 introduces a simple model of synchronous input/output machines, which will be used throughout the paper. In section 2, we show how such a machine can be designed to check the satisfaction of a safety property, and we discuss the use of such an observer in program verification. In section 3, we use an observer to restrict the behavior of a machine. This is the basic way for representing assumptions about the environment. Applications to modular and inductive verification are considered. In modular verification, one has to find, by intuition, a property of a subprogram that is strong enough to allow the verification of the whole program without fully considering the subprogram. In section 4, we consider the automatic synthesis of such a property, and in section 5, we investigate the possibility of deducing the subprogram from such a synthesized specification.

1 Synchronous I/O machines

We first define an abstract model of synchronous reactive machines. We could use a synchronous process algebra [27, 28, 1] as a basic formalism. but we will see that *non symmetric communication* is essential for the definition of observer: An observer can see the behavior of the program *without modifying it*, i.e., without additional synchronization. So, we prefer to use a notion of synchronous machine where inputs and outputs do not play a symmetric role. In the following model, as in synchronous languages, outputs are non blocking and synchronously broadcast. Moreover, we will need an explicit notion of state, which lacks in process algebras.

1.1 Definitions

Let us consider a set S of *signals*, and let $E_S = 2^S$ be the set of *events*[1] on S. An *I/O machine* M is a 5-tuple $(Q_M, q0_M, I_M, O_M, \delta_M)$ such that

[1] Events, with the union operation, will play the role of the "monoid of actions" in synchronous process algebras.

- Q_M is a set of states containing $q0_M$, the initial state;
- $I_M \subset S$, $O_M \subset S$ are the disjoint sets of input and output signals, respectively.
- $\delta_M \subseteq Q_M \times E_{I_M} \times E_{O_M} \times Q_M$ is the transition relation. When there is no ambiguity about the considered relation, we will often note "$q \xrightarrow[o]{i} q'$" instead of "$(q, i, o, q') \in \delta_M$".

Intuitively, in response to a sequence $(i_1, i_2, \ldots, i_n, \ldots)$ of input events, such a machine returns a sequence $(o_1, o_2, \ldots, o_n, \ldots)$ of output events, such that there exists a sequence $(q_0, q_1, \ldots, q_n, \ldots)$ of states, with $q_0 = q0_M$ and for all $n \geq 1$, $q_{n-1} \xrightarrow[o_n]{i_n} q_n$. The sequence $((i_1 \cup o_1), (i_2 \cup o_2), \ldots, (i_n \cup o_n), \ldots)$ will then be called a *trace* of the machine.

If $\sigma = ((i_1 \cup o_1), (i_2 \cup o_2), \ldots, (i_n \cup o_n))$ is a finite trace, and $(q_0, q_1, \ldots, q_n)$ is a corresponding sequence of states, we will note $q0_M \xrightarrow{\sigma} q_n$. For any state q, we will note *traces*(q) the set $\{\sigma \mid q0_M \xrightarrow{\sigma} q\}$ of traces leading to q. This notation is extended to sets of states: For any $X \subseteq Q_M$, $traces(X) = \bigcup_{q \in X} traces(q)$.

Let us note δ^r_M the *reaction function* from $Q_M \times E_{I_M}$ into $2^{E_{O_M} \times Q_M}$, defined by

$$\delta^r_M = \lambda(q, i).\{(o, q') \mid (q, i, o, q') \in \delta_M\}$$

A *reactive* machine cannot refuse a non-empty input event, and thus satisfies the following property: $\forall q \in Q_M, \forall i \subseteq I_M,\ i \neq \emptyset \implies \delta^r_M(q, i) \neq \emptyset$.

A *deterministic* machine has at most one possible reaction to a given input event, and thus satisfies: $\forall q \in Q_M, \forall i \subseteq I_M,\ |\delta^r_M(q, i)| \leq 1$. For a deterministic machine, we will note δ^O_M (respectively δ^Q_M) the *function* giving, for a state q and an input event i, the output event o (resp. the next state q') such that (q, i, o, q') belongs to δ_M.

We will use the usual *precondition* and *postcondition* functions, from 2^{Q_M} to 2^{Q_M}: For any $X \subseteq Q_M$,

- $post_M(X)$ is the set of successors of states belonging to X:

$$post_M(X) = \{q' \mid \exists q \in X, \exists i, o,\ q \xrightarrow[o]{i} q'\}$$

- $pre_M(X)$ is the set of states having a successor state in X:

$$pre_M(X) = \{q \mid \exists q' \in X, \exists i, o,\ q \xrightarrow[o]{i} q'\}$$

- $\widetilde{pre}_M(X)$ is the set of states having *all* their successors in X:

$$\begin{aligned} \widetilde{pre}_M(X) &= \{q \mid \forall i, \forall o, \forall q' \text{ such that } q \xrightarrow[o]{i} q',\ q' \in X\} \\ &= Q_M \setminus pre_M(Q_M \setminus X) \end{aligned}$$

1.2 Operations on I/O machines

Projection: Let M be an I/O machine, and $O' \subseteq O_M$. The *projected machine* $M \downarrow O'$ is $(Q_M, q0_M, I_M, O', \delta')$, where $\delta' = \{(q, i, o \cap O', q') \mid (q, i, o, q') \in \delta_M\}$.

Obviously, if M is reactive (respectively, deterministic), so is $M \downarrow O'$.

Synchronous product: Let M_1 and M_2 be two I/O machines, with $O_{M_1} \cap O_{M_2} = \emptyset$[2]. We define their *synchronous product* $M_1 || M_2$ to be the I/O machine M where

- $Q_M = Q_{M_1} \times Q_{M_2}$, $q0_M = (q0_{M_1}, q0_{M_2})$
- $I_M = (I_{M_1} \setminus O_{M_2}) \cup (I_{M_2} \setminus O_{M_1})$, $O_M = O_{M_1} \cup O_{M_2}$
- $((q_1, q_2), i, o, (q_1', q_2')) \in \delta_M \iff (q_1, (i \cup o) \cap I_{M_1}, o \cap O_{M_1}, q_1') \in \delta_{M_1}$ and $(q_2, (i \cup o) \cap I_{M_2}, o \cap O_{M_2}, q_2') \in \delta_{M_2}$

In other words, a transition of the product involves a transition of each machine, triggered by the global input signals *and the signals emitted by the other machine.*

1.3 Causality

With this very loose definition of the synchronous product, it can happen that the product of two deterministic (respectively reactive) machines is not deterministic (resp. reactive). This is the well-known problem of *causality paradoxes* in synchronous languages [6, 26]. For instance, let $I_{M_1} = \{x, y\}, I_{M_2} = \{x, z\}, O_{M_1} = \{z\}$ and $O_{M_2} = \{y\}$. Then:

- Assume (see Fig.1.a) that $q_1 \xrightarrow[\emptyset]{\{x,y\}} q_1'$ and $q_1 \xrightarrow[\{z\}]{\{x\}} q_1''$ are the only transitions in δ_{M_1} from state q_1, and that $q_2 \xrightarrow[\emptyset]{\{x,z\}} q_2'$ and $q_2 \xrightarrow[\{y\}]{\{x\}} q_2''$ are the only transitions in δ_{M_2} from state q_2. If the input event $\{x\}$ occurs when the product machine $M_1 || M_2$ is in the state (q_1, q_2), two different transitions can take place:
  - either M_1 performs $q_1 \xrightarrow[\{z\}]{\{x\}} q_1''$ and then the emission of z forces the transition $q_2 \xrightarrow[\emptyset]{\{x,z\}} q_2'$ in M_2. So the compound transition is $(q_1, q_2) \xrightarrow[\{z\}]{\{x\}} (q_1'', q_2')$;
  - or, conversely, M_2 performs $q_2 \xrightarrow[\{y\}]{\{x\}} q_2''$, forcing the transition $q_1 \xrightarrow[\emptyset]{\{x,y\}} q_1'$ in M_1, and the resulting global transition is $(q_1, q_2) \xrightarrow[\{y\}]{\{x\}} (q_1', q_2'')$.

So, in that case, the product of two deterministic machines is non deterministic.

- Assume now (Fig. 1.b) that $q_1 \xrightarrow[\{z\}]{\{x,y\}} q_1'$ and $q_1 \xrightarrow[\emptyset]{\{x\}} q_1''$ are the only transitions in δ_{M_1} from state q_1, and that δ_{M_2} is as before. Now, if the input event $\{x\}$ occurs in the state (q_1, q_2), the global system has no legal behavior, since:

[2] The restriction that parallel machines don't share common output signals is for simplicity only. It does not exist in Esterel [6] and Argos [26].

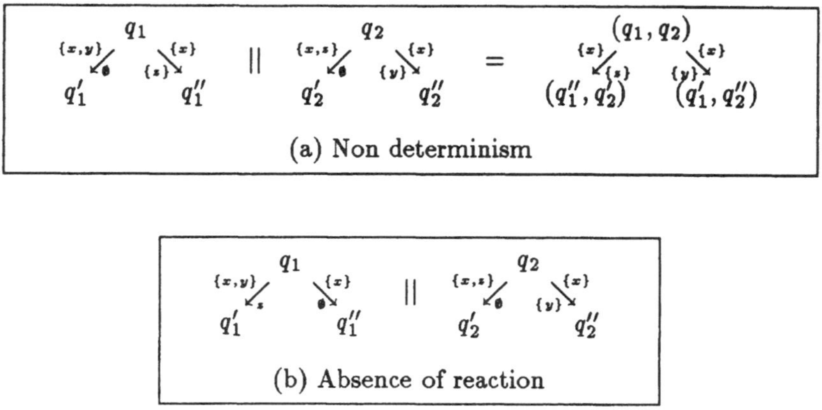
(a) Non determinism

(b) Absence of reaction

Figure 1: Synchronous product

- if M_2 performs $q_2 \xrightarrow[\{y\}]{\{x\}} q_2''$, then the emission of y forces the transition $q_1 \xrightarrow[\{z\}]{\{x,y\}} q_1'$ in M_1. But now, since z is emitted, M_2 should not have made its transition.
- Conversely if M_1 performs $q_1 \xrightarrow[\emptyset]{\{x\}} q_1''$, since z is not emitted, M_2 must perform $q_2 \xrightarrow[\{y\}]{\{x\}} q_2''$ and the emission of y forbids the transition of M_1.

So, in that case, the product of two reactive machines is not reactive.

An important feature of synchronous languages is that their parallel composition operator (synchronous product) introduces neither non-determinism nor deadlock. Compile-time consistency checks insure that the compound machine has a *unique, minimal,* reaction to each input event (see for instance [14] for details): Let M_1 and M_2 be two deterministic and reactive I/O machines, let $\delta^O_{M_1}$, $\delta^O_{M_2}$ be their respective output functions. When $M_1||M_2$ is in the state (q_1, q_2) and receives an input event i, the output event o must satisfy

$$o = \delta^O_{M_1}(q_1, (i \cup o) \cap I_{M_1}) \cup \delta^O_{M_2}(q_2, (i \cup o) \cap I_{M_2})$$

i.e., be a fixpoint of the function

$$\lambda x.\ \delta^O_{M_1}(q_1, (i \cup x) \cap I_{M_1}) \cup \delta^O_{M_2}(q_2, (i \cup x) \cap I_{M_2})$$

Causality problems come from the fact that this function is not always monotone, and thus, may admit zero or several minimal fixpoints. Compile-time consistency checks insure the existence and unicity of a least fixpoint, and the synchronous product is defined by

$$\delta^O((q_1, q_2), i) = \mu x.\ \delta^O_{M_1}(q_1, (i \cup x) \cap I_{M_1}) \cup \delta^O_{M_2}(q_2, (i \cup x) \cap I_{M_2})$$

$$\delta^Q((q_1, q_2), i) = \left(\begin{array}{l} \delta^Q_{M_1}(q_1, (i \cup \delta^O((q_1, q_2), i)) \cap I_{M_1}), \\ \delta^Q_{M_2}(q_2, (i \cup \delta^O((q_1, q_2), i)) \cap I_{M_2}) \end{array} \right)$$

(where, as usual, $\mu x.f$ denotes the least fixpoint of the function $\lambda x.f$).

2 Observers of safety properties

In this section, we show how a safety property can be specified by means of a synchronous observer. Such an observer is an I/O machine, taking as inputs both the input and the output signals of the machine under observation, and emitting an "alarm" signal as soon as the observed signals do not satisfy the property.

2.1 Safety properties

A *trace* σ on a set of signals S is a finite or infinite sequence of events on S. A *property* on S is a set of traces on S. An I/O machine M satisfies a property P if and only if each trace of M belongs to P. A property P on S is a *safety property* if and only if:

$$\sigma \in P \iff \sigma' \in P \text{ for any finite prefix } \sigma' \text{ of } \sigma$$

In other words, a safety property is a prefix-closed (as expressed by the "$\Longrightarrow$" implication above) and limit-closed (as expressed by the "$\Longleftarrow$" implication) language on the vocabulary 2^S.

2.2 Observer

Let P be a safety property on S. Let α (read "alarm") be a signal not in S. An *observer* of P is a *deterministic* and *reactive* I/O machine $\Omega_P = (Q_{\Omega_P}, q0_{\Omega_P}, S, \{\alpha\}, \delta_{\Omega_P})$, returning a sequence of empty output events as long as it receives a sequence of input events which belongs to P. More precisely, let σ be a finite trace on S belonging to P (notice that the empty trace belongs to any safety property). Let q_σ be the state that Ω_P reaches after reading σ (if σ is the empty trace, q_σ is the initial state of Ω_P). Then, for any event $e \in 2^S$,

$$\delta^O_{\Omega_P}(q_\sigma, e) = \begin{cases} \emptyset & \text{if } \sigma.e \in P \\ \{\alpha\} & \text{otherwise} \end{cases}$$

Let us assume also that any transition emitting α leads to a distinguished state q_α.

Now, a machine M satisfies a safety property P if and only if the compound machine $M||\Omega_P$ never returns any event containing α; or, equivalently, never reaches an *erroneous* state belonging to $Q_M \times \{q_\alpha\}$. We will note Q_P^M the set $Q_M \times (Q_{\Omega_P} \backslash \{q_\alpha\})$ of non erroneous states of $M||\Omega_P$.

A practical advantage of this approach, is that the properties are written in the same language as the programs, and in fact, properties are programs. As such, they can be executed and tested. An observer can be actually run with the program, thus detecting any violation of the property (run-time checks).

Notice that this approach cannot be used with only an asynchronous composition, or at least, that it cannot be applied *modularly*. For instance, consider the following property: "*the signal* b *is emitted at least once between every two successive emissions of the signal* a ". If this property is checked by an asynchronous observer, since the observer is not guaranteed to catch all the signals, it can miss any occurrence of b. So, even if the property is satisfied, the observer can emit an alarm. To check such a property of an asynchronous program, one must add some synchronization code all along the transitions of the observed program, since otherwise, the asynchronous product does not ensure that all the transitions will be observed. When verifying a program, such modifications are of course harmful, since one cannot be sure that the verified program behaves the same once the additional code is removed. This contradicts G. Berry's "WYPIWYE" principle ("*what you prove is what you execute*") which fully applies in the synchronous case.

2.3 Application to program verification

The verification that a machine M satisfies a safety property P now amounts to proving that the machine $M' = M||\Omega_P$ never returns any event containing α. So, any safety property has been translated into an *invariant*. More precisely, one has to prove that the set $Reach(M')$ of M' *reachable states* is included in the set Q_P^M of non erroneous states of M'. $Reach(M')$ is classically defined as a least fixpoint:

$$Reach(M') = \mu X.\{q0_{M'}\} \cup post_{M'}(X)$$

Let us list the advantages of this expression of the verification problem, according to various verification methods:

State enumeration: For finite state systems, state enumeration techniques (enumerative model-checking) have been widely experimented [31, 11]. In general, these techniques involve the construction of the whole state graph of the program, and its memorization for the analysis of *trace properties*. Now, since the problem has been reduced to the analysis of a *state property* (an invariant), the state graph needs only to be *traversed*. Particularly efficient techniques are available (e.g., [18]) for such a traversal.

Reduction techniques: The drawback of state enumeration techniques is the explosion of the number of states, as the size of the program increases[3]. Other approaches [7] consist in building a reduced state graph, according to some observation criteria. Now, in our approach, the machine of interest is not really $M||\Omega_P$, but rather $(M||\Omega_P) \downarrow \alpha$, since we are only interested in the presence of the signal α. This is an obvious observation criterion. So, in contrast with classic model-checking, the property is taken into account in the state graph generation. Assume the property is satisfied, then the minimal state graph of $(M||\Omega_P)\downarrow\alpha$ has only one state (it is the "always silent" automaton). Algorithms for generating a minimal state graph have been proposed [5, 25]. When applied to our simple verification problem, these algorithms amount to proving that the initial state belongs to the greatest invariant $Invar(Q_P^M)$ included in Q_P^M, i.e., the greatest part of Q_P^M from which the transition relation

[3]Notice that the state explosion is more important in an asynchronous system, because of the non deterministic interleaving of asynchronous transitions.

does not permit to go out. This greatest invariant is wellknown to be a greatest fixpoint:

$$Invar(Q_P^M) = \nu X.Q_P^M \cap \widetilde{pre}_{M||\Omega_P}(X)$$

Approximate analysis: When infinite state systems are considered, approximate methods (and, in particular, ***abstract interpretation techniques*** [9, 10]) can be applied to compute approximations of the set $Reach((M||\Omega_P) \downarrow \alpha)$. If an upper approximation of this set is included in Q_P^M, this proves that the erroneous states cannot be reached (see [13] for an application of such a method). If a lower approximation intersects the complement of Q_P^M, an error is detected.

In the remainder of the paper, we will essentially consider finite state machines, so all the considered fixpoints will be (theoretically) computable. In the following section, we will see that property observers can also be used to take into account known properties of the program environment.

3 Taking the environment into account

The main feature of reactive systems is that they tightly interact with their environment. As a consequence, the properties of the environment must be carefully taken into account in the design and verification of such a system. A reactive system is not intended to work in an ***arbitrary*** environment. In general, system specifications contain a lot of informations about the behavior of the environment, which are the hypotheses under which the design must take place. These known properties about the environment can involve not only the inputs of the system, but also its outputs, since the environment responds to the system. So, in general, among the set of traces of an I/O machine, only some of them are "realistic", i.e., satisfy the assumptions about the environment. In this section, we show how the behavior of an I/O machine can be restricted by a safety property, in order to take such assumptions into account in the verification process.

3.1 Behavior restriction

Given a safety property A (assumption) of the environment of M, our goal is to define a *restricted* machine M' having exactly the same behaviors as M composed with any environment satisfying A: the set of traces of M' must be the intersection with A of the set of traces of M.

Restriction: Let M be an I/O machine, and Ω_A be an observer of a safety property A on the set $S = I_M \cup O_M$ of input/output signals of M. Let $M' = M||\Omega_A$. We define the restriction M/Ω_A to be the I/O machine $(Q_{M'}, q0_{M'}, I_M, O_M, \delta')$, where $\delta' = \{(q, i, o, q') \in \delta_{M'} \mid \alpha \notin o\}$

Obviously, the restricted machine M/Ω_A is generally not reactive, even if M is reactive: The restriction takes into account a property of the environment, and thus, refuses some unrealistic inputs. However, it can happen that in some states of the restricted machine, ***all the input events*** are refused. So, the restricted machine deadlocks, a highly undesirable situation in reactive systems. One can consider this as an error in the expression of the assumption A. However, we adopt another point of view: When restricting a machine M with an assumption A, the user intends to consider all the *infinite traces* of M that satisfy A. So, the machine must not enter any path in M/Ω_A which *inevitably* leads to a deadlock state. We define now another restriction, called *non-blocking restriction*, which has the intended behavior:

Non-blocking restriction: Let M be an I/O machine, and Ω_A be an observer of a safety property A on the set $S = I_M \cup O_M$ of input/output signals of M. Let $M' = M||\Omega_A$. Let us call $sink_A$ the set of states of M' leading inevitably to the violation of A:

$$sink_A = \mu X.\widetilde{pre}_{M'}((Q_M \times \{q_\alpha\}) \cup X)$$

Then, if $q0_{M'} \notin sink_A$, we define $M/_{\!\infty}\, \Omega_A$ to be the I/O machine $(Q_{M'} \setminus sink_A, q0_{M'}, I_M, O_M, \delta'')$, where

$$\begin{aligned} \delta'' &= \delta_{M'} \cap ((Q_{M'} \setminus sink_A) \times E_{I_M} \times E_{O_M} \times (Q_{M'} \setminus sink_A)) \\ &= \{(q, i, o, q') \in \delta_{M'} \mid q, q' \notin sink_A \text{ and } \alpha \notin o\} \end{aligned}$$

One can notice that, if M is deterministic, $M/_{\!\infty}\Omega_A = M/\Omega_{traces(Q_{M'} \setminus sink_A)}$. So, the property A has been strengthened into the other property $A' = traces(Q_{M'} \setminus sink_A)$ which cannot block the machine M: Any finite trace satisfying A' leads to state of M which has at least one outgoing transition preserving A'.

3.2 Application

As before, a direct use of this way of expressing assumptions by an observer, is to execute the observer with the program, thus checking at run-time that the assumptions are satisfied. The restriction can also be used for program testing, to use only testcases corresponding to realistic scenarios. We consider now the use of restriction in the verification process:

Verification under assumptions: Given an I/O machine M, a safety assumption A about its environment, and a safety property P, one can prove that M satisfies P provided the environment satisfies A, by

1. proving that $(M/_{\!\infty}\Omega_A)$ has some behaviors, i.e., that the initial state of $M||\Omega_A$ does not belong to $sink_A$. Otherwise, the assumption and the program are contradictory.
2. verifying that the machine $((M/_{\!\infty}\Omega_A)||\Omega_P) \downarrow \{\alpha\}$ emits only empty events (Of course, here, α is the alarm signal of Ω_P).

Modular verification: Any sub-process of a compound system sees the remainder of the system as a part of its own environment. The ability to take the environment into account allows modular verification: Having proved a property about a sub-process, one can use this property in the verification of the remainder of the system. More precisely, let M_1, M_2 be two machines, and let P be a safety property we want to prove about $M_1||M_2$. Assume another safety property P' has been proven about M_2 alone. Then if $M_1 \angle_\infty \Omega_{P'}$ satisfies P, so does $M_1 || M_2$. This amounts to considering M_2 as the environment of M_1. Of course, assumptions about the global environment can also be taken into account. With a little additional hypothesis (see [2] and the "decomposition theorem" of [23]), which amounts to the absence of causality problems, one can even use a seemingly circular reasoning, which consists first in proving a property P_2 of M_2 under the assumption that M_1 satisfies P_1, and then in proving that M_1 satisfies P_1 assuming M_2 satisfies P_2.

Inductive proofs: Moreover, the modular verification technique can be extended to the inductive verification of regular networks of processes [34, 16]. Assume one wants to prove a safety property P of the machine

$$\underbrace{M||M||\ldots||M}_{n \text{ times}}$$

for any $n \geq 1$. This can be done by finding a property P' such that (1) M satisfies P', (2) $(M \angle_\infty \Omega_{P'})$ satisfies P', and (3) P' implies P. (1) proves that P' holds for $n = 1$, (2) proves that, if P' holds for n, then it holds for $n + 1$. So, P' holds for any n, and from (3), so does P. Point (3) can be established by proving that the machine $\chi(I, O) \angle_\infty \Omega_{P'}$ satisfies P, where

$$\chi(I, O) = (\{q\}, q, I, O, \{q\} \times E_I \times E_O \times \{q\})$$

is the "chaos" machine which completely non deterministically returns any event of E_O whatever be its input event from E_I. Of course, as for modular verification, a crucial problem is the choice of the property P'. It is considered in the next section.

4 Specification synthesis

Let us come back to modular verification: Given two machines M_1 and M_2, and a safety property P on $S = I_{M_1} \cup O_{M_1} \cup I_{M_2} \cup O_{M_2}$, one must find a property P' on $S_2 = I_{M_2} \cup O_{M_2}$ such that

1. M_2 satisfies P', and
2. $M_1 \angle_\infty \Omega_{P'}$ satisfies P

Moreover, the proof of each of the above points is expected to be easier than the global proof that $M_1 || M_2$ satisfies P.

This section deals with the synthesis of such a property P', satisfying the point (2) above by construction, when all the involved machines are finite state.

First, we need some additional definitions: Let $\sigma = (e_1, e_2, \ldots, e_n, \ldots)$ be a trace on S. We define the *projection* of σ on a set S' of signals to be the trace $\sigma \downarrow S' = (e_1 \cap S', e_2 \cap S', \ldots, e_n \cap S', \ldots)$. The projection on S' of a set T of traces is $T \downarrow S' = \{\sigma \downarrow S' \mid \sigma \in T\}$. If T is a set of *finite* traces on S, we note $\mathcal{C}(T)$ the set of traces on S which do not have any prefix in T. Obviously, $\mathcal{C}(T)$ is a safety property.

The intuitive method to find P' is the following: Replace M_2 by the "chaos" machine $\chi(I_{M_2}, O_{M_2})$. If $M_1 || \chi(I_{M_2}, O_{M_2})$ satisfies P, the machine M_2 does not influence the satisfaction of P (i.e. we can take $P' = \mathit{true}$) and we are done. Otherwise, $M_1 || \chi(I_{M_2}, O_{M_2})$ can reach some erroneous states, and the role of M_2 is to forbid the traces leading to those states. But, for doing so, M_2 can only restrict its own signals (P' cannot involve signals that M_2 cannot see).

More precisely: If $\mathit{Reach}(M_1 || \Omega_P)$ does not intersect $Q_{M_1} \times \{q_\alpha\}$, let $P' = \mathit{true}$. Otherwise let $T_{\mathrm{err}} = \mathit{traces}(Q_{M_1} \times \{q_\alpha\})$ be the set of erroneous traces. The following proposition states that $\mathcal{C}(T_{\mathrm{err}} \downarrow S_2)$ is a necessary and sufficient property that M_2 must satisfy so that $M_1 || M_2$ satisfies P:

Proposition: Let $P' = \mathcal{C}(T_{\mathrm{err}} \downarrow S_2)$. Then $M_2 \models P' \iff M_1 || M_2 \models P$.

Proof: Let $\sigma[n]$ denote the nth prefix of a trace σ.
($\Longrightarrow$): If $M_2 \models P'$, then every trace σ of $M1 || M2$ satisfies $\sigma \downarrow S_2 \in \mathcal{C}(T_{\mathrm{err}} \downarrow S_2)$. So, $\forall n, (\sigma \downarrow S_2)[n] \notin T_{\mathrm{err}} \downarrow S_2$, and since $(\sigma \downarrow S_2)[n] = (\sigma[n] \downarrow S2), \forall n, \sigma[n] \notin T_{\mathrm{err}}$. This means that $\sigma \in P$.
($\Longleftarrow$): Assume M_2 does not satisfy P', and let σ be a trace of M_2 not belonging to P'. Then, there exists n such that $\sigma[n] \in (T_{\mathrm{err}} \downarrow S_2)$, and there exists a trace $\sigma' \in T_{\mathrm{err}}$ such that $\sigma[n] = (\sigma'[n]) \downarrow (S_2)$. So, the finite trace $\sigma'[n]$ is compatible with both M_1 and M_2 and leads to the violation of P. □

Remark: $P' = \mathcal{C}(T_{\mathrm{err}} \downarrow S_2)$ is stronger than $P'' = \mathcal{C}(T_{\mathrm{err}}) \downarrow S_2$. A trace σ of M_2 can be the common projection of two traces σ' and σ'' of $M_1 || M_2$, with $\sigma' \in \mathcal{C}(T_{\mathrm{err}})$ and $\sigma'' \notin \mathcal{C}(T_{\mathrm{err}})$. In that case, σ belongs to P'' (as the projection of σ') and not to P'.

Stronger specifications: However, the necessary and sufficient property $P' = \mathcal{C}(T_{\mathrm{err}} \downarrow S_2)$ is sometimes too complicated to be interesting: As a matter of fact, an observer of P' can be as complicated as $M_1 || \Omega_P$. In that case the proof that M_2 satisfies P' is not easier than the proof that $M_1 || M_2$ satisfies P, so nothing is gained with modular proof. Now, any stronger property than P' can be tried. Such a stronger property P'' will still ensure that $M_1 /\!\!/_{\infty} \Omega_{P''}$ satisfies P, but, since it is no longer a necessary property, one cannot conclude that $M_1 || M_2$ does not satisfy P if M_2 does not satisfy P'' .

The basic technique to build such a stronger property P'' is the following: Let us note the function $\lambda T.\, \mathcal{C}(T \downarrow S_2)$ by "*avoid*". Thus, $P' = \mathit{avoid}(T_{\mathrm{err}})$. Then, for any set T of traces containing T_{err} (i.e., for any upper approximation of T_{err}), $\mathit{avoid}(T)$ is stronger than P'.

5 Module synthesis

In the preceding section, we have outlined a method to find a property P' such that, for any machine M_2 satisfying P', $M_1 || M_2$ satisfies P. P' has been only deduced from M_1 and P, so, it could be built even before M_2 is designed. So, the next question is: can M_2 be *synthesized* from P', considered as a specification? In the finite state case, this is theoretically possible: The specification must be strengthened to become *executable*. P' has been constructed so as to concern only the input/output signals of M_2. Now, an additional constraint is that M_2 must preserve P' by controlling only its output signals. In each reachable state, and whatever be the received input event (possibly satisfying an input assumption), M_2 must be able to perform a transition preserving P'.

Executability: A property P on a set of signals $S = I \cup O$ is *executable* with respect to (I, O), if and only if for any finite trace $\sigma \in P$, for any input event $i \in E_I$, there exists an output event $o \in E_O$ such that $\sigma.(i \cup o) \in P$. For any safety property P, there exists a weakest executable safety property, implying P. It will be noted $\mathcal{E}(P)$.

Relative precondition: Let P be a safety property on $I \cup O$ and Ω_P be an observer of P. For any $X \subseteq Q_{\Omega_P}$, we define

$$pre^I_{\Omega_P}(X) = \{q \mid \forall i \subseteq I, \exists o \subseteq O, \delta^Q_{\Omega_P}(q, i \cup o) \in X\}$$

In other words, $pre^I_{\Omega_P}(X)$ is the set of states which can lead into X (in one step) *whatever be the input event* received in these states.

Executable strengthening: Let $Exe = \nu X.\, pre^I_{\Omega_P}(X) \setminus \{q_\alpha\}$. Then Exe does not contain the erroneous state q_α, and

$$\forall q \in Exe,\ \forall i \subseteq I,\ \exists o \subseteq O,\ \text{such that } \delta^Q_{\Omega_P}(q, i \cup o) \in Exe$$

Moreover, Exe is the largest set of states satisfying this property. As a consequence, a restriction of Ω_P which detects any trace going out of Exe is an observer of $\mathcal{E}(P)$. Another consequence is that $\chi(O, I)/\Omega_{\mathcal{E}(P)}$ is the most general reactive machine satisfying P. Notice that Exe can be empty, which means that P is not *realizable* in the sense of [3]: There is no machine on (I, O) preserving P against any environment.

Conclusion

Many ideas that have been presented are specializations and simplifications of previous works. For instance:

- The specification of properties by means of a synchronous observer is very close to the approach of COSPAN [24], which takes also into account liveness, both in the program and the properties.
- Several verification approaches take into account the environment, e.g., [21] [2] [22], and some of them propose modular methods. The "don't care sets" considered in hardware design and verification [4, 12] are also a way of expressing assumptions about the environment.
- The synthesis problems considered in Sections 4 and 5 have been dealt with in several papers — both in control theory [32, 33, 19], and in computer science [30, 3] — and often extended to cope with liveness properties.

Our simplifications consist in considering *safety properties* of *synchronous systems*. They are suggested by the application field we have in mind: The synchronous model has been shown to be very convenient for the design of reactive systems. In general, most liveness properties are introduced for one of the following reasons:

- To abstract a real-time constraint: For instance, one replace a deadline property by the requirement that something "eventually occurs". Now, in reactive systems, such real-time constraints may not be abstracted, in general: the constraint "*an alarm must be sent within 2 milliseconds after the detection of a dangerous situation*" may not be replaced by "*the alarm must eventually occur*"!

- To restrict the asynchronous semantics: In asynchronous models, concurrency is modelled by non-deterministic interleaving, and this non-determinism must be restricted by fairness constraints. Obviously, this problem does not exist in the synchronous model. In asynchronous systems, compositionality is also achieved by allowing arbitrary (but fair) "stuttering" of processes. The synchronous model is obviously compositional thanks to zero-time, simultaneous, reactions.

Now, these simplifications are certainly fruitful, from a practical point of view. They increase the performances of the automatic tools: For instance, for finite state methods, the synchronous model drastically reduces the size of the considered state graphs; safety properties can be checked by a graph traversal, without storing any path. To specify a safety property by means of an observer, one doesn't need to use — and to learn – any other language than the programming language used to write the program. All these ideas are under implementation in the Lustre- Saga software development system [15], and actual industrial experimentations are going on.

References

[1] D. Austry and G. Boudol. Algèbre de processus et synchronisation. *TCS*, 30, April 1984.

[2] M. Abdi and L. Lamport. Composing specifications. In J.W. de Bakker, W.-P. de Roever, and G. Rozemberg, editors, *REX Workshop on Stepwise Refinement of Distributed Systems, Models, Formalisms, Correctness*. LNCS 430, Springer Verlag, May 1989.

[3] M. Abadi, L. Lamport, and P. Wolper. Realizable and unrealizable specifications of reactive systems. In G. Ausiello, M. Dezani-Ciancaglini, and S. Ronchi Della Rocca, editors, *16th ICALP*, pages 1–17. LNCS 372, Springer Verlag, July 1989.

[4] K. A. Bartlett, R. K. Brayton, G. D. Hachtel, R. M. Jacoby, R. Rudell, A. Sangiovanni-Vincentelli, and A. Wang. Multilevel logic minimization using implicit don't cares. *IEEE Transactions on CAD/ICAS*, CAD-7(6):723–739, June 1988.

[5] A. Bouajjani, J. C. Fernandez, N. Halbwachs, P. Raymond, and C. Ratel. Minimal state graph generation. *Science of Computer Programming*, 18:247–269, 1992.

[6] G. Berry and G. Gonthier. The Esterel synchronous programming language: Design, semantics, implementation. *Science Of Computer Programming*, 19(2):87–152, 1992.

[7] G. Boudol, V. Roy, R. de Simone, and D. Vergamini. Process calculi, from theory to practice: Verification tools. In *International Workshop on Automatic Verification Methods for Finite State Systems, Grenoble*. LNCS 407, Springer Verlag, 1990.

[8] F. Boussinot and R. de Simone. The Esterel language. *Proceedings of the IEEE*, 79(9):1293–1304, September 1991.

[9] P. Cousot and R. Cousot. Abstract interpretation: a unified lattice model for static analysis of programs by construction or approximation of fixpoints. In *4th ACM Symposium on Principles of Programming Languages*, January 1977.

[10] P. Cousot and R. Cousot. Abstract interpretation and application to logic programs. Research Report LIX/RR/92/08, Ecole Polytechnique, March 1992. (to appear in the Journal of Logic Programming, special issue on Abstract Interpretation).

[11] E. M. Clarke, E. A. Emerson, and A. P. Sistla. Automatic verification of finite-state concurrent systems using temporal logic specifications. *ACM TOPLAS*, 8(2), 1986.

[12] M. Damiani and G. DeMicheli. Don't care set specifications in combinational and synchronous logic circuits. Technical Report CSL-TR-92-531, Computer Systems Laboratory, Stanford University, 1992.

[13] N. Halbwachs. Delay analysis in synchronous programs. In *Fifth Int. Workshop on Computer Aided Verification, Elounda (Crete)*, July 1993.

[14] N. Halbwachs. *Synchronous programming of reactive systems*. Kluwer Academic Pub., 1993.

[15] N. Halbwachs, P. Caspi, P. Raymond, and D. Pilaud. The synchronous dataflow programming language Lustre. *Proceedings of the IEEE*, 79(9):1305–1320, September 1991.

[16] N. Halbwachs, F. Lagnier, and C. Ratel. An experience in proving regular networks of processes by modular model checking. *Acta Informatica*, 29(6/7), 1992.

[17] N. Halbwachs, F. Lagnier, and C. Ratel. Programming and verifying real-time systems by means of the synchronous data-flow programming language Lustre. *IEEE Transactions on Software Engineering, Special Issue on the Specification and Analysis of Real-Time Systems*, September 1992.

[18] G. J. Holzmann. Automated protocol validation in Argos : Assertion proving and scatter searching. *IEEE Trans. on Software Ingineering*, SE-13(6):683–696, June 1987.

[19] G. Hoffmann and H. Wong-Toi. Symbolic synthesis of supervisory controllers. In *American Control Conference, Chicago*, June 1992.

[20] Another look at real-time programming. *Special Section of the Proceedings of the IEEE*, 79(9):1293–1304, September 1991.

[21] B. Josko. MCTL - An extension of CTL for modular verification of concurrent systems. In *Workshop on Temporal Logic in Specification, Manchester*. LNCS 398, Springer Verlag, 1987.

[22] M. B. Josephs. Receptive process theory. *Acta Informatica*, 29, February 1992.

[23] R. P. Kurshan and L. Lamport. Verification of a multiplier: 64 bits and beyond. In *Fifth Int. Workshop on Computer Aided Verification, Elounda (Crete)*, July 1993.

[24] R. P. Kurshan. Analysis of discrete event coordination. In J.W. de Bakker, W.-P. de Roever, and G. Rozemberg, editors, *REX Workshop on Stepwise Refinement of Distributed Systems, Models, Formalisms, Correctness*. LNCS 430, Springer Verlag, May 1989.

[25] D. Lee and M. Yanakakis. Online minimization of transition systems. In *24th ACM Symp. on the Theory of Computing, STOC'92, Vancouver, B.C.*, 1992.

[26] F. Maraninchi. Operational and compositional semantics of synchronous automaton compositions. In *CONCUR'92, Stony Brook*. LNCS 630, Springer Verlag, August 1992.

[27] R. Milner. On relating synchrony and asynchrony. Technical Report CSR-75-80, Computer Science Dept., Edimburgh Univ., 1981.

[28] R. Milner. Calculi for synchrony and asynchrony. *TCS*, 25(3), July 1983.

[29] A. Pnueli. How vital is liveness? Verifying timing properties of reactive and hybrid systems. In *CONCUR'92, Stony Brook*. LNCS 630, Springer Verlag, August 1992.

[30] A. Pnueli and R. Rosner. On the synthesis of a reactive module. In *16th Conference on Principles of Programming Languages*. ACM, 1989.

[31] J. P. Queille and J. Sifakis. Specification and verification of concurrent systems in Cesar. In *International Symposium on Programming*. LNCS 137, Springer Verlag, April 1982.

[32] P. J. Ramadge and W. M. Wonham. Supervisory control of a class of discrete event processes. *SIAM J. Control and Optimization*, 25(1), January 1987.

[33] P. J. Ramadge and W. M. Wonham. The control of discrete event systems. *Proceedings of the IEEE*, 77(1), January 1989.

[34] P. Wolper and V. Lovinfosse. Verifying properties of large sets of processes with network invariants. In *International Workshop on Automatic Verification Methods for Finite State Systems, Grenoble*. LNCS 407, Springer Verlag, 1989.

Constraints in Term Algebras (Short Survey)

Hubert Comon
CNRS and LRI, Bât. 490
Univ. Paris-Sud
91405 Orsay cedex, France

Abstract

First, we define what is a *constraint system* and list few possible applications of them. Then, we survey recent results on constraint in term algebras. Finally, we propose a methodology of constraint solving and illustrate it on a toy example.

1 Constraints: a definition

Unification, which consists in solving equations in the (free) term algebra, is known to be a fundamental operation in many areas of computer science and, in particular, in logic programming. *Disunification*, which consists in solving more complex formulae in the (free) term algebra, also revealed to be a fundamental operation (see [29, 13] for surveys on unification and disunification respectively). Recently, these computations have been seen as *constraint solving* in term algebras and this point of view is actually fruitful.

A *constraint system* is defined by a *logical language* $\mathcal{C}$ (which is in practice a fragment of a first-order language), a *structure* M in which the formulae of $\mathcal{C}$ are interpreted and an algorithm which decides, for every $\phi \in \mathcal{C}$, whether ϕ is satisfiable in M or not. There are many examples: $\mathcal{C}$ can be a full first-order language, in which case, the third condition implies the decidability of the (first-order) theory of M. For example, the constraint system could correspond to Presburger arithmetic or the theory of real numbers. It could also be the theory of finite trees, since this theory has been shown decidable [35, 34, 18]. Many other examples will be given later.

Now, constraints can be (and have been) studied for their own mathematical interest. But, they can also be used to *constrain* other formulae. More precisely, given a logical language $\mathcal{L}$, a class of structures $\mathcal{S}$ and a satisfaction relation $\models$ on the one hand, and a constraint system $(\mathcal{C}, M, \Phi)$ on the other hand and given in addition, for each structure S in $\mathcal{S}$, a mapping H_S from the domain D of M into the domain D_S of the structure S, the *constrained logic* consists of

- the language of pairs of formulae (called *constrained formulae*) $\phi | C$ where $\phi \in \mathcal{L}$ and $C \in \mathcal{C}$
- a satisfaction relation defined as follows. Given an assignment σ of the free variables of C into D and an assignment θ of the free variables of ϕ

into D_S,

$$\sigma, \theta, S \models \phi | C \quad \text{iff} \quad \begin{cases} M \models C\sigma \\ H_S(\sigma) \circ \theta, S \models \phi \end{cases}$$

where $H_S(\sigma)$ is the assignment which associates each variable x in the domain of σ with $H_S(x\sigma)$.

This definition is somewhat complicated and is not satisfactory in many respects, but everything simplifies when we consider constraints in *term structures* (also called *symbolic constraints*). Indeed, assuming that M is a term structure and that terms of C are also terms of $\mathcal{L}$, H_S can be (and will be) chosen as the interpretation defined by S. This means that we do no longer need M to define the meaning of a constrained formula:

$$\phi | C \ \text{ represents } \ \{\phi\sigma \mid \sigma, M \models C\}$$

a constrained formula is a shorthand for the (infinite) set of its instances corresponding to assignments of its free variables which satisfy the constraint. For example, $P(x, y)|x \neq y$ could represent the set of all formulae $P(t_1, t_2)$ where t_1 and t_2 are two distinct terms. This justifies the use of the symbol | which can be read "such that": its use here does not differ from its use in set definitions (under the comprehension axiom).

Let us conclude these definitions with two remarks: first, this notion of "constraints" is coherent with what is used in practice in logic programming or artificial intelligence, but differs slightly from the "constraints" as they are used in the algebraic specification community. Let us also emphasize that constraints are different from conditions; consider for example the system

$$\begin{cases} f(x) = a \mid a = b \\ a = b \end{cases}$$

where a, b are two distinct constant symbols. Considering these formulae as constrained ones, in which the equality symbol is freely interpreted, the first constrained formula represents the set $\{f(x)\sigma = a\sigma \mid \sigma \models a = b\}$. But $a = b$ is unsatisfiable in the free algebra since a and b are distinct. Hence, this set is empty and the system collapses to the single equation $a = b$. On the contrary, if | is seen as an implication $\leftarrow$, then it is possible to prove $a = b$ using the second equation, and hence, by modus ponens, we prove that $f(x) = a$.

2 On the use of constraints

It should be clear from the definition that (symbolic) constraints can enhance the expressiveness of a logical language, since they allow for a schematization of possibly infinite sets of formulae. This ability has been used in many situations:

- in constraint logic programming (e.g. [28])
- to construct (counter)models [7]
- to forbid particular instances [30]

- to express control strategies at the formulae level [40]
- to avoid the combinatorial explosion of semantic unification (e.g. [22])

Even when the set which is schematized by a constraint is not infinite, it can be very large and might be represented in a more compact way. For example, constraints may express structure sharing (see e.g. [32]): $f(x, x, x, x) \mid x = t$ where t is a big term is a compact representation of $f(t, t, t, t)$ avoiding duplications.

Constraints are also used to store irrelevant (from the computational point of view) parts of a formula. This is the case for equational constraints and the so-called *basic strategy* (see [2, 39] for recent developments).

Finally, constraints are interpreted in a fixed domain for which dedicated efficient solving techniques can be used. Hence, it is worth characterizing some decidable fragment in a logic programming language and leave it as constraint, thus taking advantage of the knowledge on the domain (see [23] for an example of automatic detection of such fragments). This was originally one of the main motivations for adding constraints into logic programming languages: for example linear equations over the integers are not solved using the logic programming langage (which is in principle possible), but rather using another syntax and another deduction mechanism. And, as shown in [28], constraint systems can be nicely combined with any logic programming language (without equality).

3 Examples of symbolic constraints

3.1 Equations

The most well-known example of symbolic constraints is given by unification problems. In such a constraint system, the logical language consists of (disjunction of existentially quantified) conjunctions of equations between terms. The equations are interpreted in the free term algebra $T(F)$ (this is the classical interpretation) or in some quotient $T(F)/_{=_E}$ by a finitely generated congruence $=_E$. Using these constraints in logic programs or automated deductions prevents applying substitutions, which may be an expensive operation in case of duplications. That is why they are used since the very beginning in logic programming. In case of interpretations in quotient algebras, equations are also more relevant than unifiers since there might be a very large minimal complete set of unifiers (doubly exponential w.r.t. the size of the equations, in the case of associative-commutative (AC) function symbols), whereas the satisfiability of an equation system is much simpler (NP-complete in the case of AC symbols) [32]. We will not survey the equational theories for which unification is decidable, but refer to [29] instead.

Several extensions of the syntax, for example mixing integer expressions and terms, allow one to schematize infinite sets of terms (as constraints do). Solving equations over this extended syntax has been investigated in several recent papers [9, 15, 43] with applications in logic programming.

3.2 Equational formulae

More generally, *equational formulae* are arbitrary first-order formulae over an alphabet F of function symbols and the equality predicate symbol. Assuming that they are interpreted in the free term algebra, there are several decision techniques which lead to complete axiomatizations of the algebra of finite trees (see [35, 33, 34, 18, 36] and others). These axiomatizations differ, depending on the finiteness of F: when F is finite, the complete axiomatization consists of what is known as "Clark's axioms of equality" plus the *domain closure axiom*

$$\forall x, \bigvee_{f \in F} \exists \vec{x_f}. x = f(\vec{x_f}).$$

Such formulae have been used for solving various problems in rewriting theory (see [13]) and as a constraint system in automated theorem proving, searching simultaneously for a proof and for a counter-model [7].

Equational formulae can be generalized in various directions. One of them consists in adding *sort constraints*, which is studied in the next section. Another generalization consists in considering non-free interpretations: we assume a finite set of equational axioms E, generating a congruence $=_E$ on the term algebra. For example, some symbols can be assumed commutative, or associative and commutative. The first-order theory of a quotient algebra $T(F)/_{=_E}$ quickly becomes undecidable: a single associative symbol suffices [41], or an associative-commutative symbol [44]. Decidability results include the case where E is a set of flat permutative axioms [35], ground axioms [12] and E is a set of *shallow* equations, a class which encompasses the two previous ones [17].

3.3 Feature constraints

Feature trees have been introduced in order to represent linguistic information. These are rational trees whose nodes are labeled with sorts (out of an infinite set of symbols) and whose edges are labeled with *features* out of another infinite set of symbols. Contrary to constructor trees, each node may have an arbitrary number of unordered sons. The logic of feature trees (as in [5], but there are also other feature logics with different atomic formulae) involve unary predicates Ax (saying that the tree has sort A at its root), binary predicates xfy (y is a direct subtree of x, the edge relating x and y being labeled with f), unary predicates xf (x has feature f) and equality. There is however no function symbol in the logic. There are many results about feature constraints. We refer to [5] for a recent result: a complete axiomatization of the theory of feature trees.

3.4 Membership constraints

(Symbolic) constraints actually define sets of assignments which satisfy the constraints. Instead of using formulae, these sets can be defined by means of automata or grammars. For example, order-sorted signatures [25] (which are nothing but finite bottom-up tree automata) are used to constrain variables to belong to recognizable sets of trees. However, this is often hidden in the order-sorted algebra framework. The point of view "sorts as membership constraints" allows for a number of improvements. For example, there is no need of "regularity" (often required in the order-sorted framework) because unifiers are replaced with solved forms which may involve membership constraints. Another example is the design of critical pair lemmas for order-sorted rewriting [14].

Membership constraints consist of an (infinite) family of membership predicate symbols $\in \zeta$ which are interpreted as recognizable subsets of the term algebra $T(F)$. The satisfiability of equational formulae remains decidable with this additional construction [10]. These formulae have been used for solving problems in rewriting theory (e.g. "sufficient completeness" and "inductive reducibility" [13, 10]).

3.5 Ordering constraints

Ordering constraints are used as a means for expressing ordered strategies. Actually, using ordering constraints solves the old problem of non-orientable equations in rewriting theory by considering $s = t$ as two constrained rewrite rules $s \rightarrow t \mid s > t$ and $t \rightarrow s \mid t > s$. In other words, the equation can be considered as a rule from left to right or as a rule from right to left, depending on the instance which is considered. Moreover, the constraint keeps track of which instances remain to be considered in further deductions (see [40] for a completeness result in a more general setting).

Here, the logical language consists of purely existential formulae, using a set of function symbols F and the two predicate symbols $=$ and $\geq$. Several interpretations of the ordering have been considered:

- Venkataraman in [45] interprets $\geq$ as a subterm ordering, showing the decidability of the system (and undecidability of the first-order theory). However, such an ordering is useless for applications in rewriting theory, since it is not compatible with the term structure.

- The adequate orderings for the applications in automated deduction are the *reduction orderings* (see [20]) which are total on ground terms. A typical example of such an ordering is the *lexicographic path ordering* extending a total precedence, whose existential fragment has been shown decidable [11] (it is actually NP-complete [38]). This result has been extended to other total recursive path (quasi-)orderings [31]. The decidability of the full first-order theory of these orderings is an open question (problem 24 in [21]).

- The theory of partial recursive path orderings appears to be even more difficult; the Σ_4 fragment has been shown undecidable [44]. The decidability of the existential fragment of any such ordering is open. The only hint for this problem is the recent result of [6]: the *positive* existential fragment of the theory of tree embedding is decidable. (Tree embedding is the most simple recursive path ordering: it is the intersection of all simplification orderings).

- Interpreting $\geq$ as *encompassment* (a term t encompasses u if there is an instance of u which is a subterm of t), it is possible to express some properties such as *inductive reducibility* or (sometimes) *sufficient completeness* using first order formulae (see [8]). The first-order theory of a finite number of unary predicate symbols of the form $\geq t_i$ has been shown decidable in [8].

3.6 Set constraints

Many other symbolic constraints have been studied. But it is a too long work to list all of them. Let us conclude with *set constraints* for which many recent beautiful results have been obtained. (And there is still some work to do!). A *set expression* is built from a finite alphabet of function symbols, set variables and the intersection, union an complement symbols. Then, set constraints are finite conjunctions of formulae $e \subseteq e'$ where e, e' are set expressions. These formulae are interpreted assigning set variables to subsets of the term algebra $T(F)$.

Such constraints have been used for the analysis of logic and functional programs (see [26, 1, 23]). The case of *definite* constraints has been solved in [26] and the general case has been further studied by quite different means in [1, 3, 24]. There are two extensions which are still under investigation: adding negative constraints of the form $e \not\subseteq e'$ and adding the *projection* construction, which consists roughly of the inverse of applying a function symbol (see [26]). These extensions have been conjectured decidable.

4 Constraint solving

To *solve* a constraint not only means to decide its satisfiability. More precisely, a constraint solving algorithm is specified by:

- the constraint system $(\mathcal{C}, M, \Phi)$
- a subset $\mathcal{S}$ of $\mathcal{C}$ called the set of *solved forms*

$\mathcal{S}$ has to fulfill some requirements (see [13]), in particular, every formula of $\mathcal{C}$ should be equivalent (in M) to a solved form, and every solved form should be trivially satisfiable or trivially unsatisfiable. However, there is still some room for choosing the solved forms. For example, in the case of unification (in free algebras), one can choose *tree solved forms* or *DAG solved forms* as explained in [29].

Once solved forms have been chosen, constraint solving algorithms can be designed using rewriting techniques. A set of rewrite rules on formulae has to be given, their correctness proved (every formula in $\mathcal{C}$ is rewritten to an equivalent formula w.r.t. M), as well as termination (*any* rewriting sequence is finite) and completeness (every irreducible formula is a solved form). There are several advantages for this method:

- The rules can be redundant (and this is actually a desirable property). Then the termination proof may be complex, but it yields termination proof for all algorithms obtained by making the control deterministic. For example (as we will see below) tree solved forms (Robinson's unification algorithm [42, 27]) and DAG solved forms (corresponding to Martelli and Montanari's unification algorithm [37]) are obtained by strengthening the control on the same set of rules.

- There is a feed-back on the theory, since the rewrite rules are actually an axiomatization of M (see [13]).
- The constraint solving algorithms are automatically *incremental* in the following sense: in order to solve $\phi \wedge \psi$, it is possible to use the result of solving ψ.
- We expect to use rewriting tools for proving termination of the constraint solving rules, as we try to show in the following example.

A toy example

We consider the classical unification problems: formulae are conjunctions of equations between terms; they are interpreted in the free term algebra $T(F, X)$. The equality symbol is considered as symmetric (i.e. there is no difference between $s = t$ and $t = s$).

Given a conjunction of equations ϕ, the *occur-check relation* $\geq_\phi$ is the relation on the free variables of ϕ defined as the smallest reflexive-transitive relation which contains $x \geq_\phi y$ as soon as there is an equation $x = t[y]$ in ϕ. (The notation $t[y]$ means that y occurs in t). A variable is *solved* in ϕ if it has only one occurrence, as a member of an equation of ϕ. Let $U(\phi)$ be the set of unsolved variables of ϕ.

Now consider the scheme of rules for unification given below:

Decompose	$f(s_1, \ldots, s_n) = f(t_1, \ldots, t_n)$	$\rightarrow$	$s_1 = t_1 \wedge \ldots \wedge s_n = t_n$
Coalesce	$x = y \wedge P$	$\rightarrow$	$x = y \wedge P\{x \mapsto y\}$
			If $x \neq y$ and $x, y \in U(P \wedge x = y)$
Clash	$f(s_1, \ldots, s_n) = g(t_1, \ldots, t_m)$	$\rightarrow$	$\perp$
			If $f \neq g$
Eliminate	$x = s \wedge P$	$\rightarrow$	$x = s \wedge P\{x \mapsto s\}$
			If $x \in Var(P)$, $x \notin Var(s)$, $s \notin X$
Check*	$x_1 = t_1[x_2]_{p_1} \wedge \ldots \wedge x_n = t_n[x_1]_{p_n}$	$\rightarrow$	$\perp$
			If there is an i such that $p_i \neq \Lambda$
Trivial	$s = s$	$\rightarrow$	$\top$
Merge	$x = s \wedge x = t$	$\rightarrow$	$x = s \wedge s = t$

If Decompose, Coalesce, Check* do not apply, $s, t \notin X$ and x is maximal w.r.t. $\geq_\phi$ among the variables occuring at least twice as a member of an equation

In these rules we use some classical notations of [20], some of which are recalled below. *Positions* are strings of natural numbers and terms can be viewed as mappings from positions to symbols of F. The empty string is denoted Λ (the symbol at position Λ in a term t is the *root symbol* of t). $t|_p$ is the subterm of t at position p and the notation $t[x]_p$ is used either to indicate that $t|_p = x$ or for the term obtained by replacing $t|_p$ with x. $\{x_1 \mapsto t_1; \ldots; x_n \mapsto t_n\}$ is the substitution replacing the distinct variables $x_1, \ldots, x_n$ with $t_1, \ldots, t_n$ respectively. $Var(e)$ is the set of variable symbols occurring in e (whatever e can be).

Note that in these rules, we relax the classical condition on the sizes: $|s| \leq |t|$ in the merge rule (see [29]) and put instead a condition of maximality on x and assume the system decomposed. Whether these conditions can be relaxed without losing termination was stated as open problem 39 in [21]. We also assume here that there are structural rules for $\wedge$: $\bot \wedge P \rightarrow \bot$, $\top \wedge P \rightarrow P$ and $P \wedge P \rightarrow P$. Moreover $\wedge$ is assumed to be associative and commutative.

The rule system is terminating (modulo the associativity-commutativity of $\wedge$ and the commutativity of $=$). For, we use the ***associative path ordering*** [4] on formulae[1], extending the precedence on $F \cup X$ defined by:

- every variable[2] is larger than any function symbol
- every function symbol is larger than $=$ which is in turn larger than $\wedge$
- variables are compared according to the occur check relation

This last statement has to be made precise since the occur-check relation actually depends on the formula which is considered. In fact, we consider the (maybe infinite) union of all occur-check relations at any step in the computation. This definition depends on the transformation, but it does not depend on a particular formula ϕ, and we need not compute effectively this relation. It may happen that variables are *equivalent* w.r.t. this relation, in which case, they are considered as identical from the associative path ordering point of view.

Note that the associative path ordering has the subterm property and it is monotonic (see [4]). Hence, for proving the termination, we only have to prove that every left hand side of a rule is (strictly) larger than the corresponding right-hand-side:

- For the structural rules and for **Trivial**, **Check*** and **Clash** the decreasingness is obvious.
- **Decompose** is strictly decreasing because $=> \wedge$ in the precedence and

  $$f(s_1, \ldots, s_n) = f(t_1, \ldots, t_n) >_{apo} s_i = t_i$$

  by monotonicity and the subterm property.
- **Eliminate** is strictly decreasing because x is strictly larger than the variables of s (it is larger by definition, and it cannot be equivalent to any variable of s since x becomes solved after applying the rule, hence no rule can produce an equation with x in its right hand side). Moreover, variables are larger than function symbols in the precedence, which shows that $x >_{apo} s$.
- **Merge** is strictly decreasing, for the same reason as above: since x is assumed to be maximal in the decomposed system, it cannot be smaller than any variable of s or t, even after further transformations.
- **Coalesce** keeps the problem equivalent w.r.t. $\geq_{apo}$ since x and y are equivalent in the precedence. However, it can only be applied a finite number of times. Hence we can reason modulo this rule, i.e. modulo the strict equivalence on variables.

---

[1] We don't recall here the definition of associative path ordering. In this particular case, since we only have one AC symbol ($\wedge$) it coincides with the *recursive path ordering* [19] where all function symbols have a multiset status.

[2] Be careful that variables of the unification problem are seen as constants in the rewriting process! Only the *logical* variables can be instantiated.

Now, the system is terminating. If we remove the **Merge** rule, the system is complete w.r.t. tree solved forms and we can find Robinson's unification algorithm as an instance. If we remove the **Eliminate** rule, the system is complete w.r.t. DAG solved forms and we can find an instance of Martelli and Montanari's unification algorithm.

Similar techniques have been applied for the termination proofs of more powerful constraint systems [16, 14].

Acknowledgments

Thanks to A. Boudet and J.-P. Jouannaud for reading a former version of this paper.

References

[1] A. Aiken and E. Wimmers. Solving systems of set constraints. In *Proc. 7th IEEE Symp. on Logic in Computer Science*, Santa Cruz, CA, 1992.

[2] L. Bachmair, H. Ganzinger, C. Lynch, and W. Snyder. Basic paramodulation and superposition. In D. Kapur, editor, *Proc. 11th Int. Conf. on Automated Deduction, Saratoga Springs, NY, LNCS 607.* Springer-Verlag, June 1992.

[3] L. Bachmair, H. Ganzinger, and U. Waldmann. Set constraints are the monadic class. In *Proc. 8th IEEE Symp. Logic in Computer Science, Montréal*, 1993.

[4] L. Bachmair and D. A. Plaisted. Termination orderings for associative-commutative rewriting systems. *Journal of Symbolic Computation*, 1(4):329–349, Dec. 1985.

[5] R. Backofen and G. Smolka. A complete and recursive feature theory. Research Report RR–92–30, DFKI, Saarbrücken, Sept. 1992.

[6] A. Boudet and H. Comon. About the theory of tree embedding. In *Proc. CAAP 93*, 1993. LNCS 668.

[7] R. Caferra and N. Zabel. A method for simultaneous search for refutations and models by equational constraint solving. *Journal of Symbolic Computation*, 13(6):613–642, June 1992.

[8] A.-C. Caron, J.-L. Coquidé, and M. Dauchet. Encompassment properties and automata with constraints. In *Proc. RTA 93*, 1993.

[9] H. Chen and J. Hsiang. Logic programming with recurrence domains. In *Proc. 18th Int. Coll. on Automata, Languages and Programming, Madrid, LNCS 510*, 1991.

[10] H. Comon. Equational formulas in order-sorted algebras. In *Proc. 17th Int. Coll. on Automata, Languages and Programming, Warwick, LNCS 443*, Warwick, July 1990. Springer-Verlag.

[11] H. Comon. Solving symbolic ordering constraints. *International Journal of Foundations of Computer Science*, 1(4):387–411, 1990.

[12] H. Comon. Complete axiomatizations of some quotient term algebras. In *Proc. 18th Int. Coll. on Automata, Languages and Programming, Madrid, LNCS 510*, July 1991.

[13] H. Comon. Disunification: a survey. In J.-L. Lassez and G. Plotkin, editors, *Computational Logic: Essays in Honor of Alan Robinson*. MIT Press, 1991.

[14] H. Comon. Completion of rewrite systems with membership constraints. In W. Kuich, editor, *Proc. 19th Int. Coll. on Automata, Languages and Programming, LNCS 623*, Vienna, 1992. Springer-Verlag. An extended version is available as LRI Research Report number 699, Sept. 1991.

[15] H. Comon. On unification of terms with integer exponents. Research Report 770, L.R.I, Univ. Paris-Sud, Orsay, Aug. 1992. To appear in *Mathematical Systems Theory*.

[16] H. Comon and C. Delor. Equational formulas with membership constraints. Technical report, Laboratoire de Recherche en informatique, Mar. 1991. To appear in Information and Computation.

[17] H. Comon, M. Haberstrau, and J.-P. Jouannaud. Decidable properties of shallow equational theories. In *Proc. 7th IEEE Symp. Logic in Computer Science*, Santa Cruz, 1992. Also Research Report 718, Dec. 1991, Laboratoire de Recherche en Informatique, Orsay, France.

[18] H. Comon and P. Lescanne. Equational problems and disunification. *Journal of Symbolic Computation*, 7:371–425, 1989.

[19] N. Dershowitz. Termination of rewriting. *Journal of Symbolic Computation*, 3(1):69–115, Feb. 1987.

[20] N. Dershowitz and J.-P. Jouannaud. Rewrite systems. In J. van Leeuwen, editor, *Handbook of Theoretical Computer Science*, volume B, pages 243–309. North-Holland, 1990.

[21] N. Dershowitz, J.-P. Jouannaud, and J. W. Klop. Open problems in rewriting. Technical report, CWI, Amsterdam, Feb. 1991.

[22] E. Domenjoud. AC unification through order-sorted AC1 unification. *Journal of Symbolic Computation*, 14(6):537–556, Dec. 1992.

[23] T. Frühwirth, E. Shapiro, M. Vardi, and E. Yardeni. Logic programs as types for logic programs. In *Proc. 6th IEEE Symp. Logic in Computer Science, Amsterdam*, pages 300–309, 1991.

[24] R. Gilleron, S. Tison, and M. Tommasi. Solving systems of set constraints using tree automata. In *Proc. 10th Symposium on Theoretical Aspects of Computer Science, Würzburg, LNCS*, 1993.

[25] J. Goguen and J. Meseguer. Order-sorted algebra I: Partial and overloaded operators, errors and inheritance. Draft, Computer Science Lab., SRI International, 1987.

[26] N. Heintze and J. Jaffar. A decision procedure for a class of set constraints. In *Proc. 5th IEEE Symp. Logic in Computer Science, Philadelphia*, June 1990.

[27] J. Herbrand. Recherches sur la théorie de la démonstration. Thèse d'Etat, Univ. Paris, 1930. Also in: Ecrits logiques de Jacques Herbrand, PUF, Paris, 1968.

[28] J. Jaffar and J.-L. Lassez. Constraint logic programming. In *Proc. 14th ACM Symp. Principles of Programming Languages, Munich*, 1987.

[29] J.-P. Jouannaud and C. Kirchner. Solving equations in abstract algebras: A rule-based survey of unification. In J.-L. Lassez and G. Plotkin, editors, *Computational Logic: Essays in Honor of Alan Robinson*. MIT-Press, 1991.

[30] J.-P. Jouannaud and C. Marché. Termination and completion modulo associativity, commutativity and identity. *Theoretical Comput. Sci.*, 104:29–51, 1992.

[31] J.-P. Jouannaud and M. Okada. Satisfiability of systems of ordinal notations with the subterm property is decidable. In *Proc. 18th Int. Coll. on Automata, Languages and Programming, Madrid, LNCS 510*, 1991.

[32] C. Kirchner, H. Kirchner, and M. Rusinowitch. Deduction with symbolic constraints. *Revue Française d'Intelligence Artificielle*, 4(3):9–52, 1990. Special issue on automatic deduction.

[33] K. Kunen. Negation in logic programming. *Journal of Logic Programming*, 4:289–308, 1987.

[34] M. J. Maher. Complete axiomatizations of the algebras of finite, rational and infinite trees. In *Proc. 3rd IEEE Symp. Logic in Computer Science, Edinburgh*, pages 348–357, July 1988.

[35] A. I. Mal'cev. Axiomatizable classes of locally free algebras of various types. In *The Metamathematics of Algebraic Systems. Collected Papers. 1936-1967*, pages 262–289. North-Holland, 1971.

[36] G. Marongiu and S. Tulipani. Decidability results for term algebras. Preprint 9, AILA, 1991.

[37] A. Martelli and U. Montanari. An efficient unification algorithm. *ACM Transactions on Programming Languages and Systems*, 4(2):258–282, Apr. 1982.

[38] R. Nieuwenhuis. Simple LPO-constraint solving methods. Research Report LSI–93–9–R, Departament de Llenguatges i sistemes informàtics, Universitat Politècnica de Catalunya, 1993. To appear in Information Processing Letters.

[39] R. Nieuwenhuis and A. Rubio. Basic superposition is complete. In B. Krieg-Bruckner, editor, *Proc. European Symp. on Programming, LNCS 582*, pages 371–389, Rennes, 1992. Springer-Verlag.

[40] R. Nieuwenhuis and A. Rubio. Theorem proving with ordering constrained clauses. In D. Kapur, editor, *Proc. 11th Int. Conf. on Automated Deduction, Saratoga Springs, NY, LNCS 607*. Springer-Verlag, June 1992.

[41] W. V. Quine. Concatenation as a basis for arithmetic. *Journal of Symbolic Logic*, 11(4), 1946.

[42] J. A. Robinson. A machine-oriented logic based on the resolution principle. *J. ACM*, 12(1):23–41, 1965.

[43] G. Salzer. On unification of infinite sets of terms and its applications. In Voronkov, editor, *Proc. LPAR 92, LNCS 624*, pages 409–421, 1992.

[44] R. Treinen. A new method for undecidability proofs of first order theories. *Journal of Symbolic Computation*, 14(5):437–458, Nov. 1992.

[45] K. N. Venkataraman. Decidability of the purely existential fragment of the theory of term algebras. *J. ACM*, 34(2):492–510, 1987.

Joining Abstract and Concrete Computations in Constraint Logic Programming *

Roberto Giacobazzi and Giorgio Levi
Dipartimento di Informatica, Università di Pisa
Corso Italia 40, 56125 Pisa, Italy
{giaco,levi}@di.unipi.it

Saumya K. Debray
Department of Computer Science, The University of Arizona
Tucson, AZ 85721
debray@cs.arizona.edu

Abstract

The use of standard instances of the *CLP* framework (e.g. *CLP*(*Bool*) and *CLP*($\mathcal{R}$)) for non-standard (possibly abstract) interpretations, weakens the distinction between concrete and abstract computations in semantics and analysis. We formalize this idea by applying the well known approximation techniques (e.g. the standard theory of closure operators) in conjunction with a generalized notion of constraint system, supporting any program evaluation. The "generalized semantics" resulting from this process, abstracts away from standard semantic objects, by focusing on the general properties of any (possibly non-standard) semantic definition. In constraint logic programming, this corresponds to a suitable definition of the constraint system supporting the semantic definition. Both top-down and a bottom-up semantics are considered.

1 Introduction

Constraint logic programming (*CLP*) is a generalization of the pure logic programming paradigm, having similar model-theoretic, declarative and operational semantics [15]. *CLP* is then a general programming paradigm which may be instantiated on various semantic domains. The fundamental linguistic aspect of constraint logic programming is the ability of computing constraints by means of Horn-like rules. Since this aspect can be separated from the details specific to particular constraint systems, it seems natural to parameterize the semantics of *CLP* languages with respect to the underlying constraint system. We refer to such a semantics as *generalized semantics* [12]. It turns out that

*The work of R. Giacobazzi and G. Levi was supported by the Esprit Basic Research Action 3012 - Compulog and by "Progetto Finalizzato Sistemi Informatici e Calcolo Parallelo" of C.N.R. under grants no. 9100880.PF69. The work of S. Debray was supported in part by the National Science Foundation under grants CCR-8901283 and CCR-9123520.

the generalized semantics provides a powerful tool for dealing with a variety of applications relating to the semantics of *CLP* programs. For example, by considering a domain of "abstract constraints" instead of the "concrete constraints" that are actually manipulated during program execution, we obtain for free a formal treatment of abstract interpretation.

In this paper we show how abstract and concrete interpretations for logic-based languages can be joined into the unifying framework of constraint logic programming. We apply the generalized semantics introduced in [12], intended to generalize the notion of constraint logic programs as firstly introduced in [15]. The algebraic approach we take to constraint interpretation makes it easy to identify a suitable set of operators which can be instantiated in different ways to obtain both standard and non-standard interpretations, relying on some simple axioms to ensure that desirable semantic properties are satisfied. This work has a main technical contributions: to show how a wide class of analysis techniques developed for pure and constraint-based logic programs can themselves be viewed as instances of the constraint logic programming paradigm. This is obtained by considering a general notion of constraint systems which is weak enough to have general applicability and at the same time strong enough to ensure that relevant properties of the standard semantics construction for logic programs are preserved. We argue that the ability of the constraint logic programming paradigm to handle relations on a variety of semantic domains (e.g. real arithmetics, boolean algebras, *etc.*) allows this paradigm to be used in the field of program analysis both as a tool for the formal specification of abstract domains of approximate relations and for the rapid prototyping of static analysis systems. This approach has some interesting practical applications, such as the ability to compile the data-flow analysis directly to an abstract machine for constraint logic programs. This approach, which is a logical extension of the "abstract compilation" scheme discussed in [14], removes the overhead of program interpretation incurred by keeping separate abstract and concrete interpretations, and leads to significant improvements in the speed of analysis (e.g. see [14, 22]).

The paper is structured as follows: in Section 2 we introduce the basic mathematical notations used throughout the paper. Section 3 introduces the main results in [12], thus providing an incremental step-by-step algebraic specification for constraint systems and semantics. In Section 4 we consider generalized semantics for constraint logic programs as a framework for semantics-based analyses for constraint logic programs. An example, namely *ground dependency analysis*, is considered associating *boolean* constraints with standard equations on terms. Some results on approximating constraints by means of *upper closure operators* on constraint systems are also given. This approach points out how some well-known program analysis techniques can be obtained by evaluating an abstract program into a variation of some existing *CLP* systems, such as $CLP(Bool)$ for ground dependency analysis; and, as shown in Section 5: $CLP(\mathcal{R})$[1], where a weaker notion of constraint system supporting program analysis is introduced. This is accomplished by focusing on a specific application of constraint programming to data-flow analysis, namely: *linear relationships analysis*, which associates *linear* constraints with standard equations on terms. Section 6 contains a survey of the most important related works.

[1] $CLP(\mathcal{R})$ denotes the $CLP(\Re)$ (constraint logic programs on the domain of real numbers) implementation described in [16].

2 Preliminaries

The set of natural and real numbers are denoted by $\mathcal{N}$ and $\Re$ respectively. Given sets A and B, $A \backslash B$ denotes the set A where the elements in B have been removed. The powerset of a set S is denoted by $\wp(S)$. The class of finite (possibly empty) subsets of a set S is denoted $\wp^f(S)$. Let Σ be a possibly infinite set of symbols. We denote by Σ^* the family of finite-length strings (sequences) from symbols in Σ, including the empty string Λ. Sequences are typically denoted by $\langle a_1, ..., a_n \rangle$ or simply $a_1, ..., a_n$ for a_i's symbols in Σ. The *length* of s sequence s is denoted $|s|$. The set of objects a_i indexed on a set of symbols Σ is denoted $\{a_i\}_{i \in \Sigma}$. The set of n-tuples of symbols in Σ is denoted Σ^n. When the length of sequences is fixed, sequences and tuples will be often considered equivalent notions. Let $R \subseteq A \times A$ be a binary transitive relation on A, then the transitive closure of R is denoted by R^*. Syntactic identity is denoted $\equiv$.

A set P equipped with a partial order $\leq$ is said to be *partially ordered*, and sometimes written $\langle P, \leq \rangle$. A *chain* is a (possibly empty) subset X of a partially ordered set P such that for all $x, x' \in X$: $x \leq x'$ or $x' \leq x$. A *complete lattice* is a partially ordered set L such that every subset of L has a least upper bound and a greatest lower bound. A complete lattice L with partial ordering $\leq$, least upper bound $\vee$, greatest lower bound $\wedge$, least element $\bot = \vee\emptyset = \wedge L$, and greatest element $\top = \wedge\emptyset = \vee L$, is denoted $(L, \leq, \bot, \top, \vee, \wedge)$.

To specify function parameters in function definitions we often make use of Church's lambda notation. We write $f : A \longrightarrow B$ to mean that f is a total function of A into B. Let $f : A \longrightarrow B$ be a mapping, for each $C \subseteq A$ we denote by $f(C)$ the image of C by f: $\{f(x) \mid x \in C\}$. Functions from a set to the same set are usually called *operators*. The identity operator $\lambda x.x$ is often denoted *id*. Let $(L, \leq, \bot, \top, \vee, \wedge)$ be a non-empty complete lattice. Let $f : L \longrightarrow L$ be a function. The *upper ordinal powers* of f are defined as follows: $f \uparrow 0(X) = X$, $f \uparrow \alpha(X) = f(f \uparrow (\alpha - 1)(X))$ for every successor ordinal α; and $f \uparrow \alpha(X) = \bigvee_{\delta < \alpha} f \uparrow \delta(X)$ for every limit ordinal α. The first limit ordinal equipotent with the set of natural numbers is denoted by ω.

An *algebraic structure* ([13]) is a pair $(\mathcal{C}, \mathcal{Q})$ where $\mathcal{C}$ is a non-empty set, called the *universe* of the structure and $\mathcal{Q}$ is a function ranging over a (possibly infinite non-denumerable) index set $\mathcal{I}$ such that for each $i \in \mathcal{I}$, $\mathcal{Q}_i$ are finitary operations on and to elements of $\mathcal{C}$. Algebraic structures are also denoted as $(\mathcal{C}, \mathcal{Q}_i)_{i \in \mathcal{I}}$. In addition to $\mathcal{Q}_i$ operations, some special symbols (e.g. $\otimes$, $\oplus$, 0,...) will be used to denote algebraic operations, including constants. With an abuse of notation, we will often denote *distinguished elements* of $\mathcal{C}$ as constant operations $\mathcal{Q}_i$ on $\mathcal{C}$. Morphisms σ of algebraic structures $(A, \mathcal{Q}_A)$ and $(B, \mathcal{Q}_B)$, provided with a common set of basic operators, are denoted $\sigma : (A, \mathcal{Q}_A) \xrightarrow{m} (B, \mathcal{Q}_B)$.

3 Generalized semantics

In this section we recall some of the basic results on the generalized semantics in [12].

3.1 Term systems

A *term system* is an algebra of terms provided with a binary operator which realizes substitutions [4]. We are interested in term systems where every term depends only on a finite number of variables (also called *finitary term systems*). They represent the first basic definition in the semantic construction.

Definition 3.1 *[term systems [4]]*
A term system τ is an algebraic structure (τ, S, V) where we refer to the elements of τ as τ-terms (terms for short); V is a countable set[2] *of τ-variables (variables, for short) in τ; S is a countable set of binary operations on τ, indexed by V; and the following conditions are satisfied, for all $x, y \in V$ and $t, t', t'' \in \tau$:*

T_1. $s_x(t, x) = t,$ *identity*

T_2. $s_x(t, y) = y,$ *where* $x \neq y,$ *annihilation*

T_3. $s_x(t, s_x(y, t')) = s_x(y, t')$ *where* $x \neq y,$ *renaming*

T_4. $s_x(t', s_y(t'', t)) = s_y(s_x(t', t''), s_x(t', t))$ *where* $x \neq y$ *and* y *ind* t'

independent composition

where a τ-term t is independent on the τ-variable x, denoted by "x ind t", if $s_x(t', t) = t$ for any $t' \in \tau$. We say that a variable v occurs in a term t if $\neg(x$ ind $t)$. We denote the set of variables occurring in a term t as $var(t)$.

Intuitively, $s_x(t, t')$ denotes the operation "substitute t for every occurrence of the variable x in t'." For notational convenience, we often denote $s_x(t, t')$ as $[t/x]t'$. This notation can be extended to substitutions on multiple variables. Notice that, by T_2, for each $x, y \in V$: x *ind* y iff $x \neq y$. The condition that terms depend on a finite number of variables can be formalized by imposing that the *dimension set* [4]: $\{x \in V \mid [t/x]t' \not\equiv t' \text{ for some } t \in \tau\}$ is finite for every $t' \in \tau$. A *renaming* of a variable x in a term t is $[y/x]t$ for some $y \neq x$. Standard properties of term systems and substitutions, such as the properties of composition, can be found in [4].

Example 3.1 Let Σ be a finite collection of function symbols. The standard term system $\tau_{(\Sigma,V)} = (T(\Sigma, V), \mathsf{Sub}, V)$ is a term system provided that substitutions in Sub perform standard substitutions. In this case v *ind* t iff the variable v does not occur in t. ∎

Notice that the substitution operators in S do not perform in general idempotent substitutions.

Let Π be a finite collection of predicate symbols and τ be a term system. A (τ, Π)-*atom* has the form $p(t_1, ..., t_n)$ where $p \in \Pi$ and $t_i \in \tau$, $\forall i = 1, ..., n$. When clear from the context, we sometimes denote by $\bar{o}$ both a tuple and a set of syntactic objects o (terms, atoms, *etc.*). In particular we denote by $\bar{x}$ a tuple (set) of distinct variables. Let $\bar{o} = (o_1, ..., o_n)$ and $\bar{o}' = (o'_1, ..., o'_n)$ be tuples (sets) of syntactic objects. We write $\bar{o} \neq \bar{o}'$ to denote $o_i \neq o'_j$ for each i, j.

Example 3.2 Let Σ be a finite set of symbols. Let $\tau_\Sigma = (\wp^f(\Sigma), S, \Sigma)$, where S is the family of basic operators s_σ, for $\sigma \in \Sigma$, such that for each $\Delta_1, \Delta_2 \in$

[2] A more general definition that considers sets of arbitrary cardinalities is given in [4]: for our purposes, it suffices to consider countable sets.

$\wp^f(\Sigma)$:

$$s_\sigma(\Delta_1, \Delta_2) = \begin{cases} (\Delta_2 \setminus \{\sigma\}) \cup \Delta_1 & \text{if } \sigma \in \Delta_2 \\ \Delta_2 & \text{otherwise} \end{cases}$$

In this case, for each $\sigma \in \Sigma$ and finite set $\Delta \subseteq \Sigma$: σ *ind* Δ iff $\sigma \notin \Delta$. τ_Σ is a term system. ∎

3.2 Constraint systems

The process of building constraints in any fixpoint evaluation of a given *CLP* program is mainly based on set-union and conjunction. We now give an algebraic characterization of this process in order to provide a framework for generalized interpretations of constraint logic programs. We consider *closed semirings* to summarize, in an algebraic framework, all the aspects dealing with composition of terms like unification (conjunction) and set union. A weaker structure, namely a non-distributive closed semiring, will be considered in Section 5.

Definition 3.2 *[closed semirings [1]]*
A Closed Semiring is an algebraic structure $(\mathcal{C}, \otimes, \oplus, \mathbf{1}, \mathbf{0})$ satisfying the following:

1. *$(\mathcal{C}, \otimes, \mathbf{1})$ and $(\mathcal{C}, \oplus, \mathbf{0})$ are monoids.*
2. *$\oplus$ is commutative and idempotent.*
3. *$\mathbf{0}$ is an annihilator for $\otimes$, i.e., for every $c \in \mathcal{C}$, $c \otimes \mathbf{0} = \mathbf{0} \otimes c = \mathbf{0}$.*
4. *for any countable sequence of elements $a_1, \ldots, a_n, \ldots$ in $\mathcal{C}$: $a_1 \oplus a_2 \oplus \cdots \oplus a_n \oplus \cdots$ exists and is unique. Moreover associativity, commutativity and idempotence of $\oplus$ apply to countably infinite as well as to finite applications of $\oplus$.*
5. *$\otimes$ is left/right-distributive over finite and countably infinite applications of $\oplus$, i.e., if $C = \{a_1, \ldots, a_n, \ldots\}$ is a countable sequence of elements in $\mathcal{C}$ and $c \in \mathcal{C}$, then $c \otimes (\oplus C) = \oplus(\{c \otimes c' \mid c' \in C\})$ and $(\oplus C) \otimes c = \oplus(\{c' \otimes c \mid c' \in C\})$, where $\oplus C$ denotes $a_1 \oplus a_2 \oplus \cdots \oplus a_n \oplus \cdots$.*

A semantic definition necessarily implies some notion of "observable behavior": programs that have the same semantics are considered to not be observably different. Modeling the semantics of constraint logic programs in terms of answer constraints corresponds to considering answer constraints as the appropriate observable property [10]. Thus, the notion of solution for a given answer constraint has to be restricted (projected) to the variables of the corresponding query (output variables). Closed semirings are too weak to capture the notion of variable projection. We handle this notion by means of a family of "hiding" operators on the underlying algebra. The intuition here is that given a constraint c, the cylindrification operation $\exists_S(c)$ yields the constraint obtained by "projecting out" information about the variables in S from c. *Diagonal elements* [13] are considered as a way to provide parameter passing [21]. In constraint logic programming the equality symbol "=" is assumed to provide term unification in any constraint system. However, cylindric algebras, which are oriented to first-order languages without function symbols, are not adequate as an algebraic semantic framework for general constraint logic programs, so we extend diagonal elements to deal with generic terms, following the approach in [4]. Finally, for each variable x and term t, a unary operator ∂_x^t extends the substitution operation to idempotent substitutions on constraints.

Definition 3.3 *[constraint systems] A constraint system $\mathcal{A}$ is an algebraic structure $\langle \mathcal{C}, \otimes, \oplus, \mathbf{1}, \mathbf{0}, \exists_\Delta, \partial_x^t, d_{t,t'} \rangle_{\{x\},\Delta \subseteq V; t,t' \in \tau}$ where $\mathcal{C}$ is a set of $\mathcal{A}$-constraints generated by a given set of atomic constraints, and is called the universe of $\mathcal{A}$; V is a countable set of variables; τ is a term system; $\mathbf{0}, \mathbf{1}, d_{t,t'}$ are distinct (atomic) elements of $\mathcal{C}$, for each $t, t' \in \tau$; $\{\exists_\Delta\}_{\Delta \subseteq V}$ and $\{\partial_x^t\}_{x \in V; t \in \tau}$ are unary operations on $\mathcal{C}$ the latter being defined for x ind t; $\otimes, \oplus$ are binary operations on $\mathcal{C}$; such that the following postulates are satisfied for any $c, c' \in \mathcal{C}$; $\Delta, \Psi \subseteq V$ and $t, t', t'' \in \tau$:*

R_1. *the structure $\langle \mathcal{C}, \otimes, \oplus, \mathbf{1}, \mathbf{0} \rangle$ is a closed semiring;*

C_1. $c \oplus \exists_\Delta c = \exists_\Delta c$;

C_2. $\exists_\Delta(c \otimes \exists_\Delta c') = \exists_\Delta(\exists_\Delta c \otimes c') = \exists_\Delta c \otimes \exists_\Delta c'$;

C_3. $\exists_\Delta \exists_\Psi c = \exists_{(\Delta \cup \Psi)} c$;

C_4. $\exists_\Delta$ *distributes over finite and countably infinite joins;*

D_1. $d_{t,t} = \mathbf{1}$;

D_2. $\exists_{\{x\}} d_{x,t} = \mathbf{1}$;

D_3. $d_{t,t'} = d_{t',t}$;

S_1. $\partial_x^t(c) = \exists_{\{x\}}(d_{x,t} \otimes c)$;

S_2. $\partial_x^t(d_{t',t''}) = d_{[t/x]t',[t/x]t''}$;

S_3. $\partial_x^t(c \otimes c') = \partial_x^t c \otimes \partial_x^t c'$.

With an abuse of notation, when clear from the context, we denote $\partial_x^t(c)$ as $[t/x]\,c$. The meaning of cylindrification is given by the axioms from C_1 to C_4, while diagonal elements and substitutions are specified by the axioms from D_1 to S_3. Notice that Axiom S_1 and S_2 relate the notion of substitution in the term system τ with diagonal elements of $\mathcal{C}$ (which intuitively correspond to the notion of equality constraints) in the expected way. Recursively, a *simple constraint* is any atomic constraint, or the cylindrification (substitution) of a simple constraint, or a finite conjunction (meet) of simple constraints. The notions of "independence" and "occurrence" of variables extend in the obvious way from terms in τ to constraints in $\mathcal{C}$. Let $c \in \mathcal{C}$ and $x \in V$: x *ind* c iff $\partial_x^t c = c$ for any $t \in \tau$ such that x *ind* t. A variable x is *bound* in c iff it is existentially quantified in c. A variable x is *free* in c iff $x \in var(c)$ and x is not bound in c. The set of *free variables* in a constraint c is denoted by $FV(c)$. A renaming of c with respect to x is the constraint $\partial_x^y c$ such that $x \neq y$. It is *renamed apart* if also y *ind* c. Let $\{x_1, ..., x_n\} \subseteq V$, in the following we will denote $\exists_{var(c) \setminus \{x_1,...,x_n\}} c$, i.e. hiding from all the variables in c except $\{x_1, \ldots, x_n\}$, as $\exists(c)_{\{x_1,...,x_n\}}$. We often omit brackets in cylindrifications on sets of variables. We also denote by $d_{\langle t_1,...,t_n \rangle, \langle t'_1,...,t'_n \rangle}$ the element $d_{t_1,t'_1} \otimes \ldots \otimes d_{t_n,t'_n}$, where $t_1, ..., t_n, t'_1, ..., t'_n \in \tau$, and denote $\mathcal{A}$ an arbitrary constraint system $\langle \mathcal{C}, \otimes, \oplus, \mathbf{1}, \mathbf{0}, \exists_\Delta, \partial_x^t, d_{t,t'} \rangle_{\{x\},\Delta \subseteq V; t,t' \in \tau}$. $c_1 \trianglelefteq c_2$ denotes the relation $c_1 \oplus c_2 = c_2$, for $c_1, c_2 \in \mathcal{C}$. $\mathcal{C}$ is partially ordered by $\trianglelefteq$, and forms a complete lattice.

A number of important properties are shared by constraint systems. In particular, for each $\Delta \subseteq V$, $\exists_\Delta$ defines an additive *upper closure operator* on

$\mathcal{C}$[3], while the substitution operator on constraints defines an additive *retraction* on $\mathcal{C}$[4]. Notice that the substitution is not, in general, extensive. Moreover, if x is bound in c then x *ind* c, and if c is a renaming apart of c' with respect to x, then x *ind* c; and if Δ *ind* c then $\exists_\Delta(c \otimes c') = c \otimes \exists_\Delta c'$. An important property on the relation between cylindrification and renaming (with fresh variables) allows us to extend the standard approach to the semantic construction of logic programs to constraint-based programs: $c \otimes \exists_{\{x\}} c = \exists_{\{y\}}(c \otimes \hat{c}')$ where y *ind* c, c', $y \neq x$ and $\hat{c}' = \partial_x^y c'$.

Example 3.3 ($CLP(\mathcal{H})$) Let $\Sigma = \{a, b, ..., f, g, ...\}$ be a finite collection of function symbols. Atomic constraints are (one-sorted) equations on the term system $\mathcal{T}_{(\Sigma,V)}$ (see Example 3.1). The *Herbrand constraint system* $\mathcal{A}_\mathcal{H}$, is the quotient algebra

$$(\wp(\mathcal{E}_\mathcal{H}), \wedge, \cup, true, false, \exists_X, \partial_x^t, \{t = t'\})_{\{x\}, X \subseteq V; t, t' \in \mathcal{T}_{(\Sigma,V)}} / \sim_{EQ},$$

where: $\mathcal{E}_\mathcal{H}$ is the set of possibly existentially quantified finite conjunctions of equations over $\mathcal{T}_{(\Sigma,V)}$ and $\mathcal{H}$ is intended to represent the Herbrand interpretation structure, interpreting diagonal elements as unification [15]. In this case, a solution θ for a possibly quantified finite conjunction (set) of equations $\exists_X E = \exists_X\{s_1 = t_1, ..., s_n = t_n\}$ is a grounding substitution for the free variables in E such that there exists a grounding substitution for the bounded variables X: σ, and $s_1\sigma\theta \equiv t_1\sigma\theta$, ..., $s_n\sigma\theta \equiv t_n\sigma\theta$. $\mathcal{H} \models E\theta$ denotes that θ is a solution for E We extend this definition to deal with possibly infinite joins: θ is a solution for $\bigcup_{i \in I} E_i$ iff there exists $i \in I$ such that θ is a solution for E_i. $\exists$ is the existential quantification which is assumed to be distributive (as well as conjunction) over arbitrary joins: if $X \subseteq V$, θ is a solution for $\exists_X(\bigcup_{i \in I} E_i)$ iff θ is a solution for $\exists_X E_i$ for some $i \in I$; *true* denotes any constraint having every grounding substitution as a solution while *false* denotes any constraint having an empty set of solutions. ∂_x^t, for x not occurring in t, performs idempotent substitutions on constraints, by extending in the obvious way the term substitution notion to constraints. Moreover, for each $c_1 = \bigcup_{i \in I_1} E_i$ and $c_2 = \bigcup_{i \in I_2} E'_i$ denoting possibly infinite joins of (finite) quantified sets of atomic constraints (equations) E_i and E'_i:

$$c_1 \sim_{EQ} c_2 \text{ iff } \bigcup_{i \in I_1} \{ \vartheta \mid \mathcal{H} \models E_i\vartheta \} = \bigcup_{i \in I_2} \{ \vartheta \mid \mathcal{H} \models E'_i\vartheta \}.$$

∎

Example 3.4 ($CLP(\mathcal{R}_n)$) In the following $\vec{x} = (x_1...x_n)$ is a vector (point) in $\Re^n$ and x_i is its i-th element. A *hyperplane* is the set of points $\vec{x} \in \Re^n$ satisfying $a_1x_1 + ... + a_nx_n = b$, with not all a's equal to zero. Any hyperplane defines two *halfspaces* in the obvious way. A *convex polyhedron* is the (possibly unbounded) set of points constituting the intersection of a finite number of halfspaces. For any finite n, the constraint system of n-dimension linear constraints (the non-linear case is a straightforward extension), denoted by $\mathcal{R}_n$, is:

---

[3] An upper closure operator ρ on a partially ordered set $\langle A, \leq \rangle$ is a monotonic, idempotent and extensive (i.e. $\rho(x) \geq x$) operator.

[4] A retraction on a partially ordered set $\langle A, \leq \rangle$ is an operator ϱ that is idempotent and monotonic.

$(\mathcal{P}, \cap, \cup, \Re^n, \emptyset, \partial_x^t, \hat{\exists}_\Delta, [t_1 = t_2])_{\{x\}, \Delta \subseteq V_n; t, t_1, t_2 \in \tau_{Exp}}$, where $V_n = \{x_1, ..., x_n\}$ is a set of n variables, τ_{Exp} is a term system of linear expressions on V_n and $\mathcal{P}$ is the set of all space regions in $\Re^n$ defined as possibly infinite unions of *convex polyhedra* (each constraint $c \in \mathcal{P}$ can be represented as a possibly infinite set of finite conjunctions of linear equations and disequations on V_n). The *variable restriction* operation $\hat{\exists}$ is performed by *cylindrification parallel to an axis* [13]: if c is a constraint in $\Re^n$ and $i \leq n$, we define:

$$\hat{\exists}_{x_i} c = \{ \vec{y} \in \Re^n \mid y_j = x_j \ for \ \vec{x} \in c \ and \ j \neq i \ \}.$$

$\hat{\exists}_{x_i} c$ is the cylinder generated by moving the point set c parallel to the x_i axis. For any two linear expressions $t, t' \in \tau_{Exp}$ and $R \in \{=, \geq, \leq, >, <\}$ we denote by $[t \ R \ t']$ the corresponding space. The substitution operator is: $\partial_x^t = \lambda c. \hat{\exists}_{\{x\}}([x = t] \cap c)$. $\mathcal{R}_n$ is a constraint system. ∎

3.3 Operational and fixpoint semantics

Constraint logic programming was defined by Jaffar and Lassez to specify relations on a constraint language by means of constraint-based Horn clauses. We follow the approach in [12] by defining Horn-like clauses on constraint systems. Constraint logic programs are defined in the usual way: let $\mathcal{A}$ be a constraint system on the term system τ and Π be a finite set of predicate symbols. An $\mathcal{A}$-*goal* is a formula $c \,\Box\, B_1, ..., B_n$, with $n \geq 0$, where c is a simple $\mathcal{A}$-constraint and $B_1, ..., B_n$ is a sequence of (τ, Π)-atoms. An $\mathcal{A}$-*clause* is a formula of the form '$H \ :- \ c \,\Box\, B_1, ..., B_n$' where H (the *head*) is a (τ, Π)-atom and $c \,\Box\, B_1, ..., B_n$ (the *body*) is an $\mathcal{A}$-goal. If the body is empty, the clause is a *unit clause*. A *(generalized) constraint logic program*, also called $\mathcal{A}$-program, is a finite set of clauses. For notational simplicity, we will sometimes omit the superscript from the various semantic functions where the constraint system under consideration is obvious from the context. The family of $\mathcal{A}$-programs is denoted by $CLP(\mathcal{A})$. Finally, the renamings of variables in constraints and terms extend their meaning in the obvious way to any syntactic object (atoms, goals, clauses, programs *etc.*); as well as the notion of independence.

Let $\mathcal{A}$ be a constraint system and $P \in CLP(\mathcal{A})$. Define $\leadsto_P$ (an $\mathcal{A}$-*derivation step*) to be the least relation on $\mathcal{A}$-goals such that $G \leadsto_P G'$ iff

- $G = c_0 \,\Box\, p_1(\bar{t}_1), ..., p_n(\bar{t}_n)$,
- there exists a renamed version of a clause in P: $p_1(\bar{x}_1) \ :- \ c_1 \,\Box\, \bar{B}_1$, such that $var(G) \cap var(\bar{B}_1 \cup \bar{x}_1) = \emptyset$,
- $G' = c_0 \otimes d_{\bar{x}_1, \bar{t}_1} \otimes \exists(c_1)_{\bar{x}_1 \cup var(\bar{B}_1)} \,\Box\, \bar{B}_1, p_2(\bar{t}_2), ..., p_n(\bar{t}_n)$,

An $\mathcal{A}$-derivation from an $\mathcal{A}$-goal G is a finite or infinite sequence of $\mathcal{A}$-goals such that every goal is obtained from the previous one by means of a single $\mathcal{A}$-derivation step. A successful derivation is a finite sequence whose last element has an empty body. The operational semantics is then defined in terms of the *success set*, namely the set of successful computations specified by the transitive closure of the transition relation on atomic $\mathcal{A}$-goals, where ε denotes the empty sequence of goals:

$$\mathcal{O}^{\mathcal{A}}(P) = \left\{ \ p(\bar{x}) \ :- \ \bigoplus \exists(c)_{\bar{x}} \mid 1 \,\Box\, p(\bar{x}) \leadsto_P^* c \,\Box\, \varepsilon \ \right\}.$$

Goal dependent success set semantics is defined in terms of a function $\mathcal{J}_P$ that yields the computed answer constraint for any $\mathcal{A}$-goal, such that $\mathcal{J}_P(G) = \oplus\{\exists(c)_{var(G)} \mid G \leadsto_P^* c \,\Box\ \}$. The following lemma proves the AND-compositionality for the operational semantics of constraint logic programs.

Lemma 3.1 ([12])
Let $G = c_0 \Box p_1(\bar{t}_1), ..., p_n(\bar{t}_n)$ be an $\mathcal{A}$-goal and $P \in CLP(\mathcal{A})$. $\mathcal{J}_P(G) = c$ iff there exist $p_i(\bar{x}_i) \;:-\; c_i \in \mathcal{O}^{\mathcal{A}}(P)$, such that $\bar{x}_i$ *ind* G and $\bar{x}_i \neq \bar{x}_j$ for $1 \leq i, j \leq n$, $i \neq j$; and $c = \exists(c_0 \otimes d_{\bar{x}_1,\bar{t}_1} \otimes c_1 ... \otimes d_{\bar{x}_n,\bar{t}_n} \otimes c_n)_{var(G)}$. ∎

Since a constraint system can be non-meet-commutative, it is straightforward to notice that the independence on the selection rule does not hold in general in these semantic characterizations. For this reason we have assumed a left-to-right selection rule.

The fixpoint semantics is defined by allowing constrained atoms into the base of interpretations as suggested in [10]. Each constrained atom '$p(\bar{x}) \;:-\; c$' represents the set of instances $p(\bar{x})\vartheta$, where ϑ is a solution of the constraint c. We assume $FV(c) \subseteq var(A)$.
It can be shown that the unfolding of a clause is independent on the variable names used in constrained atoms. This can be expressed in the semantics by a relation $\sim$ that captures the notion of equivalence upto renaming on constrained atoms. Let $\mathcal{B}^{\mathcal{A}}$ be the set of constrained atoms of a constraint system $\mathcal{A}$. Define the binary relation $\sim$ on $\mathcal{B}^{\mathcal{A}}$ as follows: given $A_1 \equiv$ '$p(\bar{x}_1) \;:-\; c_1$' and $A_2 \equiv$ '$p(\bar{x}_2) \;:-\; c_2$' in $\mathcal{B}^{\mathcal{A}}$, $A_1 \sim A_2$ if and only if there exist "renaming apart" variables $\bar{x}'$, i.e. such that $\bar{x}' \neq \bar{x}_1$ and $\bar{x}' \neq \bar{x}_2$ ($\bar{x}'$ *ind* c_1, c_2); and $\partial^{\bar{x}'}_{\bar{x}_1} c_1 = \partial^{\bar{x}'}_{\bar{x}_2} c_2$. The *$\mathcal{A}$-base of interpretations* is $\mathcal{B}^{\mathcal{A}}/\sim$ (denoted $\mathcal{B}^{\mathcal{A}}$).

In the following, given a syntactic object o, we denote by $p(\bar{x}) \;:-\; c \ll_o I$ a constrained atom $p(\bar{x}) \;:-\; c$ such that $[p(\bar{x}) \;:-\; c]_\sim \in I$ and $\bar{x}$ *ind* o. We extend this to specify tuples of renamed apart syntactic objects.

Just as $\oplus$ expresses the notion of "merging together" the information present in two constraints, the operator $\sqcup$ captures the notion of merging together the information present in two sets of constrained atoms; i.e. the operator $\sqcup : \wp(\mathcal{B}) \times \wp(\mathcal{B}) \longrightarrow \wp(\mathcal{B})$ is defined as follows:

$I_1 \sqcup I_2 = \{[p(\bar{x}) \;:-\; \oplus\{\partial^{\bar{x}}_{\bar{x}'} c' \mid p(\bar{x}') \;:-\; c' \ll_{\bar{x}} I_1 \cup I_2\}]_\sim\}$ for any $I_1, I_2 \in \wp(\mathcal{B})$.

The relation $\sqsubseteq$, expressing the notion of a set of constrained atoms containing less information than another, is defined as follows: for any $I_1, I_2 \in \wp(\mathcal{B})$, $I_1 \sqsubseteq I_2$ iff $I_1 \sqcup I_2 = I_2$. An $\mathcal{A}$-interpretation is an element in $\wp(\mathcal{B}^{\mathcal{A}})$ containing at most one constrained atom for each predicate symbol. The set of $\mathcal{A}$-interpretations is denoted $\Im^{\mathcal{A}}$. $\langle \Im^{\mathcal{A}}, \sqsubseteq \rangle$ is a complete lattice.

The fixpoint semantics of a program P over a constraint system $\mathcal{A}$, $\mathcal{F}^{\mathcal{A}}(P)$, is defined in terms of a continuous immediate consequence operator in the style of [23], i.e. $\mathcal{F}^{\mathcal{A}}(P) = lfp(\mathcal{T}^{\mathcal{A}}_P) = \mathcal{T}^{\mathcal{A}}_P \uparrow \omega(\emptyset)$, where the mapping $\mathcal{T}^{\mathcal{A}}_P : \Im^{\mathcal{A}} \rightarrow \Im^{\mathcal{A}}$, is defined as follows:

$$\mathcal{T}^{\mathcal{A}}_P(I) = \bigsqcup_{C \in P} \left\{ [p(\bar{x}) \;:-\; \exists(\tilde{c})_{\bar{x}}]_\sim \;\middle|\; \begin{array}{c} C:\; p(t) \;:-\; c \,\Box\, p_1(\bar{t}_1), ..., p_n(\bar{t}_n), \\ \bar{x} \textit{ ind } C \text{ and for each } i = 1...n: \\ p_i(\bar{x}_i) \;:-\; c_i \ll_{C,\bar{x}_1..\bar{x}_{i-1}} I, \\ \bar{x}_i \neq \bar{x},\; c'_i = d_{\bar{x}_i,\bar{t}_i} \otimes c_i, \\ \tilde{c} = d_{\bar{x},\bar{t}} \otimes c \otimes c'_1 \otimes ... \otimes c'_n \end{array} \right\}$$

The fixpoint semantics construction requires, potentially, only a finite set of variables. This follows from the elementary properties of cylindrification with respect to substitution. Intuitively, the hiding allows to define "local environments" which cannot be influenced by substitution. As a consequence, any hidden variable in each of the c_i can be (re)used outside the scope of the hiding, thus making applicable renamings by means of the same variables. The number of variables needed to compute the semantics depends from the program structure.

Example 3.5 Consider the following program over the Herbrand constraint system:

$$\begin{array}{lll} p(x) & :- & x = [\,]. \\ p(x) & :- & x = [h|y] \,\square\, p(y). \end{array}$$

The fixpoint computation for $\mathcal{T}_P$ returns the following interpretation for p (we denote by , and ; conjunction and disjunction (set-union) of constraints):

$$\begin{array}{lll} p(x) & :- & x = [\,]; \\ & & \exists_{h,y,x'}(x = [h|y], y = x', x' = [\,]); \\ & & \exists_{h,y,x''}(x = [h|y], y = x'', \exists_{h,y,x'}(x'' = [h|y], y = x', x' = [\,])); \\ & & \exists_{h,y,x'} \left(\begin{array}{l} x = [h|y], y = x', \\ \exists_{h,y,x''} \left(\begin{array}{l} x' = [h|y], y = x'', \\ \exists_{h,y,x'}(x'' = [h|y], y = x', x' = [\,]) \end{array} \right) \end{array} \right); \\ & & etc.... \end{array}$$

The set of variables needed to compute the fixpoint is $\{x, x', x'', h, y\}$. ∎

The following result states the equivalence between the operational and the fixpoint semantics, for any constraint system $\mathcal{A}$. We need that V is a denumerable set of variables.

Theorem 3.2 ([12])
Let $\mathcal{A}$ be a constraint system and $P \in CLP(\mathcal{A})$, then $\mathcal{F}(P) = \mathcal{O}(P)/\sim$. ∎

4 Abstract constraint systems

In general, a constraint system is an interpretation (in a closed semiring) for constraint formulae. To relate constraint systems, we follow the approach to "static semantics correctness" in [3]. Correctness of non-standard semantic specifications can be handled in an algebraic way through the notion of morphism. However, the algebraic notion of morphism can be made less restrictive by assuming that the carriers of the algebras involved are partially ordered sets. We use a weaker notion of morphism between algebraic structures, capturing the approximation possibly induced by abstract interpretations or by any approximate semantics defined in the framework.

A morphism of term systems, $\kappa : \tau \xrightarrow{m} \tau'$, is a function mapping terms of τ to terms of τ' such that $\forall t_1, t_2 \in \tau$ and $x \in V$: $\kappa(s_x(t_1, t_2)) = s'_{\kappa(x)}(\kappa(t_1), \kappa(t_2))$, where s and s' are the substitution operators in τ and τ' respectively. Let $\mathcal{A}$ and $\mathcal{A}'$ be constraint systems ($\mathcal{A}' = (\mathcal{C}', \otimes', \oplus', \mathbf{1}', \mathbf{0}', \exists'_\Delta, \partial'^{t}_{x}, d'_{t_1,t_2})_{\{x\},\Delta \subseteq V';t,t_1,t_2 \in \tau'}$) be constraint systems. There exists a semimorphism $\alpha : \mathcal{A} \xrightarrow{s} \mathcal{A}'$ iff there exists a morphism of term systems $\kappa : \tau \xrightarrow{m} \tau'$ such that for each $c, c_1, c_2 \in \mathcal{C}$,

$C \subseteq \mathcal{C}$, $\{x\}, \Delta \subseteq V$ and $t, t_1, t_2 \in \tau$ such that x *ind* t: $\alpha(\mathbf{0}) = \mathbf{0}'$, $\alpha(\mathbf{1}) \trianglelefteq' \mathbf{1}'$, $\alpha(\oplus C) \trianglelefteq' \oplus' \alpha(C)$, $\alpha(\exists_\Delta c) \trianglelefteq' \exists'_{\kappa(\Delta)}\alpha(c)$, $\alpha(c_1 \otimes c_2) \trianglelefteq' \alpha(c_1) \otimes' \alpha(c_2)$ and $\alpha(d_{t_1,t_2}) \trianglelefteq' d'_{\kappa(t_1),\kappa(t_2)}$. Semimorphisms of constraint systems will be often denoted as α_κ. Notice that $\alpha(\partial^t_x c) \trianglelefteq' \partial'^{\kappa(t)}_{\kappa(x)}\alpha(c)$.

Definition 4.1
Let $\mathcal{A}$ and $\mathcal{A}'$ be constraint systems with universes $\mathcal{C}$ and $\mathcal{C}'$ and term systems τ and τ' respectively. $\mathcal{A}'$ is correct with respect to $\mathcal{A}$ iff there exists a semimorphism α_κ ($\kappa : \tau \xrightarrow{m} \tau'$ and $\alpha : \mathcal{A} \xrightarrow{s} \mathcal{A}'$) which is a surjective and additive mapping of $\langle \mathcal{C}, \trianglelefteq \rangle$ into $\langle \mathcal{C}', \trianglelefteq' \rangle$.

Additivity and surjectivity allow the semimorphism to associate the "best" approximating constraint in $\mathcal{A}'$ with any concrete constraint in $\mathcal{A}$. As usual, this is captured by the notion of *Galois insertion*, as specified by the following, where a pair of functions (α, γ) is a Galois insertion of $\langle \mathcal{C}', \trianglelefteq' \rangle$ into $\langle \mathcal{C}, \trianglelefteq \rangle$ iff α and γ are monotonic, $\alpha(\gamma(c')) = c'$ and $c \trianglelefteq \gamma(\alpha(c))$ for each $c \in \mathcal{C}$ and $c' \in \mathcal{C}'$ [7, 8]. If $\mathcal{A}'$ is correct with respect to $\mathcal{A}$ by means of a semimorphism α_κ, there exists a Galois insertion of $\langle \mathcal{C}', \trianglelefteq' \rangle$ into $\langle \mathcal{C}, \trianglelefteq \rangle$.

In the framework of abstract interpretation, correctness of fixpoint approximations require in addition some conditions on correctness of the non-standard semantics operators [7]. With the assumption of additivity, semimorphisms are adequate to specify both Galois insertions, and correctness of constraint systems. Let $\mathcal{A}'$ be a constraint system which is correct with respect to $\mathcal{A}$, by means of a semimorphism α_κ. Let $P = \{C_1, ..., C_m\}$ be a program in $CLP(\mathcal{A})$. The *corresponding program on* $\mathcal{A}'$ is a set of clauses $\{C'_1, ..., C'_m\}$ such that for each $i = 1, ..., m$ if $C_i = p(\tilde{t}) :- c \,\Box\, p_1(\tilde{t}_1), ..., p_n(\tilde{t}_n)$ then $C'_i = p(\kappa(\tilde{t})) :- \alpha(c) \,\Box\, p_1(\kappa(\tilde{t}_1)), ..., p_n(\kappa(\tilde{t}_n))$ where κ extends in the obvious way on tuples of terms. The following theorem relates the semantics of a program with the (non-standard) semantics of the corresponding program defined on a correct constraint system.

Theorem 4.1
Let $P \in CLP(\mathcal{A})$ and $P' \in CLP(\mathcal{A}')$ be the corresponding program on $\mathcal{A}'$. Assume $\mathcal{A}'$ be correct with respect to $\mathcal{A}$. There exists $\beta : \Im^{\mathcal{A}} \rightarrow \Im^{\mathcal{A}'}$ such that $\beta(\mathcal{F}^{\mathcal{A}}(P)) \sqsubseteq' \mathcal{F}^{\mathcal{A}'}(P')$. ∎

Given a (fixpoint) concrete semantics, data-flow analysis usually requires computing the limit of Kleene chains. Convergence to the least fixpoint can either be obtained by forcing the abstract domain to satisfy the *ascending chain condition* or to use *widening* and *narrowing* operators to accelerate convergence for fixpoint approximations, as suggested in [7]. In the following we consider the conditions on the constraint system that ensure the resulting abstract domain to satisfy the ascending chain condition.

Definition 4.2
A constraint system $\mathcal{A}$ is noetherian iff its universe $\mathcal{C}$ does not contain any infinite chain of free-variable bounded constraints[5].

The free-variable-boundedness condition here is crucial, for otherwise any constraint system with a denumerable set of variables is not noetherian. To see this,

[5] A set of constraints $\{c_1, ..., c_n, ..\}$ is said to be free-variable bounded iff there exists a finite set of variables $\tilde{V}$ such that $FV(c_i) \subseteq \tilde{V}$ for each $i \geq 1$.

consider the constraints $c_i \equiv X_1 \vee \cdots \vee X_i$: the set of constraints $\{c_i \mid i \geq 1\}$, ordered by entailment, forms an infinite ascending chain even on a two-valued boolean interpretation. However, it is easy to see that this set is not free-variable-bounded. Given a noetherian constraint system $\mathcal{A}$, the domain $\Im^{\mathcal{A}}$ is noetherian, and $\mathcal{F}^{\mathcal{A}}(P)$ can be computed by iterating $\mathcal{T}_P$ a finite number of times.

We illustrate this technique by means of a simple example of data-flow analysis for ***ground dependences*** in pure logic programs [2, 6].

Consider the (concrete) term system $\mathcal{T}_{(\Sigma,V)}$ being defined over a finite set of variables V. Let us consider the term system $\mathcal{T}_V$ as defined in Example 3.2. Terms are finite sets of variables. Ground terms are denoted with the empty set of variables. It is straightforward to notice that *var* is a morphism of term systems. Marriott and Søndergaard have proposed an elegant domain, named *Prop*, to represent ground dependences among arguments in atoms. This domain can be expressed as an instance of our framework using the algebra of propositional formulae with disjunction. Let $\mathcal{A}_{Prop} = (Prop_V, \wedge, \vee, true, false, \exists_X, \partial^t_x, \wedge(t) \leftrightarrow \wedge(t'))_{\{x\}, X \subseteq V; t,t' \in \mathcal{T}_V \cup \{\emptyset\}}$ be the algebra of possibly existentially quantified disjunctions of formulae, defined on the term system $\mathcal{T}_V$, by the connectives $\wedge$ and $\leftrightarrow$; where, for each finite set of variables $\{x_1, ..., x_m\} \in \mathcal{T}_V$: $\wedge(\{x_1, ..., x_m\}) = x_1 \wedge ... \wedge x_m$, and $\wedge(\emptyset) = true$.

Intuitively, the formula $x \wedge y \wedge z \leftrightarrow w \wedge v$ represents an equation $t = t'$ where $var(t) = \{x, y, z\}$ and $var(t') = \{w, v\}$; $x \wedge y$ represents a term whose groundness depends upon variables x and y; while $x \vee y$ represents a set of terms whose groundness depends upon variables x or y. Local variables are hidden by existential quantification. Since $x \leftrightarrow true$ is equivalent to x, a variable x instantiated with ground term is denoted x (i.e. the expression x denotes that x is ground). Substitution is defined in the obvious way. It is easy to prove that, because of the finiteness of V, $\mathcal{A}_{Prop}/\leftrightarrow$ is a finite (and then noetherian) constraint system.

The analysis is obtained by associating with each equational constraint in $\mathcal{A}_{\mathcal{H}}$, a boolean expression specifying groundness relationships among variables in predicates. The following example shows this technique.

Example 4.1 Consider the following program to reverse a list:

```
nrev([], []).
nrev([H|L], R) :- nrev(L, L1), append(L1, [H], R).

append([], L, L).
append([H|Y], X2, [H|Z]) :- append(Y, X2, Z).
```

The corresponding *Prop* program for groundness analysis is:

$$nrev(x_1, x_2) \ :- \ x_1 \wedge x_2.$$
$$nrev(x_1, x_2) \ :- \ x_1 \leftrightarrow (h \wedge l) \ \Box \ nrev(l, r1), append(r_1, h, r).$$

$$append(x_1, x_2, x_3) \ :- \ x_1 \wedge x_2 \leftrightarrow x_3.$$
$$append(x_1, x_2, x_3) \ :- \ x_1 \leftrightarrow (h \wedge y) \wedge x_3 \leftrightarrow (h \wedge z) \Box append(y, x_2, z).$$

The reader may verify that the abstract semantics for **append** and **nrev** can be derived by evaluating the modified program in $CLP(\mathcal{A}_{Prop})$ (which corresponds to the standard $CLP(Bool)$). They are given by:

$\{\ append(x_1, x_2, x_3) \ :- \ x_3 \leftrightarrow (x_1 \wedge x_2)\}$; and
$\{\ nrev(x_1, x_2) \ :- \ x_1 \leftrightarrow x_2\}$.

which correspond precisely with the behavious of the program with respect to groundness: in **append** the third argument is ground iff the first two is ground, while in **nrev** the first argument is ground iff the second is ground. ∎

4.1 The approximation operator on constraint systems

It is well known that the space of approximate constraints can be specified using upper closure operators ([8]). In the following we introduce the basic properties of upper closure operators on a constraint system. These properties allow the resulting algebraic structure to be a constraint system as well. In particular we characterize the approximation induced when the semimorphism α_κ behaves as a morphism of constraint systems. Section 5 discusses weaker conditions that are more useful for abstract interpretation. Following this approach, most of the well known techniques for specifying abstract domains can be extended to constraint systems.

Any upper closure approximation of a constraint system defines a partition of the universe of constraints into convex sets of constraints. As a consequence, the image of a universe of constraints $\mathcal{C}$ under a given upper closure operator ρ is a set of "abstract" constraints each representing a convex space of "concrete" solutions. However, in general, the abstract constraints so obtained may not satisfy the axioms for constraint systems: additional conditions have to be applied to ensure that they still provide a constraint system structure.

Definition 4.3
Let $\mathcal{A}$ be a constraint system with universe $\mathcal{C}$. An upper closure operator ρ on $\langle \mathcal{C}, \trianglelefteq \rangle$ is $\exists$-consistent if for each $c \in \mathcal{C}$: $\rho(\exists_\Delta c) = \exists_\Delta \rho(\exists_\Delta c)$.

$\exists$-consistency for an upper closure operator ensures that the approximation (induced by the operator) of a constraint which is hidden on a set of variables, is still hidden on the same set of variables. From this condition we prove that ρ satisfies the ∂-consistency, the $\exists$-quasi morphism condition (see Lemma 4.2) and that $\rho \circ \exists_\Delta$ is an upper closure operator. Notice that $\exists_\Delta \circ \rho$ is not idempotent, unless $\exists_\Delta$ and ρ commute. This is in accordance with a classical result of closure theory saying that any composition of two upper closure operators is an upper closure operator iff they commute [20].

Lemma 4.2
Let ρ be an $\exists$-consistent upper closure operator on the constraint system $\mathcal{A}$ with universe $\mathcal{C}$, term system τ and set of variables V. Then: for each $c \in \mathcal{C}$, $x \in V$ and $t \in \tau$ such that x *ind* t: $\rho(\partial_x^t c) = \partial_x^t \rho(\partial_x^t c)$; and for each $c \in \mathcal{C}$, $\Delta \subseteq V$: $\rho(\exists_\Delta c) = \rho(\exists_\Delta \rho(c))$. ∎

In the remainder of this section we discuss some conditions for systematically deriving abstract constraint systems from a concrete one using closure operators. As we will see, this programme is not applicable to a number of abstract interpretations. This problem is addressed in Section 5.

Definition 4.4
Let $\mathcal{A}$ be a constraint system with universe $\mathcal{C}$. A consistent upper closure operator ρ on $\mathcal{A}$ is an $\exists$-consistent upper closure operator on $\langle \mathcal{C}, \trianglelefteq \rangle$ that is a $\otimes$-quasi morphism, namely for each $c, c' \in \mathcal{C}$: $\rho(c \otimes c') = \rho(\rho(c) \otimes \rho(c'))$.

Since a consistent upper closure operator is a closure operator, it maps each constraint to one that approximates it. In addition to $\exists$-consistency, $\otimes$-quasi morphism relates meets of abstract constraints with meets of concrete constraints (recall that an upper closure operator is also a ***quasi-complete join-morphism***, namely for each $D \subseteq \mathcal{C}$, $\rho(\bigoplus_{c\in D} c) = \rho(\bigoplus_{c\in D} \rho(c)))$. It is easy to prove that for consistent upper closure operators, for each $c \in \mathcal{C}$, $x \in V$ and $t \in \tau$ such that x *ind* t: $\rho(\partial^t_x c) = \rho(\partial^t_x \rho(c))$. Notice that cylindrifications, which are (commuting) upper closure operators, are not consistent as they do not satisfy the $\otimes$-quasi morphism condition (see Axiom C_2).

Let $\mathcal{A} = (\mathcal{C}, \otimes, \oplus, \mathbf{1}, \mathbf{0}, \exists_\Delta, \partial^t_x, d_{t_1,t_2})_{\{x\},\Delta\subseteq V;t,t_1,t_2\in\tau}$ be a constraint system and ρ be a consistent upper closure operator on $\mathcal{A}$. We define:

$$\rho(\mathcal{A}) = (\rho(\mathcal{C}), \tilde{\otimes}, \tilde{\oplus}, \mathbf{1}, \rho(\mathbf{0}), \rho \circ \exists_\Delta, \rho \circ \partial^t_x, \rho(d_{t_1,t_2}))_{\{x\},\Delta\subseteq V;t,t_1,t_2\in\tau}$$

where $\rho(\mathcal{C}) = \{c \in \mathcal{C} \mid c = \rho(c)\}$, and for each $c_1, c_2 \in \rho(\mathcal{C})$: $c_1 \tilde{\otimes} c_2 = \rho(c_1 \otimes c_2)$ and $\tilde{\oplus} = \lambda C \subseteq \mathcal{C}.\rho(\oplus C)$.

Theorem 4.3
Let ρ be a consistent upper closure operator on the constraint system $\mathcal{A}$. $\rho(\mathcal{A})$ is a correct constraint system (wrt $\mathcal{A}$). ∎

As observed in [8], any Galois insertion (α, γ) defines an upper closure operator $\rho = \gamma \circ \alpha$ on the corresponding (concrete) complete lattice. In the following we characterize the consistency of upper closures induced by a Galois insertion.

Theorem 4.4
Let $\mathcal{A}$ and $\mathcal{A}^a$ be constraint systems with universes $\mathcal{C}$ and $\mathcal{C}^a$ respectively, such that $\mathcal{A}^a$ is correct with respect to $\mathcal{A}$ by means of a surjective and additive morphism α. Let $\gamma = \lambda c^a. \oplus \{c \mid \alpha(c) \trianglelefteq^a c^a\}$ and $\rho = \gamma \circ \alpha$. Then: $\rho(\mathcal{C})$ is isomorphic to $\mathcal{C}^a$ and, if $\alpha(\exists_\Delta c) = \exists^a_{\kappa(\Delta)} \alpha(\exists_\Delta c)$ for every $\Delta \subseteq V$ and $c \in \mathcal{C}$, then ρ is $\exists$-consistent. ∎

Let $\mathcal{A}$ be a constraint system and $\mathcal{A}^a$ be correct with respect to $\mathcal{A}$ by means of a surjective and additive semimorphism α_κ. Let $\gamma = \lambda c^a. \oplus \{c \mid \alpha(c) \trianglelefteq^a c^a\}$ and $\rho = \gamma \circ \alpha$.

Theorem 4.5
Let $\Delta \subseteq V$ and $c, c_1, c_2 \in \mathcal{C}$. If α_κ is a morphism on constraint systems then: (1) $\exists_\Delta \rho(c) = \rho(\exists_\Delta c)$ and (2) $\rho(\rho(c_1) \otimes \rho(c_2)) = \rho(c_1 \otimes c_2)$. ∎

In most of abstract interpretations, the concrete semantics is defined on a constraint system which is $\otimes$-idempotent and where $\mathbf{1}$ is the annihilator for $\oplus$. For this family, any meet of closed constraints is still closed: i.e., $\rho(c_1) \otimes \rho(c_2) = \rho(\rho(c_1) \otimes \rho(c_2))$ (i.e. any consistent abstraction becomes a $\otimes$-morphism). This behaviour is too restrictive for most of the abstract interpretations, where the intended meet approximation does not support the $\otimes$-quasi morphism condition. In the following we will consider $\otimes$-idempotent and commutative constraint systems where $\mathbf{1}$ is annihilator for $\oplus$, as these conditions are satisfied in most of the "concrete" constraint systems (e.g. in $CLP(\mathcal{H})$). In particular, we show that some properties (the distributivity properties) of constraint systems are affected by non-consistent closure operators.

5 Non-distributive analysis

Assume a constraint system $\mathcal{A}$ with universe $\mathcal{C}$, where the axiom of distributivity is replaced by the weaker relation: $c \otimes (\oplus C) \trianglelefteq \oplus\{c \otimes c' \mid c' \in C\}$ for $c \in \mathcal{C}$

and $C \subseteq \mathcal{C}$ (in the remainder of this section we refer to them as ***non-distributive constraint systems***). The axiom of distributivity was introduced to prove the continuity of $\mathcal{T}_P^{\mathcal{A}}$. However, by monotonicity of $\exists$ and $\otimes$, it is easy to prove that $\mathcal{T}_P^{\mathcal{A}}$ is monotone in any non-distributive constraint system $\mathcal{A}$. It follows that for noetherian non-distributive constraint systems, $\mathcal{T}_P^{\mathcal{A}}$ is continuous. Distributivity was also used to prove the equivalence between the fixpoint and operational semantics. The operational semantics is, in some sense, an "all solutions" semantics where the join is taken at the end of all the possible computations; in the fixpoint case, by contrast, the join operator is applied at each partial computation step (an equivalent operational semantics can be easily defined: this would correspond to the bottom-up execution strategy of deductive databases rather than the standard operational interpretation of logic programs [18]). In this case, as the constraint system is not distributive any more, we can only have a further approximation level by applying bottom-up instead of top-down, i.e. $\mathcal{O}(P) \sqsubseteq \mathcal{F}(P)$. We show the applicability of non-distributive constraint systems by means of an example.

Linear relationships analysis

The inference of linear size relationships between the arguments of procedures is useful for a variety of applications such as compile-time overflow detection, integer subrange checking, array bound checking, termination analysis, *etc.*, has been considered by a number of researchers [9, 17, 11, 24]. The approach of Verschaetse and De Schreye for automatic inference of linear size relations among variables in logic programs can be specified as a constraint computation in our framework.

Let $\tau_{(\Sigma,V)}$ be defined as in Example 3.1, over a finite set of variables V. Let $|..|_S$ be a norm on the term system $\tau_{(\Sigma,V)}$. We define a term system τ_{Exp} of linear expressions where terms are first order terms in the language $\{+, 0, 1, V\}$ (i.e. terms in $\tau_{(\{+,0,1\},V)}$). Substitutions are performed as standard substitutions. It is easy to see τ_{Exp} is a term system and that the mapping $Exps : \tau_{(\Sigma,V)} \rightarrow \tau_{Exp}$ which associates a linear expression with each terms in $\tau_{(\Sigma,V)}$:

$$Exps(t) = \begin{cases} t & \text{if } t \text{ is a variable} \\ c_0 + \sum\limits_{f \in F_t} Exps(f(t)) & \text{otherwise} \end{cases}$$

is a morphism.

Example 5.1 With the *length* and *size* norms:

$|t|_{length} = 0$ if t is a variable or $t = []$,
$|t|_{length} = 1 + |tail|_{length}$ if $t = [h|tail]$,

$|t|_{size} = 1$ if t is a variable or a constant,
$|t|_{size} = 1 + |t_1|_{size}, ..., |t_n|_{size}$ if $t = f(t_1, ..., t_n)$,

we have: $Exp_{length}([X[a|Z]]) = 1 + 1 + Z$ and $Exp_{size}([X[a|Z]]) = 1 + X + 1 + Z$ respectively. ∎

Karr ([17]) shows that linear relationships analysis among variables of programs can be obtained by manipulating ***affine relationships*** i.e., linear equalities of the form $c_0 = c_1X_1 + ... + c_nX_n$. In our framework, this corresponds to a constraint system as follows: the universe is a set of affine subspaces $\mathcal{K}$ on a fixed n-dimensional space; the meet operation $\otimes$ is simply intersection of affine subspaces; the join of two affine subspaces A_1 and A_2, given by $A_1 \hat{\oplus} A_2$, is the smallest affine subspace containing A_1 and A_2 (since the union of two affine subspaces is not, in general, an affine subspace); cylindrification, which corresponds to the variable restriction of Verschaetse and De Schreye, corresponds to "projection" parallel to an axis; and substitution is defined as follows: Let S be an affine subspace and $x \in V$, $t \in \tau_{Exp}$, then the substitution of x with t in S is defined as the affine subspace $\hat{\exists}_{\{x\}}(x = t \cap S)$. The elements **0** and **1** are defined as $\emptyset$ and the entire space $\Re^n$ (for some sufficiently large n) respectively. Since we are interested only in relations having finite arity, we can always represent any answer constraint as a constraint on the finite dimensional space of its free variables. Moreover, the use of a bottom-up semantics construction does not require any infinite set of variables for renamings. Therefore, the set of variables V can be assumed to be a finite set $V_n = \{x_1, ..., x_n\}$. Diagonal elements are (single) equations on the term system τ_{Exp}.

Proposition 5.1
$(\mathcal{K}, \cap, \hat{\oplus}, \Re^n, \emptyset, \hat{\exists}_\Delta, \hat{\partial}^t_x, [t = t'])_{\{x\},\Delta \subseteq V_n; t,t' \in \tau_{Exp}}$ is a non-distributive, $\cap$-idempotent and commutative constraint system, where $\Re^n$ is annihilator for $\hat{\oplus}$. ∎

As pointed out in [17], there are no infinitely ascending chains of free-variable bounded constraints (i.e. bounded dimension affine spaces), otherwise in any properly ascending chain of subspaces: $U_1 \hat{\triangleleft} U_2 \hat{\triangleleft} \ldots$ the subspaces U_i must have a dimension of at least one greater than U_{i-1}. The resulting constraint system is therefore noetherian.

Example 5.2 Consider the logic program defining the predicate *append* in Example 4.1, together with the norm *length*. The corresponding abstract program is:

$$append(x_1, x_2, x_3) \ :- \ x_1 = 0, x_2 = x_3.$$
$$append(x_1, x_2, x_3) \ :- \ x_1 = 1 + y, x_3 = 1 + z \ \Box \ append(y, x_2, z).$$

The abstract semantics can be computed in $\Re^3$:

$$\begin{aligned}
T_P^{\mathcal{K}} \uparrow 0(\emptyset) &= \emptyset \\
T_P^{\mathcal{K}} \uparrow 1(\emptyset) &= \{append(x_1, x_2, x_3) \ :- \ x_1 = 0, x_2 = x_3\} \\
T_P^{\mathcal{K}} \uparrow 2(\emptyset) &= \{append(x_1, x_2, x_3) \ :- \ (x_1 = 0, x_2 = x_3) \hat{\oplus} (x_1 = 1, x_3 = 1 + x_2)\} \\
&= \{append(x_1, x_2, x_3) \ :- \ x_1 + x_2 = x_3\}
\end{aligned}$$

The affine subspace $x_1 + x_2 = x_3$ specifies the relationship among the lengths of the arguments of the predicate *append* in the expected way.
A possible implementation can be obtained by slightly modifying the $CLP(\mathcal{R})$ interpreter in [16] to cope with affine subspaces. This corresponds to implement (at the *meta level*) the join operator $\hat{\oplus}$ for affine subspaces so as to combine the computed answer constraints generated by the interpreter. ∎

6 Related work

Abstract interpretation of constraint logic programs is considered by Marriott and Søndergaard [19]. Their treatment is based on abstracting a denotational semantics for constraint logic programs. A meta-language based on the typed λ-calculus is used to specify the semantics of logic languages in a denotational style, and both the standard and non-standard semantics are viewed as instances of the meta-language specification. In our case, instead of defining a meta-language for data-flow analysis, we consider the constraint specification on which the *CLP* paradigm is defined. Non-standard semantics for a given constraint-based program can thus be obtained by appropriately modifying the underlying constraint system. In this way, data-flow analyses of logic-based languages can be specified as a standard constraint computation. No difference is introduced between the concrete programming language and the abstract one. They both derive from the same general specification of the *CLP* paradigm.

A related approach is also considered by Codognet and Filè, who give an algebraic definition of constraint systems and consider abstract interpretation of constraint logic programs [5]. However, the algebraic structure considered by these authors is very different: only $\otimes$-composition is considered. The notion of "computation system" is introduced but the underlying structure is not provided with a join operator. Because of this construction, mainly based on a generalization of the top-down SLD semantics, a loop-checker consisting in a "tabled" interpreter is needed. In our framework, by contrast, extraneous devices such as loop checking and tabulation are not considered. Instead, finiteness is treated simply as a property of the constraint system, expressed in terms of $\trianglelefteq$-chains. This allows non-standard computations to be specified as standard *CLP* computations over an appropriate (abstract) constraint system.

Acknowledgments

The stimulating discussions with Roberto Bagnara, Roberto Barbuti, Suzanne Dietrich, Maurizio Gabbrielli, Michael Maher, Nino Salibra, Gert Smolka, and David S. Warren are gratefully acknowledged.

References

[1] A.V. Aho, J.E. Hopcroft, and J.D. Ullman. *The Design and Analysis of Computer Algorithms.* Addison Wesley Publishing Company, 1974.

[2] R. Barbuti, R. Giacobazzi, and G. Levi. A General Framework for Semantics-based Bottom-up Abstract Interpretation of Logic Programs. *ACM Transactions on Programming Languages and Systems*, 15(1):133–181, 1993.

[3] R. Barbuti and A. Martelli. A Structured Approach to Semantics Correctness. *Science of Computer Programming*, 3:279–311, 1983.

[4] J. Cirulis. An Algebraization of First Order Logic with Terms. *Colloquia Mathematica Societatis Jànos Bolyai*, 54:125–146, 1991.

[5] P. Codognet and G. Filè. Computations, Abstractions and Constraints in Logic Programs. In *Proc. Fourth Int. Conf. on Programming Languages*, 1992.

[6] A. Cortesi, G. Filè, and W. Winsborough. *Prop* revisited: Propositional Formula as Abstract Domain for Groundness Analysis. In *Proc. Sixth IEEE Symp. on Logic In Computer Science*, pages 322–327. IEEE Computer Society Press, 1991.

[7] P. Cousot and R. Cousot. Abstract Interpretation: A Unified Lattice Model for Static Analysis of Programs by Construction or Approximation of Fixpoints. In *Proc. Fourth ACM Symp. Principles of Programming Languages*, pages 238–252, 1977.

[8] P. Cousot and R. Cousot. Systematic Design of Program Analysis Frameworks. In *Proc. Sixth ACM Symp. Principles of Programming Languages*, pages 269–282, 1979.

[9] P. Cousot and N. Halbwachs. Automatic Discovery of Linear Restraints Among Variables of a Program. In *Proc. Fifth ACM Symp. Principles of Programming Languages*, pages 84–96, 1978.

[10] M. Gabbrielli and G. Levi. Modeling Answer Constraints in Constraint Logic Programs. In K. Furukawa, editor, *Proc. Eighth Int'l Conf. on Logic Programming*, pages 238–252. The MIT Press, Cambridge, Mass., 1991.

[11] A. Van Gelder. Deriving Constraints Among Argument Sizes in Logic Programs. In *Proc. of the eleventh ACM Conference on Principles of Database Systems*, pages 47–60. ACM, 1990.

[12] R. Giacobazzi, S. K. Debray, and G. Levi. A Generalized Semantics for Constraint Logic Programs. In *Proceedings of the International Conference on Fifth Generation Computer Systems 1992*, pages 581–591, 1992.

[13] L. Henkin, J.D. Monk, and A. Tarski. *Cylindric Algebras. Part I and II.* North-Holland, Amsterdam, 1971.

[14] M. Hermenegildo, R. Warren, and S.K. Debray. Global flow analysis as a practical compilation tool. *Journal of Logic Programming*, **13**(4):349–366, 1992.

[15] J. Jaffar and J.-L. Lassez. Constraint Logic Programming. In *Proc. Fourteenth Annual ACM Symp. on Principles of Programming Languages*, pages 111–119. ACM, 1987.

[16] J. Jaffar, S. Michaylov, P. Stuckey, and R. Yap. The CLP($\mathcal{R}$) Language and System. *ACM Transactions on Programming Languages and Systems*, **14**(3):339–395, 1992.

[17] M. Karr. Affine Relationships Among Variables of a Program. *Acta Informatica*, **6**:133–151, 1976.

[18] J. W. Lloyd. *Foundations of Logic Programming.* Springer-Verlag, Berlin, 1987. Second edition.

[19] K. Marriott and H. Søndergaard. Analysis of Constraint Logic Programs. In S. K. Debray and M. Hermenegildo, editors, *Proc. North American Conf. on Logic Programming'90*, pages 531–547. The MIT Press, Cambridge, Mass., 1990.

[20] Oystein Ore. Combinations of Closure Relations. *Annals of Mathematics*, **44**(3):514–533, 1943.

[21] V. A. Saraswat, M. Rinard, and P. Panangaden. Semantic Foundation of Concurrent Constraint Programming. In *Proc. Eighteenth Annual ACM Symp. on Principles of Programming Languages*, pages 333–353. ACM, 1991.

[22] Jichang Tan and I-Peng Lin. Compiling Dataflow Analysis of Logic Programs. In *ACM Programming Language Design and Implementation*, volume 27 of *SIGPLAN Notices*, pages 106–115. ACM Press, 1992.

[23] M. H. van Emden and R. A. Kowalski. The semantics of predicate logic as a programming language. *Journal of the ACM*, **23**(4):733–742, 1976.

[24] K. Verschaetse and D. De Schreye. Derivation of Linear Size Relations by abstract interpretation. In M. Bruynooghe and M. Wirsing, editors, *Proc. of PLILP'92*, volume 631 of *Lecture Notes in Computer Science*, pages 296–310. Springer-Verlag, Berlin, 1992.

Communications

Dimension-Complemented Lambda Abstraction Algebras

Don Pigozzi*
Dept. Mathematics, Iowa State University
Ames, Iowa, USA

Antonino Salibra†
Dip. Informatica, University of Bari
Bari, Italy

Abstract

Lambda abstraction algebras (LAA's) are designed to algebraize the untyped lambda calculus in the same way cylindric and polyadic algebras algebraize the first-order predicate logic. Like combinatory algebras they can be defined by true identities and thus form a variety in the sense of universal algebra, but they differ from combinatory algebras in several important respects. The most natural LAA's are obtained by coordinatizing environment models of the lambda calculus. This gives rise to two classes of LAA's of functions of infinite arity: *functional* LAA's (FLAA) and *point-relativized functional* LAA's (RLAA). It is shown that RLAA is a variety and is the smallest variety including FLAA.

Dimension-complemented LAA's constitute the widest class of LAA's that can be represented as an algebra of functions and are known to have a natural intrinsic characterization. We prove that every dimension-complemented LAA is isomorphic to RLAA. This is the crucial step in showing that RLAA is a variety.

The untyped lambda calculus is a formalization of an intensional as opposed to an extensional theory of functions; that is, it is a theory of functions viewed as "rules" rather than "sets of ordered pairs". A basic feature is the lack of distinction between functions and the elements of the domains on which the functions act. Thus a function can, in theory, take other functions, even itself, as legitimate arguments. There are two primitive notions: *application*, the operation of applying a function to an argument, and *lambda (functional) abstraction*, the process of forming a function from the "rule" that defines it. The naive, intended models of the lambda calculus are sets V that coincide with the set of functions from V into itself, symbolically, $V = V^V$. But of course there are no such sets with more than one element. However, by restricting the functions considered to a certain manageable subset of V^V it is possible to construct domains of *admissible* functions that constitute functional models of the lambda calculus in a very natural sense. The first such models were discovered by Scott [16]. They are called *environment models* in [11]. They can be characterized by means of an injective partial mapping $\lambda : V^V \circ\!\!\rightarrow V$

*Supported by National Science Foundation Grant DMS 8805870.

†Supported by a NATO Senior Fellowship Grant of the Italian Research Council.

[1] *Keywords and phrases.* lambda calculus, cylindric algebras, polyadic algebras, abstract substitution, representation theorems.

[2] 1991 *Mathematics Subject Classification.* Primary: 03G25. Secondary: 03B40, 08B05.

whose domain is the set of admissible functions. λ may be thought of as the process of *encoding* admissible functions as elements of V. With functions encoded this way, application can be viewed as a binary operation on V. Let $\mathbf{V}$ be the domain V enriched by the application operation and the encoding mapping, which we denote respectively by $\cdot^{\mathbf{V}}$ and $\lambda^{\mathbf{V}}$.

Intuitively, each admissible function f in V^V has two forms, one *intensional* and the other *extensional*. They are related by the equation

$$(\lambda^{\mathbf{V}} f) \cdot^{\mathbf{V}} v = f(v), \quad \text{for each } v \in V. \tag{1}$$

In its intensional form an admissible function is represented by a term $t(x)$ of the lambda calculus with a free variable x. For each $v \in V$, let $t^{\mathbf{V}}(v)$ be the value $t(x)$ takes in V when x is interpreted as v. Then its extensional form is the function $\langle t^{\mathbf{V}}(v) : v \in V\rangle \in V^V$, which is encoded as the element $\lambda^{\mathbf{V}}(\langle t^{\mathbf{V}}(v) : v \in V\rangle)$ of V and represented by the term $\lambda x.t(x)$. Note that $t(x)$ and $\lambda x.t(x)$ both represent the same function, but in environment models only the extensional form corresponds to an actual element of the universe of the model; this is an essential difference between the models of lambda calculus and lambda abstraction algebras.

The two forms of the function are connected by the operation of application. Intuitively, the value $t^{\mathbf{V}}(v)$ of the function at a particular argument v is obtained by applying its extensional form to v; symbolically, $\langle t^{\mathbf{V}}(v) : v \in V\rangle(v) = t^{\mathbf{V}}(v)$. Expressed in the environment model this becomes (1), i.e.,

$$\lambda^{\mathbf{V}}(\langle t^{\mathbf{V}}(v) : v \in V\rangle) \cdot^{\mathbf{V}} v = t^{\mathbf{V}}(v), \quad \text{for each } v \in V.$$

In the lambda calculus itself this relationship is represented by the fundamental axiom of *β-conversion*:

- $(\lambda x.t)s = t[s/x]$, for all terms t, s and variable x such that s is free for x in t.

$t[s/x]$ is the result of substituting s for all free occurrences of x in t. The two fundamental operations of the lambda calculus are application and lambda abstraction. Terms are defined in the usual way: every variable is a term, and if t and s are terms, so are $t \cdot s$ and $\lambda x(t)$ for each variable x. By convention we write ts for $t \cdot s$ and $\lambda x.t$ for $\lambda x(t)$. An occurrence of a variable x is *free* if it is not within the scope of any λx. s is *free for* x in t if no free occurrence of x in t lies within the scope of a lambda abstraction with respect to a free variable of s.

In addition to β-conversion, the axioms of the lambda calculus include *α-conversion:*

- $\lambda x.t = \lambda y.(\lambda x.t)y$, if y does not occur free in t,

and the standard axioms for equality. α-conversion says that bound variables can be replaced in a term under the obvious condition.

The untyped lambda calculus is formalized as a theory of equations, but it is not an equational theory in the usual algebraic sense because the equations, unlike the associative and commutative laws of group theory, for example, are not always preserved when arbitrary terms are substituted for variables. Consequently the general methods that have been developed in universal algebra and category theory, for defining the semantics of an arbitrary algebraic theory for example, are not directly applicable. There have been several attempts to reformulate the lambda calculus as a purely algebraic theory. The earliest and best known, although apparently not motivated by these considerations, are the combinatory algebras of Curry [4]. More recently, several purely algebraic theories of the lambda calculus within the context of category theory have been developed: Obtułowicz and Wieger [13] via the *algebraic theories* of Lawvere; Adachi [1] via monads; Curien [3] via categorical combinators. An algebraic theory of the lambda calculus, also modeled on cylindric and polyadic Boolean algebras and essentially the same as ours, has been introduced independently by Diskin [5].

In [14] we proposed an alternative approach in the context of universal algebra. We introduced the notion of a *lambda abstraction algebra* (LAA for short), which is intended to provide a purely algebraic theory of the lambda calculus in the same way Boolean algebras constitute an algebraic theory of classical propositional logic and, more to the point, cylindric and polyadic Boolean algebras constitute an algebraic theory of first-order predicate logic.

In the lambda calculus variables play a dual role. They serve to index the arguments of definable functions, i.e., they act as place holders; they also represent specific functions, namely the projections. This duality is preserved in the theory of LAA's by overloading the notation we use to describe the language. In their role as place holders λ-variables are represented by an infinite, countable sequence $x_1, x_2, \ldots$. The language contains a constant (i.e., nullary operation) symbol for each x_i. This constant is also denoted by x_i. Even though x_i is a constant, we shall refer to it as a *λ-variable* in order to keep the connection with the lambda calculus apparent. These constant symbols represent the λ-variables in their role as projections. In addition the language contains a unary operation symbol for each x_i that is denoted by λx_i and is called a *lambda abstraction.*

A *lambda abstraction algebra* is an algebra of the form

$$\mathbf{A} = \langle A, \cdot, \lambda x_1, \lambda x_2, \ldots, x_1, x_2, \ldots \rangle,$$

where A is a nonempty set, $\cdot$ is a binary operation (corresponding to application), $\lambda x_1, \lambda x_2, \ldots$ is an infinite system of unary operations on A, and $x_1, x_2, \ldots$ a corresponding system of distinguished elements of A. In the sequel x, y, z will represent arbitrary λ-variables. The set of all λ-variables will be denoted by I. Substitution is abstracted as a system of term-defined, binary operations $S^x_-(-)$ on A. The algebraic reformulation of β-conversion becomes the definition of abstract substitution:

$$S^x_a(b) ::= \big(\lambda x(a)\big) \cdot b, \qquad \text{for all } x \in I \text{ and all } a, b \in A.$$

An element a of a LAA is said to be *algebraically dependent* on x if $S^x_y(a) \neq a$ for some $y \neq x$. The set of all x such that a is algebraically dependent on x is called the *dimension set* of a and is denoted by $\mathbf{\Delta} a$. It can be shown on the basis of the following axioms that $x \notin \mathbf{\Delta} a$ is equivalent to any one of the equations $S^x_y(a) = a$ such that $y \neq x$.

The equational axioms of LAA's reflect α-conversion and Curry's recursive axiomatization of substitution in the lambda calculus. To make them more readable we replace $\lambda x(-) \cdot -$ everywhere by $S^x_-(-)$, and, in the last two axioms,

(β_6) and (α), the equation $S^x_y(a) = a$ is replaced by $y \notin \mathbf{\Delta} a$. Note that ($\beta_6$) and ($\alpha$) are actually quasi identities.

(β_1) $S^x_a(x) = a$;
(β_2) $S^x_a(y) = y, \quad y \neq x$;
(β_3) $S^x_x(a) = a$;
(β_4) $S^x_a(\lambda x(b)) = \lambda x(b)$;
(β_5) $S^x_a(b \cdot c) = S^x_a(b) \cdot S^x_a(c)$;
(β_6) $y \notin \mathbf{\Delta} a \Rightarrow S^x_a(\lambda y(b)) = \lambda y(S^x_a(b)), \quad x \neq y$;
(α) $y \notin \mathbf{\Delta} a \Rightarrow \lambda x(a) = \lambda y(S^x_y(a))$.

In the presence of (β_2), (β_4), and (β_5), the quasi identities (β_6) and (α) are logically equivalent to identities. So LAA is a variety. The basic theory of LAA is developed in [14]. In particular, the proofs of the following results, which are all straightforward consequences of the axioms, can be found there.

Proposition 1 1. $\mathbf{\Delta}(ab) \subseteq \mathbf{\Delta} a \cup \mathbf{\Delta} b$.
2. $\mathbf{\Delta}(\lambda x.a) = \mathbf{\Delta} a \setminus \{x\}$.
3. $\mathbf{\Delta}\big(S^x_b(a)\big) \subseteq (\mathbf{\Delta} a \cup \mathbf{\Delta} b) \setminus \{x\}$.
4. $\mathbf{\Delta} x \subseteq \{x\}$, with equality holding if $\mathbf{A}$ is nontrivial.

We list some of the basic properties of substitution that play an important role in establishing the representation results below; see Thms. 2 and 4.

For all $a, b, c \in A$ we have:

- $x \notin \mathbf{\Delta} c \Rightarrow S^y_c S^x_b(a) = S^x_{S^y_c(b)} S^y_c(a)$;
- $y \notin \mathbf{\Delta} b \Rightarrow S^y_b S^x_y(a) = S^y_b S^x_b(a)$;
- $y \notin \mathbf{\Delta} a \Rightarrow S^y_b(a) = a$;
- $x \notin \mathbf{\Delta} c, y \notin \mathbf{\Delta} b \Rightarrow S^y_c S^x_b(a) = S^x_b S^y_c(a), \quad x \neq y$;
- $z \notin \mathbf{\Delta} a \cup \mathbf{\Delta} b \Rightarrow S^x_b(a) = S^z_b S^x_z(a)$.

The functions λx are always one-one, i.e., $\lambda x(a) = \lambda x(b)$ iff $a = b$, but λx is onto iff the LAA is trivial. Thus every nontrivial LAA is infinite. We know of only two ways of constructing nontrivial LAA's. One way is as the quotient of an algebra of lambda terms by a consistent lambda theory. (Any set of lambda terms closed under β- and α-conversion and the equality axioms is called a *lambda theory*; see [11]). The LAA's that arise this way are locally-finite dimensional, reflecting the fact that there are only a finite number of λ-variables appearing in any lambda term. A LAA $\mathbf{A}$ is *locally finite-dimensional* if $\mathbf{\Delta} a$ is finite for every $a \in A$.

The most natural LAA's, the algebras that the axioms are intended to characterize, are algebras of functions. Not surprisingly, they are closely related to the environment models of lambda calculus. Indeed, they are obtained by coordinatizing environment models by the λ-variables in a natural way. We will try to explain this intuitively before we give the formal definition. The exact connection between LAA's and models of the lambda calculus is investigated in detail in [15].

Let $\mathbf{V} = \langle V, \cdot^{\mathbf{V}}, \lambda^{\mathbf{V}} \rangle$ be an environment model. $\cdot^{\mathbf{V}}$ is the application operation and $\lambda^{\mathbf{V}} : V^V \multimap V$ is the encoding of the admissible functions of $\mathbf{V}$ into V; recall that they are related by the equality (1). Let I be the set of λ-variables. An element p of V^I, i.e., an assignment of elements of V to λ-variables, is called an *environment*. p_x is the value p assigns to x for each $x \in I$. For any $v \in V$ and $x \in I$, $p(v/x)$ is the new environment defined for each $y \in I$ by

$$(p(v/x))_y = \begin{cases} v & \text{if } y = x, \\ p_y & \text{otherwise.} \end{cases}$$

Let $f \in V^{V^I}$. Each λ-variable x and environment p determines a function $f_{x,p} = \langle f(p(v/x)) : v \in V \rangle$ in V^V. f is *admissible* if each of the functions $f_{x,p}$ is admissible in $\mathbf{V}$, i.e., is in the domain of $\lambda^{\mathbf{V}}$. Every functional LAA $\mathbf{A}$ consists of a set of admissible functions in V^{V^I} for some environment model $\mathbf{V}$. $\mathbf{V}$ is called the *value domain* of $\mathbf{A}$. The lambda abstraction of a member f of $\mathbf{A}$ is defined as follows: $\lambda x^{\mathbf{A}}(f)(p) = \lambda^{\mathbf{V}}(f_{x,p})$ for every environment p.

We now give a precise definition of a functional LAA that does not depend on the notion of an environment model. After defining a functional LAA, we shall see how to define environment models in its terms.

Let $\mathbf{V} = \langle V, \cdot^{\mathbf{V}}, \lambda^{\mathbf{V}} \rangle$ be any structure, where V is a nonempty set, $\cdot^{\mathbf{V}}$ is a binary operation on V, and $\lambda^{\mathbf{V}} : V^V \circ\!\!\rightarrow V$ is a partial function. $\mathbf{V}$ is called a *functional domain* if, for every f in the domain of $\lambda^{\mathbf{V}}$, (1) holds.

Let $\mathbf{V} = \langle V, \cdot^{\mathbf{V}}, \lambda^{\mathbf{V}} \rangle$ be a functional domain and let $V_I = \{ f : f : V^I \circ\!\!\rightarrow V \}$, where I is the set of λ-variables. By the *I-coordinatization* of $\mathbf{V}$ we mean the algebra of partial functions.

$$\mathbf{V}_I = \left\langle V_I, \cdot^{\mathbf{V}_I}, \langle \lambda x^{\mathbf{V}_I} : x \in I \rangle, \langle x^{\mathbf{V}_I} : x \in I \rangle \right\rangle,$$

where for all $a, b : V^I \circ\!\!\rightarrow V$, $x \in I$, and $p \in V^I$:

- $(a \cdot^{\mathbf{V}_I} b)(p) = a(p) \cdot^{\mathbf{V}} b(p)$, provided $a(p)$ and $b(p)$ are both defined; otherwise $(a \cdot^{\mathbf{V}_I} b)(p)$ is undefined.
- $(\lambda x^{\mathbf{V}_I}.a)(p) = \lambda^{\mathbf{V}}\big(\langle a(p(v/x)) : v \in V \rangle\big)$, provided $\langle a(p(v/x)) : v \in V \rangle$ is in the domain of $\lambda^{\mathbf{V}}$ (note this implies $a(p(v/x))$ is defined for all $v \in V$); otherwise $(\lambda x^{\mathbf{V}_I}.a)(p)$ is undefined.
- $x^{\mathbf{V}_I}(p) = p_x$.

A subalgebra $\mathbf{A}$ of total functions of $\mathbf{V}_I$, i.e., a subalgebra such that $a(p)$ is defined for all $a \in A$ and $p \in V^I$, is called a *functional lambda abstraction algebra*. $\mathbf{V}$ is its *value domain*. The class of all functional LAA's and their isomorphic images is denoted by FLAA. It can be shown that FLAA is a proper subclass of LAA.

Locally finite-dimensional FLAA's are similar to the functional models of the lambda calculus developed in Krivine [10].

Environment models of the lambda calculus can now be defined as those functional domains $\mathbf{V}$ for which there exist at least one FLAA with value domain $\mathbf{V}$; Environment models are not easy to construct;[1] consequently, neither are FLAA's. However the following theorem, which is the main result of [14], shows that they can be automatically obtained from every locally finite-dimensional LAA.[2]

[1] As previously noted the first one was constructed by Scott [16].

[2] The theorem has also been independently obtained by Diskin and Beylin [6].

Theorem 2 Every locally finite-dimensional LAA is isomorphic to a FLAA with the property that each function in the domain of the algebra depends on only a finite number of arguments.

This theorem corresponds to the completeness theorem for the lambda calculus ([11]): every lambda theory consists of precisely the equations valid in some environment model. It is modeled on the functional representation theorem for locally finite-dimensional polyadic Boolean algebras ([7], Thm. (10.9)). It is also closely related to the representation theorem for locally finite-dimensional cylindric algebras ([9], Part II, Thm. 3.2.11(i)), which corresponds to the completeness theorem for first-order predicate logic (cf. the Foreward of [9], Part I).

The locally finite-dimensional LAA's correspond most closely to the other algebraic models of the lambda calculus that have appeared in the literature, for instance the *term lambda algebras* ([11]) and *syntactical models* ([2]) of combinatory logic and the *Curry theories* of [13]. On the other hand FLAA's correspond to the *environment models* ([11]) and *lambda models* ([2]) of combinatory logic and the *functional Curry theories* in [13].

The *point-relativized functional* LAA's, which we now consider, turn out to have, in some important respects, nicer properties than FLAA's.

Let $\mathbf{V}$ be a functional domain and let r be a fixed but arbitrary element of V^I. Let ${V_r}^I$ be the set of all $p \in V^I$ that differ from r at only finitely many coordinates, i.e.,

$${V_r}^I = \{ p \in V^I : |\{ p_x \neq r_x : x \in I \}| < \omega \}.$$

Let $V_{I,r}$ be the set of all partial functions $f : {V_r}^I \circ\!\!\rightarrow V$. The *$(I,r)$-coordinatization* of V,

$$\mathbf{V}_{I,r} = \langle V_{I,r},\ \cdot^{\mathbf{V}_{I,r}},\ \langle \lambda x^{\mathbf{V}_{I,r}} : x \in I \rangle,\ \langle x^{\mathbf{V}_{I,r}} : x \in I \rangle \rangle,$$

is defined just as $\mathbf{V}_I$ except that all functions are restricted to ${V_r}^I$.

A subalgebra $\mathbf{A}$ of $\mathbf{V}_{I,r}$ of total functions is called a *point-relativized functional lambda abstraction algebra*. The class of all point-relativized functional LAA and their isomorphic images is denoted by RLAA. RLAA, like FLAA, is a proper subclass of LAA. It is also known that FLAA $\subseteq$ RLAA. However, we do not know if the inclusion is proper.

Theorem 3 RLAA is a variety, i.e., it is closed under the formation of homomorphic images, subalgebras and Cartesian products. It is the smallest variety that includes all locally finite-dimensional LAA's and also the smallest variety that includes FLAA.

This theorem shows that RLAA's play a very special role in the theory of LAA's, analogous to the one representable cylindric algebras play in the theory of cylindric algebras; see [9], Part II, Cor. 3.1.108.

The notion of a dimension-complemented LAA plays a central role in the proof of Thm. 3. A LAA $\mathbf{A}$ is *dimension-complemented* if $\Delta a \neq I$ for every $a \in A$. It can be shown that, if $\mathbf{A}$ is dimension-complemented, then $\Delta a_1 \cup \ldots \cup \Delta a_n$ is coinfinite for every finite set $a_1, \ldots, a_n$ of elements of $\mathbf{A}$.

The key to the proof of Thm. 3 is the following representation result.

Theorem 4 Every dimension-complemented LAA is isomorphic to a RLAA.

Outline of proof: Let $\mathbf{A}$ be an arbitrary LAA. The functional domain $\mathbf{V} = \langle V, \cdot^{\mathbf{V}}, \lambda^{\mathbf{V}} \rangle$ *associated with* $\mathbf{A}$ is defined as follows: $V = A$ and $\cdot^{\mathbf{V}} = \cdot^{\mathbf{A}}$. The domain of $\lambda^{\mathbf{V}} : V^V \circ\!\!\rightarrow V$ is $\{ \langle S^x_v(a) : v \in V \rangle : a \in A \text{ and } x \in I \}$, and for each function in this set we define $\lambda^{\mathbf{V}}(\langle S^x_v(a) : v \in V \rangle) = \lambda x^{\mathbf{A}}(a)$. It can be shown that $\langle S^x_v(a) : v \in V \rangle = \langle S^y_v(b) : v \in V \rangle$ implies $\lambda x^{\mathbf{A}}(a) = \lambda y^{\mathbf{A}}(b)$. Thus $\lambda^{\mathbf{V}}$ is well defined. It is easily checked that $\mathbf{V}$ is a functional domain.

Let $\mathbf{A}$ be dimension-complemented and let $\mathbf{V}$ be its associated functional domain. Let $\varepsilon \in V^I$ such that $\varepsilon_x = x^{\mathbf{A}}$ for each λ-variable x. For each $p \in V_{I,\varepsilon}$ there exist lambda variables $y_1, \ldots, y_n$ and elements $v_1, \ldots, v_n$ of V such that $p = \varepsilon((v_1/y_1, \ldots, v_n/y_n))$. Define a mapping $\Psi : A \to V_{I,\varepsilon}$ as follows: for all $a \in A$,

$$\Psi(a)(\varepsilon(v_1/y_1, \ldots, v_n/y_n)) = S^{z_1}_{v_1} \ldots S^{z_n}_{v_n} S^{y_1}_{z_1} \ldots S^{y_n}_{z_n}(a),$$

for all lambda variables $y_1, \ldots, y_n$ and all $v_1, \ldots, v_n \in V$ and any set of lambda variables $z_1, \ldots, z_n$ such that $a, y_1^{\mathbf{A}}, \ldots, y_n^{\mathbf{A}}, v_1, \ldots, v_n$ are all independent of each of the z_i. It can be shown that Ψ is well defined (i.e., does not depend on the choice of $z_1, \ldots, z_n$), and that it is an isomorphism between $\mathbf{A}$ and a total subalgebra of $\mathbf{V}_{I,\varepsilon}$.

Outline of proof of first part of Thm. 3: RLAA is obviously closed under forming subalgebras; closure under quotients and Cartesian products is much more difficult to prove.

A LAA $\mathbf{A}$ is said to be a *subreduct* of a LAA $\mathbf{B}$ if $A \subseteq B$ and there is a injective mapping $\varphi : I \to I$ with coinfinite range $\varphi(I)$ such that, for all $a, b \in A$ and $x \in I$,

- $a \cdot^{\mathbf{A}} b = a \cdot^{\mathbf{B}} b$;
- $\lambda x^{\mathbf{A}}(a) = \lambda \varphi(x)^{\mathbf{B}}(a)$;
- $x^{\mathbf{A}} = \varphi(x)^{\mathbf{B}}$.

$\mathbf{A}$ is a *neat subreduct* of $\mathbf{B}$ if, in addition, $\mathbf{\Delta}^{\mathbf{B}} a \subseteq \varphi(I)$ for all $a \in A$. It is not difficult to show that RLAA is closed under neat subreducts.

Let $\mathbf{A}$ be a neat subreduct of some LAA, say $\mathbf{B}$. Since the range of φ is coinfinite, it is easy to see using Prop. 1 that the subalgebra of $\mathbf{B}$ generated by A is dimension-complemented and hence a RLAA by Thm. 4. Thus $\mathbf{A} \in$ RLAA since RLAA is closed under neat subreducts. Conversely, it is not difficult to show that every RLAA is isomorphic to a neat subreduct of some LAA. Thus RLAA coincides with the class of neat subreducts of LAA's (and their isomorphic images), and the problem of showing RLAA is closed under quotients and products reduces to establishing the same for neat subreducts of LAA's.

It is easy to see that, if $\mathbf{A}_k$ is a neat subreduct of $\mathbf{B}_k$ for each k, then $\prod \mathbf{A}_k$ is isomorphic to a neat subreduct of $\prod \mathbf{B}_k$. Finally, let $\mathbf{A}$ be a neat reduct of $\mathbf{B}$ and Θ a congruence relation on $\mathbf{A}$. Then it can be shown, using the combinatory completeness of combinatory algebras ([2], Thm.5.1.10), that there is a congruence relation $\mathbf{\Phi}$ on $\mathbf{B}$ such that $\mathbf{\Phi} \cap (A \times A) = \Theta$. Hence $\mathbf{A}/\Theta$ is isomorphic to a neat subreduct of $\mathbf{B}/\mathbf{\Phi}$.

It is an open problem if FLAA is also a variety and hence coincides with RLAA. Since RLAA is a variety, it is axiomatized by some set of identities by Birkhoff's theorem. It is conjectured that it is finitely axiomatizable and, moreover, that Curry's equational axioms for lambda algebras ([2], p. 94), together with those of LAA's, are sufficient for this purpose. In contrast the representable cylindric algebras are not finitely axiomatizable.

The reasoning behind the above conjecture is the following: By the *zero-dimensional reduct* of a LAA **A** we mean the set of zero-dimensional elements of **A**, i.e., $\{a \in A : \Delta a = \emptyset\}$, together with the restriction of the application operation of $\cdot^{\mathbf{A}}$ of **A**. In [15] it is shown that this is a lambda algebra ([2], Def. 5.2.2), and in fact that every lambda algebra arises in this way. On the basis of this characterization, it is shown in [15] that a strong categorical equivalence exists between lambda algebras and locally finite LAA's. This result, together with the fact that the variety of lambda algebras is finitely based by Curry's axioms, and that RLAA is generated as variety by the locally finite LAA's, is the basis for the above conjecture.

Dimension-complemented LAA's have a direct analogue in the theory of cylindric algebras. Thm. 4 can be compared with the representation theory for dimension-complemented cylindric algebras; see [9], Part II, Thm. 3.2.11(ii). For a detailed survey of recent results in cylindric and related algebras see [12].

References

[1] T. Adachi. *A categorical characterization of lambda calculus models*. Research Report No. C-49, Dept. of Information Sciences, Tokyo Institute of Technology, January 1983.

[2] H.P. Barendregt. *The lambda calculus. Its syntax and semantics*. North-Holland, Amsterdam, revised edition, 1985.

[3] P.-L. Curien. *Categorical combinators, sequential algorithms and functional programming*. Pitman, 1986.

[4] H.B. Curry and R. Feys. *Combinatory Logic, Vol. I*, North-Holland, Amsterdam, 1958.

[5] Z.B. Diskin. *Lambda term systems*. Preprint, Frame Inform Systems, Riga, Latvia, 1990.

[6] Z. Diskin and I. Beylin. *Lambda substitution algebras*. Preprint, Frame Inform Systems, Riga, Latvia, 1993.

[7] P. Halmos. Homogeneous locally finite polyadic Boolean algebras of infinite degree. *Fund. Math.*, 43:255–325, 1956. [Reprinted in [8].]

[8] P. Halmos. *Algebraic Logic*. Chelsea, New York, 1962.

[9] L. Henkin, J.D. Monk and A. Tarski. *Cylindric algebras, Parts I and II*. North-Holland, Amsterdam, 1971, 1985.

[10] J.L. Krivine. *Lambda-Calcul, types et modeles*. Masson, Paris, 1990.

[11] A.R. Meyer. What is a model of the lambda calculus?. *Inform. Control.*, 52:87–122, 1982.

[12] I. Németi. Algebraizations of quantifier logics. An introductory overview. *Studia Logica*, 50:485–569, 1991. [Extended version: CCSOM Report, University of Amsterdam, 1993.]

[13] A. Obtułowicz and A. Wiweger. Categorical, functorial, and algebraic aspects of the type-free lambda calculus. In T. Traczyk, editor, *Universal Algebra and Applications*, pages 399–422, Banach Center Pub., Vol. 9, Warsaw, 1982.

[14] D. Pigozzi and A. Salibra. An introduction to lambda abstraction algebras. In M. Abad, editor, *IX Simposio Latinoamericano de Logica Mathematica, Proc.* (*Bahia Blanca, Argentina, 1992*), Notas de Logica Matematica, Bahia Blanca, Argentina, to appear.

[15] D. Pigozzi and A. Salibra. *Lambda abstraction algebras: coordinatizing models of lambda calculus*. Preprint, University of Bari, Bari, Italy, 1993.

[16] D.S. Scott. Data types as lattices. *SIAM J. Computing*, 5:522–587, 1976.

Parameterized Recursion Theory - A Tool for the Systematic Classification of Specification Methods

Till Mossakowski
University of Bremen
Department of Computer Science
P.O.Box 33 04 40
D-28334 Bremen
E-mail: e13p@alf.zfn.uni-bremen.de

Abstract

We examine four specification methods with increasing expressiveness. Parameterized recursion theory allows to characterize the power of parameterization in the methods, using a computational model based on Moschovakis' search computability. The four specification methods can be characterized by four different notions of semicomputable parameterized abstract data type, which differ in the availability of the parameter algebra and of nondeterminism.

1 Introduction

Today, many different methods for the algebraic specification of abstract data types (ADTs) are proposed. They differ in various properties.
When you have a particular abstract data type in mind, which method should be used to specify it? If a certain method is not powerful enough, you have to choose a more general one. The other way round: if you use a too general method, then the available tools and proof techniques may become weaker. So it is very useful to know about which ADTs can be specified with the various methods at all.

We formalize theories as $T = (\Sigma, AX)$ with signatures $\Sigma = (S, OP, POP, REL)$ consisting of sort, total operation, partial operation and relation symbols. We compare four methods with increasing expressiveness:

1. total algebras with equations ($POP = REL = \emptyset$, AX equations, see [5])
2. total algebras with implications ($POP = REL = \emptyset$)
3. total algebras with relations and implications ($POP = \emptyset$, Horn Clause Theories, see [7, 12]) and finally
4. partial algebras with relations and implications built from existence-equations (algebraic systems in [4]).

Bergstra and Tucker [3] classify various specification methods with respect to recursion theoretic expressiveness of initial algebra semantics.
For designing modular specifications, parameterized specifications and data types are useful. We only consider parameterized data types (PADTs) which are specifiable with hidden sorts, operations and/or relations. That is, specifiable PADTs are composites of free and forgetful functors in the corresponding institution. In order to perform classifications with respect to PADTs, we first need a notion of computability over (parameter) algebras. In section 2, we adapt Moschovakis [10] computability over abstract algebras to the many-sorted case. This is the basis for the our central definition of semi-search computable PADT in section 3. By four appropriate restrictions of this notion, parameterization within the four methods can be characterized (section 4). Since the available space is limited, examples are omitted and the proofs are only sketchy. Section 5 contains some concluding remarks.

2 Computability over Abstract Algebras

In the literature, there are various notions of computability over an algebra.
Reichel [13] defines T-algorithms for a theory T by using persistent extensions. This is no algorithmical or recursion theoretical concept, since it depends already on a particular specification method.
Kaphengst [9] characterizes operations specifiable by free persistent extensions using effective numberings. But his characterization is not uniform: the extension of the parameter theory depends on the parameter algebra.
Hupbach [8] considers abstract implementations and characterizes specifiable functors by certain "uniform rules". This comes closer to our intention. The problem here is that "uniformity" is defined very technically during the proof of the characterization.
Bergstra and Klop [1] give an interesting characterization of specifiable functors with minimal total parameter algebras. But for non-minimal algebras, they again have to incorporate some specification machinery and initial semantics into their notion of computable PADT (see [2]).

For parameterized recursion theory, we want a notion of uniform algorithm over abstract algebras, which is both algorithmic (hence does not rely on algebraic specification methods) *and* uniform, i. e., does not use a particular representation of the parameter algebra. Moschovakis's search computability [10] fits into these requirements (see Ershov [6] for an overview over various approaches).

Natural numbers of ordinary recursion theory have to be replaced by elements of abstract algebras. But since recursion theory needs a pairing mechanism, we have to use S-expressions over abstract algebra elements instead: Let $\Sigma = (S, OP, POP, REL)$ be a signature and A a Σ-algebra. The set $SExpr(A)$ is defined inductively: It contains nil, $atom\text{-}s(a)$ for $s \in S$, $a \in A_s$ and $cons(t, u)$ for $t, u \in SExpr(A)$. The set $SExpr$ is the subset of S-expressions containing no atoms. Like in LISP, we can consider natural numbers and lists of S-expressions again as S-expressions, and have $first$ and $rest$ as inverses of $cons$.

Moschovakis's approach also captures nondeterminism. He considers many-valued partial maps $\mathcal{F}_A: SExpr(A)^n \longrightarrow SExpr(A)$ such that for $\bar{t}$[1] $\in SExpr(A)^n$ the values z with $\mathcal{F}_A(\bar{t}) \rightarrow z$ form a (possibly empty) subset of $SExpr(A)$. $\mathcal{F}_A(\bar{t}) \simeq \mathcal{G}_A(\bar{t})$ means $\mathcal{F}_A(\bar{t}) \rightarrow u$ if and only if $\mathcal{G}_A(\bar{t}) \rightarrow u$.

Definition 2.1 (Moschovakis) Let $\Sigma = (S, OP, POP, REL)$ be a signature and $code: OP \dot{\cup} POP \dot{\cup} REL \longrightarrow \mathbb{N}$ some numbering. We define inductively the set of Σ-*algorithms* f as subset of $SExpr$.

	definition scheme	S-expression f
C0a.	$f(\bar{x}, y_1, \ldots, y_m) = op(\bar{x})$	$(0, n+m, code(op))$
C0b.	$f(\bar{x}, y_1, \ldots, y_m) \simeq pop(\bar{x})$	$(0, n+m, code(pop))$
C0c.	$f[R, y_1, \ldots, y_m] \simeq nil$	$(0, n+m, code(R))$
C1.	$f(\bar{x}) \simeq nil$	$(1, n)$
C2.	$f(y, \bar{x}) \simeq y$	$(2, n+1)$
C3.	$f(t, u, \bar{x}) \simeq cons(t, u)$	$(3, n+2)$
C4a.	$f(\bar{y}, x) \simeq first(x)$	$(4, n+1, 0)$
C4b.	$f(\bar{y}, x) \simeq rest(x)$	$(4, n+1, 1)$
C5.	$f(\bar{x}) \simeq g(h(\bar{x}), \bar{x})$	$(5, n, g, h)$
C6.	$f(nil, \bar{x}) \simeq g(\bar{x})$	$(6, n+1, g, h_1, \ldots, h_m, k)$
	$f(atom\text{-}s_i(y), \bar{x}) \simeq h_i(atom\text{-}s_i(y), \bar{x})$	
	$f(cons(t, u), \bar{x}) \simeq k(f(t, \bar{x}), f(u, \bar{x}), t, u, \bar{x})$	
C7.	$f(\bar{x}) \simeq g(x_{j+1}, x_1, \ldots, x_j, x_{j+2}, \ldots, x_n)$	$(7, n, j, g)$
C8.	$f(e, \bar{x}, y_1, \ldots, y_m) \simeq \{e\}(\bar{x})$	$(8, n+m+1, n)$
C9.	$f(\bar{x}) \simeq \nu y(g(y, \bar{x}) \rightarrow nil)$	$(9, n, g)$ □

Definition 2.2 A Σ-algorithm f has as semantics a familiy of many-valued partial maps $\{f\}^A: SExpr(A)^n \longrightarrow SExpr(A)$ indexed by Σ-algebras A. The semantical relation $\{f\}^A(\bar{t}) \rightarrow z$ is defined as the minimal relation satisfying the following conditions:

		$f =$
C0b'.	$\{f\}^A(nil) \rightarrow nil$, $\{f\}^A(cons(t, u)) \rightarrow nil$	$(0, n+m, code(pop))$
	$pop_A(\bar{a}) = a \Rightarrow \{f\}^A(atom\text{-}\bar{s}_A(\bar{a}), u_1, \ldots, u_m) \rightarrow atom\text{-}s(a)$	
C0c'.	$\bar{a} \in R_A \Rightarrow \{f\}^A(atom\text{-}\bar{s}_A(\bar{a}), u_1, \ldots, u_m) \rightarrow nil$	$(0, n+m, code(R))$
C5'.	$\exists u\, (h(\bar{t}) \rightarrow u \wedge \{g\}^A(u, \bar{t}) \rightarrow v) \Rightarrow \{f\}^A(\bar{t}) \rightarrow v$	$(5, n, g, h)$
C8'.	$\{e\}^A(\bar{t}) \rightarrow v \Rightarrow \{f\}^A(e, \bar{t}, u_1, \ldots, u_m) \rightarrow v$	$(8, n+m+1, n)$
C9'.	$\{g\}^A(u, \bar{t}) \rightarrow nil \Rightarrow \{f\}^A(\bar{t}) \rightarrow u$	$(9, n, g)$

(with similar translations to semantical conditions for the other cases) □

Schemes C0 to C7 allow to express *primitive recursiveness*, schemes C0 to C8 *prime computability* and schemes C0 to C9 *search computability*. Both prime and search computability reduce to partial recursiveness when Σ is empty.

Definition 2.3 We call a family $\mathcal{R} = (\mathcal{R}_A)_{A \in Alg(\Sigma)}$ of relations ($\mathcal{R}_A \subseteq SExpr(A)^n$) *primitive recursive (semi-search computable)*, if there is a primitive recursive (search computable) Σ-algorithm f with $\bar{t} \in \mathcal{R}_A$ iff $\{f\}^A(\bar{t}) \rightarrow nil$ for all $A \in Alg(\Sigma), \bar{t} \in SExpr(A)^n$. We call $\mathcal{R}$ *primitive recursively enumerable*, if there is a total primitive recursive Σ-algorithm f (i. e. f **does not use C0b or C0c**) such that for all $A \in Alg(\Sigma)$, $range(\{f\}^A) = \mathcal{R}_A$. □

[1] We abbreviate $t_1, \ldots, t_n$ by $\bar{t}$, $x_1, \ldots, x_n$ by $\bar{x}$ and so on

Semi-search computability has the following features:

- the algorithms deal with abstract algebra elements, no particular representation of the algebra is used
- algorithms are formulated uniformly for all Σ-algebras
- the equality relation and constant functions are not computable in general
- unbounded search (including and nondeterminism and OR-parallelism) is made explicit (via the ν-operator in C9)
- because of the nondeterministic search (C9), there is no single-valuedness theorem (cf. [14]). For our purposes, the problem of defining single valued functions can be solved with congruence relations (see definition 3.2)
- the strongest notion of computability relative to partial functions is used, namely reducibility with enumeration operators (see [14])

3 Computable PADTs

With the computational model of Moschovakis, we can generalize the notion of semi-computable algebra (see [3]) to the parameterized case.

Since the equality relation is not necessarily search computable, we have to add explicitly relation symbols $EQ\text{-}s : s\ s$ for $s \in S$ to parameter signatures $\Sigma = (S, OP, POP, REL)$. The resulting signature is denoted by $EQ(\Sigma)$, and the algebra $EQ(A)$ interprets $EQ\text{-}s$ as equality on A_s.

Definition 3.1 Let $\Sigma \subseteq \Sigma 1$ be a parameterized signature ($\Sigma = (S, OP, POP, REL)$, $\Sigma 1 = (S1, OP1, POP1, REL1)$). An algorithm p for a semi-search computable $(\Sigma, \Sigma 1)$-PADT is a quintuple $p = ((\chi_s)_{s \in S1}, (eq_s)_{s \in S1}, (\Phi_{op})_{op \in OP1}, (\Xi_{pop})_{pop \in POP1}, (\Psi_R)_{R \in REL1})$, where χ_s and Ψ_R (resp. eq_s) are $EQ(\Sigma)$-algorithms for unary (resp. binary) semi-search computable families of relations, the Φ_{op} (resp. Ξ_{pop}) are $EQ(\Sigma)$-algorithms for primitive recursive (resp. search computable) families of maps of appropriate arity, such that the construction of definition 3.2 below is well-defined.

Definition 3.2 Let $\Sigma \subseteq \Sigma 1$ be a parameterized signature and p an algorithm for a semi-search computable $(\Sigma, \Sigma 1)$-PADT. The semantics of p is the PADT $\{p\} = (\eta_{\{p\}}, F)$ with $\eta_{\{p\}}: Id_{Alg(\Sigma)} \longrightarrow U_\Sigma \circ F^2$ and for each $A \in Alg(\Sigma)$

$$
\begin{array}{ll}
\equiv_s := < \{eq_s\}^{EQ(A)} > & s \in S1 \\
(FA)_s := \{\chi_s\}^{EQ(A)} / \equiv_s & s \in S1 \\
op_{FA}([\overline{t}]_{\equiv_{\overline{s}}}) := [\{\Phi_{op}\}^{EQ(A)}(\overline{t})]_{\equiv_s} & op: \overline{s} \longrightarrow s \in OP1 \\
pop_{FA}([\overline{t}]_{\equiv_{\overline{s}}}) \simeq [\{\Xi_{pop}\}^{EQ(A)}(\overline{t})]_{\equiv_s} & pop: \overline{s} \longrightarrow s \in POP1 \\
[\overline{t}]_{\equiv_{\overline{s}}} \in R_{FA} \text{ iff } \{\Psi_R\}^{EQ(A)}(\overline{t}) \rightarrow nil & R \in REL1 \\
\eta_{\{p\},A,s}(a) := [atom\text{-}s(a)]_{\equiv_s} & s \in S
\end{array}
$$

[2] U_Σ yields the Σ-reduct of a $\Sigma 1$-algebra

where $< R >$ is the p-congruence generated by R, that is, the least relation which contains R, is an equivalence relation and satisfies

$$(\bar{t},\bar{t}')\in\, < R >_{\bar{s}} \Rightarrow (\{\Phi_{op}\}^{EQ(A)}(\bar{t}), \{\Phi_{op}\}^{EQ(A)}(\bar{t}'))\in\, < R >_{s} \qquad \square$$

4 The characterization

Theorem 4.1 Let $T \subseteq T1$ be a parameterized theory in method i ($i = 1, \ldots, 4$) and (η, F) a persistent[3] PADT with $F\colon Alg(T) \longrightarrow Alg(T1)$ and $\eta\colon Id_{Alg(T)} \longrightarrow U_T \circ F$. Then the following are equivalent[4]

(1) (η, F) is –up to isomorphism– computable by an algorithm p of the model of semicomputable PADT defined in row i below.

(2) (η, F) is specifiable with method i. That is, there is a theory $T2$ with $T \subseteq T1 \subseteq T2$ such that for each T-algebra A, there is a natural isomorphism $\epsilon_A\colon U_{T1}\, F_{(T,T2)} A \longrightarrow F\, A$ with $\eta_A = U_T(\epsilon_A) \circ \eta_{(T,T2)_A}$ [5].

Method	Model of semicomputable PADT				Example
	data χ_s	congruence on data eq_s	relations Ψ_R	partial operations Ξ_{pop}	PADT separating the methods
1	pr.	p.e.	–	–	lists, trees etc. over some data
2	pr.	s.c.c.	–	–	making some Abelian group torsion free
3	pr.	s.c.c.	s.c.c.	–	transitive closure of some relation
4	s.c.c	s.c.c.	s.c.c.	s.c.	set of paths over some graph

In the table, a "pr." means primitive recursiveness, an "(s.)s.c." means (semi-) search computability and a "p.e." means primitive recursive enumerability. The total operations Φ_{op} always can be chosen primitive recursive. □

To prove theorem 4.1, we encode primitive recursive definitions into theories.

Definition 4.2 Let $\Sigma = (S, OP, POP, REL)$ be a signature. Then

$SEXPR(\Sigma) = \Sigma +$
sorts sexpr
opns nil : ⟶sexpr; atom-s : s⟶sexpr (for each $s \in S$)
first : sexpr⟶sexpr; cons : sexpr sexpr⟶sexpr
rest : sexpr⟶sexpr
axioms first(cons(x,y)) = x; rest(cons(x,y)) = y

[3] that is, η is a natural isomorphism

[4] For method 1 to 3, the target carrier sets have to be non-empty. The case with empty carriers is treated in [11] exactly.

[5] $(\eta_{(T,T2)}, F_{(T,T2)})$ is the free construction corresponding to the parameterized theory $T \subseteq T2$

first(nil) = nil rest(nil) = nil
first(atom-s(x)) = cons(nil,nil) rest(atom-s(x)) = cons(nil,nil)

Let f be a total primitive recursive algorithm over Σ. Inductively over the definition of f by clauses C0a and C1 to C7, we define $Def(f)$, which includes

1. all $Def(g)$ for all algorithms g used for the definition of f,
2. a total operation symbol $imppr^f: sexpr^n \longrightarrow sexpr$, where n is the arity of f, and
3. the following equations (missing cases treated similarly):

C0a". $imppr^f(atom\text{-}\overline{s}(\overline{x}), y_1, \ldots, y_m) = atom\text{-}s(op(\overline{x}))$
$imppr^f(nil) = nil,\ imppr^f(cons(x, y)) = nil$ □
C5". $imppr^f(\overline{x}) = imppr^g(\overline{x}, imppr^h(\overline{x}))$

Sketch of proof of theorem 4.1, row 1, (1)⇒(2): Let $T1 = ((S1, OP1, \emptyset, \emptyset), AX1)$ and (η, F) be computable by $p = ((\chi_s)_{s\in S1}, (eq_s)_{s\in S1}, (\Phi_{op})_{op\in OP1})$. The $\{eq_s\}$ are enumerations of binary relations. We assume without loss of generality that the $\{\chi_s\}^{EQ(A)}$ comprise all of $SExpr(A)$: if not, $\{eq_s\}^A$ simply identifies all S-expressions outside $\{\chi_s\}^{EQ(A)}$ with a fixed element.

Now let $T_{Def} := SEXPR(\Sigma) + \bigcup_{op\in OP1} Def(\Phi_{op})$ and

$T2 := T_{Def} + (T1 - T) +$
opns $build_s: sexpr \longrightarrow s \quad (s \in S1)$
axioms

$$build_s(atom\text{-}s(x)) = x \qquad s \in S1 \quad (1)$$
$$build_s(first(imppr^{eq_s}(x))) = build_s(rest(imppr^{eq_s}(x))) \qquad s \in S1 \quad (2)$$
$$op(build_{\overline{s}}(\overline{x})) = build_s(imppr^{\Phi_{op}}(\overline{x})) \qquad op \in OP1 \quad (3)$$

Then the parameterized theory $(T, T2)$ can be shown to specify p. □

Sketch of proof of theorem 4.1, row 1, (2) ⇒ (1): Let $T = (\Sigma, AX)$, $T1 = (\Sigma1, AX1)$, $\Sigma = (S, OP, \emptyset, \emptyset)$ and $\Sigma1 = (S1, OP1, \emptyset, \emptyset)$. For a T-algebra A, let $\Sigma1(A)$ be $\Sigma1$ augmented by constants $c^a :\longrightarrow s$ for each $a \in A_s$ and $T1(A)$ be the $\Sigma1(A)$-theory containing axioms from $T1$ and all equations

$$op(c^{\overline{a}}) = c^{op_A(\overline{a})} \quad (op: \overline{s} \longrightarrow s \in OP)$$

Following [5], theorem 7.16, $F_{(T,T1)}(A)$ is isomorphic to the $T1$-reduct of the initial $T1(A)$-algebra.

To compute this initial algebra, we represent terms from $T_{\Sigma1(A)}$ and valuations $\alpha: X \longrightarrow T_{\Sigma1(A)}$ uniformly in A as S-expressions. We denote the representation function by $[\![\_]\!]$ and only require that $[\![c^a]\!] = atom\text{-}s(a)$ for $a \in A_s$. Now an algorithm $p = ((\chi_s)_{s\in S1}, (eq_s)_{s\in S1}, (\Phi_{op})_{op\in OP1})$ which computes $F_{(T,T1)}$ must have the components

- χ_s checks if its argument is the representation of a term from $T_{\Sigma1(A)}$ of sort $s \in S1$

- $eq_s((0, code1(op), atom\text{-}s(\overline{a}))) = ([\![op(c^{\overline{a}})]\!].[\![c^{op_A(\overline{a})}]\!])$
  $eq_s((1, code2(t_1 = t_2), [\![\alpha\colon X \longrightarrow T_{\Sigma 1(A)}]\!])) = ([\![\alpha^{\#}(t_1)]\!].[\![\alpha^{\#}(t_2)]\!])$
  $eq_s(u) = ([\![t^s]\!].[\![t^s]\!])$, otherwise
  where t^s is a fixed $\Sigma 1$-term of sort s, $code1$ is a numbering of OP and $code2$ is a numbering of $AX1$.
- $\Phi_{op}([\![\overline{t}]\!]) = [\![op(\overline{t})]\!]$ □

Sketch of proof of theorem 4.1, row 2, (1) ⇒ (2): In contrast to row 1, here we have to specify semi-search computable families of relations, which cannot be fully represented with theories. Only a one-sided representation is possible. This is achieved using the theory

ONE-SIDED-BOOL =
sorts *osbool* **opns** $ostrue : \longrightarrow osbool$

The axioms of definition 4.2 have to be modified, for example:
C9"'. $impsc^g(y, \overline{x}, nil) \stackrel{e}{=} ostrue \longrightarrow impsc^f(\overline{x}, y) \stackrel{e}{=} ostrue$
By a normal form theorem (see [10]), scheme C8 can be omitted. □

Sketch of proof of theorem 4.1, row 2, (2) ⇒ (1): Here, in comparison to row 1, eq_s has to be modified: $eq_s(x, y) \rightarrow nil$ iff $x = [\![t_1]\!]$, $y = [\![t_2]\!]$ and there exists a proof of $T1(A) \vdash t_1 = t_2$. Checking if a list of equations (term pairs) actually represents a proof in $T1(A)$ is no longer primitive recursive: We need to check equations $op(c^{\overline{a}}) = c^{op_A(\overline{a})} \in T1(A)$, and this requires applying the one-sided A-equality. Moreover, proofs are guessed with the ν-operator. □

Sketch of proof of theorem 4.1, row 4: The introduction of partial operations causes a distinction between interpretable and non-interpretable terms, which can be distinguished by partial equational deduction (see [4]). This corresponds to χ_s being semi-search computable.

5 Conclusion

We have examined the recursion theoretic expressiveness of parameterization in four methods for the specification of abstract data types. Therefore, we first have introduced a computational model for parameterized abstract data types, which is based on Moschovakis' prime and search computability (see [10]) and avoids difficulties of previous notions in the literature.

In the unparameterized case, both primitive recursive enumerability and semi-search computability reduce to semirecursiveness. With appropriate simulations, the methods 2–4 then all have the same power. In contrast to this, our characterization of persistent parameterized abstract data types allows to distinguish the methods by characteristic features. Given the problem of specifying a particular PADT, it helps to find out a method of appropriate generality.

The methods do not differ with respect to semi-computability versus computability. *Within* various notions of semicomputability, they differ in the availability of unbounded search and parameter relations. In comparison to the first method, which has only limited access to the parameter (see also [15]), the second method allows to generate *equalities* nondeterministically from parameter equalities, which corresponds to the availability of implications as axioms. The third methods allows *relation members* to be generated nondeterministically, while using the fourth method, new *data elements* may be generated nondeterministically from parameter relations (including parameter equality).

References

[1] J.A. Bergstra and J.W. Klop. Algebraic specifications for parametrized data types with minimal parameter and target algebras. In *Proc ICALP 1982*, volume 140 of *SLNCS*, pages 23–34. Springer Verlag, 1982.

[2] J.A. Bergstra and J.W. Klop. Initial algebra specifications for parametrized data types. *Elektronische Informationsverarbeitung und Kybernetik*, 19:17–32, 1983.

[3] J.A. Bergstra and J.V. Tucker. Algebraic specifications of computable and semicomputable data types. *TCS*, 50:137–181, 1987.

[4] P. Burmeister. Partial algebras — survey of a unifying approach towards a two-valued model theory for partial algebras. *Algebra Universalis*, 15:306–358, 1982.

[5] H. Ehrig and B. Mahr. *Fundamentals of Algebraic Specification 1*. Springer Verlag, Heidelberg, 1985.

[6] A.P. Ershov. Abstract computability on algebraic structures. In A.P. Ershov and D.E. Knuth, editors, *Algorithms in Modern Mathematics and Computer Science*, volume 122 of *SLNCS*, pages 397–420. Springer Verlag, 1981.

[7] J. A. Goguen and J. Meseguer. Eqlog: Equality, types, and generic modules for logic programming. In D. DeGroot and G. Lindstrom, editors, *Logic Programming. Functions, Relations and Equations*, pages 295–363. Prentice-Hall, Englewood Cliffs, New Jersey, 1986.

[8] U.L. Hupbach. Abstract implementation of abstract data types. In P. Dembiński, editor, *Proc. MFCS 1980*, volume 88 of *SLNCS*, pages 291–304. Springer Verlag, 1980.

[9] H. Kaphengst. What is computable for abstract data types? In *Proc. FCT 1981*, volume 117 of *SLNCS*, pages 173–181. Springer Verlag, 1981.

[10] Y.N. Moschovakis. Abstract first order computability I. *Transactions of the AMS*, 138:427–464, 1969.

[11] T. Mossakowski. Spezifizierbarkeit und Berechenbarkeit parametrischer partieller Datentypen. Master's thesis, Universität Bremen, 1992.

[12] P. Padawitz. *Computing in Horn Clause Theories*. Springer Verlag, Heidelberg, 1988.

[13] H. Reichel. *Initial Computability, Algebraic Specifications and Partial Algebras*. Oxford Science Publications, 1987.

[14] Hartley Rogers, Jr. *Theory of Recursive Functions and Effective Computability*. McGraw-Hill 1967. Reprint: MIT Press, Cambridge, Massachusetts 1987.

[15] J.W. Thatcher, E.G. Wagner, and J.B. Wright. Data type specification: Parameterization and the power of specification techniques. 10th ACM STOC, pages 119–132. 1978.

Increasing the Level of Abstraction in Traditional Functional Languages by Using Compile-time Reflection

Tim Sheard*
Oregon Graduate Institute of Science & Technology
Beaverton, Oregon, USA
sheard@cse.ogi.edu

Abstract

Abstraction is the key to reuse in software technology. Traditional functional languages support greater levels of abstraction than imperative languages, yet cannot express certain new kinds of abstraction recently identified. In this paper we report on a simple technique we call *Compile-time Reflection* and show how this technique can be added to traditional functional languages by the addition of an explicit user programmable phase distinction in their compilation. This distinction implements the *2-level λ-Calculus* of Nielson and Nielson[11], and supports the algebraic approach to programming exemplified in the *Squigol* school of programming, all in a traditional functional language.

1 Introduction

Recent work by Malcom [8], Meijer, Fokkinga, and Paterson [9], and Cockett with the programming language **Charity** [1, 2] has suggested a high level of modularity and abstraction may be obtained by the use of generic control structures that capture patterns of recursion for a large class of algebraic types in a uniform way. This is important for several reasons.

- **Abstraction.** It allows the specification of algorithms independent of the type of data structures they are to operate on, since the control structure of the algorithm is generated for each datatype.
- **Genericity.** It allows the statement, proof, and use of type parametric theorems independant of any particular type.
- **Structure.** Functional programs are often the target of transformation and optimization. These techniques generally search for patterns of structure in programs to satisfy hypothesis of particular transformations. If structure is explicit, rather than implicit, the job of the transformation system is made easier.

Unfortunately it is hard to reap these benefits when using a traditional functional programming language as there is no mechanism for defining type

*Tim Sheard is supported in part by a grant from OACIS and Tektronix

parametric abstractions, which are the heart of these methods. This shortcoming can be overcome by the use of Compile-time reflection in a typed language.

A programming language supports reflection if it has a distinguished class of values that correspond to syntactic fragments of the language and operations to manipulate these representation as data or programs, either by computing over them, evaluating them or injecting them into the value space. Typically these operations are called $\underline{reify}$: $value \rightarrow rep$, $\underline{reflect}$: $rep \rightarrow value$, and $\underline{eval}$: $rep \rightarrow rep$. In this paper we concentrate on the uses of $\underline{reflect}$ at compile-time.

Reflection is classified as either "compile-time" or "run-time" depending on when the semantic actions are expected to take place. Semantically, compile-time reflection is the most straightforward since every compile-time reflective program has the same meaning as a program that does not use reflection which is obtained by executing all of the reflection operations. The *2-Level λ-Calculus* of Nielson and Nielson[11] exploits these ideas by performing reductions at compile-time when both parts of a redex are available at compile-time. This is also the idea behind Danvy's reduction of *administrative redexes*[3]. Since type information *is* available at compile-time we can use this information to construct specific functions tailored for any type. The next section details this process in a language independant manner, while the following section outlines an implementation of these ideas for ML.

2 Type Parametric Combinators

Algebraic operators can be added to traditional functional languages by the disciplined use of compile-time reflection. Algebraic operators like *fold* can be created by computing over the representations of type declarations to build the representation of operators for these types, then reflecting over these representations to obtain the actual operators. This could be done in the following way. Consider type constructors defined by using recursive equations of the form:

$$T(\alpha_1, \ldots, \alpha_p) = C_1(t_1) \mid \cdots \mid C_n(t_n)$$

where $\alpha_1, \ldots, \alpha_p$ denote type variables, the C_i are names of value constructor functions with type $t_i \rightarrow T(\alpha_1, \ldots, \alpha_p)$, and the t_i are either:

- primitive types such as *int* or *string*
- type variables (in the set $\alpha_1, \ldots, \alpha_p$)
- type formulas constructed using primitive type constructors: cross $(t_1 \times t_2)$ and arrow, $(t_1 \rightarrow t_2)$
- instantiations of defined types other than T
- the instantiation, $T(\alpha_1, \ldots, \alpha_p)$, of T itself.

where each t_i is covariant in the type $T(\alpha_1, \ldots, \alpha_p)$.

Functions manipulating values of these types will use a pattern of recursion related to the pattern of recursion in the type definitions. Algebraic methods often capture these patterns using the categorical notion of a functor. The functor, E^T[6, 1, 16] defined below, is the morphism part of a categorical functor. There exists an E^T for each type constructor, T, above. Category theorists would say that T is defined in terms of the fix point of E^T. Functional programmers are used to defining types by the use of recursive equations, so we follow this path.

Using E^T it is possible to describe the generalized *fold* (catamorphism [9]) operator for any type constructor by defining a set of recursive equations, one for each constructor, C_i:

$$\text{fold}^T(\overline{h}) \circ C_i = h_i \circ E_i^T(id_1, \ldots, id_p, \text{fold}^T(\overline{h}))$$

where $\overline{h} = (h_1, \ldots, h_n)$ (we call each h_i an *accumulating function*) and for each index j, id_j is the identity function.

To make this definition precise we must provide a definition of E^T in terms of the data type equation defining T. The functor E^T is constructed from the n-fold sum of functors, E_i^T. Each, E_i^T is a $(p+1)$-adic functor [1] associated with the corresponding constructor, $C_i : t_i \rightarrow T(\overline{\alpha})$.

$$E_i^T(\overline{f}, g_{Rec}) = K^{T(\overline{\alpha})}[\overline{f}, g_{Rec}, t_i]$$

where $T(\overline{\alpha}) = T(\alpha_1, \ldots, \alpha_p)$, and $\overline{f} = f_{\alpha_1}, \ldots, f_{\alpha_p}$ and K is the type parametric combinator:

$$\begin{array}{lcl}
K^{T(\overline{\alpha})}[\overline{f}, g, \alpha_k] & = & f_{\alpha_k} \\
K^{T(\overline{\alpha})}[\overline{f}, g, T(\overline{\alpha})] & = & g \\
K^{T(\overline{\alpha})}[\overline{f}, g, S(t_1, \ldots, t_q)] & = & \text{map}^S\ (K^{T(\overline{\alpha})}[\overline{f}, g, t_1], \ldots, K^{T(\overline{\alpha})}[\overline{f}, g, t_q]) \\
K^{T(\overline{\alpha})}[\overline{f}, g, t_1 \times \ldots \times t_n] & = & K^{T(\overline{\alpha})}[\overline{f}, g, t_1] \times \ldots \times K^{T(\overline{\alpha})}[\overline{f}, g, t_n] \\
K^{T(\overline{\alpha})}[\overline{f}, g, u \rightarrow v] & = & \lambda\, h.\ (K^{T(\overline{\alpha})}[\overline{f}, g, v]) \circ h \circ (K^{T(\overline{\alpha})}[\overline{f}, g, u]) \\
K^{T(\overline{\alpha})}[\overline{f}, g, ()] & = & id
\end{array}$$

where the $\times$ notation represents a function: $(h_1 \times \ldots \times h_n)(x_1, \ldots, x_n) = (h_1\ x_1, \ldots, h_n\ x_n)$

We may also use E^S to generate the the morphism part of the categorical functor, often called the *map* for S:

$$(\text{map}^S(f_1, \ldots, f_p)) \circ C_i = C_i \circ (E_i^S(f_1, \ldots, f_p, \text{map}^S(f_1, \ldots, f_p)))$$

3 Compile-time Reflection

These mechanisms can easily be added to traditional functional languages by adding a phase distinction to the processing of functional programs. This distinction includes *compile-time* and *run-time* phases. The compile-time phase includes an elaboration or expansion phase (prior to type checking) in which user defined operators may manipulate information, such as type and symbol table information, normally available only to the compiler. Since this user directed transformation phase happens prior to type checking all accepted functions are type safe, yet the system provides a remarkable degree of flexibility, and levels of abstraction normally found only in untyped languages.

Language tools usually consist of an *object language* in which the programs that are being manipulated are expressed, and a *meta language* which is used to describe the manipulation. A compile-time reflective language has features that allow it to be its own meta-language. We have built an implementation

[1] Where p is the number of universally quantified type variables in the left hand side of T's type equation.

of compile-time reflection for a subset of ML we call CRML (Compile-time Reflective ML). In CRML the object language is "encoded" (represented) in an ML datatype. There is a datatype for each syntactic feature of ML. Object language manipulations are described by manipulations of this "representation" datatype. CRML contains syntactic sugar (object brackets **<< >>**, and escape **‘**) for constructing and pattern matching program representations which *mirror the corresponding represented programs*. Thus, meta-programs manipulating object programs may either be expressed directly with the explicit constructors of the representation type or with this "object-language" extension to ML's syntax. Text within the object-language brackets (<< >>) is parsed but not compiled. Its representation is returned as the value. Meta-language expressions may be included in the object-language text by "escaping" them with a backquote character (‘). Samples of this feature are illustrated in the table below.

Concrete syntax	Constructor based	Object bracket based
`x`	`Id "x"`	`<< x >>`
`f x`	`App(Id "f",Id "x")`	`<< f x >>`
	`App(g,y)`	`<< ‘g ‘y >>`
`(x,y)`	`Tuple [ Id "x", Id "y" ]`	`<< (x,y) >>`
	`Tuple [x, y]`	`<< ‘x * ‘y >>`

The object bracket notation encodes the overlining and underlining notation of the *2-level λ-Calculus* of Nielson and Nielson.

By using reflection, generic operators, such as *map* and *fold*, have straightforward implementations by computing over the representations of datatype declarations. In CRML a *template* defines a function which, when invoked, is mapped over all the constructors (and their corresponding types) of a datatype declaration, constructing the object language value for the representation of a function declaration. For example the template below defines a function `mapf` which generates the representation of a function declaration from a string (representing the name of a type constructor).

```
fun template mapf T =
    map f ((Ci of d -> r) X) = ‘Ci (‘(K r <<f>> <<map f>> d) ‘X);
```

The expression in the constructor position of the function definition, `((Ci of d -> r) X)`, is treated as a pattern. Thus upon invocation of the template the variables in this pattern will be bound to object language values particular to each constructor. `Ci` is bound to an object language expression for the constructor function, `X` to an object language tuple expression (of the appropriate "shape" to be `Ci`'s argument), `d` to the object language type of `Ci`'s domain, and `r` to the object language type of `Ci`'s range (which is the type `T`).

The rest of the expression is taken literally to compute one of the equations defining a function, except that escaped expressions are evaluated at invocation time and "spliced" into the equation.

While an escape character inside object brackets or a template definition allows the results of meta-computations to be "spliced" into object programs, an unbracketed, escaped expression is a simple interface to compile-time reflection. It indicates that the escaped expression should be evaluated (at compile-time) to compute the expression (or type, pattern, declaration, etc.) that replaces the escaped expression (much like macro expansion).

Thus, using the `mapf` meta-program the program below calculates and defines the map for list.

```
val maplist = let '(mapf "list") in map end;
```

as if the user had typed the following instead:

```
val maplist = let fun map f [] = []
                    | map f (a1::a2) = Cons(f a1,map f a2)
              in  map end
```

4 Monadic Composition

We have used methods similar to the templates for *map* and *fold* in automating the generation of polymorphic functions to realize the *monadic* structure of datatype declarations [7]. Moggi has shown that monads can be used to structure semantics [10]. Other researchers, including Wadler [15] and our group [7] have explored the use of monads to structure specifications and programs. Many algorithms may be expressed solely in terms of the monadic operations. When this can be done, changes to the details of the data type do not require changes in the specification of the algorithms. They also support a very powerful notion of composition that allows programs to be decomposed into more easily understood and maintained modules.

For example, let the type constructor *Maybe* be defined by $Maybe(x) = Nothing \mid Just(x)$. Spivey[13] has used this type to model exceptional computations. *Maybe* has the structure of a monad[14, 7]. The ***binary product distribution*** for *Maybe*, with type $(Maybe(a) \times Maybe(b)) \rightarrow Maybe(a \times b)$, is defined as:

$$\tau_2^{Maybe}(x,\, y) \;=\; \{\, (a,b) \mid a \leftarrow x;\; b \;\leftarrow y\}^{Maybe}$$

Using the usual translation[14] for monad comprehensions we get:

$$\tau_2^{Maybe}(x,\, y) \;=\; mult^{Maybe}\,(map^{Maybe}\,(\lambda\, a.(map^{Maybe}\,(\lambda\, b.(a,b))\, y))\; x)$$

Let the type $T(\alpha) = S(Maybe(\alpha))$, where S is any type constructor. Then T has the structure of a monad[7]. The distribution function $\pi^S_{Maybe} : S(Maybe(\alpha)) \rightarrow Maybe(S(\alpha))$ can be given in terms of the operator fold^S,

$$\pi^S_{Maybe}\; x \;=\; \text{fold}^S\; (f_1 \ldots f_n)\; x$$

where f_i is an accumulating function for each constructor, $C_i : \sigma_i \rightarrow S$. If C_i is a nullary constructor (i.e. $\sigma_i = ()$), then $f_i\;() = unit^{Maybe}\; C_i$. If C_i is not a nullary constructor, then the corresponding accumulating function, f_i, can be defined as

$$f_i = (map^{Maybe}\; C_i) \circ \tau^{Maybe}_{m_i} \circ H^S_i(unit^{Maybe}, id, id)$$

where H^S_i is defined in a manner similiar to E^T_i as follows:

$$H^S_i(f_{non}, f_\alpha, f_{rec}) \;=\; \hat{K}[\sigma_i]$$

and $\hat{K}$ is the type parametric combinator:

$$\begin{array}{lcl}
\hat{K}[t] & = & f_{non} \text{ when neither } \alpha \text{ nor } S(\alpha) \text{ occurs in t} \\
\hat{K}[\alpha] & = & f_{\alpha} \\
\hat{K}[S(\alpha_1, \ldots, \alpha_p)] & = & f_{Rec} \\
\hat{K}[U(t_1, \ldots, t_q)] & = & \text{map}^U \ (\hat{K}[t_1], \ldots, \hat{K}[t_q]) \\
\hat{K}[t_1 \times \ldots \times t_n] & = & \hat{K}[t_1] \times \ldots \times \hat{K}[t_n]
\end{array}$$

For example, the type composition distribution function, π^{List}_{Maybe}, is a function with type $List(Maybe(\alpha)) \rightarrow Maybe(List(\alpha))$, and is defined as follows:

$$\pi^{List}_{Maybe}\ x \ = \ \text{fold}^{List}\ (f_{Nil}, f_{Cons})\ x$$

$$\text{where } \left\{ \begin{array}{lcl} f_{Cons}(x, xs) & = & \text{map}^{Maybe}\ Cons\ \ (\tau_2^{Maybe}(x, xs)) \\ f_{Nil}() & = & unit^{Maybe} Nil \ = \ Just(Nil) \end{array} \right.$$

This function, which can be generated for any datatype, S, allows us to "lift" a function, $f : \alpha \rightarrow Maybe(\beta)$ to a function, $g : S(\alpha) \rightarrow Maybe(S(\beta))$.

$$g = \pi^{S}_{Maybe} \circ (map^S\ f)$$

Using other type parametric combinators we have implemented algebraic generators for structural equality, and unification over data structures which represent abstract terms.

In addition we have defined an *normalization algorithm* [4, 5, 12] which automatically calculates improvements to programs whose only contol structures are folds. It reduces these programs to a canonical form. Based upon a generic *promotion theorem* [8, 9], the algorithm is facilitated by the explicit structure of fold programs rather than using an analysis phase to search for implicit structure. Canonical programs are minimal in the sense that they contain the fewest number of fold operations. Because of this property the improvement algorithm has important applications in program transformation, optimization, and proving properties of functional programs.

5 Example: The CPS Transformation

While some may conclude that the full power of compile-time reflection provides more than enough rope to hang ones self, the expressive power allows for succinct expression of powerful ideas. For example Danvy's two level Continuation Passing Style transformation[3] is easily expressed in CRML

```
fun cpst x =
let fun C e k =
        case e of
          Id(n) => k e
        | <<fn 'n => 't>>  =>k (<<fn 'n => '(cpst t)>>)
        | <<t't 't1>> =>
              C t (fn v =>
                      C t1 (fn v1 =>
                               let val Z = Rename "v"
                               in << ('v 'v1)
                                     (fn '(PId Z) =>
                                         '(k (Id Z))) >> end))
   and  T e k =
        case e of
          Id(n) => << 'k 'e >>
        | <<fn 'n => 't>> => (<<'k (fn 'n => '(cpst t))>>)
        | <<'t 't1>> =>
             C t (fn v => C t1 (fn v1 => << 'v 'v1 'k >>))

in <<fn c => '(T x <<c>>) >> end;
```

6 Conclusion

A compile-time reflective programming environment is an appropriate choice when computations over programs is necessary. Meta-programs can access the types of objects in the environment, retrieve representations of types or functions as data, generate representations of the derivative functions for types, or apply optimizations or transformations to functions, and then submit these representations to the compiler. This allows the incremental expansion of traditional functional languages to include algebraic methodologies based upon formal foundations in a straight forward manner.

The ability to compute over representations of programs and to inject these representations into the value space vastly increases the level of abstraction available to programmers.

References

[1] J. Cockett and D. Spencer. Strong Categorical Datatypes I. In R. Seely, editor, *International Meeting on Category Theory 1991*, Canadian Mathematical Society Proceedings, Vol. 13, pp 141-169. AMS, Montreal, 1992.

[2] J. Cockett and T. Fukushima. About Charity. The University of Calgary, Department of Computer Science, Research Report No. 92/480/18. June 1992.

[3] O. Danvy. Three Steps for the CPS Transformation. Technical report CIS-92-02, Department of Computing and Information Sciences, Kansas State University, February 1992

[4] L. Fegaras. *A Transformational Approach to Database System Implementation.* PhD thesis, Department of Computer Science, University of Massachusetts, Amherst, February 1993. Also appeared as CMPSCI Technical Report 92-68.

[5] L. Fegaras, T. Sheard, and D. Stemple. Uniform Traversal Combinators: Definition, Use and Properties. In *Proceedings of the 11th International Conference on Automated Deduction (CADE-11), Saratoga Springs, New York*, pp 148–162. Springer-Verlag, June 1992.

[6] T. Hagino. *A Categorical Programming Language.* PhD thesis, University of Edinburgh, 1987.

[7] James Hook, Richard Kieburtz, and Tim Sheard. Generating Programs by Reflection. Oregon Graduate Institute Technical Report 92-015.

[8] G. Malcolm. Homomorphisms and Promotability. In *Mathematics of Program Construction*, pp 335–347. Springer-Verlag, June 1989.

[9] E. Meijer, M. Fokkinga, and R. Paterson. Functional Programming with Bananas, Lenses, Envelopes and Barbed Wire. In *Proceedings of the 5th ACM Conference on Functional Programming Languages and Computer Architecture, Cambridge, Massachusetts*, pp 124–144, August 1991.

[10] Eugenio Moggi. Notions of computations and monads. *Information and Computation*, 93(1):55–92, July 1991.

[11] F. Nielson. aand H.R. Nielson. Two-Level Functional Languages. Cambridge Tracts in Theoretical Computer Science 34. 1992 Cambridge University Press, Cambride CB2 1RP, UK

[12] T. Sheard. and L. Fegaras. A Fold for All Seasons. In *Conference on Functional Programming Languages and Computer Architecture*, Copenhagen, pp 233-242, June 1993.

[13] M. Spivey. A Functional Theory of Exceptions. In *Science of Computer Programming*, 14:25-42, 1990.

[14] P. Wadler. Comprehending Monads. In *Proc. 1990 ACM Conference on Lisp and Functional Programming*, pp 61-78, 1990.

[15] Philip Wadler. The essence of functional programming. In *Conference Record of the Nineteenth Annual ACM Symposium on Principles of Programming Languages.* ACM Press, January 1992.

[16] G. C. Wraith. A note on categorical datatypes. In D. H. Pitt, D. E. Rydeheard, P. Dybjer, A. M. Pitts, and A. Poigné, editors, *Category Theory and Computer Science*, volume 389 of *Lecture Notes in Computer Science*, pages 118,127. Springer-Verlag, 1989.

A Coherent Type System for a Concurrent, Functional and Imperative Programming Language *

Dominique Bolignano Mourad Debabi

Bull Corporate Research Center,
78340 Les Clayes-Sous-Bois, FRANCE
D.Bolignano@frcl.bull.fr, M.Debabi@frcl.bull.fr

1 Motivation, Background and Related Work

The ultimate goal of this work is the definition of a wide-spectrum specification language that supports both data and concurrency descriptions. The design of this specification language follows the same approach as the one used in the design of Extended ML [14]. The starting point is the design of an implicitly typed, polymorphic, concurrent and functional programming language. Axioms are then added in the signatures and structures as in Extended ML. The resulting specification language is thus highly expressive though it embodies a restricted number of concepts. More concisely our language can be viewed as a sugared version of typed λ-calculus that safely incorporates imperative and concurrent extensions.

Aim of this paper is to focus on the theoretic foundations of the underlying programming language. The latter unifies three computational paradigms which we refer to as concurrent, functional and imperative programming. A great deal of interest has been expressed in each of these programming styles and their foundations have been deeply investigated, albeit generally separately.

The language described here supports polymorphic types. It supports also both functional and process abstractions as in CML [13] and FACILE [7]. Functions, processes, references and communication channels are first-class values and thus can be passed along channels. Consequently, the mobility of these values is supported.

Modern languages have been proposed that reconcile the functional, concurrent and imperative styles. For instance one can cite CML [13], FACILE [7] and LCS [4]. All the three languages emerged from the idea of combining an SML-like language [12] as a functional and imperative core, with a CCS or CSP-like process algebra for process abstraction. They support polymorphism, functional and process abstractions, dynamic behaviors and higher order objects.

The static semantics (typing semantics) in CML, FACILE and LCS rests on the type inference discipline. It is well known that this discipline is problematic in the presence of non referentially transparent constructs. More precisely, the

*This work is partially supported by the LaCoS Esprit project 5383.

problem is relevant to type generalization in the presence of mutable data. Therefore, many extensions of Milner's [11] have been proposed.

The classical way to deal with this issue is the imperative type discipline [16]. An extension of this approach has been used in the implementation of Standard ML of New Jersey. In [10], another method is proposed that consists in detecting some so called dangerous type variables (the ones occurring in the types of imperative objects), and labeling function types accordingly.

Later, in [15], the type and effect discipline is introduced. The latter yields as a result of the static evaluation of an expression, not only its principal type, but also all the minimal side effects. A decidable and consistent typing system w.r.t. the operational semantics is advanced [15]. Notice, that the inference typing system was devised for an ML-like language with imperative constructs. The idea of considering the effects as part of the static evaluation of an expression, was suggested in [9] and adopted in the **FX** project [8].

One of the aims addressed here is to propose a dynamic semantics for our language. Elaborating a dynamic semantics for such languages is somewhat complicated, for we have to deal with, and integrate, various aspects of the language: concurrent, functional, imperative. Mostly, the dynamic semantics proposed for these languages (Concurrent ML-like) are operational as for instance, with CML [6, 13] and FACILE [7]. In this paper, we present an operational semantics of our language, but also a denotational model has been devised. The model is discussed in[3], its foundations are investigated in [1].

2 Informal presentation

The syntactic constructions allowed in our language are close to those allowed in CML and FACILE. The set of expressions includes:

- Literals such as integers, booleans, a distinguished value (), a constant **skip** which models an expression that immediately terminates successfully.
- Three binding operations that is: abstraction, recursion and let definition.
- Imperative aspects are supported by the notion of reference. An expression of the form **ref** (E) stands for the allocation of a new reference and assignment to it of the value of the expression E. We will use the unary operator ! for dereferencing and the binary operator := for assignment.
- Expressions may communicate through channels. The expression **channel**() means allocate a new channel. The expression $E!E'$ means: evaluate E', evaluate E and then send the result of E' evaluation on the channel resulting from the evaluation of E. The whole expression evaluates then to (). The expression $E?$ evaluates to any value received on the channel resulting from the evaluation of E. Communications are synchronized as in CCS and CSP.
- Four concurrency combinators "; ,$\sqcap$, $\Box$, $||$" which stand respectively for sequencing, internal choice, external choice and parallel composition.

  More formally the BNF syntax of our language is:

$$E ::= ()|true|false|ident\ x|\mathbf{skip}|\lambda x \bullet E|E\ E|E \sqcap E|\ E \Box E|E||E|E;E|$$
$$\mathbf{ref}\ E\ |!E|E := E|\mathbf{channel}()|E?|E!E|\mathbf{let}\ x = E\ \mathbf{in}\ E\ |\ \mathbf{rec}\ x \bullet E$$

In the following, we will use $\mathcal{P}_f(E)$ to stand for the finite powerset of the set E.

3 Static semantics

The choice of adopting the type and effect discipline in order to give a static semantics to our language is motivated by the following reasons:

- As shown in [15], the type and effect discipline is more appropriate than the other type systems [16, 10] in integrating efficiently functional and imperative programming.
- The type generalization in let expressions is more efficient due to the use of the effect information and the observation criterion.
- The strongest reason for us is purely technical and is relevant to the foundations of the denotational model. If we attempt naively to construct the process domain, this will lead to reflexive domain definitions that have no solution. In order to get round this difficulty, we make a dependence between the static and the dynamic semantics by typing the dynamic domains by the hierarchy laid down by the static domains. At this level we need to know type, communication and store effects of the expressions exactly.

The type and effect discipline reported in [15] does not support communication effects. Thus the work reported hereafter is an extension of this discipline. We define the following static domains:

- The domain of *Reference regions*: Reference regions are introduced to abstract the memory locations. Every data structure corresponds to a region. The domain consists of the disjoint union of a countable set of constants and variables noted γ. We use $\rho, \rho', \ldots$ to represent reference regions.
- The domain of *Reference effects*: Reference effects abstracts the memory side-effects. We define the following basic effects: $\emptyset$ for the absence of effect, ς for a reference effect variable, $init(\rho, \tau)$ for the reference allocation, $read(\rho)$ for reading in the region ρ and $write(\rho)$ for assignments of values to references in the region ρ. We introduce also a union operator $\cup$ for effects.

$$\sigma ::= \emptyset | \varsigma | init(\rho, \tau) | read(\rho) | write(\rho) | \sigma \cup \sigma$$

We will write $\sigma \sqsupseteq \sigma' \Leftrightarrow \exists \sigma'', \sigma = \sigma' \cup \sigma''$. Equality on reference effects is modulo ACI (Associativity, Commutativity and Idempotence) with $\emptyset$ as the neutral element.

Analogously, we introduce the following static domains:

- The domain of *Channel regions*: As with reference regions, channel regions are intended to abstract channels. Their domain consists in the disjoint union of a countable set of constants and variables noted δ. We will use $\chi, \chi', \ldots$ to represent values drawn from this domain.
- The domain of *Channel effects* is inductively defined by:

$$\kappa ::= \emptyset | \eta | chan(\chi, \tau) | in(\chi) | out(\chi) | \kappa \cup \kappa$$

We will use η to stand for a channel effect variable. The basic channel effect $chan(\chi, \tau)$ represents the creation of a channel of type τ in the channel region χ. $in(\chi)$ denotes the effect resulting from an input on a channel of the channel region χ while $out(\chi)$ denotes an output on the channel of the region χ. We will write $\kappa \sqsupseteq \kappa' \Leftrightarrow \exists \kappa'', \kappa = \kappa' \cup \kappa''$. Equality on effects is modulo ACI with $\emptyset$ as the neutral element.

(unit) $\mathcal{E} \vdash () : Unit, \emptyset, \emptyset$

(true) $\mathcal{E} \vdash \mathbf{true} : Bool, \emptyset, \emptyset$

(false) $\mathcal{E} \vdash \mathbf{false} : Bool, \emptyset, \emptyset$

(skip) $\mathcal{E} \vdash \mathbf{skip} : Unit, \emptyset, \emptyset$

(var) $$\frac{\tau \prec \mathcal{E}(x)}{\mathcal{E} \vdash x : \tau, \emptyset, \emptyset}$$

(abs) $$\frac{\mathcal{E}_x \dagger [x \mapsto \tau'] \vdash E : \tau, \sigma, \kappa}{\mathcal{E} \vdash \lambda x \bullet E : \tau' \xrightarrow{\sigma,\kappa} \tau, \emptyset, \emptyset}$$

(op) $$\frac{\mathcal{E} \vdash E : \tau, \sigma, \kappa \qquad \mathcal{E} \vdash E' : \tau, \sigma', \kappa'}{\mathcal{E} \vdash E \; op \; E' : \tau, \sigma \cup \sigma', \kappa \cup \kappa'}$$

where: op=$\sqcap$,$\square$,$\|$

(ref) $$\frac{\mathcal{E} \vdash E : \tau, \sigma, \kappa}{\mathcal{E} \vdash \mathbf{ref}\; E : ref_\rho(\tau), \sigma \cup init(\rho, \tau), \kappa}$$

(deref) $$\frac{\mathcal{E} \vdash E : ref_\rho(\tau), \sigma, \kappa}{\mathcal{E} \vdash !E : \tau, \sigma \cup read(\rho), \kappa}$$

(ass) $$\frac{\mathcal{E} \vdash E : ref_\rho(\tau), \sigma, \kappa \qquad \mathcal{E} \vdash E' : \tau, \sigma', \kappa'}{\mathcal{E} \vdash E := E' : Unit, \sigma \cup \sigma' \cup write(\rho), \kappa \cup \kappa'}$$

(chan) $\mathcal{E} \vdash \mathbf{channel}() : chan_\chi(\tau), \emptyset, chan(\chi, \tau)$

(in) $$\frac{\mathcal{E} \vdash E : chan_\chi(\tau), \sigma, \kappa}{\mathcal{E} \vdash E? : \tau, \sigma, \kappa \cup in(\chi)}$$

(out) $$\frac{\mathcal{E} \vdash E : chan_\chi(\tau), \sigma, \kappa \qquad \mathcal{E} \vdash E' : \tau, \sigma', \kappa'}{\mathcal{E} \vdash E!E' : Unit, \sigma \cup \sigma', \kappa \cup \kappa' \cup out(\chi)}$$

(seq) $$\frac{\mathcal{E} \vdash E : \tau, \sigma, \kappa \qquad \mathcal{E} \vdash E' : \tau', \sigma', \kappa'}{\mathcal{E} \vdash E \; ; \; E' : \tau', \sigma \cup \sigma', \kappa \cup \kappa'}$$

(rec) $$\frac{\mathcal{E}_x \dagger [x \mapsto \tau] \vdash E : \tau, \sigma, \kappa}{\mathcal{E} \vdash \mathbf{rec}\; x \bullet E : \tau, \sigma, \kappa}$$

(app) $$\frac{\mathcal{E} \vdash E : \tau \xrightarrow{\sigma,\kappa} \tau', \sigma', \kappa' \qquad \mathcal{E} \vdash E' : \tau, \sigma'', \kappa''}{\mathcal{E} \vdash (E\; E') : \tau', \sigma \cup \sigma' \cup \sigma'', \kappa \cup \kappa' \cup \kappa''}$$

(let) $$\frac{\mathcal{E} \vdash E' : \tau', \sigma', \kappa' \qquad \mathcal{E}_x \dagger [x \mapsto Gen(\sigma', \kappa', \mathcal{E})(\tau')] \vdash E : \tau, \sigma, \kappa}{\mathcal{E} \vdash \mathbf{let}\; x = E' \;\mathbf{in}\; E : \tau, \sigma \cup \sigma', \kappa \cup \kappa'}$$

(obs) $$\frac{\mathcal{E} \vdash E : \tau, \sigma, \kappa \qquad \sigma' \sqsupseteq Observe(\mathcal{E}, \tau, \sigma) \qquad \kappa' \sqsupseteq Observe(\mathcal{E}, \tau, \kappa)}{\mathcal{E} \vdash E : \tau, \sigma', \kappa'}$$

Table 1: The static semantics

- The domain of *types* is inductively defined by:

$$\tau ::= Unit | Bool | \alpha | ref_\rho(\tau) | chan_\chi(\tau) | \tau \xrightarrow{\sigma,\kappa} \tau$$

Unit is a type with only one element "()", α a type variable, $ref_\rho(\tau)$ is the type of references in the region ρ to values of type τ, $chan_\chi(\tau)$ is the type of channels in the communication region χ that are intended to be media for values of type τ, $\tau \xrightarrow{\sigma,\kappa} \tau'$ is the type of functions that take parameters of type τ to values of type τ' with a *latent* reference effect σ and a latent channel effect κ. We mean by latent effect, the effect generated when the corresponding expression is evaluated.

We also define type schemes of the form $\forall v_1, ..., v_n, \tau$ where v_i can be a type, a reference region, a channel region, a reference effect or a channel effect variable. A type τ' is an instance of $\forall v_1, ..., v_n, \tau$ noted $\tau' \prec \forall v_1, ..., v_n, \tau$ if there exists a substitution θ defined over $v_1, ..., v_n$ such that $\tau' = \theta\tau$.

Our static semantics contains sequents of the form $\mathcal{E} \vdash E : \tau, \sigma, \kappa$ which state that under some typing environment $\mathcal{E}$ the expression E has a type τ, a reference effect σ and a channel effect κ. Type environments $\mathcal{E}$ map identifiers to type schemes.

4 Operational semantics

In this section we present the operational semantics. For that, first, let us introduce the notion of *computable values* of the language.

Definition 4.1 The set $\mathcal{V}$ of computable values is the least set which satisfies:

- $\mathcal{V}$ contains literals such as (), **true**, **false**, integers, or references, or channels.
- If Γ is an environment, then the closure $[\![\lambda x \bullet E,\ \Gamma]\!] \in \mathcal{V}$.

Let us denote by R the set of references and by K the set of channels. Now, we need to define the notion of *store*. The set of possible stores *Store* is made of *store actions*. The latter stands for both the current associations of the references and values, and the different actions on the store (read, write operations and the channel creations). The formal definition is:

$$Store = \mathcal{P}_f(Store\_Action)$$
$$Store\_Action = \{init(r, v) \mid r \in R \text{ and } v \in \mathcal{V}\} \cup \{read(r) \mid r \in R\} \cup \{write(r) \mid r \in R\} \cup \{chan(c) \mid c \in K\}$$

The store action $init(r, v)$ means that the reference r is bound to the value v. The store actions $read(r)$ and $write(r)$ model respectively a read and a write operation on the reference r. Finally, the store action $chan(c)$, corresponds to the creation of a channel c. We will write $s, s', \ldots$ to denote stores drawn from the set *Store*. We write s_r to denote the store s excluding store actions of the form $init(r, v)$. We say that s is included in s', or s' extends s, noted $s \subseteq s'$, if and only if there exists s'' such that $s' = s \cup s''$. We note $dom(s) = \{r \mid \exists v, init(r, v) \in s\}$ the domain of store s.

We note $\mathcal{EV}$ the set of expressions and computable values. We will use $v, v', \ldots$ to represent values drawn from $\mathcal{V}$, $t, t', \ldots$ to represent values drawn from $\mathcal{EV}$ and E, $E_i, \ldots$ to represent expressions.

Our operational semantics is based on the evolution of special *configurations* defined hereafter. First, we distinguish the set of *basic* (initial) configurations:

Definition 4.2 The set of basic configurations $\mathcal{BC}$ is defined as:

$$\mathcal{BC} \ = \ \{\langle t, s\rangle \mid t \in \mathcal{EV} \wedge s \in Store\}$$

Definition 4.3 The set of configurations, $\mathcal{C}$, is the least set, such that:

1. $\mathcal{BC} \subseteq \mathcal{C}$
2. $\alpha \in \mathcal{C}$ implies $\mathbf{ref}\,\alpha$, $\alpha?$, $!\alpha$, $\alpha; E$, $E!\alpha$, $E := \alpha$, $E\ \alpha \in \mathcal{C}$
3. $\alpha, \beta \in \mathcal{C}$ implies $\alpha\ op\ \beta$, $\alpha||s||\beta$, $\alpha||s||s'$, $s'||s||\alpha \in \mathcal{C}$ where: op = $\sqcap$,$\square$
4. $\alpha \in \mathcal{C}$ implies $\alpha!v$, $\alpha := v$, $\alpha\ v$, $[\![\lambda id : \tau \bullet \alpha, \Gamma]\!]\ v$, $\mathbf{let}\ x = \alpha\ \mathbf{in}\ E \in \mathcal{C}$

where E, E_1, E_2 denote expressions, s, s' denote stores and v denotes a computable value.

We will use $\alpha, \alpha', \ldots, \beta, \beta', \ldots$ to denote configurations drawn from $\mathcal{C}$.

The operational semantics is presented in the usual way, by defining a labeled transition system on configurations. There are two kinds of events, ranged over respectively by a and ε:

- Visible events: They consist of input events of the form $\langle ?, c, v, s\rangle$ and output events of the form $\langle !, c, v, s\rangle$ where c is a channel, v is a value in $\mathcal{V}$ and s is the current operational dynamic store. Let $\bar{a}$ denote the complement action of a, e.g. the complement of $\langle ?, c, v, s\rangle$ is $\langle !, c, v, s\rangle$. Note that $\bar{\bar{a}}$ is a.

- A silent event noted ε that is used to denote internal moves such as synchronizations on complementary actions.

We will use $\diamond, \diamond', \ldots$ as events drawn from the set of visible and invisible events. We will write $\alpha \xrightarrow{\diamond} \beta$ to denote the evolution of α into β after performing the event $\diamond$. The transition relation is defined as the smallest relation satisfying the axioms and rules given in the figures 2 and 3. The functions "*merge*" and "*pass*" that perform respectively the store merging and the value passing are not detailed here for lack of space—see [2] for a detailed explanation.

5 Consistency Theorem

Aim of this section is to prove that the static semantics is consistent w.r.t. the dynamic semantics. Due to lack of space only the main steps will be presented—see [2] for detailed proofs. The primary objective underlying the consistency theorem is to ensure that an expression and the value it evaluates into, have the same type. It ensures also that the evaluation of an expression only leads to observable effects of the store that are compatible with that of its original static effect.

Definition 5.1 (Slice Models) A slice model $\mathcal{L}$ is a pair of two finite functions $(\mathcal{S}, \mathcal{K})$ where $\mathcal{S}$ maps dynamic references to static regions and $\mathcal{K}$ maps dynamic channels to channel regions. We say that $\mathcal{L} = (\mathcal{S}, \mathcal{K})$ extends $\mathcal{L}' = (\mathcal{S}', \mathcal{K}')$ and we note $\mathcal{L} \subseteq \mathcal{L}'$ when:

$$\mathcal{S} \subseteq \mathcal{S}' \Leftrightarrow dom(\mathcal{S}) \subseteq dom(\mathcal{S}') \ \wedge \ \forall r \in dom(\mathcal{S}), \mathcal{S}(r) = \mathcal{S}'(r)$$
$$\mathcal{K} \subseteq \mathcal{K}' \Leftrightarrow dom(\mathcal{K}) \subseteq dom(\mathcal{K}') \ \wedge \ \forall r \in dom(\mathcal{K}), \mathcal{K}(r) = \mathcal{K}'(r)$$

Definition 5.2 (Consistent Types) The consistency relation $s : \sigma, \kappa, \mathcal{L} \models v : \tau$ between values v and types τ w.r.t. the slice model $\mathcal{L} = (\mathcal{S}, \mathcal{K})$, the dynamic store s, the reference effect σ and the communication effect κ is inductively defined by:

$$\begin{array}{lll}
s : \sigma, \kappa, \mathcal{L} & \models & () : Unit \\
s : \sigma, \kappa, \mathcal{L} & \models & r : ref_{\mathcal{S}(r)}(\tau) \ \text{ iff} : init(\mathcal{S}(r), \tau) \in \sigma \text{ and there exists } v \\
 & & \text{such that: } init(r, v) \in s \text{ and} s : \sigma, \kappa, \mathcal{L} \models v : \tau \\
s : \sigma, \kappa, \mathcal{L} & \models & c : chan_{\mathcal{K}(c)}(\tau) \ \text{ iff} : chan(\mathcal{K}(c), \tau) \in \kappa \\
s : \sigma, \kappa, \mathcal{L} & \models & [\![\lambda x \bullet E, \ \rho]\!] : \tau \ \text{ iff} : \text{there exists } \mathcal{E} \text{ such that:} \\
 & & \mathcal{E} \vdash \lambda x \bullet E : \tau, \emptyset, \emptyset \text{ and } s : \sigma, \kappa, \mathcal{L} \models \rho : \mathcal{E}
\end{array}$$

We note $s : \sigma, \kappa, \mathcal{L} \models \rho : \mathcal{E}$ when $dom(\rho) = dom(\mathcal{E})$ and $s : \sigma, \kappa, \mathcal{L} \models \rho(x) : \tau$ for every $x \in dom(\rho)$ and type τ such that $\tau \prec \mathcal{E}(x)$

Definition 5.3 (Consistent Effects: store effects and channel creation) The extended store $S = (C, s)$ and the effects σ and κ are consistent w.r.t. the slice model $\mathcal{L} = (\mathcal{S}, \mathcal{K})$, noted $\mathcal{L} \models S : \sigma, \kappa$ iff: $\forall read(r) \in s, read(\mathcal{S}(r)) \in \sigma$ and $\forall write(r) \in s, write(\mathcal{S}(r)) \in \sigma$ and $\forall init(r, v) \in s, \exists \tau, init(\mathcal{S}(r), \tau) \in \sigma$ and $s : \sigma, \kappa, \mathcal{L} \models v : \tau$ and $\forall chan(c) \in C, \exists \tau, chan(\mathcal{K}(c), \tau) \in \kappa$

Definition 5.4 (Consistent Effects: channel communications) The set of visible events E, and the set of communication effects κ are consistent w.r.t. the slice model $\mathcal{L} = (\mathcal{S}, \mathcal{K})$, noted $\mathcal{L} \models E : \kappa$ iff: $\forall e \in E, \exists \tau$, if $e = c?v$ for some

Constants:

$$\frac{\Box}{\Gamma \vdash \langle \mathbf{skip}, s\rangle \xrightarrow{\varepsilon} \langle (), s\rangle}$$

Configuration Fork:

$$\frac{\Box}{\Gamma \vdash \langle E_1\ op\ E_2, s\rangle \xrightarrow{\varepsilon} \langle E_1, s\rangle\, op\, \langle E_2, s\rangle}$$

where: $op = \sqcap, [\,]$

Id Evaluation:

$$\frac{\Box}{\Gamma \dagger [x \mapsto v] \vdash \langle x, s\rangle \xrightarrow{\varepsilon} \langle v, s\rangle}$$

Internal Choice:

$$\frac{\Box}{\begin{array}{llll}\Gamma \vdash & \alpha \sqcap \beta & \xrightarrow{\varepsilon} & \alpha \\ & & \xrightarrow{\varepsilon} & \beta\end{array}}$$

External Choice:

$$\frac{\Gamma \vdash \alpha \xrightarrow{a} \alpha'}{\begin{array}{llll}\Gamma \vdash & \alpha [\,] \beta & \xrightarrow{a} & \alpha' \\ & \beta [\,] \alpha & \xrightarrow{a} & \alpha'\end{array}}$$

$$\frac{\Gamma \vdash \alpha \xrightarrow{\varepsilon} \alpha'}{\begin{array}{llll}\Gamma \vdash & \alpha [\,] \beta & \xrightarrow{\varepsilon} & \alpha' [\,] \beta \\ & \beta [\,] \alpha & \xrightarrow{\varepsilon} & \beta [\,] \alpha'\end{array}}$$

$$\frac{\Box}{\begin{array}{llll}\Gamma \vdash & \langle v, s\rangle [\,] \alpha & \xrightarrow{\varepsilon} & \langle v, s\rangle \\ & \alpha [\,] \langle v, s\rangle & \xrightarrow{\varepsilon} & \langle v, s\rangle\end{array}}$$

Parallel Composition:

$$\frac{\Box}{\Gamma \vdash \langle E_1 \| E_2, s\rangle \xrightarrow{\varepsilon} \langle E_1, s\rangle \|s\| \langle E_2, s\rangle}$$

$$\frac{\Gamma \vdash \alpha \xrightarrow{a} \alpha', \quad \Gamma \vdash \beta \xrightarrow{\bar{a}} \beta'}{\begin{array}{llll}\Gamma \vdash & \alpha \|s\| \beta & \xrightarrow{\varepsilon} & \alpha' \|s\| \beta' \\ & \beta \|s\| \alpha & \xrightarrow{\varepsilon} & \beta' \|s\| \alpha'\end{array}}$$

$$\frac{\Gamma \vdash \alpha \xrightarrow{\diamond} \alpha'}{\begin{array}{llll}\Gamma \vdash & \alpha \|s\| \beta & \xrightarrow{\diamond} & \alpha' \|s\| \beta \\ & \beta \|s\| \alpha & \xrightarrow{\diamond} & \beta \|s\| \alpha'\end{array}}$$

$$\frac{\Box}{\begin{array}{llll}\Gamma \vdash & \alpha \|s\| \langle v, s'\rangle & \xrightarrow{\varepsilon} & \alpha \|s\| s' \\ & \langle v, s'\rangle \|s\| \alpha & \xrightarrow{\varepsilon} & s' \|s\| \alpha\end{array}}$$

$$\frac{\Gamma \vdash \alpha \xrightarrow{\diamond} \alpha'}{\begin{array}{llll}\Gamma \vdash & \alpha \|s\| s' & \xrightarrow{\diamond} & \alpha' \|s\| s' \\ & s' \|s\| \alpha & \xrightarrow{\diamond} & s' \|s\| \alpha'\end{array}}$$

$$\frac{\Box}{\begin{array}{llll}\Gamma \vdash & \langle v, s''\rangle \|s\| s' & \xrightarrow{\varepsilon} & \langle v, merge(s, s', s'')\rangle \\ & s' \|s\| \langle v, s''\rangle & \xrightarrow{\varepsilon} & \langle v, merge(s, s', s'')\rangle\end{array}}$$

Sequencing:

$$\frac{\Box}{\Gamma \vdash \langle E_1 ; E_2, s\rangle \xrightarrow{\varepsilon} \langle E_1, s\rangle ; E_2}$$

$$\frac{\Gamma \vdash \alpha \xrightarrow{\diamond} \alpha'}{\Gamma \vdash \alpha ; E \xrightarrow{\diamond} \alpha' ; E}$$

$$\frac{\Box}{\Gamma \vdash \langle v, s\rangle ; E \xrightarrow{\varepsilon} \langle E, s\rangle}$$

Function:

$$\frac{\Box}{\Gamma \vdash \langle \lambda x \bullet E, s\rangle \xrightarrow{\varepsilon} \langle [\ \lambda x \bullet E, \Gamma\ ], s\rangle}$$

$$\frac{\Box}{\Gamma \vdash \langle E_1\ E_2, s\rangle \xrightarrow{\varepsilon} E_1\ \langle E_2, s\rangle}$$

$$\frac{\Gamma \vdash \alpha \xrightarrow{\diamond} \alpha'}{\Gamma \vdash E\ \alpha \xrightarrow{\diamond} E\ \alpha'}$$

$$\frac{\Box}{\Gamma \vdash E\ \langle v, s\rangle \xrightarrow{\varepsilon} \langle E, s\rangle\ v}$$

$$\frac{\Gamma \vdash \alpha \xrightarrow{\diamond} \alpha'}{\Gamma \vdash \alpha\ v \xrightarrow{\diamond} \alpha'\ v}$$

$$\frac{\Box}{\Gamma \vdash \langle [\ \lambda x \bullet E, \Gamma_1\ ], s\rangle\ v \xrightarrow{\varepsilon} [\ \lambda x \bullet \langle E, s\rangle, \Gamma_1\ ]\ v}$$

$$\frac{\Gamma_1 \dagger [x \mapsto v] \vdash \alpha \xrightarrow{\diamond} \alpha'}{\Gamma \vdash [\ \lambda x \bullet \alpha, \Gamma_1\ ]\ v \xrightarrow{\diamond} [\ \lambda x \bullet \alpha', \Gamma_1\ ]\ v}$$

$$\frac{\Gamma_1 \dagger [x \mapsto v] \vdash \alpha \xrightarrow{\diamond} \langle v', s\rangle}{\Gamma \vdash [\ \lambda x \bullet \alpha, \Gamma_1\ ]\ v \xrightarrow{\diamond} \langle v', s\rangle}$$

Let Expressions:

$$\frac{\Box}{\begin{array}{l}\Gamma \vdash \langle \mathbf{let}\ x = E_1\ \mathbf{in}\ E_2, s\rangle \xrightarrow{\varepsilon} \\ \quad \mathbf{let}\ x = \langle E_1, s\rangle\ \mathbf{in}\ E_2\end{array}}$$

$$\frac{\Gamma \vdash \alpha \xrightarrow{\diamond} \alpha'}{\Gamma \vdash \mathbf{let}\ x = \alpha\ \mathbf{in}\ E \xrightarrow{\diamond} \mathbf{let}\ x = \alpha'\ \mathbf{in}\ E}$$

$$\frac{\Box}{\Gamma \vdash \mathbf{let}\ x = \langle v, s\rangle\ \mathbf{in}\ E \xrightarrow{\varepsilon} \langle E[v/x], s\rangle}$$

Recursion:

$$\frac{\Box}{\Gamma \vdash \langle \mathbf{rec}\ x \bullet E, s\rangle \xrightarrow{\varepsilon} \langle E[\mathbf{rec}\ x \bullet E/x], s\rangle}$$

Channel Creation:

$$\frac{\Box}{\Gamma \vdash \langle \mathbf{channel}(), s\rangle \xrightarrow{\varepsilon} \langle c, s \cup \{chan(c)\}\rangle}$$

Table 2: Operational semantics: Part I

channel c and some value v then $in(\mathcal{K}(c)) \in \kappa$ else $e = c!v$ for some channel c and some value v and $out(\mathcal{K}(c)) \in \kappa$.

Definition 5.5 (Expression extraction) Let us define the function *expr* that extracts an expression from a given configuration. It is defined by:

$$
\begin{array}{lrcl}
expr(\alpha) = \textbf{case}\ \alpha\ \textbf{of} & & & \\
& \langle E, \sigma\rangle & \rightarrow & E \\
& \langle [\![\lambda x \bullet E, \rho]\!], \sigma\rangle & \rightarrow & \lambda x \bullet E \\
& \alpha_1\ op\ \alpha_2 & \rightarrow & expr(\alpha_1)\ op\ expr(\alpha_2) \\
& \alpha_1; E & \rightarrow & expr(\alpha_1); E \\
& \alpha_1? & \rightarrow & expr(\alpha_1)? \\
& E!\alpha_1 & \rightarrow & E!expr(\alpha_1) \\
& \alpha_1!v & \rightarrow & expr(\alpha_1)!v \\
& E := \alpha_1 & \rightarrow & E := expr(\alpha_1) \\
& \alpha_1 := v & \rightarrow & expr(\alpha_1) := v \\
& E\ \alpha_1 & \rightarrow & E\ expr(\alpha_1) \\
& \textbf{ref}\ \alpha_1 & \rightarrow & \textbf{ref}\ expr(\alpha_1) \\
& \left\{ \begin{array}{l} \textbf{let}\ x = \alpha_1 \\ \textbf{in}\ E \end{array} \right\} & \rightarrow & \left\{ \begin{array}{l} \textbf{let}\ x = expr(\alpha_1) \\ \textbf{in}\ E \end{array} \right\} \\
\textbf{end} & & &
\end{array}
$$

Actually the expressions extracted by the previous definition are not syntactical expressions. They may embody some computable values such as references or channels. At specific points in the proof of the consistency theorem, we need to type such expressions. For that, we extend the type system as follows:

Definition 5.6 (Typing Intermediate Expressions)
Let I be an intermediate expression. We say that, under some typing environment $\mathcal{E}$, I is of type τ, with σ and κ as reference and communication effects iff the sequent $\mathcal{E} \vdash I : \tau, \sigma, \kappa$ is provable in the typing inference system obtained from the static semantics (see the table 1), by replacing expressions $E, E', ...$ by intermediate expressions $I, I', ...$, and by adding the following rule:

$$\frac{s : \sigma', \kappa', \mathcal{S}, \mathcal{K} \models v : \tau}{\mathcal{E} \vdash v : \tau, \emptyset, \emptyset}$$

where s is a dynamic store, $\mathcal{S}$ a reference model, $\mathcal{K}$ a channel model.

Definition 5.7 (Store Extraction)
The function *store* that returns the store of a given configuration.

$$
\begin{array}{lrcl}
store(\alpha) = & & & \\
\textbf{case}\ \alpha\ \textbf{of} & & & \\
& \langle E, s\rangle \text{ or } \langle [\![\lambda x \bullet E, \rho]\!], s\rangle & \rightarrow & s \\
& \alpha_1\ op\ \alpha_2 & \rightarrow & store(\alpha_1) \cup store(\alpha_2) \\
& \alpha_1; E \text{ or } \alpha_1? \text{ or } E!\alpha_1 \text{ or } \alpha_1!v \text{ or } E := \alpha_1 & \rightarrow & store(\alpha_1) \\
& \alpha_1 := v \text{ or } E\ \alpha_1 \text{ or } \textbf{ref}\ \alpha_1 \text{ or } \left\{ \begin{array}{l} \textbf{let}\ x = \alpha_1 \\ \textbf{in}\ E \end{array} \right\} & \rightarrow & store(\alpha_1) \\
\textbf{end} & & &
\end{array}
$$

Theorem 5.8 (Consistency)
Let α be a configuration, suppose that $\mathcal{S}, \mathcal{K} \models store(\alpha) : \sigma, \kappa$ and $store(\alpha) : \sigma, \kappa, \mathcal{S}, \mathcal{K} \models \Gamma : \mathcal{E}$. If $\mathcal{E} \vdash expr(\alpha) : \tau, \sigma', \kappa'$ and $\Gamma \vdash \alpha \overset{\diamond}{\rightarrow} \alpha'$ then, provided that whenever $\diamond$ is an input event its value matches the type of the involved

channel (i.e. whenever $\diamond = \langle ?, c, v, s\rangle$ for some channel c and some value v, then $s : \sigma, \kappa, \mathcal{S}, \mathcal{K} \models v : \tau_1$ and $s : \sigma, \kappa, \mathcal{S}, \mathcal{K} \models c : chan_{\mathcal{K}(c)}(\tau_1)$), there exist $\mathcal{S}'$ and $\mathcal{K}'$ extending $\mathcal{S}$ and $\mathcal{K}$, and unobservable effects σ'' and κ'' i.e. $Observe(\mathcal{E}, \tau, \sigma'') = \emptyset$ and $Observe(\mathcal{E}, \tau, \kappa'') = \emptyset$, such that:

- If $exp(\alpha')$ is a value then:
  1. $\mathcal{S}', \mathcal{K}' \models store(\alpha') : \sigma \cup \sigma' \cup \sigma'', \kappa \cup \kappa' \cup \kappa''$ and,
  2. $store(\alpha') : \sigma \cup \sigma' \cup \sigma'', \kappa \cup \kappa' \cup \kappa'', \mathcal{S}', \mathcal{K}' \models expr(\alpha') : \tau$ and,
  3. $\mathcal{K}' \models \diamond : \kappa' \cup \kappa''$
- Else there exist σ_1', σ_2', κ_1' and κ_2', such that:
  $\sigma_1' \cup \sigma_2' = \sigma'$ *and* $\kappa_1' \cup \kappa_2' = \kappa'$ *and*
  $\mathcal{S}', \mathcal{K}' \models store(\alpha') : \sigma \cup \sigma_1' \cup \sigma'', \kappa \cup \kappa_1' \cup \kappa''$ *and* $\mathcal{K}' \models \diamond : \kappa_1' \cup \kappa''$ *and*
  $\mathcal{E} \vdash expr(\alpha') : \tau, \sigma_2', \kappa_2'$ *and* $store(\alpha') : \sigma \cup \sigma_1' \cup \sigma''$ *and* $\kappa \cup \kappa_1' \cup \kappa'', \mathcal{S}', \mathcal{K}' \models \Gamma : \mathcal{E}$

Furthermore if $\diamond$ is an output event, its value is conform to the type of the involved channel.

Reference Creation:

$$\frac{\Box}{\Gamma \vdash \langle \mathbf{ref}(E), s\rangle \xrightarrow{\varepsilon} \mathbf{ref}\ \langle E, s\rangle}$$

$$\frac{\Gamma \vdash \alpha \xrightarrow{\diamond} \alpha'}{\Gamma \vdash \mathbf{ref}\ \alpha \xrightarrow{\diamond} \mathbf{ref}\ \alpha'}$$

$$\frac{\Box}{\Gamma \vdash \mathbf{ref}\ \langle v, s\rangle \xrightarrow{\varepsilon} \langle r, s \cup \{init(r, v)\}\rangle}$$

Input:

$$\frac{\Box}{\Gamma \vdash \langle E?, s\rangle \xrightarrow{\varepsilon} \langle E, s\rangle ?}$$

$$\frac{\Gamma \vdash \alpha \xrightarrow{\diamond} \alpha'}{\Gamma \vdash \alpha? \xrightarrow{\diamond} \alpha'?}$$

$$\frac{\Box}{\Gamma \vdash \langle c, s\rangle ? \xrightarrow{\langle ?, c, v, s'\rangle} \langle v, pass(s', s, v)\rangle}$$

Dereferencing:

$$\frac{\Box}{\Gamma \vdash \langle !E, s\rangle \xrightarrow{\varepsilon} !\langle E, s\rangle}$$

$$\frac{\Gamma \vdash \alpha \xrightarrow{\diamond} \alpha'}{\Gamma \vdash !\alpha \xrightarrow{\diamond} !\alpha'}$$

$$\frac{\Box}{\Gamma \vdash !\langle r, s\rangle \xrightarrow{\varepsilon} \langle v, s \cup \{read(r)\}\rangle}\ init(r, v) \in s$$

Output:

$$\frac{\Box}{\Gamma \vdash \langle E_1 ! E_2, s\rangle \xrightarrow{\varepsilon} E_1 ! \langle E_2, s\rangle}$$

$$\frac{\Gamma \vdash \alpha \xrightarrow{\diamond} \alpha'}{\Gamma \vdash E!\alpha \xrightarrow{\diamond} E!\alpha'}$$

$$\frac{\Box}{\Gamma \vdash E!\langle v, s\rangle \xrightarrow{\varepsilon} \langle E, s\rangle !v}$$

$$\frac{\Gamma \vdash \alpha \xrightarrow{\diamond} \alpha'}{\Gamma \vdash \alpha!v \xrightarrow{\diamond} \alpha'!v}$$

$$\frac{\Box}{\Gamma \vdash \langle c, s\rangle !v \xrightarrow{\langle !, c, v, s\rangle} \langle (), s\rangle}$$

Assignment:

$$\frac{\Box}{\Gamma \vdash \langle E_1 := E_2, s\rangle \xrightarrow{\varepsilon} E_1 := \langle E_2, s\rangle}$$

$$\frac{\Gamma \vdash \alpha \xrightarrow{\diamond} \alpha'}{\Gamma \vdash E := \alpha \xrightarrow{\diamond} E := \alpha'}$$

$$\frac{\Box}{\Gamma \vdash E := \langle v, s\rangle \xrightarrow{\varepsilon} \langle E, s\rangle := v}$$

$$\frac{\Gamma \vdash \alpha \xrightarrow{\diamond} \alpha'}{\Gamma \vdash \alpha := v \xrightarrow{\diamond} \alpha' := v}$$

$$\frac{\Box}{\Gamma \vdash \langle r, s\rangle := v \xrightarrow{\varepsilon} \langle (), s_r \cup \{write(r),\ init(r, v)\}\rangle}$$

Table 3: Operational Semantics: Part II

6 Conclusion

We have reported in this paper the complete definition of an implicitly strongly typed polymorphic concurrent and functional language that supports data accepting in-place modification. We have presented a complete static semantics that rests on an extension of the type and effect discipline to handle communication effects, and a transitional semantics of the language. The consistency of the typing system w.r.t. the operational semantics has been established.

As a future research, we plan to investigate refinement issues as well as structuring and modularity mechanisms. We are particularly interested in experimenting some new approaches in modularity from the algebraic specification world such as the loose stratified semantics proposed by [5].

References

[1] D. Bolignano and M. Debabi. Higher order communicating processes with value-passing, assignment and return of results. In *Proceedings of the ISAAC'92 Conference, Lecture Notes in Computer Science 650*. Springer Verlag, December 1992.

[2] D. Bolignano and M. Debabi. A coherent type system for a concurrent, functional and imperative programming language. Technical report, Bull-ORDA, January 1993.

[3] D. Bolignano and M. Debabi. A denotational model for the integration of concurrent functional and imperative programming. In *Proceedings of the ICCI'93 Conference*. IEEE, May 1993.

[4] B. Berthomieu. Implementing CCS, the LCS experiment. Technical Report 89425, LAAS CNRS, 1989.

[5] M. Bidoit. *PLUSS, un Langage pour le Développement de Spécifications Algébriques Modulaires*. PhD thesis, Paris Sud, July 1989.

[6] D. Berry, A.J.R.G. Milner, and D. Turner. A semantics for ML concurrency primitives. In *Proc. 17th ACM Symposium on Principles of Programming Languages*, 1992.

[7] A. Giacalone, P. Mishra, and S. Prasad. Facile: A symmetric integration of concurrent and functional programming. *International Journal of Parallel Programming*, 18(2):121–160, April 1989.

[8] J.M. Lucassen and D.K. Gifford. Polymorphic effect systems. In *Proc. 15th ACM Symposium on Principles of Programming Languages*, 1988.

[9] J.M. Lucassen. *Type and Effects: Towards an Integration of Functional and Imperative Programming*. PhD thesis, Laboratory of Computer Science, MIT, 1987.

[10] X. Leroy and P. Weis. Polymorphic type inference and assignment. In *Proceedings of the seventeenth ACM Symposium on Principles of Programming Languages*, 1991.

[11] A.J.R.G. Milner. A theory of type polymorphism in programming. *Computer and systems sciences*, 17:348–375, 1978.

[12] A.J.R.G. Milner, M. Tofte, and R. Harper. *The Definition of Standard ML*. MIT Press, 1990.

[13] J.H Reppy. An operational semantics of first-class synchronous operations. Technical Report TR 91-1232, Department of Computer Science, Cornell University, August 1991.

[14] D. Sannella and A. Tarlecki. Program specification and development in standard ML. In *Proc. 12th ACM Symposium on Principles of Programming Languages*, 1985.

[15] J. Talpin and P. Jouvelot. The type and effect discipline. In *Proc. Logic in Computer Science*, 1992.

[16] M. Tofte. *Operational semantics and polymorphic type inference*. PhD thesis, Department of Computer Science, University of Edinburgh, 1987.

Peirce Algebras*

Chris Brink[†] Katarina Britz[†]

Renate A. Schmidt[†§]

[†]Department of Mathematics, University of Cape Town
7700 Rondebosch, South Africa

[§]Max-Planck-Institut für Informatik
66123 Saarbrücken, Germany

Extended Abstract

In its modern form the algebra of relations has been under investigation by mathematicians since Tarski's seminal paper of (1941). The main line of development has been the study of a class of algebras called *relation algebras* (Chin and Tarski 1951, Jónsson 1982), in parallel with developments such as Boolean algebras with operators (Jónsson and Tarski 1951/1952) and cylindric algebras (Henkin, Monk and Tarski 1985). Since the early seventies the algebra of relations has increasingly become of interest to computer scientists. Just as the notion of a partial function provides a natural model for deterministic programs, so the more general notion of a (binary) relation provides a natural model for nondeterministic programs. This idea has been exploited by various authors. For example, it is evident in Floyd-Hoare logic for program verification, it has been extended to specification in Hoare and He, Jifeng (1987), it figures in logics of programs such as dynamic logic (Parikh 1981, Harel 1984), and it was used in the early seventies to model recursive procedures (de Bakker and de Roever 1973, Hitchcock and Park 1972). Recently the algebra of relations has been extensively used in a graph-theoretic approach to programs by Schmidt and Ströhlein (1991). In modal logic, relation algebra features strongly in the Dutch-Hungarian cooperation on van Benthem's (1991) new *arrow logic* (see *Logic at Work, Proceedings of the Applied Logic Conference* (1992)). Venema (1992) is another interdisciplinary study of relation algebra and multi-modal logic. The proof theory of relations is also of interest to computer scientists, and several relational inference systems are available (Wadge 1975, Hennessy 1980, Maddux 1983, Orlowska 1991).

In many applications it has become clear that we need, not just an algebra of relations as distinct from an algebra of sets, but an algebra of relations *interacting* with sets. (For example, if we view a program as effecting a transition on a state space, we may wish to model this by a binary relation acting on a set of states.) Such an algebra was presented in Brink (1981) under the name of *Boolean modules*. A Boolean module is defined (Brink 1988) as a two-sorted algebra $\mathcal{M} = (\mathcal{B}, \mathcal{R}, :)$, where $\mathcal{B}$ is a Boolean algebra, $\mathcal{R}$ is a relation algebra and $:$ is a mapping $\mathcal{R} \times \mathcal{B} \longrightarrow \mathcal{B}$ written $r:a$ such that for any $r, s \in \mathcal{R}$ and $a, b \in \mathcal{B}$:

*The full version of this paper is due to appear in 'Formal Aspects of Computing', vol. 6, Springer-Verlag, London (1994).

M1 $r:(a+b) = r:a + r:b$
M2 $(r+s):a = r:a + s:a$
M3 $r:(s:a) = (r;s):a$
M4 $e:a = a$
M5 $0:a = 0$
M6 $r^{\smile}:(r:a)' \leq a'$.

The symbols $+$, $:$, $;$, e, 0, $^{\smile}$, $'$ and $\leq$ respectively denote join, Peirce product, relational composition, identity, zero, converse, complementation and the usual partial ordering. Let A be any subset of some non-empty set U and let R, S be any binary relations over U. In the standard models (i.e., in *proper Boolean modules*) the join is set-theoretic union. The *Peirce product* $R:A$ is the set of elements x related by R to some element y in A. The relational composition $R;S$ is the set of pairs (x,y) for which there is a z such that $(x,z) \in R$ and $(z,y) \in S$. The identity is the identity relation over U. The zero is the empty set. The converse of a relation R is the set $R^{\smile}$ of pairs (y,x) for which $(x,y) \in R$. Complementation of sets (respectively relations) is with respect to U (respectively $U \times U$). And, $\leq$ is interpreted as the subset relation.

Though independent of the computer science context, Boolean modules are very similar to *dynamic algebras*, introduced by Kozen (1980) as the algebraic version of dynamic logic. And both of these are quite similar to the *extended relation algebras* introduced by Suppes (1976) in a linguistic context. However, Boolean modules and dynamic algebras both have the drawback of not treating relations (programs) and sets equally: there is a set-forming operator on relations, but no relation-forming operator on sets. Extended relation algebras do not have this drawback, but they do have the drawback of being as yet unformalized as algebras.

We present here a two-sorted algebra, called a *Peirce algebra*, of relations and sets interacting with each other. In a Peirce algebra, sets (or rather, the variables representing sets) can combine with each other as in a Boolean algebra, relations can combine with each other as in a relation algebra, and in addition we have both a set-forming operator on relations and a relation-forming operator on sets. The former is the Peirce product used in Boolean modules; the latter is the operation of *cylindrification*. Peirce algebras thus present a natural next step after Boolean algebras, relation algebras and Boolean modules.

Formally, we define a *Peirce algebra* to be a Boolean module $(\mathcal{B}, \mathcal{R}, :)$ enriched with an operation ^{c} from the underlying Boolean algebra $\mathcal{B}$ to the underlying relation algebra $\mathcal{R}$ such that for every $a \in \mathcal{B}$ and $r \in \mathcal{R}$:

P1 $a^c:1 = a$
P2 $(r:1)^c = r;1$.

In the standard models (i.e., in *proper Peirce algebras*) applying the cylindrification operation to a set A yields the relation A^c given by the Cartesian product $A \times U$. An example of a Peirce algebra is any extended relation algebra. Another example is any relation algebra. We show that the underlying Boolean algebra $\mathcal{B}$ of any Peirce algebra can be embedded in its underlying relation algebra $\mathcal{R}$ in two ways: as the Boolean algebra of so-called right ideal elements in $\mathcal{R}$, and as the Boolean algebra of elements below the identity of $\mathcal{R}$. These results reiterate the point made by Maddux (1990) that Peirce algebra is not a mathematical requisite for modelling interactions between relations and sets, in the sense that these can be modelled in relation algebras (as interactions with right ideal elements, for example). However, we argue that Peirce algebra provides a more natural framework for doing so. In a Peirce algebra one can actually manipulate both sets and relations simultaneously. From an applications-oriented point of view this is an advantage, and we present two (sets of) sample applications to substantiate this point.

The first shows how three programming constructs in the calculus of weakest prespecification of Hoare and He, Jifeng (1987) can be modelled naturally in Peirce algebras. This comes about through the isomorphism in any Peirce algebra $(\mathcal{B}, \mathcal{R}, :, ^c)$ between the Boolean algebra $\mathcal{B}$ and the Boolean algebra of right ideal elements of the relation algebra $\mathcal{R}$ and the isomorphism between $\mathcal{B}$ and the Boolean algebra of identity elements in $\mathcal{R}$. First, Hoare and He, Jifeng (1987) use right ideal elements to model conditional statements in logics representing programs as binary relations. Second, subsets of the identity relation are used to model a test operation (Parikh 1981). Third, left ideal elements can be used to model the initialization of abstract data types as defined in Hoare, He, Jifeng and Sanders (1987).

The second application points out that the so-called *terminological logics* arising in knowledge representation based on the system KL-ONE (Woods and Schmolze 1992) have evolved a semantics best described as a calculus of relations interacting with sets. Brink and Schmidt (1992) show that the terminological representation language $\mathcal{ALC}$ of Schmidt-Schauß and Smolka (1991) can be captured in the context of Boolean modules. In this paper we extend this idea and use Peirce algebra to accommodate terminological representation languages even more expressive than $\mathcal{ALC}$.

Terminological representation languages have two syntactic primitives, called *concepts* and *roles*. Concepts are usually interpreted as sets and roles as binary relations. As sets and relations have simple calculi that can be presented, respectively, in the context of Boolean algebra and relation algebra, concepts can be modelled in Boolean algebra and roles in relation algebra. Concepts and roles also interact in certain ways, and these can be modelled as interactions between relations and sets. More specifically, concept-forming operations on roles can be interpreted as variants of Peirce product (with two exceptions), and an algebraic characterization for such interactions are Boolean modules. (The exceptions involve numerical quantification.) Role-forming operators on concepts can be interpreted in terms of cylindrification. A natural algebraic presentation for such interactions is then Peirce algebra. The advantages for doing so are: First, Peirce algebra provides a formal mathematical framework for KL-ONE-based knowledge representation, the development of which has, by and large, been implementation-driven and rather *ad hoc*. Second, Peirce algebra provides a natural (equational) axiomatization for reasoning about information represented in a terminological language. Third, terminological representation can be linked to other areas of application of Peirce algebra. Schmidt (1993), for example, exploits the link between Peirce algebra and extended relation algebra and shows how terminological representation can benefit from Suppes' (1976) linguistic analysis of English language sentences.

References

Brink, C. (1981), Boolean modules, *Journal of Algebra* 71(2), 291–313.

Brink, C. (1988), On the application of relations, *S. Afr. J. Philos.* **7**(2), 105–112.

Brink, C. and Schmidt, R. A. (1992), Subsumption computed algebraically, *Computers and Mathematics with Applications* **23**(2–9), 329–342.

Chin, L. H. and Tarski, A. (1951), Distributive and modular laws in the arithmetic of relation algebras, *Univ. Calif. Publ. Math.* **1**(9), 341–384.

de Bakker, J. W. and de Roever, W. P. (1973), A calculus for recursive program schemes, *in* M. Nivat (ed.), *Symposium on Automata, Formal Languages and Programming*, North Holland, Amsterdam.

Harel, D. (1984), Dynamic logic, *in* D. Gabbay and F. Guenther (eds), *Handbook of Philosophical Logic*, Vol. II, Reidel Publ. Co., Dordrecht, Holland, pp. 497–604.

Henkin, L., Monk, J. D. and Tarski, A. (1985), *Cylindric Algebras: Part II*, Vol. 115 of *Studies in Logic and the Foundations of Mathematics*, North-Holland, Amsterdam.

Hennessy, M. C. B. (1980), A proof-system for the first-order relational calculus, *Journal of Computer and System Sciences* **20**, 96–110.

Hitchcock, P. and Park, D. (1972), Induction rules and termination proofs, *in* M. Nivat (ed.), *Automata, Languages and Programming*, North-Holland, Amsterdam.

Hoare, C. A. R. and He, Jifeng (1987), The weakest prespecification, *Information Processing Letters* **24**, 127–132.

Hoare, C. A. R., He, Jifeng and Sanders, J. W. (1987), Prespecification in data refinement, *Information Processing Letters* **25**, 71–76.

Jónsson, B. (1982), Varieties of relation algebras, *Algebra Universalis* **15**(3), 273–298.

Jónsson, B. and Tarski, A. (1951/1952), Boolean algebras with operators, Part I/II, *American Journal of Mathematics* **73/74**, 891–939/127–162.

Kozen, D. (1980), A representation theorem for models of ∗-free PDL, *in* J. De Bakker and J. van Leeuwen (eds), *Automata, Languages and Programming*, Vol. 85 of *Lecture Notes in Computer Science*, Springer-Verlag, Berlin, pp. 351–362.

Logic at Work, Proceedings of the Applied Logic Conference (1992), University of Amsterdam. Preprint. To appear.

Maddux, R. D. (1983), A sequent calculus for relation algebras, *Annals of Pure and Applied Logic* **25**, 73–101.

Maddux, R. D. (1990). Personal communication with C. Brink.

Orlowska, E. (1991), Relational interpretation of modal logic, *in* H. Andréka, J. D. Monk and I. Németi (eds), *Algebraic Logic*, Vol. 54 of *Colloquia Mathematica Societatis János Bolyai*, North-Holland, Amsterdam, pp. 443–471.

Parikh, D. (1981), Propositional dynamic logic of programs: A survey, *in* E. Engeler (ed.), *Logic of Programs*, Vol. 125 of *Lecture Notes in Computer Science*, Springer-Verlag, Berlin, pp. 102–144.

Schmidt, G. and Ströhlein, T. (1991), *Relations and Graphs*, Springer-Verlag, Berlin.

Schmidt, R. A. (1993), Terminological representation, natural language & relation algebra, *in* H. J. Ohlbach (ed.), *Proceedings of the sixteenth German AI Conference (GWAI-92)*, Vol. 671 of *Lecture Notes in Artificial Intelligence*, Springer-Verlag, Berlin, pp. 357–371.

Schmidt-Schauß, M. and Smolka, G. (1991), Attributive concept description with complements, *Artificial Intelligence* **48**, 1–26.

Suppes, P. (1976), Elimination of quantifiers in the semantics of natural language by use of extended relation algebras, *Rev. Int. de Philosophie* **30**(3–4), 243–259.

Tarski, A. (1941), On the calculus of relations, *Journal of Symbolic Logic* **6**(3), 73–89.

van Benthem, J. (1991), Logic and the flow of information, *Technical Report, ILLC Prepublication Series for Logic, Semantics and Philosophy of Language LP-92-11*, Institute for Logic, Language and Computation, University of Amsterdam. To appear.

Venema, Y. (1992), *Many-Dimensional Modal Logic*, PhD thesis, University of Amsterdam.

Wadge, W. W. (1975), A complete natural deduction system for the relational calculus, *Theory of Computation Report 5*, University of Warwick.

Woods, W. A. and Schmolze, J. G. (1992), The KL-ONE family, *Computers and Mathematics with Applications* **23**(2–5), 133–177.

Comparing Two Different Approaches to Products in Abstract Relation Algebra

R. Berghammer* A. Haeberer† G. Schmidt* P. Veloso†

† Departamento de Informática, PUC, Rio de Janeiro, RJ 22453 (Brazil)

* Fakultät für Informatik, Bundeswehr-Univ., 85577 Neubiberg (Germany)

1. Introduction

During the development of relation algebra as a formal programming tool, the need of some form of "categorical product" of relations became apparent, whether as a type or as an operation. Two approaches arose in the late 70's and the early 80's which will be referred here as the "Munich approach" (see, e.g., [18, 7]) and the "Rio approach" (see, e.g., [13, 12, 22]).

Both of them rely more or less on relation algebras as presented in [9]. The former introduces heterogeneous relations and undertakes the *product-extension* as being a data type defining the product in terms of two projections π and ρ. With this approach, it was possible to give relational semantics to programming language constructs and to construct semantic domains by relation-algebraic means. Introducing the point axiom in [17], questions of representability have been discussed. Defining the symmetric quotient ([6, 16, 23]) made it possible to handle set and function comprehension.

The latter group uses homogeneous relations and introduces axioms for a *fork*-operation ∇, thus extending relation algebra in the same way Jónsson and Tarski in [14] extended a Boolean algebra. The introduction of ∇ induces poses some interesting representability questions discussed in [2]. This approach tackled first the problem—posed in [19] and formally treated in [20]—of the impossibility of expressing first-order formulae with four or more variables in abstract relation algebra. As it was shown in [21, 22], the expressive power of the extension of relation algebra with the ∇-operation encompasses that of first-order logic.

This paper reports research work under joint development by the two groups. Some parts of the proofs presented here were developed with RALF, a relation-algebraic formula manipulation system and proof checker developed in Munich [8] and under re-implementation by the Rio group.

2. Homogeneous Relation Algebras

The following definition, in essence due to [9], applies to homogeneous relations, in which case all operations are total:

Definition 1. A **(homogeneous abstract) relation algebra** $(\mathcal{R}, \sqcup, \sqcap, \overline{}, \circ, {}^{\mathsf{T}})$ consists of a set $\mathcal{R} \neq \emptyset$, whose elements are called relations, such that

- $(\mathcal{R}, \sqcup, \sqcap, \overline{})$ is a complete, atomic Boolean algebra with zero element O, universal element L, and ordering $\subset$,
- $(\mathcal{R}, \circ)$ is a semigroup with precisely one unit element I,
- the Schröder equivalences $QR \subset S \iff Q^{\mathsf{T}}\overline{S} \subset \overline{R} \iff \overline{S}R^{\mathsf{T}} \subset \overline{Q}$ and the Tarski rule $R \neq O \implies LRL = L$ hold[1]. □

When dealing with programming, one has to handle several sorts or types of elements. Even then, one can stay within the framework of homogeneous relation algebra and try to find a universe containing all the elements in question, where sorts or types may then be distinguished by partial identities.

3. Heterogeneous Relation Algebras

An alternative is to switch to heterogeneous relations, where $\sqcup, \sqcap$ and $\circ$ are *partial* operations. With regard to applicability, one can let oneself be guided by the calculus of $m \times n$-matrices or by category theory. For reasons of economy, when considering a relation algebra, we want to say as little as possible about the question of whether relations can be joined, intersected, or multiplied. In practical problems, these operations will be permitted if this can be deduced from some corresponding union, intersection, or product given in the first place. We now give a definition of a heterogeneous relation algebra.

Definition 2. A **(heterogeneous abstract) relation algebra** is a category $\mathcal{R}$ consisting of a set $\mathcal{O}$ of objects and sets $\mathtt{Mor}(A, B)$ of morphisms, where $A, B \in \mathcal{O}$. Composition is denoted by juxtaposition (or, in rare cases by $\circ$) while identities are denoted by $I_A \in \mathtt{Mor}(A, A)$. In addition, there is a totally defined unary operation ${}^{\mathsf{T}}_{A,B} : \mathtt{Mor}(A, B) \longrightarrow \mathtt{Mor}(B, A)$ between morphism sets. The operations satisfy the following rules:

i) Every set $\mathtt{Mor}(A, B)$ carries the structure of a complete, atomic boolean algebra with operations $\sqcup_{A,B}, \sqcap_{A,B}, \overline{}_{A,B}$, zero element $O_{A,B}$, universal element $L_{A,B}$ (the latter two non-equal), and inclusion ordering $\subset$.

ii) The Schröder equivalences $QR \subset S \iff Q^{\mathsf{T}}\overline{S} \subset \overline{R} \iff \overline{S}R^{\mathsf{T}} \subset \overline{Q}$ (where the definedness of one of the three formulae implies that of the other two) and the Tarski rule $R \neq O_{A,B} \implies L_{C,A}RL_{B,D} = L_{C,D}$ hold for all $R \in \mathtt{Mor}(A, B)$ and $C, D \in \mathcal{O}$.

All the indices of elements and operations are usually omitted for brevity and can easily be reinvented. □

A categorical formalism for the partial operations has first been used in [4]. The following computational rules—well-known in the homogeneous case—may be proven from these axioms without applying the Tarski rule; see [16].

Proposition 3. i) $OR = RO = O$;

ii) $R \subset S \implies QR \subset QS,\ RQ \subset SQ$; (monotonicity);

[1] Ernst Schröder (1841–1902), Alfred Tarski (1911–1983).

iii) $Q(R \sqcap S) \subset QR \sqcap QS, \quad (R \sqcap S)Q \subset RQ \sqcap SQ$ ($\sqcap$-subdistributivity),
$Q(R \sqcup S) = QR \sqcup QS, \quad (R \sqcup S)Q = RQ \sqcup SQ$ ($\sqcup$-distributivity);

iv) $(R^\top)^\top = R$;

v) $(RS)^\top = S^\top R^\top$;

vi) $R \subset S \iff R^\top \subset S^\top$;

vii) $\overline{R}^\top = \overline{R^\top}$;

viii) $(R \sqcup S)^\top = R^\top \sqcup S^\top$;
$(R \sqcap S)^\top = R^\top \sqcap S^\top$;

ix) $QR \sqcap S \subset (Q \sqcap SR^\top)(R \sqcap Q^\top S)$. (Dedekind rule) □

We call a relation R **univalent** (or functional) if $R^\top R \subset I$. If R satisfies $I \subset RR^\top$ (or equivalently if $L \subset RL$), then R is said to be **total**. If these requirements are both satisfied, i.e., if R resembles a total and univalent function, we will often speak of a **mapping**. A relation R is called injective, surjective and bijective, if $R^\top$ is univalent, total, or both, respectively. From the results concerning partial functions, we need the following:

$$Q \text{ univalent} \implies RQ \sqcap S = (R \sqcap SQ^\top)Q \text{ for all relations } R, S, \tag{1}$$

$$Q \text{ univalent} \implies \begin{array}{l}\text{For every relation } R\text{:}\\ R \subset Q, RL \supset QL \text{ if and only if } R = Q,\end{array} \tag{2}$$

$$R \text{ mapping} \implies R\overline{S} = \overline{RS} \text{ for all relations } S. \tag{3}$$

4. Direct Product

Most operations involve several arguments and not just one. Using relational algebra as a programming calculus, therefore, requires a means to deal with n-ary functions. First we study direct products in a heterogeneous setting.

Definition 4. Given two relations π and ρ, we call

$$(\pi, \rho) \quad \text{a } \mathbf{direct\ product} \quad :\iff \quad \begin{cases} \pi^\top \pi = I, & \rho^\top \rho = I, \\ \pi\pi^\top \sqcap \rho\rho^\top = I, & \pi^\top \rho = L. \end{cases}$$ □

In particular, π, ρ are mappings; usually called **natural projections.**

While in category theory the universal characterization of a direct product works second-order as an infimum definition, the present one is in equational style. It becomes a first-order definition if interpreted in the usual way.

The concept of projections and of some kind of product in connection with algebras of first-order logic and, especially, with relational algebras appears as early as 1946 with the work on Projective Algebra [11] and since 1953 by Tarski in papers one should now access via [20]. Later on, de Roever [10], Schmidt [18], Schmidt and Ströhlein [16], Zierer [23], Berghammer and Zierer [7], and Backhouse et al. [1], introduced the product and projections either as data types or as operations.

5. Homomorphisms and Isomorphisms

We introduce a notion of homomorphism inside a relation algebra (not between relation algebras). If some structure is to be mapped homomorphically into another one, so that *its structure is preserved*, one needs mappings (these mappings are relations) to relate the structures (the structure is a relation). The structures in question may be relational (as graphs or orderings) or algebraic (as groups or fields). They may consist of more than one relation; although, in order to present the principle, a structure given by one relation will suffice.

Definition 5. If B and B' are relations, we call the pair Φ, Ψ a **homomorphism** from B to B', provided Φ, Ψ are mappings and $B \subset \Phi B' \Psi^{\mathsf{T}}$. □

Using $\Phi^{\mathsf{T}}\Phi \subset I$ and $I \subset \Phi\Phi^{\mathsf{T}}$, one immediately sees that $B \subset \Phi B' \Psi^{\mathsf{T}}$ is equivalent to each of the following three inclusions $B\Psi \subset \Phi B', \Phi^{\mathsf{T}} B \Psi \subset B'$, $\Phi^{\mathsf{T}} B \subset B' \Psi^{\mathsf{T}}$. So the equivalent conditions for homomorphy are produced in a cyclic way by suitably multiplying by Φ, Ψ.

Definition 6. Let relations B, B', and Φ, Ψ be given. We call the pair Φ, Ψ an **isomorphism** if both Φ, Ψ and $\Phi^{\mathsf{T}}, \Psi^{\mathsf{T}}$ are homomorphisms. □

Thus, an isomorphism is characterized by the following conditions

$$\Phi, \Psi \text{ are bijective mappings}, \qquad B\Psi \subset \Phi B', \qquad B'\Psi^{\mathsf{T}} \subset \Phi^{\mathsf{T}} B.$$

The two inclusions on the right may equally well be replaced by those, cyclically produced, equivalent conditions from above. If Φ, Ψ is an isomorphism, then each of the cyclically produced homomorphy conditions becomes an equality:

$$B = \Phi B' \Psi^{\mathsf{T}}, \quad B\Psi = \Phi B', \quad \Phi^{\mathsf{T}} B \Psi = B', \quad \Phi^{\mathsf{T}} B = B' \Psi^{\mathsf{T}}.$$

However, these four equations are no longer equivalent to one another if Φ, Ψ are not bijective.

6. Homomorphisms of Algebraic Structures

As we have seen, our homomorphisms of relational structures are not characterized by equations. Now we consider an *algebraic* structure, as opposed to a relational structure, i.e. we assume that the relations considered are mappings.

Proposition 7. Let mappings B and B' be given and let Φ, Ψ be mappings.

i) $$B\Psi \subset \Phi B' \iff B\Psi = \Phi B'.$$

ii) *Each* of the following three equations implies $B\Psi = \Phi B'$:

$$B = \Phi B' \Psi^{\mathsf{T}}, \quad \Phi^{\mathsf{T}} B \Psi = B', \quad \Phi^{\mathsf{T}} B = B' \Psi^{\mathsf{T}}.$$

For any other two of the four equations there exist examples where one is satisfied while the other is not.

Proof: i) In $B\Psi \subset \Phi B'$, the relation $\Phi B'$ is univalent, since Φ and B' are mappings. The domains $B\Psi L = L = \Phi B' L$ of $B\Psi$ and $\Phi B'$ coincide, because all the relations are mappings total. So we may use (2) and obtain $B\Psi = \Phi B'$.

ii) From any of the equations, $B\Psi \subset \Phi B'$ may be obtained by cyclic permutation, so that using (i) we have $B\Psi = \Phi B'$. □

The condition $B\Psi \subset \Phi B'$ for homomorphy, therefore, may be used for algebraic as well as for relational structures. The use of the equation $B\Psi = \Phi B'$ is restricted to algebraic structures.

Now, we return to the direct product. For the Cartesian product to be uniquely determined, we need to show that there can be no two essentially distinct pairs of natural projections π, ρ and π', ρ'. Being not essentially distinct means that they are equal *up to isomorphism.* We leave the question open whether projections π, ρ do at all exist—in a given relation algebra they need not. Assuming that two different direct products are given with isomorphic component sets, we now establish an isomorphism between them.

Proposition 8. (*Monomorphic characterization of direct products*). Let direct products (π, ρ) and (π', ρ') and bijective mappings Φ, Ψ be given. Whenever the products $\pi\Phi\pi'^{\mathsf{T}}$, $\rho\Psi\rho'^{\mathsf{T}}$ are defined, then $\Xi := \pi\Phi\pi'^{\mathsf{T}} \sqcap \rho\Psi\rho'^{\mathsf{T}}$ is a bijective mapping satisfying $\pi\Phi = \Xi\pi'$ and $\rho\Psi = \Xi\rho'$. Therefore, Ξ gives rise to an isomorphism with respect to the direct product structure: The pair Φ, Ξ is an isomorphism from π to π' and Ψ, Ξ from ρ to ρ', respectively.

Proof: Using (1) and univalence of π', we obtain

$$\Xi\pi' = (\pi\Phi\pi'^{\mathsf{T}} \sqcap \rho\Psi\rho'^{\mathsf{T}})\pi' = \pi\Phi \sqcap \rho\Psi\rho'^{\mathsf{T}}\pi' = \pi\Phi \sqcap \rho\Psi L = \pi\Phi.$$

Other isomorphism formulae for π and ρ may be derived similarly. We now show that Ξ is a mapping. Since π' and ρ' are mappings, we can use (3):

$$\begin{aligned}\Xi\overline{I} = \Xi\overline{\pi'\pi'^{\mathsf{T}} \sqcap \rho'\rho'^{\mathsf{T}}} &= \Xi(\pi'\overline{\pi'^{\mathsf{T}}} \sqcup \rho'\overline{\rho'^{\mathsf{T}}}) = \Xi\pi'\overline{\pi'^{\mathsf{T}}} \sqcup \Xi\rho'\overline{\rho'^{\mathsf{T}}}\\ &= \pi\Phi\overline{\pi'^{\mathsf{T}}} \sqcup \rho\Psi\overline{\rho'^{\mathsf{T}}} = \overline{\pi\Phi\pi'^{\mathsf{T}} \sqcap \rho\Psi\rho'^{\mathsf{T}}} = \overline{\Xi}.\end{aligned}$$

Due to symmetry, Ξ^{T} is a mapping and Ξ a bijective mapping. □

7. ∇-Extended Abstract Relational Algebra

Let us now introduce an axiomatization for products in a homogeneous algebra.

Definition 9. A ∇-**extended (homogeneous abstract) relational algebra** is a structure $(\mathcal{R}, \sqcup, \sqcap, ^-, \circ, ^{\mathsf{T}}, \nabla)$ over a non-empty set $\mathcal{R}$, such that

i) $(\mathcal{R}, \sqcup, \sqcap, ^-, \circ, ^{\mathsf{T}})$ is a homogeneous relation algebra in the sense of Def. 1,
ii) $R\nabla S = R(I\nabla L) \sqcap S(L\nabla I)$,
iii) $(R\nabla S)(P\nabla Q)^{\mathsf{T}} = RP^{\mathsf{T}} \sqcap SQ^{\mathsf{T}}$,
iv) $(I\nabla L)^{\mathsf{T}}\nabla(L\nabla I)^{\mathsf{T}} \subset I$. □

With regard to ∇, the following basic results can easily be proven:

$$X \subset U,\ Y \subset V \implies (X\nabla Y) \subset (U\nabla V) \qquad \text{isotonicity,}$$
$$R(X\nabla Y) \subset (RX\nabla RY) \qquad \text{subdistributivity,}$$
$$(((I\nabla L)^{\mathsf{T}}R)\nabla((L\nabla I)^{\mathsf{T}}S))^{\mathsf{T}} = ((I\nabla L)^{\mathsf{T}}R^{\mathsf{T}})\nabla((L\nabla I)^{\mathsf{T}}S^{\mathsf{T}}) \qquad \text{transposition rule.}$$

It is a result of Tarski (see [19, 20]) that a predicate logic formula can be expressed relation-algebraically, if and only if its predicate-logic form can be expressed using at most 3 variables. So relational algebra is inferior in expressive power to predicate logic. However, extended with a product using the above ∇-extension, it has the full expressive power of predicate logic. Everett and Ulam (and, later, Bednarek and Ulam [3]) when defining projective algebra, already extended Boolean algebra with three fundamental operations: two projections p_1 and p_2 and a product $\Box$. In doing so, they did not recognize—at least did not explicitly mention—the power of their combination with Peircean operations for the construction of a relational algebra over locally finite trees. Researchers involved in Computer Science starting from a categorical viewpoint were not aware of the fundamental character of the projections.

We now investigate the concept of homomorphism in the homogeneous setting. Given two relations B, B' we call the pair φ, ψ of univalent relations a **homomorphism** from B to B', if

$$B\psi \subset \varphi B', \quad B^{\mathsf{T}}L \subset \psi L, \quad BL \subset \varphi L.$$

This is closely related to the heterogeneous formalism, however, the totality of φ, ψ has been taken care of separately. Again, the rolled variants of the homomorphism condition can be used.

Let now two relations R, S be given and relations R', S' such that φ, ψ is an isomorphism from R to R' and φ, γ is an isomorphism from S to S'. We are going to prove that defining $\zeta := ((I\nabla L)^{\mathsf{T}}\psi)\nabla((L\nabla I)^{\mathsf{T}}\gamma)$ we obtain an isomorphism φ, ζ from $R\nabla S$ to $R'\nabla S'$.

First we show that ζ is univalent. To this end we start with

$$\begin{aligned}
\zeta^{\mathsf{T}}\zeta &= ((I\nabla L)^{\mathsf{T}}\psi)\nabla((L\nabla I)^{\mathsf{T}}\gamma)^{\mathsf{T}}\ ((I\nabla L)^{\mathsf{T}}\psi)\nabla((L\nabla I)^{\mathsf{T}}\gamma) \\
&= ((I\nabla L)^{\mathsf{T}}\psi^{\mathsf{T}})\nabla((L\nabla I)^{\mathsf{T}}\gamma^{\mathsf{T}})\ ((I\nabla L)^{\mathsf{T}}\psi^{\mathsf{T}})\nabla((L\nabla I)^{\mathsf{T}}\gamma^{\mathsf{T}})^{\mathsf{T}} \\
&= (I\nabla L)^{\mathsf{T}}\psi^{\mathsf{T}}\psi(I\nabla L) \sqcap (L\nabla I)^{\mathsf{T}}\gamma^{\mathsf{T}}\gamma(L\nabla I) \\
&\subset (I\nabla L)^{\mathsf{T}}(I\nabla L) \sqcap (L\nabla I)^{\mathsf{T}}(L\nabla I) = (I\nabla L)^{\mathsf{T}}\ \nabla\ (L\nabla I)^{\mathsf{T}} \subset I.
\end{aligned}$$

Next, we prove one of the homomorphism conditions:

$$\begin{aligned}
(R\nabla S)\zeta &= (R\nabla S)\ (((I\nabla L)^{\mathsf{T}}\psi)\nabla((L\nabla I)^{\mathsf{T}}\gamma)) \\
&= (R\nabla S)\ (((I\nabla L)^{\mathsf{T}}\psi^{\mathsf{T}})\nabla((L\nabla I)^{\mathsf{T}}\gamma^{\mathsf{T}}))^{\mathsf{T}} \\
&= R\psi(I\nabla L) \sqcap S\gamma(L\nabla I) = \varphi R'(I\nabla L) \sqcap \varphi S'(L\nabla I) \\
&= \varphi(R'(I\nabla L) \sqcap S'(L\nabla I)) = \varphi(R'\nabla S').
\end{aligned}$$

Finally, one of the totality conditions is proved leaving the other to the reader:

$$\begin{aligned}
(R\nabla S)L &\subset (\varphi R'\psi^{\mathsf{T}}\nabla\varphi S'\gamma^{\mathsf{T}})L = (\varphi R'\psi^{\mathsf{T}}(I\nabla L) \sqcap \varphi S'\gamma^{\mathsf{T}}(L\nabla I))L \\
&= \varphi(R'\psi^{\mathsf{T}}(I\nabla L) \sqcap S'\gamma^{\mathsf{T}}(L\nabla I))L \subset \varphi L.
\end{aligned}$$

8. π, ρ via ∇

We are now going to compare the product axiomatizations of the two approaches. This is a little bit complicated as it means a comparison of results in a homogeneous and in a heterogeneous relation algebra. So when simulating one feature in the other type of algebra, we cannot in all cases expect textually equal results. While, in the homogeneous algebra, we work with partial identities such as δ_X, δ_Y resembling the identity on the domain and on the range side of a relation, we let applicability of operations in the heterogeneous algebra be regulated by the ordinary category mechanism.

Let now a ∇-extended homogeneous relation algebra be given in which we consider partial identities, i.e., relations contained in I. Certain partial identities show an additional structure specific for products. It is easy to prove that transposition of partial identities is the identical operation and that composition of a partial identity with itself is idempotent, i.e., $\delta \subset I$ implies $\delta^{\mathsf{T}} = \delta = \delta\delta$.

Proposition 10. Let three partial identities $\delta_X, \delta_Y, \delta_P$ be given satisfying

$$\delta_P = (\delta_X \nabla L)^{\mathsf{T}}(\delta_X \nabla L) \sqcap (L \nabla \delta_Y)^{\mathsf{T}}(L \nabla \delta_Y).$$

Then it is possible to define two relations $\pi_\delta := (\delta_X \nabla L)^{\mathsf{T}}, \rho_\delta := (L \nabla \delta_Y)^{\mathsf{T}}$ such that the intentions of Definition 4 are met in the following form:

$$\pi_\delta \pi_\delta^{\mathsf{T}} \sqcap \rho_\delta \rho_\delta^{\mathsf{T}} = \delta_P, \quad \pi_\delta^{\mathsf{T}} \pi_\delta = \delta_X, \quad \rho_\delta^{\mathsf{T}} \rho_\delta = \delta_Y, \quad \pi_\delta^{\mathsf{T}} \rho_\delta = \delta_X L \sqcap L \delta_Y.$$

Proof. Applying (9.iii) we derive, e. g., for π_δ:

$$\pi_\delta^{\mathsf{T}} \pi_\delta = ((\delta_X \nabla L)^{\mathsf{T}})^{\mathsf{T}}(\delta_X \nabla L)^{\mathsf{T}} = (\delta_X \nabla L)(\delta_X \nabla L)^{\mathsf{T}} = \delta_X \delta_X^{\mathsf{T}} \sqcap L L^{\mathsf{T}} = \delta_X \sqcap L = \delta_X.$$

From the definition of π_δ, ρ_δ, our hypotheses on $\delta_X, \delta_Y, \delta_P$, and reducing double transposition, we have

$$\pi_\delta \pi_\delta^{\mathsf{T}} \sqcap \rho_\delta \rho_\delta^{\mathsf{T}} = (\delta_X \nabla L)^{\mathsf{T}}((\delta_X \nabla L)^{\mathsf{T}})^{\mathsf{T}} \sqcap (L \nabla \delta_Y)^{\mathsf{T}}((L \nabla \delta_Y)^{\mathsf{T}})^{\mathsf{T}} = \delta_P.$$

Finally, eliminating double transposition and applying (9.iii) yields

$$\pi_\delta^{\mathsf{T}} \rho_\delta = (\delta_X \nabla L)(L \nabla \delta_Y)^{\mathsf{T}} = \delta_X L^{\mathsf{T}} \sqcap L \delta_Y^{\mathsf{T}} = \delta_X L \sqcap L \delta_Y. \qquad \square$$

For relations $R \subset L\delta_X, S \subset L\delta_Y$, we can now prove that $R \nabla S = R\pi_\delta^{\mathsf{T}} \sqcap S\rho_\delta^{\mathsf{T}}$.

9. ∇ via π, ρ

Let a heterogeneous relation algebra be given and let π, ρ be a direct product. We define for this product an operation with the full notation ${}_\pi\nabla_\rho^C$ adapting the ∇-operation to the heterogeneous setting.

If we say that an element p of a relation algebra is a **point** if $O \neq p = pL$ and $pp^{\mathsf{T}} \subset I$, we have a means of characterizing *elements* of a set—a task often occurring in practice. A relation algebra is said to satisfy the point axiom provided that for every relation $R \neq O$ there exist points x, y such that $xy^{\mathsf{T}} \subset R$. Relation algebras with point axiom are known to be representable.

Proposition 11. If a direct product (π, ρ) is given such that $\pi \in \mathtt{Mor}(P, A)$ and $\rho \in \mathtt{Mor}(P, B)$, then for all objects C of the category the following operation can be defined

$${}_\pi\nabla_\rho^C : \mathtt{Mor}(C, A) \times \mathtt{Mor}(C, B) \longrightarrow \mathtt{Mor}(C, P), \qquad R \;{}_\pi\nabla_\rho^C\; S := R\pi^{\mathsf{T}} \sqcap S\rho^{\mathsf{T}}.$$

For these operations, the intention of (9.ii) is met in the following form:

$$R \;{}_\pi\nabla_\rho^C\; S = R(I_A \;{}_\pi\nabla_\rho^A\; L_{A,B}) \sqcap S(L_{B,A} \;{}_\pi\nabla_\rho^B\; I_B).$$

Condition (9.iv) reads as

$$(I_A \;{}_\pi\nabla_\rho^A\; L_{A,B})^\top \;{}_\pi\nabla_\rho^P\; (L_{B,A} \;{}_\pi\nabla_\rho^B\; I_B)^\top \subset I_P.$$

If the point axiom is satisfied, we have (9.iii) as

$$(R \;{}_\pi\nabla_\rho^C\; S)(X \;{}_\pi\nabla_\rho^D\; Y)^\top = RX^\top \sqcap SY^\top.$$

Proof. First we show that $I_A \;{}_\pi\nabla_\rho^A\; L_{A,B} = I_A\pi^\top \sqcap L_{A,B}\rho^\top = \pi^\top \sqcap L_{A,P} = \pi^\top$ and, by analogy, $L_{B,A} \;{}_\pi\nabla_\rho^B\; I_B = \rho^\top$. With these two identities, the first statement reduces to the definition of the operator. The second is proven by

$$(I_A \;{}_\pi\nabla_\rho^A\; L_{A,B})^\top \;{}_\pi\nabla_\rho^P\; (L_{B,A} \;{}_\pi\nabla_\rho^B\; I_B)^\top = \pi^{\top\top} \;{}_\pi\nabla_\rho^P\; \rho^{\top\top} = \pi\pi^\top \sqcap \rho\rho^\top = I_P.$$

The third statement needs an additional assumption. Using the point axiom, however, the proof is rather trivial. It is left to the reader. □

It is, therefore, possible to prove (9.iii) in a representable algebra. For relation algebras without point axiom, however, only "$\subset$" can be proven instead of "$=$" in (9.iii). One might ask whether this statement could be proven without assuming the point axiom, i.e., for nonrepresentable algebras. We have tried this very hard over the years. The extensive work on conjugate quasi-projections in [20] shows that Tarski and Givant also felt that such a result was necessary.

At first sight, it might seem that the axiomatization of heterogeneous relation algebras is too weak compared with that of a ∇-extended abstract relational algebra. However, it turns out that there is a difficult model-theoretic problem. Following this AMAST conference, Roger Maddux has indeed shown (see [15]) that according to Gunther Schmidt's unsharpness conjecture, there exist models of heterogeneous relation algebras that fail to satisfy (9.iii). Among these models, some are to be expected to closely resemble Computer Science problems of concurrency and observability in the presence of parallelism.

10. Representability of ∇-Extended Relational Algebras

The question discussed before is closely related to the representability problem for ∇-extended abstract relational algebras which is an object of ongoing research. As was discussed in [2], ∇-extended abstract relational algebras are representable if we add to the above mentioned axioms the following one,

$(*)\qquad O \neq R \subset (L\nabla L) \quad \Longrightarrow \quad$ There exist v, w with $O \neq (v\nabla w) \subset R$.

Then representability can be proven in the following way:

Proposition 12. If α is an atom, so is $(\alpha\nabla\alpha)$, provided $(*)$ holds.

Proof. Assume a relation $O \neq \beta \subset (\alpha\nabla\alpha)$ to be given. By $(*)$ there are v, w such that $O \neq (v\nabla w) \subset \beta$. It is an easy consequence that by (9.iii)

$$v \sqcap wL = (v\nabla w)(I\nabla L)^\top \subset \beta(I\nabla L)^\top \subset (\alpha\nabla\alpha)(I\nabla L)^\top = \alpha \sqcap \alpha L = \alpha.$$

Since α is an atom and $v \sqcap wL \neq O$, we obtain $\alpha = v \sqcap wL \subset v$ and, similarly, $\alpha \subset w$. Now, $(\alpha \nabla \alpha) \subset (v \nabla w) \subset \beta$, or actually $\beta = (\alpha \nabla \alpha)$. □

Proposition 13. Every atom is a univalent relation.

Proof. First we prove that for any atom α we have $\alpha(I \nabla I) = (\alpha \nabla \alpha)$. We have "$\subset$" by ∇-subdistributivity and "$=$" since α is an atom for which $O \neq \alpha(I \nabla I)$. Having this result in mind, we prove

$$\alpha\overline{I} \sqcap \alpha I = (\alpha \nabla \alpha)(\overline{I} \nabla I)^{\mathsf{T}} = \alpha(I \nabla I)(\overline{I} \nabla I)^{\mathsf{T}} = \alpha(I\overline{I} \sqcap II) = O,$$

which is obviously equivalent with univalence of α. □

Hence, by a well-known result (see [14]), the ∇-extended abstract relational algebra is representable, provided axiom $(*)$ is satisfied, since its atoms are functional (i.e., univalent).

11. Comparison

We have shown that one approach may more or less directly simulate the other; so either one could be taken, the Rio approach with partial identities, as well as the Munich approach using heterogeneous relations. Using partial identities, products of nonfitting relations will yield the null relation, whereas a supporting computer system such as RALF ([8]) or RELVIEW ([5]) should refuse to operate on nonfitting relations.

A second difference between the two approaches is with respect to the existence of models. In the heterogeneous case, on can work with small models such as the set of all boolean $n \times n, m \times m, n \times m, m \times n$-matrices, which certainly exists. In contrast, already the very first example in the other case is burdened with the question of whether the base set of all the partial identities is free of set-theoretical antinomies.

Furthermore, heterogeneous relations fit neatly to the way of thinking with sorts or types in Computer Science. Working with matrices and vectors might contribute for engineers to feel comfortable since they are accustomed to them.

There is one further difference. When working with relations $R \subset X \times Y$ between sorts and types, one has the possibility of distinguishing the categorical object X from the domain RL where the relation is defined. This difference, to which computer scientists are very much accustomed is usually hidden when using partial identities, since then one would have to manipulate *two* partial identities to handle R fully.

Acknowledgement. We gratefully acknowledge the comments of Claudia Hattensperger, Wolfram Kahl, Peter Kempf, Michael Winter, and not least Roger Maddux for detailed comments and suggestions.

12. References

[1] R. C. Backhouse, P. J. de Bruin, P. Hoogendijk, G. Malcolm, J. van der Woude: Polynomial relators. Computing Science Notes, Dept. Mathematics and Computing Science, Eindhoven Univ. of Technology, May 1991

[2] G. BAUM, A. HAEBERER, P. VELOSO: On the Representability of the Abstract Relational Algebra, IGPL Newsletter 1, 3 (September 1992) European Foundation for Logic, Language, and Information, Interest Group on Programming Logic

[3] A. R. BEDNAREK, S. ULAM: Projective algebra and the calculus of relations. J. Symb. Logic 43, 56–64 (1978)

[4] R. BERGHAMMER, G. SCHMIDT: A relational view on gotos and dynamic logic. In: Schneider, H.J., Göttler, H. (eds.): Proc. Conf. Graphtheoret. Concepts in Comput. Sci., June 16–18, 1982, Neunkirchen a. Br., 13–24, Hanser 1982

[5] R. BERGHAMMER, G. SCHMIDT: The RELVIEW-System. Notes to a system presentation. In: Choffrut, C., Jantzen, M. (Eds.): Proc. 8th Ann. Symp. Theoret. Aspects of Comput. Sci. Lect. Notes Comput. Sci. 480, 535 - 536, Springer 1991

[6] R. BERGHAMMER, G. SCHMIDT, H. ZIERER: Symmetric quotients and domain constructions. Inform. Proc. Letters 33, 3, 163–168 (1989/90)

[7] R. BERGHAMMER, H. ZIERER: Relational algebraic semantics of deterministic and nondeterministic programs. Theoret. Comput. Sci. 43, 123–147 (1986)

[8] R. BRETHAUER: Ein Formelmanipulationssystem zur computergestützten Beweisführung in der Relationenalgebra, Univ. der Bundeswehr München, Diplomarb. (1991)

[9] L. CHIN, A. TARSKI: Distributive and modular laws in the arithmetic of relation algebras. University of California Publications in Mathematics (new series) 1 (1951)

[10] W. P. DE ROEVER: Recursive program schemes: semantics and proof theory. Ph. D.-Thesis, Math. Centrum Tracts, Amsterdam, 1974

[11] C. J. EVERETT, S. ULAM: Projective algebra I. Amer. J. Math. 68, 77–88 (1946)

[12] A. HAEBERER, P. VELOSO: Partial relations for program derivation: Adequacy, Inevitability, and Expressiveness. In: Möller, B. (ed.): Constructing programs from specifications. Proc. IFIP TC 2/WG 2.1, Pacific Grove, USA, North-Holland 1991

[13] A. HAEBERER, P. VELOSO, P. ELUSTONDO: Towards a relational calculus for software construction. Doc. 640-BUR-5, 41st IFIP WG 2.1, Chester, GB (1990)

[14] B. JÓNSSON, A. TARSKI: Boolean algebras with operators, Part II. Amer. J. Math. 74, 127–167 (1952)

[15] R. MADDUX: On the derivation of identities involving projection functions. Draft paper July 29, 1993

[16] G. SCHMIDT, T. STRÖHLEIN: Relation and Graphs – Discrete Mathematics for Computer Scientists. EATCS Monographs on Theoret. Comput. Sci., Springer 1993

[17] G. SCHMIDT, T. STRÖHLEIN: Relation algebras: Concept of points and representability, Discrete Math. 54, 83–92 (1985)

[18] G. SCHMIDT: Programs as partial graphs I: Flow equivalence and correctness. Theoret. Comput. Sci. 15, 1–25 (1981)

[19] A. TARSKI: On the calculus of relations. J. Symb. Logic 6, 73–89 (1941)

[20] A. TARSKI, S. GIVANT: A formalization of set theory without variables. Amer. Math. Soc. Coll. Publ. 41, Providence, Rhode Island, 1987

[21] P. VELOSO, A. HAEBERER: A finitary relational algebra for classical first-order logic. Bull. of the Section on Logic of the Polish Academy of Sciences 20, 52–62 (1991)

[22] P. VELOSO, A. HAEBERER, G. BAUM: Formal program construction within an extended calculus of binary relations. J. Symb. Comp. (to appear)

[23] H. ZIERER: Relation algebraic domain constructions. Theoret. Comput. Sci. 87, 163–188 (1991)

Specifying Type Systems with Multi-Level Order-Sorted Algebra

Martin Erwig
FernUniversität Hagen, Praktische Informatik IV
58084 Hagen, Germany, erwig@fernuni-hagen.de

Abstract

We propose to use order-sorted algebras (OSA) on multiple levels to describe languages together with their type systems. It is demonstrated that even advanced aspects can be modeled, including, parametric polymorphism, complex relationships between different sorts of an operation's rank, the specification of a variable number of parameters for operations, and type constructors using values (and not only types) as arguments.

The basic idea is to use a signature to describe a type system where sorts denote sets of type names and operations denote type constructors. The values of an algebra for such a signature are then used as sorts of another signature now describing a language having the previously defined type system. This way of modeling is not restricted to two levels, and we will show useful applications of three-level algebras.

1 Introduction

The concept of multi-level algebra (MLA) was initiated from our work on extending data models by new data types [2]. Although many-sorted algebra can be conveniently used to describe non-standard data models many important aspects remain unformalized. Even the generalization to OSA, though nicely expressing subtypes and the notions of inheritance and overloading (Section 2), is not able to model the powerful concept of parametric polymorphism. Parametric order-sorted algebra [4] offers a partial solution, but there are still dependencies that cannot be expressed. For example, it is not clear, in general, how to define a parametric module that is not allowed to accept an instance of itself as a parameter. This is needed, for instance, to define a sequence constructor that is not allowed to be nested. In contrast, this is possible with *two levels* of OSA which is demonstrated in Section 3. After introducing the notion of *lifting* in Section 4 we will consider three-level algebras in Section 5. In Section 6 we use the formalism developed thus far to specify type systems of data models. Finally, concluding remarks and a comparison with other approaches is given in Section 7.

2 Order-Sorted Algebra: Modeling Subtype Polymorphism and Overloading

An operation symbol that is used to denote different functions is said to be *overloaded*. When these functions are only loosely related, this is also called *ad hoc polymorphism*. On the other hand, the types on which the different functions operate may be related by subtyping, i.e., one argument type is a subset of another argument type for the same operation symbol. Then, no matter which function is taken, an application (whenever this makes sense) for one argument always yields the same result.[1] Such a situation is called *subtype polymorphism*. If a function is applicable to a class of types without needing to know the exact extent or structure of any type, this is an example of *parametric polymorphism*. This includes the identity function (applicable to all types) and the length function (applicable to all sequences). The code for such functions is independent of the type parameter since it does not inspect objects of that type.

For standard definitions of OSA refer to [3]. Now, consider the following signature (on the left) for the polymorphic operation +.

types nat, int	**types** nat, int
order nat $\leq$ int	**order** nat $\leq$ int
funs 0: $\rightarrow$ int	**funs** 0: $\rightarrow$ nat
0: $\rightarrow$ nat	+: int $\times$ int $\rightarrow$ int
+: int $\times$ int $\rightarrow$ int	+: nat $\times$ nat $\rightarrow$ nat
+: int $\times$ nat $\rightarrow$ int	
+: nat $\times$ int $\rightarrow$ int	
+: nat $\times$ nat $\rightarrow$ nat	

Even this small example indicates that repeating an operation with many different ranks may become very cumbersome. Instead, it would be nice to define an operation with a "high" rank (with respect to the subtype order $\leq$) once and let the lower ranks be inferred automatically. This can be achieved by using a *signature specification* (shown on the right).

Definition 1 Any order-sorted signature $(S, \leq, \Sigma)$ is at the same time a *signature specification*. The *induced signature* $(S, \leq, IND(\Sigma))$ is defined by $IND(\Sigma) = \Sigma \cup \{\sigma_{w'',s} \mid \exists\, \sigma \in \Sigma_{w,s} : (w'' \leq w \wedge \forall\, \sigma \in \Sigma_{w',s'} : w' \leq w \Rightarrow w' \leq w'')\}$ □

Using signature specifications means to factorize operations' types along a $\leq$-chain of their arguments. The induced signature amounts to a feature which is termed *inheritance* in object-oriented languages.

Now suppose we have to define an operation "<" on numbers and strings (which are assumed to be not related by $\leq$). One approach is to give each signature entry separately. This becomes tedious as the number of data types for which "<" is defined grows. So it is much more convenient to group all the sorts in a *kind* [1], e.g., ORD = {nat, int, str}, and then to define all signature entries by a type scheme:

$$\forall\, ord \in \mathsf{ORD}.\ <:\ ord \times ord \rightarrow \mathsf{bool}$$

Apart from saving space, this notation is more descriptive w.r.t. the language being defined since the overloading of "<" is not "scattered" over different places in the signature. To use such type schemes in signatures we need the notion of an *extended signature specification*. Therefore, let K be the set of kinds where a kind is a set of sorts. The idea is to allow kind variables to be used like sorts in signatures.

[1] For example, the + operation is defined on $\mathbb{N}$ and $\mathbb{R}$. Formally, we have two different functions $+_{\mathbb{N}}$ and $+_{\mathbb{R}}$, but their behavior is identical on $\mathbb{N} \cap \mathbb{R}$.

Definition 2 Given a set of sorts S and a kind-sorted family $Y = \{Y_k \mid k \in K\}$ of disjoint sets of variables, an *Y-extended signature specification* is an order-sorted signature $(S', \leq, \Sigma)$ with $S' = S \cup Y$ and $\leq \subseteq S' \times S'$. The *induced signature* $(S', IND(\leq), IND(\Sigma))$ is defined by[2]

$$IND(\Sigma) = \{\sigma_{w',s'} \mid \exists\, \sigma \in \Sigma_{w,s} : (w', s') = [s''/y](w, s) \wedge y \in Y_k \wedge s'' \in k\}$$
$$IND(\leq) = \{(s', t') \mid \exists\, (s, t) \in \leq\colon\ (s', t') = [s''/y](s, t) \wedge y \in Y_k \wedge s'' \in k\} \quad \square$$

Note that we now have two levels of signature specification available, i.e., the order-sorted signature induced by an extended signature specification can again be regarded as a signature specification (in the sense of Definition 1) which itself induces an order-sorted signature.

We observe that the $\leq$ order relates types in a way that induces kinds similarly to the above example: Each type s defines a kind SUB_s which contains s and all subtypes (with respect to $\leq$) of s. Subtype polymorphism can then be expressed by using kind variables ranging over such SUB kinds, or, to put it in other words, we could, in principle, define OSA in terms of many-sorted algebra plus an appropriate kind structure.

3 Two-Level Algebra: Describing Parametric Polymorphism and Type Constructors

A type constructor takes one or more types as arguments and produces a new type as result. The sequence constructor (seq), e.g., takes a type, say, int, and produces the type containing all sequences of integers. Of course, seq may be applied to other types as well, but in some languages where nested sequences are not allowed (for instance, database languages) it must not be applied to sequence types. In that case, the argument types for seq are a proper subset of all types and can be grouped into an appropriate kind. Similarly, the result types form a kind, too.

We can regard kinds and type constructors as sorts and operations, respectively, of an order-sorted signature. The example of unnested sequences can then be expressed as shown below (nesting of sequences could be allowed by simply defining SEQ $\leq$ ARG).

typesystem UNNESTED
kinds ARG, SEQ
tcons int, str, bool: $\rightarrow$ ARG
    seq: ARG $\rightarrow$ SEQ

language LISTS
types from UNNESTED
funs nil: $\rightarrow$ *seq*
    cons: *arg* $\times$ seq(*arg*) $\rightarrow$ seq(*arg*)
    hd: seq(*arg*) $\rightarrow$ *arg*
    tl: seq(*arg*) $\rightarrow$ seq(*arg*)
    length: *seq* $\rightarrow$ int

Note that "$\forall$ *seq* $\in$ SEQ. *seq*" denotes the same types as "$\forall$ *arg* $\in$ ARG. seq(*arg*)". Thus, we can use *seq* in the type specifications for nil and length since we do not need to refer to the argument type of the respective sequences.

Also note carefully that type expressions containing variables like *seq* are not types themselves, but simply specifications of sets of types. One impact is that expressions like nil or cons(nil, nil) are not type-correct since the type of

[2] The notation $[s/y]t$ denotes the substitution of all occurrences of the variable y in t by s.

the overloading of nil cannot be resolved. This situation is called *predicative polymorphism* [10] and is certainly a somewhat restricted form of parametric polymorphism. The good thing about it is that we can have set-theoretical models, which is not true for more general forms of polymorphism.

The signature UNNESTED defines merely the typing of type constructors. The semantics usually consists of two parts: On the one hand, algebraic properties of type constructors can be specified by equations (for instance, associativity of a product operator). The set of sorts is then taken modulo such a specification (in our example this was not necessary). On the other hand, the effects of type constructors on the carrier sets need to be given by additional functions.

Definition 3 An order-sorted signature is a 1st-*level signature*, and an order-sorted algebra is a 1st-*level algebra*. Given an nth-level signature $(S', \leq', \Sigma')$ and an nth-level Σ'-algebra $\mathcal{B}$, an order sorted signature $(S, \leq, \Sigma)$ is an $n+1^{st}$-*level signature* depending on Σ' and $\mathcal{B}$ if $S = \bigcup_{s \in S'} s^{\mathcal{B}}$. A Σ-algebra $\mathcal{A}$ is an $n+1^{st}$-*level algebra* if for each $\sigma_{w,s} \in \Sigma'$ there is a functor $\overline{\sigma}_{w,s}$ (called *type constructor*) and if for each $s \in S$ such that $s = \sigma^{\mathcal{B}}_{w,s}(t_1, \ldots, t_n)$ (with $w = s_1 \ldots s_n$ and $t_i \in s_i^{\mathcal{B}}$ for $1 \leq i \leq n$) we have $s^{\mathcal{A}} = \overline{\sigma}_{w,s}(t_1^{\mathcal{A}}, \ldots, t_n^{\mathcal{A}})$. The functions $\overline{\sigma}_{w,s}$ define the *constructor semantics* for Σ', and $\mathcal{A}$ *depends* on (the higher level) $\mathcal{B}$ and the constructor semantics for Σ'. □

Note that the individual algebra levels are denoted by counting backwards (with regard to the construction history), i.e., an $n+1^{st}$-level algebra $\mathcal{A}$ depending on the nth-level algebra $\mathcal{B}$ is said to be on the first level whereas $\mathcal{B}$ is said to be on second level, etc.. In particular, when Σ' is used to describe types, we also say that Σ' is on *type level* and Σ is on *language level*. In the following we will always work with term algebras, i.e., we have, e.g., $\mathsf{ORD}^{\mathcal{B}} = \{\mathsf{nat}, \ldots\}$.

The constructor semantics for the seq constructor is defined by:

$$\mathsf{seq}(s)^{\mathcal{A}} = \overline{\mathsf{seq}}(s^{\mathcal{A}}) = (s^{\mathcal{A}})^*$$

4 Algebra Lifting

All type constructors presented so far have built new types from other types. But there are some type constructors that are also based on *values*. The array constructor, e.g., takes in addition to the component type two values of a scalar type. Other examples are constructors for fixed length strings or subranges.

In order to retain the clear separation of the kind/type/value levels Cardelli [1] proposes to "lift" values onto the type level. For instance, introduce for each value $n \in \mathsf{nat}$ a new type $\underline{n}$ with the carrier being $\underline{n}^{\mathcal{A}} = \{n\}$. Moreover, create a new kind, $\underline{\mathsf{nat}}$, with $\underline{\mathsf{nat}}^{\mathcal{B}} = \{\underline{n} \mid n \in \mathsf{nat}^{\mathcal{A}}\}$. Then array can be used exclusively on the type level, as in $\mathsf{array}(\underline{1}, \underline{9}, \mathsf{bool})$.

Let Σ'_L denote the set of type constructors that need lifted types. In order to specify a type system and a language using Σ'_L the following steps have to be performed (for a two-level algebra):

(i) Define the type system without Σ'_L. Call the signature Σ'_0.
(ii) Define Σ_0, the part of the language not needing types constructed by Σ'_L.
(iii) Perform lifting of Σ'_0 and Σ_0, and add Σ'_L to $\underline{\Sigma'_0}$, i.e., let $\Sigma' = \underline{\Sigma'_0} \cup \Sigma'_L$.
(iv) Finally, define Σ with regard to Σ'.

We can specify Σ_L together with Σ_0 in one step. Thus, array is defined by:[3]

typesystem ARRAYS
kinds ARR, ANY
order ARR $\leq$ ANY
tcons nat, int, str, bool: $\rightarrow$ ANY
array: $\underline{\text{nat}} \times \underline{\text{nat}} \times$ ANY $\rightarrow$ ARR

The constructor semantics is given by:

$$\text{array}(\underline{n}, \underline{m}, t)^{\mathcal{A}} = \overline{\text{array}}(\underline{n}^{\mathcal{A}}, \underline{m}^{\mathcal{A}}, t^{\mathcal{A}}) = \overline{\text{array}}(\{n\}, \{m\}, t^{\mathcal{A}}) = \{n, \ldots, m\} \rightarrow t^{\mathcal{A}}$$

Array operations can be defined by (assume quantifications "$\forall\ \underline{n}, \underline{m} \in \underline{\text{nat}}$"):

types from ARRAYS
order nat $\leq$ int
funs newarray: nat $\times$ nat $\times$ *any* $\rightarrow$ array($\underline{n}, \underline{m}$, *any*)
select: array($\underline{n}, \underline{m}$, *any*) $\times$ nat $\rightarrow$ *any*
update: array($\underline{n}, \underline{m}$, *any*) $\times$ nat $\times$ *any* $\rightarrow$ array($\underline{n}, \underline{m}$, *any*)

Note that with the above definition range checking (for select/update) is not expressible on the type level since an expression select(newarray(1,9,true),15) is type correct w.r.t. to the above signature. This can be remedied by using three levels of algebras. Another application of lifting arises in the modeling of operations with a variable numbers of parameters. Note that lifting of operations is also conceivable. Then type constructors taking predicates and denoting subtypes w.r.t. theses predicates can be defined.

5 Three-Level Algebras

Consider the function [ ] for constructing sequences, which is defined for an arbitrary number of arguments. The signature entries are:

[ ]: $\rightarrow$ *seq*
[ ]: *arg* $\rightarrow$ seq(*arg*)
[ ]: *arg* $\times$ *arg* $\rightarrow$ seq(*arg*)
...

To denote these signature entries we need for each argument type t a kind containing all product types over t. This can be achieved as follows: We define a *kind constructor* list (this is an operation on level three with the same semantics as seq). Now, list(K) denotes for a kind K all sequences of sorts from K. If, e.g., $K^{\mathcal{B}}_{\text{nat}} = \{\text{nat}\}$[4], the quantification "$\forall$ *natlist* $\in$ list(K_{nat})" binds the sequences $\langle\rangle$, $\langle\text{nat}\rangle$, $\langle\text{nat}, \text{nat}\rangle$, ... to *natlist*. The desired product types can be obtained by "inserting" a "$\times$" type constructor between each two adjacent types in a sort sequence. This is done by the higher order function fold:

$$\begin{aligned}
\overline{\text{fold}}(\sigma, \langle\rangle) &= \epsilon \\
\overline{\text{fold}}(\sigma, \langle t_1\rangle) &= t_1 \\
\overline{\text{fold}}(\sigma, \langle t_1, t_2, \ldots, t_n\rangle) &= \sigma(t_1, \overline{\text{fold}}(\sigma, \langle t_2, \ldots, t_n\rangle))
\end{aligned}$$

Now the type of [ ] (for nat-sequences only) can be specified by:

[ ]: fold($\times$, *natlist*) $\rightarrow$ seq(nat)

---

[3] We do not list lifted kinds explicitly.

[4] K_{nat} can be obtained by lifting.

A more precise account of this kind of specification requires higher order algebras [8] and lifting on higher levels. Finally, for the convenient specification of multi-level algebras we need a language that allows for the use of terms of all levels in the definition of operations' ranks. This is covered in the long version of this paper.

6 Specifying Data Models

A relation is a set of tuples, and the components of the tuples each have a fixed type and are named. In the "flat" relational model, relations are built only over atomic types, whereas in the NF^2 model tuples may contain whole relations. The relational model demonstrates the use of two languages on different levels:

(i) The first is the language of schemas, or, tuple types. A schema is a type, and we have operations on schemas (i.e., type constructors), such as adding an identifier/type pair or merging two schemas. Another type constructor builds relation types from schemas.
(ii) The second language is that of relational algebra working on relations that are instances of relation types. Operations on relations, such as **natjoin** or **select**, belong to the language level.

The following type system defines the operations on schemas and, of course, the **rel** constructor. The **fun** constructor will be needed for selection expressions.

typesystem RELMODEL
kinds TUP, REL, ATOM, FUN
tcons null: → TUP
  int, str, bool: → ATOM
  add: <u>str</u> × ATOM × TUP → TUP
  merge: TUP × TUP → TUP
  mix: TUP × TUP → TUP
  names: TUP → list(<u>str</u>)
  rel: TUP → REL
  fun: TUP × <u>bool</u> → FUN

Note that we use lifted strings as identifiers in tuples. **add**, **merge**, and **mix** are type constructors which will be used on the language level to perform pattern matching on relational schemas, and **names** yields the sequence of identifiers of a tuple.

As it stands, the structure of schemas is specified only very loosely. This would be sufficient as long as we considered only schemas (in fact, the constructor semantics for schema type constructors is not really needed since schemas are used on the language level only to build relations over them). However, being faced with the need to describe the constructor semantics of **rel** it is very helpful to fix a concrete representation for schemas, in particular, it is convenient to think of a schema as a sequence of (identifier, type name) pairs. This can be done by introducing on the third level a kind constructor **schema** which is defined to provide just this representation (see full paper). For now we just presume that representation of schemas. We have:

$$\langle (i_1, t_1), \ldots, (i_n, t_n) \rangle^{\mathcal{A}} = i_1^{\mathcal{A}} \times t_1^{\mathcal{A}} \times \ldots \times i_n^{\mathcal{A}} \times t_n^{\mathcal{A}}$$

Now we can assign a constructor semantics to **rel**.

$$\text{rel}(\langle(i_1,t_1),\ldots,(i_n,t_n)\rangle)^{\mathcal{A}} = \overline{\text{rel}}(i_1^{\mathcal{A}} \times t_1^{\mathcal{A}} \times \ldots \times i_n^{\mathcal{A}} \times t_n^{\mathcal{A}}) = 2^{i_1^{\mathcal{A}} \times t_1^{\mathcal{A}} \times \ldots \times i_n^{\mathcal{A}} \times t_n^{\mathcal{A}}}$$

With the auxiliary function *isect* we can give the following definitions for the remaining type constructors.

$$\begin{aligned} isect(s,s') &= \langle (i,a') \in s' \mid \exists a : (i,a) \in s \rangle \\ \text{add}(i,t,s) &= \text{merge}(\langle (i,t) \rangle, s) \\ \text{merge}(s,s') &= s \cdot (s' - isect(s,s')) \\ \text{mix}(s,s') &= \text{merge}(s,s') \cdot \langle (i',a) \mid \exists (i,a) \in isect(s,s') \rangle \\ \text{names}(s) &= \langle i \mid \exists (i,a) \in s \rangle \end{aligned}$$

(For simplicity we assume in the definition of mix that i' does not occur as an identifier in s or s'. Since i is a lifted string, say, $\underline{s}$, we can think of i' as a suitable renaming of s, say, s', resulting in $\underline{s'}$.)

Finally, we can define the language of relational algebra (we only give operations on relations and omit, e.g., comparison operators). The function tuple is needed to construct (one-tuple) relations from lifted strings and atomic values.

language RELALG
types from RELMODEL
funs tuple: $tup \to \text{rel}(tup)$
union: $rel \times rel \to rel$
project: $\text{rel}(\text{merge}(tup_1, tup_2)) \times \text{names}(tup_1) \to \text{rel}(tup_1)$
product: $\text{rel}(tup_1) \times \text{rel}(tup_2) \to \text{rel}(\text{mix}(tup_1, tup_2))$
natjoin: $\text{rel}(tup_1) \times \text{rel}(tup_2) \to \text{rel}(\text{merge}(tup_1, tup_2))$
select: $\text{rel}(tup) \times \text{fun}(tup, \text{bool}) \to \text{rel}(tup)$
attrib: $\text{add}(\underline{str}, atom, tup) \times \underline{str} \to atom$

The definition of an NF^2 model [14] can be obtained by simply adding an order specification REL $\leq$ ATOM to the type system. This means that attributes need not be atomic values any more. Otherwise, type system and language require no changes.

The two operations nest and unnest are defined by:

funs nest: $\text{names}(tup_1) \times \underline{str} \times \text{rel}(\text{merge}(tup_1, tup_2))$
$\to \text{rel}(\text{add}(\underline{str}, \text{rel}(tup_1), tup_2))$
unnest: $\text{rel}(\text{add}(\underline{str}, \text{rel}(tup_1), tup_2)) \times \underline{str} \to \text{rel}(\text{mix}(tup_1, tup_2))$

Note how nicely these typings reflect the fact that unnest is the inverse operation of nest.

7 Conclusions and Related Work

Two-level algebras were already used in [13] to specify categories with certain properties for theoretical investigation and in [7] for the formalization of the composition of specifications. Meinke [9] gives a categorical semantics for two-level specifications. In contrast, our concern is the specification of type systems, more specifically, the formal description of data models and query languages.

Unlike [13, 7, 9] MLA is not limited to two levels, and we have indicated that especially a third level can be extremely helpful: One usage is to describe overloading of operations with functions on different numbers of parameters. Another application is the generalization of certain type constructors (e.g., the definition of an array type constructor not only for a fixed index type but for a class of scalar index types). In some cases this also results in sharper type descriptions (the generalized array definition prevents out-of-range errors).

Another difference between [13, 7] and our work is that we employ more than only one sort on level two. This is necessary, for instance, to facilitate the description of a type constructor for unnested sequences.

Focusing on two levels and ignoring extensions, such as lifting, the work in [9] is in a sense more general than MLA since the first level (called "combinator signature") is fully parameterized by a second level whereas in MLA, a second level is fixed and a first level is constructed w.r.t. such a fixed second level; the dependency is "encapsulated" by construction. The advantage of our approach is that theorems which have to be proved in [9] are trivially true in MLA.

Finally, let us summarize some points counting in favor of using MLA and exhibiting its scope.

- All kinds of polymorphism (subtype, ad hoc, parametric) are describable within one formalism.
- Type systems can be easily extended by new structures. This is important to meet changing requirements of new applications.
- The definition of properties of type constructors (e.g., associativity) is separated from the constructor semantics.
- Recently, general approaches to the type checking of languages that use overloading in a systematic way have become available [11, 6, 12]. In many cases these methods are directly applicable to languages defined by MLA.

References

[1] L. Cardelli. Types for Data Oriented Languages. In *Conf. on Extending Database Technology*, LNCS 303, pp. 1–15, 1988.

[2] M. Erwig and R. H. Güting. Explicit Graphs in a Functional Model for Spatial Databases. Report 110, FernUniversität Hagen, 1991.

[3] M. Gogolla. Partially Ordered Sorts in Algebraic Specifications. In *9th Coll. on Trees in Algebra and Programming*, pp. 139–153, 1984.

[4] J. A. Goguen. Higher-Order Functions Considered Unnecessary for Higher-Order Programming. In D. A. Turner, ed., *Research Topics in Functional Programming*, pp. 309–352. Addison-Wesley, 1990.

[5] J. A. Goguen and J. Meseguer. Order-Sorted Algebra I. Report, SRI Int., 1989.

[6] S. Kaes. Type Inference in the Presence of Overloading, Subtyping and Recursive Types. In *ACM Conf. on Lisp and Functional Programming*, pp. 193–204, 1992.

[7] J. Leszczylowski and M. Wirsing. Polymorphism, Parameterization and Typing: An Algebraic Specification Perspective. In *STACS 91*, LNCS 480, pp. 1–15, 1991.

[8] K. Meinke. Universal Algebra in Higher Types. In *Workshop on Specification of Abstract Data Types*, LNCS 534, pp. 185–203, 1990.

[9] K. Meinke. Equational Specification of Abstract Types and Combinators. In *5th Workshop on Computer Science Logic*, LNCS 626, pp. 257–271, 1991.

[10] J. C. Mitchell. Type Systems for Programming Languages. In J. van Leeuwen, ed., *Handbook of Theoretical Computer Science, Vol. B*, pp. 367–458. Elsevier, 1990.

[11] T. Nipkow and C. Prehofer. Type Checking Type Classes. In *ACM Symp. on Principles of Programming Languages*, pp. 409–418, 1993.

[12] T. Nipkow and G. Snelting. Type Classes and Overloading Resolution via Order-Sorted Unification. In *Conf. on Func. Progr. and Comp. Arch.*, LNCS 523, pp. 1–14, 1991.

[13] A. Poigné. On Specifications, Theories, and Models with Higher Types. *Information and Control*, 68:1–46, 1986.

[14] H.-J. Schek and M. H. Scholl. The Relational Model with Relation-Valued Attributes. *Information Systems*, 11:137–147, 1986.

An Overview of the SODA System

Peter Thiemann
thiemann@informatik.uni-tuebingen.de
Wilhelm-Schickard-Institut, Universität Tübingen
Sand 13, D-72076 Tübingen, Germany

1 Introduction

We propose a system for software development which is aimed at merging the advantages of using methods from algebraic specification with features known from object-oriented systems, namely rapid prototyping, evolutionary programming, and reusability. Our proposal is a refinement of earlier work where we proposed to access functionally specified abstract data types from imperative modules [4].

A project is composed from modules with the usual operations of selective import and export, parametrization, and renaming. There are three kinds of modules. Modules can be either functional, state machine, or imperative.

Functional modules are specified in the executable first-order specification language SODA (specification in order-sorted data algebras). Data algebras are initial algebras of a modest extension of order-sorted algebra [2] by sort constructors and parametric polymorphism [5]. Derived functions are defined by recursive definitions as a conservative extension of the data algebra.

The other kinds of modules (state machine and imperative) describe the non-functional parts of a project (*e.g.*, interaction, database access). Their operations can not be used from functional modules. A state machine module defines a state and operations to destructively manipulate the state and/or provide information about the state to the outside.

Imperative modules play an important rôle for our system to be interesting for real world projects. At any point of the design process the implementation of a functional or state machine module can be replaced by an imperative module. Of course there is the requirement that replacements of functional modules remain side effect free and cannot have internal state.

For reasons of space we focus our attention here just to the data part of the underlying algebraic model[1]. The data algebra for functional and state machine modules is an extension of order-sorted algebra (OSA). While ordinary OSA provides parameterization only through module instantiation, we follow Hanus and others [3, 6, 1] by extending OSA with parametric polymorphic sort constructors and with a mechanism similar to record extensions as proposed by Wirth for the language Oberon [8, 9]. While Hanus and Smolka define two-level semantics for polymorphic structures, we give a one-level semantics as an algebra that employs truly polymorphic data values.

[1] A full version of the paper which also contains some proofs that have been omitted will be available as a technical report.

2 Preliminaries

$\wp^{fin}(M)$ denotes the set of finite subsets of M. M^* denotes the set of finite sequences (or words) over M. For a relation $R \subseteq A \times B$, $R^{-1} = \{(b,a) \in B \times A \mid (a,b) \in R\}$ denotes the inverse relation. For a relation $R \subseteq A \times A$, R^* denotes the reflexive and transitive closure of R.

Definition 2.1 (Ranked alphabet) A ranked alphabet $\Theta = (\Theta^{(l)})_{l \in \mathbb{N}}$ is a disjoint family of finite sets of *operator symbols*.

An operator symbol $\chi \in \Theta^{(l)}$ has *arity* l.

Definition 2.2 (Terms) Let V be a denumerable set of *variables*. The set $T_\Theta(V)$ of *Θ-terms over V* is the smallest subset of $(V \cup \bigcup_{l \in \mathbb{N}} \Theta^{(l)} \cup \{(,),,\})^*$ where $V \cup \Theta^{(0)} \subseteq T_\Theta(V)$, and for all $k > 0$ and $\chi \in \Theta^{(k)}$ and for all $t_i \in T_\Theta(V)$, $1 \leq i \leq k$, it holds that $\chi(t_1, \ldots, t_k) \in T_\Theta(V)$.

We write T_Θ for $T_\Theta(\emptyset)$. The function var: $T_\Theta(V) \to \wp^{fin}(V)$ yields the set of all variables occurring in a term. The *depth* of a term $d\colon T_\Theta(V) \to \mathbb{N}$ is inductively defined by $d(v) = 0$ for $v \in V$, $d(\chi) = 1$ for $\chi \in \Theta^{(0)}$ and $d(\chi(t_1, \ldots, t_k)) = 1 + d(t_1) + \cdots + d(t_k)$ for $\chi \in \Theta^{(k)}$, $k > 0$, $t_i \in T_\Theta(TV)$.

Definition 2.3 (Substitutions) A *substitution* is a function $\vartheta\colon V \to T_\Theta(V)$ where $\vartheta(v) \neq v$ only for finitely many $v \in V$. Denote the set of substitutions with range $T_\Theta(V)$ by Subst(Θ, V). We write $[t_1/v_1, \ldots, t_n/v_n]$ for the substitution that maps each v_i to t_i and leaves all other variables fixed. A substitution ϑ is extended to a function $\hat{\vartheta}\colon T_\Theta(V) \to T_\Theta(V)$ by $\hat{\vartheta}(v) = \vartheta(v)$ for all $v \in V$, for all $\chi \in \Theta^{(0)}$: $\hat{\vartheta}(\chi) = \chi$, and for all $k > 0$, $\chi \in \Theta^{(k)}$, and $t_i \in T_\Theta(V)$ for $1 \leq i \leq k$: $\hat{\vartheta}(\chi(t_1, \ldots, t_k)) = \chi(\hat{\vartheta}(t_1), \ldots, \hat{\vartheta}(t_k))$. For convenience we write ϑ instead of $\hat{\vartheta}$.

Let t_1 and $t_2 \in T_\Theta(V)$ for some V. The term t_2 is an *instance* of t_1, written $t_1 \leq t_2$, if there is a substitution $\vartheta \in$ Subst(Θ, V) with $t_2 = \vartheta(t_1)$.

A *renaming* is a substitution that only permutes the variables.

Remark 2.4 Renamings induce an equivalence relation $\equiv\ \subseteq T_\Theta(V) \times T_\Theta(V)$ where $\equiv\ =\ \leq \cap \leq^{-1}$. The equivalence class of a term t is denoted by $[t]_\equiv$ and the set of all equivalence classes is $T_\Theta(V)_\equiv$. Note however that $\equiv$ is not a congruence, since for distinct variables α and $\beta \in V$ and $\chi \in \Theta^{(2)}$ we have $\alpha \equiv \beta$ but $\chi(\alpha, \alpha) \not\equiv \chi(\alpha, \beta)$.

Definition 2.5 (Tuples of terms) Let $k \in \mathbb{N}$ and $(t_1, \ldots, t_k) \in T_\Theta(V)^k$. The depth function is extended to $d\colon T_\Theta(V)^k \to \mathbb{N}$ by $d(t_1, \ldots, t_k) = d(t_1) + \cdots + d(t_k)$. A substitution $\vartheta \in$ Subst(Θ, V) is extended componentwise to tuples of terms, *i.e.*, $\vartheta(t_1, \ldots, t_k) = (\vartheta(t_1), \ldots, \vartheta(t_k))$. The instance relation $\leq$ is extended in the obvious way and $\equiv$ is defined as $\leq \cap \leq^{-1}$.

3 Signatures

In the following we use the terms over a ranked alphabet to provide a set of sorts for a sorted algebra. Let *TSYM*, *VSYM*, and *TV* be disjoint countably infinite sets of *type constructor symbols*, *value constructor symbols*, and *type variables*, respectively. Furthermore the symbols α, β, γ always denote type variables (elements of *TV*).

Definition 3.1 A partially ordered set $(M, \sqsubseteq)$ is an *lower quasi-lattice* if for all elements a and $b \in M$ there is a greatest lower bound $a \sqcap b \in M$ whenever a and b have a common lower bound. $(M, \sqsubseteq)$ is a *upper quasi-lattice* if there is a least upper bound $a \sqcup b \in M$ whenever a and b have a common upper bound. $(M, \sqsubseteq)$ is a *quasi-lattice* if it is both an upper and a lower quasi-lattice.

Definition 3.2 A partially ordered set $(M, \sqsubseteq)$ is *locally downward filtered* if every $\sim$-connected component of M has a least element, where $\sim\ = (\sqsubseteq \cup \sqsubseteq^{-1})^*$.

Definition 3.3 $\Sigma = (\Theta, \sqsubseteq, \Delta)$ is a *polymorphic order-sorted signature* if

- Θ is a ranked alphabet of *sort constructors*,
- $\sqsubseteq$ is a partial order on $T_\Theta(TV)_\equiv$ that makes $(T_\Theta(TV)_\equiv, \sqsubseteq)$ into a quasi-lattice, and
- Δ is a finite set of *operator symbols* with a total function $a\colon \Delta \to D\setminus\{\emptyset\}$ for $D = \wp^{fin}(\bigcup_{n\in\mathbb{N}} D_n)$ and $D_n = \{(\tau_1 \ldots \tau_n, \tau_0) \mid \tau_i \in T_\Theta(TV), 0 \leq i \leq n\}$, for $n > 0$, and $D_0 = \{(\varepsilon, \tau) \mid \tau \in T_\Theta(TV)\}$. For a symbol $\delta \in \Delta$ the set $a(\delta)$ denotes the possible arities.

Example 3.4 Since the instance ordering $\leq$ makes $T_\Theta(TV)_\equiv$ into a quasi-lattice for any ranked alphabet Θ, $(\Theta, \leq, \Delta)$ is a polymorphic order-sorted signature for any set Δ of operator symbols.

3.1 Sort rewriting

Definition 3.5 For all $l \in \mathbb{N}$, a ranked alphabet Θ, and $\alpha_i \in TV$ define the set $RHS^l_\Theta(\alpha_1, \ldots, \alpha_l) = \{atom_1 + \cdots + atom_m \mid m \geq 0, atom_i \in ATOM_\Theta(\{\alpha_1, \ldots, \alpha_l\}), 1 \leq i \leq m\} \cup EXTD^l_\Theta(\alpha_1, \ldots, \alpha_l)$ where

$$\begin{aligned} ATOM_\Theta(V) &= COND_\Theta(V) \cup INCD_\Theta(V) \\ COND_\Theta(V) &= \{(c(\tau_1, \ldots, \tau_k)) \mid c \in VSYM, k \in \mathbb{N}, \tau_i \in T_\Theta(V), 1 \leq i \leq k\} \\ INCD_\Theta(V) &= \{\tau_1 + \cdots + \tau_m \mid m > 0, \tau_i \in T_\Theta(V) \setminus V, 1 \leq i \leq m\} \end{aligned}$$

and for all $l \in \mathbb{N}$: $EXTD^l_\Theta(\alpha_1, \ldots, \alpha_l) = \{\chi(\alpha_1, \ldots, \alpha_l)\langle \tau_1, \ldots, \tau_n\rangle \mid \chi \in \Theta^{(l)}, n \in \mathbb{N}, \tau_i \in T_\Theta(\{\alpha_1, \ldots, \alpha_l\}), 1 \leq i \leq n\}$.

The elements of $COND_\Theta(V)$ are called *constructor declarations*, $INCD_\Theta(V)$ is the set of *inclusion declarations*, and elements of $EXTD_\Theta(\ldots)$ are *extension declarations*.

Definition 3.6 A *polymorphic data structure declaration* (PDSD) P is a set of equations of the form $\chi(\alpha_1, \ldots, \alpha_l) = rhs$ where $\chi \in TSYM$, $l \in \mathbb{N}$, $\alpha_i \in TV$ for $1 \leq i \leq l$, $rhs \in RHS^l_\Theta(\alpha_1, \ldots, \alpha_l)$, and each χ may appear at most once in the left hand side of an equation in P.

The ranked alphabet Θ of *sort constructors* induced by P is defined to be $\Theta = (\Theta^{(l)})_{l\in\mathbb{N}}$ where $\Theta^{(l)} = \{\chi \mid \chi(\alpha_1, \ldots, \alpha_l) = rhs \in P\}$.

Similar as described by Smolka [6, 7] a PDSD defines a rewrite relation on $T_\Theta(TV)$. He only considers inclusion declarations in his work. The rewrite relation is used to describe an inclusion relation on the sorts.

Definition 3.7 Given a PDSD P and its induced sort constructors Θ, we define the rewrite relation $\Rightarrow$ on $T_\Theta(TV)$.

If there is an inclusion declaration $\chi(\alpha_1,\ldots,\alpha_l) = \cdots + \sigma + \ldots$ in P and $\tau' = [\tau_i/\alpha_i \mid 1 \le i \le l](\sigma)$ then $\chi(\tau_1,\ldots,\tau_l) \Rightarrow \tau'$.

If there is an extension declaration $\chi(\alpha_1,\ldots,\alpha_l) = \chi'(\alpha_1,\ldots,\alpha_l)\langle\sigma_1,\ldots,\sigma_n\rangle$. in P then $\chi'(\tau_1,\ldots,\tau_l) \Rightarrow \chi(\tau_1,\ldots,\tau_l)$.

The relation $\rightarrow$ is the Θ-compatible closure of $\Rightarrow$.

Definition 3.8 For all $k \in \mathbb{N}$ the rewrite relation $R \in \{\Rightarrow, \rightarrow\}$ is extended to $T_\Theta(TV)^k \times T_\Theta(TV)^k$ by $(\sigma_1,\ldots,\sigma_k)\ R\ (\tau_1,\ldots,\tau_k)$ if $\exists j,\ 1 \le j \le k$, where $\tau_i = \sigma_i$ for $i \ne j$, $1 \le i \le k$, and $\sigma_j\ R\ \tau_j$ (as rewriting of terms).

Definition 3.9 Let P, Θ, and $\Rightarrow$ be as in definition 3.7. Define the relation $\sqsubseteq' \subseteq \Theta \times \Theta$ as follows. For $\chi \in \Theta^{(l)}$ and $\chi' \in \Theta^{(l')}$ $\chi' \sqsubseteq' \chi$ holds iff there exist terms $\tau_1,\ldots,\tau_{l'} \in T_\Theta(TV)$ such that $\chi(\alpha_1,\ldots,\alpha_l) \Rightarrow^* \chi'(\tau_1,\ldots,\tau_{l'})$.

Definition 3.10 A PDSD is *well-formed* if the induced rewrite relation $\Rightarrow$ (cf. definition 3.7) fulfills the conditions

- **(Termination)** there are no infinite chains $\tau_1 \rightarrow \tau_2 \rightarrow \ldots$,
- **(Coherence)** for every $\tau \in T_\Theta(TV)$, $l \in \mathbb{N}$, and $\chi \in \Theta^{(l)}$ there is at most one tuple $(\tau_1,\ldots,\tau_l)$ where $\tau \Rightarrow^* \chi(\tau_1,\ldots,\tau_l)$,
- **(Completeness)** Θ forms a quasi-lattice under the order $\sqsubseteq'$,
- **(Filteredness)** Θ is locally downward filtered under $\sqsubseteq'$.

Theorem 3.11 It is decidable whether a PDSD is well-formed.

Proof: Smolka proves the decidability of $\sqsubseteq'$ and the decidability of the termination, coherence, and completeness properties [7]. Since $\sqsubseteq'$ is decidable the components of $(\sqsubseteq' \cup {\sqsubseteq'}^{-1})^*$ can be computed and the least element of each component can be found by a combinatorial test. □

From now on we assume that every PDSD is well-formed, that $\Rightarrow$ is induced by a well-formed PDSD, and that $\rightarrow$ is its Θ-compatible closure. Furthermore, the symbols $\chi, \chi', \ldots$ always denote sort constructors (elements of Θ), $\sigma, \tau \in T_\Theta(TV)$ range over *sort terms*, and $\vartheta \in \mathrm{Subst}(\Theta, TV)$ denotes substitutions.

Lemma 3.12 Rewriting of tuples of terms with $\Rightarrow$ is terminating, componentwise coherent, complete, and filtered.

3.2 An ordering on sort terms

Definition 3.13 Given a rewrite relation $\Rightarrow$ on $T_\Theta(TV)$ the relation $\sqsubseteq$ on $T_\Theta(TV) \times T_\Theta(TV)$ is defined by $\sigma \sqsubseteq \tau$ if $\exists \tau'$, $\tau \rightarrow^* \tau'$ and $\sigma \le \tau'$.

This extends to tuples of length $l > 0$ by $(\sigma_1,\ldots,\sigma_l) \sqsubseteq (\tau_1,\ldots,\tau_l)$ if $\exists(\tau_1',\ldots,\tau_l'),\ (\tau_1,\ldots,\tau_l) \rightarrow^* (\tau_1',\ldots,\tau_l')$ and $(\sigma_1,\ldots,\sigma_l) \le (\tau_1',\ldots,\tau_l')$.

In the following, let $\sqsubseteq$ denote a relation obtained from a well-formed PDSD by definitions 3.13 and 3.7.

Lemma 3.14 Let $l > 0$, $\overline{\sigma} = (\sigma_1,\ldots,\sigma_l)$, and $\overline{\tau} = (\tau_1,\ldots,\tau_l)$.

1. If $\overline{\sigma} \sqsubseteq \overline{\tau}$ then $\overline{\sigma} \sqsubseteq \vartheta(\overline{\tau})$ for all substitutions ϑ.
2. For all $\chi \in \Theta^{(l)}$: $\overline{\sigma} \sqsubseteq \overline{\tau}$ if and only if $\chi\overline{\sigma} \sqsubseteq \chi\overline{\tau}$.

Proof: 1. Let $\overline{\sigma} \sqsubseteq \overline{\tau}$, *i.e.*, there is $\overline{\tau}'$ with $\overline{\tau} \to^* \overline{\tau}'$ and a substitution ϑ' with $\vartheta'(\overline{\sigma}) = \overline{\tau}'$. By induction on the number of rewrite steps $\vartheta(\overline{\tau}) \to^* \vartheta(\overline{\tau}')$ follows from $\overline{\tau} \to^* \overline{\tau}'$. Now $(\vartheta \circ \vartheta')(\overline{\sigma}) = \vartheta(\overline{\tau}')$ and hence $\overline{\sigma} \sqsubseteq \vartheta(\overline{\tau})$.

2. Let $\chi(\overline{\sigma}) \sqsubseteq \chi(\overline{\tau})$. This means there is τ' with $\chi(\tau_1, \ldots, \tau_l) \to^* \tau'$ and $\chi(\sigma_1, \ldots, \sigma_l) \leq \tau'$. Since $\to^*$ is terminating $\tau' = \chi(\tau_1', \ldots, \tau_l')$ holds. Thus $\tau_i \to^* \tau_i'$ and $\sigma_i \leq \tau_i'$ for $1 \leq i \leq l$. But this is equivalent to the definition of $(\sigma_1, \ldots, \sigma_l) \sqsubseteq (\tau_1, \ldots, \tau_l)$ (cf. definition 3.13). □

Lemma 3.15 $\sqsubseteq$ is a partial order on $T_\Theta(TV)_\equiv$.

Proof: We show the stronger assumption that $\sqsubseteq$ extended to tuples over $T_\Theta(TV)$ is a partial order modulo renaming of variables.

The reflexivity of $\sqsubseteq$ is obvious. For transitivity suppose there are tuples $\overline{\tau}_1$, $\overline{\tau}_2$, and $\overline{\tau}_3$ of equal length such that $\overline{\tau}_1 \sqsubseteq \overline{\tau}_2$ and $\overline{\tau}_2 \sqsubseteq \overline{\tau}_3$. By definition, there is some $\overline{\tau}_3'$ with $\overline{\tau}_3 \to^* \overline{\tau}_3'$ and ϑ_2 with $\overline{\tau}_3' = \vartheta_2(\overline{\tau}_2)$. From $\overline{\tau}_1 \sqsubseteq \overline{\tau}_2$ we obtain by Lemma 3.14 (1) $\overline{\tau}_1 \sqsubseteq \vartheta_2(\overline{\tau}_2) = \overline{\tau}_3'$. By definition there is some $\overline{\tau}_3''$ with $\overline{\tau}_3' \to^* \overline{\tau}_3''$ and ϑ_1 such that $\overline{\tau}_3'' = \vartheta_1(\overline{\tau}_1)$. Since $\overline{\tau}_3 \to^* \overline{\tau}_3' \to^* \overline{\tau}_3''$ we have proved $\overline{\tau}_1 \sqsubseteq \overline{\tau}_3$.

For anti-symmetry suppose there are tuples $\overline{\tau}_1$ and $\overline{\tau}_2$ where $\overline{\tau}_1 \sqsubseteq \overline{\tau}_2$ and also $\overline{\tau}_2 \sqsubseteq \overline{\tau}_1$. The proof proceeds by induction on the depth of the tuple $\overline{\tau}_2$. If $d(\overline{\tau}_2) = 0$ then all components of $\overline{\tau}_2$ are variables and so are all components of $\overline{\tau}_1$. So the assumption reduces to $\overline{\tau}_1 \leq \overline{\tau}_2$ and $\overline{\tau}_2 \leq \overline{\tau}_1$. By definition 2.5 this means $\overline{\tau}_1 \equiv \overline{\tau}_2$. Now suppose $d(\overline{\tau}_2) > 0$ and let τ^j denote the jth component of a tuple $\overline{\tau}$. Let n be the length of the tuples $\overline{\tau}_2$ and $\overline{\tau}_1$. Since $d(\overline{\tau}_2) > 0$ there exists some j with $1 \leq j \leq n$ such that τ_2^j has the form $\chi(\overline{\mu}_2)$ for some $l \in \mathbb{N}$ and $\overline{\mu}_2 \in T_\Theta(TV)^l$. Thus τ_1^j cannot be a variable, since this would contradict to $\overline{\tau}_2 \sqsubseteq \overline{\tau}_1$. Furthermore τ_1^j must have the form $\chi(\overline{\mu}_1)$, for $\overline{\mu}_1 \in T_\Theta(TV)^l$, since otherwise $\Rightarrow$ could not be terminating (which is required by the well-formedness of the PDSD). By lemma 3.14(2) we have $\tau_1^j \sqsubseteq \tau_2^j$ iff $\overline{\mu}_1 \sqsubseteq \overline{\mu}_2$ (and vice versa). By a similar argument, for $\overline{\tau}_1' = (\tau_1^1, \ldots, \tau_1^{j-1}, \mu_1^1, \ldots, \mu_1^l, \tau_1^{j+1}, \ldots, \tau_1^n)$ and $\overline{\tau}_2' = (\tau_2^1, \ldots, \tau_2^{j-1}, \mu_2^1, \ldots, \mu_2^l, \tau_2^{j+1}, \ldots, \tau_2^n)$ we have $\overline{\tau}_1 \sqsubseteq \overline{\tau}_2$ iff $\overline{\tau}_1' \sqsubseteq \overline{\tau}_2'$ and also $\overline{\tau}_2 \sqsubseteq \overline{\tau}_1$ iff $\overline{\tau}_2' \sqsubseteq \overline{\tau}_1'$. But $d(\overline{\tau}_2') = d(\overline{\tau}_2) - 1$, so we conclude by induction that $\overline{\tau}_1' \equiv \overline{\tau}_2'$ and thus, by lemma 3.14(2), $\overline{\tau}_1 \equiv \overline{\tau}_2$. □

Theorem 3.16 The partial order $(T_\Theta(TV)_\equiv, \sqsubseteq)$ is a quasi-lattice.

In the proof of the theorem we need to compare two terms ν and λ where it is known that there is an instance of λ which is greater than ν wrt. the order $\sqsubseteq$. The comparision is accomplished with the auxiliary function *collect*: $T_\Theta(TV) \times T_\Theta(TV) \to \wp(TV \times T_\Theta(TV))$. *collect* is defined as follows for σ and $\tau \in T_\Theta(TV)$.

$$
collect(\sigma, \tau) = \begin{cases}
\{(\alpha, \tau)\} & \sigma = \alpha \in TV, \tau \in T_\Theta(TV) \\
\{(\beta, \beta) \mid \beta \in \mathrm{var}(\tau)\} & \sigma \in T_\Theta(TV) \setminus TV, \tau \in TV \\
\bigcup_{i=1}^{l} collect(\sigma_i', \tau_i) & \sigma = \chi(\sigma_1, \ldots, \sigma_k), \tau = \chi'(\tau_1, \ldots, \tau_l), \\
 & \chi \in \Theta^{(k)}, \chi' \in \Theta^{(l)}, k, l \in \mathbb{N}, \\
 & \sigma \Rightarrow^* \chi'(\sigma_1', \ldots, \sigma_l') \\
\text{undefined} & \text{otherwise}
\end{cases}
$$

Lemma 3.17 Suppose $\nu, \lambda \in T_\Theta(TV)$ and $\vartheta \in \mathrm{Subst}(\Theta, TV)$ such that $\nu \sqsubseteq \vartheta(\lambda)$. If $(\alpha, \tau) \in \mathit{collect}(\lambda, \nu)$ then $\tau \sqsubseteq \vartheta(\alpha)$.

Notice that *collect* is a partial function and is undefined on arguments ν and λ if there is no substitution ϑ such that $\nu \sqsubseteq \vartheta(\lambda)$.

Lemma 3.18 $\forall \sigma \in T_\Theta(TV)$: $S(\sigma) = \{\tau \in T_\Theta(TV)_\equiv \mid \tau \sqsubseteq \sigma\}$ is finite.

Proof: Follows from the termination property. □

Lemma 3.19 Let $k \in \mathbb{N}$, $K = \{1, \ldots, k\}$, $(\alpha_1, \ldots, \alpha_k)$ and $(\beta_1, \ldots, \beta_k) \in TV^k$ be tuples of type variables (not necessarily all different). For $i, j \in K$ let $i \sim j$ iff $\alpha_i = \alpha_j \vee \beta_i = \beta_j$ and let $K_\sim$ denote the set of equivalence classes of the transitive closure of $\sim$. Choose a set $\{\gamma_1, \ldots, \gamma_n\} \subseteq TV$ where $n = |K_\sim|$ and a fixed bijection $\zeta\colon K_\sim \to \{\gamma_1, \ldots, \gamma_n\}$. Now for $1 \le i \le k$ let $\sigma_i = \zeta([i]_\sim)$.

$\overline{\sigma} = (\sigma_1, \ldots, \sigma_k)$ represents the least upper bound of $\overline{\alpha}$ and $\overline{\beta}$ with respect to $\le$ and $\sqsubseteq$.

Proof: (of theorem 3.16) First we need to show that for all $k > 0$ the partial order $(T_\Theta(TV)^k_\equiv, \sqsubseteq)$ is an upper quasi-lattice, *i.e.*, for all $k \in \mathbb{N}$ and $\overline{\sigma}, \overline{\tau}, \overline{\rho} \in T_\Theta(TV)^k$ with $\overline{\sigma} \sqsubseteq \overline{\rho}$ and $\overline{\tau} \sqsubseteq \overline{\rho}$ there is a least upper bound $\overline{\sigma} \sqcup \overline{\tau} \in T_\Theta(TV)^k$

The proof is by induction on the well-founded partial order $\preceq\ \subseteq T_\Theta(TV)^* \times T_\Theta(TV)^*$ where $(\tau_1, \ldots, \tau_{j-1}, \sigma_1, \ldots, \sigma_k, \tau_{j+1}, \ldots, \tau_n) \preceq (\tau_1, \ldots, \tau_n)$ if $\tau_j \to^* \chi(\sigma_1, \ldots, \sigma_k)$ for $1 \le j \le n$, $k \in \mathbb{N}$, and $\chi \in \Theta^{(k)}$. This order is well-founded since $\to$ is terminating. The induction is applied to $\overline{\rho}$ and the cases are as follows.

1. If $\overline{\sigma}, \overline{\tau} \in TV^k$ they have a least upper bound by Lemma 3.19.
2. If there exists $m \in \mathbb{N}$, $1 \le m \le k$, with $\sigma^m = \chi_1(\overline{\nu}_1)$ and $\tau^m = \chi_2(\overline{\nu}_2)$ and $\rho^m = \chi(\ldots)$ then by the completeness condition there is a least upper bound $\chi' \in \Theta^{(l)}$ for χ_1 and χ_2 wrt. $\sqsubseteq'$. By coherence there is exactly one tuple $\overline{\rho}' = (\rho'_1, \ldots, \rho'_l)$ where $\rho^m \Rightarrow^* \chi'(\overline{\rho}')$. Furthermore, there are unique tuples $\overline{\mu}_1$ and $\overline{\mu}_2$ such that $\chi'(\overline{\rho}') \Rightarrow^* \chi_1(\overline{\mu}_1)$ and $\chi'(\overline{\rho}') \Rightarrow^* \chi_2(\overline{\mu}_2)$ uniquely, again by coherence.

   Now define $\vartheta = [\rho'_1/\alpha_1, \ldots, \rho'_l/\alpha_l]$ for some l-tuple $(\alpha_1, \ldots, \alpha_l)$ of distinct variables that do not occur in $\overline{\tau}$, $\overline{\sigma}$, or $\overline{\rho}$. By coherence, there are unique tuples $\overline{\lambda}_1$ and $\overline{\lambda}_2$ of length l_1 and l_2, respectively, such that $\chi'(\overline{\alpha}) \Rightarrow^* \chi_1(\overline{\lambda}_1)$ and $\chi'(\overline{\alpha}) \Rightarrow^* \chi_2(\overline{\lambda}_2)$. Since getting from χ' to χ_1 (or χ_2) involves only top level rewriting steps ($\Rightarrow$) it holds that $\overline{\mu}_j = \vartheta(\overline{\lambda}_j)$, for $j = 1, 2$.

   Since $\overline{\nu}_j \le \overline{\mu}_j$ and $\overline{\mu}_j = \vartheta(\overline{\lambda}_j)$ *collect* can be applied to $\overline{\lambda}_j$ and $\overline{\nu}_j$, for $j = 1, 2$. Let $CC_j = \bigcup_{i=1}^{l_j} \mathit{collect}(\lambda^i_j, \nu^i_j)$, for $j = 1, 2$, and $A^i_j = \{\tau \mid (\alpha_i, \tau) \in CC_i\}$, for $1 \le i \le l$ and $j = 1, 2$. Each of the A^i_j is a finite set which is bounded by ρ'_i by lemma 3.17. For $1 \le i \le l$ and $j = 1, 2$ let $A^{i\,\prime}_j = A^i_j$ if $A^i_j \ne \emptyset$, and $A^{i\,\prime}_j = \{\alpha_i\}$ if $A^i_j = \emptyset$. By definition of $\preceq$ we have $(\rho'_1, \ldots, \rho'_l) \preceq \rho^m$, so also $\overline{\rho}'' = (\rho_1, \ldots, \rho_{m-1}, \rho'_1, \ldots, \rho'_l, \rho_{m+1}, \ldots, \rho_k) \preceq \overline{\rho}$. Thus by induction we can obtain least upper bounds for the two finite non-empty sets of tuples $\{(\sigma_1, \ldots, \sigma_{m-1}, v_1, \ldots, v_l, \sigma_{m+1}, \ldots, \sigma_k) \mid v_i \in A^i_1\}$ and $\{(\tau_1, \ldots, \tau_{m-1}, v_1, \ldots, v_l, \tau_{m+1}, \ldots, \tau_k) \mid v_i \in A^i_2\}$. Since both bounds are bounded by $\overline{\rho}''$ they possess, by induction, a least upper bound $(\tau^o_1, \ldots, \tau^o_{m-1}, v_1, \ldots, v_l, \tau^o_{m+1}, \ldots, \tau^o_k)$ and the least upper bound of $\overline{\sigma}$ and $\overline{\tau}$ can be constructed as $(\tau^o_1, \ldots, \tau^o_{m-1}, \chi'(v_1, \ldots, v_l), \tau^o_{m+1}, \ldots, \tau^o_k)$.

3. In the final case we have to consider, for all $m \in \mathbb{N}$ with $1 \leq m \leq k$ at least one of σ^m and τ^m is a type variable.

   So let $m \in \mathbb{N}$ with $1 \leq m \leq k$ where wlog. $\sigma^m = \alpha \in TV$ and $\tau^m \in T_\Theta(TV) \setminus TV$. Let $\tau' = \vartheta(\tau)$ for a renaming ϑ such that the variables of τ' do not appear in $\overline{\sigma}$ or $\overline{\tau}$. Also, take $\tau_\perp \in T_\Theta(TV) \setminus TV$ as $\tau^m \rightarrow^* \tau_\perp$ and no further $\rightarrow$ is applicable to $\tau_\perp$ which exists by termination. Define $\overline{\sigma}' = (\sigma'_1, \ldots, \sigma'_k)$ by $\sigma'_m = \tau'$ and $\sigma'_i = \sigma^i[\tau_\perp/\alpha]$ for $1 \leq i \leq k$ and $i \neq m$. Obviously $\overline{\sigma} \sqsubseteq \overline{\sigma}'$. Now the least upper bound of $\overline{\sigma}$ and $\overline{\tau}$ is the same as the least upper bound of $\overline{\sigma}'$ and $\overline{\tau}$, if it exists.

   Now case 2 of the proof is applicable to $\overline{\sigma}'$ and $\overline{\tau}$ which leads to a decrease of $\overline{\rho}$, so we obtain the least upper bound by induction.

Finally we show that $T_\Theta(TV)$ also forms a lower quasi-lattice. If τ_1 and τ_2 have a common lower bound the set $S = \{\tau \mid \tau \sqsubseteq \tau_1 \land \tau \sqsubseteq \tau_2\}$ is non-empty and, by lemma 3.18, finite. Since S has an upper bound its least upper bound $\bigsqcup S$ exists and is equal to the greatest lower bound $\tau_1 \sqcap \tau_2$. □

Smolka defines the partial order on terms as follows ([7]): $\tau_1 \sqsubseteq \tau_2$ if $\tau_2 \rightarrow^* \tau_1$. In order to make T_Θ into an upper quasi-lattice he has to assume the existence of a least sort $\perp$.

Definition 3.20 A PDSD $P = \{\chi_j(\alpha_1, \ldots, \alpha_{l_j}) = rhs_j \mid 1 \leq j \leq N\}$ defines a polymorphic order-sorted signature $(\Theta, \sqsubseteq, \Delta)$ in the following way.

Θ is the ranked alphabet of sort constructors induced by P as defined in 3.6. $\sqsubseteq$ is the relation obtained by definition 3.13 from the rewrite relation obtained by definition 3.7 from P. $\Delta \subseteq VSYM$ is the set of all symbols that appear in some rhs as part of a constructor declaration $COND_\Theta(V)$ for some $V \subseteq TV$.

The arity function a is defined in two steps. First define $a_0(c)$ inductively as the least set such that

1. $(\tau_1 \ldots \tau_k, \tau_0) \in a_0(c)$ if there is an equation $\chi(\alpha_1, \ldots, \alpha_l) = rhs$ in P where rhs contains an atom $(c(\tau_1, \ldots, \tau_k)) \in COND_\Theta(\{\alpha_1, \ldots, \alpha_l\})$ and $\tau_0 = \chi(\alpha_1, \ldots, \alpha_l)$,
2. if there is an extension declaration $\chi(\alpha_1, \ldots, \alpha_l) = \chi'(\alpha_1, \ldots, \alpha_l)\langle\tau_1, \ldots, \tau_m\rangle$ in P and $(\sigma_1 \ldots \sigma_k, \sigma_0) \in a_0(c)$, $\chi'(\alpha_1, \ldots, \alpha_l) \rightarrow^* \sigma'_0$ where none of the rewrite steps is induced by an extension declaration and $\sigma_0 \equiv \sigma'_0$ with $\vartheta(\sigma_0) = \sigma'_0$ then $(\vartheta(\sigma_1) \ldots \vartheta(\sigma_k)\tau_1 \ldots \tau_m, \sigma'_0) \in a_0(c)$.

$a(c) = \{(\sigma_1 \ldots \sigma_k, \tau_0) \mid (\tau_1 \ldots \tau_k, \tau_0) \in a_0(c) \land (\tau_1, \ldots, \tau_k) \rightarrow^* (\sigma_1, \ldots, \sigma_k)\}$.

4 Examples

Polymorphic lists are defined as usual in OSA.

```
Empty     = (nil)
NeList(X) = (cons(X, List(X)))
List(X)   = Empty + NeList(X)
```

`Empty` and `NeList(X)` denote the sort constructors for empty and non-empty lists, while `List(X)` is the sort constructor for empty or non-empty lists. The first two are constructor declarations, `List(X)` is an inclusion declaration.

However this signature is not downward filtered, so it has to be completed by adding some extra sorts. The complete signature is

```
ListBot   = ()
Empty     = ListBot + (nil)
NeList(X) = ListBot + (cons(X, List(X)))
List(X)   = Empty + NeList(X)
```

Here we have a for `Empty` and `NeList(X)` right hand sides that contain constructor declarations as well as inclusion declarations.

The tedious process of downward filtering can be automated since downward filteredness is a technical requirement which is not very interesting for the programmer. The following signatures will not be downward filtered either. It is easy though to add the necessary declarations.

If we also want to pass around error messages we define

```
Error = (error)
ListOrError(X) = List(X) + Error
```

Now we can add our own error information to this by taking

```
MyError = Error < String >
```

This is an example of an extension declaration. Assuming the foregoing declarations the sort `MyError` declares just one constructor symbol, namely `error` of arity $\{(\varepsilon, \texttt{Error}), (\texttt{String}, \texttt{MyError})\}$. We can also have a sort of anything or error by saying

```
Just(X)  = (just(X))
AnythingOrError(X) = Just(X) + Error
```

References

[1] Christoph Beierle. Logic programming with typed unification and its realization on an abstract machine. *IBM Journal of Research and Development*, 36(3):375–390, May 1992.

[2] Joseph A. Goguen and José Meseguer. Order-sorted algebra I: Equational deduction for multiple inheritance, overloading, exceptions and partial operations. Technical Report SRI-CSL-89-10, SRI International, Menlo Park, CA, July 1987.

[3] Michael Hanus. Parametric order-sorted types in logic programming. In *Proc. TAPSOFT 1991*, pages 181–200, 1991. LNCS 394.

[4] Herbert Klaeren and Peter Thiemann. A clean Modula-2 interface to abstract data types. *Structured Programming*, 11:69–77, April 1990.

[5] Robin Milner. A theory of type polymorphism in programming. *Journal of Computer and System Sciences*, 17:348–375, 1978.

[6] Gert Smolka. Logic programming with polymorphically order-sorted types. In *Proc. First International Workshop on Algebraic and Logic Programming*, pages 53–70, Gaussig, G.D.R., 1988. Springer Verlag. LNCS 343.

[7] Gert Smolka. *Logic Programming over Polymorphically Order-Sorted Types*. PhD thesis, Fachbereich Informatik, Universität Kaiserslautern, 1989.

[8] Niklaus Wirth. The programming language Oberon. *Software, Practice and Experience*, 18(7):671–690, July 1988.

[9] Niklaus Wirth. Type extensions. *ACM Transactions on Programming Languages and Systems*, 10(2):204–214, April 1988.

Category Theory for the Configuration of Complex Systems

Gillian Hill
Department of Computing, Imperial College of Science and Technology and
Department of Computer Science, City University, London, Great Britain

Abstract

The abstract framework of category theory is shown to provide a precise semantics for the configuration of complex systems from their component parts. Diagrams express configuration by representing the results of applying combinators to recursively defined system components. Although modularity has been described as an essential property of complex systems, no clear and simple definition of a module has emerged at this general level. In this paper a new module concept is defined to represent reusable system components, at any level of development.

1 Introduction

A category theoretic semantics was given in [1] for putting theories together to make specifications. The activity of specification was viewed as theory-building in [5, 7] and interpretation between theories was formalized in a categorial framework in [3]. Category theory was used to define an abstract specification theory for refining specifications in [6]. In this paper these ideas are extended to provide a precise semantics for both structuring and implementing system components to configure the architecture of a final executable system.

In [2] a language for configuration is designed, that is at a meta-level to a specification language and describes the operations of combinators on the objects that represent the system components. High-level combinators are used to express both the structuring of objects, by extension and parameterization, and the implementation of objects that takes place in the design process of software development. The possible relationships between the component parts of systems are identified at an intuitive level initially in order to choose appropriate high-level combinators for configuration. The high-level combinators have then been formally defined in terms of more primitive combinators: interpretation, extension and conservative extension.

The aim of this paper is to present a category-theoretic framework for the configuration of modular systems that is independent of any particular specification approach, design methodology or programming paradigm. It is important that the logic chosen for configuration guarantees the preservation of structure as defined by the strong Craig interpolation property. First-order logic, which possesses the strong Craig interpolation property, is chosen for configuration and is used to express new operations for adding structure and for implementation within a conceptual framework that is both simple and natural for engineers to use. System components are represented in a uniform development space by recursively defined objects with sorts from the set {*specification, module*}.

In [2] specifications are presented as objects in textual form that record the history of configuration as a sequence of operations by the combinators on recursively defined objects. The semantics of each primitive object is given by the underlying theory. The focus of this paper is the abstract category-theoretic semantics of configuration which is based on morphisms between theories in a logical category. The primitive combinators that operate on specifications are represented by morphisms between recursively defined diagrams. Morphisms that represent conservative extension play an important role within the mathematical workspace that we provide for software engineers to use.

Our new module concept is proposed as an aid to managing the complexity of large systems by focusing on building systems from reusable components at any stage in system development. A module is created by a combinator from the textual specification of an object, and the semantics of module creation is based on the construction of a colimit for the diagram of that configured specification.

Our approach is intended to be flexible. The engineer is able to choose, at each stage in building a system, between building from specifications or modules. The final configured object of a software system will be a structured object that is implemented and in the form of an executable module.

This paper is arranged as follows. In Section 2, we present an intuitive view of system configuration and introduce the high-level configuration language within a framework of first-order logic. The mathematical workspace for configuration is introduced in Section 3. Finally conclusions are drawn in Section 4.

2 System Components are Configured by Combinators

The key idea for the configuration of complex systems is that the activity of configuration is carried out at a meta-level to the activities of specification and the implementation of specifications. The components of a system are represented by recursively defined objects and configured by combinators.

2.1 The Language for Configuration

The high-level configuration language, presented in [2], has been defined at an intuitive level, and without reference to an underlying mathematical framework. Our aim has been to design a language that is easy to use and involves concepts that seem natural to software engineers. The configuration language is not an extension of a specification language; instead it is at a meta-level to existing specification languages.

We have identified the 'combining' relationships between the component parts of a system. Again at an intuitive level, we have identified the component parts as uniform objects, in a development space, which are of two sorts: specification or module. From the 'combining' relationships we have defined the combining operations, or combinators, that progressively build objects into more structured concrete objects until the complete system has been configured. The combinators are: extension and parameterization to add structural information; implementation to add concrete details; and the creation of unique module instances from a specification at any stage in the development space.

The process of system configuration records the information about the structuring and the implementation used to form the final most concrete object (which is a module). The object that results from the process of configuration is also referred to as the configured system, or, confusingly, the configuration. A snapshot view of system configuration will record the configuration at different stages in the development of each component part of the system. The complete configuration program expresses the action of the combinators on the objects that represent the component parts. Some of the objects will be specifications that are used as patterns before their modules are created.

By identifying explicit combinators between objects rather than one general notion of compositionality between modules, we have simplified the module construct itself to be an instance of a specification; the module is without the structural information concerning the combinators used to build that specification. Our notion of a module is not an implementation of an abstract data type; it can itself be implemented by the combinator for implementation.

The combinators that we have identified are our high-level combinators. We have noticed that parameterization and implementation are themselves composed of more basic operations that we identify as primitive, or low-level combinators:

- conservative extension between objects that preserves the properties of the extended object and does not allow the deduction of new properties about the extended object in the extension
- interpretation between objects that adds details of primitive operations by translating to a new and more concrete language.

The objects that are configured are of two sorts: specifications as named and finite representations of theories; and modules as the uniquely named instances of a specification.

Any number of module instances can be created from a (possibly configured) specification at any stage in system configuration. Modules may be created from primitive specifications before they are configured, or alternatively from complex specifications at the end of the configuring process. Similarly modules may be created from abstract specifications before they are implemented, or alternatively they may be created from concrete specifications at the end of the refinement process. Modules encapsulate the structure of previous configurations but lose the history of the structuring.

Example 2.1.1 A house structured by rooms may be represented by the object 'housestructure'. The textual specification for this object will express the high-level structuring by parameterization as **spec house[spec room]**. In terms of the primitive combinators the object is structured by conservatively extending the specification for a room as the parameter to the specification for a house. Instantiation of a room as a generic parameter requires the addition of more concrete detail and is defined by the primitive combinator for interpretation. The expression **spec house** $_{\textbf{spec room}}$ **[spec bedroom]** is the result of instantiating a room by a bedroom. □

Example 2.1.2 The number of rooms in the house is specified by creating the required number of module instances of a room as the parameters to a house.

It follows that **obj one_roomed_house** is fixed in its structure by applying the create combinator to **spec room** to form a single module instance of a room and then conservatively extending this module to configure the parameterized structure **spec house[module room1]**. Instantiation of the module instance of a room by a module instance of a bedroom is recorded in **spec one_roomed_house** by the expression **spec house** $_{\textbf{module room1}}$ **[module bedroom]**. □

Example 2.1.3 The instantiation of **obj two_roomed_bungalow**, structured as **spec house[module room1, module room2]**, to **obj new_bungalow** with a kitchen and a bedroom is expressed in the specification for **obj new_bungalow**. Instantiation is carried out by interpreting **module room1** to **module kitchen** and **module room2** to **module bedroom** in **spec two_roomed_bungalow** to form **spec house**$_{\textbf{module room1, module room2}}$**[module kitchen,module bedroom]**. □

Example 2.1.4 The module instance of the one-bedroomed house specified as **spec house** $_{\textbf{module room1}}$ **[module bedroom]** will be structurally identical to the module instance of **spec house** $_{\textbf{specroom}}$ **[spec bedroom]**. Their textual specifications would record different histories of specification, however: the first with instantiation by a module; the second by a specification. □

2.2 The Logic for System Configuration

In this paper we fix the logic for configuration as first-order logic and present a specific definition of the general notion of a theory. A similarity type, analogous to the algebraic concept of a signature, is used to define both relation and function symbols in the language of a first-order theory.

Definition 2.2.1 (A Many-Sorted Similarity Type) A *many-sorted similarity type* is the triple (S, ar_r, ar_f) where S is a non-empty set of *sorts* and ar_r and ar_f are *arity functions*. The elements in the domains of ar_r and ar_f are the *relation symbols* and the *function symbols* respectively. If the similarity type is called σ then we denote the domains by *rel* σ and *func* σ. The arity functions assign the sorts of the arguments to each symbol in *rel* $\sigma \cup$ *func* σ and, in addition, for symbols in *func* σ the result sort. □

A similarity type σ determines a first-order language whose formulae will be all the well-formed formulae with sorts from S and the connectives of first-order logic. We assume the usual relation of consequence for first-order logic.

Notation 2.2.2

1. A *first-order language* is a pair $(\sigma,\ Form_\sigma)$ where σ is a similarity type and $Form_\sigma$is the set of *well-formed formulae* for σ. The language determined by σ will be denoted by L_σ.
2. The consequence relation is $\vdash_\sigma\ \subseteq \mathcal{P}\ (Form_\sigma) \times Form_\sigma$ and satisfies the usual properties of cut, weakening and inclusion. □

Within our logic many theories can be specified to express the properties of particular software applications. We specify a many-sorted theory in terms of the similarity type of the language and the set of non-logical axioms that express the properties of the application. This definition of a theory within a linguistic system is sometimes given as a theory presentation. Our intention is to distinguish between those formulae which are axioms and those which are derived from the axioms and are closed under the consequence relation.

Definition 2.2.3 (A Theory) Let σ be a similarity type. Then a *theory* over the similarity type σ is the pair $T = (\sigma, \Gamma)$ where $\Gamma \subseteq Form_\sigma$ is a set of formulae called the non-logical axioms. □

2.3 The Craig Interpolation Property

The work of structuring objects within our formal system for configuration will depend on some precisely defined notion of structure that must be preserved by the operations of each of the combinators that we define for our system. We show in [2] that the structure of objects that have been extended conservatively *is* preserved if the underlying logic of the configuration system possesses the strong Craig interpolation property. It is vital to preserve the properties of objects already structured by conservative extension and subsequently operated on under interpretation. First-order logic has this structural property and is also simple and natural for software engineers to use. We have identified other logics that have the Craig interpolation property in [2] and explained why equational logic lacks the *strong* form of the interpolation property that is essential for specification building. In our view, [2, 5, 3], the lack of the strong interpolation property in equational logic has led to increasing complexity, such as the need for concepts like persistency, in the algebraic approach to specification,

The strong form of the interpolation property, (*), that does not hold in equational logic is called a combined interpolation and *splitting* property in [4] and is derived from the interpolation property in predicate logic. The algebraic notion of the signature of a set of equations X, denoted by $\Sigma\ (X)$, defines the sorts and the function symbols in X.

(*) if $A \cup B \vdash \Gamma$, then there is a set I with $\Sigma(I) \subseteq \Sigma(A) \cap (\Sigma(B) \cup \Sigma(\Gamma))$ such that $A \vdash I$ and $B \cup I \vdash \Gamma$.

If equational logic is used as a finite system of deduction, it is required that the set I is finite. By setting $B = \emptyset$, a weaker form of the interpolation theorem can be formed which does hold in equational logic. This form holds because the problem of constructing $A \vdash \bigwedge B \rightarrow \Gamma$ by the Deduction theorem with possibly infinite conjunctions no longer exists.

2.4 The Combinators

The high-level combinators are defined in [2] in terms of the primitive combinators for the extension, conservative extension and interpretation of objects. These primitive combinators are denoted by e, $c\ .\ e$ and i respectively. Extension is defined in terms of e or $c\ .\ e$, whereas parameterization is defined only in terms of $c\ .\ e$. The instantiation of parameters is defined in terms of i, which is itself defined in terms of the interpretation of a theory in another theory. The low-level combinators $c\ .\ e$ and e are defined in terms of the extension of theories. Our aim has been to establish correct 'connections' between theories in order to define the high-level combinators.

The extension of a theory involves an addition to the language of a theory, rather than a translation to the symbols of a new language. It is, in fact, an interpretation where the language translation is inclusive. In an extension of a theory we can prove everything that was provable before the theory was extended.

Definition 2.4.1 (Extension of a Theory) Let $T_1 = (\sigma_1, \Gamma_1)$ and $T_2 = (\sigma_2, \Gamma_2)$ be theories. Then T_2 is an *extension* of T_1 if $\sigma_1 \subseteq \sigma_2$ and for every $\varphi \in Form(\sigma_1, V_S)$, $\Gamma_1 \vdash \varphi$ implies $\Gamma_2 \vdash \varphi$.

An extension that is conservative ensures that any properties deduced in the extension that are expressed in the language of the original theory also hold in the original theory.

Definition 2.4.2 (Conservative Extension of a Theory) Let $T_2 = (\sigma_2, \Gamma_2)$ be an extension of the theory $T_1 = (\sigma_1, \Gamma_1)$. Then T_2 is a *conservative extension* of T_1 if for every $\varphi \in Form_{\sigma_1}$, $\Gamma_2 \vdash \varphi$ implies $\Gamma_1 \vdash \varphi$. □

Checking that an extension of a theory is conservative is not easy. It involves proof, at a meta-level to the logic, concerning all the theorems in the extension that are expressed in the language of the extended theory. The aim of our configuration system is to construct objects in such a way that the extensions are *guaranteed* to be conservative.

A parameterized object may be structured by fitting objects together, by use of another object or by genericity.

Example 2.4.3 (Parameterization by fitting objects together) The specification for the object room will contain the rules about fitting the walls to the floor and finally the ceiling to all the walls. In our configuration language, the structuring of the room is expressed within the textual specification for the composite object by the structure **spec** room[**spec** ceiling, **spec** wall, **spec** floor] and specified as $T_{\text{roomstructure}} = (\sigma_{\text{roomstructure}}, \Gamma_{\text{roomstructure}})$. The specification expresses the conservative extension of the parameters by the object room to form the composite object 'roomstructure'. The axioms that describe the fitting together of the parameters are given in **spec** room by Γ_{room}. □

Implementation, as a high-level combinator, has been defined in [5] by the pair $(i,\ c\ .\ e)$. The structurality of an implementation is preserved if the underlying logic possesses the Craig interpolation property which itself depends on the more primitive property of structurality under interpretation. Clearly there is no unique implementation for an object. The configuration of a concrete object involves choosing appropriate $(i,\ c\ .\ e)$ pairs and composing implementations that have already been configured. The composition of implementations is dependent on the property of Craig interpolation in the underlying logic.

Example 2.4.4 The implementation of a set by a sequence is by interpretation from **obj** set to **obj** extseq which is constructed as the conservative extension of **obj** seq. □

3 The Mathematical Workspace for Configuration

In this section we define the categorical framework for the configuration of recursively defined objects. Diagrams represent the configured objects and natural transformations between diagrams represent the primitive combinators for interpretation and extension (as a special case of interpretation).

3.1 A Category of Configured Objects

We define a diagram as a functor from a finite graph, as a category, to the finitely cocomplete category $\mathcal{C}$ of configured objects. The functor labels a graph, which has a only a shape, by the specifications or modules, as the objects, at the nodes and by the morphisms between the objects as the arrows. The natural transformations that join objects, represented by diagrams, to form more structured diagrams become the morphisms between objects in the diagrams of the more structured objects. The semantics of the high-level combinators is given by the construction of colimit diagrams that express the joining together of structured objects that may share common parts. The construction of these colimit diagrams is completed by morphisms that represent the primitive combinator for conservative extension. The intuition behind the requirement for the cocompleteness of $\mathcal{C}$ is that the existence of colimits ensures constructivity enabling objects to be joined together in order to construct new structured objects.

The creation of a unique module from a specification is expressed by constructing the colimit of the diagram representing the structured specification.

3.2 A Categorical Framework for Configuration

The power of category theory is that it provides a mathematical workspace within which a unified view is held not only of logical structures as objects in a category but also of mappings between these objects as morphisms in the category. Specifications, as named theories, are represented by the objects in our mathematical workspace for configuration, and the primitive combinators are represented by the morphisms between the categorical objects. Since parameterization and implementation are defined only in terms of the primitive combinators for interpretation and conservative extension, we must identify those morphisms which are conservative and essential for building safely.

Definition 3.2.1 (A Configuration Theory) Let $\mathcal{C}$ be a category that is finitely cocomplete, and **Cons** a sub-category of $\mathcal{C}$ such that *Obj* **Cons** = *Obj* $\mathcal{C}$. Then a *configuration theory* is the pair ($\mathcal{C}$, **Cons**) if for any diagram

$$\begin{array}{ccc} \cdot & \xrightarrow{c} & \\ {\scriptstyle f}\downarrow & & \\ \cdot & & \end{array}$$

where $c \in$ *Mor* **Cons**, there exists its colimit

$$\begin{array}{ccc} \cdot & \xrightarrow{c} & \cdot \\ {\scriptstyle f}\downarrow & & \downarrow{\scriptstyle f'} \\ \cdot & \xrightarrow{c'} & \cdot \end{array}$$

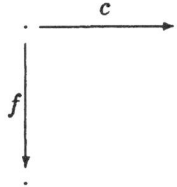

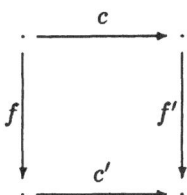

such that c' also belongs to *Mor* **Cons**. This property in the configuration theory represents the Craig interpolation property of the logic. □

Definition 3.2.2 (Objects and Morphisms of $\mathcal{C}$) Any element of *Obj* $\mathcal{C}$ represents a specification of a configured object and is denoted by *spec*. If $f : spec_1 \rightarrow spec_2$ is a morphism of $\mathcal{C}$ then f is called an *interpretation*. A morphism $c : spec_1 \rightarrow spec_2$ is a *conservative extension* of $spec_1$ iff $c \in Mor$**Cons**. □

Definition 3.2.3 (A Configured Object) Let $\mathcal{G}$ be a finite category. A *configured object* (of shape $\mathcal{G}$) in $\mathcal{C}$ is a diagram $D : \mathcal{G} \rightarrow \mathcal{C}$. □

We fix as our configuration theory the category of all first-order theories and theory morphisms between them, paired with its sub-category of all conservative theory morphisms. In this workspace each object is configured (recursively) by the use of morphisms that represent the primitive combinators.

4 Conclusions

We have suggested a solution to the problem of constructing systems-in-the-large. Our solution provides an architecture for the configuration of systems that is independent of the variety of approaches that exist for the specification, design and coding of systems. The key idea is to focus on configuring systems from reusable modules at any stage in system development. The module is precisely defined as an instance of a textual specification. Configuration takes place within a mathematical workspace that is based on category theory.

Acknowledgments

The many discussions with Tom Maibaum have been very valuable. Mike Johnson, Paulo Veloso, Steve Vickers and Mark Ryan have also made helpful comments. Paul Taylor's macros were used for the diagrams.

References

[1] R. M. Burstall and J. A. Goguen. Putting theories together to make specifications. In *Proceedings of the 5th. International Joint Conference on Artificial Intelligence*, pages 1045–1058, Cambridge, Mass., 1977.

[2] Gillian Hill. *A Language for System Configuration*. PhD thesis, Department of Computing, Imperial College, University of London, 1993. draft.

[3] T. Maibaum and J. Fiadeiro. Stepwise program development in Π institutions. Technical report, Imperial College, November 1990. with Martin Sadler.

[4] P. H. Rodenburg and R. J. van Glabbeek. An interpolation theorem in equational logic. Technical Report CS-R8838, Department of Computer Science, Centre for Mathematics and Computer Science, Amsterdam, 1988.

[5] Wladyslaw M. Turski and Thomas S. E. Maibaum. *The Specification of Computer Programs*. International Computer Science Series. Addison Wesley, 1987.

[6] László Úry and Tamás Gergely. A constructive specification theory. In G. David, R. T. Boute, and B. D. Shriver, editors, *Declarative Systems*. Elsevier Science Publishers B. V. (North Holland) IFIP, 1990.

[7] Paulo A. S. Veloso. Program development as theory manipulations. Technical report, PUC/RJ Departamento de Informatica, Rio de Janeiro, Brazil, May 1985. Series: Monografias em Ciencia da Computacao No4/85.

Algebraic-Oriented Institutions *

M. Cerioli and G. Reggio
DISI - Dipartimento di Informatica e Scienze dell'Informazione
Viale Benedetto XV, 3 – 16132 Genova – Italy

Introduction

In many recent applications of algebraic paradigms to formal specification methodologies, already known algebraic frameworks are endowed with features tailored for special purposes ([4, 7, 8, 2]). Although it is often the case that these new features are parametric on the underlying framework and that the same construction applies to any sufficiently expressive formalism, in practice *ad hoc* theories are developed. This lack of generality is conflicting with the ability of changing the basic formalism, and hence with the reuse of methodologies, seen as high-level theoretical tools for the software development.

Here we propose a modular construction of algebraic frameworks, formalized by operations on institutions in order to build richer formalisms by adding one feature at a time. But, as many constructions used in practice have meaning only for those institutions representing "algebraic formalisms", in order to give sound foundations for the treatment of such operations, a preliminary step is the formal definition of the institutions corresponding to algebraic frameworks and we devote to this task the first 3 sections of our paper.

The main idea is to characterize such institutions by standard algebraic specifications, so that both the theoretical and software tools of the usual algebraic machinery are at hand for modularly defining the operations on the institutions; moreover this approach should look more friendly, in contrast to more abstract and categorical ones, for algebraic specification users who already have the know-how to understand and manipulate metaoperations building algebraic formalisms. Three kinds of operations can be introduced, respectively modifying signatures, models and sentences, that can be easily described as enrichments of the specifications defining the basic framework.

In the last section we show that for operations modifying the signatures a general property holds: they return an algebraic formalism, when applied to a formalism of the same kind. Therefore using these operations we can modularly define a framework as complex as needed by the current application. Moreover this result is instantiated for the particularly interesting case of an operation that endows an algebraic framework with sorts of *dynamic* elements.

This work continues and adds to [3, 2], where some operations on institutions were proposed to deal with uniform enrichments of logical formalisms.

*This work has been partially supported by Esprit-BRA W.G. n.6112 Compass, Progetto Finalizzato Sistemi Informatici e Calcolo Parallelo of C.N.R. (Italy), MURST-40% Modelli e Specifiche di Sistemi Concorrenti

1 Algebraic-Based Institutions

We take the view that the signatures used in algebraic worlds are characterized by a set of *sorts*, classifying the model elements, a set of *operation symbols* and (possibly) a set of *predicate symbols*, stating the properties of the model elements; moreover for each operation or predicate symbol, its *arity* (the sorts of the arguments) is known and each operation symbol has a *result sort*. Then some different algebraic approaches structure and enrich those basic ingredients in several ways; e.g. the order-sorted approach [5] endows the sort set with a subsorting relation, compatible with the operation and predicate symbols.

A natural formalization of these intuitions, by algebraic techniques, is to see the signatures of an algebraic framework as the models of a specification including a standard part, corresponding to the minimal ingredients, like the types "sort", "operation symbol", or the operation symbol "arity".

Although the basic operations are total, partial operations are needed, even in easy and classical cases, in order to structure the signature elements; hence in this paper we use partial specifications, adopting a standard notation. Moreover in the sequel $\mathcal{I} = (\mathbf{Sign}, Sen, Mod, \models)$ is a generic institution.

We call $\underline{\text{sign}}$ the standard part of the signature specification, $\underline{\text{stream}}(S)$ being the specification of the streams of elements of sort S, whose main sort is $S^\star$.

spec $\underline{\text{sign}}$ = **enrich** $\underline{\text{stream}}(S)$ **by**
sorts Op, P
opns $Arity: Op \to S^\star$ (total)
$P\text{-}arity: P \to S^\star$ (total)
$R\text{-}type: Op \to S$ (total)

A subcategory $\mathbf{D}$ of $\mathbf{C}$ is *object-full* iff $|\mathbf{D}| = |\mathbf{C}|$, i.e. iff $\mathbf{D}$ and $\mathbf{C}$ have the same objects.

Def. 1.1 Let $\underline{\text{SIGN}}$ be a specification enriching $\underline{\text{sign}}$; then $\mathcal{I}$ is *algebraic-based on* $\underline{\text{SIGN}}$ iff **Sign** is (isomorphic to) a object-full subcategory of the category of models of $\underline{\text{SIGN}}$. In this case **Sign** is said an *algebraic signature category*. □

In most cases the usual (strengthening) homomorphisms between the models of the specification describing the signatures correctly represent the signature morphisms; however sometimes they are too liberal. Indeed there are algebraic frameworks, where, for instance, the allowed signature morphisms should have surjective generalizations to contexts at least for some sorts, representing the visible part of data types. Thus we require the signature category to be isomorphic to a subcategory of the specification model category with the same objects, so that deductive tools, if any, can correctly be used.

It is immediate to verify that the signature category of many-sorted logic is isomorphic to the model category of $\underline{\text{sign}}$; but it is also easy to enrich $\underline{\text{sign}}$ by axioms to qualify the usual many-sorted signatures without predicates (using the axiom $p \neq p$, with p variable of sort P, that is satisfied iff the corresponding carrier is empty) and the homogeneous logic (using a constant Srt of sort S and the axiom $s = Srt$, with s variable of sort S). Even more complex kinds of signatures can be defined enriching $\underline{\text{sign}}$; consider indeed the following (incomplete) specification of the order-sorted signatures. Moreover also many non-standard cases used in the concurrency field fit the framework as well.

spec $\underline{\text{OSAsign}}$ = **enrich** $\underline{\text{sign}}$ **by**
sorts $Opname, Predname$

opns	$Name: Op \rightarrow Opname$ (total)	
	$Pname: P \rightarrow Predname$ (total)	
preds	$\_ \leq \_: S \times S$	
	$\_ \leq^{\star} \_: S^{\star} \times S^{\star}$	– extension of $\leq$ on streams
axioms	$s \leq s \quad s \leq s' \wedge s' \leq s \supset s = s' \quad s \leq s' \wedge s' \leq s'' \supset s \leq s''$	
	$\Lambda \leq^{\star} \Lambda \quad \neg(\Lambda \leq^{\star} s \cdot w) \quad \neg(s \cdot w \leq^{\star} \Lambda)$	
	$w \leq^{\star} w' \wedge s \leq s' \equiv s \cdot w \leq^{\star} s' \cdot w'$	
–	monotonicity condition	
	$Name(f_1) = Name(f_2) \wedge Arity(f_1) \leq^{\star} Arity(f_2) \supset R\text{-}type(f_1) \leq R\text{-}type(f_2)$	
–	regularity condition for operations ... □	

2 Algebraic-Oriented Institutions

The acceptable structures (models) of an algebraic-oriented institution interpret sorts, operation and predicate symbols respectively as sets, functions and predicates; this is formalized, as we did for signatures, by a specification. To achieve this, the syntax specification is enriched by the sorts corresponding to "semantic objects" and by "semantic interpretation" operations. In particular sorts for representing models and homomorphisms are introduced, together with (auxiliary sorts, operations and) the standard operations needed to have a category structure. Then, for each signature, an algebra on this enriched meta-signature is chosen, whose carriers of "model" and "homomorphism" sorts are the objects and the arrows of the model category[1].

Note that while the specification representing the signatures had directly as models (a representation of) the concrete signatures, the specification representing the structures has models whose carriers and operations are used to canonically build the category of structures. In this way we avoid to fix a particular kind of algebras and have tools to define the structure homomorphisms, having a particular relevance in all algebraic approaches.

As for signatures, the specification representing model categories has a standard part, defined as follows [2].

spec <u>alg</u> =	**enrich** <u>sign</u>, <u>stream</u>(U), <u>stream</u>($U\text{-}Set$) **by**	
sorts	$Obj, Hom, Pred, Fun$	
opns	$\_\_: Hom \times S \rightarrow Fun$ (total)	– homomorphism components
	$Id: Obj \rightarrow Hom$ (total)	– identity homomorphism
	$\delta_0, \delta_1: Hom \rightarrow Obj$ (total)	– homomorphism source and target
	$\_;\_: Hom \times Hom \rightarrow Hom$	– homomorphism composition
	$\mathsf{S}: S \times Obj \rightarrow U\text{-}Set$ (total)	– sort interpretation
	$\mathsf{O}: Op \times Obj \rightarrow Fun$ (total)	– operation symbol interpretation
	$\mathsf{P}: P \times Obj \rightarrow Pred$ (total)	– predicate symbol interpretation
	$\mathsf{S}^{\star}: S^{\star} \times Obj \rightarrow U\text{-}Set^{\star}$	– sort interpretation extended on streams
	$Dom: Fun \rightarrow U\text{-}Set^{\star}$ (total)	– function domain
	$Cod: Fun \rightarrow U\text{-}Set$ (total)	– function codomain
	$A: Fun \times U^{\star} \rightarrow U$	– function application
	$PDom: Pred \rightarrow U\text{-}Set^{\star}$ (total)	– predicate domain
preds	$\_\epsilon\_: U \times U\text{-}Set$	

[1] In this way the objects of the model category form a set (being a carrier in an algebra) and cannot be a proper class. This restriction is immaterial from a pragmatic point of view, as just finite models are used in practice and hence they form a set, and can be overcome by slightly generalizing the notion of algebra, fixing a universe U and allowing the carriers to be classes of elements in U.

[2] The sort $U\text{-}Set$ is characterized in a non-constructive way by the membership predicate

$$\begin{array}{ll} & Holds(\_(\_)) : Pred \times U^\star \\ \textbf{axioms} & \delta_0(Id(x)) = x \quad \delta_1(Id(x)) = x \quad f; Id(\delta_1(f)) = f \quad Id(\delta_0(f)); f = f \\ & \delta_0(g) = \delta_1(f) \supset D(f;g) \wedge \delta_0(f;g) = \delta_0(f) \wedge \delta_1(f;g) = \delta_1(g) \\ & D(f;g) \supset \delta_0(g) = \delta_1(f) \qquad (f;g);h = f;(g;h) \\ & \mathsf{S}^\star(\Lambda, x) = \Lambda \qquad \mathsf{S}^\star(s \cdot u, x) = \mathsf{S}(s,x) \cdot \mathsf{S}^\star(u,x) \\ & Dom(\mathsf{O}(op,x)) = \mathsf{S}^\star(Arity(op),x) \qquad Cod(\mathsf{O}(op,x)) = \mathsf{S}(R\text{-}type(op),x) \\ & PDom(\mathsf{P}(p,x)) = \mathsf{S}^\star(P\text{-}arity(p),x) \\ & Dom(h_s) = \mathsf{S}(s,\delta_0(h)) \cdot \Lambda \qquad Cod(h_s) = \mathsf{S}(s,\delta_1(h)) \end{array}$$

Non-strict operations and error recovery can be treated, because no axioms are imposed on function application and so a defined and correctly typed output can be obtained even on an incomplete (or incorrectly typed) input. Neither it is required that the application of an operation to correctly typed inputs yields a correctly typed output and hence partial operations can be defined too. However it is easy to impose strictness and/or totality, by a predicate $ok: U^\star \times U\text{-}Set^\star$, representing the correct typing of a tuple w.r.t. a set sequence, and by axioms of the form

$$\begin{array}{llll} ok(\Lambda,\Lambda) & \neg ok(t \cdot w, \Lambda) & \neg ok(\Lambda, k \cdot a) & ok(w,a) \wedge t \in k \equiv ok(t \cdot w, k \cdot a) \\ D(A(f,w)) \supset ok(w, Dom(f)) & & - \textit{strictness} & \\ ok(w, Dom(f)) \supset D(A(f,w)) & & - \textit{totality} & \end{array}$$

Def. 2.1 Let $\mathcal{I}$ be algebraic-based on <u>SIGN</u> and <u>ALG</u> be a specification enriching <u>alg</u> and <u>SIGN</u>. If for each signature $\Sigma \in |\mathbf{Sign}|$ a model $Alg^\sharp(\Sigma)$ of <u>ALG</u> exists s.t. the restriction of $Alg^\sharp(\Sigma)$ to the signature of <u>SIGN</u> is (isomorphic to) Σ and $Mod(\Sigma)$ is isomorphic to the category with: $Obj^{Alg^\sharp(\Sigma)}$ as objects, $\{h \mid h \in Hom^{Alg^\sharp(\Sigma)}, {\delta_0}^{Alg^\sharp(\Sigma)}(h) = a, {\delta_1}^{Alg^\sharp(\Sigma)}(h) = b\}$ as morphisms from a into b, $Id^{Alg^\sharp(\Sigma)}$ as identity and $\_;\_^{Alg^\sharp(\Sigma)}$ as composition, then $\mathcal{I}$ is *algebraic-oriented on* <u>SIGN</u>, <u>ALG</u> *and* $Alg^\sharp$. □

Axioms can be given in order to easily characterize homomorphism behaviour, so that different algebraic frameworks can be captured, using an auxiliary operation $A^\star: Hom \times U^\star \times S^\star \to U^\star$ generalizing A to tuples; let us consider the paradigmatic examples of strengthening homomorphisms, that in partial and non-strict frameworks preserve (but non-necessarily reflect) the element structure, and the truth preserving homomorphisms.

$$\begin{array}{l} A^\star(f,\Lambda,\Lambda) = \Lambda \qquad \neg D(A^\star(f, u \cdot w, \Lambda)) \qquad \neg D(A^\star(f,\Lambda, s \cdot k)) \\ A^\star(f, u \cdot w, s \cdot k) = A(f_s, u) \cdot A^\star(f, w, k) \\ - \textit{strengthening} \quad R\text{-}type(op) = s \wedge D(A(\mathsf{O}(op,\delta_0(h)),a)) \supset \\ \qquad A(h_s, A(\mathsf{O}(op,\delta_0(h)),a)) = A(\mathsf{O}(op,\delta_1(h)), A^\star(h,a,Arity(op))) \\ - \textit{truth preserving} \quad Holds(\mathsf{P}(p,\delta_0(h)),a) \supset Holds(\mathsf{P}(p,\delta_1(h)), A^\star(h,a,P\text{-}arity(p))) \end{array}$$

It is immediate to see that the standard "algebraic" institutions (as many-sorted/one-sorted, total/partial/order-sorted algebras, with and without predicates, with homomorphisms preserving or not the truth) are algebraic-oriented.

3 Logic-Oriented Institutions

In most algebraic frameworks, sentences are a fragment of first-order formulas, possibly with further features (e.g. temporal, higher-order); in any case, the sentences are inductively built starting from *terms*, by logical connectives and quantifiers, and accordingly the validity definition is based on *term evaluation*.

Following the principle of internalizing, we want to describe logic sentences as model classes of suitable specifications. Such specifications consist of a standard part, with symbols for variables, terms and so on, and of a user-defined part, characterizing the logical connectives and variable binders needed by the particular application. Let us define the standard part.

$$
\begin{array}{ll}
\textbf{spec } \underline{\text{sen}} = & \textbf{enrich } \underline{\text{sign}}, \underline{\text{stream}}(Term) \textbf{ by} \\
\quad \textbf{sorts} & F, Var, Atom \\
\quad \textbf{opns} & sort_V\colon Var \to S \quad \text{(total)} \\
 & sort_T\colon Term \to S \quad \text{(total)} \\
 & sort^*_T\colon Term^* \to S^* \quad \text{(total)} \\
 & \_\colon Var \to Term \quad \text{(total, injective)} \\
 & \_(\_)\colon Op \times Term^* \to Term \\
 & \_(\_)\colon P \times Term^* \to Atom \\
 & \_\colon Atom \to F \quad \text{(injective)} \\
\quad \textbf{axioms} & sort_T(x) = sort_V(x) \qquad D(f(w)) \supset sort_T(f(w)) = R\text{-}type(f) \\
 & sort^*_T(\Lambda) = \Lambda \qquad sort^*_T(t \cdot w) = sort_T(t) \cdot sort^*_T(w) \\
 & sort^*_T(w) = Arity(f) \equiv D(f(w)) \qquad sort^*_T(w) = P\text{-}arity(p) \equiv D(p(w))
\end{array}
$$

Thus the sentence functor definition is factorized in two steps: first with each signature the algebraically structured sentences on the signature are associated and then their structure is forgotten, keeping only the formula carrier. To define the sentence validity on the basis of term evaluation, as usual in algebraic framework, the sentences have to be *free*, so that for all variable valuations there exists a unique evaluation for both terms and formulas.

Def. 3.1 Let **Sign** be an algebraic signature category described by SIGN, SEN be a specification enriching sen and SIGN, and $Sen^\sharp$: **Sign** $\to$ $PAlg$(SEN) be a functor s.t. $PAlg(e) \cdot Sen^\sharp$ is the **Sign** identity and $Sen^\sharp$ is the left adjoint of the forgetful functor $PAlg(e)$, with e the embedding of SIGN into SEN.

A functor Sen: **Sign** $\to$ **Set** is *logic-oriented* iff $Sen(\Sigma)$ is the carrier of sort F in $Sen^\sharp(\Sigma)$ and $Sen(\sigma)$ is the component of sort F of $Sen^\sharp(\sigma)$. □

It is worth noting that if the axioms used in both SIGN and SEN are (first-order equivalent) to positive Horn-Clauses (built on existential equalities and predicates), then such a free construction $Sen^\sharp$ exists, as the institution of partial algebras with positive conditional axioms is *liberal* [1]. Moreover if the enrichment of sen and SIGN is hierarchically consistent and partially complete [6], then the first condition on $Sen^\sharp$ is satisfied, too. In particular, in order to avoid introducing new elements of sort S, the syntax of variables and their typing must be axiomatized. Moreover, as the left adjoint, if any, is unique (up to isomorphism), SEN implicitly defines $Sen^\sharp$, too.

The main intuition is that atomic sentences are built starting from terms and predicate symbols and then used to construct more complex formulas; as a simple example, let us consider the positive Horn Clause fragment of typed first-order logic. The standard syntax $x_{n,s}$, where $n \in \mathbb{N}$, is fixed for variables of sort s, so that for each sort a denumerable set of variables is available.

$$
\begin{array}{ll}
\textbf{spec } \underline{\text{HCsen}} = & \textbf{enrich } \underline{\text{sen}}, \underline{\text{nat}} \textbf{ by} \\
\quad \textbf{sorts} & AtomSet \\
\quad \textbf{opns} & x_{\_,\_}\colon S \times Nat \to Var \quad \text{(total)} \\
 & \_\colon Atom \to AtomSet \quad \text{(total, injective)} \\
 & \_ \wedge \_\colon AtomSet \times AtomSet \to AtomSet \quad \text{(total)} \\
 & \_ \supset \_\colon AtomSet \times Atom \to F \quad \text{(total)}
\end{array}
$$

Validity is defined on the basis of *term evaluation*: for each signature Σ, first any Σ-structure M is extended to a model $Ext(\Sigma, M)$ of the structured sentence specification, by interpreting the standard part in the usual way, and then the evaluation is defined as a homomorphism from $Sen^\sharp(\Sigma)$ into $Ext(\Sigma, M)$.

It is interesting to note that, as validity (and hence sentence evaluation) is not preserved by model homomorphisms, the required extension cannot take in account the morphisms and hence is a plain function instead of a functor.

Def. 3.2 Let $\mathcal{I}$ be algebraic-oriented on SIGN, ALG and $Alg^\sharp$, and Sen be a logic-oriented sentence functor, described by SEN (and $Sen^\sharp$).

Let $\mathbb{B}$ be $\{\mathbf{true}, \mathbf{false}\}$, $Mod^\sharp$ be the class of pairs (Σ, M), where $\Sigma \in |\mathbf{Sign}|$ and $M \in |Mod(\Sigma)|$, and, for each $(\Sigma, M) \in Mod^\sharp$, C be $Alg^\sharp(\Sigma)$, F be $Sen^\sharp(\Sigma)$ and Env be the set of *environments in* M (sort preserving partial functions from the variable set into the carriers of M), i.e.

$\text{Env} = \{f\colon Var^F \underset{p}{\rightarrow} U^M \mid f(x) \notin U^M \text{ or } f(x) \epsilon^C \mathsf{S}^C(sort_V{}^F(x), M) \text{ for all } x\}$

Then $\mathcal{I}$ is *logic-oriented on* SIGN, ALG, $Alg^\sharp$ *and* SEN iff

- A function $Ext\colon Mod^\sharp \to |PAlg(\underline{\text{SEN}})|$ exists s.t. for all $(\Sigma, M) \in Mod^\sharp$ the following properties are satisfied, using M' to denote $Ext(\Sigma, M)$:
  Carriers
  - $S^{M'} = \{\mathsf{S}^C(s, M) \mid s \in S^\Sigma\}$;
  - $Op^{M'} = \{\mathsf{O}^C(f, M) \mid f \in Op^\Sigma\}$;
  - $P^{M'} = \{\mathsf{P}^C(p, M) \mid p \in P^\Sigma\}$;
  - $Var^{M'} = Var^F$
  - $Term^{M'} =$
    $\{f\colon \text{Env} \underset{p}{\rightarrow} U^M \mid f(e) \notin U^M \text{ or } f(e) \epsilon^C \mathsf{S}^C(sort_T{}^{M'}(f), M) \text{ for all } e\}$;
  - $F^{M'} = \{bf \mid bf\colon \text{Env} \underset{p}{\rightarrow} \mathbb{B}\}$.

  Operations
  - $sort_V{}^{M'}(x) = \mathsf{S}^C(sort_V{}^F(x), M)$
  - if $D(g(t_1 \cdot \ldots \cdot t_n \Lambda)^{M'})$, then for all $e \in \text{Env}$
    $g(t_1 \cdot \ldots \cdot t_n \cdot \Lambda)^{M'}(e) = A^C(g, t_1(e) \cdot \ldots \cdot t_n(e) \cdot \Lambda)$;
  - if $D(q(t_1 \cdot \ldots \cdot t_n \Lambda)^{M'})$, then for all $e \in \text{Env}$
    $q(t_1 \cdot \ldots \cdot t_n \Lambda)^{M'}(e) = \mathbf{true}$ iff $Holds^C(q(t_1(e) \cdot \ldots \cdot t_n(e) \cdot \Lambda))$;
  - the inclusion of a variable x in the term set is the function f_x defined by $f_x(e) = e(x)$ for all $e \in \text{Env}$.

  Valuation A *valuation* morphism $V\colon \Sigma \to PAlg(e)(M')$ exists in **Sign** s.t.:
  - $V_S(s) = \mathsf{S}^C(s, M)$ for all $s \in S^\Sigma$;
  - $V_{Op}(f) = \mathsf{O}^C(f, M)$ for all $f \in Op^\Sigma$;
  - $V_P(p) = \mathsf{P}^C(p, M)$ for all $p \in P^\Sigma$.
- For all $M \in |Mod(\Sigma)|$ and all $\xi \in Sen(\Sigma)$ $M \models \xi$ iff for all $e \in \text{Env}$, $\text{eval}_{(\Sigma,M)}(\xi^F)(e)$ either yields **true** or is undefined, where $\text{eval}_{(\Sigma,M)}$ is the free extension of the above valuation morphism. □

4 Building algebraic-oriented institutions

With the algebraic machinery defined so far, three kinds of operations, respectively modifying signatures, sentences and models, are easily definable as enrichment of the specification describing the corresponding part of the institution. Thus the signature modifying operations can be defined on any algebraic-based institution, while in order to be able to modify the models (sentences), the argument should be algebraic (logic)-oriented.

The easier kind of operation consists of enriching the signature specification and building a new institution whose signatures are the models of the enriched specification and whose sentences and models on a fixed signature are those of the starting institution on the same signature (forgetting the extrastructure introduced by the enrichment). These operations preserve algebraic-basedness, algebraic-orientedness and logic-orientedness.

Def. 4.1 Let OP be a specification of form **enrich** X, sign **by** ..., where X is a variable. An operation OP on institutions is *algebraic-based* on OP if on each $\mathcal{I}$ algebraic-based on SIGN yields $\texttt{OP}(\mathcal{I}) = (\mathbf{Sign}', Sen', Mod', \models')$ s.t.:

1. denoting OP[SIGN/X] by OPsign, the embedding of SIGN into OPsign by e and the functor $PAlg(e)$ by F, $\mathbf{Sign}'$ is a object-full subcategory of $PAlg$(OPsign) s.t. for each arrow σ in $\mathbf{Sign}'$ the image $F(\sigma)$ is an arrow in **Sign**. In the sequel F denotes the restriction of F to $\mathbf{Sign}'$, too.
2. $Mod' = Mod \cdot F$;
3. $Sen' = Sen \cdot F$;
4. $\models'_\Sigma$ is $\models_{F(\Sigma)}$ for all $\Sigma \in |\mathbf{Sign}'|$. □

As **Sign** is a object-full subcategory of $PAlg$(SIGN), F on each object of **Sign** yields an object of $\mathbf{Sign}'$ and hence the requirement on arrows in condition 1 suffices for F to be a well-defined functor from $\mathbf{Sign}'$ into **Sign**.

Prop. 4.2 Using the notation of def. 4.1 we have that:

1. $\texttt{OP}(\mathcal{I})$ is an institution algebraic-based on OPsign;
2. if $\mathcal{I}$ is algebraic-oriented on SIGN, ALG and $Alg^\sharp$, then $\texttt{OP}(\mathcal{I})$ is algebraic-oriented on OPsign, OPalg = OP[ALG/X] and $Alg^\sharp{}_{\texttt{OP}}$, defined by $Alg^\sharp{}_{\texttt{OP}}(\Sigma) = \Sigma + Alg^\sharp(F(\Sigma))$;
3. if $\mathcal{I}$ is logic-oriented on SIGN, ALG, $Alg^\sharp$ and SEN, then $\texttt{OP}(\mathcal{I})$ is logic-oriented on OPsign, OPalg, $Alg^\sharp{}_{\texttt{OP}}$ and OPsen = OP[SEN/X]. □

As an example let us consider the **Dyn** operation, yielding, on each algebraic-based institution $\mathcal{I}$, a new institution for specifying processes by labelled transition systems where the static parts are specified using $\mathcal{I}$, see e.g. [4, 7, 8]. To define **Dyn** it suffices to enrich the signature structure as follows.

spec DYN = **enrich** sign, X **by**
opns $\texttt{trans}: S \to P$
$\texttt{label}: S \to S$
preds $\texttt{Dyn}: S$
axioms $P\text{-}arity(\texttt{trans}(s)) = s \cdot \texttt{label}(s) \cdot s$
$\texttt{Dyn}(s) \equiv D(\texttt{label}(s)) \equiv D(\texttt{trans}(s))$
– `label` and `trans` are defined only for dynamic sorts

If the signatures of the argument $\mathcal{I}$ cannot have predicate symbols, then $\texttt{Dyn}(\mathcal{I})$ is isomorphic to $\mathcal{I}$ (no dynamic sorts allowed).

Because of prop. 4.2, $\texttt{Dyn}(\mathcal{I})$ is algebraic-based and if $\mathcal{I}$ is algebraic (logic)-oriented, then $\texttt{Dyn}(\mathcal{I})$ is algebraic (logic)-oriented, too. However if $\mathcal{I}$ is non-algebraic-oriented, then $\texttt{trans}(s)$ may be not interpreted as a ternary relation, so we cannot build the labelled transition tree associated with a process; while if $\mathcal{I}$ is non-logic-oriented, then the atoms built by **trans** may be non-available to specify the process activity.

As a simple example of a more complex kind of operation enriching the sentences of a logic-oriented institution with particular combinators, let us consider the addition of a built-in equality. This is achieved by enriching the structured sentence specification, providing the syntax for the equalities, and then defining the equality interpretation in any model, by generalizing *Ext* in the obvious way. The same technique applies to many cases of sentence enrichment by standard combinators; the key point is the capability of defining the model extension to give the semantic interpretation of the new sentences. Let us first define the enrichment of sentence syntax.

spec $\underline{\text{EQ}}$ = **enrich** $\underline{\text{sen}}, X$ **by**
opns $\_ \doteq \_ : Term \times Term \to Atom$
axioms $D(t \doteq t') \equiv sort_T(t) = sort_T(t')$
– equality is defined between terms of the same sort

Let $\mathcal{I}$ be logic-oriented on $\underline{\text{SIGN}}$, $\underline{\text{ALG}}$, $Alg^\sharp$ and $\underline{\text{SEN}}$; in general we are not guaranteed of the existence of a free construction on the forgetful functor $PAlg(e)$, where e is the embedding of $\underline{\text{SIGN}}$ into $\underline{\text{EQsen}} = \underline{\text{EQ}}[\underline{\text{SEN}}/X]$ (the limit case is if $\underline{\text{EQsen}}$ is inconsistent). Let us assume that the specification $\underline{\text{SEN}}$ is positive conditional; thus there exists a free right inverse $Sen^\sharp{}_{\text{EQ}}$ of $PAlg(e)$ and it is the composition of $Sen^\sharp$ and the free construction on the forgetful defined by the embedding of $\underline{\text{SEN}}$ into $\underline{\text{EQsen}}$.

For all $\Sigma \in |\mathbf{Sign}|$ and all $M \in |Mod(\Sigma)|$ we define $Ext_{\text{EQ}}(\Sigma, M)$ as:

- each symbol in the $\underline{\text{SEN}}$ signature is interpreted as in $Ext(\Sigma, M)$;
- for all $f, g \in Term^M$, $f \doteq^M g$ is the function that on each environment e yields **true** if $f(e) = g(e)$ and **false** otherwise.

With these ingredients it is immediate to build a logic-oriented institution $\text{EQ}(\mathcal{I})$ on $\underline{\text{SIGN}}$, $\underline{\text{ALG}}$, $Alg^\sharp$, and $\underline{\text{EQsen}}$.

References

[1] A.Tarlecki. Quasi-varieties in abstract algebraic institutions. *J. of Comp. and Syst. Science*, (33), 1986.

[2] R. Burstall and R.Diaconescu. Hiding and behaviour: an institutional approach. Tech. Rep. ECS-LFCS-92-253, Univ. of Edinburgh, 1992.

[3] M. Cerioli and G. Reggio. Institutions for very abstract specifications. Submitted.

[4] G. Costa and G. Reggio. Abstract dynamic data types: a temporal logic approach. In *Proc. MFCS'91*, number 520 in L.N.C.S. Springer Verlag, 1991.

[5] J. Goguen and J. Meseguer. Order-sorted algebra I: Equational deduction for multiple inheritance, overloading, exceptions and partial operations. *T.C.S.*, 105(2), 1992.

[6] M.Broy, C.Pair, and M.Wirsing. A systematic study of models of abstract data types. *T.C.S.*, (33), 1984.

[7] G. Reggio. Entities: an institution for dynamic systems. In *Recent Trends in Data Type Specification*, number 534 in L.N.C.S. Springer Verlag, 1991.

[8] G. Reggio. Event logic for specifying abstract dynamic data types. In *Recent Trends in Data Type Specification*, number 655 in L.N.C.S. Springer Verlag, 1993.

On the Correctness of Modular Systems

Marisa Navarro[†]
Fernando Orejas[*]
Ana Sánchez[†]

[†] Universidad del Pais Vasco. San Sebastian, Spain
[*] Universidad Politécnica de Cataluña. Barcelona, Spain

Given a requirements specification for a software system, a simple (modular) software development process can be represented by a tree, as follows:

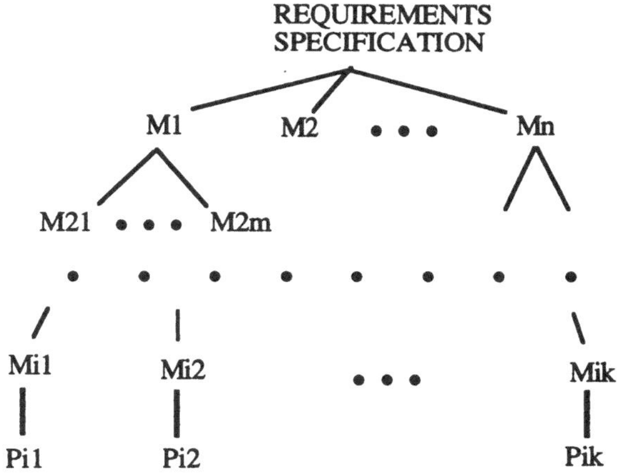

Here, the (informal or semi-formal) requirements specification is transformed into a detailed (formal) specification consisting of the specification modules M1,...,Mn. Then, the development phase starts and each of the specification modules is refined into a new set of modules. The process continues until all the specification modules describe objects that can be directly coded in the given programming language, obtaining as a result the set of program modules Pi1,..., Pik. Modular correctness means that the set of program modules Pi1,..., Pik should be a correct implementation of the given system if every refinement step applied to any module is correct.

To ensure modular correctness, Goguen and Burstall in [9] defined the properties of horizontal and vertical composition. Horizontal composition ensures that if a modular system S is transformed into another system S' by means of a correct development step (applied on one module from S) then the whole system S' is a "correct implementation" of S. Vertical composition ensures the transitivity of implementation correctness. In this sense, if the development process is represented as a sequence:

$$S0 \rightsquigarrow S1 \rightsquigarrow S2 \rightsquigarrow \ldots \rightsquigarrow Sj$$

where Si $\leadsto$ Si+1, means that Si+1 is obtained from Si by applying a refinement operation over a module from Si. The horizontal composition property would ensure that, for every i, Si+1 is a correct implementation of Si, provided that the module refinement operation is correct. Similarly, the vertical composition property would ensure that Sj is a correct implementation of S0.

However, a number of seemingly reasonable specification frameworks do not satisfy these properties (see [12]). Actually, as we show below, the problem is not related to the way of defining the composition but with the fact that the semantics of these specifications is not "compatible" with implementation. In particular, we show that given a development sequence, it may happen that Si+1 is an inconsistent system even if Si is consistent and if the development step Si $\leadsto$ Si+1 is defined in terms of a correct module refinement. However, we also show that if the programming language is *stable* [15,17], with respect to the given behavioural equivalence underlying refinements, then we can ensure that, independently of the specification language, modular correctness is satisfied. That is, the reason for this "local inconsistency is that many specification languages are not stable. To obtain our results with full generality, we introduce an abstract framework for reasoning about modular systems. This framework is independent of the underlying specification and programming languages and it allows us to deal with modular software development for incompletely specified systems.

Our work follows the lines of [15,17]. However we believe that it goes beyond theirs. First, the role of stability in modular correctness gets clearer by integrating in the same framework specification and software modules. Then, our approach to define the semantics of modular systems is simpler but, at the same time, more powerful since we are able to handle incompletely specified systems. This allows us to study in the same framework specification and program development. Finally, in the full version of this paper, we study the property of stability showing that is just a compact formulation of the horizontal and vertical composition properties.

1. Basic Definitions

In this section we briefly review the basic notions on algebraic specification needed in the paper (for further detail see e.g. [7, 18,10]).

Definition 1 An *institution* $\mathcal{L}$ consists of four parts, $\mathcal{L}$ = (Sig, Sen, Mod, $\models$), Sig is the category of *signatures*; Sen: Sig $\rightarrow$ Set is a functor defining the set of *sentences* associated to a given signature; Mod: Sig $\rightarrow$ $\underline{CAT}^{op}$ is a functor defining the category of models associated to every signature and, for each Σ in Sig, $\models_\Sigma \subseteq$ Mod(Σ)xSen(Σ) is a relation that states when a model satisfies a given sentence. In addition, $\models$ is assumed to satisfy the *satisfaction condition*: for every signature Σ, every α in Sen(Σ), every signature morphism h: $\Sigma \rightarrow \Sigma'$ and every A in Mod(Σ')

$$A \models_{\Sigma'} \mathrm{Sen}(h)(\alpha) \text{ iff } U_h(A) \models_\Sigma \alpha$$

where U_h is a more standard notation for Mod(h). Additionally, we assume that the institutions we work with are equipped with a notion of signature inclusion (see [5]).

$\mathcal{L}$ is *exact* (*semiexact*) iff Sig has finite limits (pushouts) and, in addition, Mod transforms finite limits (pushouts) in Sig into colimits (pullbacks) in $\underline{CAT}^{op}$.

Given an institution $\mathcal{L}$, one can define specifications (programs) over $\mathcal{L}$, in an obvious way. On the other hand we consider the simplest kind of specification morphism:

Definition 2 Given an institution $\mathcal{L}$ = (Sig, Sen, Mod, $\models$), we define the *category of specifications* over $\mathcal{L}$, $\mathrm{Spec}_{\mathcal{L}}$ (or just Spec if $\mathcal{L}$ can be inferred from the context), as the class of all pairs (Σ,E) where Σ is in Sig and E is a set of Σ-sentences (called the *axioms* of the specification) together with specification morphisms h: (Σ,E)→ (Σ',E') consisting of a signature morphism h: Σ → Σ' satisfying Sen(h)(E) ⊆ E'.

Inclusions of signatures can be extended to define inclusions of specifications in an obvious way: (Σ,E) ↪ (Σ',E') iff Σ ↪ Σ' and E ⊆ E'.

2. Modular Systems: Assumptions and Constructs

Software systems, as studied in this paper, may include specifications and programs. Then, they are defined over two institutions, $\mathcal{SPEC}$ and $\mathcal{PROG}$, underlying the specification and programming languages, respectively. For simplicity, *we assume that both institutions share the same category of signatures and the same model functor*, i.e. they only differ in the Sen functor and on the satisfaction relation. *We also assume that $\mathcal{SPEC}$ and $\mathcal{PROG}$ are semiexact institutions*. Intuitively, this means that the result of "combining" two specifications (programs) is another specification (program) and that the semantics of this combination is compositional.

Modules are the only construction that we consider for structuring software systems, both at the specification and at the program levels.

Definition 3 A *module* M is an inclusion of specifications, M = IMP ↪ EXP. IMP and EXP are called, respectively, the *import* and *export* specifications of M.

This definition covers all the module constructions that we know [1, 3, 8, 11, 15, 17]. This may seem surprising for some notions (eg. [8, 17]) since they may seem more complex than ours, but this is shown in the full version of the paper.

We assume that the meaning of a module M is some kind of mapping, κ_M, called a *constructor*, from Mod(IMP) to $2^{\mathrm{Mod(EXP)}}$. We do not make any specific assumption on how κ_M is defined: we only assume that κ_M is fixed by the underlying concrete framework. It must be noted that we assume that the such framework may be loose, in the sense that if A is in Mod(IMP) then κ_M(A) may include several non-isomorphic models. If the underlying framework is monomorphic, this means that κ_M(A) only includes one model up to isomorphism.

Definition 4 A *system of modules* over an institution $\mathcal{L}$, $\mathcal{MOD}_{\mathcal{L}}$, is a mapping associating a constructor $\kappa_{\mathcal{MOD}_{\mathcal{L}}}$(M): Mod(IMP) → $2^{\mathrm{Mod(EXP)}}$ to every module M.

From now on, if $\mathcal{MOD}_{\mathcal{L}}$ is implicit we will just write κ_M. According to the literature, different candidates for the choice of the module system would define κ_M(A) as:

a) The free construction F_M: Mod(IMP) → Mod(EXP), associated to the inclusion IMP ↪ EXP, whenever we may ensure the existence of such a free construction.

b) The behavioural closure of the free construction, i.e. $\kappa_M(A) = \{B \in \mathrm{Mod(EXP)} / A \equiv_{Beh} B\}$, for an appropriate notion of behavioural equivalence.

c) All conservative extensions of A, i.e. $\kappa_M(A) = \{B \in \mathrm{Mod(EXP)} / V_M(B) = A\}$.

We do not make assumptions on *MODSPEC*, but with respect to program modules:

1. If M = IMP $\hookrightarrow$ EXP is a program module then *we assume that the "import interface" of the module includes no axioms*, since checking that a given actual parameter satisfies the requirements in the import interface would need theorem proving capabilities in a compiler. This is equivalent to assuming that κ_M is defined from Mod(ΣIMP) to $2^{Mod(EXP)}$, where ΣIMP is the signature of IMP.

2. According to our intuition about programming languages, we *assume that programs and program modules are monomorphic*.

3. Finally, *we assume that κ_M is always strongly persistent* in the sense that for every A1 there is an A2$\in \kappa_M$(A1) such that U_M(A2) = A1.

In this context, a modular system may be seen as a set of program and specification modules together with some global description on the system, e.g. the services or operations offered by the system and the *global properties* that must be satisfied.

Definition 5 A *modular software system* S is assumed to be a triple (SP, MSPEC, MPROG), where SP = (Σ,E) is a requirements specification, including the signature of the whole system and the "global properties" that must be satisfied. MSPEC and MPROG are, respectively, (finite) sets of specification and program *modules on SP*, i.e. if IMP $\hookrightarrow$ EXP $\in$ MSPEC$\cup$MPROG, then ΣEXP $\hookrightarrow$ Σ.

Usually, the semantics of a modular system is defined as some form of composition of the semantics of each all the modules in the system. This is not possible in our framework for various reasons. The most important one is that we assume that systems may be *unfinished*. For instance, the signature of SP may not necessarily be the "union" of all the signatures of the modules in MSPEC, i.e. some components of the system may be not specified yet. In this situation it may not be sensible to assume the existence of such a "composition". For example, suppose that we are defining a text processing system with various facilities and suppose that up to now we have defined two specification modules M1 and M2, such that M1 describes the form of the texts and M2 specifies the structure of a dictionary that we know that is needed. The problem is how to define the semantics of this system. Obviously, it makes no sense to try to "compose" this two modules. The solution we have found consists in regarding the modules as "constraints" over the given system. That is, in the above example, we consider that the semantics of the text processing system is the class of all models over the global signature that satisfy the global axioms and such that the text and the dictionary "parts" of the models "follow" the definition of the given module, i.e. in this sense, we say that the models of a system must *satisfy* the modules of the system. This idea is a generalization of the one used in [4, 13] where data constraints ([14, 2]) were used to deal with "incomplete" specifications.

Definition 6 Given a specification SP and a module M= IMP $\hookrightarrow$ EXP over SP, a model *A$\in$Mod(SP) satisfies M*, denoted A$\models$ M iff $U_M(U_i(A))\in$ Mod(IMP) and, in addition, $U_i(A)\in \kappa_M(U_M(U_i(A)))$ where i is the inclusion i:ΣEXP $\hookrightarrow$ Σ.

The *semantics of a modular system* S = (SP, MSPEC, MPROG) is defined:

$$[S] = \{A\in \text{Mod(SP)} \,/\, \forall M \in \text{MSPEC}\cup\text{MPROG}\ A\models M\}$$

This technique not only allows us to define the semantics of a modular system at any stage of development but, even for finished systems, it can be considered a more adequate semantic definition. The reason is that this semantics is really modular, in the sense that the meaning of the whole system is given in terms of the meaning of its parts without having to compute the composition of all the modules of the system. However, we can prove that for finished systems both semantics coincide.

Definition 7 A set of (program or specification) modules on SP, MSPEC, is *(SP0,SP)-complete*, with $SP0 \hookrightarrow SP$, iff MSPEC = $\{M_k\}_{k=1,n}$ and given the sequence of pushout diagrams:

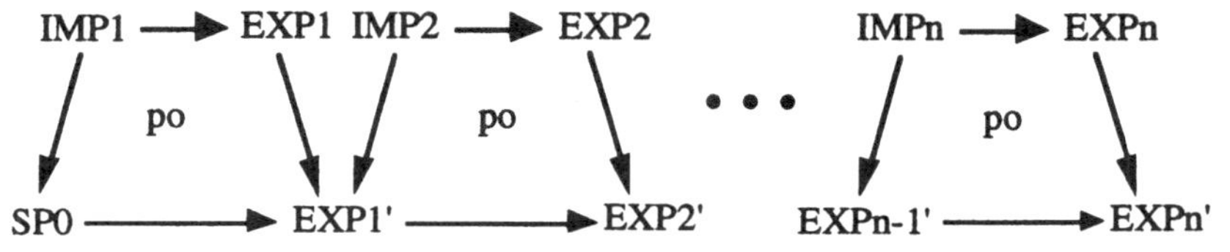

we have that $SP \hookrightarrow EXPn'$

The intuition behind this definition is that a system (SP0,SP)-complete is a system which completely defines all the components of the specification SP, except those that belong to a some basic predefined specification SP0. Actually, we may consider SP0 to be the empty specification, if we can identify such an object in our institution. In order to define the meaning of a (SP0,SP)-complete set of modules by means of the successive application of the modules in the system, we have first to define the meaning of applying a module M to a model A whose signature is larger than ΣIMP:

Definition 8 Given a module $M = IMP \hookrightarrow EXP$ and a set of Σ-models S, with $\Sigma IMP \hookrightarrow \Sigma$ the *application of M to S*, denoted M[S] is the amalgamation (see [6]):

$$M[S] = S +_{S0} \kappa_M(S0)$$

where $S0 = U_i(S)$. Now, if MSPEC = $\{M_k\}_{k=1,n}$ is (SP0,SP)-complete then the *semantics of MSPEC*, denoted [MSPEC], is a mapping from Mod(SP0) to $2^{Mod(EXPn')}$ defined:

$$\forall A \in Mod(SP0) \quad [MSPEC](A) = M_n[\ldots M_1[A]\ldots]$$

where EXPn' is defined as in Definition 7.

Theorem 9 Given a software system S = (SP, MSPEC, MPROG) such that MSPEC = $\{M_k\}_{k=1,n}$ is (SP0,SP)-complete,then:

$$\{A \in Mod(SP) \;/\; \forall M \in MSPEC \; A \models M\} = \{A \in [MSPEC](A0) \;/\; \forall A0 \in Mod(SP0)\}$$

This theorem states that the models satisfying all the modules in MSPEC are exactly the models that can be built by successive application of the modules over all the possible interpretations of the base specification.

3. Operations for the Development of Modular Systems

We consider three operations for system development: adding a new specification module to the given system; adding a new program module *translating* a specification module in the system, and, finally, specifying a *simulation implementation* [12]. Due to lack of space, we only describe in detail the last operation associated to refinement implementations. On the other hand, module translation is quite simple since we consider that a module M' is a translation of a specification module M, with $\Sigma IMP = \Sigma IMP'$, iff for every $A \in Mod(IMP)$ $\kappa_{M'}(A) = \kappa_M(A)$.

In order to define the operation below we need to assume that our institutions *SPEC* and *PROG*, are equipped with some suitable notion of behavioural equivalence (see e.g. [12]), i.e. we assume that for every Σ in Sig an equivalence relation on $Mod(\Sigma)$, denoted $\equiv_{Beh(\Sigma)}$ (or just $\equiv_{Beh}$ if Σ can be inferred), is defined.

Definition 10 Given a system S = ((Σ,E), MSPEC, MPROG) and two modules M1= IMP1$\hookrightarrow$EXP1 and M2= IMP1$\hookrightarrow$EXP2 in MSPEC, the module M3= EXP2 $\hookrightarrow$ EXP3, with i:ΣEXP1 $\hookrightarrow$ ΣEXP3, is an *implementation of M1 by means of M2*, if $\forall A \in Mod(IMP1)$ $\forall B \in \kappa_{M3}(\kappa_{M2}(A))$ $\exists B' \in \kappa_{M1}(A)$ such that $U_i(B) \equiv_{Beh} B'$

Then, the result of the operation:

Implement M1 **by** M3 **by means** of M2 **in** S

is the new modular system S' = (SP', MSPEC-{M1}$\cup${M3}, MPROG), where SP' = (Σ',E) and Σ' is defined by the following pushout diagram:

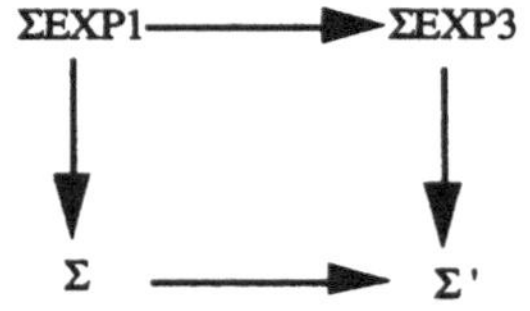

Remarks and interpretation

1. The intuition behind this implementation is that the modules M2 and M3 refine M1 in two ways. On the one hand, M2 and M3 together may be seen as a thighter version of M1. In this sense, if we identify the class of models of a given implementation with the different ways of "realizing" this specification, then the development step associated to this operation implies taking some design decision ruling out some of this realizations. On the other hand, the models built by M2 and M3 may be not exactly equal to models built by M1, but just behaviourally equivalent. In this sense, for instance, M1 may specify sets, M2 may specify strings and M3 may enrich strings with set operations defining the standard implementation of sets by strings.

4. Correctness Results for Modular Systems

If S is a consistent system and we perform one of the operations described above obtaining a new system S' it would be desirable to prove that S' is a correct refinement of S. Unfortunately, it may be shown that it is not even sure that S' is consistent, as the following counter-example shows:

Let us assume that we work in the institution of equational logic and that the associated module system maps every module M= IMP$\hookrightarrow$ EXP into the associated free construction F_M. Now let NAT be the specification of the natural numbers and let SP1, SP2 and SP3 be the following specifications:

SP1 = NAT + **sorts** s
opns a,b : s
f: s $\rightarrow$ nat
eqns a = b
f(x) = 0

SP2 = **sorts** nat, s
opns a : s

SP3 = SP2 + **opns** g: s $\rightarrow$ nat
eqns g(a) = f(a)

Let S be the system formed by the modules M1 = (∅,NAT), M2 = (NAT,SP1) and M3 = (SP2,SP3). It can be shown that the algebra A defined $A_{nat} = \mathbb{N}$, $A_s = \{a\}$, $a_A = b_A = a$, $f_A(a) = 0$, $g_A(a) = 0$ satisfies the three modules. Now, let SP1' be:

$$\begin{array}{lll} SP1' = NAT + & \textbf{sorts} & s \\ & \textbf{opns} & a,b : s \\ & & f: s \rightarrow nat \\ & \textbf{eqns} & f(x) = 0 \end{array}$$

and let M2' be the module (NAT,SP1'). It can be easily proved that M2' is a correct implementation of M2, if we assume the sort s to be non-observable. Now, if in the given system we substitute module M2 by M2' then the result becomes inconsistent.

The problem with this example is that the semantics considered is incompatible with behavioural equivalence. We may argue, that then the given semantics is not adequate. The problem is that, to make it adequate, we would have to "embed" behavioural equivalence into our semantics which would probably result in a complication of the underlying logic and of the associated verification tools. However we can still prove modular correctness if the programming language has the right properties.

Definition 11 A module system on a given program institution is stable iff for any module M = (IMP,EXP), any signature Σ such that $i:\Sigma IMP \hookrightarrow \Sigma$ and any A, A', with $A,A' \in Mod(\Sigma)$, such that $A \equiv_{Beh} A'$, then it must hold that $M[A] \equiv_{Beh} M[A']$

Related notions of stability [15, 17] are essentially equivalent. In the next theorem we show that if S' is a system, whose set of program modules is complete, obtained after a series of correct steps from a completely specified system S then the meaning of the composition of all the program modules in S' can be shown to be a *realization* of S, independently of the inconsistency of some "intermediate" systems. In the full version of the paper, similar results are shown for incompletely specified systems.

Theorem 12 Let S = (SP, MSPEC, MPROG) be a consistent system such that MPROG = ∅ and let S' = (SP', MSPEC', MPROG'), such that MPROG' is (SP0-SP')-complete and S' has been obtained obtained after applying a sequence of translation and implementation steps over S, then:

$$[MPROG] = \{A \in Mod(SP') / \forall M \in MPROG'\ A \models M\} \neq \emptyset,$$

moreover $\forall A \in [MPROG]\ \exists B \in Sem(S)$ such that $U_{SP}(A) \equiv_{Beh} B$

5. Conclusions

The results presented in this paper show that modular correctness depends only on the properties of the programming language used and is independent of the satisfaction of similar properties by the given specification language. Hence, modular correctness depends on the adequacy of the programming language to the notion of refinement (behavioural equivalence) used in the development process. In particular, given a notion of behavioural equivalence, if our programming language is not stable then we can either choose to use a weaker notion of behavioural equivalence (for which the language is stable) or else use only a "save" (stable) subset of the language. A typical example of this can be seen with respect to the programming language Ada. If we consider all private types as non-observable then Ada is a non-stable language. The problem is related to non-"limited" types. Then, to ensure modular correctness we may either weaken behavioural equivalence (by considering that all non-limited types are observable) or else we may choose to use only types which are limited private.

ACKNOWLEDGEMENTS

The writing of this paper took place, partially, during a stay of F. Orejas in Paris, at the E. Normal Superieur invited by Michel Bidoit. In this context, the paper improved as a consequence of several discussions with him. Also, discussions with H. Ehrig, D. Sannella and A. Tarlecki have been very fruitful. This work has been partially supported by ESPRIT Working Groups CCL (Ref. 6026) and COMPASS (Ref. 6112).

References

1. Bernot G, Bidoit M. Proving the correctness of Algebraically Specified Software: Modularity and Observability Issues. Report LIENS-91-8, D.M.I., Ecole Normale Superieur, Paris (1991).
2. Burstall R, Goguen J. The semantics of Clear, a specification language, Proc. Copenhagen Winter School on Abstract Software Specification, Springer LNCS 86, pp. 292-332, 1980.
3. Bidoit M., Hennicker R. A general framework for modular implementations of modular system specifications, in Proc. TAPSOFT 93 (Orsay, France), Springer LNCS 668 (1993), 199-214.
4. Clérici S, Orejas F. GSBL: an algebraic specification language based on inheritance. Proc. 1988 Eur. Conf. on Object Oriented Prog. Springer LNCS 322, 78-92 (1988).
5. Diaconescu R, Goguen J, Stefaneas P. Logical support for modularisation, Report Prog. Res. Group, Oxford University, 1991.
6. Ehrig H, Baldamus M, Cornelius F, Orejas F. Theory of algebraic module specifications including behavioural semantics and constraints, Proc. AMAST 91.
7. Ehrig H, Mahr B. Fundamentals of Algebraic Specifications 1, Springer 1985.
8. Ehrig H, Mahr B. Fundamentals of Algebraic Specifications 2, Springer 1989.
9. Goguen J, Burstall R. CAT, a system for the structured elaboration of correct programs from structured specifications. Technical report CSL-118, Comp. Sc. Laboratory, SRI Int. (1980).
10. Goguen J, Burstall R. Institutions: Abstract model theory for specification and programming, Journ. of the ACM 39, 1 (1992) 95-146.
11. Goguen J, Meseguer J. Universal realization, persistent interconnection and implementation of abstract modules. Proc. 9th ICALP, Aarhus. Springer LNCS 140, 265-281 (1982).
12. Orejas F, Navarro M, Sánchez A. Implementations and behavioural equivalence: a survey.8th Workshop on Specification of Abstract Data Types. Springer LNCS 655 (1993), 93-125.
13. Orejas F, Sacristan V, Clérici S. Development of algebraic specifications with constraints. in 'Categorical Methods in Computer Science'. Springer LNCS 393, 102-123 (1989).
14. Reichel H. Initially restricting algebraic theories, Proc. MFCS 80, Springer LNCS 88 (1980), pp. 504-514.
15. Schoett O. Data Abstraction and the Correctness of Modular Programming. Ph.D. thesis; Report CST-42-87, Dept. of Computer Science, Univ. of Edinburgh (1987).
16. Sannella DT, Tarlecki A. Toward formal development of programs from algebraic specifications: implementations revisited. Acta Informatica 25, 233-281 (1988).
17. Sannella DT, Tarlecki A. Toward formal development of ML programs: foundations and methodology. LFCS Report Series, Univ. of Edinburgh ECS-LFCS-89-71(1989).
18. Wirsing M. Algebraic Specification. Handbook of Theoretical Computer Science, Vol 2: Formal Models and Semantics, Elsevier (1991) 675 - 788.

Interaction between Algebraic Specification Grammars and Modular System Design

Hartmut Ehrig
Fachbereich Informatik, Technische Universität Berlin
D-10587 Berlin Germany

Francesco Parisi-Presicce
Dip. di Matematica Pura ed Applicata, Universitá degli Studi L'Aquila
I-67100 L'Aquila Italy

Abstract
The problem of designing a modular system with given interfaces can be reduced to the generation of a specification in an algebraic specification grammar and the subsequent translation of the derivation into design. The need to obtain more general interconnections has motivated a different notion of derivation in algebraic specification grammars, namely restricting derivation sequences where each specification produced can be reduced using a specification morphism. On the other hand, recent results on canonical derivations for algebraic specification grammars can be used to check the equivalence of modular systems by reducing them to the normal form obtained from the canonical derivation

1 Introduction

For the last 20 years, abstract data types have been (usefully) described using algebraic specifications, within different frameworks including equational institutions, and with diverse semantics, from initial to loose to stratified to behavioral. An extension of the original formulation which allows to isolate a *variable* part (thus generalizing parametrized specifications) and to *hide* details of the specification from the outside (to model encapsulation mechanisms such as modules, clusters and classes) has been defined in [8, 1, 6]. A module specification in such a framework consists of four parts : an export interface EXP specifying what the module specification *produces*, an import interface IMP describing what the module specification *consumes* or needs, a body part BOD describing how the module specification uses the imported items to construct the exported ones and containing hidden implementation details, and a parameter part PAR which can be *actualized* by different actual specifications and which is left unchanged by the semantics of the module specification.

Each module is seen as a self-contained unit developped independently and interconnected with other modules. Three basic interconnection mechanisms have been defined [6] to construct complex systems : a *union* $MOD1 +_{MOD0} MOD2$ where each part is the union of the corresponding ones in MOD1 and MOD2, identifying the MOD0 part; an *actualization* $act_h(PS, MOD)$, where a parametrized specification PS is substituted via the specification morphism h for PAR in each component of MOD; and a *composition* $MOD1 \circ_h MOD2$, where the import IMP1 is matched via the specification morphism h with the export EXP2. The semantics of such mechanisms can be easily given by viewing each interconnection as an operation on module specifications which preserves correctness and which produces a module specification whose semantics can be expressed in terms of those of the operands.

An important problem is to determine whether there is a way to interconnect some of the module specifications of a library LIB so that the import and export interfaces of the overall system are some given specifications BASE and GOAL. This problem has been tackled in [9, 10, 11] by considering the visible part of MOD, i.e., the specifications PAR, IMP and EXP, as a production $p : IMP \leftarrow PAR \rightarrow EXP$ similar to those of the algebraic theory of graph grammars [2]. The problem of designing the desired modular system is reduced to finding a way to generate GOAL in the algebraic specification grammar defined by the initial specification BASE and by the productions extracted from the module specifications. There is a systematic way of constructing the modular system from the derivation. Unfortunately, the induced interconnection is limited to actualization and identity composition and thus the nonexistence of a derivation does not imply the nonexistence of a modular system. In particular, general composition allows one to take only part of a module export interface: this has suggested to revise the notion of derivation sequence by inserting between two direct derivations an 'inverse morphism' representing the possibility of taking only a view of the modular system obtained after the first derivation. This idea of restricting derivation sequences has been extended to graph grammars [12] and can be defined in High Level Replacement Systems (HLRS) [3].

As modular system design has motivated an extension of algebraic specification grammars, so recent extensions to HLRS of canonical derivation sequences for graphs have motivated the notion of a canonical structuring of a modular system, which allows not only the manipulation of interconnections to reach a design with certain properties, but also the testing of equivalence between two arbitrary systems by comparing their unique canonical forms. For simplicity of presentation, we use simple algebraic specifications, but it is easy to see that the development can be generalized to other institutions or logical frames, provided they satisfy the basic general properties of HLRS as presented in [3].

2 Reducing Derivation Sequences

We assume that the reader is familiar with the notions of ***algebraic specification*** $SPEC = (S, OP, E)$ and of ***specification morphism*** $f = (f_S, f_{OP}, f_E) : SPEC \rightarrow SPEC'$ as in [5]. In our examples we use a more intuitive notation listing under the keywords **sorts**, **opns**, **eqns** the elements of the three components of the specification. In particular,
FS-PAR = **bool** +
sorts $f^*, dest, dep$
opns $Eqf : f^*\ f^* \rightarrow bool$; $Nodep : \rightarrow dep$
eqns $Eqf(F^*, F^*) = True$
denotes the specification obtained by adding to the standard specification of boolean values the set of sorts $\{f^*, dest, dep\}$, the operation symbol Eqf and the constant $Nodep$ and an equation universally quantified over all the F^* ranging over elements of sort f^*.

As mentioned in the Introduction, a *module specification* consists of four algebraic specifications and four specification morphisms as in the following com-

$$\begin{array}{ccc} PAR & \xrightarrow{e} & EXP \\ {\scriptstyle i}\downarrow & & \downarrow{\scriptstyle v} \\ IMP & \xrightarrow{s} & BOD \end{array}$$

mutative diagram
The items *not* in the image of v are to be considered hidden and thus not visible from other modules. In all our examples, the four specification morphisms of a module are taken to be inclusions.

We (re)use the example of a specification of a module for a flight schedule with flight number (f^*) , destination ($dest$) and departure time (dep) from [8, 6] with minor modifications to define
FS-MOD = (FS-PAR, FS-EXP, FS-IMP, FS-BOD) where FS-PAR is as given above, FS-IMP = FS-PAR,
FS-EXP = FS-PAR +
sorts fs
opns $Createfs :\to fs$; $Addfs : f^*\ dest\ dep\ fs \to fs$;
$Searchfs : f^*\ fs \to bool$; $Returnfs : f^*\ fs \to dep$; $Wherefs : f^*\ fs \to dest$
eqns $Searchfs(F^*, Createfs) = False$;
$Searchfs(F^*, FS) = True \Rightarrow Addfs(F^*, DES, DEP, FS) = FS$;
$Wherefs(F^*, Addfs(F^*, DES, DEP, FS)) = DES$
FS-BOD = FS-EXP +
opns $Tab : f^*\ dest\ dep\ fs \to fs$
eqns $Addfs(F^*, DES, DEP, Createfs) = Tab(F^*, DES, DEP, Createfs)$;
$Addfs(F*, DES, DEP, Tab(F1^*, DES1, DEP1, FS)) =$
if $Eqf(F^*, F1^*)$ **then** $Tab(F1^*, DES1, DEP1, FS)$
else $Tab(F1^*, DES1, DEP1, Addfs(F^*, DES, DEP, FS))$

There are three basic ways of interconnecting module specifications [6]: *union* $MOD3 = MOD1 +_{MOD0} MOD2$, *actualization* $act_h(PS, MOD)$ and *composition* $MOD1 \circ_h MOD2$. Having an interconnection mechanism for the modules, the problem is how to design a modular system which will produce a model of a desired specification (the overall export interface of the system) given a model of a set of predefined data type specifications (the overall import interface). The approach proposed in [9] is to view the visible part (PAR,EXP,IMP) of a module specification MOD as a *production* $p = (IMP \leftarrow PAR \to EXP)$ and to reduce the problem of designing a system using a set LIB of module specifications to the problem of formally deriving the desired specification GOAL from the predefined specification BASE using the interfaces of the modules in LIB as productions. A direct derivation $p : SPEC \Rightarrow SPEC'$ with such a production p is a double pushout diagram

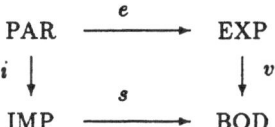

$$\begin{array}{ccccc} \text{IMP} & \longleftarrow & \text{PAR} & \longrightarrow & \text{EXP} \\ \downarrow & & \downarrow & & \downarrow \\ \text{SPEC} & \longleftarrow & \text{CON} & \longrightarrow & \text{SPEC'} \end{array}$$

where CON is the context specification unchanged by the *transformation*. As usual $\Rightarrow^\star$ denotes the reflexive and transitive closure of $\Rightarrow$.
The interfaces of FS-MOD form a production FS-PRO which can be applied to
nat + string = bool +
sorts *nat*, *str*, *alph*
opns $0 :\rightarrow nat$; $Succ : nat \rightarrow nat$; $Eq : nat\ nat \rightarrow bool$;
$Empty :\rightarrow str$; $Make : alph \rightarrow str$; $Conc : str\ str \rightarrow str$
eqns $Eq(X, X) = True$; $Eq(Succ(X), Succ(Y)) = Eq(X, Y)$;
$Eq(Succ(X), 0) = False$; $Eq(0, Succ(Y)) = False$;
$Conc(Conc(X, Y), Z) = Conc(X, Conc(Y, Z))$;
$Conc(X, Empty) = X = Conc(Empty, X)$
via the specification morphism which maps f^* and *dep* to *nat*, *dest* to *str*,*Nodep* to 0, *Nodest* to *Empty*, etc. to produce the specification
SPEC1' = **nat + string +**
sorts *fs*
opns $Createfs :\rightarrow fs$; $Addfs : nat\ str\ nat\ fs \rightarrow fs$;
$Searchfs : nat\ fs \rightarrow bool$; $Returnfs : nat\ fs \rightarrow nat$; $Wherefs : nat\ fs \rightarrow str$
eqns $Searchfs(N, Createfs) = False$;
$Searchfs(N, FS) = True \Rightarrow Addfs(N, DES, N', FS) = FS$;
$Wherefs(N, Addfs(N, STR, DEP, FS)) = STR$

It has been shown in [10, 11] that, given a library LIB of module specifications represented by their interfaces $PRO = \{p_i : IMP_i \leftarrow PAR_i \rightarrow EXP_i, i \in I\}$, then $BASE \Rightarrow^\star GOAL$ using PRO *if and only if* there exists an interconnection, using only actualization and composition with identity, of (some of) the module specifications of LIB such that BASE and GOAL are the overall import and export interfaces, respectively. This result can be seen as a way to construct a prototype of a system which, given a (built-in) realization of BASE, provides a realization of GOAL (which can be used to test the adequacy of the specification) since there is a systematic way of translating a derivation sequence $BASE \Rightarrow^\star GOAL$ into the appropriate combination of the interconnections.

This solution is not satisfactory for two reasons. The first one is that not every interconnection of the module specifications can be obtained from a derivation sequence and, in particular, general compositions with non-identity matching morphism $IMP1 \rightarrow EXP2$ cannot be obtained by "translating" a derivation sequence. The second one is that an occurrence morphism $IMP \rightarrow SPEC$ from the left hand side to a specification does not guarantee [9] the applicability of the production to the specification, while from the point of view of modular system design it should be possible to use only part (namely $h(IMP)$) of a specification SPEC as the input of a module specification MOD.

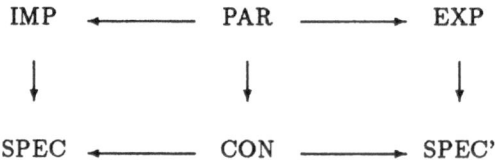

Let the production $APSPRO = (APSIMP \leftarrow APSPAR \rightarrow APSEXP)$ be defined by $APSPAR = FS - PAR +_{\mathbf{bool}} FS - PAR$
and, indicating by ps, p^*, typ and sea the duplicates of fs, f^*, $dest$ and dep, respectively, in the previous 'union',
$APSIMP = APSPAR +$
sorts fs, ps
opns $Createfs :\rightarrow fs$; $Addfs : f^*\ dest\ dep\ fs \rightarrow fs$;
$Searchfs : f^*\ fs \rightarrow bool$; $Returnfs : f^*\ fs \rightarrow dep$; $Wherefs : f^*\ fs \rightarrow dest$;
$Createps :\rightarrow ps$; $Addps : p^*\ typ\ sea\ ps \rightarrow ps$;
$Searchps : p^*\ ps \rightarrow bool$; $Returnps : p^*\ ps \rightarrow sea$
eqns $Searchfs(F^*, Createfs) = False$; $Searchps(P^*, Createps) = False$;
$Searchfs(F^*, FS) = True \Rightarrow Addfs(F^*, DES, DEP, FS) = FS$;
$Wherefs(F^*, Addfs(F^*, DES, DEP, FS)) = DES$;
$Searchps(P^*, PS) = True \Rightarrow Addfs(P^*, TYP, SEA, PS) = PS$;
$APSEXP = APSPAR +$
sorts aps
opns $Create :\rightarrow aps$; $Schedule : f^*\ dest\ dep\ p^*\ typ\ sea\ aps \rightarrow aps$;
$Search : f^*\ aps \rightarrow bool$; $Return : f^*\ aps \rightarrow dep$;
eqns $Search(F^*, Create) = False$;
$Search(F^*, APS) = True \Rightarrow$
$Schedule(F^*, DES, DEP, P^*, TYP, SEA, APS) = APS$.

The production APSPRO cannot be applied to the specification SPEC1' even if there is an obvious specification morphism from APSIMP to SPEC1', because such morphism does not satisfy the Gluing Condition [2, 9]. On the other hand, if there is a modular system which produces SPEC1', then it can be composed with the module specification APSMOD of which APSPRO is the visible part, to produce a system with APSEXP as overall export. A restricting step - corresponding to the morphism needed in the composition - allows one to remove the items which interfere with the Gluing Condition and to apply the production APSPRO. This suggests the notion of *restricting derivation sequences* $SP0 \gg SPn$ with

$$SP0 \leftarrow SP1 \Rightarrow SP1' \leftarrow SP2 \Rightarrow \ldots \leftarrow SPn$$

where, having generated $SP0$, we can generate $SP1'$ provided that there exist $SP1$ and a specification morphism $SP1 \rightarrow SP0$ such that $SP1 \Rightarrow SP1'$, and so on. We then have

Theorem 1 *$BASE \gg GOAL$* via the productions PRO **if and only if** there exists an interconnection with general composition and actualization using LIB with overall interfaces BASE and GOAL.

It is direct to show that if $SP \Rightarrow^* SP'$, then $SP \gg SP'$ but not necessarily viceversa.

The specification
$GOAL = \mathbf{nat} + \mathbf{string} +$
sorts sc
opns $New :\rightarrow sc$; $Extend : nat\ str\ nat\ nat\ str\ nat\ sc \rightarrow sc$;
$Give : natsc \rightarrow nat$; $Find : natsc \rightarrow bool$
eqns $Find(N, New) = False$;
$Find(N, SC) = True \Rightarrow Extend(N1, ST1, M1, N2, ST2, M2, SC) = SC$

can be generated by the set of productions PRO which consists of the interfaces of FS-MOD and APSMOD, starting from **nat + string**. First apply FS-PRO to obtain SPEC1' : in this case, SPEC0 and SPEC1 coincide since FS-PRO is directly applicable. Then, with a restricting step h eliminate the operation $Wherefs$ and duplicate the sort fs and the operations $Createfs$, $Searchfs$, $Addfs$ and $Returnfs$ to obtain SPEC2. Now there is a morphism from APS-IMP to the specification SPEC2, mapping the *fs-part* to the *fs-part* and the *ps-part* to the duplicated items. An application of APSPRO to generate SPEC2', via the context specification CON, followed by the appropriate restricting step (which accomplishes the renaming of sorts and operations as well) provides the required specification.

The modular system can be extracted from the derivation : first we construct $act(\mathbf{nat+string}, FS-MOD)$ which has **nat + string** and SPEC1' as interfaces; then construct $act(CON, APSMOD)$ from the second derivation step; finally we take their composition via the specification morphism h to obtain $act(CON, APSMOD) \circ_h act(\mathbf{nat+string}, FS-MOD)$ from which we take the appropriate "view" using the inclusion $GOAL \rightarrow SPEC2'$.
The approach can be extended in a straightforward manner to High Level Replacement Systems [3]. Such systems have been defined to generalize, in an axiomatic way to arbitrary categories, the Parallelism Theorem, the Concurrency Theorem and other similar results typical of the algebraic theory of graph grammars [2]. By selecting a distinguished subset M of morphisms to be used in the productions, High Level Replacement Systems can be classified (at least) as HLR0, HLR0.5, HLR0.5*, HLR1 and HLR1* depending on which set of generic properties on the underlying category they satisfy and which are sufficient to guarantee properties such as local confluence of independent derivations or replacing a sequence $p_1 \circ p_2$ of independent derivations with one step using their disjoint union $p_1 + p_2$.

3 Canonical System Design

In this section, we investigate how ideas of algebraic specification grammars can suggest notions in modular system design which can exploit results from High Level Replacement Systems. Recently [4], results on canonical derivation sequences for graph grammars have been extended to HLR systems. Before defining canonical derivations, we need the notion of *equivalence* of derivations.
Given a derivation $s : G \Rightarrow_* G0 \Rightarrow_{p1} G1 \Rightarrow_{p+p2} G3 \Rightarrow_* G'$
where $p1$ and p are sequentially independent in $G0 \Rightarrow_{p1} G1 \Rightarrow_p G2$
the derivation sequence
$s' : G \Rightarrow_* G0 \Rightarrow_{p1+p} G2 \Rightarrow_{p2} G3 \Rightarrow_* G'$ is called a **shift** of p in s.
Two derivations s and s' are *equivalent* if they are related by the reflexive, transitive and symmetric closure of the **shift** relation.

A canonical derivation is a derivation which does not contain two steps $p_1 : G0 \Rightarrow G1$ and $p + p_2 : G1 \Rightarrow G3$ where $p_1 : G0 \Rightarrow G1$ and $p : G1 \Rightarrow G2$ are sequentially independent. For non canonical derivations in which such a situation occurs, the application of p could be shifted earlier to obtain the equivalent derivation sequence $p+p_1 : G0 \Rightarrow G2$, $p_2 : G2 \Rightarrow G3$ which increases the leftmost parallelism. Thus, canonical derivations are derivations with optimal leftmost parallelism. It has been shown in [4] that canonical derivations exist for High Level Replacement Systems based on HLR0.5 categories (i.e., where the morphisms of a production are from a distinguished class **M** of morphisms of a category **CAT**, pushouts of **M**-morphisms and generic morphisms exist and 'inherit' **M**-morphisms, **M** is closed under binary coproducts, which exist for all morphisms) and are unique for HLRS based on HLR1* categories.

The way morphisms between two algebraic specifications are defined determines the crucial properties needed for Algebraic Specification Grammars. Of the three possible ways of defining the category of algebraic specifications considered [7, 4] only the one (defining the category **LAB**) which allows one to distinguish, through labels, equations between terms guarantees unique canonical derivations, while if the specification morphisms $f : SPEC1 \rightarrow SPEC2$ are such that $f^{\#}(E1)$ is either derivable (in some calculus) or syntactically contained in $E2$ (defining the categories **DER** and **INCL**, respectively) then every derivation has an equivalent canonical one, which is not necessarily unique.

Canonical derivation sequences correspond to modular designs and can be used to check the equivalence of modular systems. There are several ways of defining equivalence between modular systems, among which:

- $S1 equiv_1 S2$ if the flattened versions obtained by applying as operations the interconnections have isomorphic interfaces
- $S1 equiv_2 S2$ if, in addition, the corresponding semantical functors are naturally isomorphic
- $S1 equiv_3 S2$ if the flattened versions are isomorphic (not only the interfaces are isomorphic but also the body parts and therefore the corresponding free functors)

If we limit our attention to the systems which are constructed using only disjoint union, actualization and identity composition we have the following result.

Theorem 2
- Every modular system based on the category **INCL** has a canonical equivalent one.
- Every modular system based on the category **LAB** has a *unique* canonical equivalent system

It is easy to see that the equivalence of the theorem is 'at least' what we have called $S1 equiv_1 S2$ since each **shift** step leaves unchanged the initial and final specifications. It can be shown that in fact the results hold for the more restrictive form of equivalence $S1 equiv_3 S2$. What needs to be done is to extend this result to systems built using general composition.

We illustrate the last theorem with a simple example taken from [10]. First we modify the production FS-PRO used earlier by eliminating the operations *Returnfs* and *Wherefs* in FS-EXP to obtain the production SFSPRO. Let OUT be the specification consisting of **nat + string** and the following sorts, operations and axioms (where for readibility we have maintained the intended meaning instead of replacing *title*, *author* and *type* by the sort *str* and *duedate*, *patno* and *phone* by *nat*)

sorts *books, patrons, library*

opns $Create : \rightarrow books$; $Reserved : title\ author\ duedate\ books \rightarrow books$; $Look : title\ books \rightarrow bool$; $Nodate : \rightarrow duedate$; $Eqt : title\ title \rightarrow bool$; $New : \rightarrow patrons$; $Find : patno\ patrons \rightarrow bool$; $Add : patno\ type\ phone\ patrons \rightarrow patrons$;

$Initial : \rightarrow library$; $Search : title\ library \rightarrow bool$;
$Borrow : title\ author\ duedate\ patno\ type\ phone\ library \rightarrow library$
eqns $Search(TI, Initial) = False$; $Eqt(TI, TI) = True$;
$Search(TI, LIB) = True \Rightarrow$
$Borrow(TI, AUT, DD, PN, TYP, PHO, LIB) = LIB$
$Look(TI, BO) = True \Rightarrow Date(TI, Update(TI, DD, BO)) = DD$
$Look(TI, BO) = True \Rightarrow Reserved(TI, AUT, DD, BO) = BO$
$Look(TI, Create) = False$; $Find(PN, New) = False$,
$Find(PN, PAT) = True \Rightarrow Add(PN, TYP, PHO, PAT) = PAT$

It is a simple exercise to check that there exists a modular design with overall import **nat + string** and overall export interface OUT obtained as $act(\mathbf{nat + string}, SFSMOD) \circ act(CON1, SFSMOD) \circ$
$act(CON2, APSMOD) \circ act(CON3, SFSMOD) \circ act(CON4, SFSMOD)$ for appropriate specifications CONi.
If we let $FOUR$ be the disjoint union of 4 copies of $SFSMOD$, the corresponding canonical derivation sequence is
$\mathbf{nat + string} \Rightarrow_{FOUR} SP \Rightarrow_{APS} OUT$
which corresponds to the modular design
$act(\mathbf{nat + string}, FOUR) \circ act(CON, APSMOD)$ for an appropriate CON.

References

[1] E.K.Blum, H.Ehrig, F.Parisi-Presicce: Algebraic Specifications of Modules and their Basic Interconnections. J. Comput. Syst. Sci. **34** (1987) 293-339

[2] H.Ehrig: Introduction to the Algebraic Theory of Graph Grammars. First International Workshop on Graph Grammars, Springer Lect. Notes Comp. Sci. 73 (1979) 1-69

[3] H.Ehrig, A.Habel,H.-J.Kreowski,F.Parisi-Presicce: Parallelism and Concurrency in High Level Replacement Systems. Math. Struct.in Comp. Science 1 (1991) 361-406

[4] H.Ehrig,H.-J.Kreowski, G.Taentzer: Canonical Derivations for High-level Replacement Systems. Techn.Report 6/92, Univ. Bremen, FB Mathematik und Informatik, Dec 1992

[5] H.Ehrig, B.Mahr: Fundamentals of Algebraic Specification 1.Equations and Initial Semantics. EATCS Monograph on Theoret. Comp. Sci., vol 6,Springer Verlag 1985

[6] H.Ehrig, B.Mahr: Fundamentals of Algebraic Specification 2.Module Specifications and Constraints. EATCS Monograph on Theoret. Comp. Sci., vol 21,Springer Verlag 1990

[7] H.Ehrig, F.Parisi-Presicce: High Level Replacement Systems for Equational Algebraic Specifications. Proc. 3rd Int. Conf. on Algebraic and Logic Programming, Springer Lect. Notes Comp. Sci. 632 (1992) 3-20.

[8] H.Ehrig H.Weber: Algebraic Specification of Modules. in "Formal Models in Programming" (E.J.Neuhold and G.Chronist, eds.), North-Holland (1985) 231-258

[9] F.Parisi-Presicce: Modular System Design applying Graph Grammar Techniques. Proc. ICALP 89, Springer Lect. Notes Comp. Sci. 372 (1989) 621-636

[10] F.Parisi-Presicce: A Rule Based Approach to Modular System Design. Proc. 12th Internat. Conf. Soft. Engin. (1990) 202-211

[11] F.Parisi-Presicce: Foundations of Rule-Based Design of Modular Systems. Theoret. Comp. Sci. **83** (1991) 131-155

[12] F.Parisi-Presicce: Single vs. Double Pushout Derivations of Graphs. Proc. 18th Int. Workshop on Graph Theoretic Concepts in Comp. Sci. Springer Lect. Notes Comp. Sci. 657 (1993) 248-262

Specification of Hybrid Systems in CRP

R.K. Shyamasundar*
Tata Institute of Fundamental Research
Homi Bhabha Road, Bombay 400 005, India
e-mail: shyam@turing.tifr.res.in

Abstract

In this paper, we show that the paradigm of *Communicating Reactive Processes* (CRP) unifying asynchronous and perfectly synchronous mechanisms can be naturally extended for the specification of *continuous* computations and provide a convenient formalism for specifying hybrid systems. Further, it can be used for specifying asynchronous systems operating in dense real-time domains.

1 Introduction

Programming languages based on the *perfect synchrony paradigm* have proven useful for programming reactive systems. Perfect synchrony paradigm essentially states that the considered reactive programs respond in no time and produce their outputs synchronously with their input. One of the main reasons for its success is that it permits the programmer to focus on the logic of reactions and makes it possible to use several automata-based verification systems for correctness proofs. Further, the correctness proofs of programs follow their implementation very closely and hence, are more robust and reliable. However, the application is limited to clocked systems. If we look at complex reactive system specifications such as process control systems and robotic applications, the need for features such as (i) asynchronous events (events that can happen arbitrarily close to each other), (ii) integration of discrete and continuous components (continuous components may cause continuous change in the values of some state variables according to some physical law), and (iii) explicit clock times, become apparent. In [4], a paradigm referred to as *Communicating Reactive Processes* (CRP) that provides a unification of perfect synchrony and asynchrony has been presented. In this paper, we discuss an extension of CRP, referred to as *Timed* CRP, that

- models *continuous* computations and thus, provides a convenient formalism for specifying hybrid systems, and
- models asynchronous systems operating in dense real-time domains.

Consider specifying hybrid systems that combine discrete and continuous components possibly with the need to reference clocks explicitly. For consistency, it is necessary to have a consistent assumption about the progress of the computation as the system evolves. In the timed CRP, it has been possible to provide such a consistent assumption through the clocked semantics of ESTEREL and the interpretation of the clocks in terms of the **exec** primitive. One of the

*The work was partially supported by IFCPAR (Indo-French Centre for the promotion of Advanced Research), New Delhi, India.

interesting features is that hybrid systems without explicit references to clocks can be specified by a subset of timed CRP consisting of just the statements of ESTEREL and the **exec** primitive. The full version of timed CRP can specify dense asynchronous systems with explicit references to clocks.

2 Hybrid Systems

Hybrid systems are systems that combine discrete and continuous computations. Hybrid system model contains activities that modify their variables continuously over intervals of positive duration in addition to the familiar transitions that change the values of variables instantaneously, representing the discrete components. Many systems that interact with a physical environment such as a digital module controlling a process or a manufacturing plant, a digital-analog guidance of transport systems, control of a robot, flexible manufacturing systems etc., can benefit from the study of hybrid models. In the sequel, we use the word *asynchronous* to mean that initiation and completion cannot happen simultaneously; in other words, the initiation and completion of an asynchronous activity are observable. Various abstract models for systems for handling real-time and *continuous* computations have been proposed recently in [6,7,8]. An extension of Statecharts for the specification of hybrid systems has been described in [6]. In this paper, we broadly use the definitions of hybrid systems as defined in [6,7] and the main characteristics of the hybrid model is briefed below.

A *continuous or a hybrid* component is defined as an *asynchronous activity* characterized by $(\mathcal{V}, \mathcal{A}, \Theta, \mathcal{F}, \mathcal{E})$ where:

- $\mathcal{V}$ is the set of *continuous*, V_c and *discrete*, V_d, variables that are modified by continuous and discrete activities respectively.
- $\mathcal{A}$ is a finite set of activities: Each activity, $\alpha \in \mathcal{A}$ is a conditional differential equation of the form, $p \rightarrow \dot{x} = e$, where p is a predicate over V_d called the activation condition of α, $x \in V_c$ is a continuous state variable and e is an expression over V. We say that the activity α governs variable x. Activity α is said to be *active* in state s if its activation condition p holds in s; otherwise, α is said to be *passive*. It is required that the activation conditions of the activities that govern the same variable x be exhaustive and exclusive, i.e., exactly one of them holds on any state.
- $\mathcal{E}$ is a set of important events: These are all the observable discrete events relative to the finite set of activities.
- Θ defines the initial condition.
- $\mathcal{F}$ is the set of differential equations satisfying the conditions given in [7].

3 Timed CRP

A CRP program consists of a network $M_1 \ // \ M_2 \ \cdots \ // \ M_n$ of ESTEREL reactive programs or *nodes*, each having its own input/output reactive signals and its own notion of an instant. The network is asynchronous and node M_i is locally reactively driving a part of a complex network which is handled globally by the network. Asynchronous communication between nodes is achieved through the

exec primitive and **channel** declarations. The informal and formal semantics of some of the important constructs of the language are given below.

3.1 Informal Semantics

3.1.1 Basic ESTEREL

The execution of an ESTEREL program associates a sequence of output events with a sequence of input events. The program repeatedly receives an input event E_i from its environment and reacts by building an output event E'_i. The events E_i and E'_i are synchronous in the sense that the external observer observes the input/output event as a single event $E_i \cup E'_i$. The production of an output event from an input event is called a *reaction*. The flow of time is defined by the sequence of reactions and hence,*reaction* is also termed an *instant*. Note that at any instant there is at least one input signal. A signal is present at an instant if and only if it is received as input from the environment or emitted by the program itself at that instant. At each instant, each input or local signal is consistently seen as present or absent by all statements - thus, ensuring determinism. By default, signals are absent. The notion of an instant leads to consistent definitions of temporal expressions.

In order to provide the ability to quantify the progress of computation as the system evolves, we assume that every input event or instant consists of a special clock signal of type *real* referred to as **tick**.

The list ESTEREL kernel statements is given below:

```
nothing
halt
emit S
stat1; stat2
loop stat end
present S then stat1 else stat2 end
do stat watching S
stat1 || stat2
trap T in stat end
exit T
signal S in stat end
```

The kernel statements are imperative in nature, and most of them are classical in appearance. Instantaneous control transmission appears everywhere. The **nothing** statement is purely transparent: it terminates immediately when started. An **emit** S statement is instantaneous: it broadcasts S and terminates right away, making the emission of S transient. In **emit** S1; **emit** S2, the signals S1 and S2 are emitted simultaneously. In a signal-presence test such as **present** S ..., the presence of S is tested for right away and the **then** or **else** branch is immediately started accordingly. In a **loop** *stat* **end** statement, the body *stat* starts immediately when the loop statement starts, and whenever *stat* terminates it is instantaneously restarted afresh; to avoid infinite instantaneous looping, it is required that the body of a loop should not terminate instantaneously when started.

The **watching** and **trap-exit** statements deal with behavior preemption – the most important feature of ESTEREL. In the watchdog statement **do** *stat* **watching** S, the statement *stat* is executed normally up to proper termination or up to future occurrence of the signal S, which is called the guard. If *stat* terminates strictly before `S` occurs, so does the whole `watching` statement; then the guard has no action; otherwise, the occurrence of `S` provokes immediate preemption of the body *stat* leading to immediate termination of the whole watching statement. Note that nesting watching statements provides for priorities. For details on `trap`, the reader is referred to [3].

3.1.2 Asynchronous Tasks

In a very general way, asynchronous tasks are those tasks which do take time; that is, the time between initiation and completion is observable. In the terminology of ESTEREL , this can be interpreted to mean that there will be at least one instant between initiation and completion. The `exec` primitive provides the interface between ESTEREL and asynchronous tasks.

Task Declaration

An asynchronous task is declared as follows:

`task task_id (par_lst) [(CONT: DE; var_lst)] return signal_nm (type);`

where

- `par_lst` gives the list of *discrete* parameters (reference or value);
- the signal returned by the task is given by the `signal_nm` with its type after the keyword `return`; it is possible to have multiple return signals.
- the optional phrase `[CONT:DE ; var_lst]` is used if the underlying task has a *continuous* component. Here, `DE` denotes the underlying differential equation and `var_lst` denotes the list of *continuous* variables. If the differential equation of the form $\dot{x} = e$ satisfies the conditions stated earlier, then the value of the continuous variables can be computed at various instants (e.g., linear hybrid systems).

A typical example of the declaration of a hybrid component is given by:

`task MOUSE (y) (CONT:` $\dot{X}_m = -V_m$; x_m`) return Mouse ({sanct,kill})`

Task Instantiation

Instantiation of the task is done through the primitive `exec`. For example, the above task can be instantiated from an ESTEREL program as follows:

`exec MOUSE (y) (`x_m`)`

The execution of the above statement starts task `MOUSE` and waits for its termination; of course, the number and type of arguments, and the return signal type should match with the task declared. In other words, `exec` requests the environment to start the task and then waits for the return signal (which also indicates the termination of the task).

Since there can be several occurrences of `exec T` in a module for the same task `T`, several simultaneously active tasks having the same name can coexist. To avoid confusion among them one can assign an explicit label to each `exec` statement; a labeled `exec` statement is of the form `exec L:T`. The label name must be distinct from all other labels and input signal names. An implicit distinct label is given to `exec` statements.

The primitive **exec** provides an interface between ESTEREL and the asynchronous environment can be seen by the following interpretation. Given an **exec** statement labeled L, the asynchronous task execution is controlled from ESTEREL by three implicit signals **sL** ((output signal), L (input signal), and **kL** (output signal) corresponding to starting the task, completion and killing the execution of the task respectively. The output *start* signal **sL** is sent to the environment when the **exec** statement starts. It requests the start of an asynchronous incarnation of the task. The input *return signal* L, is sent by the environment when the task incarnation is terminated; it provokes instantaneous termination of the **exec** statement. the output *kill signal* **kL** is emitted by ESTEREL if the **exec** statement is preëmpted before termination, either by an enclosing watching statement or by concurrent exit from an enclosing trap. The return signals corresponding to the **exec** label can be used for declaring incompatibility with other input signals (this becomes handy in declaring channels).

3.1.3 Interpretation of a Global Clock in terms of **exec**

Consider a task CLOCK which accesses a global clock and sends the alarm signals at the times requested. Declaration of the task CLOCK in timed CRP takes the form:

```
task CLOCK(d) return alarm ({real})
```

Now, an alarm after ℓ units can be instantiated by

```
exec CLOCK(ℓ)
```

Since the **exec** statement is not instantaneous, it follows that $\ell > 0$. The semantics of **exec** permits the use of multiple instantiations on the same and different nodes. This feature makes it possible to use CLOCK as a global clock for the different components.

3.1.4 Timed Statements

The primitive timed statements of Timed CRP are given below where `tick` denotes the clock signal.

a. *await* with *ticks*:
   await tick(d): This statement delays the next reaction till the instant $t + d$ is crossed where t is the value of CLOCK at the current instant. In other words, it corresponds to a delay of d. **await tick(0)** is not valid as it instantaneously terminates. In ESTEREL **await tick** corresponds to awaiting for the next input signal or the instant.

b. *watching with ticks*:
   do *stat* **watching tick(d)**: This statement gives the *time limit* to the execution of its body *stat*. Let us assume $d > 0$. In this case, the body starts as soon as the **watching** statement starts. If the body terminates or exits a trap strictly before a timeout of d from the current instant, so does the **watching** statement; otherwise the **watching** statement terminates as soon as the value of `tick` signal reaches $t + d$. As the **watching** statement is active at the current instant, $d = 0$ corresponds to the instantaneous termination of the body without being executed.

Restrictions: As `tick` is always present, the following restrictions are placed:

1. It is not permitted to use **tick** in expressions of **await Immediate** and **watch immediate** statement constructs.
2. The expressions in the **present** statement constructs are not allowed to reference clocks explicitly.

3.1.5 Using Timed Statements

1. *Specifying Time Bounds*
   (a) **await tick(ℓ)** specifies a delay of ℓ.
   (b) Specifying timeout (maximum duration) of u can be done by:
   do S watching tick(u) end
   (c) Enforcing a time interval of $[\ell, u]$ for producing a *good_part* in the usual producer-consumer problem (cf. [6]) is given below:

```
do
  [exec good_part || await tick(ℓ)]
  watching tick(u)
end
```

2. Actual time for the transition/task with a timeout of **d** is specified below:

```
x:=0;
do
 exec T; (* Let us assume that rT is the return signal *)
watching tick(d)
 emit abort ; (* aborted due to timeout *)
end
present rT then x := ?tick
```

   In the above program, **x** would have the actual value of time taken on proper termination; if aborted due to timeout then x will have value zero and also signal **abort** will be emitted.
3. Specifying time for multiple rendezvous and interrupt servicing can be done in the same manner.

3.1.6 Illustrative Example

Let us consider a variant of the Cat and Mouse problem described in [6] with the addition of a reward. The addition reflects the use of continuous variables during the computation. The variant of the problem is defined below.

At time $t = 0$, a mouse starts running from a certain position on the floor in a straight line towards a hole in the wall, which is at a distance X_0 from the initial position. The mouse runs at a constant velocity V_m. After Δ time units, a cat is released at the same initial position and chases the mouse at velocity V_c along the same path. The competition is as follows:

- CAT: It has to catch the MOUSE before it reaches the hole; reward is the MOUSE itself.
- MOUSE: It has to find a sanctuary in the hole before the CAT catches; it gets a reward of FOOD proportional to the distance the CAT did not cover.

Program in timed CRP is given below: (EXP denotes some pure function):

```
module WATCHER;
  task MOUSE (x) (CONT: Ẋ  =  −V) return MOUSE()
  task CAT (y) (CONT: Ẏ  =  −V) return CAT()
   loop
   do
     do
       [   exec MOUSE (x)
              ||
           await tick(Δ);
           exec CAT (y)
       ]
     watching  CAT
     timeout emit CAT_Wins;
     end;
    watching MOUSE
    timeout  emit MOUSE_WINS (FOOD(EXP(?tick,y))
    end;
    end
end module
```

In the programs there is a priority for the MOUSE; that is, if both reach the destination at the same time, MOUSE is declared the winner.

3.1.7 Formal Semantics

Given a module M and an input event I, the behavioral semantics determines a transition $M \underset{I}{\overset{O}{\longrightarrow}} M'$ where O is the generated output event and M' is another module suited to perform further reactions. The derivative M' has the same interface as M and differs only by its body. The reaction to a sequence of input events is computed by chaining such elementary transitions. The transition relation is defined by using an auxiliary inductive relation

$$< stat, \rho_C > \xrightarrow[E\cup\{\mathtt{tick}\}]{E',L.k} < stat', \rho'_{C'} >$$

on statements where

1. The old and the new signal environments are defined by,
   - E is the current event to which *stat* reacts; the return signal (input signal) of **exec** appears in E.
   - E' is the event emitted by *stat* in response to E; the start and kill signals (output signals) of **exec**'s appear in E'.
   - L is the set of labels of the **exec** statements currently active in *stat*;
   - The integer *termination level* k (cf. [3]) determines how control is handled. In each reaction, any statement can behave in three ways: it can terminate and release the control, it can retain the control and wait for further events, or it can exit a trap. We set $k = 0$ for proper termination, and $k = 1$ for waiting; other values correspond to trap-statements.
   - Since signals are broadcast, *stat* receives the signals it emits and E' will always be contained in E.
2. The old and the new states are defined by,

- ρ_C is the memory environment with C denoting the set of continuous variables corresponding to the active continuous tasks at the beginning of the transition.
- $\rho'_{C'}$ is the memory environment with C' denoting the value of continuous variables immediately at the end of the transition.
- For each $x \in C$, x is assigned a value given by the differential equation (say, $\dot{X} = exp$).

The relation between the two transition systems is given by $M \xrightarrow[I]{O} M'$ iff $< stat, \rho > \xrightarrow[I \cup O\{tick\}]{O,L.k} < stat', \rho' >$ where $stat$ and $stat'$ are the bodies and ρ and ρ' are the states of M and M' respectively; we assume the harmless restriction that $stat$ cannot internally emit input signals.

With respect to the set $\mathcal{L}$ of active **exec** labels, we use the notation,
$E\#L = E \cup \{kL | L \in \mathcal{L} \text{ and } sL \notin E\} \; - \; \{sL | L \in \mathcal{L} \text{ and } sL \in E\}$
to denote the set obtained from E by killing **exec** 's started before the current instant and ignoring the one's started at the current instant.

Transition Rules for Constructs without explicit time

For lack of space, we describe only the transition rules for **exec**, **watching** and **present** statements ignoring the state component.

The rule (*exec_start*) is used to start an **exec** statement. A distinct label is used for keeping track of several instances and the statement is rewritten into an auxiliary **exec_wait** statement which has been introduced for the sake of convenience. The rule (*exec_wait1*) expresses the termination of the asynchronous task with the receipt of the return signal from the task. The (*exec_wait2*) rule reflects the waiting for the arrival of the return signal from the task.

(exec_start) $\texttt{exec } L : P \xrightarrow[E]{sL,\{L\},1} \texttt{exec\_wait L : P}$
(exec_wait1) $\dfrac{L \in E,\ P \in TASK}{\texttt{exec\_wait } L : P \xrightarrow[E]{\emptyset,\emptyset,0} \texttt{nothing}}$
(exec_wait2) $\dfrac{L \notin E,\ P \in TASK}{\texttt{exec\_wait } L : P \xrightarrow[E]{\emptyset,\{L\},1} \texttt{exec\_wait } L : P}$

The rule for **watching** statement is given using a **present** statement that will behave as the required guard at future instants. For remembering the particular **exec**'s that should be killed if preemption occurs because of the presence of the signal S at some future instant, the **present** statement is decorated with the set of currently active exec-labels L. It can be seen that the set L is used in rule *present1* to generate the appropriate kill signals when the then-branch is taken (that is at preemption time).

(watching)

$$\frac{stat \xrightarrow[E]{E',L,k} stat'}{stat \ \texttt{watching}\ S \xrightarrow[E]{E',L,k} \texttt{present}_L\ S\ \texttt{else}\ stat'\ \texttt{watching}\ S}$$

(present1)

$$\frac{S \in E, \quad stat_1 \xrightarrow[E]{E_1',L_1,k_1} stat_1'}{\texttt{present}_L\ S\ \texttt{then}\ stat_1\ \texttt{else}\ stat_2\ \texttt{end} \xrightarrow[E]{E_1'\#L,L_1,k_1} stat_1'}$$

(present2)

$$\frac{S \notin E, \quad stat_2 \xrightarrow[E]{E_2',L_2,k_2} stat_2'}{\texttt{present}_L\ S\ \texttt{then}\ stat_1\ \texttt{else}\ stat_2\ \texttt{end} \xrightarrow[E]{E_2',L_2,k_2} stat_2'}$$

Transitions Rules for Constructs with Time

Let $\texttt{tick}(\delta_+)$ denote the incremental increase from the previous reading of the signal **tick**. Then the basic rules using time are given below:

(watching_t1)

$$\frac{stat \xrightarrow[E\cup\{\texttt{tick}(\delta_+)\}]{E',\{L\},k} stat', \ d > 0, \ d-\delta > 0}{\texttt{do}\ stat\ \texttt{watching}\ \texttt{tick}(d) \xrightarrow[E\cup\{\texttt{tick}(\delta_+)\}]{E',L,k} \texttt{do}\ stat'\ \texttt{watching}\ tick(d-\delta)}$$

(watching_t2)

$$\frac{stat \xrightarrow[E\cup\{\texttt{tick}(\delta_+)\}]{E',\{L\},k} stat', \ d > 0, \ d-\delta = 0}{\texttt{do}\ stat\ \texttt{watching}\ tick(d) \xrightarrow[E\cup\{\texttt{tick}(\delta_+)\}]{E'\#L,\emptyset,k} \texttt{nothing}}$$

The rule (*watching_t1*) reflects the perceiving of the advancement of the clock by the task whenever an event happened in the system. Every task perceives the same time. The time/alarm at d units from the point of watching becomes an input signal.

Rule (watching_t2) corresponds to timeout d. At this instant, the statement is preempted along with the asynchronous tasks L it is awaiting for.
Note: In the full ESTEREL notation (cf. [3]) $s^+(v1)$ is used to denote the value, $v1$, for signal, s, at the present instant and $s^-(v2)$ to denote the value in the previous instant. Using this notation, the expression $d - \delta > 0$ in the premise of (*watching_t1*), corresponds to $(d - |\mathtt{tick}^+(v_1)| - |\mathtt{tick}^-(v_2)|) > 0$; in other words, $v_2 - v_1 = \delta$.

Continuous Components

Let **exec** $L : \dot{Y} = e$ denote an asynchronous task denoting a continuous component where L is the label associated with the task and Y_L denotes the continuous variables associated with the task. In the following, rules for the basic transitions are given showing the changes to the continuous variables explicitly. In rule **exec_H_start**, the expression $\rho[Y_L \leftarrow \theta_L]$ denotes the assignment to the continuous variables when the task is initiated; signal environments remaining the same as given earlier. In rules **exec_H_wait1**, and **exec_H_wait2**, the expression $\rho[Y_L \leftarrow e(Y_L, \delta)]$ denotes updating of the continuous variables after the time advances by δ as per the differential equation given. In case, the continuous component is based on handshake communications, we need to have an additional rule to keep track of the instant at which the actual handshake/rendezvous starts (such a rule is not necessary in pure CRP).

(exec_H_start)

$$< \mathtt{exec}\ L : \dot{Y} = e,\ \rho > \xrightarrow[E]{sL,\{L\},1} < \mathtt{exec\_wait}\ L : \dot{Y} = e,\ \rho[Y_L \leftarrow \theta_{L_0}] >$$

(exec_H_wait1)

$$\frac{L \in E,\ P \in TASK}{< \mathtt{exec\_wait}\ \ L : \dot{Y} = e,\ \rho > \xrightarrow[E \cup \mathtt{tick}(\delta_+)]{\emptyset,\emptyset,0} < \mathtt{nothing}, \rho[Y_L \leftarrow e(Y_L, \delta)] >}$$

(exec_H_wait2)

$$\frac{L \notin E,\ P \in TASK}{< \mathtt{exec\_wait}\ L : \dot{Y} = e,\ \rho > \xrightarrow[E \cup tick(\delta_+)]{\emptyset,\{L\},1} < \mathtt{exec\_wait}\ L : \dot{Y} = e,\ \rho[Y_L \leftarrow e(Y_L, \delta)] >}$$

4 Behaviour of Timed CRP Programs

In this section, we illustrate that a timed CRP defines a hybrid transition system [6] and show the relation to other models. For lack of space, we only state the propositions with an informal sketch of the ideas without proof.

Definition 1: A *history* of a CRP node is a sequence of events $E_1, \cdots, E_n, \cdots$; for convenience, we denote E_i by $I_i.O_i$ where I_i and O_i denote the input and the output events in the ith instant respectively. In the *timed CRP* node every instant consists of the input signal `tick`.

Definition 2: A *history* is said to be *timed CRP valid* if it satisfies the following properties:

1. The history satisfies all the declared exclusion relations.
2. $\forall i$, `tick` $\in I_i$, every input instant contains the special signal `tick` with values. For instance, the signal `tick(v)` in I_n indicates an elapse of $\mathtt{v} \in \mathcal{R}$ units of time from the last occurrence of `tick`.
3. Signals from asynchronous/hybrid components satisfy:
   - An event is received only after requested (which has not been killed).
   - The start- and receive- of an asynchronous request cannot happen in the same instant.
4. $\forall i$, $|I_i| + |O_i| < \infty$. That is, it satisfies the property of *finite variability*, namely, the state changes only finitely often throughout any finite interval of time. That is, between any two consecutive input instants containing `tick` there can be only a finite sequence of events.

Definition 3: A progressive time sequence is an infinite sequence of time elements $\theta : t_0, t_1, \cdots$, where $t_i \in T$, for each $i = 0, 1, \cdots$ satisfying

- $t_0 = 0$
- Time does not decrease. That is, for every $i \geq 0, t_i \leq t_{i+1}$.
- Time eventually increases beyond any bound. That is, for every time element $t \in T, t_i > t$ for some $i \geq 0$; this ensures the non-Zeno requirement.

Theorem 1: The history of timed CRP valid programs forms a progressive time sequence.
Proof: The proof is based on considering the sets of sequences of accumulated `tick`'s at each instant (i.e., the global time at each instant) and show that each sequence is progressive and hence, non-Zeno.

Using properties of the timed CRP execution sequences (history) such as confluency, relation between halted execution sequences and causal freeness etc., we establish the relationship of timed CRP with other models such as *timed transition systems, hybrid traces* and *timed graphs* (cf. [1,6,7,8]).

Theorem 2: The timed CRP defines a hybrid transition system [6].
Proof: The proof is based on showing that time and discrete variables are not changed at the same time and time progresses synchronously on all processes.

Theorem 3: *Causally correct* timed CRP programs defines *timed graphs*.

5 Conclusions

We have described timed extensions of the CRP and shown that it can be conveniently used for specifying asynchronous timed systems and hybrid systems. Additionally, it can be used to specify and check the continuous presence of signals for a given duration [5]. One of the distinct features is that hybrid systems that do not reference clocks explicitly can be specified using timed CRP without the timed statements. Further, it is possible to relax the conditions on $\mathcal{F}$ used in the hybrid model, if there is no need to compute the values of continuous variables in other components.

As mentioned already, [6] describe an extension of Statecharts for specifying hybrid systems; in their language extension, they achieve the power through the addition of features such as **watching** on variables, channel variables and preemption constructs to Statecharts. In timed CRP the availability of the CLOCK as an asynchronous task avoids the need of watching variables – thus, conforming with the ESTEREL philosophy. We feel that the availability of asynchronous tasks and rendezvous communications makes it convenient to specify classes of hybrid systems naturally, even those requiring multiple rendezvous. Many implementations for the asynchronous tasks are possible leading to natural specifications for hybrid systems. Currently, we are investigating the possible protocols that would be best suited for a variety of applications. From the point of view of specification of hybrid systems, it is not clear whether there is a need to use the power of specifying nondeterminism of the network. A study in this direction is being taken as a positive answer would enable the adaptation of verification tools.

Acknowledgment

The work on synchronous programming has been due to the inspiration of Gèrard Berry. It is a pleasure to thank Amir Pnueli whose lectures on hybrid systems at TIFR clarified various subtle aspects of hybrid system specification and F. Boussionot and S. Ramesh for many valuable discussions.

References

[1] R. Alur, C. Courcoubetis, and D. Dill, *Model Checking for Real-time Systems*, 5th IEEE LICS, pp. 414-425, June 1990.

[2] G. Berry (1992), *A hardware implementation of pure Esterel*, *Sadhana*: Academy Proceedings in Engineering Sciences, Indian Academy of Sciences, Special Issue on Real Time edited by RK Shyamasundar, 17 (1):95-139, 1992.

[3] G. Berry and G. Gonthier (1988), *The Esterel synchronous programming language: Design, semantics, Implementation*, Rapport de Recherche 842, INRIA 1988, Science of Computer Programming, Vol. 19, No.2, Nov. 92, pp. 87-152.

[4] G. Berry, S. Ramesh and R.K. Shyamasundar, *Communicating Reactive Processes*, 20th ACM Symposium on Principles pf Programming Languages, South Carolina, Jan. 1993, pp. 85-99.

[5] L.Y. Liu and R.K. Shyamasundar, *RT-CDL: A real time design language and its semantics*, IFIP 89, North-Holland Publishing Co., pp. 21-26.

[6] Y. Kesten and A. Pnueli, *Timed and hybrid Statecharts and their textual presentation*, LNCS 571, pp. 591-619, 1992.

[7] Z. Manna and A. Pnueli, *Models for Reactivity*, to appear in Acta Informatica, 1993 (an earlier version presented at the 25th Anniversary of INRIA).

[8] X. Nicollin, J. Sifakis, and S. Yovine, *From ATP to timed graphs and hybrid systems*, LNCS 600, pp. 549-572, 1992.

Real-Time Program Synthesis from Specifications

Cornell, A.[†], Knaack, J.[‡], Nangia, A.[†], Rus, T.[‡]
[†] Brigham Young University, Department of Computer Science
Provo, Utah

[‡] The University of Iowa, Department of Computer Science
Iowa City, IA 52242

1 Introduction

Real-time systems are characterized by their umbilical connection to the environment [11]. They are most often modeled as event driven systems where the occurrence of events dictates a timed response by the system [3]. Such a behavior is naturally described by a state transition diagram [1]. The goal of this paper is to initiate an algebraic methodology for real-time program development that is convenient for the programmer and allows easy proofs of the correctness of real-time programs. This methodology is algebraic in nature in the sense that program development is closer to the development of algebraic computations rather than to the development of programs using conventional languages. Following this methodology a real-time program is developed in two steps: first the behavior of a real-time system is specified using a real-time system specification language and then, this behavior is automatically transformed into a semantic driven automaton [9, 6] that implements the real-time program. Consequently, no programming activity in the usual sense is involved. A similar approach for real-time program development is described in [8]. The difference is that our real-time system specification language is a regular language on the alphabet of conditional-actions similar to guarded commands [4] while in [8] a language of timed processes [7] is used. In addition, the abstract time used to model the time is different in the two approaches.

2 Real-Time System Specification

We consider that any specification language must be provided with a capability for abstraction manipulation that consists of three parts: a mechanism for type definition, a mechanism for object declaration, and a mechanism for application specification. We propose a language capable of specifying the behavior of a real-time application where each specification contains three sections: a definition section which specifies the types that are needed, a declaration section which specifies the variables of those types that will be used, and a behavior specification section which specifies the application in terms of the declared variables, as seen below. The declaration section specifies the *state* of the system seen as the interpretation of the collection of names used in the real-time system, $\sigma : Names \rightarrow Values$. Let Σ be the collection of states of a given real time system. The behavior of the system is stepwise specified in terms of two well-understood constructions, state transitions and their composition. State transitions, $\tau : \Sigma \rightarrow \Sigma$, are expressed by named conditional actions of the form $\tau : \langle Condition \rightarrow Action \rangle$ interpreted as "when Condition holds the Action is performed". Composition of state transitions is performed by using regular operators. That is, if a and b are state transitions then (1) the concatenation of a and b denoted $a\ b$, (2) the choice of a or b denoted $a|b$, and (3) the repetition of a state transition a known as Kleene star and denoted by a^* are state transitions.

2.1 Type Definition Section

The real-time system specification language discussed here allows one to express the behavior of the real-time system as a continuous interaction between the system and its environment. During this interaction the system receives data from the environment that determines the system state transitions; during the state transition the system may receive or send data to/from the environment affecting it as well as changing the state. This behavior is accomplished by considering the environment as a collection of *typed communication channels*. Conceptually, typed channels are predefined abstract data types; as such a channel consists of a data carrier and the operations defined on that carrier. In addition, the typed channels can have as operations the following, where α is a channel:

- $send(x, \alpha)$ evaluates x, an expression of type α, and sends that value on the channel α,
- $receive(x, \alpha)$ assigns to a variable x of type α the current value on the channel α,
- $set(x, t)$ evaluates an expression t of type α and sets the variable x, also of type α, to that value. We denote this by $x := t$, since the *set* operation is an assignment. Note that the *set* operation does not involve the channel α, it only affects a variable of type α.

There are three channel types, input, output, and input/output. An input channel provides data from the environment. The valid operations on objects of this type (i.e. variables or constants) are *set*, *receive*, and the operations defined on the data carrier of the channel. An output channel sends data into the environment. The valid operations on objects of this type that are *set*, *send*, and the operations defined on the data carrier of the channel. An I/O channel can both provide data from the environment and also send data into the environment. The valid operations on objects of this type are *set*, *send*, *receive*, and the operations defined on the data carrier of the channel.

¿From the viewpoint of an application development there are two kind of channels: *predefined* typed channels that are given for the real-time system, and *defined* typed channels that are implemented as connections to actual devices in the environment specific to the real-time system. The predefined typed channels are I/O channels and are represented by the usual types **boolean, integer, character, string, real**, with the usual carriers and operations defined on those carriers; in addition the three channel operations are defined as follows, where α is one of these types:

1. *send*(x, α) evaluates x; thus the value of x can be examined.
2. *receive*(x, α) initializes the variable x to some arbitrary value; alternatively some chosen (by the implementor) value may be assigned to x.
3. *set*(x, t) evaluates t and assigns that value to the variable x.

The predefined channels can be thought of as interacting with an abstract environment consisting of just those values appropriate for the channel type. The defined types specific to real-time applications considered here are:

Time: time is an algebraic structure $\mathbf{T} = \langle T, 0, +, \leq \rangle$ as in [8] where

1. $\langle T, 0, + \rangle$ is a commutative monoid and $\forall t_1, t_2 \in T\ [t_1 + t_2 = t_1 \Rightarrow t_2 = 0]$.
2. $\leq$ is a total order on T such that $\forall t_1, t_2 \in T\ [t_1 \leq t_2] \equiv \exists t_3 \in T\ [t_1 + t_3 = t_2]$.

Practically, the time is implemented by an input channel on which the real time is continuously ticking. This is usually realized in hardware by a clock register T that is continuously incremented by a time unit. When T overflows, an interrupt is generated. This interrupt can be treated either by hardware, resetting T, or by software, performing the timed actions measured by the value set in T when the real-time application starts. This allows us to look at the time as an input channel implemented by an infinite register T that is set when the real-time application starts. Then at any instance a *receive* operation on this channel returns an object of type time that represents the real time elapsed from the starting of the application until the moment when the *receive* operation has been executed. We assume here that the data carrier of the time channel is the set of positive real numbers, R^+, although according to the application any infinite set satisfying the axioms of the time can be used. Since the time is an input channel it supports the operations *receive* and *set*:

1. if x is a variable of type *Time* where *Time* is a channel of type *time* then *set*(x, t) assigns the value of t of type *Time* to x.
2. *receive*$(x, Time)$ sets x to the value $t + \delta$ where δ is the real time elapsed since the last set of x to the time t.

The functioning model of a real-time system in this paper is considered as taking place in real time and independently of the time. That is, while state transitions of the real-time system take place as described by the equations specifying the system, the time continuously ticks independently. The time becomes visible only when a variable x of type *Time* is checked by a *receive*$(x, Time)$ operation.

Text: is an I/O channel whose data carrier are objects of type string.

Analog: An analog channel could be Input, Output, or I/O, depending upon the application. This type describes analog devices that are controlled by the real-time system, or that are used to sense the real world. The data carrier of an analog channel must be consistent with the type of control exercised through the channel. A *receive* operation on an input analog channel returns an analog value that represents the current measured quantity as sensed by the device, such as temperature, density, speed, etc. A *send* operation on an output analog channel may activate a device such as a stepping motor or audible tone generator. A *set* operation, as noted above, is just an assignment to the variable and does not activate the channel.

Digital: A digital channel could be Input, Output, or I/O, depending upon the application. This type describes analog devices used to sense the environment, or to be controlled by the environment. A digital input channel may be a switch whose status can be read and that is operated by a human, and a digital output channel may be a control which starts a fan, turns on a heating element, etc. The operations *send*, *receive* and *set* operate the same as those for an analog channel.

A type definition specification has the syntax

TypeName ChannelType NameList DataCarrier

where

- *TypeName* is one of the names of the types defined above, i.e., one of the names *time*, *text*, *digital*, *analog*, *integer*, *boolean*, *real*, *character*, *string*.
- *ChannelType* is one of {*input*, *output*, *i/o*}.
- *NameList* is a list of user-defined names of the channel type.
- *DataCarrier* is the name of a predefined or already defined data type that specifies the data carrier for the channel type. In this manner the type of the data expected to be transferred over the channel is specified, and the operations that are valid for that type of data are known.

The ChannelType parameter is optional for the predefined types, as well as for the *time* defined types, as they can only be of one given channel type. Similarly, the data carriers of the predefined types can be omitted, since the carrier of a predefined type is usually given. Other supplementary information can be added to the definition specifying hardware characteristics, device drivers, ranges of values over which the carrier is valid, etc. All these are application- and concrete implementation-dependent. Example of the definition of an input channel named *Temperature* which is connected to a thermometer that continuously senses the temperature of its environment (returning integers) would be *analog input Temperature integer*. A definition of a real-valued timer type named *Timer* would be *time Timer real*.

2.2 Variable Declaration Section

The variables in terms of which system behavior is specified are of the types of channels defining the system. The variable declarations in a real-time system are analogous to variable specifications in a conventional language, i.e. variables are defined over the types (some of them unique to real-time systems). The declaration of a variable has the syntax *TypeName VarList* where *TypeName* is one of the names defined as a type, and *VarList* is a list of variable names to be declared.

2.3 Behavior Specification Section

The behavior of the real-time application is represented by a system of conditional equations [6, 10] specifying a semantic driven automaton, denoted by *SDA*. Since the primary behavior of an SDA depends on the content of the data it receives from its environment, the SDA must check conditions on these data in order to know when to move from one state of the real-time application machine to the next and also what actions to perform as it changes state. That is, a state transition is a description of the conditions that allow a move from one state to another. The description consists of a test of real-world conditions in the application's environment and of actions to perform while changing state.

A *condition* is a predicate which tests properties of the current state of the real-time system. For example, let *Temperature* be a channel and *Temp* be a variable of type *Temperature*. Then if the SDA must perform some action if the temperature exceeds 350 degrees, we can write the condition $Temp > 350$. In order to evaluate this condition, the SDA must first perform the operation $receive(Temp, Temperature)$ and then if $Temp > 350$ the SDA will change state performing the specified action, such as shutting off a heating element, as it does so. Thus, the evaluation of a variable in a condition requires an implicit *receive* operation in order to get the current value from the channel into that variable. Conditional expressions [6] consist of either single conditions or conditions connected by logical operators *and*, *or* and *not*. Thus, information from multiple channels can be tested in the same conditional expression. The *actions* that can be performed by an SDA are the following:

1. send data x to the channel α, $send(x, \alpha)$.
2. receive data x from a channel α, $receive(x, \alpha)$.
3. Do nothing, denoted by *idle*. This action never terminates. The only way to get out of it is through a preempt operation [5] (i.e., an interrupt).
4. Skip action, denoted by *skip*. This action does nothing and terminates in a single execution.
5. Wait for a condition C to be satisfied, denoted by $wait(C)$. This action terminates only when C becomes true.
6. Assignment action, denoted by $x := t$ where x is a variable, t is an expression (possibly including a function call) and the type of x is the same as the type of t.

A transition has two parts:

1. A conditional expression which is a predicate over the language of conditions on variables of the types defining the real-time system. An empty condition is interpreted as always true.
2. A list of actions to perform when the condition is satisfied. This is a list of the actions specified above.

A transition in this language has the form $id : \langle condition \rightarrow action \rangle$ where *id* is a transition name, *condition* is a conditional expression as defined above, and *action* is a list of actions which actually control the channels making up the real-time system. In this manner each transition defined is represented by a name. The collection of transition names used in a real-time specification is called the *alphabet of transitions*.

The specification of a real-time system consists of a set of conditional equations over the alphabet of transitions. The equations are of the form *id* = *regular expression* where *id* is either a transition name, one of the names "Start", "Stop", "Error", denoting the start state, terminate state, and calling an error manager, respectively, or the left-hand side of a previously defined equation. The *regular expression* utilizes the usual regular operations of concatenation, choice, and Kleene star over the set of transition names to specify a finite-state machine. A complete example follows. It is derived from the set of equations that specifies the behavior of an oven [2]; this is a simpler version of the oven specified in that paper.

Analog	Input	Temperature, Thermostat
Digital	Input	OnOffSwitch
Digital	Output	HeatSwitch
Integer	I/O	HystType
Temperature	T1	
Thermostat	T2	
OnOffSwitch	OnOff	
HeatSwitch	Heat	
HystType	Hyst	

$T_0 : \langle \rightarrow \boldsymbol{skip} \rangle$
$T_1 : \langle \rightarrow Heat := 0; \boldsymbol{send}(Heat, HeatSwitch); Hyst := 10 \rangle$
$T_2 : \langle OnOff = 1 \rightarrow \boldsymbol{skip} \rangle$
$T_3 : \langle OnOff = 1 \wedge T1 > T2 + Hyst \rightarrow Heat := 0; \boldsymbol{send}(Heat, HeatSwitch) \rangle$
$T_4 : \langle OnOff = 1 \wedge T1 < T2 - Hyst \rightarrow Heat := 1; \boldsymbol{send}(Heat, HeatSwitch) \rangle$
$T_5 : \langle OnOff = 1 \wedge T1 \leq T2 + Hyst \wedge T1 \geq T2 - Hyst \rightarrow \boldsymbol{skip}) \rangle$
$T_6 : \langle OnOff = 0 \rightarrow Heat := 0; \boldsymbol{send}(Heat, HeatSwitch) \rangle$
$Start = T_1(T_0(T_2(T_3|T_4|T_5)^*\ T_6)^*)^*$

3 Expressive Power

A semantic driven automaton is controlled by the properties of the tokens it recognizes instead of being controlled by their syntax. The semantic driven automaton that recognizes transition equations specifying the real-time system is described by a two-level transition table [6] and is equivalent to the program controlling the real-time application. Since time is a type of a real-time system, variables of type *time* can be defined and initialized in the systems specification part. These variables can be set, their values can be tested and used in various conditions defining the transitions of the real-time application. Therefore, a semantic driven automaton that uses time-conditions in its transitions is a timed-automaton [8]. However, any kind of real-time device and condition can be easily integrated in the real-time specification language defined in this paper. Therefore, the semantic driven automata provide a unifying mechanism for real-time program synthesis from specification.

We define a transition $id : \langle C \rightarrow A \rangle$ to be equivalent to the statements

$$\textbf{while } (\neg C) \textbf{ do } \text{skip};\ A$$

In order to show the expressive power of semantic driven automata we use this definition to sketch here the proof that a computation can be expressed using a conventional language iff that computation can be expressed by regular expressions over transitions specifying a semantic driven automaton. For that we will consider the statement as the unit of computation specified by conventional languages and will show the equivalence of the constructs expressing control-flow on statements and regular expressions using transitions as defined previously.

First, let S be a statement label. Then the named transition $S' : \langle \rightarrow S \rangle$ expresses the statement **while** $(\neg True)$ **do** *skip*; S since an empty condition evaluates to True. Now let S_1 and S_2 be statement labels and E be a boolean expression. Without showing all the steps, we have:

1. The *concatenation* of S_1; S_2 is a regular expression $S'\ S''$, where $S' : \langle \rightarrow S_1 \rangle$ and $S'' : \langle \rightarrow S_2 \rangle$. Conversely, if transitions $S' : \langle C' \rightarrow A' \rangle$ and $S'' : \langle C'' \rightarrow A'' \rangle$, where C' and C'' are conditions and A' and A'' are actions, then the regular expression $S'\ S''$ is expressed by the code

   while $(\neg C')$ **do** *skip*; A'; **while** $(\neg C'')$ **do** *skip*; A'';

2. The *branching* statement **if** E **then** S_1 **else** S_2 can be expressed by the regular expression $S = S'|S''$, where $S' : \langle E \rightarrow S_1 \rangle$ and $S'' : \langle \neg E \rightarrow S_2 \rangle$. Conversely, if $S' : \langle C' \rightarrow A' \rangle$ and $S'' : \langle C'' \rightarrow A'' \rangle$, then the regular expression $S'|S''$ is expressed by the code

   if C' **then** A' **else if** C'' **then** A''

3. The *while* loop **while** E **do** S_1 can be expressed by the regular expression $(S')^*$, where $S' : \langle E \rightarrow S_1 \rangle$. Conversely, if the transition $S' : \langle C' \rightarrow A' \rangle$ is given then the expression $(S')^*$ is expressed by the code

   while (C') **do** A';

We used here only regular operators to express conditional equations due to their well understood semantics and well-known methodology of mapping regular expressions into programs. However, the approach we use to implement semantic driven automata allows us to use other operators than the regular ones and therefore we can easily generalize introducing equations of the form $S = S_1||S_2$ where $||$ denotes the parallel composition of S_1 and S_2 thus obtaining a mechanism for parallel program synthesis from specifications.

Example: From the example oven specification given earlier, we can use this expressibility to obtain the code that is expressed by the regular expression $T_1(T_0(T_2(T_3|T_4|T_5)^*\ T_6)^*)^*$. The final program that is equivalent to the entire regular expression is shown below, with all conditions and actions expressly given (some statements that were effectively null have been removed).

```
Heat := 0; send(Heat, HeatSwitch); Hyst := 10;
while (True) do
  begin
   while (OnOff = 1) do
     begin
      while (OnOff = 1 ∧
               (T1 > T2 + Hist ∨ T1 < T2 − Hist ∨
                T1 ≤ T2 + Hist ∧ T1 ≥ T2 − Hist) ) do
        begin
         if (T1 > T2 + Hist) then
           Heat := 0; send(Heat, HeatSwitch)
         else if (T1 < T2 − Hist) then
           Heat := 1; send(Heat, HeatSwitch)
         else if (T1 ≤ T2 + Hist ∧ T1 ≥ T2 − Hist)
           skip
        end
      Heat := 0; send(Heat, HeatSwitch);
     end
   end
```

The main purpose of this development, however, is not merely to define a way of creating code from a specification; rather it is to show that *a regular expression over transitions is equivalent to a program.* The equivalence goes both ways; thus any program can also be expressed as a regular expression, and since we have a large body of knowledge about regular expressions, we may be able to deduce some correctness theorems from this knowledge. This is an area that deserves further study.

The major advantages of this methodology for program synthesis from specifications are:

1. It allows stepwise program development in terms of simple actions, well-understood by programmers, and their automatic composition through the mechanism of transforming regular expressions in programs.
2. It allows a formal proof of the program correctness by first proving the correctness of the simple actions making up the program and by automatically preserving this correctness by the translator mapping regular expressions in programs.
3. The automatic mapping of regular expressions in efficient programs is feasible and well-understood.
4. It unifies the methodology of program synthesis from specification, and opens a new field of research.

References

[1] A. Bestavros. Specification and Verification of Real-Time Embedded Systems using Time Constrained Reactive Automata. *Proceedings IEEE 12th Real-Time Systems Symposium*, pages 244-253, Dec 4-6, San Antonio, Texas, 1991.

[2] A. Cornell. Oven. *Research Report 7*, Department of Computer Science, Brigham Young University, 1992.

[3] B. Dasarathy. Timing Constraints of Real-Time Systems. *IEEE Transactions on Software Engineering*, Volume 11, Number 1:80-86, 1985.

[4] E.W. Dijkstra. Guarded Commands, Nondeterminacy, and Formal Derivation of Programs. *Communications of the ACM*, Volume 18, Number 8:453-457, 1975.

[5] Y. Kesten and A. Pnueli. Timed and Hybrid Statecharts and their Textual Representations. *Formal Techniques in Real-Time and Fault-Tolerant Systems*, Lecture Notes in Computer Science 571:591-619, 1992.

[6] J. Knaack and T. Russ. TwoLev: A Two Level Scanner. In M. Nivat, C.M.I. Rattray, T. Rus, and G. Scollo, editors, *Proceedings of AMAST'91*, pages 264-276, Workshops in Computing Series, Springer Verlag, 264-276, 1992.

[7] X. Nicollin and J. Sifakis. An Overview and Synthesis on Timed Process Algebra. *Proceedings Third Workshop on Computer-Aided Verification*, pages 1-21, Alborg, Denmark, July 1991.

[8] X. Nicollin, J. Sifakis and S. Yovine. Compiling Real-Time Specifications into Extended Automata. *IEEE Transactions on Software Engineering*, Volume 18, Number 9:794-804, 1992.

[9] T. Rus. Algebraic Construction of Compilers. *Theoretical Computer Science*, Volume 90:271-308, 1991.

[10] T. Rus. *Computation Specification by Semantic Driven Automata*, Unpublished Paper, The University of Iowa, Department of Computer Science, Iowa City, IA 52242, 1992.

[11] N. Wirth. Toward a Discipline of Real-time Programming. *Communications of the ACM*, Volume 20, Number 8:577-583, 1977.

On the coverage of partial validations

Ed Brinksma
Faculty of Computer Science, University of Twente
Enschede, The Netherlands
brinksma@cs.utwente.nl

Abstract

The validation of implementations is an essential part of the design of both hardware and software systems in order to establish the correctness of such systems. As such it has been an important application area for all kinds of formal methods to support this activity. Many of such methods, however, aim at a complete proof of correctness, which become unmanageable in the case of larger, realistic designs. In practice, therefore, attention is limited to such methods that can be applied partially or in an approximative manner. Albeit more pragmatic, these approaches usually lack a good measure for the extent to which correctness is established. Such *coverage* measures are needed to compare and assess different strategies for partial validation in the context of a given specification. In this article we propose to follow a measure-theoretic approach in which an exogenous *cost* function (quantifying the effect of certain properties in an implementation) is integrated over a measure that is induced by the probability of error occurrences in implementations. In this way, in fact, we do not only obtain a notion of coverage, but a general way of assigning measures to specification theories in the context of a given class of implementation structures.

1 Introduction

It is widely recognized that a completely rigourous treatment of the correctness of designs of realistic information-processing systems is beyond the scope of the formal methods currently at our disposal. While for some aspects of this predicament improvements can be expected through the development and use of more powerful formalisms, theories, and supporting software tools, there are structural problems related to managing the combinatorial complexity of correctness proofs for large systems. In essence, the huge complexity of such proofs reintroduces the correctness problem at the meta-level, viz. the validation of such proofs themselves. The investment done to prove correctness should also be measured against the remaining possibility that errors are introduced in the ultimate realization phase of the design, where formal methods may no longer be applicable (e.g. silicon compilation). As a result in practice mostly methods that deal with *approximate* correctness criteria are used, such as testing and the verification of particular properties. This should also be seen against the background that complete correctness of systems in not required in most cases: in reality one tries to make the occurrence of important errors sufficiently unlikely.

In recent years there has been also a growing theoretical interest in the question of partial validation, which has led to much new work on topics like *model checking* and *testing theory*, e.g. [12, 7, 4, 3]. This has given rise to new algorithms for the validation of given properties and for the generation of tests, whereas the related question concerning the *coverage* of partial validation methods, i.e. how much the validation of a particular property contributes to the overall correctness of the design, has received considerably less attention. Such measures are needed to guide the selection of properties that should be validated, and can be used to quantify the quality of a validation procedure, and, indirectly, of the implementations that succeed in passing them. Unfortunately, it is not straightforward how to obtain such measures.

In the literature it has been proposed to use the probability of the occurrence of an error as a guiding principle for partial validations, viz. by ignoring improbable errors (see e.g. [9]). This would seem to suggest that the coverage of such a partial validation method could be calculated as a sum of the probabilities of independent errors that are exposed by the method. This approach has the drawback that often it may be the absence of less frequent errors that determines the quality of a design. Moreover, the appreciation of the role of a particular error may depend more on the application of a system than on its specified abstract functionality. The occurrence of the same software bug in a computer game and in the operating system of a nuclear plant could be of a radically different importance, and this should preferably be reflected in a coverage measure.

In an earlier paper we have therefore proposed that coverage should be based on so-called *valuations* that assign weights to error classes corresponding to their gravity [5]. Probability distributions over error classes being special instances of valuations, this yielded a generalization of the probability induced notion of coverage. This approach has the drawback, however, that it was not clear how, in view of their subjective nature, such valuations could be obtained or approximated for given applications. For the probability induced notion of coverage there exists at least the wealth of statistical methodology to estimate the distributions involved.

In this paper we refine our idea of valuations. Measurements of the probability of error occurrences in implementations can be used to improve our estimates of valuations, while still maintaining a possibility to account for the difference between the probability and the gravity of an error. We follow a measure-theoretic approach in which an exogenous *cost* function (quantifying the effect of certain properties in an implementation) is integrated over a measure that is induced by the probability of error occurrences. In this way, in fact, we do not only obtain a notion of coverage, but a general way of assigning measures to specification theories in the context of a given class of implementation structures.

2 Main formalizations

The correctness of an implementation I with respect to a specification S is usually formalized by means of an *implementation* or *refinement* relation R such that I is a correct implementation of S iff $\langle I, S\rangle \in R$. We will in fact assume that this relation R can be formalized in terms of the satisfaction of a logical theory, viz. $R = \{\langle I, S\rangle \mid I \models Th(S)\}$, where $Th(S)$ is the theory in some logical language $\mathcal{L}$ specified by S and $\models$ denotes a satisfaction relation. Many implementation relations can in fact be characterized in this way, including those using constructive specification formalisms (see e.g. [10]).

As indicated above we view the design process as a stochastic experiment that produces an implementation $\underline{I}$ on the basis of a given specification S. In order to model this correctly we need to define a Borel space in which $\underline{I}$ takes its value (see e.g. [2]). Let $\mathcal{I}$ be the set of all potential implementations of S, and $\Phi_{\mathcal{L}}$ the set of formulae in $\mathcal{L}$, then we are particularly interested in the sets

$$V_{\Phi} =_{df} \{I \in \mathcal{I} \mid I \models \Phi\} \quad \text{for } \Phi \subseteq \Phi_{\mathcal{L}} \tag{1}$$

We say that $\mathcal{I}$ has the *Borel* property w.r.t. $\mathcal{L}$ iff $\mathcal{V} =_{df} \{V_{\Phi} \mid \Phi \subseteq \Phi_{\mathcal{L}}\}$ is a Borel set for $\mathcal{I}$, i.e. (*i*) $\emptyset \in \mathcal{V}$, and (*ii*) $\mathcal{V}$ is closed under arbitrary unions and complementation (w.r.t. $\mathcal{I}$). Requirement (*i*) is often directly fulfilled, viz. if $\mathcal{L}$ is sufficiently rich to allow for *inconsistent* theories Φ, as that implies $V_{\Phi} = \emptyset$.[1] The closure property w.r.t. complementation is more involved as for each $\Phi \subseteq \Phi_{\mathcal{L}}$ there need not exist a $\Phi' \subseteq \Phi_{\mathcal{L}}$ such that $V_{\Phi'} = \overline{V_{\Phi}} = \{I \in \mathcal{I} \mid I \not\models \Phi\}$. As the latter set could be characterized by the disjunction over the negations of all $\varphi \in \Phi$, one solution would be to work with languages that have negation and either explicit generalized disjunctions, such as e.g. $\mathcal{L}_{\omega_1\omega}$ [8], or implicit ones, e.g. in the form of fixpoint constructions [10]. Another option is to restrict the class of implementations $\mathcal{I}$. In practice, for example, one can often restrict the attention to a *finite* set $\mathcal{I}$ where each $I \in \mathcal{I}$ is completely characterized by a *finite* theory $\Phi_I \subseteq \Phi_{\mathcal{L}}$. This is typically the case when testing the control aspects of systems, where because of finite resources only finite fragments of system behaviour are tested, see e.g. the example in [5]. In such cases ordinary negation and disjunction suffice to warrant the desired closure properties.

Assuming that $\mathcal{I}$ has the Borel property w.r.t. $\mathcal{L}$ we can now introduce for each specification S a measure P_S over $\mathcal{I}$, viz. by putting

$$P_S(V_{\Phi}) =_{df} Pr\{\underline{I} \in V_{\Phi}\} \tag{2}$$

i.e. assigning V_{Φ} the probability that the implementation satisfies Φ.

As we have observed above we wish to modify this measure by also taking the *cost* of errors into account. To do so, we first assume there exists a function $k : \mathcal{P}(\Phi_{\mathcal{L}}) \longrightarrow \mathbf{R}_{\geq 0}$ that determines the cost $k(\Phi)$ of *satisfying* the properties of Φ. This function has to satisfy the intuitive property that cost increases with logical strength, i.e. $\Phi \models_{\mathcal{I}} \Psi$ implies that $k(\Phi) \geq k(\Psi)$, where $\Phi \models_{\mathcal{I}} \Psi$ means that for all $I \in \mathcal{I}$ $I \models \Phi$ implies $I \models \Psi$. If we put $Th(I) =_{df} \{\varphi \in \Phi_{\mathcal{L}} \mid I \models \varphi\}$ then we can overload k to denote also a function of type $\mathcal{I} \longrightarrow \mathbf{R}_{\geq 0}$ by putting $k(I) =_{df} k(Th(I))$. It can be shown quite easily that this function is integrable w.r.t. each measure P_S. This result allows us to define the *valuation* measure μ_S on $\mathcal{V}$ as the measure-theoretic integral

$$\mu_S(V) =_{df} \int_{\overline{V}} k(I)\, dP_S \quad \text{for all } V \in \mathcal{V} \tag{3}$$

Note that in order to calculate $\mu_S(V)$ we integrate the cost of its complement $\overline{V}$. This can be understood by realizing that once we have established, by (partial)

[1] Here, we mean inconsistency in the conventional sense when a negation is present, e.g. as in $p \wedge \neg p$. Inconsistencies in, for example, *equational* logics are different as they give rise to trivial rather than empty models, e.g. as that generated by $true = false$.

validation, that $I \models \Phi$, or equivalently that $I \in V_\Phi$, it follows that $I \notin \overline{V_\Phi}$ so that the cost related to implementations in $\overline{V_\Phi}$ has been avoided. This seems a natural way to measure the value of having established Φ. Another way of looking at it is that μ_S must increase with logical strength, as k does: if $\Phi \models_{\mathcal{I}} \Psi$ then Φ contains more information than Ψ, and should consequently have a higher valuation. This follows as $\Phi \models_{\mathcal{I}} \Psi$ implies $V_\Phi \subseteq V_\Psi$ implies $\overline{V_\Psi} \subseteq \overline{V_\Phi}$ implies $\mu_S(V_\Psi) \leq \mu_S(V_\Phi)$.

Because of the generally non-continuous nature of $\mathcal{I}$ the integral in (3) will in practice be evaluated as a, possibly infinite, summation. Nevertheless, equation (3) gives us the most compact representation of the definition of the measure in full generality.

Having established the measure μ_S for given specifications S it is now straightforward to produce the definition of the coverage of a partial validation w.r.t. S as a normalization of μ_S. Let $\Phi \subseteq Th(S)$ then a procedure for establishing that $I \models \Phi$ has a *coverage* α, with $0 \leq \alpha \leq 1$, iff

$$\mu_S(V_\Phi) \;\geq\; \alpha.\mu_S(V_{Th(S)}) \tag{4}$$

We also say that an implementation I is α-correct, or, alternatively, has a margin of error of $1-\alpha$, iff there exists a $\Phi \subseteq Th(S)$ with $I \in V_\Phi$ for which equation (4) holds. Note that 1-correctness does not necessarily coincide with total correctness in the classical sense, as errors with measure 0 are ignored if the measure that is used admits their existence.

It should be noted that the above definition of coverage applies even in the pathological case where $\mu_S(V_{Th(S)}) = 0$, by (4) trivially yielding coverage 1 for any Φ. In the normal case, i.e. when $\mu_S(V_{Th(S)}) \neq 0$, the normalisation can be applied directly to the definition of the measure itself by putting

$$\mu_S^*(V) \;=_{df}\; \mu_S(V)/\mu_S(V_{Th(S)}) \tag{5}$$

In this way μ_S^* has become insensitive to the absolute value of applications of the cost function k, taking only its proportional variation into account. Inequality (4) then simplifies to $\mu_S^*(V_\Phi) \;\geq\; \alpha$.

3 Elaboration in Boolean algebras

In [5] an elaborated example of the application of our theory can be found, although as part of a less formally developed framework. In the present setting the work presented there can be understood as explained below. It is applicable in those cases where the relevant logical theory is finitely generated with respect to Boolean operations. In [5] this condition applies for the selection of test cases for implementations of a specification of finite behaviour in a process algebraic setting.

Consider the Boolean algebra $\mathcal{B}$ generated by the finite number of (logically) independent properties $F_1, \ldots, F_n$, each expressing potential error cases occurring (stochastically) independently with a probability $\alpha_i \neq 0$ $(1 \leq i \leq n)$.

The disjunctive normal form theorem (see e.g. [11]) states that all non-zero elements of $\mathcal{B}$ can be written as exclusive disjunctions of elements of the set

$$MinTerms_{\mathcal{B}} =_{df} \{P_1 \wedge \ldots \wedge P_n \mid P_i = F_i \text{ or } \neg F_i \ (1 \leq i \leq n)\} \tag{6}$$

This representation is unique up to permutation of the disjuncts.

Note that the assumption of stochastic independence of the F_i can be made if for each $F \in MinTerms_{\mathcal{B}}$ there exists an implementation $I \in \mathcal{I}$ with $I \models F$, i.e. $\mathcal{I}$ must be sufficiently rich as a collection of models. Under the given assumptions, in fact, $MinTerms_{\mathcal{B}}$ induces a partition of $\mathcal{I}$, viz. that with partition classes $V_F =_{df} \{I \in \mathcal{I} \mid I \models F\}$ for $F \in MinTerms_{\mathcal{B}}$.

We assume that each potential error F_i has an associated cost $k_i \in \mathbf{R}_{\geq 0}$. For each $P_1 \wedge \ldots \wedge P_n \in MinTerms_{\mathcal{B}}$ we calculate the cumulative cost as

$$k(P_1 \wedge \ldots \wedge P_n) =_{df} \sum_{P_i = F_i} k_i \tag{7}$$

Since the theory of a given implementation $I \in \mathcal{I}$ is completely characterized by a unique $F_I \in MinTerms_{\mathcal{B}}$ we kan immediately lift the definition of k to implementations by putting

$$k(I) =_{df} k(F_I) = \sum_{I \models F_I} k_i \tag{8}$$

We can now elaborate the meaning of definition 3 in this context

$$\begin{aligned}
\mu_S(V_G) &= \int_{V_{\neg G}} k(I)\, dP_S \\
&= \sum_{\substack{F \in MinTerms_{\mathcal{B}} \\ F \Rightarrow \neg G}} \int_{V_F} k(I)\, dP_S \\
&= \sum_{\substack{F \in MinTerms_{\mathcal{B}} \\ F \Rightarrow \neg G}} \Big(\sum_{F \Rightarrow F_i} k_i\Big) \prod_{F \Rightarrow F_i} \alpha_i \prod_{F \Rightarrow \neg F_i} (1 - \alpha_i)
\end{aligned} \tag{9}$$

In the chosen setting it is reasonable to assume that the specification S is given by $S = \neg F_1 \wedge \ldots \wedge \neg F_n$. It follows that $k(S) = \sum_{\emptyset} k_i = 0$ and therefore that

$$\begin{aligned}
\mu_S(\mathcal{I}) &= \sum_{F \in MinTerms_{\mathcal{B}}} \Big(\sum_{F \Rightarrow F_i} k_i\Big) \prod_{F \Rightarrow F_i} \alpha_i \prod_{F \Rightarrow \neg F_i} (1 - \alpha_i) \\
&= \sum_{\substack{F \in MinTerms_{\mathcal{B}} \\ F \Rightarrow \neg S}} \Big(\sum_{F \Rightarrow F_i} k_i\Big) \prod_{F \Rightarrow F_i} \alpha_i \prod_{F \Rightarrow \neg F_i} (1 - \alpha_i) \\
&= \int_{V_{\neg S}} k(I)\, dP_S \\
&= \mu_S(V_S)
\end{aligned} \tag{10}$$

We conclude that the expression for coverage in this setting is given by

$$\mu_S^*(V_G) = \frac{1}{\mu_S(\mathcal{I})} \sum_{\substack{F \in MinTerms_B \\ F \Rightarrow \neg G}} \left(\sum_{F \Rightarrow F_i} k_i\right) \prod_{F \Rightarrow F_i} \alpha_i \prod_{F \Rightarrow \neg F_i} (1 - \alpha_i) \tag{11}$$

4 Conclusion

In this paper we have proposed a general stochastic framework for the quantification of the coverage of validation procedures, given the probability distribution of errors in implementations. We have argued that the probability of an error occurring is, by itself, not an adequate measure of its importance as frequent errors may be insignificant and rare errors can be catastrophic. In our approach we therefore suggest to obtain the desired coverage measure by integrating the cost of errors, given by an exogenous cost assignment function that is a design parameter, with respect to the measure induced by the error probability distribution.

We have presented our proposal in a very general framework, and have elaborated it in the special case of logical theories that form finitely generated Boolean algebras. An application of this elaboration in the domain of test selection can be found in [5], although it is presented there in terms of a more restricted, and pragmatic model.

The application of the proposed model requires that the specifiable sets of implementations form a Borel space. In practice, this requirement need not be prohibitive, as it often suffices to consider the Borel space that is *generated* by the specifiable sets of implementations to obtain useful results. In any case, it seems an interesting model-theoretic question to characterize those (logical) specification languages that have the associated Borel property as defined in section 2.

It should be noted that our use of probability is in principle very different from that in probabilistic processes (see e.g. [6]), where it is the *behaviour* of the processes that is stochastic in nature. Nevertheless it seems useful to study the connection between these different notions of probability. Our notion of coverage quantifies the information that is obtained when a part of the implementation is validated with complete precision. The theory of probabilistic processes can be used to quantify the imprecision that is present when observing probabilistic processes. Given the probabilistic behaviour of many practical (distributed) systems (e.g. communication media), the definition of a well-chosen combination of these notions is an interesting topic for further research.

Of course, an important point in the application of our definition of coverage is how to obtain reliable estimates of the probability distribution of potential errors, i.e. $Pr\{\underline{I} \in V_\Phi\}$. At first sight the standard application of statistical methods to estimate such distributions seems to fail, as on the basis of a given specification usually only very few final implementations are developed. If one views this question not in terms of entire design trajectories, however, but at the level of smaller design steps as part of a general design methodology, then perhaps statistical significance can be obtained. One could try to measure the effects of such design steps as parts of many different design experiments.

Under the hypothesis of the independence of design steps as error generators, one could then calculate the error distributions of complete designs as the cumulative effect of the design steps applied. Not surprisingly, reliable coverage measures are thus tied to the application of well-defined design methods.

Even if it proves hard to obtain reliable estimates of the probability distributions involved, we think that our proposal may be used to lend precision to coverage claims under the hypothesis of a given distribution and cost assignment. As we have tried to show, an adequate measure of coverage is necessarily context-dependent, and it is therefore essential that coverage claims are made with respect to an explicit error-model. As shown in [5] even quite crude assumptions can lead to useful results in order to decide what subset of tests to select out of a larger test suite, or vice versa, how to enlarge a given test suite with extra tests that significantly increase its coverage. One interesting direction of research would therefore be to study coverage as a function of the probability distributions and cost assignements involved, i.e. how variations over well-defined classes of these parameters affect the coverage value that is obtained for a given validation problem.

Our notion of coverage works with a notion of *area* in the space of implementations. It is also possible to approach the question by trying to define a (pseudo-)metric space of implementations, i.e. working from a notion of *distance*. Interesting work in this direction, with applications to the problem of tests selection, can be found in [1].

References

[1] J. Alilovic-Curgus, S.T. Vuong, A Metric Based Theory of Test Selection and Coverage, in: A. Danthine, G.Leduc, and P. Wolper (eds.), *Protocol Specification, Testing, and Verification, XIII*, North-Holland (*to appear*).

[2] H. Bauer, *Probability Theory and Elements of Measure Theory*, Holt, Rinehart, and Winston.

[3] G. Bernot, Testing against formal specifications: a theoretical view. In: S. Abramsky and T.S.E. Maibaum (eds.), *TAPSOFT'91*, Volume 2, 99–119. LNCS 494, Springer-Verlag, 1991.

[4] E. Brinksma, A Theory for the derivation of tests. In: S.Aggarwal and K. Sabnani (eds.), *Protocol Specification, Testing, and Verification VIII*, 63–74, North-Holland, 1988.

[5] E. Brinksma, J. Tretmans, and L. Verhaard, A framework for test selection. In: B. Jonsson, J. Parrow, and B. Pehrson (eds.), *Protocol Specification, Testing, and Verification XI*, 233–248, North-Holland, 1991.

[6] R. van Glabbeek, S.A. Smolka, B. Steffen, C. Tofts, Reactive, generative, and stratified models of probabilistic processes, in: *Proceedings LICS 1990*.

[7] P. Godefroid and P. Wolper, Using Partial orders for the Efficient Verification of Deadlock Freedom and Safety Properties. In: K.G. Larsen and A. Skou (eds.), *Computer Aided Verification '91*, 332–342. LNCS 575, Springer-Verlag, 1992.

[8] H.J. Keisler, *Model Theory for Infinitary Logic*, North-Holland.

[9] N.F. Maxemchuk and K. Sabnani, Probabilistic Verification of Communication Protocols. In: H. Rudin and C. West (eds.), *Protocol Specification, Testing, and Verification VII*, North-Holland, 1987.

[10] C. Stirling, Modal and Temporal Logics for Processes, *LFCS Report Series*, ECS-LFCS-92-221, Dept. of Computer Science, University of Edinburgh, 1992.

[11] J.P. Tremblay and R. Manohar, *Discrete Mathematical Structures with Applications to Computer Science*, McGraw-Hill, 1975.

[12] A. Valmari, Error detection by reduced reachability graph generation. In: *Proc. 10th International Conference on Application and Theory of Petri Nets*, volume 2, 1–22, Bonn, 1989.

Verifying communication protocols via testing-projection

Khalil DRIRA, Pierre AZEMA
LAAS-CNRS, 7 avenue du Colonel Roche F-31077 Toulouse Cedex

Abstract
A method is provided to reduce a labeled transition system while preserving testing equivalence. This method uses the refusal graph, an abstract structure for representing communicating systems, and two transformations for deriving a refusal graph from a labeled transition system and vice-versa. The reduced systems are in normal form for the testing equivalence and are minimal with respect to the bisimulation equivalence.

1 Introduction

Protocol projection is an efficient approach for the analysis of communication protocols. It consists of deriving from an initial automaton the minimal one, while preserving specific equivalence relations. According to the OSI model, the basic architecture consists of two protocol entities communicating via an underlying service. The global service, the protocol provides, corresponds to the behavior as observed from both Service Access Points only. Using LOTOS notations, this service can be described by the following expression where SAP_i are the service access points, and Γ_i designates the interaction point that synchronizes entity i and the communication medium:

$$service[SAP_1, SAP_2] = \textbf{hide}\ \Gamma_1, \Gamma_2\ \textbf{in}$$
$$((entity[SAP_1, \Gamma_1]\ |||\ entity[SAP_2, \Gamma_2])|[\Gamma_1, \Gamma_2]|medium[\Gamma_1, \Gamma_2])$$

Compiling such expression produces a Labeled Transition System (LTS) which describes the service. This LTS is generally so complex that it is very difficult for the designer to decide whether this service is the expected one for the specified protocol.

Verifying a protocol specification can be carried out by using an equivalence relation. The specification is correct when the provided service is equivalent to the expected one. This equivalence-based verification approach is well known (see for example [4]).

In practice, it is not always possible to have a reference model (the so-called expected service). This is often due to the difficulty to describe this service in a monolithic style where composition operator is not used. Projection is then a convenient alternative to protocol verification. It consists of furnishing a reduced model of the protocol service while preserving some properties: the more the properties are strong the more the reduced model is complex.

Such a reduced model can be obtained using equivalence induced by the weak bisimulation (the observational equivalence) [7, 9]. Projection of LTS according to this equivalence produces a minimal LTS in the sense that it contains no (weakly)-bisimilar distinct states. The size of the so-reduced system can be such that it is still not possible to analyze it. Currently, this problem is solved by substituting trace equivalence (known also as language equivalence in the automata theory) for observational equivalence. The projection supplies a deterministic LTS (with only observable events) which is minimized w.r.t. the (strong) bisimulation equivalence (see Fig. 1). Unfortunately, the size reduction is accompanied by a loss of relevant properties: the preserved properties are only those concerning event ordering. That is the reduced system accepts the same strings (sequences of events) as the initial system.

We propose here a tradeoff between the complexity of the reduced system and the interest of the preserved properties . We propose to define a new projection relying on another equivalence. This equivalence is known as testing equivalence (te) in Brinksma's testing theory for LOTOS [1] and is a simplification of Hoare's failure equivalence used for CSP [5] : like observational equivalence, testing equivalence considers that loops of internal transitions are not interpreted as divergent executions of the described system. This equivalence is less discriminating than observational equivalence but more discriminating than trace equivalence. It preserves the traces and the failures of a system, that is properties dealing with the possibilities of deadlock with the system environment.

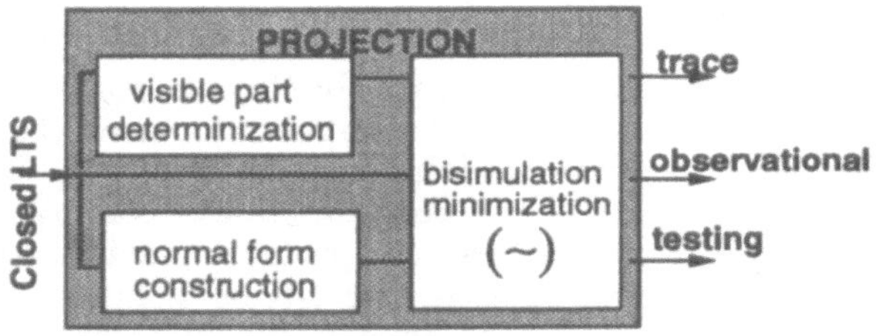

Figure 1: *Trace, observational and testing projections. The closed LTS is obtained by considering* $\stackrel{a}{\Rightarrow}=\stackrel{\tau^* a \tau^*}{\longrightarrow}$

Unlike bisimulation-based equivalences it is not sufficient to minimize the system by identifying testing equivalent states. For example, the LTS described by the transitions $(1,\tau,2)$, $(1,\tau,3)$, $(1,\tau,4)$, $(2,a,1)$, $(3,a,1)$, $(3,b,1)$, $(4,b,1)$ has no testing equivalent states, but the state 2 and the related transitions can be removed without breaking the testing equivalence to the initial LTS. We propose here to solve this difficulty for the testing equivalence. For this purpose a transformation (designated as *normal form* for testing equivalence) of LTS is defined. This transformation simplifies an LTS and preserves the testing equivalence. This transformation is defined using recursive algebraic definitions. This makes it support rigorous and simple proofs of correctness.

This paper is composed of this introduction and four other sections. The next section recalls standard definitions related to LTSs and testing equivalence. The testing projection is then introduced. Before conclusion, the three projections are compared on a small simple example.

2 Basic definitions

Labeled Transition Systems (shortly LTS) are the basic structure commonly used to represent dynamic behavior of communicating systems.

A Labeled Transition System can be viewed as a set of processes (S) executing actions in Σ. The behavior of a process $s \in S$ is specified by the set of actions it can perform. The behavior following an action is specified by the set of transitions Δ.

A finite Labeled Transition System (LTS) is a quadruple: $\mathcal{S} = (S, \Sigma, \Delta, s_0)$ where:

- S is a finite set of states, and s_0, $s_0 \in S$, is the initial state of $\mathcal{S}$.
- Σ is a finite set of visible actions, or labels
- $\Delta \subseteq S \times (\Sigma \cup \{\tau\}) \times S$: the transitions set, $\tau \notin \Sigma$ is called internal or invisible action. An element $(x, \mu, y) \in \Delta$ is denoted: $x \xrightarrow{\mu} y$

Another transition relation, $\{\overset{\mu}{\Rightarrow}\}_{\mu \in \Sigma \cup \{\varepsilon\}}$ is defined in a standard way by:

- $s \overset{\varepsilon}{\Rightarrow} s'$: $s = s'$ or $s \xrightarrow{\tau} s_1 \xrightarrow{\tau} \cdots \xrightarrow{\tau} s_n \xrightarrow{\tau} s'$: this means that internal moves of a system cannot be distinguished.
- $s \overset{a}{\Rightarrow} s'$: $s \overset{\varepsilon}{\Rightarrow} s_1 \xrightarrow{a} s_2 \overset{\varepsilon}{\Rightarrow} s'$: this means that observable moves are not distinguished by internal moves that encapsulate them.

The output of a state s denotes the set of visible actions that can be performed by the system at the state s. Formally $out(s) = \{a \in \Sigma \mid s \overset{a}{\Rightarrow}\}$.
This relation is extended to sequences (i.e. words or strings over Σ: $\sigma \in \Sigma^*$) by:

- if σ is the sequence $a_1 \cdots a_n$ write $s \overset{\sigma}{\Rightarrow} s'$ when $s \overset{a_1}{\Rightarrow} s_1 \overset{a_2}{\Rightarrow} \cdots \overset{a_{n-1}}{\Rightarrow} s_{n-1} \overset{a_n}{\Rightarrow} s'$

The empty sequence is denoted ε. As in the case of a state output, "traces of a state" refer to the set of all sequences of (visible) actions, $\sigma \in \Sigma^*$, that can be performed from this state: $Tr(s) = \{\sigma \in \Sigma^* \mid s \overset{\sigma}{\Rightarrow}\}$. By convention, the traces of LTS are those of its initial state: $Tr(\mathcal{S}) = Tr(s_0)$. Two LTSs are said to be trace equivalent when the have the set of traces.

Using LTS, we recall now the formal definition of conformance introduced in the testing theory of LOTOS [1]

In the following, we consider that all the LTSs have their actions in a given set designated by L (i.e. $\forall \Sigma, \Sigma \subseteq L$). Let A be a set of visible actions: $A \subseteq L$; σ is a sequence of actions: $\sigma \in L^*$, P denotes a behavior expression associated with a finite Labeled Transition System whose initial state is P and whose alphabet is contained in L.

- P **ref** A when $\forall a \in A$ $P \overset{a}{\not\Rightarrow}$ (i.e. $\neg(\exists P', P \overset{a}{\Rightarrow} P')$). P has no derivation by any action a among A. Then it is said that P refuses A. Note that if P refuses A then P refuses all subsets of A (i.e. $B \subseteq A$ implies P **ref** B)
- P **after** σ=$\{P' : P \overset{\sigma}{\Rightarrow} P'\}$. set of all derivations of P via sequence σ. If $\sigma \notin Tr(P)$ then P has no derivate via σ and then P **after** $\sigma = \emptyset$.
- (P **after** σ) **ref** A when ($\exists P' \in P$ **after** σ , P' **ref** A). At least one of the derivations of P refuses A.

Definition 1 (testing equivalence [1]) Two LTSs $P_i = (S_i, \Sigma, \Delta_i, P_i)$ $i = 1, 2$ are said to be testing equivalent (denoted P_1 <u>te</u> P_2) when
$\forall \sigma \in L^*, \forall A \subseteq \Sigma$, ($P_1$ (**after** σ) **ref** A) **iff** (P_2(**after** σ) **ref** A) □

Definition 2 (Bisimulation) A bisimulation (over S, the state space of an LTS) is a binary relation $\mathbf{R} \subseteq S \times S$ such that: if p $\mathbf{R}$ q then $\forall \mu \in \Sigma \cup \{\tau\}$:
(i)*if* $p \xrightarrow{\mu} p'$ *then* $q \xrightarrow{\mu} q'$ *and* ($p'\mathbf{R}q'$) (ii)*if* $q \xrightarrow{\mu} q'$ *then* $p \xrightarrow{\mu} p'$ *and* ($p'\mathbf{R}q'$) □

Two LTSs are said bisimilar, denoted by $\mathcal{S}_1 \sim \mathcal{S}_2$, when there exists a bisimulation $\mathbf{R} \subseteq S_1 \times S_2$ which contains their initial states.

The weak bisimulation is defined by substituting the weak transition relation $(\{\overset{\mu}{\Rightarrow}\}_{\mu \in \Sigma \cup \{\epsilon\}})$ for the strong one $(\{\overset{\mu}{\rightarrow}\}_{\mu \in \Sigma \cup \{\tau\}})$in the definition of the bisimulation.

3 The testing projection

The testing projection of LTS S is an $\approx$-minimized normal form of this system: $(nf(S))_{\approx}$, where $\approx$ is the bisimulation equivalence.

The resulting system verifies the following expected properties:

- A projection of an LTS is testing equivalent to this LTS: $(nf(S))_{\approx}$ $\underline{\text{te}}$ S
- Two testing-equivalent LTSs have the same projection. In other words testing equivalence is an isomorphism over the subset of LTSs which are $\approx$-minimal normal forms.

3.1 LTS in normal form

Definition 3 (LTSs in normal form) An LTS, $\mathcal{S} = (S, L, \Delta, s_0)$, is said to be in normal form for the testing-equivalence if
(i) its initial state s_0 verifies the following equation:

$$s = (\sum_{X \in R(s)} \tau; \sum_{a \in out(s) \setminus X} a; f_a(s)) \; [] \sum_{b \in \bigcap_{X \in R(s)} X} b; f_b(s) \qquad \textbf{(P1)}$$

Where $R(s)$ is a (non-empty) set of subsets of $out(s)$ which verifies the following minimality (w.r.t. cardinality) property:

$$\forall X, Y \in R(s) : (Y \subseteq X) \Rightarrow (X = Y). \qquad \textbf{(P2)}$$

(ii) The states, $f_a(s)$ et $f_b(s)$, specified in equation **P1** verify also **(i)** et **(ii)**. □

The Lotos operators ";" and "[]" designate respectively action prefix and choice. The Lotos expression $\sum_{i \in I = \{1,\cdots,n\}} P_i$ denotes the expression $P_1[]$ $P_2[] \cdots []P_n$. Semantics of these operators is defined by the following rules:

$$\forall a \in L \cup \{\tau\} \qquad \text{(i)} \; \frac{}{a; P \xrightarrow{a} P} \qquad \text{(ii)} \; \frac{k \in I, P_k \xrightarrow{a_k} P'_k}{\sum_{i \in I} P_i \xrightarrow{a_k} P'_k}$$

Property 4 (normal Form) If an LTS , $\mathcal{S}$, is in normal form (for the testing equivalence) then for every sequence of actions $\sigma = a_1 \cdots a_n \in Tr(\mathcal{S})$, and for all set of actions $A \subseteq L$ the following properties hold

1. there exists a unique state s_σ and a unique sequence of states $(s_1, .., s_{n-1})$ such that
$$s_0 \xrightarrow{a_1} s_1 \xrightarrow{a_2} \cdots s_{n-1} \xrightarrow{a_n} s_\sigma$$
Where the transition relation (simple arrow) $\xrightarrow{a}$ is defined by : $s \xrightarrow{a} s' \equiv_{def}$ $(s \xrightarrow{a} s') \vee (s \xrightarrow{\tau} s'' \xrightarrow{a} s')$

2. if $s \xrightarrow{a}$ then $\nexists s'(s \xrightarrow{\tau} s' \xrightarrow{a})$.

   This property implies the determinism of the relation (simple arrow) $\xrightarrow{a}$.

3. if ($\mathcal{S}$ **after** σ **ref** A) then
   - there exists a successor of s_σ by τ. (i.e. s' such that $s_\sigma \xrightarrow{\tau} s'$) which

     is stable : that is $s' \stackrel{\tau}{\not\rightarrow}$

     and which refuses all actions of A : $\forall a \in A, s' \stackrel{a}{\not\rightarrow}$
   - furthermore, if A verifies the following maximality property:

$$(\forall a \in L, a \notin A, \ \neg(\mathcal{S}\ \textbf{after}\ \sigma\ \textbf{ref}\ A \cup \{a\})),$$

   then the state s' is **unique**.

□

Remark 5 The definition of the normal form particularizes (by explicitly naming them) certain states of the LTS. These are states of the set $P(S) \subseteq S$ defined by the following equation:

$$P(S) = \{s_0\} \cup \{s' \in S | \exists s \in P(S), \exists a \in L \ : \ s \xrightarrow{a} s'\}.$$

These are the unique states that can have invisible transitions (i.e. τ transitions). The remaining states of the LTS are those that are reached from stable states (i.e. elements of $P(S)$) by a τ transition.

$$Stables(S) = S \setminus P(S) = \{s' | \exists s \in S, \ s \xrightarrow{\tau} s'\}.$$

This set is denoted $Stables(S)$ because its elements cannot be the origin of a τ transition.

Proposition 6 If two LTS, $\mathcal{S}_1$ and $\mathcal{S}_2$, in normal form are testing equivalent then the following properties are verified: $\forall \sigma \in Tr(\mathcal{S}_1) = Tr(\mathcal{S}_2)$

1. $out(s^1_\sigma) = out(s^2_\sigma)$
2. $R(s^1_\sigma) = R(s^2_\sigma)$

Where s^i_σ, $i = 1, 2$, is the unique successor of s^i_0 (see property 4). $R(\_)$ is the set of subsets of $out(\_)$ of the normal form definition. ■

The following proposition shows that testing equivalence and observational equivalence (i.e. weak bisimulation equivalence) are identical over LTSs in normal form.

Proposition 7 If $\mathcal{S}_1$ et $\mathcal{S}_2$ are in normal form (def. 3) then ($\mathcal{S}_1$ **te** $\mathcal{S}_2$) $\Leftrightarrow$ ($\mathcal{S}_1 \approx \mathcal{S}_2$) ■

Proof

$\Leftarrow$ always holds (even if the two systems are not in normal form).

$\Rightarrow$ To prove that the two LTSs are observationally equivalent, we will build a bisimulation relating their initial states. Let's consider the relation

$$\mathbf{B} = \bigcup_{n \geq 0} \mathbf{B}_n$$

where $(\mathbf{B}_n)_{n\geq 0}$ is the series (of binary relations contained in $S_1 \times S_2$) defined by:

$$\mathbf{B}_n = \mathbf{B}_n^1 \cup \mathbf{B}_n^2$$

with:
$\mathbf{B}_0^1 = \{(s_0^1, s_0^2)\}$ and for $n \geq 1$ $\mathbf{B}_n^1 = \{(f_a(s^1), f_a(s^2)), a \in L, \ (s^1, s^2) \in \mathbf{B}_{n-1}^1\}$.

$$\mathbf{B}_n^2 = \left\{ \left(\overbrace{\sum_{a \in out \setminus X} a; f_a(s^1)}^{s_X^1}, \overbrace{\sum_{a \in out \setminus X} a; f_a(s^2)}^{s_X^2} \right), (s^1, s^2) \in \mathbf{B}_n^1, X \in R(s^1) = R(s^2) \right\}$$

$n \geq 0$. It is not difficult to show that $\mathbf{B}$ exists and is a bisimulation. □

3.2 Normal form of an LTS

Definition 8 (Refusal Graph) A refusal graph, denoted RG, is a bilabeled graph represented by a 5-tuple $(G, \Sigma, \Delta, g_0, Ref)$ where:
• (G, Σ, Δ, g_0) is a deterministic LTS. That is which verifies : $\forall g \in G$, $\forall a \in \Sigma$; $\exists$ at the most one $g' \in G$ such that $(g, a, g') \in \Delta$. This successor can then be denoted $f_a(g)$ which means that the set of transitions is described using a family of functions $\{f_a : G \longrightarrow G\}_{a \in \Sigma}$.
• $Ref : G \longrightarrow \mathcal{P}(\mathcal{P}(\Sigma))$ is a mapping which defines for each state, the sets of actions that may be refused after the sequence leading to this state. □

To avoid redundancy, refusal sets must be minimal w.r.t. set inclusion: $\forall g \in G, \forall X, Y \in Ref(g) : (Y \subseteq X) \Rightarrow (X = Y)$.

And to avoid describing imaginary systems, the following hypotheses is imposed on the refusal graph structure: $\forall X \in Ref(g)$, $X \subseteq out(g)$. Only refused parts of the output set are considered.

Let $\mathcal{S}$ be the transition system (S, Σ, Δ, s_0) and the two following functions, whose domain is the set of subsets $\mathcal{P}(S)$,

$$\delta_a(P) = \bigcup_{p \in P} \delta_a(p) \quad \text{and} \quad out(P) = \bigcup_{p \in P} out(p)$$

where P is a subset of S, and $\forall s \in S$, $\delta_a(s) = \{s' \in S | s \stackrel{a}{\Rightarrow} s'\}$.

Definition 9 ("rg" transformation) The refusal graph $rg(\mathcal{S})$, associated with transition system $\mathcal{S} = (S, \Sigma, \Delta, s_0)$ is defined by the 5-tuple $\mathcal{G} = (G, \Sigma, \Delta', Ref, g_0)$, where

- $g_0 = \delta_\varepsilon(s_0) = \{s \mid s_0 \stackrel{\varepsilon}{\Rightarrow} s\}$
- $\langle G \subseteq \mathcal{P}(S), \Sigma, \Delta' \subseteq G \times \Sigma \times G \rangle$ is the labeled graph $rg(g_0)$, where for all $g \subseteq S$, $rg(g)$ is recursively defined by the following Lotos expression :

$$rg(g) = \sum_{a \in out(g)} a; rg(\delta_a(g))$$

- and for all $g \in G$, $Ref(g) = \{out(g) \setminus out(s), s \in g\} \setminus \{X \in Ref(g), \exists Y \in Ref(g) : (X \subseteq Y \text{ and } X \neq Y)\}$. (This is denoted $\mathrm{Min}(\{out(g) \setminus out(s), s \in g\})$)

□

Definition 10 ("lts" transformation) From a refusal graph g_0, an LTS $lts(g_0)$ may be derived according to the following recursive definition :

$$lts(g) = \sum_{X \in Ref(g)} \tau; \sum_{a \in out(g)\setminus X} a; lts(f_a(g)) \ [] \sum_{b \in \bigcap_{X \in Ref(g)} X} b; lts(f_b(g))$$

□

Proposition 11 The LTS associated with a refusal graph using the transformation *lts* is in normal form. ■

Proof On the one hand, thanks to the determinism property of the refusal graph, the following holds : $\forall g \in G,\ f_a(g) \stackrel{def}{=} \{g' | g \stackrel{a}{\Rightarrow} g'\}$ is at the most a singleton. This means that f_a is a function. On the other hand, the property **P2** (see definition 3) holds for the sets that label the nodes of the graph. □

In [2] a new bisimulation was defined over the so-called Tgraphs and proposed to provide a decision procedure for the testing equivalence of [8].

We will now establish a similar result[1] by introducing (without more investigation) bisimulation over refusal graphs. This result can be viewed as an instance of the one yet introduced by Cleaveland and Hennessy, and will be used further to prove the theorem introduced in the next section.

Definition (Bisimulation) A relation $\mathbf{B} \subseteq G \times G$ is a bisimulation when it verifies:

$$p\ \mathbf{B}\ q \text{ implies } \begin{cases} (i)\ \lceil Ref(p) \rceil = \lceil Ref(q) \rceil \text{ and} \\ (ii)\ \forall a \in \Sigma,\ (p \stackrel{a}{\Rightarrow} p' \textbf{ iff } q \stackrel{a}{\Rightarrow} q') \text{ and } (p'\ \mathbf{B}\ q'). \end{cases}$$

Definition (Bisimulation equivalence)

Two refusal graphs $(\mathcal{G}_i = \langle G_i, L, \Delta_i, Ref_i, g_i^0 \rangle,\ i = 1,2)$ are bisimilar when there exists a bisimulation $B \subseteq G_1 \times G_2$ such that $g_1^0\ \mathbf{B}\ g_2^0$. (Denoted $g_1^0 \asymp g_2^0$ or $\mathcal{G}_1 \asymp \mathcal{G}_2$)

The next proposition shows that the testing equivalence can be computed as bisimulation over refusal graph:

Proposition 12 $\mathcal{S}_1\ \underline{\text{te}}\ \mathcal{S}_2 \Longleftrightarrow rg(\mathcal{S}_1) \asymp rg(\mathcal{S}_2)$. ■

Definition (isomorphism) Let $\mathcal{G}_i = (G_i, L, \Delta_i, Ref_i, g_i^0)$ be two refusal graphs, they are isomorphic, denoted by $\mathcal{G}_1 \leftrightarrow \mathcal{G}_2$, if there exists a bijective mapping

$$\phi : G_1 \longrightarrow G_2 \text{ such that : } \begin{cases} (i) \phi(g_1^0) = g_2^0 \textit{ and } \forall g_1 \in G_1 : \\ (ii) \begin{cases} \bullet Ref_1(g_1) = Ref_2(\phi(g_1)) \\ \bullet \forall a \in L, g_1 \stackrel{a}{\Rightarrow} g_1' \text{ iff } \phi(g_1) \stackrel{a}{\Rightarrow} \phi(g_1') \end{cases} \end{cases}$$

Definition 13 ("nf" transformation) The normal form of an LTS $\mathcal{S}$ is the LTS $nf(\mathcal{S})$ derived from the refusal graph of $\mathcal{S}$, that is $rg(\mathcal{S})$, by using transformation *lts*. That is : $nf(\mathcal{S}) = lts(rg(\mathcal{S}))$. □

Theorem 14 Every LTS is testing-equivalent to its normal form: $\mathcal{S}$ te $nf(\mathcal{S})$.
■

To show that the normal form of an LTS is testing equivalent to this LTS, it is sufficient to verify that they have the same (isomorphic) refusal graphs. In other words it is sufficient to show that the refusal graph of the normal form is isomorphic to the one which served to obtain this normal form.

---

[1] the two testing equivalences of [8] and [1] are identical to Hoare's failure equivalence when considering only strongly convergent processes.

The next proposition can be deduced from the proposition 7 and the theorem 14. It provides an alternative (to the Π-bisimulation of [2]) of verification of testing equivalence allowing (weak) bisimulation equivalence over standard LTSs to be used.

Proposition 15 $\mathcal{S}_1$ **te** $\mathcal{S}_2 \Leftrightarrow nf(\mathcal{S}_1) \approx nf(\mathcal{S}_2)$ ∎

Proposition 16 For every LTS, we have:
$\mathcal{S} \approx \mathcal{S}_{\approx}$. And $\mathcal{S}_1 \approx \mathcal{S}_2$ iff $(\mathcal{S}_1)_{\approx} \leftrightarrow (\mathcal{S}_2)_{\approx}$. Where $\leftrightarrow$ denotes the isomorphism over LTSs. ∎

Finally, using the fact that $\approx$ is compatible with <u>te</u> (i.e. $\approx \subset$ <u>te</u>) and using the standard results of proposition17, we deduce from proposition 16

Proposition 17 For every LTS, we have:
$\mathcal{S}$ <u>te</u> $(nf(\mathcal{S}))_{\approx}$. And
$\mathcal{S}_1$ <u>te</u> $\mathcal{S}_2$ iff $(nf(\mathcal{S}_1))_{\approx} \leftrightarrow (nf(\mathcal{S}_2))_{\approx}$. Where $\leftrightarrow$ denotes the isomorphism over LTSs. ∎

Proposition 18 All the previous propositions still hold when substituting the strong bisimulation equivalence (denoted $\sim$ as usual) for the weak bisimulation' equivalence ($\approx$). ∎

4 Optimization

The minimization part of the testing-projection can be conducted by means of strong bisimulation equivalence. This provides easier minimization and is possible by slightly modifying (the definition of the normal form and) the "lts" transformation.

Definition 19 (LTSs in optimized normal form) An LTS, $\mathcal{S} = (S, L, \Delta, s_0)$, is said to be in (optimized) normal form for the testing-equivalence if the equation **P1** of the definition 3 is replaced by
If $R(s) = \{\emptyset\}$ then

$$\sum_{a \in out(s)} a; f_a(s)$$

otherwise

$$s = \sum_{X \in R(s)} \tau; \sum_{a \in out(s) \backslash X} a; f_a(s) \quad [] \quad \sum_{b \in \bigcap_{X \in R(s)} X} b; f_b(s)$$

□

This new definition assure that if an LTS is in normal form then all the states of an LTS in normal form (not only unstable states) are also in normal form.

As a consequence the strong bisimulation-based minimization[2] of (the state space of) an LTS in normal form provides an LTS which is minimal with respect to the weak bisimulation.

Formally this result is presented by the following proposition, where nf denotes the transformation of an LTS into its optimized normal form (defined by changing the *lts* transformation in accordance with the new definition).

[2]is a more efficient procedure for minimizing LTS, because no transition closure (i.e. computation of the relations $\{\xrightarrow{\tau^*}\xrightarrow{a}\xrightarrow{\tau^*}\}_{a \in L \cup \{\tau\}}$) is needed.

Proposition 20 $\sim$-minimal normal form and $\approx$-minimal normal of an LTS are isomorphic: $nf(S)_{\sim} \leftrightarrow nf(S)_{\approx}$. ∎

5 Example

The next Figure presents an example of the three former projections. This example shows that testing projection may provide an LTS less reduced than trace projection and more reduced than observation projection.Observational projection does not reduce the initial LTS. This is due to the fact that states s_2 and s_3 are not observationally equivalent because their behaviours are respectively of the form $\tau; (P[]Q)[]\tau; P$ and $\tau; P[]Q$ which are not observationally equivalent. The system depicted by these LTSs can be viewed as the local service provided by a data transfer connection-oriented protocol which locally uses a rendez-vous communication between a protocol entity (i.e., service provider) and its user. The trace projection shows that initially the system can allocate a connection (ConReq), and then transmit data (DataReq) or accepts disconnection (DisInd). The testing projection shows that, after connection, data transmission is not always possible. This is due to the presence of an internal transition ($p_2 \xrightarrow{\tau} p_3$) that system may execute without communicating with its environment compelling the latter to stop data transfer. Abstraction made by this projection consists of ignoring the origin of this internal transition. It can either represent a remote or a local disconnection decision.

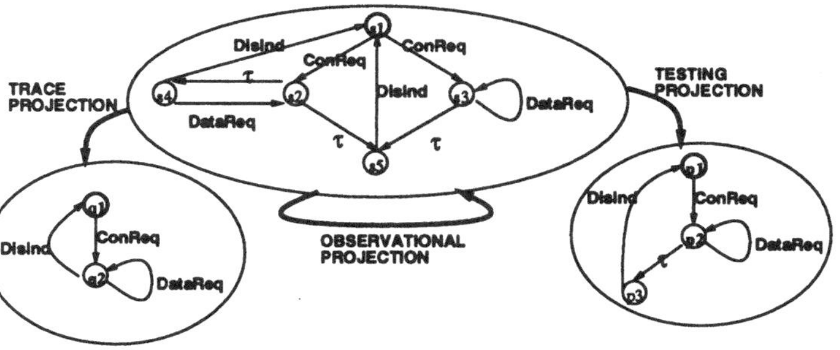

6 Conclusion

The underlying idea of the testing-projection can be summarized by the following:

- we characterize a particular family of LTS called LTS in normal form. For this family we prove that (weak) bisimulation equivalence is identical to testing equivalence.
- we provide a transformation of an LTS to a testing equivalent LTS which is in normal form. This transformation relies on an abstract structure (we refer to as Refusal graph [3]) that eliminates redundancy related to information that does not concern trace and deadlock properties.
- $\sim$-minimization of this normal form preserves testing equivalence and reduces the state space of the LTS.

This technique has been experimented on several communication protocols, namely MMS and OSI-TP [6]. These experiences showed that in the first design steps the so-reduced system is useful for modeling error detection and correction.

References

[1] E. Brinksma, G. Scollo, and C. Steenbergen. Lotos Specifications, their implementations and their tests. In B. Sarikaya and G.V. Bochmann, editors, *Protocol Specification Testing and Verification*, volume VI. Elsevier Science Publishers B.V., North-Holland, 1987.

[2] R. Cleaveland and M. Hennessy. Testing Equivalence as Bisimulation Equivalence. In J. Sifakis, editor, *Automatic Verification Methods for Finite State Systems*, number 407 in Lecture Notes in Computer Science, pages 11–23, Grenoble-france, June 1989. Springer-Verlag.

[3] K. Drira, P. Azéma, B. Soulas, and A.M. Chemali. Testability of a communicating system through an environment. In *Proc. 4th International Join Conference on the Theroy and Practice of Software Development. TAPSOFT'93 (LNCS 668)*, ORSAY, FRANCE, April 1993.

[4] Jean-Claude Fernandez, Hubert Garavel, Laurent Mounier, Anne Rasse, Carlos Rodríguez, and Joseph Sifakis. A toolbox for the verification of lotos programs. In Lori A. Clarke, editor, *Proceedings of the 14th International Conference on Software Engineering ICSE'14 (Melbourne, Australia)*, New-York, May 1992. ACM.

[5] C.A.R. Hoare. *Communicating Sequential Processes*. Prentice-Hall, 1985.

[6] R. Jacinto, G. Juanole, and K. Drira. On the application to OSI-TP of a Structured Analysis and Modelling Methodologie Based on Petri Nets Models. In *Proceedings of the 4th IEEE Workshop on Future Trends in Distributed Computing Systems (FTDCS)*, Lisboa-Portugal, September 22-24 1993. To appear.

[7] R. Milner. *Communication and Concurrency*. Prentice-Hall, 1989.

[8] R. De Nicola and M.C.B. Hennessy. Testing equivalences for processes. *Theoretical Computer Science*, 34:83–133, 1984.

[9] D. Park. Concurrency and automata on infinite sequences. In *Lecture Notes in Computer Science*, volume 104. Springer-Verlag, Berlin Heidelberg, 1981.

Equivalences of Transition Systems in an Algebraic Framework

Pasquale Malacaria
LIENS, Ecole Normale Superieure,
Paris, France

Department of Computing, Imperial College
London, Great Britain

Abstract

We study the category of transition systems and the notions of equivalence by simulation and by bisimulation. In order to study the notion of simulation we introduce a monad on the category of transition systems. Bisimulation is studied in an algebraic way, by introducing a category of algebras which turns out to be the "Stone dual" of the category of transition systems. This category of algebras seems to be a natural framework for reasoning about bisimulation equivalence; in particular we argue an equivalence between the concepts of minimal transition system in a bisimulation class and minimal subalgebra.

1 Introduction

Transition systems provide a model for systems whose state evolves in time. This model is rather concrete and in order to formulate and to prove properties of such systems, several tools have been proposed. In this context, Hennessy-Milner modal logic [4] which has successfully characterised properties of systems in logical terms has played a major role.

The problem of equivalence of transition systems has a place of its own. Indeed if we have a notion of equivalence and we want to prove a property of a system, we can try to prove the property in the smallest system equivalent to the given one. If this equivalence preserves the features we want in a system, then the consequence is a general decrease of the complexity in proving properties of systems.

The bisimulation equivalence [8, 4] has this property w.r.t. observable features of a system. Despite its simple formulation, it seems difficult to work with this equivalence directly on transition systems. An important contribution of Hennessy-Milner logic is to have given an abstract framework facilitating reasoning about bisimulation.

In this paper we study transition systems from an algebraic point of view. For the simulation equivalence, the algebras are the free algebras of a monad on the category of transition systems. These algebras are however "concrete" because they are an "algebraic completion" of a system. A more interesting category of algebras seems to be the one we will propose for studying bisimulation; being related to the category of transition systems by a Stone duality [5] it is in some sense canonical. Here by canonical we mean that the algebra associated to a transition system is as close as possible to the structure of the system (roughly speaking they are the space of ultrafilters on the systems). Stone duality makes it possible to establish an equivalence between categories having a very different structure, for example between categories of algebras and categories of topological spaces [5] or between categories of domains and categories of algebras and logics [1, 3].

The Stone duality we present in this paper relates the category of transition systems to a category of algebras underlying a generalised Hennessy-Milner logic, that is algebras which contain Tarsky-Lindembaum algebras of this logic. As a test for the validity of abstract reasoning (i.e. algebraic tools) about transition systems, we will prove the equivalence of the notions of subalgebra and bisimulation relation, that is we will prove that two systems are in bisimulation if and only if they have isomorphic subalgebras. It will follow then that the minimal subalgebra of the algebra of a system T corresponds by duality to the smallest transition system (w.r.t. number of states) which is in bisimulation with T.

2 Categories of action algebras and transition systems

A complete atomic Boolean algebra (CBA for short) is a Boolean algebra A in which the g.l.b. and l.u.b. operations are defined for all subsets of A and such that there exists a subset $\mathrm{At}(A) \subseteq A$ such that $A \simeq \wp(\mathrm{At}(A))$ (the power algebra generated by $\mathrm{At}(A)$). Elements of $\mathrm{At}(A)$ are called *atoms*.

Let **CBA** denote the category whose objects are complete atomic Boolean algebras and whose arrows are the structure preserving maps. Note that if $\phi : A \rightarrow A'$ is an arrow in **CBA** , then there exists a unique set theoretical map

$$\phi^* : \mathrm{At}(A') \rightarrow \mathrm{At}(A)$$

such that (under the isomorphism $A \simeq \wp(\mathrm{At}(A))$) we have $(\phi^*)^{-1} = \phi$. The map ϕ^* is the *underlying map for* ϕ.

Let A be a CBA and X a set; a *linear action* of X on A is given by a map $\alpha : X \times A \rightarrow A$ (we write $x.v$ instead of $\alpha(x, v)$) such that:

- $x.0 = 0$,
- $x.\bigvee V = \bigvee_{v \leq V}(x.v)$.

The *category of actions of X over complete atomic boolean algebras* (which we will note $\mathcal{AL}$) has as objects pairs (A, α) (lets call such a pair an *action algebra*) where A is a CBA and α is a linear action of X over A. An arrows $\phi : (A, \alpha) \rightarrow (A', \alpha')$ is a **CBA** morphisms between A and A' which satisfies the inequality:

$$x.\phi(v) \leq \phi(x.v)$$

A transition system is a pair $T = (S, T)$ (we use the same letter T to indicate the set of transitions and the transition system) where S is the set of *states* and $T \subseteq S \times X \times S$ is the set of *transitions* whose elements we denote as $s \xrightarrow{x} s'$. A transition system map f from (S, T) to (S', T') is a set theoretic map $f : S \rightarrow S'$ such that

$$s \xrightarrow{x} s' \in T \Rightarrow f(s) \xrightarrow{x} f(s') \in T'$$

Let $\mathcal{TS}$ denote the *category of transition systems over a set of actions X*. The categories $\mathcal{TS}$ and $\mathcal{AC}$ are related by two contravariant functors $\mathbf{Ts} : \mathcal{AC} \rightarrow \mathcal{TS}$ and $\mathbf{Ac} : \mathcal{TS} \rightarrow \mathcal{AC}$.

- The functor **Ts** is defined as follows:
  $\mathbf{Ts}(A, \alpha) = (\mathrm{At}(A), T_A)$ where $a_1 \xrightarrow{x} a_2 \in T_A$ iff $a_1 \leq x.a_2$
  $\mathbf{Ts}(\phi) = \phi^*$ (the underlying map before defined)
- The functor **Ac** is defined in the following way:
  $\mathbf{Ac}(T) = (\wp(S), \alpha)$ where $\alpha(x, v) = \{s_1 \in S | \exists s_2 \in v \text{ such that } s_1 \xrightarrow{x} s_2\}$
  $\mathbf{Ac}(f) = f^{-1}$

Proposition 1 The categories $\mathcal{TS}$ and $\mathcal{AC}$ are duals (i.e. $\mathcal{TS} \simeq \mathcal{AC}^{\mathrm{Op}}$)

2.1 Categorical properties of $\mathcal{TS}$

We list here some categorical properties of $\mathcal{TS}$ which could be useful in the following:

- The category $\mathcal{TS}$ has small limits; This can be proved by showing that $\mathcal{TS}$ has small products and equalizers:
- the *product* of a family $(T_i)_{i \in I}$ is the transition system $\times T = (\times S, \times T)$ where
  $\times S$ is the set theoretical product of the family $(S_i)_{i \in I}$ i.e.

$$\{V : I \rightarrow \bigcup_{i \in I} T_i | \forall i \in I (V(i) \in T_i)\}$$

  $V_1 \xrightarrow{x} V_2 \in \times T$ iff for any $i \in I$ $V_1(i) \xrightarrow{x} V_2(i) \in T_i$
- The *equalizer* of $f, g \in \mathcal{TS}(T, T')$ is given by the system T_0 such that $S_0 \subseteq S$ and $s \xrightarrow{x} s' \in T_0$ iff $f(s) \xrightarrow{x} f(s') \in T'$ and $g(s) \xrightarrow{x} g(s') \in T'$. The map which "equalizes" f and g is of course the inclusion map from S_0 to S.
- The category $\mathcal{TS}$ has *sums* as well. The sum of the family $(T_i)_{i \in I}$ is the transition system $+T = (+S, +T)$ where
  $+S$ is the disjoint union of the family $(S_i)_{i \in I}$
  $(s, i) \xrightarrow{x} (s', j) \in +T$ iff $i = j$ and $s \xrightarrow{x} s' \in T_i$
- The *terminal object* in $\mathcal{TS}$ is the system $(\{*\}, \{* \xrightarrow{x} * | x \in X\})$
- The *initial object* in $\mathcal{TS}$ is the system $(\{*\}, \emptyset)$
- Given two transistion systems T, T' we can construct the *weak exponential* $T^{T'}$ as follows:
  The set of states of $T^{T'}$ is the set $\mathcal{TS}(T', T)$.
  Given $f, g \in \mathcal{TS}(T', T)$ the transition $f \xrightarrow{x} g$ is a transition in $T^{T'}$ iff for all $s \in S$ $f(s) \xrightarrow{x} g(s) \in T'$

The object $T^{T'}$ is not an exponential in categorical terms; for if it were the evaluation map $\epsilon(T', T) : T^{T'} \times T' \rightarrow T$ associating $(f, s) \xrightarrow{x} (g, s') \in T^{T'} \times T'$ to its value $f(s) \xrightarrow{x} g(s')$ should esists. However this transition is in general not in T since the definition of product and weak exponential only allows for $f(s) \xrightarrow{x} g(s)$ and $g(s) \xrightarrow{x} g(s')$ in T. Hence in order to have a true exponential it is sufficient to require a transitivity property of transition, i.e. if $s_1 \xrightarrow{x} s_2$ and $s_2 \xrightarrow{x} s_3$ are in T then $s_1 \xrightarrow{x} s_3 \in T$.

3 Stone duality between $\mathcal{TS}, \mathcal{AL}$

Indeed the duality between $\mathcal{TS}$ and $\mathcal{AL}$ is a Stone duality : Roughly speaking this means that there exists an action algebra $\Omega_{\mathcal{AL}}$ and a transition system $\Omega_{\mathcal{TS}}$ such that the functor **Ts** is naturally isomorphic to the Hom enriched [1] functor $\mathcal{AL}(-,\Omega_{\mathcal{AL}})$ and that the functor **Ac** is naturally isomorphic to the Hom enriched functor $\mathcal{TS}(-,\Omega_{\mathcal{TS}})$.

For example the transition system $\Omega_{\mathcal{TS}}$ is shown in the following picture:

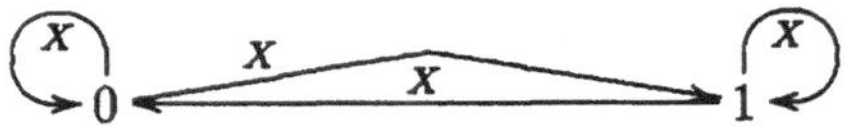

That is $\Omega_{\mathcal{TS}} = (\{0,1\}, \{s_1 \xrightarrow{x} s_2 | s_1, s_2 \in \{0,1\}, x \in X\})$

The action algebra $\Omega_{\mathcal{AL}}$ is pictured as follows:

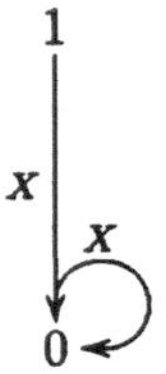

That is $\Omega_{\mathcal{AL}} = (\{0,1\}, \alpha)$ where α is defined by $x.a = 0$ for $a \in \{0,1\}$

Proposition 2
- The functors **Ac** and $\mathcal{TS}(-,\Omega_{\mathcal{TS}})$ are naturally isomorphic.
- The functors **Ts** and $\mathcal{AL}(-,\Omega_{\mathcal{AL}})$ are naturally isomorphic.

Proof:

- This means that the functor $\mathcal{TS}(-,\Omega_{\mathcal{TS}})$ associates a transition system T to an algebraic structure. This can be proved as follows:
  1 Any set theoretic map $f : S \to \{0,1\}$ is in $\mathcal{TS}(T,\Omega_{\mathcal{TS}})$, and any map $f : \mathcal{TS}(T,\Omega_{\mathcal{TS}})$ is the characteristic map χ_V of a subset V of S
  2 The set of characteristic maps on S has an algebraic structure: For a boolean operation $\omega \in \{\bigcup, \bigcap\}$ we put $\omega(\chi_{V_i})_{i\in I}(s) = 1$ iff $s \in \omega(\chi_i^{-1}(1))_{i\in I}$, similarly for negation. We have that $\omega(\chi_{V_i})_{i\in I} = \chi_{\omega(V_i)_{i\in I}}$ We only have to define the actions, i.e. $x.\chi_V$; we put

$$x.\chi_V(s) = 1 \text{ iff } s \in x.(\chi_V^{-1}(1))$$

  Again it is easy to verify that $x.\chi_V = \chi_{x.V}$ The isomorphism is then $\Psi : \mathcal{TS}(-,\Omega_{\mathcal{TS}}) \to \mathbf{Ts}$ defined by $\Psi(T)(\chi_V) = V = [\chi_V^{-1}](1)$; it is natural since

[1] By "enriched" we mean that the functor $\mathcal{AL}(-,\Omega_{\mathcal{AL}})$ associates to an action algebra A the set $\mathrm{HOM}_{\mathcal{AL}}(A,\Omega_{\mathcal{AL}})$ equipped with a transition system structure

for any $f : T' \to T, V \subseteq S$ the following identities hold:

$$\begin{array}{rcll} [\Psi(T') \circ \mathcal{TS}(f, \Omega_{\mathcal{TS}})](\chi_V) & = & [\mathcal{TS}(f) \circ \Psi(T)](\chi_V) & \text{iff} \\ \Psi(T')(\chi_V \circ f) & = & f^{-1}(V) & \text{iff} \\ f^{-1}(\chi_V^{-1}(1)) & = & f^{-1}(V) & . \end{array}$$

Which completes the proof.

- We first remark that the set $\mathcal{AL}((A, \alpha), \Omega_{\mathcal{AL}})$ is the same as **CBA** $(A, \{0,1\})$ since each morphism ϕ in **CBA** $(A, \{0,1\})$ satisfies the inequality

$$x.\phi(v) \leq \phi(x.v)$$

Now it is well known that the set **CBA** $(A, \{0,1\})$ is in bijection with the set of ultrafilters on A i.e. the set of sets of the shape $\uparrow a \stackrel{\text{def}}{=} \{v \in A | a \leq v\}$ (the bijection is $\phi \mapsto \phi^{-1}(1)$. Seen as a map $(\uparrow a)(v) = 1$ iff $a \leq v$). Hence we define the transition system $(\mathcal{AL}((A, \alpha), \Omega_{\mathcal{AL}}), T_{(A,\alpha)})$ by putting $\uparrow a \xrightarrow{x} \uparrow a' \in T_{(A,\alpha)}$ iff $a \leq x.a'$.
We can then prove that the map $\iota : \mathbf{Ac} \to \mathcal{AL}(-, \Omega_{\mathcal{AL}})$ defined by $\iota(A)(a) = \uparrow a$ is a natural isomorphism. It is a bijective transition system isomorphism since $a \xrightarrow{x} a' \in T_A$ iff $\uparrow a \xrightarrow{x} \uparrow a' \in T_{(A,\alpha)}$. Eventually to prove naturality is a routine exercise.

∎

4 Simulation equivalence and Kleisli category

Given two transition systems $T = (S, T), T' = (S', T')$ a *simulation* between T and T' is a relation $\mathcal{R} \subseteq S \times S'$ such that:

1 For any $s \in S$ there exists $s' \in S'$ such that $(s, s') \in \mathcal{R}$.

2 For any $s_1 \xrightarrow{x} s_2 \in T$ if $(s_1, s'_1) \in \mathcal{R}$ then there exists $s'_2 \in S'$ such that $s'_1 \xrightarrow{x} s'_2 \in T'$ and $(s_2, s'_2) \in \mathcal{R}$.

A *bisimulation* between T and T' is a simulation $\mathcal{R}$ between T and T' such that $\mathcal{R}^{-1}$ is a simulation between T' and T.

Let consider the functor $\mathbf{Sm} : \mathcal{TS} \to \mathcal{TS}$, defined on objects by $\mathbf{Sm}(S, T) = (\wp^+(S), T^+)$ where :

- $\wp^+(S)$ is the set of non empty subset of states of S
- $V_1 \xrightarrow{x} V_2 \in T^+$ iff for any $s_1 \in V_1$ there exists $s_2 \in V_2$ such that $s_1 \xrightarrow{x} s_2 \in T$.

Sm is defined on arrows by $\mathbf{Sm}(f) = f^+$, f^+ being the extension of $f : (S, T) \to (S', T')$ to the subsets of S. Intuitively the functor **Sm** maps a transition system T in the space of all possible simulations on T.

The functor **Sm** has a natural structure of monad $(\mathbf{Sm}, \eta, \mu)$ so that we can consider the Kleisli category of **Sm** on $\mathcal{TS}$, noted as $\mathcal{TS}_{\mathbf{Sm}}$. We characterise then simulation equivalence as follows:

Proposition 3 Let T, T' two transition systems. Then there exists a simulation between T and T' iff there exists an arrow between T and T' in $\mathcal{TS}_{\mathbf{Sm}}$.

Proof: Given a simulation $\mathcal{R} \subseteq S \times S'$ we define $\rho : S \rightarrow \wp^+(S')$ by putting $\rho(s) = \{s' | (s, s') \in \mathcal{R}\}$. It is easily seen that ρ is transition system map.

On the other hand an arrow $\rho : T \rightarrow \mathbf{Sm}(T')$ seen as $\{(s, s') | s' \in \rho(s)\}$ is a relation between S, S' that satisfies $\mathcal{R}1$ since the empty set is not in $\wp^+(S)$ and satisfies $\mathcal{R}2$ because it is a transition system map ∎

5 Action algebras and Bisimulation

A *subalgebra* A' of an action algebra (A, α) is given by a subset of elements of A which is closed under the operations. By using the isomorphism between A and $\wp(At(A))$, we can consider set theoretic operations on atoms of A; hence we define a subalgebra of (A, α) as a subset A' of elements of A such that: For any $v \in V \subseteq A'$ and for any $x \in X$ the elements $\emptyset, A, \bigcup V, \bigcap V, \neg v, \alpha(x, v)$ are in A'

We can prove then:

Theorem 1 Two transition systems T, T' are in bisimulation iff $\mathbf{Ac}(T), \mathbf{Ac}(T')$ have some isomorphic subalgebras.

The subalgebras of a given algebra are closed under arbitrary intersections; in particular the intersection of all subalgebras of A is (as we will see) a subalgebra which is the smallest (w.r.t. inclusion) subalgebra of A. This minimal subalgebra has a very interesting property:

Theorem 2 Let T be a transition system and let A_0 be the minimal subalgebra of $\mathbf{Ac}(T)$. Then the smallest transition system (w.r.t. number of states) which is in bisimulation with T is the transition system $\mathbf{Ts}(A_0)$

This section is devoted to prove theorems 1,2; the key tool is the following:

A *strong morphism* between two algebras A and A' is a one to one morphism satisfying the following equality:

$$\phi(x.v) = x.\phi(v)$$

The following is a well known result [2].

Lemma 1 Let $f : T \rightarrow T'$ be a transition system map which is onto; then f^{-1} is a strong morphism iff for all transition $f(s) \xrightarrow{x} s' \in T'$ there exists a $s'' \in S$ such that $f(s'') = s'$ and $s \xrightarrow{x} s'' \in T$.

Theorem 3 Two transition systems T_1, T_2 are equivalent by bisimulation iff there exists an algebra A and two strong morphisms $\phi_1 : A \rightarrow \mathbf{Ac}(T_1)$ and $\phi_2 : A \rightarrow \mathbf{Ac}(T_2)$.

Proof: (**Sketch,** for the full proof see [7])

$(\Leftarrow)$: Let $T = \mathbf{Ts}(A)$ and f_1, f_2 be the transition system maps such that ${f_1}^{-1} = \phi_1 : A \rightarrow \mathbf{Ac}(T_1)$ and ${f_2}^{-1} = \phi_2 : A \rightarrow \mathbf{Ac}(T_2)$.

Let consider the maps

$$h_1 : T_1 \rightarrow \wp(T_2),\ h_2 : T_2 \rightarrow \wp(T_1)$$

defined by: $h_1(s_1) = \phi_2\{f_1(s_1)\}$, $h_2(s_2) = \phi_1\{f_2(s_2)\}$.

By using lemma 1 it can be proven that the maps h_i (for $i \in \{1, 2\}$) are arrows in $\mathcal{TS}_{\mathbf{Sm}}$ (i.e. are simulations) .

In order to prove that T_1 and T_2 are equivalent by bisimulation, it suffices then to show that the relations induced by h_1, h_2 are inverses one of the other.

This is true since for all $s \in S_1, s' \in S_2$ we have:

$$s' \in h_1(s) \iff s \in h_2(s')$$

$(\Rightarrow)$: Let us define $\mathcal{B}_* \stackrel{\text{def}}{=} \mathcal{B} \bigcup \mathcal{B}^{-1}$ where $\mathcal{B}$ is an arbitrary bisimulation between T_1, T_2.

Let then define an equivalence relation $s \sim s'$ on elements of $S_1 \bigcup S_2$ (the equivalence classe of s will be noted by $[s]$) as follows:

$s \sim s'$ if and only if

$$\exists s_1, \ldots, s_n (s = s_1,\ s' = s_n,\ (s_1, s_2) \in \mathcal{B}_*, \ldots (s_{i-1}, s_i) \in \mathcal{B}_*, \ldots, (s_{n-1}, s_n)) \in \mathcal{B}_*$$

Let us now define a transistion system T by defining the set of states of T as $S = (S_1 \bigcup S_2)/\sim$ and the set of transistions of T as :

$[s_1] \xrightarrow{x} [s_2] \in T$ if and only if for all $s \in [s_1]$ there exists a $s' \in [s_2]$ such that $s \xrightarrow{x} s' \in T_1 + T_2$.

The action algebra A is then $\mathbf{Ac}(T)$. The strong morphisms are the inverse images of the following transition system maps: $\iota_1 : S_1 \rightarrow S$, $\iota_2 : S_2 \rightarrow S$ defined by $\iota_1 : s_1 \mapsto [s_1]$ and $\iota_2 : s_2 \mapsto [s_2]$ (for all $s_1 \in S_1, s_2 \in S_2$). ∎

Lemma 2 Let A be an algebra

- Let $\mathcal{A}$ be a family of subalgebras of A; then $\bigcap \mathcal{A}$ is a subalgebra of A. In particular there is a *minimal subalgebra* of A
- If $\phi : A \rightarrow A'$ is a strong morphism, then $\phi(A)$ is a subalgebra of A'.

Proof: Trivial. ∎

Let (A', α') be a subalgebra of (A, α) and define on $\text{At}(A)$ the following equivalence relation:

$$a \simeq a' \text{ iff } \forall v \in A'(a \in v \iff a' \in v)$$

We will write the equivalence class of a as $[a]$.

Lemma 3 For any $a \in \text{At}(A)$ the element $[a] \in A'$

Proof: Let $v \stackrel{\text{def}}{=} \bigcap\{v' \in A' | a \in v'\}$ ($v \neq \emptyset$ because $a \in 1 \in A'$); assume that there exists $b \in v - [a]$; since $b \notin [a]$ there exists $v_1 \in A'$ such that $b \in v_1, a \notin v_1$; hence $a \in v - v_1, b \notin v - v_1$ and since $v \subseteq v - v_1$ we conclude $b \notin v$, which is absurd; hence $v = [a]$. ∎

Now we can prove the following proposition:

Proposition 4 Let A, A_1 be algebras and A' a subalgebra of A. The following are true:

- A' is atomic.
- A strong morphism $\phi : A_1 \rightarrow A$ is an isomorphism between A_1 and $\phi(A_1)$.

Proof:

- It easily seen that the atoms in A' are the classes $[a]$ for $a \in A$.

- We will show that $[b]_{\phi(A_1)} = \phi(\phi_*(b))$. We have $b' \in \phi(\phi_*(b))$ iff $\phi_*(b') = \phi_*(b)$, hence for any $u \in A_1$ ($b \in \phi(u) \Longleftrightarrow b' \in \phi(u)$) which proves equivalence of b, b'.
  On the other hand if $b' \simeq b$ then $b' \in \phi(\phi_*(b))$ because $b \in \phi(\phi_*(b))$. ∎

Proof of theorem 1: Immediate by theorem 3 and proposition 4.

Proof of theorem 2: As A_0 is a subalgebra of $\mathbf{Ac}(T)$, from theorem 1 we deduce that $T_0 = \mathbf{Ts}(A_0)$ and T are equivalent by bisimulation. Now if T' is in bisimulation with T then it is in bisimulation with T_0 too (again by theorem 1). Now the number of states in T' is the cardinal of the set of atoms in $\mathbf{Ac}(T')$ which is greater then the cardinal of the set of atoms in $\mathbf{Ac}(T_0) = A_0$ which is the number of states of T_0.

6 Skeleton of an action algebra

Note that in the case of a CBA the notion of minimal subalgebra is trivial, the latter always being the algebra $\{0, 1\}$. The presence of actions in the category $\mathcal{AL}$ makes this notion not trivial since for any $x \in X$ the element $x.1$ (which in general is not 0) must be in the minimal algebra. Hence we are looking for a set Σ_A, the *skeleton* of the algebra A, that is the smallest subset of A containing 1 and closed under linear actions.

Σ_A is included in the minimal subalgebra of A and has moreover a natural structure of transition system (note that Σ_A is a rooted transitions system, the root being the 1 of the algebra).

We define then a *skeleton* homomorphism between two skeletons Σ, Σ' as a transition systems morphism which preserve the root and investigate the equivalence induced by skeleton isomorphism which we note $\simeq_\Sigma$. This is a rather weak equivalence. Indeed we have:

Proposition 5 Let T and T' be two transition systems such that for any $s \in S$ there exists a trace-equivalent state $s' \in S'$ and for any $s' \in S'$ there exists a trace equivalent state $s \in S$: Then $T \simeq_\Sigma T'$.

References

[1] S. Abramsky. Domain theory in logical form. *Proceedings of the 2nd annual symposium on Logic in Computer Science* IEEE Computer Society Press 1987.

[2] A. Arnold. *Systemes de transitions finis et semantique des processus comunicants.* Masson, 1992.

[3] T. Ehrhard, P. Malacaria. Stone duality for stable functions. *Proceedings of Category Theory in Computer Science.* Springer Verlag L.N.C.S. 530.

[4] M. Hennessy, R. Milner. Algebraic laws for nondeterminism and concurrency. *Journal of A C M.* vol 32, 1985.

[5] P. Johnstone. *Stone Spaces.* Cambridge University Press 1982.

[6] S. MacLane. *Categories for the working mathematician.* Springer Verlag 1971.

[7] P. Malacaria *Deux contributions de la dualité de Stone à l'informatique théorique* Ph.D. thesis, University of Paris VII, 1993.

[8] D. Park Concurrency and automata on infinite sequences. *Proceedings 5th GI conference on Theoretical Computer Science.* Springer Verlag L.N.C.S. 104.

Semantics frameworks for a class of modular algebraic nets

E. Battiston, V. Crespi, F. De Cindio, G. Mauri
Dipartimento di Scienze dell'Informazione -Università degli Studi di Milano
Milan, Italy

Among the various proposals for an 'Algebraic Specification of Concurrency' [1], OBJSA Nets [3] are a class of algebraic high-level nets which combine Superposed Automata (SA) nets, a modular class of Petri nets, and the algebraic specification language OBJ. OBJSA Nets together with their support environment ONE (OBJSA Net Environment), constitute a specification language for distributed systems which is called OBJSAN as each OBJSAN specification is mapped by ONE into an OBJSA Net [4].

To enhance specification modularity and reusability, an OBJSAN specification is obtained by composing, via transition fusion (i.e., superposition), some OBJSAN (open) components. An OBJSAN component is a couple which consists of a net and an OBJ module. The net part expresses the control of the system to be specified and the OBJ part describes data modification through occurrence of events modelled by net transitions. An OBJSAN component is either *closed,* if all of its transitions are closed, or *open* if it contains at least one open transition, i.e., a transition which is only partially extensionally specified, since couples of its input/output places have to be identified through superposition of the transition itself with other transition(s). Open transitions represent the interface of the component toward other components, and are specified by non executable modules (in OBJ called theories), while closed transitions are specified by executable modules (in OBJ called theories).

With the aim of defining a formal semantics for this class of algebraic high-level Petri nets, two operators have been defined in [5]: Spec(_) and Unf(_). They map an OBJSAN closed component (in the following called OBJSAN system) C respectively to an OBJ module Spec(C) called the *Specification module* (by translation of the net scheme into conditional equations and operators) and to a 1-safe SA labelled pure net Unf(C) (an Elementary Net system) called the *Unfolding net* (by translation of the OBJ specification into net elements).
While Unf(_) well supports concurrency since it produces Elementary Net (EN) systems, whose categorical semantics has been defined in [8], Spec(_) is less satisfactory because of the loss of concurrency due to the OBJ3 sequential semantics. The idea is therefore to turn on the specification language MAUDE.
Let us recall that MAUDE is a specification language syntactically similar to OBJ3 whose operational and denotational semantics were defined by Meseguer in [9]. In MAUDE there exist essentially two kinds of modules: functional modules (whose syntax is entirely identical to OBJ3) and system modules. While operational semantics is concurrent rewriting for both of kinds of modules, denotational

semantics is different. For the functional modules it is the usual initial algebra associated with the equational specification (so MAUDE has OBJ3 as sublanguage). For the system modules it is a categorical model which describes the system whose local behaviour is specified by the rewriting rules.

More precisely let us consider a case that will be useful in the following. Suppose to have a MAUDE system module M which imports a functional module M'. M codes a rewrite theory $R = (\Sigma, E, L, R)$ while M' codes a rewrite theory $R' = (\Sigma', E', L', R')$ where Σ (resp., Σ') is an equational signature, E (resp., E') is a set of Σ_equations (resp. of Σ'_equations), L (resp., L') is a set of labels, R (resp., R') is a set of conditional rewriting rules of the type l: $[t]_E \rightarrow [t']_E$ if Cond, with $l \in L$ and $[t]_E \in T_{\Sigma,E}(X)$ (resp. for R'). The operational semantics of the global specification is given by a categorical model in which objects are the elements of $T_{\Sigma\cup\Sigma',E\cup E'}(X)$ and arrows are all the possible sequents $[t]_{E\cup E'} \rightarrow [t']_{E\cup E'}$ inductively generated by the rewriting logic inference rules starting from $R \cup R'$. In practice this means that we have concurrent rewriting modulo $E \cup E'$ on terms $T_{\Sigma\cup\Sigma'}(X)$ by using $R \cup R'$ as rewriting rules [9], i.e. concurrent rewriting in both the system module (called supermodule in the following) and the functional module (called submodule).
The denotational semantics is given by a categorical model in which the objects are the elements $T_{\Sigma\cup\Sigma',E\cup E'\cup Unlabel(R')}(X)$ and arrows are all the possible sequents $[t]_{E\cup E'\cup Unlabel(R')} \rightarrow [t']_{E\cup E'\cup Unlabel(R')}$ inductively generated by the rewriting logic inference rules starting from R. So the denotational semantics treats the rewriting rules in the functional module as equations whose semantics is the initial algebra. Then only the rewriting rules in the system supermodule are interpreted as arrows of the categorical model.

According to these considerations, here we redefine Spec(_) as the operator which maps an OBJSAN system C=(N,A) to a MAUDE system module which imports functional modules: a (conditional) rewriting rule in the system module is associated with each transition $t \in T$, whereas the functional submodules contain the coded specification of the data structure of C (the information in A).

As we are now able to associate a MAUDE module Spec(C) and an EN system Unf(C) with each OBJSAN system C, to give it a semantics we consider the categorical models developed for MAUDE modules (by Meseguer [9], see above) and for Petri nets (by Meseguer&Montanari [11]). As we shall see, both of the categorical semantics result to be redundant. The reason is that OBJSAN systems introduce, for modelling purposes, constraints on the marking: tokens are couples <a_name;some_data>, where the name represents the token identity which cannot change by transition occurrence and is unique in each elementary subnet of an OBJSAN system. Therefore, the net markings are multisets of tokens without multiplicity (i.e., multisets in which there are not two or more identical tokens) and the Unf(_) operation maps an OBJSAN system C to a 1-safe SA labelled net without slip-knots [5], which is a particular contact-free EN system [7] (while proper multisets at the higher level would require a P/T system at the lower level).

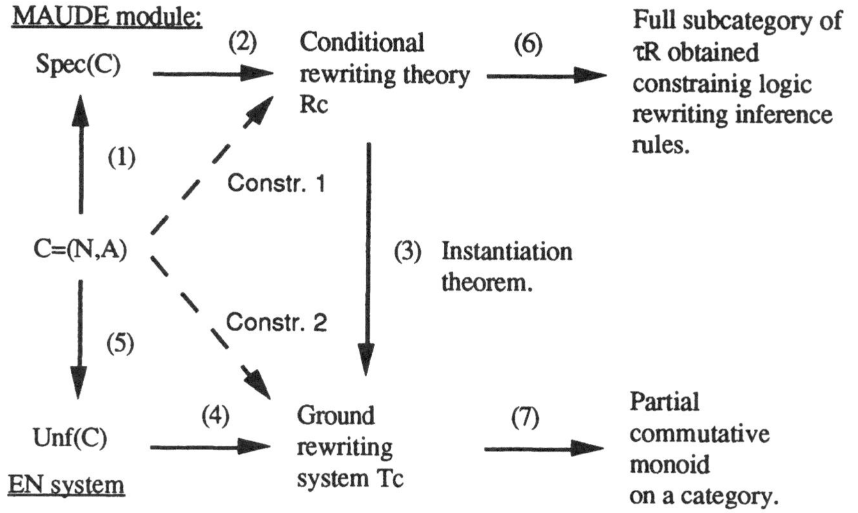

fig 1

The relationship between Spec(_) and Unf(_) is stated by a theorem that we call 'instantiation theorem' as it proves that by instantiating the rewriting rules of the system part of Spec(C) with ground terms and considering only those rules whose predicates are reduced to true (representing transitions with a chance of occurring), we get the transitions of Unf(C). This result is the starting point to prove the isomorphism between the two semantics (resp. the reducted Meseguer's model for Spec(C) and the reducted Meseguer&Montanari's model for Unf(C)); both the proves [6] are not included in this short paper as they take too much space, anyway, they will be given just in the next full version.

More formally, let C=(N,A) be an OBJSAN system:
$N=(S,T,\Pi,F,\Theta,W)$ is an OBJSA net where S is the finite set of places, T is the finite set of transitions, F is the flow relation on $S \times T \cup T \times S$, $\Theta=\{T_{op},T_{cl}\}$ is a partition of transitions into open and close transitions (in our case T_{op} is empty), $W:F \rightarrow N^+$ is the weight function and at the end $\Pi=\{\Pi_1,...,\Pi_n\}$ is a partition of places S into "elementary subnets" such that:

$$\forall ji\ \forall t \in T\ \Sigma_{s \in \bullet t \cap \Pi ji} W(s,t) = \Sigma_{s \in t \bullet \cap \Pi ji} W(t,s) \text{ (balance condition)}$$

with Π_{ji} the ji_th elementary subnet connected to t. This further condition is necessary for the Unf() operation to return a 1-safe SA labelled net, i.e. a net obtained by the composition of two or more state machines by superposition of transitions [7].
A is an OBJ3 module which codes an algebraic specification that defines the following three elements:

1) For each elementary subnet Π_i the carrier of structured tokens flowing in its places. So it is implicitly defined a map from Π to a set of sorts O.

2) With each place $p \in \Pi_i$ is associated a multiset of tokens without multiplicity of the proper carrier (net initial Marking). We will denote with $T_{<SPEC>}$ the O_sorted family of sets of tokens of the entire system and with $T_{m<SPEC>}$ the O_sorted family of sets of multisets without multiplicity (represented by formal sums).
3) For each transition t the arc inscriptions:
a set of O_sorted variables $Ty_t = \{ty_i\}$ one for each input arc $(s_i,t) \in F$; a set of operators $Ty'_t = \{ty'()\}$ in the variables ty one for each output arc $(t,s_j) \in F$. The ty'() operators transforms only the data part of the tokens in the firing mode during the transition firing and satisfy the balance condition (see the equation above); the names of the tokens are left unchanged.
4) Firing predicates: logical formulas tpr in the variables ty that enable the corresponding transition when they are evaluated to True under instantiation.

Let $t \in T$ be a transition such that $\bullet t = \{s_{j1,1},..,s_{j1,a1},..,s_{jn,1},..,s_{jn,an}\}$ and $t\bullet = \{s'_{j1,1},..,s'_{j1,b1},..,s'_{jn,1},..,s'_{jn,bn}\}$ ($s_{ji,k}$ belongs to the subnet Π_{ji}) then the firing rule of t is defined below:
Given a marking M and a substitution $\theta : Ty_t \rightarrow T_{m<SPEC>}$ to the t input variables ty say

$$\theta = \{ty_{j1,1} \rightarrow ms_{j1,1},..,ty_{j1,a1} \rightarrow ms_{j1,a1},..,ty_{jn,1} \rightarrow ms_{jn,1},.., ty_{jn,an} \rightarrow ms_{jn,an}\}$$

with $\{ms_{jk,l}\}$ formal sums of tokens of the proper cardinality (i.e. according to the weight of the input arcs) such that $\forall u,v \; ms_{jk,u} \cap ms_{jk,v} = \varnothing$ (in the following we will always assume this conditions when treating with substitutions), then t has concession to fire in mode md at marking M if and only if

1) $tpr()\theta \rightarrow^* True$,
2) $[ms_{j1,1},..,ms_{j1,a1},..,ms_{jn,1},..,ms_{jn,an}] <= M$.

In that case we write $M[t_{md} > M'$ where

$$M' = M - [ms_{j1,1},..,ms_{j1,a1},..,ms_{jn,1},..,ms_{jn,an}] + [ty'_{j1,1}()\theta,..,ty'_{jn,bn}()\theta]$$

and md is the term $mode(ty_{j1,1},..,ty_{j1,a1},..,ty_{jn,1},..,ty_{jn,an})\theta$ called "firing mode". Furthermore we can define:

$$MODES(t) = \{md \;/\; md = mode(ms_{j1,1},..,ms_{j1,a1},..,ms_{jn,1},..,ms_{jn,an}) \; tpr(md) = true\}$$

so each firing mode md is a term which represents a substitution θ_{md} to the input arc inscriptions of the transition which verifies the predicate tpr().
Let us now derive from C its MAUDE Specification module Spec(C) and its Unfolding net Unf(C) (arrows 1 and 5 in fig.1).

As we have seen, Spec(C) codes two rewrite theories $\mathcal{R}=(\Sigma, E, L, R)$ and $\mathcal{R}'=(\Sigma', E', L', R')$, respectively associated with the system module and with the functional submodules. The rewriting theory $R_c=(\Sigma\cup\Sigma', E\cup E'\cup Unlabel(R'), L, R)$ (arrow 2) gives the denotational semantics of Spec(C), according to [9].

According to the construction given in [8] which specializes the Meseguer&Montanari's work for P/T nets to EN systems, Unf(C) can be translated into a set of ground rewriting rules which we name Tc (arrow 4). For example, a transition t in an EN system is translated into the rewriting rule $s_1\oplus..\oplus s_n \rightarrow s'_1\oplus..\oplus s'_m$ (with $\oplus$ commutative and associative operator of parallel sum) where $\bullet t=\{s_1,..,s_n\}$ and $t\bullet=\{s'_1,..,s'_m\}$. T_c gives the denotational semantics of Unf(C), according to [8].

Then, the instantiation theorem (arrow 3) states that by instantiating the open (conditional) rewriting rules in R_c with ground terms and considering only the conditional equations whose predicates are reduced to true we get T_c. In the following we sketch its proof, whose kernel consists of the constructions related as shown in fig.2.

$$\begin{aligned} rt:\ & C_{j1}t_my_{j1}\oplus..\oplus C_{jn}t_my_{jn} \rightarrow \\ & C_{j1}t_my'_{j1}(md_m())\oplus..\oplus C_{jn}t_my'_{jn}(md_m() \\ & \text{if } t_mpr(md_m()) \\ & \theta_m : T_my_t \rightarrow T'_{m<SPEC>} \end{aligned}$$

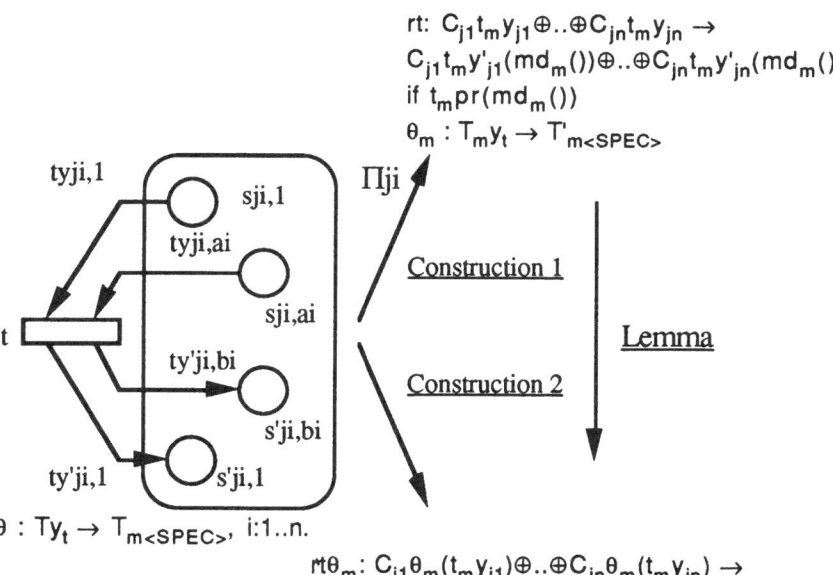

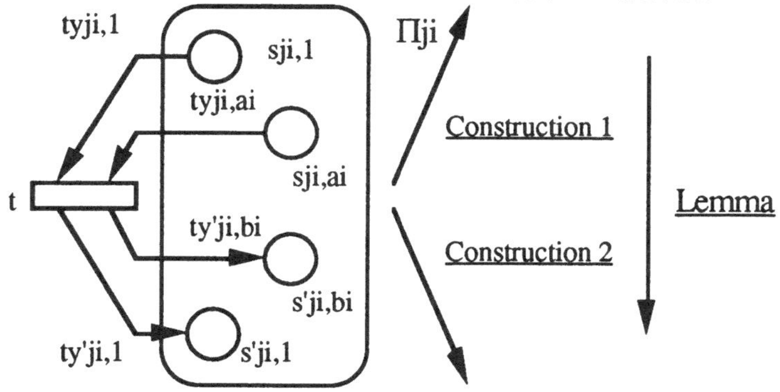

$\theta : Ty_t \rightarrow T_{m<SPEC>}$, i:1..n.

$$\begin{aligned} rt\theta_m:\ & C_{j1}\theta_m(t_my_{j1})\oplus..\oplus C_{jn}\theta_m(t_my_{jn}) \rightarrow \\ & C_{j1}t_my'_{j1}(md_m()\theta_m)\oplus..\oplus C_{jn}t_my'_{jn}(md_m()\theta_m) \end{aligned}$$

$$\begin{aligned} t\theta:\ & Unf_{\Pi j1}(\theta(ty_{j1,1}),s_{j1,1})\oplus..\oplus Unf_{\Pi jn}(\theta(ty_{jn,an}),s_{jn,an})\rightarrow \\ & Unf_{\Pi j1}(ty'_{j1,1}(md()\theta),s'_{j1,1})\oplus..\oplus Unf_{\Pi jn}(ty'_{jn,bn}(md()\theta),s'_{jn,bn}) \end{aligned}$$

with $md_m() = mode(t_my_{j1},..,t_my_{jn})$, $md()=mode(ty_{j1,1},..,ty_{jn,an})$.

fig 2

Taken a transition $t \in T$ of an OBJSAN system C and a ground substitution θ of the input arc inscriptions which satisfies the occurrence predicate (representing an occurrence mode enabling t in a certain marking) we get, via construction 1, a conditional rewriting rule rt with a corresponding ground substitution θ_m for var(rt) and, via construction 2, a ground rewriting rule $t\theta$. The lemma closes the cycle: by instantiating rt with θ_m we get $t\theta$. Formally:

<u>**Construction 1:**</u> Let C=(N,A) be an OBJSA component with $N=(S,T,\Pi,F,\Theta,W)$ OBJSA net, A obj3 Module; let $t \in T$ be a net transition and $\theta: Ty_t \rightarrow T_{m<SPEC>}$ a ground substitution, then we can associate with t a (conditional) open rewriting rule rt with a corresponding ground substitution θ_m adapted for var(rt).

<u>proof:</u>

Let us take a generic transition t as in figure 2 and let us describe how we associate with it a conditional rewriting rule to obtain at the end a conditional rewrite theory according to Meseguer definition.

For this purpose we first perform a net transformation to simplify the net structure. Substantially we collapse each elementary subnet on a single place transferring the sacrified net information into the tokens data parts (cf. fig. 3). In such a way we obtain a sort "minimal" model (cf [5]), where for each ji $W'(s_{ji},t) = \Sigma_{k \in \bullet t \cap \Pi_{ji}} W(s_{ji,k},t)$ (idem for the output case).

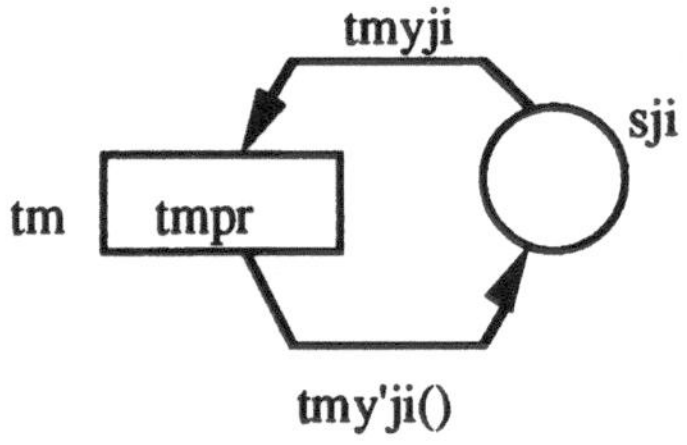

fig 3

The substitutions (i.e. the firing modes) for the variables ty must be transformed for the new variables $t_m y$ (input arc inscriptions for the transition in the minimal model) as follows. Let us first define a new operator MIN: $T_{m<SPEC>} \times S \rightarrow T'_{m<SPEC>}$

$$MIN(<N_1,V_1><+><N_2,V_2><+>..<+><N_k,V_k>,s) =$$
$$<N_1,<<V_1,s>>><+><N_2,<<V_2,s>>><+>..<+><N_k,<<V_k,s>>>$$

where <+> is the overloaded associative operator with identity which takes two formal sums of tokens and returns a unique formal sum [3].
Given the generic substitution θ on the input variables of t:

$\theta = \{ty_{j1,1} \rightarrow ms_{j1,1},..,ty_{j1,a1} \rightarrow ms_{j1,a1},..,ty_{jn,1} \rightarrow ms_{jn,1},.., ty_{jn,an} \rightarrow ms_{jn,an}\}$

we have a corresponding substitution θ_m: $T_m y_t \rightarrow T'_{m<SPEC>}$ on the input variables of t_m:

$$\theta_m = \{t_m y_{j1} \rightarrow MIN(ms_{j1,1},s_{j1,1})<+>..<+>MIN(ms_{j1,a1},s_{j1,a1}),..,\ t_m y_{jn} \rightarrow MIN(ms_{jn,1},s_{jn,1})<+>..<+>MIN(ms_{jn,an},s_{jn,an})\}$$

This generic transition t_m can be expressed by the following conditional rewriting rule:

$$rt: C_{j1}t_m y_{j1} \oplus .. \oplus C_{jn}t_m y_{jn} \rightarrow C_{j1}t_m y'_{j1}(mode(t_m y_{j1},..,t_m y_{jn})) \oplus .. \oplus C_{jn}t_m y'_{jn}(mode(t_m y_{j1},..,t_m y_{jn})) \quad \text{if } t_m pr(mode(t_m y_{j1},..,t_m y_{jn}))$$

where $card(t_m\, y_{ji}) = W(s_{ji},t)$, $t_m\, y'_{ji}(md_m) = \Sigma_{k \in \Pi ji \cap t\bullet} MIN(ty'_{ji,k}(md),s_{ji,k})$ for md and md_m the firing modes associated respectively with θ and with θ_m.

◊

Some comments are necessary.

Symbols C_{ji} are unary operators which apply to formal sums of tokens belonging to the ji_th elementary subnet. If an OBJSA component C has $\Pi = \{\Pi_1,..,\Pi_m\}$ elementary subnets, then a generic marking $M: P \rightarrow [T_{<SPEC>} \rightarrow \{0,1\}]$ with $M(s_{ij}) = ms_{ij}$ (s_{ij} is place j of the subnet Π_i) is denoted by the term:

$$C_1 \Sigma_{j \in \Pi 1} MIN(ms_{1j},s_{1j}) \oplus .. \oplus C_n \Sigma_{j \in \Pi n} MIN(ms_{nj},s_{nj}).$$

If md is an occurrence mode, i.e. $md \in MODES(t)$ with $md = mode(m's_{j1,1},..,m's_{jn,an})$ and
$m's_{ji,k} <= ms_{ji,k}$, i:1..n, k=1,..,ai
then the substitution

$$\theta_m = \{t_m y_{j1} \rightarrow MIN(ms_{j1,1},s_{j1,1})<+>..<+>MIN(ms_{j1,a1},s_{j1,a1}),..,\ t_m y_{jn} \rightarrow MIN(ms_{jn,1},s_{jn,1})<+>..<+>MIN(ms_{jn,an},s_{jn,an})\}$$

is a matching modulo commutativity and associativity of <+> and ⊕ for the conditional rewriting rule rt on the marking term. (The <+> and ⊕ operatorts are related by the equations $C_i A<+>B = C_i A \oplus C_i B$ for each operator C_i with A and B variables for formal sums of tokens of the proper sort).

Construction 2: Let C=(N,A) be an OBJSA component with N=(S,T,Π,F,Θ,W) OBJSA net, A obj3 Module; let $t \in T$ be a net transition and θ: $Ty_t \rightarrow T_{m<SPEC>}$ be a ground substitution which satisfies the occurrence predicate of t, then we can associate with t a ground rewriting rule $t\theta$. Furthermore we associate with t exatly card(MODES(t)) ground rewriting rules.

proof:

Let $t \in T$ be the transition whose topological structure is described in fig.2 and $\theta: Ty_t \rightarrow T_{m<SPEC>}$ be a ground substitution satisfying the occurrence predicate of t. We have seen that θ represents a firing mode $md \in MODES(t)$, say $md=mode(ms_{j1,1},..,ms_{j1,a1},..,ms_{jn,1},..,ms_{jn,an})$ with tpr(md)=true.
Let us recall, from [5], the operator $Unf_{\Pi ji}: T_{m<SPEC>} \times S \rightarrow S'^{<+>}$ defined as:

$$Unf_{\Pi ji}(<N_1,V_1><+><N_2,V_2><+>..<+><N_k,V_k>,s) = s_{N1V1s}<+>s_{N2V2s}<+>..<+>s_{NkVks}$$

where $s \in \Pi_{ji}$ and s_{N1V1s} is a place of the Unfolding net Unf(C) (cf. [5]).
According to the style proposed by Montanari and Meseguer in [11], the low level transition we want is expressed by the ground rewriting rule:

$$t\theta : Unf_{\Pi j1}(ms_{j1,1},s_{j1,1})<+>..<+>Unf_{\Pi jn}(ms_{jn,an},s_{jn,an}) \rightarrow Unf_{\Pi j1}(ty'_{j1,1}(md),s'_{j1,1})<+>..<+>Unf_{\Pi jn}(ty'_{jn,bn}(md),s'_{jn,bn})$$

Thus we have a ground rewriting rule for each firing mode (resp. ground substitution), i.e. globally, we get card(MODES(t)) different ground rewriting rules.

◊

The rewriting system T_c is obtained directly by applying the construction 2 to the transitions of C.
The rewriting rules in $R_c=(\Sigma_1, E_1, L_1, R_1)$ are obtained directly by applying the construction 1 to the transitions of C, while the equations E_1 concern the data part of C and the associativity, commutativity and ditributivity axioms for ⊕ (and C_i operators). As we have said, the MAUDE functional modules specify data, i.e., the tokens carriers, the occurrence predicates $t_m pr$ and the arc inscriptions containing variables $t_m y$ and operators $t_m y'()$. In fact the carriers of tokens together with the operations defined on them are abstract data types. We instead use system modules to specify control, i.e., local transitions.
The idea is that concurrent term rewriting in system modules captures the concurrency expressed by the control part of the net, while concurrent term rewriting in functional modules performs the parallel computation of the operators ty'.
R_c and T_c are related by the following result whose proof is omitted due to space constraints.

Lemma: Let $R_c = (\Sigma_1,E_1,L_1,R_1)$ be the rewrite theory associated with the OBJSA component C=(N,A) as seen before; let $rt \in R_1$ be a conditional open rewriting rule:

rt: w → w' if Cond

let θ_m: var(rt) → $T'_{m<SPEC>}$ be an istantiation function of formal sums of tokens to the variables $t_m y$ such that Cond$\theta_m \rightarrow^*$ true, then rtθ_m is a ground rewriting rule of T_c. rt$\theta_m =_{def}$ wθ_m → u and w'$\theta_m \rightarrow^*$ u with u ground term (canonical representative of w'θ_m).

The lemma proves the semantic equivalence between Spec(C) and Unf(C), namely between the concurrency expressed by the system module, captured by R_c, and the concurrency expressed by the Unfolding EN system, captured by T_c. Besides, the lemma proves that the concurrent application of two conditional rewriting rules in R_c r_1 and r_2 to a marking term s (with substitutions θ_{m1} and θ_{m2}) represents the concurrent occurrence of the two corresponding low level transitions $r_1\theta_1$ and $r_2\theta_2$ in T_c in the marking represented by s.

Let us now discuss the redundancy of the two categorical models due to the constraints which characterize OBJSAN systems.

a) The categorical model proposed by Meseguer, when applied to our case (R_c), is redundant because the inductive process generation of the category (by rewriting logic inference rules) would produce arrows without corresponding net computations. We get the correct model constraining the logic rewriting inference rules. What we obtain is a full subcategory of the Meseguer's original model in which objects are associated with admissible net states only (arrow 6). Such states are denoted by terms not containing two or more identical tokens: this is because OBJSAN system markings do not allow multisets of tokens with multiplicity. From the operational point of view, proofs in this *modified* Meseguer's formal system, represent the simultaneous application of several rewrite rules in R_c to a correct marking term, so that the concurrent term rewriting models concurrent transition occurrence. In practice, since we can consider only marking terms s without multiplicity then it is possible to apply concurrently two or more rewriting rules ri of R_c to s if and only if the corresponding matching substitutions θ_{mi} do not share any token (i.e., the occurrence modes are disjoint).

b) The categorical model for P/T nets defined in [11] is redundant when applied to EN systems, as shown in [8]. The redundancy is eliminated by reducing the parallel sum carrier, leading to a partial commutative monoid on a category (arrow 7) (cf. in [8] the EN category).

By removing the constraints characterizing OBJSAN systems we fall in the more general class of SPEC-inscribed nets [12] to which Unf(_) and Spec(_) can be extended: in that case the Meseguer's and Meseguer&Montanari's categorical models would not be redundant. Nevertheless, as a counterpart, SPEC-inscribed nets do not support modularity and therefore they have not a notion of parameterized open component. Indeed, our current effort is extending the approach to OBJSAN open components semantics towards using the categorical frameworks presented here for characterizing concurrent object-oriented languages (cf. [2] and [10]).

Acknowledgements

This work has been supported by the ESPRIT Working Groups CALIBAN and ASMICS2 and by the CNR-Progetto Finalizzato "Sistemi Informatici e Calcolo Parallelo", sottoprogetto 4, LRC LAMBRUSCO.

References

1. E. Astesiano, G. Reggio. Algebraic Specification of Concurrency. In: M. Bidoit, C. Choppy (eds.), Recent Trends in Data Type Specification, LNCS 655, Springer-Verlag, 1993.
2. E. Battiston, P. Consolaro, F. De Cindio, L. Rapanotti. POTS, POLS, OBJSA Nets. From object-based to class-based net formalisms. CNR-Progetto Fin. "Sistemi Informatici e Calcolo Parallelo", Tech. Rep.n.° i/4/59, 1992.
3. E. Battiston, F. De Cindio, G. Mauri. A class of high level nets having objects as domains. In: G. Rozenberg (eds.), Advances in Petri nets. LNCS 340, Springer-Verlag, 1988.
4. E. Battiston, F. De Cindio, G. Mauri. Specifying concurrent systems with OBJSA Nets. CNR-Progetto Fin. "Sistemi Informatici e Calcolo Parallelo", Tech. Rep.n.° i/4/72, 1992.
5. E. Battiston, F. De Cindio, G. Mauri, L. Rapanotti. Morphisms and Minimal Models for OBJSA Nets. In: Proc.12th Int. Conference on Application and Theory of Petri nets, Gjern (DK) June 1991.
6. V. Crespi. Un approccio categoriale alla semantica dei sistemi OBJSA. Grad thesis, University of Milan, Dipartimento Scienze dell'informazione, 1992.
7. F. De Cindio, G. De Michelis, L. Pomello, C. Simone. Superposed Automata Nets. In: C. Girault, W. Reisig (eds.), Application and Theory of Petri Nets, IFB 52, Springer-Verlag, Berlin, 1982.
8. C. Diamantini, S. Kasangian, L. Pomello, C. Simone. Elementary Nets and 2-Categories. CNR-Progetto Fin. "Sistemi Informatici e Calcolo Parallelo", Tech. Rep. n.° i/4/29, March 1991.
9. J. Meseguer. Conditional rewriting logic. deduction, models and concurrency. In: S.Kaplan and M.Okada, (eds.), Conditional and Typed Rewriting Systems, LNCS 510, Springer-Verlag, 1991.
10. J. Meseguer. Multiparadigm logic programming. In: H. Kirchner and G. Levi (eds), Algebraic and Logic Programming, LNCS 632, Springer-Verlag, 1992.
11. J. Meseguer, U. Montanari. Petri nets are monoids. In: Information and Computation, Volume 88, fascicolo 2, 1990.
12. W. Reisig. Petri Nets and Algebraic Specifications. In K. Jensen and G. Rozemberg (eds), High-Level Petri Nets. Theory and Applications, Springer-Verlag, 1991.

A Characterization of LOTOS Representable Networks of Parallel Processes *

David de Frutos-Escrig
Departamento de Informática y Automática
Facultad de Ciencias Matemáticas - Universidad Complutense
28040 Madrid, Spain

Abstract
We compare graphic and algebraic representations of parallel networks of processes. More exactly we characterize the class of graphically definable networks that can be represented in LOTOS, by means of an expression which combines the processes in the network by instances of the LOTOS parallel operator. The characterization is defined by means of an efficient algorithm that tests the given graphic representation trying to construct the equivalent LOTOS expression.

1 Introduction

Graphic formalisms have proved very useful to specify and study distributed systems. Petri Nets [8] are probably the most well known graphically inspired formalism to define that kind of systems. People that develop systems using Petri Nets are usually familiar with graphical developping tools like *Design/CPN* [5] which make their job easier and much more productive.

Graphical approaches are not so much used in connection with process algebras. Nevertheless, already Robin Milner in his first book on CCS [6], based most of his examples on some kind of graphical representations of the systems to be developped. However, those diagrams do not contain all the semantical information of the represented process, because they only give *static information*. Thus they are adequate to represent the *static combinators* (see [7]) but not the dynamic ones. But if we restrict ourselves to networks in which only the parallel structure of processes is considered, we have that the graphical framework is adequate, since the parallel operator is a static operator. This will be the kind of networks that we will study in this paper.

The present work was motivated by some previous joint work with T. Bolognesi and Y. Ortega, in the framework of the ESPRIT II project LOTOSPHERE [3, 2], exploring the (partial) associativity properties of the LOTOS parallel operator. It was T. Bolognesi who introduced in [1] a simplified version of the process-gate nets which we study in this paper. Later, we generalized in [3] those nets in order to cope with the *hiding* operator (which is also a static operator.) Finally, in [2] the case was considered in which the maximal cooperation restriction is not imposed.

Another contribution to the study of the subject is [4], giving a simple example that shows that not every parallel network is LOTOS representable.

*This work has been partially supported by ESPRIT Project 2304: LOTOSPHERE

We characterize in this paper the class of graphically definable networks that can be represented in LOTOS, by means of an expression which combines the processes in the network by instances of the LOTOS parallel operator.

Unfortunately the obtained characterization is far from trivial. In fact, what we have obtained is an efficient algorithm to decide if a given network is representable. But if finally we have decided to use the word *characterization*, it is mainly to emphasize the efficiency of the obtained algorithm, which ought to be appreciated against the combinatorial flavour of the solved problem.

2 Main Definitions

Definition 1 A general process-gate net GPGN is an undirected bipartite graph (P,G,E), where P is a set of meaning process-nodes, G is a set of gate-nodes, and E is a set of arcs $E \subseteq P \times G$. □

This definition only captures the architecture of the net: neither process-nodes nor gate-nodes are labelled by concrete processes or gate names. This generality is adequate concerning the process component, but not for gate-nodes, since we want that they express, not only the existence of a shared gate between several processes, but also the different possibilities that have the processes in the net to synchronize through them. Thus we need a possibly non-injective function which labels each gate-node by the name of the (physical) gate to which it corresponds. Hence we consider a universe of gate-names *Gates*.

Definition 2 A labelled process-gate net LPGN is a pair (GN,GL) where GN = (P,G,E) is a GPGN and $GL : G \rightarrow Gates$ is a labelling function. For each process-node $P_i \in P$ we define its alphabet $AL(P_i)$ by $AL(P_i) = \{a \in Gates \mid \exists e = (P_i, g) \in E \mid GL(g) = a\}$. □

As we will see, when we say that a net is LOTOS representable, we are not thinking on an individual net in which both process-nodes and gate-nodes are instantiated, but in general ones. Thus a representation of some net, if any exists, should be valid for any (coherent) instantiation of its process-nodes, by LOTOS-processes. We we will denote the set of LOTOS-processes by *Proc*, and for each $B \in Proc$ we will denote its set of gates by $Alphabet(B)$.

Definition 3 A concrete process-gate net CPGN is a coherently instantiated GPGN, which means a pair (LN,PL) where LN = (GN,GL), with GN = (P,G,E), is a LPGN, and $PL : P \rightarrow Proc$, is a function which verifies $Alphabet(PL(P_i)) \subseteq AL(P_i)$, for each $P_i \in P$. □

We have forbidden the execution of actions out of the set of gates labelling gate-nodes, which is a too strong restriction. But it has been imposed because it simplifies the forthcoming definitions and proofs. Besides, it is easy to generalize all our results to the general case, in which any process is allowed to execute its private actions. For we only have to consider the extended net which is obtained by adding for any of the private gates of each process a new node, which is only connected with the corresponding process-node.

The semantics of concrete nets is defined by

Definition 4 Let CPGN = (LN,PL) a concrete process-gate net with LN = (GN,GL) and GN = (P,G,E). For each $g \in G$, if all the processes B_i labelling process-nodes connected with g can execute the action $GL(g)$, evolving into B_i', then CPGN can also execute that action, evolving into CPGN' = (LN,PL'), where PL' is defined as PL, but taking $PL'(P_i) = B'_i$, for each process node P_i connected with g . □

Thus, just the processes labelling the process-nodes ***connected with the corresponding gate-node*** evolve, but the structure of the net remains the same.

Now we can formalize the problem which we will study in this paper. It is to decide if, given a certain LPGN, we can construct an equivalent LOTOS representation LRep(LN), which just combines the process variables in P, by parallel operators $|[S]|$, with $S \subseteq Gates$. Equivalency means here that for any concrete instance of LN, CN = (LN,PL), we have $CN \sim LRep(LN)[PL(P_i)/P_i]$, where by $[B_i/P_i]$ we denote the substitution of all the appearances of the variables P_i by the corresponding processes B_i , and $\sim$ means equality between the corresponding abstract operational semantics. The notion of ***abstract operational semantics*** is obtained from the corresponding operational semantics, by abstracting the process information that it contains.

Remark: It is true that any LPGN can be represented by a LOTOS expression, if the use of the renaming operator is allowed. In fact, to obtain a representation of each concrete net is not too difficult. But note that to obtain a common solution valid for all the instances of a LPGN, is much more involved. Try it!

3 Checking LOTOS-representability

To solve the problem we have followed a three-step procedure.

In the first step we consider the case in which the given network has a single gate. The reason to study this too restrictive case, is that if we project a representable network over a subset of its set of gates, we obtain another representable net. Thus, a necessary condition for a network to be representable, is that its projections over each one of its gates be representable. But this condition is not in general sufficient. Whenever a network is representable, all the representations of the projections over each gate could be obtained by projecting the representation of the net, and this means that those representations must be somehow coherent. Thus, a reasonable way to cope with the general case of the problem, would be first to solve the instances of the problem which correspond to the projections of the given net over each one of its gates, and then to check if all the obtained representations are coherent.

Unfortunately, this reduction of the problem to a family of problems corresponding to single gates, only works whenever all the alphabets of the process nodes of the network are the same. This is the case that we have studied in the second step of our procedure.

We tried to solve the general case by somehow reducing it to the adequate instance of the particular case solved in the second step of the procedure, but we did not succeed. Instead, we had to directly develop the appropriate generalization of the algorithm. Thus the second step of the procedure could be removed. But we prefer to keep it, since both the general algorithm and its correctness proof are absolutely inspired by the corresponding ones for that particular case, but their generality make them much more difficult to be understood.

Due to space limitations, we can only include in the present version of the paper the details corresponding to the first step of the procedure.

3.1 Networks with a single gate

We consider in this section the case in which the system has a single gate, that is to say $|GL(G)| = 1$. In such a case the kind of parallel expressions in which we are interested, can be represented, as already suggested by T. Bolognesi in [2], by arithmetic expressions, rewriting $|||$ into $+$ and $|[a]|$ into $\cdot$.

We will consider two kind of such arithmetic expressions: those whose atoms are ***pairwise different*** process-names representing arbitrary processes, which we will call ***general expressions;*** and those whose atoms are LOTOS-processes, which will be called ***concrete expressions.*** We will denote the set of process-names in a general expression E by $Proc(E)$.

We can translate the definition of the operational semantics of the parallel operators of LOTOS, to this arithmetic framework, obtaining the rules

$$\frac{E_1 \xrightarrow{a} E_1'}{E_1+E_2 \xrightarrow{a} E_1'+E_2} \quad \frac{E_2 \xrightarrow{a} E_2'}{E_1+E_2 \xrightarrow{a} E_1+E_2'} \quad \frac{E_1 \xrightarrow{a} E_1' \;\; E_2 \xrightarrow{a} E_2'}{E_1\cdot E_2 \xrightarrow{a} E_1'\cdot E_2'}$$

It is also easy to check that commutativity and associativity of both operators and the distributive axiom $(E_1+E_2)\cdot E_3 = (E_1\cdot E_2)+(E_1\cdot E_3)$ are also correct in this framework. Then we will prove that our problem reduces to check if the arithmetic version of the given network can be rewritten into another (equivalent) expression, by application of commutativity and associativity of both operators, and of the distributive axiom in the ***right to left*** way.

To prove this fact we use an auxiliary result, whose statement needs the following definitions:

Definition 5 i) Two general expressions are ***essentially equivalent*** iff we can rewrite each one in the other just by applying commutativity and associativity of the addition and the product.
ii) Two general expressions are ***semantically equivalent*** iff by instantiating in the same way its set of process-variables by LOTOS-processes, we always obtain a pair of expressions with the same abstract operational semantics.
iii) We call ***flat*** form of an expression the ***sum of products*** expression which is obtained from it, by expanding as much as possible all the products in the expression, by applying distributivity of the product with respect to addition. We will denote the flat form of an expression E by $Flat(E)$. □

Remark: Since we are working modulo commutativity, flats forms are in fact sets of products of process-names. Thus, sometimes we will write $E' \in Flat(E)$, to express the fact that E' is some of the summands of $Flat(E)$.

Theorem 1 If E_1 and E_2 are two general expressions that are not essentially equivalent, then they are not semantically equivalent either.

Proof:. By induction on the cardinal of the set of processes $\mathcal{P} = \{P_1, \ldots, P_n\}$ which occur in each one of the expressions.

If $n = 1$ then we have $E_1 = P_1 = E_2$.

If E_1 and E_2 are nontrivial expressions, we distinguish several subcases:

1. If $E_1 = E_{11} + E_{12}$ and $E_2 = E_{21} \cdot E_{22}$, we take $P_1 \in Processes(E_{11})$, $P_2 \in Processes(E_{12})$. There is no expression X such that $P_1P_2X \in Flat(E_1)$, and thus we can conclude that all the processes are either included in $Processes(E_{21})$ or in $Processes(E_{22})$.

2. Let us suppose that $E_1 = E_{11} \cdot \ldots \cdot E_{1n_1}$ and $E_2 = E_{21} \cdot \ldots \cdot E_{2n_2}$, where for all i, j we have either $E_{ij} = P_{ij}$ or $E_{ij} = E_{ij1} + E_{ij2}$. Then, if for any j we have $E_{1j} = P_{1j}$, we must also have some j' such that $E_{2j'} = P_{1j}$, and we can apply the induction hypothesis.
   Otherwise we take any P from $Processes(E_{11})$ and remove it from E_1 to obtain expression $E_1^{-P} = E_{11}^{-P} \cdot \ldots \cdot E_{1n_1}$. P must be included in some E_{2j}. Assume $j = 1$. Then $E_{21} = X_2 \cdot P + Y_2$ for some subexpressions X_2 (which could be empty) and Y_2, and if we remove P from E_2, we obtain the expression $E_2^{-P} = E_{21}^{-P} \cdot \ldots \cdot E_{2n_2}$, where $E_{21}^{-P} = X_2 \cdot Y_2$.
   Then we apply the induction hypothesis to expressions E_1^{-P} and E_2^{-P}, to conclude that the subexpression E_{12} must be essentially equivalent to some of the factors of E_2^{-P}. We will see that this factor must be some of the expressions E_{2j}. We consider the case in which X_2 is empty. Then the factors of E_2^{-P} are the subexpressions E_{2j} with $j \in \{2, \ldots, n_2\}$ and the factors of the expression Y_2. But E_{12} cannot be essentially equivalent to any of the factors of Y_2, since $\forall P' \in Processes(E_{12})\ \exists Z\ PP'Z \in Flat(E_1)$ but $\forall P' \in Processes(Y_2)\ \not\exists Z\ PP'Z \in Flat(E_2)$, and if that would be the case, E_1 and E_2 would not be essentially equivalent.
   Thus E_{12} must be essentially equivalent to some subexpression E_{2j}, hence we can remove both subexpressions from E_1 and E_2 and apply the induction hypothesis to infer that both expressions are essentially equivalent.
   The case in which X_2 is not empty is similar.
3. If $E_1 = E_{11} + \ldots + E_{1n_1}$ and $E_2 = E_{21} + \ldots + E_{2n_2}$ the proof is similar.

□

Next we present the algorithm to decide if a process network with a single gate is LOTOS representable. It is based on the fact that networks with a single gate can be represented by an equivalent general expression.

Definition 6 Let LPGN = (GN,GL) with GN = (P,G,E) a *lpgn* with a single gate a ($\forall g \in G\, GL(g) = a$.) We define the (flat) arithmetic expression representing it, $Arith(LPGN)$, by $Arith(LPGN) = \sum_{g \in G} \prod_{(P_i,g) \in E} P_i$. □

Proposition 1 For any *lpgn* LPGN with a single gate, we have $LPGN \sim Arith(LPGN)$ where again $\sim$ denotes equivalence with respect to the corresponding abstract operational semantics. □

Algorithm 1: Let E be an arithmetic expression representing a process network with a single gate. The algorithm will decide if the corresponding network is LOTOS representable, defining the value of the predicate *Rep?*, and returning the corresponding representation *LOTOS(E)* whenever it exists. Note that as a consequence of the previous theorem, it is correct to talk, up to essential equivalence, about *the* representation of a network.

If $E = P$ then we return $Rep?(E) =$ TRUE and $LOTOS(E) = P$.

Otherwise we select some $P \in Processes(E)$ and we rewrite the expression E into an equivalent expression $P \cdot E_P + E_{-P}$ where E_{-P} is a possibly empty expression, such that $P \notin Processes(E_{-P})$. If E_{-P} is empty, we return $Rep?(E) = Rep?(E_P)$ and, if it is representable, $LOTOS(E) = P \cdot LOTOS(E_P)$.

Otherwise, we recursively apply the algorithm to both E_P and E_{-P}, and if we have $\neg Rep?(E_P) \wedge Rep?(E_{-P})$ we return $Rep?(E) =$ FALSE . If this is not the case, we consider the decomposition of $LOTOS(E_{-P})$ into a sum of products $E^1_{-P}+\ldots+E^n_{-P}$, and compute the number N of components which include some process in $Processes(E_P)$, $N = |\{i \mid Processes(E^i_{-P}) \cap Processes(E_P) \neq \emptyset\}|$. Then,

- If $N = 0$ we return $Rep?(E) =$ TRUE and $LOTOS(E) = P \cdot LOTOS(E_P) + LOTOS(E_{-P})$.
- If $N > 1$ we return $Rep?(E) =$ FALSE .
- If $N = 1$, let us assume that $Processes(E^1_{-P}) \cap Processes(E_P) \neq \emptyset$. Then we consider the decomposition of $E^1_{-P} = E^{11}_{-P} \cdot \ldots \cdot E^{1m}_{-P}$, and we consider the set J of indexes i such that E^{1i}_{-P} is a factor of E_P, $J = \{i \mid \exists R_i : E^{1i}_{-P} \cdot R_i = E_P\}$. We will assume $J = \{1, \ldots, j\}$. Then
  - If $J = \emptyset$ we return $Rep?(E) =$ FALSE.
  - If $J \neq \emptyset$ and $\forall i \notin J\ Processes(E^{1i}_{-P}) \cap Processes(E_P) = \emptyset$ we return $Rep?(E) =$ TRUE and $LOTOS(E) = (P \cdot X + E^{1j+1}_{-P} \cdot \ldots \cdot E^{1m}_{-P}) \cdot E^{11}_{-P} \cdot \ldots \cdot E^{1j}_{-P} + E^2_{-P} + \ldots + E^n_{-P}$, where X is such that $LOTOS(E_P) = P \cdot (E^{11}_{-P} \cdot \ldots \cdot E^{1j}_{-P}) \cdot X$.
  - Finally, if $J \neq \emptyset$ but $\exists i \notin J\ Processes(E^{1i}_{-P}) \cap Processes(E_P) \neq \emptyset$, we consider the expression $E' = P \cdot X + E^{1j+1}_{-P} \cdot \ldots \cdot E^{1m}_{-P}$ with X as before, and we recursively apply the algorithm to decide if E' is LOTOS representable. Then we return $Rep?(E) = Rep?(E')$, and $LOTOS(E) = LOTOS(E') \cdot E^{11}_{-P} \cdot \ldots \cdot E^{1j}_{-P} + E^2_{-P} + \ldots + E^n_{-P}$

Theorem 2 The previous algorithm is a correct algorithm to test LOTOS representability of process networks with a single gate. Its complexity is polynomial (quadratic with adequate data structures) on the network size.

Proof: It is easy to check that whenever the algorithm succeedes the computed LOTOS expression is indeed a representation of the given network. Thus we will concentrate on the cases in which the algorithm fails.

- The first such situation corresponds to the case in which the computed value for N is greater than 1. Then, if E could be represented by means of the expression L, there would be two possible cases:
  $L = L_1 + \ldots + L_n$ where each $L_i = L_{i1} \cdot \ldots \cdot L_{in_i}$ (we maintain the convention of representing $|||$ by $+$ and $|[a]|$ by $\cdot$.) Suppose $P \in Processes(L_{11})$. We will consider $L'_1 = L_2 + \ldots + L_n$ and $L'_{11} = L_{12} \cdot \ldots \cdot L_{1n_1}$. Then, if $L_{11} = P$ we should have $E_{-P} = L'_1$ and thus $N = 0$.
  Otherwise we have $E_{-P} = L'_{11} \cdot X + L'_1$ for some X, and thus $N = 1$.
  The case $L = L_1 \cdot \ldots \cdot L_n$ where each $L_i = L_{i1} + \ldots + L_{in_i}$, is similar.
- If the algorithm fails because J is empty, let us suppose that E is representable, and let us concentrate (the other case is similar) on the case in which $L = L_1 + \ldots + L_n$ where each $L_i = L_{i1} \cdot \ldots \cdot L_{in_i}$. Then we would obtain $E_P = L'_{11} \cdot X_1$ and $E_{-P} = L'_{11} \cdot X_2 + L'_1$ for some X_1 and X_2, and the common presence of L'_{11} implies $J \neq \emptyset$.
- Finally, once our algorithm has computed the corresponding set J, if we concentrate on the same case as before, we would have $L'_1 = E^2_{-P} + \ldots + E^n_{-P}$ and $L'_{11} = E^{11}_{-P} \cdot \ldots \cdot E^{1j}_{-P}$, and the remaining factor E' would correspond to the term L_{11} and thus it must be LOTOS representable.

Concerning the complexity of the algorithm, we give the intuitive idea on which it is based. What roughly the algorithm does is to study one by one all the process variables in the arithmetic expression representing the net, trying to eliminate repeated occurrences by application of the distributive axiom. Since the procedure needs no backtracking at all, each one of those steps has a linear cost, and thus the total cost of the algorithm is quadratic. □

3.2 All the process nodes have a common alphabet

We begin by applying the algorithm for the previous case to the projections of the given network over each one of its gates. If any of them is not LOTOS representable, neither the full network is. Otherwise we have to check if all the obtained expressions could be obtained by projecting over each gate, the same LOTOS expression (that we are looking for.) For we have to study if the different *hierarchical relations* between the process variables, induced by the expressions corresponding to each gate of the network, are not *contradictory*.

To check that consistency, we use the fact that for each set of gates A, the corresponding parallel operator $|[A]|$ is associative. Then we can write the involved expressions in what we call *normal form*, which is defined by

Definition 7 a) If $P_1, \ldots, P_n$ are process variables and $A \subseteq \mathit{Gates}$, then the expression $E = |[A]|(P_1, \ldots, P_n)$ is in normal form, and we will say that the set A is its *root synchronization set*, which we will denote by $rss(E)$.
b) If $E_1, \ldots, E_k$ are expressions in normal form, with $rss(E_i) = A_i$, and $A \subseteq \mathit{Gates}$ satisfies $A \neq A_i$, for each $i \in \{1, \ldots, k\}$, then the expression $E = |[A]|(E_1, \ldots, E_k)$ is also in normal form, and we take $rss(E) = A$. □

Then, in order to check the consistency of two expressions in normal form, $E = |[A]|(E_1, \ldots, E_m)$ and $F = |[B]|(F_1, \ldots, F_n)$, which combine the processes in the set $\mathcal{P}$ we first study if this set can be partitioned in a family of subsets $\mathcal{P}^1, \ldots, \mathcal{P}^t$, in such a way that for each $i \in \{1, \ldots, t\}$ either there exist some $j \in \{1, \ldots, m\}$ with $\mathit{Processes}(E_j) = \mathcal{P}^i$ and some $K \subseteq \{1, \ldots, n\}$ with $\bigcup_{k \in K} \mathit{Processes}(F_k) = \mathcal{P}^i$, or we have the symmetrical situation. If this is the case our problem reduces to a family of instances of the same problem, with one instance for each $i \in \{1, \ldots, t\}$; otherwise the given expressions are not consistent. Those instances of the problem are the following ones:

- If $\exists j_1 \in \{1, \ldots, m\}\ \exists j_2 \in \{1, \ldots, n\} \mid \mathit{Processes}(E_{j_1}) = \mathit{Processes}(F_{j_2}) = \mathcal{P}^i$, we check the consistency of E_{j_1} and F_{j_2}.
- If $\exists j \in \{1, \ldots, m\}\ \exists K \subseteq \{1, \ldots, n\} \mid |K| > 1 \wedge \mathit{Processes}(E_j) = \bigcup_{k \in K} \mathit{Processes}(F_k) = \mathcal{P}^i$, we have to compare E_{j_1} and $|[B]|_{k \in K}(F_k)$.
- If $\exists j \in \{1, \ldots, n\} \exists K \subseteq \{1, \ldots, m\} \mid |K| > 1 \wedge \mathit{Processes}(F_j) = \bigcup_{k \in K} \mathit{Processes}(E_k) = \mathcal{P}^i$, we compare $|[A]|_{k \in K}(E_k)$ and F_j.

The cost of this procedure is quadratic on the size of the given expressions, so the cost of the algorithm to test LOTOS-representability in this case is cubic.

3.3 The General Case

As in the previous case we begin by solving the problems corresponding to each gate in isolation. But in this case, when considering the subproblem corresponding to a gate g, the process nodes which do not contain that gate in their alphabet, are ignored. However, once we have the corresponding solution, we add those processes as new sons of the root of the solution.

It is clear that whenever $|[g]|$ is the operator labelling the root of the obtained expression, we have an *impossible synchronization*, since g is not a gate of any of the added processes. But the key idea in order to guarantee the correctness of the algorithm, is that the obtained LOTOS expressions are not interpreted in the ordinary way. Instead we base our reasoning on a modified semantics for the parallel operator, which considers that if we have an expression $E = |[A]|(E_1, \ldots, E_n)$, and $a \in A$, only those processes P_i including a in their alphabets have to cooperate to execute it.

This change implies that the hierarchical structure induced by an expression is no longer unique, since the processes which do not contain the corresponding action in their alphabet could have been added anywhere, and not just below the root of the expression. This implies that whenever we check the compatibility of two expressions, if any of them contains under its root several *independent* subexpressions, which means that their alphabets are disjoint, then we must allow that they will be combined into a single subexpression, if that is necessary in order to match the structure induced by the other expression.

Thus, the second step of the algorithm for this general case is obtained from the corresponding step of the algorithm for the previous case, by relaxing the condition which imposes that for each set $\mathcal{P}^i$ in the considered partition, we have either to find some single subexpression E_j (or F_j) with $Processes(E_j) = \mathcal{P}^i$ (or equivalently for F_j), allowing now to have a family $\{E_j \mid j \in J\}$ (or equivalently for F's), of independent processes instead.

Finally, if the algorithm succeedes, those impossible synchronizations remaining in the obtained solution are removed, since they were only added to keep the algorithm as close as possible to that solving our second case, and the obtained expression would be the representation of the given network.

References

[1] T. Bolognesi *A Graphical Composition Theorem for Networks of LOTOS Processes* in Proceedings of the 10th International Conference on Distributed Computing Systems, IEEE Computer Society Press, 1990.

[2] T. Bolognesi (Ed.) *Catalogue of LOTOS Correctness Preserving Transformations* LOTOSPHERE Task 1.2 Final Deliverable Lo/WP1/T1.2/N0045 ESPRIT 2304: LOTOSPHERE (1992)

[3] T. Bolognesi, D. de Frutos, Y.Ortega *Graphical Composition Theorems for Parallel and Hiding Operators* in Formal Description Tecniques III, (Procs. FORTE'90) North Holland (1991)

[4] J. Hinterplattner, H. Nirschl, H. Saria *Process Topology Diagrams* in Formal Description Tecniques III, (Procs. FORTE'90) North Holland (1991)

[5] K. Jensen, S. Christensen, P. Huber, M. Holla *Design/CPN. A Reference Manual* Meta Software Corporation, Cambridge MA USA (1991)

[6] R. Milner *A Calculus of Communicating Systems* Springer Verlag LNCS Vol. 92 (1980)

[7] R. Milner *Communication and Concurrency* Prentice Hall (1989)

[8] W. Reisig *Petri Nets: An Introduction* EATCS Monographs on Theoretical Computer Science Vol. 4 Springer Verlag (1985)

Towards Performance Evaluation in Process Algebras *

Roberto Gorrieri Marco Roccetti
Dipartimento di Matematica, Università di Bologna
Piazza di Porta San Donato 5, I – 40127 Bologna (Italy)

Abstract

A new bisimulation based semantics, called *performance* equivalence, is proposed for a finite process algebra. It equates systems whenever they perform the same actions in the same amount of time, thus introducing a simple form of performance evaluation in process algebras. A comparison with other equivalences is provided; in particular, we show that performance equivalence is strictly finer than step bisimulation equivalence and strictly coarser than partial ordering bisimulation equivalence.

1 Introduction

Process algebras, such as CCS [10] and TCSP [4], are widely used formalisms for the "functional" specification of concurrent systems, where functional means that a process term specifies *what* actions the system should do. Bisimulation [10] is a standard tool for the definition of a behavioural equivalence on process terms which, besides the actions, considers the structure of the alternative choices (the so-called *branching-time* semantics). Another, not less relevant, aspect of the specification of a system is its "performance", i.e., the measure of the time consumed for execution. It may be argued that performance is only a matter of efficient implementation. This is debatable: For applications whose functionality is performance-dependent (i.e., alterable by the flow of time), it is reasonable to require that a specification does not allow implementations which do not have an adequate performance.

Our work gives a contribution in the direction of integrating the two needs by presenting a new bisimulation-based semantics, called *performance equivalence*, for a finite process algebra where systems are equated if they perform the same actions in the same time (i.e., they have the same functional and performance behaviour).

The basic assumptions on which this semantics relies are the following. Any action a has a duration – a natural number $f(a)$ – which represents the time units needed for its execution. Every sequential subsystem is equipped with a clock, whose elapsing is set by the execution of actions: whenever an action a is executed by a sequential subcomponent P, the value n of the local clock of P is incremented to $n + f(a)$, whilst the local clocks of those sequential components not involved in the execution of a are unaffected. Each sequential subsystem is always *eager* to perform an executable action, as the time value is incremented locally only when the executable action is performed. The only exception is

*This work has been partially supported by Esprit Basic Research project BROADCAST n.6360 and by Italian CNR, grant n. 92.00069.CT12.115.25585.

concerned with synchronization. Two processes can synchronize when they perform the same action at the same time; if one of the two is able to execute such an action before the other one, then a form of "busy waiting" is allowed. This shows that the local clocks are locally replicated, possibly inconsistent, versions of the unique physical global time. Indeed, the time is the same for all the sequential components, even if we do not pretend that all the local views be consistent during the simulation. This assumption is rather natural if we are interested in performance evaluation only. In a simulation there is no need of having a tight agreement between the *time of execution* (i.e., the number attached to the executed actions) and the *time of observation* (i.e., the time of "generation" of the action during the simulation).

A simple example may help in clarifying the basic idea. Consider the term $a.g.\underline{0} \parallel b.\underline{0}$. Since the clock is set to 0 before starting, the initial state of the transition system is $(0 \Rightarrow a.g.\underline{0}) \parallel (0 \Rightarrow b.\underline{0})$, where the auxiliary operator $n \Rightarrow P$ means that the execution of P begins exactly after n time units. A transition out of it is labelled $\langle a, f(a)\rangle$ and reaches $(f(a) \Rightarrow g.\underline{0}) \parallel 0 \Rightarrow b.\underline{0}$. By executing b, we reach $f(a) \Rightarrow g.\underline{0} \parallel f(b) \Rightarrow \underline{0}$; finally, a transition labelled $\langle g, f(a)+f(g)\rangle$ with target state $(f(a)+f(g) \Rightarrow \underline{0}) \parallel f(b) \Rightarrow \underline{0}$. The time needed for the complete execution of the system is $max\{f(a) + f(g), f(b)\}$. Bisimulation equivalence over this labelled transition system is finer than interleaving bisimulation: the equation $a.\underline{0} \parallel b.\underline{0} = a.b.\underline{0} + b.a.\underline{0}$ does not hold

$$0 \Rightarrow a.\underline{0} \parallel 0 \Rightarrow b.\underline{0} \stackrel{\langle a,f(a)\rangle}{\longrightarrow} f(a) \Rightarrow \underline{0} \parallel 0 \Rightarrow b.\underline{0} \stackrel{\langle b,f(b)\rangle}{\longrightarrow} f(a) \Rightarrow \underline{0} \parallel f(b) \Rightarrow \underline{0}$$

$$0 \Rightarrow a.b.\underline{0} + b.a.\underline{0} \stackrel{\langle a,f(a)\rangle}{\longrightarrow} f(a) \Rightarrow b.\underline{0} \stackrel{\langle b,f(a)+f(b)\rangle}{\longrightarrow} f(a) + f(b) \Rightarrow \underline{0}$$

as the execution of b after a in the right-hand-side term is performed with a higher clock value. Notice that, if $f(a) > f(b)$, the execution of a before b in $a.\underline{0} \parallel b.\underline{0}$ generates two transitions where the clock value is decreased in the second transition. This phenomenon has been criticized in real-time literature (e.g., [2]), because in this context the time of execution and the time of observation are required to agree tightly; however, a recent report [1] shows that this view can be reasonably accepted also in real-time applications, provided that those "ill-timed" traces are "well-caused", as we do here.

The paper is organised as follows. In the next section, we introduce the language together with its operational semantics, which exploits additional information on *location* of actions. A location may be interpreted as an "abstract name" for a sequential subagent. In our operational semantics, an action has, besides its time of completion, the "name" of the subagents involved in the execution. Locations are needed because the "busy-waiting" mechanism needs a precise knowledge of the subagents involved in the synchronisation. Section 3 is devoted to the behavioural semantics, hence to performance equivalence. This is an abstraction step on the operational semantics, because the location part of the label is forgotten (as we have done in the example above). Here we show that the new equivalence is not a congruence for the TCSP parallel composition operator. Despite of the lack of a congruence result, performance equivalence is equipped with a complete proof system. Section 4 deals with "comparative concurrency semantics". We show that performance equivalence is strictly finer than step equivalence and strictly coarser than partial ordering equivalence [5]. Some other comparative results are simply stated (more details in [8]). Then some concluding remarks are reported in Section 5.

2 The Language and its Semantics

Let *Act* be a set of actions, ranged over by a, b, ... Let $f : Act \to \mathbf{N}$ be the *action duration function*, where $\mathbf{N}$ is the set of nonzero natural numbers, which associates to each action the number of time units needed for its execution. The finite process algebra $\mathcal{L}$ we study has operators borrowed from CCS and TCSP:

$$E ::= \underline{0} \mid a.E \mid E + E \mid E \parallel_A E \mid E[\Phi]$$

where, for the sake of simplicity, we assume that Φ relabels actions with the same duration, i.e., $f(a) = f(\Phi(a))$ holds for any a. The terms generated through prefixing and sum are called *sequential*. We often write $E_1 \parallel E_2$ for $E_1 \parallel_\emptyset E_2$. $\mathcal{L}$ is equipped with an SOS [12] semantics in terms of labelled transition systems. The states are terms of an extended syntax, comprising also the *clock prefixing* operator, $n \Rightarrow \_$, on sequential terms.

Definition 1 *The* states *are terms generated by the following syntax:*

$$s ::= n \Rightarrow \underline{0} \mid n \Rightarrow a.E \mid s + s \mid s \parallel_A s \mid s[\Phi]$$

where E denotes any $\mathcal{L}$ term. S denotes the set of states. A state is sequential when the parallel and relabelling operators do not occur at top level.

When an agent E is prefixed with a clock value n, $n \Rightarrow E$, we mean that n distributes over the operators, till to the sequential components (see the *clock distribution equations* in Table 1). Hence, a term $n \Rightarrow E$ can be "canonically" reduced to a state, when interpreting these equations as rewrite rules from left to right. This will be used in the operational rule for prefixing where the target term becomes a state after clock distribution rewriting.

Each transition is labelled by triples of the form $\langle a, n\rangle \star \omega$. The *observable part* is $\langle a, n\rangle$, meaning that action a has been completed exactly after n time units, while the *location part* ω is a term pointing out which sequential subagents have been involved in the execution of action a itself.

Definition 2 *The terms generated by the following syntax:*

$$\omega ::= \bullet \mid \omega\rfloor \mid \lfloor\omega$$

are called locations. *The set of all locations is denoted Ω. A preorder relation $\sqsubseteq$ is defined on locations according to the following:*

$$(a)\ \bullet \sqsubseteq \omega \qquad (b)\ \frac{\omega_1 \sqsubseteq \omega_2}{\omega_1\rfloor \sqsubseteq \omega_2\rfloor} \qquad (c)\ \frac{\omega_1 \sqsubseteq \omega_2}{\lfloor\omega_1 \sqsubseteq \lfloor\omega_2}$$

We use the convenient shorthand expression $\omega_1 \parallel \omega_2$ to denote the set $\{\omega_1\rfloor, \lfloor\omega_2\}$. Using $\parallel$ as an additional term constructor, we yield location-set *terms, which denote sets of locations. A relation of* space-sharing $\trianglelefteq$ *on location-sets is defined as follows: $\omega_1 \trianglelefteq \omega_2$ iff there exists a location ω_1' in ω_1 and a location ω_2' in ω_2 such that $\omega_1' \sqsubseteq \omega_2'$. The* labels *of the transitions belong to the set $\Pi = (Act \times \mathbf{N}) \star \Omega$.*

$$\begin{aligned} n \Rightarrow (E + E') &= (n \Rightarrow E) + (n \Rightarrow E') \\ n \Rightarrow (E \parallel_A E') &= (n \Rightarrow E) \parallel_A (n \Rightarrow E') \\ n \Rightarrow (E[\Phi]) &= (n \Rightarrow E)[\Phi] \end{aligned}$$

Table 1: The Clock Distribution Equations

$$\frac{}{n \Rightarrow a.E \overset{\langle a,k\rangle\star\bullet}{\longrightarrow} k \Rightarrow E}\; k = n + f(a) \qquad \frac{s \overset{\langle a,n\rangle\star\omega}{\longrightarrow} s'}{s[\Phi] \overset{\langle \Phi(a),n\rangle\star\omega}{\longrightarrow} s'[\Phi]}$$

$$\frac{s_1 \overset{\langle a,n\rangle\star\omega}{\longrightarrow} s_1'}{s_1 + s_2 \overset{\langle a,n\rangle\star\omega}{\longrightarrow} s_1'} \qquad \frac{s_2 \overset{\langle a,n\rangle\star\omega}{\longrightarrow} s_2'}{s_1 + s_2 \overset{\langle a,n\rangle\star\omega}{\longrightarrow} s_2'}$$

$$\frac{s_1 \overset{\langle a,n\rangle\star\omega}{\longrightarrow} s_1'}{s_1 \parallel_A s_2 \overset{\langle a,n\rangle\star(\omega\rfloor)}{\longrightarrow} s_1' \parallel_A s_2}\; \text{if } a \notin A \qquad \frac{s_2 \overset{\langle a,n\rangle\star\omega}{\longrightarrow} s_2'}{s_1 \parallel_A s_2 \overset{\langle a,n\rangle\star(\lfloor\omega)}{\longrightarrow} s_1 \parallel_A s_2'}\; \text{if } a \notin A$$

$$\frac{s_1 \overset{\langle a,n_1\rangle\star\omega_1}{\longrightarrow} s_1' \quad s_2 \overset{\langle a,n_2\rangle\star\omega_2}{\longrightarrow} s_2'}{s_1 \parallel_A s_2 \overset{\langle a,n_1\rangle\star(\omega_1\parallel\omega_2)}{\longrightarrow} s_1' \parallel_A ([k,\omega_2]s_2')}\; \text{if } a \in A,\ n_1 \geq n_2 \text{ and } k = n_1 - n_2$$

$$\frac{s_1 \overset{\langle a,n_1\rangle\star\omega_1}{\longrightarrow} s_1' \quad s_2 \overset{\langle a,n_2\rangle\star\omega_2}{\longrightarrow} s_2'}{s_1 \parallel_A s_2 \overset{\langle a,n_2\rangle\star(\omega_1\parallel\omega_2)}{\longrightarrow} ([k,\omega_1]s_1') \parallel_A s_2')}\; \text{if } a \in A,\ n_2 > n_1 \text{ and } k = n_2 - n_1$$

Table 2: The Structural Rules for Operational Semantics

The intuition behind locations is as follows: $\bullet$ stands for a sequential system; $\omega\rfloor$ ($\lfloor\omega$) means that the system is composed of two main parts and that ω comes from the *left* (*right*) part. The location of a subagent is its *access path* in the abstract syntax tree where only parallel operators are kept into account. The preorder relation $\sqsubseteq$ expresses an evolution in the structure of the space: a sequential subsystem can be replaced by two subsystems acting in parallel. Relation $\trianglelefteq$ denotes a form of overlapping of the space, as one of the locations of the former set is part (or has evolved to a location) of the latter.

The rules for the operational semantics are listed in Table 2. The rule for prefixing states that an action a, executable at time n, is completed at time $k = n + f(a)$; the number k denotes the time which passed for all the sequential subsystems of E. The rules for nondeterminstic choice and relabelling are standard. The rule for the asynchronous execution of an action a (not belonging to A) from the left subagent is almost standard; notice, however, that the location label ω of the transition in the premise of the rule is enriched with the context information, yielding the label $\omega\rfloor$ for the transition in the conclusion.

The rule for synchronisation needs some explanation. Assume that s_1 completes the communication action a at time n_1 and s_2 the same action a at n_2; assume also $n_1 \geq n_2$, as in the first rule for synchronisation. Since s_2 has completed its action first, it must wait for $k = n_1 - n_2$ time units before syn-

$$
\begin{array}{rcl}
[k,\bullet](m \Rightarrow \underline{0}) & = & m+k \Rightarrow \underline{0} \\
[k,\bullet](m \Rightarrow a.E) & = & m+k \Rightarrow a.E \\
[k,\bullet](m \Rightarrow E_1 + E_2) & = & m+k \Rightarrow E_1 + E_2 \\
[k,\omega](s[\Phi]) & = & ([k,\omega]s)[\Phi] \\
[k,\omega\rfloor](s_1 \parallel_A s_2) & = & ([k,\omega]s_1) \parallel_A s_2 \\
[k,\lfloor\omega](s_1 \parallel_A s_2) & = & s_1 \parallel_A ([k,\omega]s_2) \\
[k,\omega_1 \parallel \omega_2](s_1 \parallel_A s_2) & = & ([k,\omega_1]s_1) \parallel_A ([k,\omega_2]s_2)
\end{array}
$$

Table 3: Equations Defining the Time Update Operator

chronising with s_1. As in s_2' the clock number of the locations involved in the executions of a is set to n_2, it is necessary to update this value, increasing it to n_1, by exploiting the location information stored in ω_2. This is performed by the auxiliary *time update* operator $[k,\omega]\_$, the definition of which is given in Table 3. It is essentially a clock prefixing substitution operation. Note that the result of applying $[k,\omega]\_$ to a state is a state, again.

Similarly to the time update operator, one can define a function, $\_\{\_\} : S \times \Omega \to P(S)$, which, given a state s and a location term ω, yields the set of the substates sited at the locations in ω. All these substates are sequential.

Proposition 3 *Let* $s_1 \stackrel{\langle a,n\rangle\star\omega}{\longrightarrow} s_2$ *be derivable with the rules in Table 2. If* $s \in s_2\{\omega\}$, *then* s *is of the form* $n \Rightarrow E$, *where* E *is sequential.*

3 Behavioural Semantics

The observational semantics we are interested in does not consider the location information, as two systems should be equated whenever they perform the same actions at the same time. To this aim, we introduce the "forgetful" operator, $F(\_)$, which forgets about the additional location part on the labels.

$$
\frac{s \stackrel{\langle a,n\rangle\star\omega}{\longrightarrow} s'}{F(s) \stackrel{\langle a,n\rangle}{\longrightarrow} F(s')}
$$

Definition 4 *Given* $E_1, E_2 \in \mathcal{L}$, E_1 *and* E_2 *are* performance equivalent, *denoted* $E_1 \sim_p E_2$, *iff* $F(0 \Rightarrow E_1)$ *is (strong) bisimilar to* $F(0 \Rightarrow E_2)$.

Example 5 *In the introduction it was shown that* $a.\underline{0} \parallel b.\underline{0} \not\sim_p a.b.\underline{0} + b.a.\underline{0}$. *The validity of the following equalities strictly depends on forgetting locations:*

$$
\begin{array}{rcl}
E_1 \parallel_A E_2 & \sim_p & E_2 \parallel_A E_1 \\
(E_1 \parallel_A E_2) \parallel_A E_3 & \sim_p & E_1 \parallel_A (E_2 \parallel_A E_3) \\
E \parallel \underline{0} & \sim_p & E
\end{array}
$$

Proposition 6 *Given* $E_1, E_2 \in \mathcal{L}$, *if* $E_1 \sim_p E_2$ *then:*

(*i*) $a.E_1 \sim_p a.E_2$ *for any action* $a \in Act$;

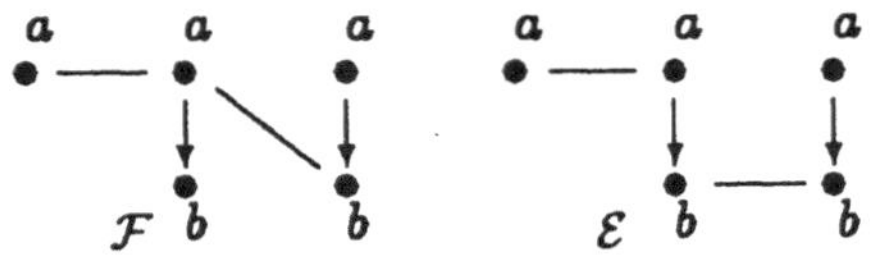

Figure 1: Two performance equivalent event structures

(ii) $E + E_1 \sim_p E + E_2$ *and* $E_1 + E \sim_p E_2 + E$ *for any* $\mathcal{L}$ *term* E;

(iii) $E_1[\Phi] \sim_p E_2[\Phi]$ *for any relabelling* Φ;

(iv) $E_1 \parallel E \sim_p E_2 \parallel E$ *and* $E \parallel E_1 \sim_p E \parallel E_2$ *for any* $\mathcal{L}$ *term* E.

Example 7 *Parallel composition* with communication *does not preserve performance equivalence. The counter-example is the same proposed by A. Rabinovich to show that partial ordering bisimulation [5] is not a congruence for the TCSP parallel composition operator. For simplicity sake, the example is described in terms of prime event structures [11], but it can be translated to the language* $\mathcal{L}$. *Consider the two labelled prime event structures depicted in Figure 1.* [1] *It is easy to see that the two structures* $\mathcal{E}$ *and* $\mathcal{F}$ *are performance equivalent. However, if we compose each of them with the event structure* $\mathcal{G}$ *of* $a.a.\underline{0}$ *(two events, labelled a, the former of which causing the latter) by forcing the communication on a, then we obtain two structures,* $\mathcal{E} \parallel_a \mathcal{G}$ *and* $\mathcal{F} \parallel_a \mathcal{G}$, *which are not performance equivalent.*

A complete proof system for performance equivalence can be provided with the help of some auxiliary operators. Besides the usual laws for strong bisimulation, there are axioms which transform each state in a tree labelled over Π, and some more axioms that, taken such a tree, forget the location information. Hence, the procedure for checking if two $\mathcal{L}$ terms are performance bisimilar is as follows: first, generate a tree out of a state; second, forget the location part; third, check their equivalence according to the usual axioms of strong bisimulation. The axiom system $\mathcal{A}$ over the extended algebra is reported in [8]. Here we simply present a few relevant axioms:

$$n \Rightarrow a.E \;=\; (\langle a,k\rangle \star \bullet).(k \Rightarrow E) \quad \text{for } k = n + f(a)$$

$$s_1 \parallel_A s_2 \;=\; s_1 \rfloor_A s_2 + s_1 \lfloor_A s_2 + s_1 \mid_A s_2$$

$$(\langle a,n\rangle \star \omega.s_1)\rfloor_A s_2 \;=\; (\langle a,n\rangle \star \omega\rfloor).(s_1 \parallel_A s_2) \quad \text{if } a \notin A$$

$$(\langle a,n_1\rangle \star \omega_1.s_1) \mid_A (\langle a,n_2\rangle \star \omega_2.s_2) \;=\; (\langle a,n_1\rangle \star \omega_1 \parallel \omega_2).s_1 \parallel_A ([k,\omega_2]s_2)$$
$$\text{if } a \in A,\ n_1 \geq n_2 \text{ and } k = n_1 - n_2$$

$$[k,\omega](\langle a,n\rangle \star \omega'.s) \;=\; \langle a,n+k\rangle \star \omega'.([k,\omega]s) \quad \text{if } \omega \trianglelefteq \omega'$$

$$[k,\omega](\langle a,n\rangle \star \omega'.s) \;=\; \langle a,n\rangle \star \omega'.([k,\omega]s) \quad \text{if } \omega \not\trianglelefteq \omega'$$

$$F(\langle a,n\rangle \star \omega.s) \;=\; \langle a,n\rangle.F(s)$$

Proposition 8 *Two terms* E_1 *and* E_2 *are performance equivalent,* $E_1 \sim_p E_2$, *if and only if* $\mathcal{A} \vdash F(0 \Rightarrow E_1) = F(0 \Rightarrow E_2)$.

[1] Events, labelled on $\{a,b\}$, are denoted by circles in the plane; the straight lines joining two events are used to represent conflict; the arrows, instead, stand for causality.

4 Comparative Concurrency Semantics

Performance equivalence is a non-interleaving semantics which is based on the notion of time-consumption. It is interesting to see what is the rank of this equivalence in the large spectrum of non-interleaving semantics proposed in the literature. It can be proved that performance equivalence is strictly contained in between step semantics, $\sim_{step}$, and partial ordering bisimulation [5], $\sim_{po}$.

Proposition 9 *Given two terms E_1 and E_2, the following hold:*

i) $E_1 \sim_p E_2$ implies $E_1 \sim_{step} E_2$;

ii) $E_1 \sim_{po} E_2$ implies $E_1 \sim_p E_2$.

The proof of point *i*) is based on the fact that the execution of independent actions generates a "diamond" (i.e., a square diagram where opposite transitions have the same label) in the operational performance semantics. Hence, a performance bisimulation is also a step bisimulation. Point *ii*) is similarly easy: $\sim_{po}$ is finer than $\sim_p$ as causality gives enough information to recover the time needed for execution.

The reverse of *i*) does not hold. Consider the two agents $E = a.\underline{0} \parallel b.\underline{0}$ and $E' = a.\underline{0} \parallel b.\underline{0} + a.b.\underline{0}$. It is clear that $E \sim_{step} E'$, but $E \not\sim_p E'$, as only the latter can complete an action b at time $f(a) + f(b)$. The counter-example for the reverse of *ii*) is presented in the full version of this abstract [8]. [2]

Performance equivalence and ST equivalence [9], $\sim_{ST}$, are incomparable. Consider the two event structures in Figure 1. They are performance equivalent but not ST equivalent. More interesting is the counter-example showing that $\sim_{ST}$ does not imply $\sim_p$. Consider the two terms $E = a.\underline{0} \parallel b.\underline{0}$ and $E' = ((a.c.\underline{0} \parallel_c (b.\underline{0} + c.\underline{0}))[^b/_c]$. These are ST bisimilar but not performance bisimilar, as in E', action b can be completed also after $f(a) + f(b)$ time units, when synchronisation on c takes place. This example may also help in clarifying in which sense our semantics is not "real-time", according to some papers in the literature (see, e.g., [13]). A different operational semantics for synchronisation, which is claimed "real-time", requires that both agents are ready to perform the same action at the same time, without any busy-waiting. This solution, proposed in a process algebra by [1], forbids several executions that we prefer to keep (for instance, the synchronisation over c in the example above), and thus produces a semantics which is incomparable even with interleaving bisimulation. (Our view is shared by other researchers, proposing similar ideas in different contexts [3,6].)

Still open is the problem of finding a natural characterisation of the coarsest congruence contained in $\sim_p$, denoted $\sim_p^c$. Since history preserving equivalence ($\sim_{hp}$) is finer than $\sim_{po}$ and $\sim_{hp}$ is a congruence, we know that $\sim_p^c$ cannot be finer than $\sim_{hp}$. In [8], we show that $\sim_p^c$ is incomparable with $\sim_{po}$, and also that $\sim_{hp}$ is strictly finer than $\sim_p^c$.

[2] In that paper, we also prove that if systems are *time-deterministic* (there are no reachable states with two outgoing transitions labelled by the same action at the same time), then performance equivalence induces a semantics which is even finer than $\sim_{po}$.

5 Concluding Remarks

The semantics we propose is *a priori* of timed calculi and real-time is not an issue of this paper. Nonetheless, we feel that our approach to time in system executions can be helpful for a formal description of time-dependent programming constructs such as timeout, watchdog, and so on.

In conclusion, our aim is to provide an approach able to incorporate time into formal specifications, in order to capture functional and performance behaviour of distributed and parallel systems. Nevertheless we are aware that, because of the ineherent random nature of the investigated problems, the concepts of random variables and stochastic processes represent the unique well-founded discipline able to describe performance aspects of computer systems. Thus, even if other alternative approaches can be studied (e.g., Stochastic Petri Net), our next purpose will be to replace deterministic duration values with probabilistic distribution duration functions, in order to provide a uniform integration of the theories of process algebras and performance evaluation (see, e.g., [7] for a preliminary study). This justifies the title of the paper.

Acknowledgements

We are grateful to Luca Aceto, Enrico Stancampiano and the anonymous referees for their useful comments.

References

[1] L. Aceto, D. Murphy, *On the Ill-timed but Well-caused*, to appear in Proc. CONCUR'93, Hildesheim, LNCS, Springer, August 1993.

[2] J. Baeten, J.A. Bergstra, *Real Time Process Algebra*, Formal Aspects of Computing 3(2):142-188, 1991.

[3] E. Best, *Weighted basic Petri Nets*, Concurrency'88, LNCS 335, 257-276, 1988.

[4] S.D. Brooks, C.A.R. Hoare, A.W. Roscoe, *A Theory of Communicating Sequential Processes*, J.ACM 31(3), 560-599, 1984.

[5] P. Degano, R. De Nicola, U. Montanari, *Observational Equivalences for Concurrency Models*, in Formal Des. of Prog. Con. III, North-Holland, 105-132, 1987.

[6] G.L. Ferrari, U. Montanari, *Observing Time-Complexity of Concurrent Programs*, submitted for publication.

[7] N. Gotz, U. Herzog, M. Rettelbach, *TIPP- Introduction and Application to Protocol Performance Analysis*, in Proc. Performance '93, October 1993.

[8] R. Gorrieri, M. Roccetti, E. Stancampiano, *The Theory of Performance Equivalence*, in preparation.

[9] R.J. van Glabbeek, F. Vaandrager, *Petri Net Models for Algebraic Theories of Concurrency*, in Proc. PARLE II, LNCS 259, Springer, 224–242, 1987.

[10] R. Milner, *Communication and Concurrency*, Prentice-Hall, 1989.

[11] M. Nielsen, G. Plotkin, G. Winskel, *Petri Nets, Event Structures and Domains: part I*, Theoretical Computer Science 13 (1), 85-108, 1981.

[12] G. Plotkin, *A Structural Approach to Operational Semantics*, Tech. Rep. DAIMI FN 19, Aarhus University, Dept. of Computer Science, Aarhus, 1981.

[13] W. Vogler, *Timed Testing of Concurrent Systems*, to appear in Proc. ICALP'93, LNCS, Springer, July 1993.

Translation Results for Modal Logics of Reactive Systems

F. Laroussinie[1], S. Pinchinat[1,2] and Ph. Schnoebelen[1]
(1) Laboratoire LIFIA-IMAG
Grenoble, France
and
(2) School of Computing & Cognitive Sciences, Univ. of Sussex
Brighton,UK

Introduction

Modal logics are an important tool in the analysis, specification and verification of reactive systems [12]. Among many other applications, logics like HML have been used as a benchmark for semantic equivalences [9], as the specification language used in model checking tools [1], and as a language in which to explain why two systems are not semantically equivalent [11].

Regarding modal characterizations of semantic equivalences, the classical result is the adequacy theorem of Hennessy and Milner who showed that two states in a (finitely branching) transition system are bisimilar, written $p \underline{\leftrightarrow} q$, iff they satisfy the same HML formulas, written $p \equiv_{HML} q$, where

$$p \equiv_L q \overset{\text{def}}{\Leftrightarrow} \forall f \in L\, (p \models f \;\Leftrightarrow\; q \models f)$$

Here we are mostly interested in modal logics with past-time (backward) operators. A few exist. They have been used (among other applications) to capture non-continuous properties of *generalized* transitions systems (J_T in [10]), to capture history-preserving bisimulation in causality-based models (L_P in [2]) and to capture branching bisimulation by mimicking back-and-forth τ-bisimulation (L_B in [5]).

In this paper we give three non-trivial translation theorems of the generic form $L \preceq L'$ showing, given any formula f from some modal logic L, how to build an equivalent $f' \in L'$. This kind of problem has not received much attention in modal logics of reactive systems and the existing results in temporal logics with past mostly deal with linear-time logics.

Our translations are defined by rewrite rules (to apply with a given strategy) over formulas. A consequence is that the translations are easy to implement. Our motivations are not only theoretical. For example, by showing how to translate HML_{bf} (HML with past-time connectives) into its future-time fragment HML, we show how to easily expand the input language of any software tool (e.g. a verifier) handling HML properties.

All the logics we consider are variants of HML:

HML_{bf}: a back-and-forth version of HML, in a framework with only visible labels,

L_U: a version of HML with an "Until" modality, in a framework with invisible labels (τ's),

L_{BF}: a version of HML_{bf} incorporating τ's.

Section 1 presents a translation from HML_{bf} into HML. Section 2 presents a translation from L_U into L_{BF}. Section 3 presents a translation from L_{BF} into L_U.

1 Backward modalities

We consider a fixed set $A = \{a, b, \ldots\}$ of *labels*. A *labeled transition system* (LTS) is an edge-labeled graph $\langle Q, \rightarrow\rangle$ where $Q = \{p, q, \ldots\}$ is a set of *states* and $\rightarrow \subseteq Q \times A \times Q$ is the *transition relation*. We assume a fixed LTS S.

1.1 Syntax of HML_{bf}

HML_{bf} (read "HML back-and-forth") is HML with past-tense modalities[1] and has the following grammar:

$$HML_{bf} \ni f, g ::= \top \mid \neg f \mid f \wedge g \mid \langle a\rangle f \mid \overline{\langle a\rangle} f$$

where a is any action from A.

HML is the fragment of HML_{bf} where the $\overline{\langle a\rangle}$ operators are not allowed.

We use $f, g, \alpha, \beta, \varphi, \psi, \ldots$ to denote HML formulas and we use the standard abbreviations: $f \vee g$, $\perp$, $[a]f$ (for $\neg\langle a\rangle\neg f$) and $\overline{[a]}f$ (for $\neg\overline{\langle a\rangle}\neg f$).

1.2 Semantics of HML_{bf}

A modal logic with backward modalities states properties of a *run* $\pi = [q_0 \xrightarrow{a_1} q_1 \cdots \xrightarrow{a_n} q_n]$ of S. A run like π is a partial computation of S starting from state q_0 and currently in state q_n. This partial computation can be extended (if q_n is not a final state) and we write $\pi \xrightarrow{a} \pi'$ when run π' is π with a transition $q_n \xrightarrow{a} q_{n+1}$ added. If $n > 0$ the run has a past (a history) and the backward modalities in HML_{bf} can be used to state properties of this past.

Formally, for a run π and an HML_{bf} formula f, we define $\pi \models f$ by induction on the structure of f:

$$\begin{array}{ll}
\pi \models \top & \text{always,} \\
\pi \models \neg f & \text{iff } \pi \not\models f, \\
\pi \models f \wedge g & \text{iff } \pi \models f \text{ and } \pi \models g, \\
\pi \models \langle a\rangle f & \text{iff there is a } \pi \xrightarrow{a} \pi' \text{ s.t. } \pi' \models f, \\
\pi \models \overline{\langle a\rangle} f & \text{iff there is a } \pi' \xrightarrow{a} \pi \text{ s.t. } \pi' \models f.
\end{array}$$

[1] It was introduced in [5] for systems with τ's (but note that HML_{bf} is a subset of J_T defined in [10].)

In this framework, there is some asymmetry between past and future because (1) past is finite, while future needs not be, and (2) past is "deterministic", or fixed by the history, while future is branching.

In practice, we use HML_{bf} to express properties of states (mainly the initial state of the system) and not runs. For a state $q \in Q$, the derived notion $q \models f$ is given by

$$q \models f \stackrel{\text{def}}{\Leftrightarrow} [q] \models f$$

$[q]$ is just state q seen as a run, with no past.

[5] mention that $p \equiv_{HML_{bf}} q$ iff $p \leftrightarrow q$ because (strong) bisimulation coincides with (strong) back-and-forth bisimulation [3]. This entails

$$p \equiv_{HML} q \text{ iff } p \equiv_{HML_{bf}} q \tag{1}$$

We are looking for a more detailed comparison of the expressive power of HML and HML_{bf}. We consider whether formulas of HML_{bf} can be translated into HML. Of course, a formula like $\overline{\langle a \rangle}\top$, which says that the last step was an a-step cannot be written in HML where only properties about the possible futures can be expressed. But when we are expressing properties of states (without a past), we know that we never have $q \models \overline{\langle a \rangle}\top$. That is $\overline{\langle a \rangle}\top$ can be translated into $\bot$.

This requires some definitions:

Definition 1 Two formulas are *globally equivalent*, written $f \equiv_g f'$, iff $\pi \models f \Leftrightarrow \pi \models f'$ for all runs in all LTS's.

They are *initially equivalent*, written $f \equiv_i f'$, iff $q \models f \Leftrightarrow q \models f'$ for all states in all LTS's.

For example, we have $\overline{\langle a \rangle}\top \equiv_i \bot$ but $\overline{\langle a \rangle}\top \not\equiv_g \bot$.

Clearly, $f \equiv_g f'$ implies $f \equiv_i f'$ but the converse is not true as we just saw. $\equiv_g$ is a congruence: when $f \equiv_g f'$ with f a subformula of g then $g \equiv_g g[f'/f]$. This does not hold for $\equiv_i$ which is not a congruence w.r.t. the $\langle a \rangle$ operators.

Now we can define two different notions of translations between logics.

Definition 2 A logic L can be translated (resp. initially translated) into L', written $L \preceq_g L'$ (resp. $L \preceq_i L'$), iff for any $f \in L$ there is a $f' \in L'$ with $f \equiv_g f'$ (resp. $f \equiv_i f'$).

Clearly, $L \preceq_g L'$ implies $L \preceq_i L'$. Also $L \preceq_i L'$ implies $\equiv_{L'} \subseteq \equiv_L$. In both cases, the reverse implication is not true in general.

HML_{bf} can be translated into HML:

Theorem 1 $HML_{bf} \preceq_i HML$.

The proof is in two steps.

Say a formula is *pure-past* (resp. *pure-future*) if it does not contain forward (resp. backward) modalities. Say it is *separated* if no backward modality occurs in the scope of a forward modality (and write HML_{bf}^{sep} for the fragment of HML_{bf} that contains only separated formulas).

Lemma 1 Any $f \in HML_{bf}$ is equivalent to a separated formula.
Proof By structural induction on f. The cases when f has the form $\top$, $g_1 \wedge g_2$, or $\neg g$ are obvious.

$f = \overline{\langle a \rangle} g$: g can be separated (by ind. hyp.) into some g'. Then $f \equiv_g f' \stackrel{\text{def}}{=} \overline{\langle a \rangle} g'$ is separated.

$f = \langle a \rangle g$: g can be separated (by ind. hyp.) into some g'. There are two subcases:

- Assume g' has the form $\overline{\langle b_1 \rangle}\varphi_1 \wedge \cdots \wedge \overline{\langle b_n \rangle}\varphi_n \wedge \neg\overline{\langle c_1 \rangle}\varphi'_1 \wedge \cdots \wedge \neg\overline{\langle c_m \rangle}\varphi'_m \wedge \psi^+$ where ψ^+ is pure future. Write $c_{i_1}, \ldots, c_{i_k}$ for the c_i's that are equal to a. Then $\langle a \rangle g' \equiv_g g''$ with

$$g'' \stackrel{\text{def}}{=} \begin{cases} \varphi_1 \wedge \cdots \varphi_n \wedge \neg\varphi_{i_1} \wedge \cdots \neg\varphi_{i_k} \wedge \langle a \rangle \psi^+ & \text{if } a = b_1 = \ldots = b_n, \\ \bot & \text{otherwise.} \end{cases}$$

  $f \equiv_g g''$ and g'' is separated.
- In the general case, g' can be put in disjunctive normal form $\bigvee_i \bigwedge_j g_{i,j}$ where every $\bigwedge_j g_{i,j}$ has the form $\overline{\langle b_1 \rangle}\varphi_1 \wedge \cdots \wedge \overline{\langle b_n \rangle}\varphi_n \wedge \neg\overline{\langle c_1 \rangle}\varphi'_1 \wedge \cdots \wedge \neg\overline{\langle c_m \rangle}\varphi'_m \wedge \psi^+$. Then $f \equiv_g \langle a \rangle g' \equiv_g \bigvee_i \langle a \rangle \left(\bigwedge_j g_{i,j}\right)$ and each $\langle a \rangle \left(\bigwedge_j g_{i,j}\right)$ falls in the previous subcase and can be separated.

□

Proposition 1 **(Separation Lemma for** HML_{bf}**)**

$$HML_{bf} \preceq_g HML_{bf}^{sep} \tag{2}$$

is the immediate corollary.

Remark 1 Note that, in a linear-time framework, [7, 8] use a different, less general, definition of separated formulas: a formula is *separated (in Gabbay's sense)* if it is a boolean combination of pure-past and pure-future formulas. In branching-time frameworks our definition is required. Indeed (2) does not hold for Gabbay's definition of separated formulas: $\overline{\langle a \rangle}\langle b \rangle \top$ has no equivalent as a boolean combination of pure-past and pure-future formulas.

Now we conclude the proof of Theorem 1 with

Proposition 2 $HML_{bf}^{sep} \preceq_i HML$.

Proof Use $\overline{\langle a \rangle} f \equiv_i \bot$ to eliminate (modulo $\equiv_i$) any past-time modality which is not in the scope of a future-time modality. □

2 τ-moves, from L_U to L_{BF}

For transition systems labeled over $A_\tau \stackrel{\text{def}}{=} A \cup \{\tau\}$, [5] introduces L_U and L_{BF}, two modal logics characterizing branching bisimulation.

2.1 Syntax of L_{BF}

L_{BF} is a version of HML_{bf} adapted to systems with silent moves. Its grammar is

$$L_{BF} \ni f, g ::= \top \mid \neg f \mid f \wedge g \mid \langle\langle k \rangle\rangle f \mid \overline{\langle\langle k \rangle\rangle} f$$

where k is any label from $A_\epsilon \stackrel{\text{def}}{=} A \cup \{\epsilon\}$. We use $[[k]]f$ and $\overline{[[k]]}f$ as standard abbreviations.

2.2 Semantics of L_{BF}

The semantics of the new modalities is given by:

$$\begin{array}{lll} \pi \models \langle\langle a\rangle\rangle f & \text{iff} & \text{there is a } \pi \overset{\epsilon}{\Rightarrow}\overset{a}{\rightarrow}\overset{\epsilon}{\Rightarrow} \pi' \text{ s.t. } \pi' \models f, \\ \pi \models \langle\langle \epsilon\rangle\rangle f & \text{iff} & \text{there is a } \pi \overset{\epsilon}{\Rightarrow} \pi' \text{ s.t. } \pi' \models f, \\ \pi \models \overline{\langle\langle a\rangle\rangle} f & \text{iff} & \text{there is a } \pi' \overset{\epsilon}{\Rightarrow}\overset{a}{\rightarrow}\overset{\epsilon}{\Rightarrow} \pi \text{ s.t. } \pi' \models f, \\ \pi \models \overline{\langle\langle \epsilon\rangle\rangle} f & \text{iff} & \text{there is a } \pi' \overset{\epsilon}{\Rightarrow} \pi \text{ s.t. } \pi' \models f. \end{array}$$

where $\overset{\epsilon}{\Rightarrow}$ is the reflexive and transitive closure of $\overset{\tau}{\rightarrow}$.

2.3 Syntax of L_U

L_U has no backward modalities but it has a so-called "until" operator which is more powerful than the simple future-time operator of L_{BF}. The grammar of L_U is

$$L_U \ni f, g ::= \top \mid \neg f \mid f \wedge g \mid f\langle k\rangle g$$

with $k \in A_\epsilon$.

2.4 Semantics of L_U

The semantics of the new modalities is given by

$$\begin{array}{lll} \pi \models f\langle a\rangle g & \text{iff} & \exists n > 0,\ \pi = \pi_0 \overset{\tau}{\rightarrow} \pi_1 \overset{\tau}{\rightarrow} \cdots \pi_{n-1} \overset{a}{\rightarrow} \pi_n \\ & & \text{s.t. } \pi_n \models g \text{ and } \pi_i \models f \text{ for } i < n, \\ \pi \models f\langle \epsilon\rangle g & \text{iff} & \exists n \geq 0,\ \pi = \pi_0 \overset{\tau}{\rightarrow} \pi_1 \overset{\tau}{\rightarrow} \cdots \pi_{n-1} \overset{\tau}{\rightarrow} \pi_n \\ & & \text{s.t. } \pi_n \models g \text{ and } \pi_i \models f \text{ for } i < n. \end{array}$$

For technical reasons, we introduce L_{BU} [13], a logic built by combining all modalities of L_U and of L_{BF}, so that both L_{BF} and L_U are fragments of a common superset:

$$L_{BU} \ni f, g ::= \top \mid \neg f \mid f \wedge g \mid \langle\langle k\rangle\rangle f \mid \overline{\langle\langle k\rangle\rangle} f \mid f\langle k\rangle g$$

with $k \in A_\epsilon$. In L_{BU}, the $\langle\langle k\rangle\rangle$ is not really needed because

$$\langle\langle k\rangle\rangle f \equiv_g \top\langle k\rangle(\top\langle\epsilon\rangle f) \tag{3}$$

Considering that $\equiv_{L_U}$ and $\equiv_{L_{BF}}$ coincide because they both coincide with branching bisimulation [5], a natural question is whether L_U or L_{BF} can be translated into the other. This question is discussed (but not answered) in [6]. At first, the authors of [5] tried to simply embed L_U into L_{BF} (see Theorem 2.19 in [4]) but later found a mistake in their proof. A translation exists but it is not trivial:

Theorem 2 $L_U \preceq_g L_{BF}$.

We prove the result for a larger logic. Say an L_{BU} formula is an FB-formula (FB is for "forward-backward") if (1) no until modality is in the scope of a backward modality, and (2) every backward modality is immediately (but disregarding boolean combinators) under a forward L_{BF} modality (i.e. a $\langle\langle k\rangle\rangle$, not an until). For example, $\langle\langle a\rangle\rangle\overline{\langle\langle b\rangle\rangle}\langle\langle c\rangle\rangle(f\langle d\rangle g)$, $f\langle a\rangle(\overline{\langle\langle b\rangle\rangle}g)$ and $\langle\langle a\rangle\rangle\overline{\langle\langle b\rangle\rangle}\,\overline{\langle\langle c\rangle\rangle}f$ are not FB-formulas.

Lemma 2 Any FB-formula f in L_{BU} is equivalent to an FB-formula in L_{BF}.
Proof We proceed by induction on f. The only interesting case is when f is an until-formula. Assume f is $f_1\langle k\rangle f_2$. Then f_1 and f_2 are FB and by ind. hyp., we can find equivalent FB-formulas $f_1', f_2' \in L_{BF}$. Write ψ instead of f_2' and put f_1' in disjunctive normal form. We get the general form:

$$f \equiv_g f_1'\langle k\rangle\psi = \left[\bigvee_{i=1}^{n}\Big(\bigwedge_{j\in J_i}[[k_{ij}]]\varphi_{ij} \;\wedge\; \bigwedge_{j\in J_i'}\langle\langle k_{ij}'\rangle\rangle\varphi_{ij}'\Big)\right]\langle k\rangle\,\psi \tag{4}$$

for which we introduce the following simplifying abbreviations:

$$[\alpha_i] \stackrel{\text{def}}{=} \bigwedge_{j\in J_i}[[k_{ij}]]\varphi_{ij} \qquad\qquad \langle\alpha_i'\rangle \stackrel{\text{def}}{=} \bigwedge_{j\in J_i'}\langle\langle k_{ij}'\rangle\rangle\varphi_{ij}'$$

We show by induction over n how to rewrite (4) into an FB-formula in L_{BF}.

1. First, consider the simpler case where $n = 1$ in f. Then if $k = a \in A$ we have
$$f \equiv_g [\alpha_1] \;\wedge\; \langle\langle a\rangle\rangle\Big(\overline{[[\epsilon]]}\psi \wedge \overline{[[a]]}\langle\alpha_1'\rangle\Big)$$
while if $k = \epsilon$ we have
$$f \equiv_g \psi \vee \Big[[\alpha_1] \wedge \langle\langle\epsilon\rangle\rangle\Big(\psi \wedge \overline{[[\epsilon]]}(\psi \vee \langle\alpha_1'\rangle)\Big)\Big]$$

2. Now in the general case with $n > 1$, we show how to rewrite (4) into a formula where the until is eliminated by introducing new until-formulas having $n-1$-ary disjunctions in their left-hand sides.
If $k = a \in A$ we have
$$f \equiv_g \bigvee_{i=1}^{n}\left[[\alpha_i] \wedge \left(\begin{array}{c}\langle\langle a\rangle\rangle(\overline{[[\epsilon]]}\psi \wedge \overline{[[a]]}\langle\alpha_i'\rangle)\\ \vee\;\langle\langle\epsilon\rangle\rangle(\psi_i \wedge \overline{[[\epsilon]]}(\psi_i \vee \langle\alpha_i'\rangle))\end{array}\right)\right]$$
where
$$\psi_i \stackrel{\text{def}}{=} \Big(\bigvee_{\substack{k=1\ldots n\\ k\neq i}}[\alpha_k] \wedge \langle\alpha_k'\rangle\Big)\langle\epsilon\rangle\psi \qquad\qquad \text{(for any } i \in I)$$
are the new until-formulas containing only $n-1$ members in the disjunction.
Similarly, if $k = \epsilon$, we have
$$f \equiv_g \psi \vee \bigvee_{i=1}^{n}\Big([\alpha_i] \wedge \langle\langle\epsilon\rangle\rangle\Big(\psi_i \wedge \overline{[[\epsilon]]}(\psi_i \vee \langle\alpha_i'\rangle)\Big)\Big)$$

Observe that all the formulas we introduce are FB. They are all in L_{BF} except for the ψ_i's. But by our second induction hypothesis, every ψ_i can be rewritten into an FB formula $\psi_i' \in L_{BF}$. With this we are done. □

Corollary 1 $L_{BU}^{FB} \preceq_g L_{BF}$.

where L_{BU}^{FB} is the set of all FB-formulas in L_{BU}. It only remains to see that L_U is a subset of L_{BU}^{FB} to conclude the proof of Theorem 2. (In fact we have $L_{BU} \preceq_g L_{BF}$. But this needs new arguments. See Theorem 4 below.)

3 From L_{BF} to L_U

Theorem 3 $L_{BF} \preceq_i L_U$.

This problem was considered in [13] where a partial solution is proposed. Our approach was developed independently and uses our separation techniques. Write L^{sep}_{BU} for the set of separated L_{BU} formulas, i.e. of formulas with no backward modality under the scope of a forward (or until) modality. We show how to rewrite any L_{BU} formula into an equivalent separated formula. The most difficult part here is to find a strategy which ensures termination. For this we use an approach inspired from [7].

In this section, we will use (3) and consider that "until" is the only forward combinator in L_{BU}. We will also need to introduce variables $x_1, \ldots, x_n$ in our formulas. Classically, $f[x_1]$ denotes a formula f where x_1 occurs (possibly several times). Then $f[\varphi]$ is f where x_1 has been replaced by φ. We write $f[x_1, \ldots, x_n] \equiv_g g[x_1, \ldots, x_n]$ when $f[\varphi_1, \ldots, \varphi_n] \equiv_g g[\varphi_1, \ldots, \varphi_n]$ for all $\varphi_1, \ldots \in L_{BU}$.

Lemma 3 If $f[x]$ is a pure-future L_{BU} formula, then $f[\overline{\langle\langle\epsilon\rangle\rangle}x]$ is equivalent to some separated $f'[x, \overline{\langle\langle\epsilon\rangle\rangle}x]$ with $f'[x, y]$ pure-future.

Proof By induction on $f[x]$. The only interesting case is when $f[x]$ is an until-formula. First apply Lemma 3 to the arguments of the until. Now assume $\overline{\langle\langle\epsilon\rangle\rangle}x$ occurs in the right-hand side of the until. First of all, we need not consider disjunctions in the right-hand side because

$$\varphi\langle k\rangle(\psi_1 \vee \psi_2) \equiv_g \varphi\langle k\rangle\psi_1 \vee \varphi\langle k\rangle\psi_2$$

Then conjunctions in the right-hand side can be dealt with using

$$\begin{aligned}
\alpha\langle a\rangle(\overline{\langle\langle\epsilon\rangle\rangle}x \wedge \beta) &\equiv_g \alpha\langle a\rangle(x \wedge \beta) \\
\alpha\langle a\rangle(\neg\overline{\langle\langle\epsilon\rangle\rangle}x \wedge \beta) &\equiv_g \alpha\langle a\rangle(\neg x \wedge \beta) \\
\alpha\langle \epsilon\rangle(\overline{\langle\langle\epsilon\rangle\rangle}x \wedge \beta) &\equiv_g (\overline{\langle\langle\epsilon\rangle\rangle}x \wedge \alpha\langle\epsilon\rangle\beta) \ \vee\ \alpha\langle\epsilon\rangle(x \wedge \alpha\langle\epsilon\rangle\beta) \\
\alpha\langle \epsilon\rangle(\neg\overline{\langle\langle\epsilon\rangle\rangle}x \wedge \beta) &\equiv_g \neg\overline{\langle\langle\epsilon\rangle\rangle}x \ \wedge\ (\alpha \wedge \neg x)\langle\epsilon\rangle(\beta \wedge \neg x)
\end{aligned} \tag{5}$$

Now if $\overline{\langle\langle\epsilon\rangle\rangle}x$ occurs in the left-hand sides of the until, we only consider the general form:

$$\Big((\overline{\langle\langle\epsilon\rangle\rangle}x \wedge \varphi) \vee (\neg\overline{\langle\langle\epsilon\rangle\rangle}x \wedge \varphi') \vee \beta\Big)\langle k\rangle\alpha \tag{6}$$

which can always be obtained by boolean manipulations. We use

$$\begin{aligned}
&\Big((\overline{\langle\langle\epsilon\rangle\rangle}x \wedge \varphi) \vee (\neg\overline{\langle\langle\epsilon\rangle\rangle}x \wedge \varphi') \vee \beta\Big)\langle k\rangle\alpha \\
&\quad \equiv_g \begin{array}{l} \overline{\langle\langle\epsilon\rangle\rangle}x \wedge (\varphi \vee \beta)\langle k\rangle\alpha \ \vee\ \neg\overline{\langle\langle\epsilon\rangle\rangle}x \wedge (\neg x \wedge (\varphi' \vee \beta))\langle k\rangle\alpha \\ \vee\ \neg\overline{\langle\langle\epsilon\rangle\rangle}x \wedge (\neg x \wedge (\varphi' \vee \beta))\langle\epsilon\rangle(x \wedge (\varphi \vee \beta)\langle k\rangle\alpha) \end{array}
\end{aligned}$$

We have no room here to show the rules for the general cases where $\overline{\langle\langle\epsilon\rangle\rangle}x$ occurs in both sides of the until (4 distinct combinations of (5) and (6)). In almost all cases, separation is achieved by a combination of the previous transformations. In some cases we need new transformations in the same spirit. □

Now we can generalize Lemma 3 into:

Lemma 4 If $f[x]$ is a pure-future L_{BU} formula, then $f[\overline{\langle\langle k\rangle\rangle}x]$ is equivalent to some separated $f'[x, \overline{\langle\langle k\rangle\rangle}x, \overline{\langle\langle \epsilon\rangle\rangle}x]$ with $f'[x,y,z]$ pure-future.

Proof We have already proved the result when $k = \epsilon$. If $k = b \neq \epsilon$, we follow the lines we used in the proof of Lemma 3 except that we may introduce some $\overline{\langle\langle \epsilon\rangle\rangle}x$ subformulas in the scope of until modalities. Let's consider the induction step assuming that $f[x]$ is an until-formula:

If $\overline{\langle\langle b\rangle\rangle}x$ only appears in the right-hand side of the until, we use

$$\alpha\langle a\rangle\big(\overline{\langle\langle b\rangle\rangle}x \wedge \beta\big) \equiv_g \begin{cases} \bot & \text{if } a \neq b, \\ (\alpha\langle\epsilon\rangle(x \wedge \alpha\langle a\rangle\beta)) \vee (\overline{\langle\langle \epsilon\rangle\rangle}x \wedge \alpha\langle a\rangle\beta) & \text{if } a = b. \end{cases}$$

$$\alpha\langle a\rangle\big(\neg\overline{\langle\langle b\rangle\rangle}x \wedge \beta\big) \equiv_g \begin{cases} \alpha\langle a\rangle\beta & \text{if } a \neq b, \\ \neg\overline{\langle\langle \epsilon\rangle\rangle}x \wedge (\alpha \wedge \neg x)\langle a\rangle\beta & \text{if } a = b. \end{cases}$$

$$\alpha\langle\epsilon\rangle\big(\overline{\langle\langle b\rangle\rangle}x \wedge \beta\big) \equiv_g \overline{\langle\langle b\rangle\rangle}x \wedge \alpha\langle\epsilon\rangle\beta$$

$$\alpha\langle\epsilon\rangle\big(\neg\overline{\langle\langle b\rangle\rangle}x \wedge \beta\big) \equiv_g \neg\overline{\langle\langle b\rangle\rangle}x \wedge \alpha\langle\epsilon\rangle\beta$$

Now if $\overline{\langle\langle b\rangle\rangle}x$ occurs in the left-hand sides of the until, we use

$$\begin{aligned}&\Big((\overline{\langle\langle b\rangle\rangle}x \wedge \varphi) \vee (\neg\overline{\langle\langle b\rangle\rangle}x \wedge \varphi') \vee \beta\Big)\langle k\rangle\alpha \\ &\qquad \equiv_g \Big(\overline{\langle\langle b\rangle\rangle}x \wedge (\varphi \vee \beta)\langle k\rangle\alpha\Big) \vee \Big(\neg\overline{\langle\langle b\rangle\rangle}x \wedge (\varphi' \vee \beta)\langle k\rangle\alpha\Big)\end{aligned}$$

Again, we omit the rules for the general cases where $\overline{\langle\langle b\rangle\rangle}x$ occurs in both sides of the until.

Once we are finished, we get some $f'[x, \overline{\langle\langle k\rangle\rangle}x, \overline{\langle\langle \epsilon\rangle\rangle}x]$ where $f'[x,y,z]$ is pure-future. Here y is not in the scope of until modalities but z may be. We use Lemma 3 to rewrite $f'[x, \overline{\langle\langle k\rangle\rangle}x, \overline{\langle\langle \epsilon\rangle\rangle}x]$ into some separated $f''[x, \overline{\langle\langle k\rangle\rangle}x, \overline{\langle\langle \epsilon\rangle\rangle}x]$. □

We can build on this basic step:

Lemma 5 If $f[x_1,\ldots,x_n]$ is a pure-future L_{BU} formula, then $f[\overline{\langle\langle k_1\rangle\rangle}x_1,\ldots,\overline{\langle\langle k_n\rangle\rangle}x_n]$ is equivalent to some separated $f'[x_1, \overline{\langle\langle k_1\rangle\rangle}x_1, \overline{\langle\langle \epsilon\rangle\rangle}x_1, \ldots, x_n, \overline{\langle\langle k_n\rangle\rangle}x_n, \overline{\langle\langle \epsilon\rangle\rangle}x_n]$ where $f'[x_1,y_1,z_1,\ldots,x_n,y_n,z_n]$ is pure-future.

Proof By induction on n and using Lemma 4. □

Lemma 6 If $f[x_1,\ldots,x_n]$ is a pure-future L_{BU} formula and if $\psi_1,\ldots,\psi_n$ are pure-past L_{BU} formulas, then $f[\psi_1,\ldots,\psi_n]$ is equivalent to a separated formula.

Proof By induction on the maximum number of nested backward modalities in the ψ_i's, and using Lemma 5. □

Lemma 7 If $f[x_1,\ldots,x_n]$ is a pure-future L_{BU} formula and if $\psi_1,\ldots,\psi_n$ are separated L_{BU} formulas, then $f[\psi_1,\ldots,\psi_n]$ is equivalent to a separated formula.

Proof The ψ_i's may contain forward modalities in the scope of (nested) backward modalities. So that f is some $f[\psi_1[f_{1,1},\ldots,f_{1,k_1}],\ldots,\psi_n[f_{n,1},\ldots,f_{n,k_n}]]$ where the $f_{i,j}$'s are pure-future and where the $\psi_i[z_{i,1},\ldots,z_{i,k_i}]$'s are pure-past.

We apply Lemma 6 to $f[\psi_1[z_{1,1},\ldots,z_{1,k_1}],\ldots,\psi_n[z_{n,1},\ldots,z_{n,k_n}]]$ and get a separated $f'[z_{1,1},\ldots,z_{n,k_n}]$. Then $f \equiv_g f'[f_{1,1},\ldots,f_{n,k_n}]$ which is separated. □

Lemma 8 Any f in L_{BU} is equivalent to a separated formula.

Proof By induction on f. The difficult step has been dealt with in the previous lemma. □

Proposition 3 **(Separation Lemma for L_{BU})**

$$L_{BU} \preceq_g L_{BU}^{sep}$$

is the immediate corollary.

Proposition 4 $L_{BU}^{sep} \preceq_i L_U$.

Proof Use $\overline{\langle\langle a\rangle\rangle}\varphi \equiv_i \bot$ and $\overline{\langle\langle\epsilon\rangle\rangle}\varphi \equiv_i \varphi$. □

These two propositions combine with the fact that L_{BF} is a fragment of L_{BU} to complete the proof of Theorem 3.

Incidentally, we can now generalize Theorem 2 with

Theorem 4 $L_{BU} \preceq_g L_{BF}$.

Proof Consider $f \in L_{BU}$. Then f is equivalent to some $f' \in L_{BU}^{sep}$ (Proposition 3). f' is separated and thus has the form $\psi[\varphi_1,\ldots,\varphi_n]$ where $\psi[x_1,\ldots,x_n]$ is pure-past (and then in L_{BF}) and the φ_i's are pure-future (and then in L_U). Theorem 2 implies that the φ_i's are equivalent to some φ_i''s in L_{BF}. Finally, $f \equiv_g \psi[\varphi_1',\ldots,\varphi_n'] \in L_{BF}$. □

Conclusion

Translations between modal logics have not been investigated in the literature. Our three theorems clearly show that many interesting results can be found when modal logics with backward modalities are considered. We intend to pursue this line of research

1. by investigating complexity issues (not dealt with in this introductory paper),
2. by relaxing our rewriting strategies and simplifying our proofs,
3. and especially by considering other richer logics: HML with recursion, logics for "truly parallel" models, ...

This last point seems promising. For example, F. Cherief, F. Laroussinie and S. Pinchinat proved that the logic L_P from [2] can be translated into a variant of HML_{bf} with $\langle\rho\rangle$ modalities for pomsets ρ. Regarding HML with recursion, we do not expect to develop translation algorithms based on rewrite rules. As an indication, let us mention that the linear-time μ-calculus with backward modalities can be translated (modulo $\equiv_i$) into the pure-future fragment [14] but the proof uses automata-theoretic techniques and it is not clear how to develop a translation operating on logic formulas.

Acknowledgments

We would like to thank F. Vaandrager and an anonymous referee for the many helpful comments they provided.

References

[1] R. Cleaveland, J. Parrow, and B. Steffen. The concurrency workbench: A semantics-based tool for the verification of concurrent systems. *ACM Transactions on Programming Languages and Systems*, 15(1):36–72, January 1993.

[2] R. De Nicola and G. L. Ferrari. Observational logics and concurrency models. In *Proc. 10th Conf. Found. of Software Technology and Theor. Comp. Sci. Bangalore, India, LNCS 472*, pages 301–315. Springer-Verlag, December 1990.

[3] R. De Nicola, U. Montanari, and F. Vaandrager. Back and forth bisimulations. In *Proc. CONCUR'90, Amsterdam, LNCS 458*, pages 152–165. Springer-Verlag, August 1990.

[4] R. De Nicola and F. Vaandrager. *Three logics for branching bisimulation.* Research Report CS-R9012, CWI, 1990.

[5] R. De Nicola and F. Vaandrager. Three logics for branching bisimulation (extended abstract). In *Proc. 5th IEEE Symp. Logic in Computer Science, Philadelphia, PA*, pages 118–129, June 1990.

[6] R. De Nicola and F. Vaandrager. *Three logics for branching bisimulation.* Research Report SI-92/07, Dipartimento di Scienze dell'Informazione, Università degli Studi di Roma La Sapienza, November 1992.

[7] D. Gabbay. The declarative past and imperative future: Executable temporal logic for interactive systems. In *Proc. Temporal Logic in Specification, Altrincham, UK, LNCS 398*, pages 409–448. Springer-Verlag, April 1987.

[8] D. Gabbay, A. Pnueli, S. Shelah, and J. Stavi. On the temporal analysis of fairness. In *Proc. 7th ACM Symp. Principles of Programming Languages, Las Vegas, Nevada*, pages 163–173, January 1980.

[9] M. Hennessy and R. Milner. Algebraic laws for nondeterminism and concurrency. *Journal of the ACM*, 32(1):137–161, January 1985.

[10] M. Hennessy and C. Stirling. The power of the future perfect in program logics. *Information and Control*, 67:23–52, 1985.

[11] M. Hillerström. *Verification of CCS processes.* M.Sc. Thesis, Aalborg University, 1987.

[12] C. Stirling. *Modal and temporal logics.* Research Report ECS-LFCS-91-157, Lab. for Foundations of Computer Science, Edinburgh, May 1991. To appear in, S. Abramsky, D. Gabbay and T. S. E. Maibaum (eds), "Handbook of Logic in Computer Science", Oxford University Press.

[13] F. Vaandrager. *Translating back and forth logic to HML with until operator.* Unpublished note, 1992.

[14] M. Vardi. A temporal fixpoint calculus. In *Proc. 15th ACM Symp. Principles of Programming Languages, San Diego, CA*, pages 250–259, January 1988.

Modal Action Logic in a Practical Specification Language

Ismar Neumann Kaufman*

Silvio Lemos Meira†

Department of Informatics – Federal University of Pernambuco
Recife-PE, Brazil

Abstract

It is now considered important that formal methods should express properties of concurrence and time in the abstract languages to which developers are used. This article shows how modal action logic was incorporated in an object-oriented dialect of Z, respecting, as much as possible, the original syntax. We explain the specific modal action logic used and MaMooZ, the resulting language, is described.

Keywords: formal specification, modal action logic, concurrence, time, object-orientation.

1 Introduction

The need for formal specification languages in the requirements phase of software engineering has been recognized by scientists and practitioners alike. The Z language [12], particularly, is widely accepted as a medium to express software requirements, with its schemas providing modularity to build new specifications by composition of elements already defined. Z has been tested in a number of industrial projects.

Nevertheless, schemas are means of functional decomposition; in the last few years it was shown that object oriented decomposition is more suitable for the development of large software systems. Object oriented software tends to be more stable through time and enforces extendibility and reusability. Among other ways to bring object orientation to Z [13], MooZ [8, 9] was proposed and experimented.

MooZ has many new features, but "respects" Z semantics – based on set theory and first-order predicate calculus – making its application restricted, because temporal ordering of events and concurrency are not easy to describe within such formalisms. The problem gets worse if the language is used for the logical design of software, when we augment the problem universe with elements of the chosen solution. Temporal and concurrency properties appear more often in the solution than in the requirements space.

On the other hand, if we want formalism to permeate software development, we need to extend its application from the requirements phase to later steps of the software life cycle. A practical approach to formal logical design, based

*Research funded by a CNPq postgraduate scholarship. email ink@di.ufpe.br.

†Research funded by CNPq research grant number 300.133/85 CC. email srlm@di.ufpe.br.

upon the MooZ (and Z) experience, capable of treating time and concurrence, among other properties, is the key issue of this work.

The semantic foundation is given by modal action logic (**MAL**) [5, 4], a very comprehensive and expressive linguistic framework. In particular, **MAL**'s object structured version is adequate for the purpose in hand and is described below.

This article reports on a way to incorporate **MAL** in object oriented Z and demonstrates that the approach may be general enough to enrich model based specification languages with stronger semantics. The semantics of MaMooZ, given as a translation to **MAL**, is indicated in [7, Ch.5].

2 Object structured modal action logic

The application of modal and temporal logics in the specification of software systems has been advocated for more than a decade [1, 2, 11, 10]. The logic shown herein, **MAL**, is adapted from the work of Fiadeiro and Maibaum [5, 4].

A **MAL** specification is a set of related object descriptions, each one being a pair (θ, Φ), where θ is an object signature and Φ is a set of formulas over θ. If an object description is viewed as a theory, the signature and formulas are the language and axioms of the theory, respectively.

An object signature θ is a triple (Σ, α, Γ) where $\Sigma = (S \cup \{E\}, \Omega)$ is the universe signature (a usual algebraic signature with a special sort for events) and α and Γ are families of attribute and action symbols, respectively. The rigid and non-rigid symbols are syntactically distinguished, the former coming from the universe signature and the latter from the attributes and actions. Every function symbol from the universe algebra and every attribute is $S^* \times S$-indexed; every action is S^*-indexed.

Terms include variables (introduced via classifications), function application (either from universe functions or attributes) and modal qualification of terms. This last and unusual construction was introduced in [6], in order to make formulas more intuitive, because very often one needs to express the changes in individual entities, not in whole formulas. Languages like VDM and Z have similar features. The translation from MaMooZ to **MAL** is made easier by having modal qualification of terms in **MAL**. To express change, there are also action terms resulting from the application of action symbols to arguments.

Let t_1, t_2 be terms of some sort s, e a term of sort E (event), g an action term (application of a symbol from Γ to arguments) and p, q state propositions. The following constructions are state propositions:

- $g(e)$ – application of action terms to terms of sort event;
- $(t_1 =_s t_2)$ – equality between terms;
- $\mathsf{Per}(e)$ and $\mathsf{Obl}(e)$ – permissions and obligations of events;
- $([e]p)$ and $([]p)$ – modal qualification of state propositions;
- $p \vee q$ and $p \wedge q$ – conjunction and disjunction of state propositions and
- $(\forall\, x : s)p$ and $(\exists\, x : s)p$ – quantification of variables over state propositions.

Formulas are built from pairs of sets of state propositions, connected by the relational symbol $\rightarrow_\Xi$, like $(P_1 \rightarrow_\Xi P_2)$, where Ξ is a classification.

The semantics of an object signature $\theta = (\Sigma, \alpha, \Gamma)$ is given by an interpretation structure $(\mathcal{U}, \mathcal{J}, \mathcal{P}, \mathcal{O})$, where:

- $\mathcal{U}$ is a Σ-algebra such that $E_{\mathcal{U}}$ (the interpretation of E, the sort of events, in $\mathcal{U}$) is not empty.
- $\mathcal{J}$ maps:
  - $f \in \alpha_{\langle s_1,\ldots,s_n\rangle,s}$ to
    $\mathcal{J}(f) : s_{1\mathcal{U}} \times \ldots \times s_{n\mathcal{U}} \times E_{\mathcal{U}}^* \to s_{\mathcal{U}}$
  - $g \in \Gamma_{\langle s_1,\ldots,s_n\rangle}$ to
    $\mathcal{J}(g) : s_{1\mathcal{U}} \times \ldots \times s_{n\mathcal{U}} \times E_{\mathcal{U}}^* \to \wp(E_{\mathcal{U}})$
- $\mathcal{P}$ and $\mathcal{O}$ are relations over $E_{\mathcal{U}} \times E_{\mathcal{U}}^*$.

The relations $\mathcal{P}$ and $\mathcal{O}$ state in which event an action is permitted or obligatory. Sequences of actions form trajectories, which can be safe and/or live, following a deontic style of specification that *does not prescribe* behavior. Separating normativeness from inconsistency is richer than the pure temporal logic approach, since it allows the specification of error recovery, punishment, etc. Implementations are either normative or else treat non-normative traces explicitly.

We may define special interpretation structures that guarantee locality, i.e., that satisfy the locality axiom: objects can be modified iff one of their actions occur in a given event; otherwise, the event is silent in relation to that object and not observed by it. Events that respect locality are called local events. We call *θ-locus* an interpretation structure where every non-local event in every trace (finite sequence of events) does not affect any attribute. Locality plays a very important role, assuring that encapsulation of information will be part of the theory presentation. The semantics of modal qualification of terms and state propositions are given over traces, constituting a Kripke semantics, where traces are the "possible worlds".

Satisfaction of propositions is defined in terms of an interpretation structure, an assignment and a trace. A θ-formula $(P_1 \to_{\Xi} P_2)$ is *true* in a θ-structure $\mathbb{S}$ iff for all assignments $\mathbb{A}$ and traces ω, if *every* proposition in P_1 is satisfied by $\mathbb{S}$ and $\mathbb{A}$ in ω, then *there is* a proposition P_2 that is satisfied by $\mathbb{S}$ and $\mathbb{A}$ in ω. The relation $\to_{\Xi}$ allows reasoning about information in a state. There is another consequence relation $(\Rightarrow_\theta)$ intended to reason about the consequences of a specification: an assertion $(F \Rightarrow_\theta f)$ is valid iff every θ-object that makes every formula of F true also makes f true.

Object descriptions are related to each other by morphisms. For example, let (θ_1, F_1) and (θ_2, F_2) be two algebraic signatures. There is a morphism $\sigma_v : \Sigma_1 \to_{\Xi} \Sigma_2$ that relates the two algebraic signatures. There is also a mapping from each attribute or action symbol from θ_1 to the corresponding symbol in θ_2. The morphism between the object descriptions, besides these mappings, has to assure that every translation of a formula from F_1 into the language of θ_2 is also a theorem of (θ_2, F_2), that is:

$$F_2 \Rightarrow_{\theta_2} \sigma(f), \quad \forall f \in F_1$$

Particularly, morphisms must preserve locality, to allow for compositional development, or, in other words, the locality axiom of the first object must be a theorem of the second.

Class ⟨*Class_Name*⟩

givensets ⟨*type_names_list*⟩

superclasses
⟨*class_references_list*⟩
⟨*auxiliary_definitions*⟩

private ⟨*definition_names_list*⟩
or
public ⟨*definition_names_list*⟩

constants
⟨*axiomatic_descriptions_list*⟩
⟨*auxiliary_definitions*⟩

state
⟨*anonymous_schema*⟩ or
⟨*constraint*⟩

initialstates
⟨*schema*⟩
⟨*auxiliary_definitions*⟩

operations
⟨*definitions*⟩

EndClass ⟨*Class_Name*⟩.

Figure 1: General structure of a class.

3 A MAL Based Language

The modularization of Z specifications is based on *schemas*, syntactical structures that aggregate variable declarations and an optional first-order predicate over those variables. Some decoration conventions are used to represent input, output and next-state variables. For example, the following Z schemas specify square root operations for positive natural numbers: the first one inputs a number and outputs its square root, the second transforms a state component.

$SquareRoot_1$

$num? : \mathbb{N}$
$sqrt! : \mathbb{N}$

$num? > 0$
$sqrt! * sqrt! = num?$

$SquareRoot_2$

$num, num' : \mathbb{N}$

$num > 0$
$num' * num' = num$

Modular object oriented Z (MooZ) [9] enriches Z with object-oriented concepts (classes and inheritance) keeping as much as possible Z's syntax. Like Z, MooZ's semantics is based on set theory and classical first-order logic. The language does not allow for definitions outside classes, so that any relation between classes must be either clientship or inheritance. The language is intended at the "specification-in-the-large" and the general format of a MooZ class is shown in fig. 1.

MaMooZ[7] is a modal logic enrichment of MooZ, where the syntax is close to the latter's but the semantics is given in terms of **MAL**. The next section describes the language and the translation method is given in [7, Ch.5].

3.1 MaMooZ in Brief

A method may be defined by a schema or by a semantic operation (an axiomatic description which involves state components). The definition of a *method* in a MaMooZ class means an action that can be performed by an object in an event. The *events* occur constantly and eternally: there is a *global* event sequence, called *trace*, unique for all the system. Operationally, we can think of events as clock ticks heard by all objects. In some ticks some objects perform an action, like communicating with other objects or altering their private memory. Such actions are specified by methods.

The methods of an object occur in some subset of the event set. This subset may contain events dispersed throughout the trace. Two methods occurring in the same event are simultaneous; if they come from distinct objects there is a *synchronization* between the objects, maybe with *information exchange*.

A component of an object changes only when one or more methods of the object occur. This restriction means that every translation of a MaMooZ class into a **MAL** object description includes a locality axiom for every component of the class (attribute of the translation).

As a working example, let's take a phone box partially described by the following MaMooZ class:

Class *PhoneBox*

givensets *PhoneNumber*

state

$phoneLine : PhoneLine$
$dialedNumber : PhoneNumber$
$tokens : \mathbb{N}$

operations

. . .

EndClass *PhoneBox*.

The state includes, among other (omitted) components, an object representing the phone line, capable of answering to messages like *AvailableLine?*. The components *dialedNumber* and *tokens* represent the last dialed number and the number of tokens inserted by the current user.

A switchboard class built using *PhoneBox*es should have a set of them in its state. When a switchboard needs to operate over a specific object, say *pb*, a message is sent to it: *pb mes*. The implicit locality axiom then guarantees that no other phone box will be affected by such a message.

In MooZ, a method takes in account the object's current state (say s) and the next (s'). This is still valid in MaMooZ: the translation of a decorated component is the component modally qualified by the event in which the method occurs, meaning the value of the component after the method's occurrence.

For example, we show below the MaMooZ specification and its **MAL** translation of a phone box operation that accepts a new token put into the phone by the user.

Accept
$\Delta(tokens)$
$tokens' = tokens + 1$

$$\overrightarrow{_{x:E}} Accept(x) \wedge [x]tokens = tokens + 1$$

where E stands for the sort of events.

This proposition could be read as:

When Accept occurs in an event x, the value of tokens after the event is the value of tokens before the event plus one.

The notation $\Delta(c)$ means that the state component c may be changed during this operation. Syntactically it declares two components: c and c'. The notation $\Xi(c)$ – used below – states that $c = c'$, that is, the component is used in the operation but it is not changed.

Another operation could state that if the user gives up calling then the phone box should give his tokens back:

GiveUp
$\Delta(tokens)$
$change! : \mathbb{N}$
$tokens' = 0$
$change! = tokens$

Since the component *change!* represents an output element, the translation of this operation has a parameter to denote the exchange of information:

$$\overrightarrow{_{x:E, c:NAT}} \ GiveUp(c)(x) \wedge c = tokens \wedge [x]tokens = 0$$

The natural reading of this proposition is:

When GiveUp occurs in an event x with parameter c, which equals the current value of tokens, the value of tokens after the event is 0.

The two deontic predicates Per and Obl are present in MaMooZ. To express that some of the methods $a_1, \ldots, a_n$ *may* happen in the next event observed by the object, we write $\mathsf{Per}(a_1, \ldots, a_n)$, meaning that the methods in the list have *permission* to occur,

It is important to distinguish preconditions from permissions: none of the implementations of a class may call an operation when its precondition is false, while the occurrence of a not permitted operation is possible, although it should be avoided, because it may drives the execution to an undesirable state.

Phone boxes do not allow a call to be completed when there are no tokens, but may react in two different ways:

1. switch off the dial, so the user dials but nothing happens or else
2. allow the dial to work but cut the call if no tokens are present when the connection is established.

We show how to specify the two different behaviors using MaMooZ.

The first approach uses a precondition on the *Dial* operation:

Dial
$\Xi(tokens)$
$\Delta(dialedNumber)$
$num? : PhoneNumber$
$tokens > 0$
$dialedNumber' = num?$

The second approach defines a class invariant stating that whenever there are no tokens the *Dial* operation is not permitted. The new state clause of the *PhoneBox* class is:

$phoneLine : PhoneLine$
$dialedNumber : PhoneNumber$
$tokens : \mathbb{N}$
$tokens = 0 \Rightarrow \neg \mathsf{Per}(Dial)$

The predicate $\mathsf{Obl}(a_1, \ldots, a_n)$ establishes that in future events the methods $a_1, \ldots, a_n$ will occur. There is no restriction about how many events will fill the trace between the setting of an obligation and its satisfaction. The semantics of an obligation is analogous to that of the operator $\Diamond$ (or **F**) in temporal logic: the obligation will be eventually discharged by the occurrence of the method.

Obligations may be used to express liveness conditions, like expressing that after a *Dial* operation either the user gets a connection or hears a busy tone. Without this specification, we should have to accept an implementation of *Dial* that halts instead of signaling the user. The following *Dial* definition expresses these constraints (*Connection* and *BusyTone* are operations of the *PhoneBox* class):

$$
\begin{array}{|l}
\hline
\multicolumn{1}{c}{\textit{Dial}} \\
\Delta(\textit{dialedNumber}) \\
\textit{num?} : \textit{PhoneNumber} \\
\hline
\textit{dialedNumber}' = \textit{num?} \\
\mathsf{Obl}(\textit{Connection}) \vee \\
\quad \mathsf{Obl}(\textit{BusyTone}) \\
\hline
\end{array}
$$

Both for Per and Obl there is no relation between the several methods listed as arguments: they are grouped only for brevity and the order is unimportant. So $\mathsf{Per}(a_1, \ldots, a_n)$ is an abbreviation for $\mathsf{Per}(a_1) \wedge \ldots \wedge \mathsf{Per}(a_n)$.

Besides Per and Obl, some few words are introduced in the language to name special sorts. The methods in a class, whether defined or inherited, have sort Method. This sort has "local" meaning, its elements being distinct in each context. Attribute is the sort of a class' state components and Event is the (global) sort of events.

A construct like *object* Method could be used to obtain a set with the names of the methods of a class. The same holds for attributes. All these constructs are well founded in **MAL** and, as far as possible, compatible with Z (and MooZ) style.

MaMooZ specifications are organized in documents and chapters (coarse grain modules) and classes (fine grain). Operations in the classes may be defined by schemas and axiomatic descriptions. The predicates defining an operation may use deontic predicates (permission and obligation) in order to deal with time and concurrence, but there is no explicit modal qualification of terms, since this is the resource used in the semantics to map components of the operations representing "next state values".

4 Conclusion

Other approaches that incorporate modal logics in Z are restricted to temporal logics [3]. Richer languages, like **MAL**, may be used too, without many changes to the syntax, with the semantics given in a translational approach, instead of ZF theory.

One of the problems still to be dealt with is to "upgrade" the proposed calculus for MAL to cater for a more abstract syntactical and semantical discourse.

The adoption of explicit temporal operators should be studied, but care must be taken to avoid conflicts between the deontic and temporal facets. In particular, modal qualification of temporal operators is impossible and should be refrained from. Surely, the two tasks are connected: if temporal operators are used, so the calculus must be refined to deal with them.

References

[1] H. Barringer. The use of temporal logic in the compositional specification of concurrent systems. In A. Galton, editor, *Temporal Logics And Their Applications*. Academic Press, 1987.

[2] M. Danelutto and A. Masini. A temporal logic approach to specify and prove properties of finite state concurrent systems. In E. Börger, H.K. Büning, and M.M. Richter, editors, *Proc. CSL'88 2nd Workshop on Computer Science Logic*, Lecture Notes in Computer Science, 1988.

[3] R. Duke, P. King, G. Rose, and G. Smith. The Object-Z Specification Language. Technical Report 91 - 1, SVRC - Software Verification Centre, The University of Queensland, May 1991.

[4] J. Fiadeiro and T. Maibaum. Describing, structuring and implementing objects. In *School/Workshop on Foundations of Object-Oriented Languages, REX/FOOL*, Netherlands, 1990.

[5] J. Fiadeiro and T. Maibaum. Towards Object Calculi. In *IS-CORE Workshop*, London, 1990.

[6] J. Fiadeiro and A. Sernadas. Logics of Modal Terms for Systems Specification. *Journal of Logic and Computation*, 1(2):187–227, 1990.

[7] I. N. Kaufman. On the Application of Formal Specifications to the Logical Design of Software. Master's thesis, Universidade Federal de Pernambuco, Recife-PE, Brazil, August 1992. In Portuguese.

[8] S. R. L. Meira and A. L. C. Cavalcanti. Modular Object-Oriented Z Specifications. In *Z Users & Technical Meeting, Workshops in Computing*, Oxford - UK, December 1990. Springer-Verlag.

[9] S. R. L. Meira and A. L. C. Cavalcanti. The MooZ Specification Language. Technical report, Universidade Federal de Pernambuco, Departamento de Informática, Recife - PE, 1992.

[10] A. Pnueli. The temporal logic of programs. In *Proc. 18th Ann. Symp. on Foundations of Computer Science*, pages 46–57, 1977.

[11] G. Saake and U.W. Lipeck. Using finite-linear temporal logic for specifying database dynamics. In E. Börger, H.K. Büning, and M.M. Richter, editors, *Proc. CSL'88 2nd Workshop on Computer Science Logic*, Lecture Notes in Computer Science, 1988.

[12] J. M. Spivey. *Understanding Z: A Specification Language and Its Formal Semantics*. C. A. R. Hoare, Series Editor. Prentice Hall, 1988.

[13] S. Stepney, R. Barden, and D. Cooper, editors. *Object Orientation in Z*. Workshops in Computing. Springer-Verlag, 1992.

[14] D.A. Watt. *Programming Language Syntax and Semantics*. Prentice-Hall, 1990.

On using a Composition Principle to Design Parallel Programs

Abdelillah Mokkedem
Dominique Méry*
CRIN-CNRS & INRIA-Lorraine, BP239
54506 Vandœuvre-lès-Nancy, France

Abstract

We briefly present a rigorous and modular method, we are developing to design concurrent systems starting from their desired properties. This method is based on a mechanization of Manna-Pnueli's modular validity concept and on a modular temporal language in which properties are invariant under *stuttering* [1]. A compositional proof system is established to support both specification verification and modular program construction. Each program is developed together with the proof that it meets its specification. A refinement relation is defined by using rules in backward, while the proof is constructed by using the same rules in forward. Constrained by a limited space, we focus attention on the underlying concepts and leave a complete presentation of the proof systems (soundness, relative completeness, modular completeness, and adaptation completeness) in a future paper.

1 Introduction

The temporal logic as presented in [10] provides a powerful tool for *global* specification and *non-compositional* verification of *existing* concurrent programs. However, this logic offers a very poor support for *systematic* design of concurrent programs because of lack of modularity. More recently new concepts have been introduced to make more *modular* the language of temporal logic and the temporal proof system more *compositional* [2, 4, 8]. In the present work we explore these new concepts and we present a *modular* specification method together with a *compositional* temporal proof system. We show how our logic offers a rigorous support for the systematic design of concurrent programs.

Our logic aims to provide a mixed verification and development strategy (*top down* and *bottom up*) of concurrent programs. Proof rules should (1) preserve some desired properties (safety and certain liveness properties), (2) be compositional, and (3) be possibly mechanizable. The first feature aims to guarantee that whenever the starting abstract specification expects the system to operate according to some safety properties (partial correctness, deadlock freedom, mutual exclusion, ...) then so behaves the derived implementation. We show that liveness properties are in general more difficult to preserve whenever we want to define the proof rules according to a composition principle. But such a principle is of a great importance when we want to adopt both the *modular verification* and *stepwise refinement* concepts in the concurrency setting. Given

*on sabbatical leave at the department of Computing Science University of Stirling under the European Science Exchange Programme Royal Society - CNRS

the correctness proofs of some small modules, ***composition principles*** allow the verifier to establish the correctness of bigger modules. Conversely, given the specification of a big module to be implemented, ***composition principles*** allow the designer to reduce the implementation problem to the subproblems of implementing smaller modules.

Traditionally, composition principles for both specification, verification and refinement of concurrent systems are hard to obtain. However, previous work [4, 6] have shown that this difficulty mainly lies in the formulation of a compositional rule for parallel composition. In our opinion, if one wants to formulate a compositional rule for parallel composition, then the first step is to be careful at the stage of the definition of the specification language semantics. Especially, we believe that ***invariance under stuttering*** of properties[1] is one of the key requirements needed for, in the one hand, parallel composition to be ***conjunction*** and, in the other hand, to be able to implement a coarser-grained program by a finer-grained one in the setting of the temporal logic [2].

2 The logic

The full purpose of this work is to provide a complete methodology for ***compositional*** specification, verification and development of concurrent programs. For we first introduce a programming notation (**IPL**) for concurrent modules of large systems and define a computational model to represent semantics of modules. The obtained semantics is compositional in the sense that the semantics of a composite concurrent system is a function of semantics of its sub-modules. We then define the temporal logic MTL and derive from it a specification language by establishing a closed connection between computations of IPL programs and models of MTL formulas. Our logic is ***state-based*** oriented. A system may be specified at many level of abstraction; highest-level properties are described in terms of stuttering invariant temporal formulae, while implementations are programs in the intermediate programming language IPL. A highest-level specification must deal only with the expected behaviour of the system, avoiding references to efficiency or architectural details of its implementation. Such details can be introduced only in the last stage of the ***design*** process when a parallel algorithmic solution is already built.

2.1 A programming notation for concurrent systems

Concurrent systems are described using the language IPL. This language is a slight modification of the language introduced in [11]. The introduced modifications aim to reach a compositional semantics for IPL programs. For instance, usual laws like commutativity and associativity of concatenation and parallel constructs are conserved. The central notion of IPL is the one of ***module*** statement. Here is an excerpt of the syntax. A module statement has the form M :: [**module**; *interface*; *body*] where,

---

[1]A property P is said to be invariant under stuttering if whenever a model σ satisfies P then every model τ, stuttering equivalent (this concept will be defined below) to σ satisfies P.

$interface$ ::= $\{modes\ dcl\}^*$
$modes$ ::= $\{$**in**$|$ **out**$|$ **consum**$|$ **external**$\}^+$
$body$ ::= [**local** dcl;] $statement$
dcl ::= $\{variable \mid channel\}^+ : type$ [**where** : $init$]
$statement$ ::= $action \mid statement; statement$
| **IF** $[]_{i=1}^{n} guard \rightarrow statement$ **FI**
| **DO** $[]_{i=1}^{n} guard \rightarrow statement$ **OD** | $[label:]statement[: label]$
$action$ ::= $skip \mid assignment \mid send \mid receive$
$guard$ ::= $expression \mid receive$
$send$ ::= $channel!expression$
$receive$ ::= $channel?variable$

A concurrent system *Net* has the following syntax:

$$Net ::= M \mid Net||Net \mid \nu c.\ Net \mid Net[d/c]$$

Concurrent modules communicate by asynchronous message passing via unbounded channels. Each module should communicate with the environment (other modules) through its interface according to the *modes* assigned to channels. Local variables are not visible outside, thus all variables of a module are implicitly hidden. Throughout the remainder of this paper we assume the syntactic restriction that variables in different modules are distinct, while we give more attention to channels. Hiding of channels must be done explicitly using the binder ν. We define the viewed channels of a module M be channels that are not hidden, we denote $View(M)$ the set of viewed channels of M. $N[d/c]$ represents *channel renaming* of c into d.

Let c be a channel declared in M, a statement of M may have reading (resp. writing) reference to c only if c is declared with the mode **in** (resp. **out**). A statement in a module parallel to M may have a reading (resp. writing) reference to c only if c is declared as viewed in M with the mode **consum** (resp. **external**).

Definition 2.1 (Interface compatibility) Let M_1 and M_2 be two modules, we say that M_1 and M_2 are interface compatible (we denote by M_1 *compat_with* M_2) if the declaration for any channel c that is declared as viewed in both M_1 and M_2 satisfy the following requirements: the types of c in both declarations match, the conjunction of the **where** clauses (supposed true when is not specified) is consistent, and if one of the declarations specifies an **out** (resp. **in**) mode, the other specifies an **external** (resp. **consum**) mode.

Semantics. The basic computational model we use to assign meanings to concurrent programs is that of fair transition system (FTS for short). We associate with each IPL module M a fair transition system $S_M = (\Pi_M, \Sigma_M, \mathcal{T}_M, \Theta_M, \mathcal{J}_M, \mathcal{F}_M)$ whose components represent, respectively, *state variables, states, transitions, initial condition, just transitions,* and *fair transitions.* A (possible) computation of M is an infinite sequence of states $\sigma : s_0, s_1, \ldots$ such that (1) s_0 satisfies the initial condition Θ_M, (2) for each $i \geq 0, s_{i+1} \in \tau(s_i)$ for some $\tau \in \mathcal{T}_M$, (3) σ satisfies *justice* and *fairness* requirements imposed by the sets $\mathcal{J}_M$ and $\mathcal{F}_M$. We recall that we are adopting an *open* semantic model, and finite computations are represented by infinite sequences by adding an infinite number of stuttering steps (τ_I) which takes the halting state into itself. A behaviour of a module M is the set $open(M)$ of all possible computations.

The semantics of a concurrent system $N_1||\ldots||N_n$ is a *fair* transition system resulting from a *fair* composition of transition systems associated with modules N_i, in notation, $S_{N_1||\ldots||N_n} = S_{N_1} \otimes \ldots \otimes S_{N_n}$. Executions in $S_{N_1||\ldots||N_n}$ are represented as *interleaving* concurrent actions in the different modules under *fairness* constraints (together with the *limited-critical-reference*, *LCR*, restriction [11]) in order to capture a closed connection between *interleaving* and *overlapped* executions (The *LCR* restriction is satisfied by all programs in the class of asynchronously communicating modules we consider).

A complete definition of IPL' semantics is given in [12] and several *good* properties (like commutativity-associativity of parallel composition, compositionality *w.r.t* constructors, etc.) are proven. We state here only compositionality *w.r.t* parallel composition.

Definition 2.2 (compatible computations) Let M_1 and M_2 be two compatible modules such that $V_1 = View(M_1)$ and $V_2 = View(M_2)$, and σ_1 and σ_2 be two computations of S_{M_1} and S_{M_2} respectively, σ_1 and σ_2 are said to be compatible iff $\sigma_1|_{V_1 \cap V_2} = \sigma_2|_{V_1 \cap V_2}$.

Proposition 2.1 (Compositionality) Let M_1 and M_2 be two compatible modules, $M = [M_1||M_2]$ and S_M the FTS associated with M according to the relation $S_M = S_{M_1} \otimes S_{M_2}$, the two following propositions are equivalent:
(1) *σ is a computation of S_M*
(2) $\sigma|_{\Pi_1}$ *and* $\sigma|_{\Pi_2}$ are two *compatible* computations of S_{M_1} and S_{M_2} respectively.

2.2 To get over stuttering in temporal logic

We are convinced that we must be careful at the design decision stage if we want to define a temporal logic for concurrent programs which should be compositional. Linear discrete temporal logic has been perceived to be an appropriate tool for both description of semantics of concurrent (and sequential) programs and reasoning about them. This relies on the fact that concurrent program behaviour can be easily modeled by all possible interleavings of the discrete, linear, execution sequences arising from the separate 'sequential' processes of the concurrent program (interleaving semantics). In [3], Barringer *et al.* proposed a compositional temporal logic for the specification and verification of concurrent systems. They use a *floating* version of the linear temporal logic with the fixpoint operators and still represent actions by the classical *Next* operator $\bigcirc$. However, temporal logics based on this operator have been strongly criticized from different points of view. Our study of a refined temporal logic, namely MTL, starts from a list of valid claims made by the pioneers of the temporal logic of programs and compositional verification:

- In [7], Lamport objects the use of the *Next* operator to be the origin of some trouble in abstraction, which forces too much irrelevant detail to be present in the semantic description. It appears that the lowest level of atomicity is forced to be visible, which a properly abstract semantics should not make.

- Still for abstraction, quantification over flexible variables turned out to be very useful [9], and has been shown to be necessary for attaining compositional completeness. But, with its classical definition, flexible quantification also enforces some lowest level of atomicity to be visible.

- In [9], Manna and Pnueli gave some points of dissatisfaction of the regular temporal logic presented in [10] due to the *floating* interpretation which does not assign any special significance to the initial state so that satisfiability and validity are evaluated at *all* positions in the computations. This interpretation needs the generalization rule in the proof system which violates the *deduction* rule (a powerful tool in the predicate calculus) and, in the other hand, requires the *suffix* closure property for the set of computations when one needs to interpret formulas over computations of a given program. In fact, they presented an *anchored* temporal logic in [9] in which they consider that a formula φ is defined to be *valid* (resp. *satisfiable*) over a set of sequences $\mathcal{C}$, if it holds at position 0 of *every* (resp. some) sequence of $\mathcal{C}$.

2.3 The Logic MTL

Our present contribution is concerned with the investigation of such remarks and the proposition of a refined *future*-temporal logic MTL in which (1) we consider the *anchored* interpretation, (2) flexible quantification is defined modulo finite stuttering, and (3) actions are formulated in terms of a new *Next* operator which is insensitive to finite stuttering and sensitive to infinite stuttering. Note that our design decisions have especially been motivated by the need to reach a sufficient abstraction for the the temporal language semantics which should enable us to design composition principles for modular reasoning about concurrent programs. Moreover, we are interested with an *open* semantical model in which the temporal semantics of a program M describes the execution sequences of M in all (possible) environments. The resulting logic does not require *suffix* closure of program computations, and guarantees *invariance under stuttering* of properties. Besides allowing semantic description of open systems, it provides a good abstraction for compositional specification and verification of concurrent systems and also offers a good support for systematic design of reactive and concurrent programs.

State formulas and models. State formulas describe properties at individual states and can be expressed in some fragment of the first order language. We assume a countable set of flexible variables[2] $\mathcal{V}_s$ $(x, y, z, \ldots \in \mathcal{V}_s)$ which represent quantities that may change in different states of the model, and a countable set of logical variables $\mathcal{V}_l$ $(u, v, n, \ldots \in \mathcal{V}_l)$ which represent quantities that do not change in different states of the model.

We assume a set **Val** of *values* including the booleans *true* and *false*, natural numbers, strings, ... We will assume that **Val** contains all the values we need. A state s over V $(V \subseteq \mathcal{V}_s)$ is an assignment (that respects typing) of values to variables in V– that is, a mapping from V to **Val**. We denote by $s[x]$ the value that s assigns to the variable x. We denote by **St** the set of all states. Let s, s' be two states over V and x be a variable, we say that s' is an x-variant of s ($s' =_x s$ in notation) if $s[y] = s'[y]$ for every $y \in V - \{x\}$. Mappings are

[2]We shall call flexible variables simply variables

extended to state formulas in the usual way [11, 8]. Logical are often used for specification ends in practice and, thus, they are always bounded. For we consider logical variables exactly as constants (i.e. $s[\![u]\!]$ for any s). Since constant expressions are ordinary mathematical formulas whose semantics is the basis of predicate calculus, which is well known, we will assume the meaning of constant expressions. Under such an assumption we can define states as assigning values to only flexible variables. A model (σ, i) consists of an infinite sequence of states $\sigma : s_0, s_1, \ldots$ together with a positive index i to be used as *now*, i.e. (σ, i) represents the sequence $s_i, s_{i+1}, \ldots$; we write σ as an abbreviation of $(\sigma, 0)$ and σ_i denotes the ith state s_i in σ. We denote by $\mathbf{St}^\infty$ the set of all models. Let $\sigma : s_0, s_1, \ldots$ and $\sigma' : s'_0, s'_1, \ldots$ be two models over V, and $x \in$V be a flexible variable, we say that σ' is an x-variant of σ (we write this $\sigma' =_x \sigma$) if for each $j \geq 0$, $s'_j =_x s_j$. Let σ be a model and w be a set of variables ($w \subseteq \mathcal{V}_s$), we denote by $\sigma|_w$ the sequence $s_1|_w, s_2|_w, \ldots$ where $s_i|_w$ denotes the projection of the state s_i onto the set of variables w (i.e., the restriction of the mapping s_i to the set $w \subseteq \mathcal{V}_s$). A step (s_{i-1}, s_i) in σ is called a *stuttering* step iff $s_{i-1} = s_i$. We define $\natural\sigma$ to be the model obtained from σ by removing all stuttering steps.

Definition 2.3 let $(\sigma, j) : s_j, s_{j+1}, s_{j+2}, \ldots$ be a model,

$$\natural(\sigma, j) = \text{if } \forall i > j,\ s_i = s_j \text{ then } (\sigma, j)$$
$$\text{else if } s_j = s_{j+1} \text{ then } \natural(\sigma, j+1)$$
$$\text{else } (s_j) \bullet \natural(\sigma, j+1)$$

Definition 2.4 (w-stuttering) Two models σ, τ are said to be w-stuttering equivalent (in notation $\sigma \simeq_w \tau$) if $\natural(\sigma|_w) = \natural(\tau|_w)$. We simply say that σ and τ are stuttering equivalent for the case $w = \mathcal{V}_s$ and we write this $\sigma \simeq \tau$.

The new and central concept in the definition of MTL consists in introducing a new kind of *Next* operator, denoted $\bigotimes_w$, (and its dual, denoted $\bigoplus_w$). An important feature of $\bigotimes_w$ is being *insensitive* to finite w-stuttering and *sensitive* to infinite w-stuttering (with respect to a given set of variables w), while its dual, $\bigoplus_w$, is *insensitive* to both finite and infinite w-stuttering. Another new concept, similar to Lamport's one recently introduced in [8], consists of flexible quantification modulo stuttering steps. We then define the other temporal operators (*unless, stable, leads-to*, etc.) in terms of these new concepts in order to obtain a temporal logic that will enable semantic descriptions which are *invariant* under finite w-stuttering, where w shall represent the set of variables viewed by the component. This is one of the major results to ensure a *desired* level of abstraction necessary for modular specification and compositional verification of concurrent systems. The syntax and semantics of MTL are summarized in figure 1. Assuming the meaning of state formulas, which can easily be defined in the setting of the predicate logic (see [11]), figure 1 provides all one needs to understand MTL formulas. In [12] we give a proof system providing rules for proving theorems within MTL. The theorems derived with this proof system are formulas which are valid over any model (it thus mechanize the *general validity* relation $\models$ defined in figure 1). We present later additional rules, namely *program* part, for proving theorems about IPL programs; they consist of MTL formulas that are valid over the set of models restricted to the computations of the program.

Definition 2.5 A formula F is said to be valid, written $\models F$, iff it is satisfied by all possible models at the position 0.

Syntax:

$$\begin{array}{lll} <formula> ::= & <state\_formula> \mid \bigotimes_{<w>} <formula> \mid \Box <formula> \\ & \mid \neg <formula> \mid <formula> \vee <formula> \\ & \mid \exists_{<w>} <variable><formula> \\ <variable> ::= & <flexible\_variable> \mid <logical\_variable> \\ <w> ::= & \{<flexible\_variable>\}^* \end{array}$$

Semantics:

$$\begin{array}{l} (\sigma, j) \models p \text{ iff } \sigma_j[\![p]\!] \quad \text{for a state formula } p \\ (\sigma, j) \models \bigotimes_w p \text{ iff } \textit{there is some } k > j \textit{ s.t } \sigma_k|_w \neq \sigma_j|_w \textit{ and } (\sigma, k) \models p \\ \qquad\qquad \textit{and for every } i,\ j \leq i < k,\ \sigma_j|_w = \sigma_i|_w \\ (\sigma, j) \models \Box p \text{ iff } (\sigma, k) \models p \textit{ for every } k \geq j \\ (\sigma, j) \models \exists_w x.\ p \text{ iff } \exists \rho, \tau \in \mathbf{St}^\infty.\ \rho \simeq_w (\sigma, j) \textit{ and } \tau =_x \rho \textit{ and } \tau \models p \\ (\sigma, j) \models \exists_w u.\ p \text{ iff } \exists u \in \mathbf{Val}.\ (\sigma, j) \models p \\ (\sigma, j) \models \neg p \text{ iff } (\sigma, j) \not\models p \\ (\sigma, j) \models p \vee q \text{ iff } (\sigma, j) \models p \textit{ or } (\sigma, j) \models q \end{array}$$

where w includes all variables that appear in p, p is a w-indexed formula, x is a flexible variable, and u is a logical variable.

Figure 1: The logic MTL

Each MTL formula F has an index (possibly more) w which indicates the abstraction level of F. We give an inductive definition of the the indexes of any MTL formula F. We shall call an MTL formula F_w to state that w is an index of the formula F.

Definition 2.6 (Indexes of MTL formulas) Let F be an MTL formula,

1- *if* F is a state formula *then* any w *s.t.* $w \subseteq V_s \wedge Var(F) \subseteq w$ is an index of F
2- *if* $F = \bigotimes_w f$ *then* F has the index w if w is an index of f
3- *if* $F = \Box f$ *then* each index of f is an index of F
4- *if* $F = \exists_w x.\ f$ *then* F has the index w if w is an index of f
5- *if* $F = \neg f$ *then* each index of f is an index of F
6- *if* $F = f \vee g$ *then* each index of both f and g is an index of F

Proposition 2.2 (Fully abstraction) For every property F_w in **MTL** and every pair of models σ, τ *such that* $\sigma \simeq_w \tau$, *then* $\sigma \models F_w$ iff $\tau \models F_w$.

Proof 1 One proceeds as follows: we first show by induction on the structure of formula F_w that $\sigma \models F_w$ iff $\natural(\sigma|_w) \models F_w$; the general result will be straightforward (the complete proof is given in [12]).

2.4 Properties of IPL programs

In order to relate an MTL formula to the IPL module it is supposed to specify, it is necessary that the computations of the module can serve as *models* (in the logical sense) for the formula, which means that we can evaluate the formula on each of these computations and find whether it holds on the computation. We thus should introduce a more specific *program-validity* considering computations. For we augment the MTL logic by some specific predicates and functions, referring to the additional IPL domains and constructs needed to fully describe a state in IPL program's computations, for instance, functions upon integers, booleans, lists, like $\geq, +, \bullet, hd, tl, \ldots$, *control*-predicates like at_{-M}, $after_{-M}$.

Let $S = (\Pi, \Sigma, \mathcal{T}, \Theta, \mathcal{J}, \mathcal{F})$ be the FTS associated with the IPL module N, V be a vocabulary that contains Π, and $\sigma : s_0, s_1, s_2, \ldots$ a model over V, we say that σ corresponds to the computation $\rho : s'_0, s'_1, s'_2, \ldots$ of S iff $\sigma \simeq_{\Pi} \rho$, and we refer to σ as a V-model of N. We denote by $open_V[N]$ the set of all $V-$models of N.

Definition 2.7 Let F be an MTL formula and denote its vocabulary by V_F, we define F to be N-valid or, equivalently, F is valid over the program N ($N \supset\!\!= F$ in notation), if every model in $open_V[N]$ satisfies F, where $V = V_F \cup \Pi_N$.

Note that our program-validity $\supset\!\!=$ is defined according to the open semantics $open_V[N]$. We can therefore establish a relationship between this strong notion of program-validity and the classical one defined according to the close semantics (usually denoted $\models$). Also, we can establish a close relationship between our program-validity $\supset\!\!=$ and the modular-validity relation in the sense of Manna and Pnueli [11]. They define a property F to be ***modularly valid*** for a module M_1 if $M_1 || M_2 \models F$ for any module M_2, interface compatible with M_1. The following theorem quite justifies this informel notes.

Theorem 2.1

1. $M \models F \;\; iff \;\; \nu\bar{c}.\ M \supset\!\!= F$ where $\nu\bar{c} = View(M)$
2. $M \supset\!\!= F \;\; iff \;\; M||M' \models F$ for all M' interface compatible with M

2.5 Modular specification

Large systems are built up of several components (modules) and a separate specification is given for each component specifying its desired behaviour in the whole system. For specifying concurrent modules in a convenient way we explore Lamport's modular specification method [7] and similar notions introduced in [11]. We emphasize, in particular, the relevance to complement a specification module by the specification of the *interface*—the mechanism by which the module communicates with its environment. The interface specification of a module stipulates the constrains the environment must satisfy for a correct interaction with the module. The information that should contain the interface is especially essential for the completeness of the specification module and is intended to eliminate the need for any communication between the user of the module and its implementor. Thereby while the ***behavioural*** part can be a highest-level specification the *interface* part will be a low-level specification.

Specification module. A module specification is an object of the form $(\Psi =) \; < inter, F_w >$ where *inter* specifies the interaction constraints on the environment and F_w is an MTL formula that specifies intial states, safety properties, and liveness properties of the expected behaviour of the module M when it runs within an environment interacting according to *inter*. Since we want to be sensitive to all changes about viewed channels, the index set w should contain all the variables or channels appearing in *inter*. For syntactic simplification, instead of using the IPL' syntax to write the interface part '*inter*' of the specification module Ψ we define a mapping Pr that translates an IPL interface onto an equivalent predicative form. For example, $Pr($**external in c** : *channel*[1..] of integer$) = ext\text{-}in(c) \wedge c \in \mathbb{N}^{\infty}$.

Definition 2.8 (correctness formulas) Let M be an IPL module and $< inter, F >$ be a specification module, we define the correctness formula written $M < inter, F >$ as follows :

$$\models M < inter, F > \quad \text{iff } inter = Pr(interface(M)) \text{ and } M \sqsupseteq F$$

2.6 A compositional proof system for IPL

The proof system for MTL [12], not presented in this paper, provides rules to derive temporal tautologies, i.e. MTL formulas that are true regardless of the meanings of their elementary formulas. We augment the logic MTL with a collection of composition rules to deal with MTL formulas whose elementary formulas are instantiated by assertions about domains and control of IPL programs. This extension will permit us to derive, for a given IPL program M, theorems that are valid over the set of models corresponding to the behaviour of M. Clearly, every temporal tautology of the basic logic MTL is a theorem for any program M, but there are formulas that are valid for a given program M but not valid in general. For the seek to establish a proof system that should support both compositional verification and incremental (and modular) construction of IPL programs, we need composition rules whose both program part and specification part of correctness formulas in premisses reduce in complexity *w.r.t* the conclusion. According to this criterion, given a big specification to be implemented, rules allow the implementor to decompose it into more elementary ones that can be implemented separately. Conversely, given the correctness proofs of some small modules, allow the verifier to establish the correctness of bigger modules. We give only few rules, essentially some of those we have used to develop a Ping-Pong program from a temporal specification of the game [12]. The full proof system and its soundness are studied in [12].

Rules for networks :

$$(\textbf{PAR})\ \frac{\begin{array}{l} M_1 < inter_1, F_1 > \\ M_2 < inter_2, F_2 > \end{array}}{[M_1 \| M_2]_M < inter_1 \oplus inter_2, F_1 \wedge F_2 >} \quad if \left\{ \begin{array}{l} M_2\ compat\_with\ M_1 \\ Free(F_1) \cap Free(F_2) \\ \subseteq var(inter_1, inter_2) \\ \pi_M = (\pi_{M_1}, \pi_{M_2}) \end{array} \right.$$

$$(\textbf{Bind})\ \frac{M < inter, F_w >}{\nu\overline{c}.\ M < inter \ominus \overline{c}, \exists_w \overline{c}.\ (F_w \wedge unchange_w(\pi_M) \Rightarrow unchange_w(\overline{c}))>}$$

$$(\textbf{Rename})\ \frac{M < inter, F >}{M[d/c] < inter[d/c], F[d/c] >}$$

Adaptation rules :

$$(\textbf{Conjunction})\ \frac{M < inter, F_1 > \qquad M < inter, F_2 >}{M < inter, F_1 \wedge F_2 >}$$

$$(\textbf{Consequence})\ \frac{M < inter, F > \qquad F \rightarrow G}{M < inter, G >}$$

3 Discussion

In this paper we presented the preliminary concepts of a refined temporal logic that guarantee a fully abstract semantics *w.r.t* to the chosen level of observation. We then shown how a compositional temporal proof system for concurrent programs can be derived. The resulting full logic should provide a practicable method for both compositional verification and modular construction of concurrent programs.

We believe that Lamport's TLA [8] is the first logic in which programs are described by formulas that are invariant under stuttering. Another attempt to tackle the problem of stuttering within the classical temporal logic is done by Pnueli in [13]. The main difference between Pnueli's work and the own one lies in the fact that, contrary to our *discrete* temporal logic, Pnueli dealt with the temporal logic TLR [5] which is based on a *dense* time domain (isomorphic to reals). Our current contribution lies in achieving results equivalent to Lamport's ones (for TLA) and Pnueli's ones (for TLR) for discrete temporal logic (TL [11]). We thus define a discrete temporal logic that supports refinement and systematic development of concurrent system.

References

[1] M. Abadi and L. Lamport. The existence of refinement mappings. In *Third Annual Symposium on Logic In Computer Science*, pages 165–177, Edinburgh, July 1988.

[2] M. Abadi and L. Lamport. Composing specifications. In J. W. de Bakker, W. P. de Roever, and G. Rozenberg, editors, *Stepwise Refinement of Distributed Systems: Models, Formalisms, Correctness*. Springer Verlag, 1990. LNCS 430.

[3] H. Barringer. The use of temporal logic in the compositional specification of concurrent systems. In A. Galton, editor, *Temporal logics and their applications*, pages 53–90, London, 1987. Academic Press.

[4] H. Barringer, R. Kuiper, and A. Pnueli. Now you may compose temporal logic specifications. In *Sixteenth ACM Symposium on Theory of Computing*, pages 51–63, April 1984. ACM.

[5] H. Barringer, R. Kuiper, and A. Pnueli. A really abstract concurrent model. In *13th ACM Symp. Princ. of Prog. Lang.*, pages 173–183, 1986. ACM.

[6] L. Lamport. The 'Hoare Logic' of concurrent programs. *Acta Informatica*, 14:21–37, 1980.

[7] L. Lamport. A simple approach to specifying concurrent systems. *Communications of ACM*, 1(32):32–45, January 1989.

[8] L. Lamport. The temporal logic of actions. Technical report, DEC Palo Alto, December 1991.

[9] Z. Manna and A. Pnueli. The anchored version of teh temporal framework. In J.W. de Bakker, W.-P. de Roever, and G. Rozenberg, editors, *Linear Time, Branching Time and Partial Order in Logics and Models for Concurrency*, pages 201–284, New York, 1981. Spinger Verlag. LNCS 354.

[10] Z. Manna and A. Pnueli. Verification of concurrent programs: A temporal proof system. In *4th School on Advanced Programming*, pages 163–255, June 1982.

[11] Z. Manna and A. Pnueli. *The Temporal Logic of Reactive and Concurrent Systems.* Springer-Verlag, 1991. ISBN 0-387-97664-7.

[12] A. Mokkedem and D.Méry. On compositionality to reach a uniform proof system for verification and design of reactive systems. Technical report, crin, 1993. Internal note.

[13] A. Pnueli. System specification and refinement in temporal logic. In *FSTTCS 92*, pages 1–38. Spinger Verlag, 1992. LNCS 652.

A notion of refinement for automata

N. Sabadini, S. Vigna
Dipartimento di Scienze dell'Informazione,
Università di Milano, Via Comelico 39/41, I-20135 Milano MI, Italy
e_mail: sabadini@imiucca.csi.unimi.it, vigna@ghost.dsi.unimi.it

R.F.C. Walters
School of Mathematics and Statistics, University of Sydney,
N.S.W. 2006, Australia; e_mail: walters_b@maths.su.oz.au

1. Introduction

The notion of *refinement* of concurrent and distributed systems is a crucial one in any concurrency model. There are (at least) two distinct notions under the name of refinement, namely *refinement of specifications* and *refinement of machines* (automata). It is important to keep these two concepts distinct since their properties, and their mathematical formulation, are, or should be, quite different. A specification describes a whole class of machines and refinement here yields a smaller class of models, whereas a refinement of a machine yields a new, more complex, machine. It is not always clear which of these two notions is under consideration, because sometimes a mixture of the two approaches is appropriate and even because some formalisms allow different interpretations [1], [4], [16].

This paper is concerned with the second notion, refinement of machines, where we refine both actions and the state space, in the context of the model of concurrency based on distributive automata, introduced by Sabadini and Walters in [15]. We leave to a later paper the discussion of refinement of specification in this context.

Action refinement [16], [3] is motivated by top-down design, and hence it is considered desirable that the refinement be performed in such a disciplined way that the behaviour and properties of a refined system are deducible from the unrefined one. For example, it is claimed that a semantic equivalence should be a congruence with respect to refinement.

However, there is another, more objective, notion of refinement, which arises from the need of a deeper analysis of a system, in which further information is introduced. Our definition of refinement captures precisely this idea. For example, on deeper analysis atomic actions may be seen to be non-atomic, actions which are conflicting for resources may be seen to be conflicting only part of the time, and actions which are parallel may be seen to be in fact not parallel. Notice again a problem with names, since the word conflict which we use in relation to resources, is often used for the idea of a choice, in a specification, between different possible behaviours. Ideas similar to ours occur in [6], [8].

With our definition, the refined system may have a much richer structure than the unrefined one. Thus we can study such issues as efficiency in time and resources. This implies that at each stage of refinement it is necessary to prove again, if possible, that desired properties of the system are preserved. This is not unreasonable, because the desired properties are properties of the *final* object of these refinement process, and at an earlier stage it may happen that it is not even possible to define them. This approach is advocated, for instance, by Chandy and Misra in [2]. Further, in contrast to the requirement that a semantic equivalence should be a congruence with respect to refinement, we expect that two systems which become equivalent on refinement should in fact be equivalent.

The notion of refinement is an integral part of any model of concurrency, one reason being that concurrency is concerned with the delay independent behaviour of systems. To introduce a delay into an atomic component (action) it is necessary to refine it. The resulting system should also be a refinement, in the sense that the set of its behaviours, restricted to the old states, should be exactly the same of those of the unrefined system, without delays. We prove in this paper that distributive automata are delay-insensitive in this precise sense. Note also that the encapsulation mechanism central to our model is just the replacement of a refined machine by an unrefined one, hence making a non atomic action atomic. It is also through the refinement notion that we are able to avoid non deterministic machines—the uncertainty of the occurence of an action is analysed in terms of refinements instead of non-determinism, as we will discuss later.

Formally, our definition is based on considering the automata as categories of transitions, and then a morphism is a functor between transition categories, and a refinement is an embedding of the category of one automaton in another one. The elementary categorical concepts used in this paper may be found in Walters [17].

This work has been supported by the Australian Research Council, Esprit BRA ASMICS, Italian MURST 40%, and the Italian CNR.

2. Distributive Automata

In [15] a model of distributed systems, *distributive automata*, was given in terms of a calculus for structured deterministic automata. Distributive automata are automata constructed from a given finite family of sets and function (data types and data operations) using the operations of a distributive category. Both the alphabet and state space of a distributive automaton are formed by the operations of sum and product from some given basic sets. The actions of a distributive automaton are formed from basic functions by composition, sum, and product of functions, projections, injections, the diagonal and codiagonal, and the distributive isomorphism $X \times (Y + Z) \cong X \times Y + X \times Z$. Thus, the alphabet and state space have a rich structure reflecting parallel or conflicting, synchronous or asynchronous actions. There is one further operation. A distributive automaton whose alphabet is one letter and whose state space is of the form $X + U + Y$ may compute by iteration a (total) function from X to Y; such automata we call pseudofunctions. In the construction of distributive automata we may use the function computed by a pseudofunction. This operation allows hiding of state, encapsulation of iteration, and making atomic a non-atomic action. The notion of pseudofunction has a precursor in Elgot's iteration theories [5] and Heller's work on recursion categories [7]. A similar definition can also be found in [9], and [13].

Remarks on the model

One way to view our model is that our machines are finitary hierchical nets of deterministic automata, where, as we have mentioned above, non deterministic features are dealt with by requiring that constructions be delay insensitive.

The usual reasons for taking a non deterministic model for concurrency are that full knowledge of states is too complicated to deal with, and there is uncertainity in the timing of actions. Again, notice a problem with names: the fact that there is a lack of knowlege about which external actions occur is sometimes called non determinism, but it is a sort of "non determinism" already existing in finite state deterministic automata.

Moreover, once properly organized, states are not too complicated, and in any case there are far more possible behaviours of a system than states.

Another reason for the simplicity of our model is that, for example, there is no special mechanism for synchronizing processors. However there *is* a synchronization mechanism, which is purely mathematical in nature, namely the product of functions. The fundamental synchronization assumption is that atomic actions occur completely in parallel, or completely separated. The function $f \times g$ is the synchronized parallel product of f and g. For two actions to overlap non-trivially means that at least one is not atomic.

3. Refinement of automata

Definition 3.1 Suppose M is a monoid and $\mathbf{X}$ an M-automaton; that is, a set X together with an action of M on X, $M \times X \to X : (m, x) \mapsto m \cdot x$; the action is required to satisfy the usual axioms $m_1 \cdot (m_2 \cdot x) = (m_1 m_2) \cdot x$ and $1 \cdot x = x$. Define the category *Trans*$(\mathbf{X})$ (the *transition category of* X) as follows:

(i) objects are states (that is, elements) of X;

(ii) arrows from x to y are state transitions; that is, elements $m \in M$ such that $m \cdot x = y$;

(iii) composition is monoid multiplication.

A morphism of automata, or, in short, a *mapping* from $\mathbf{X}$ to $\mathbf{Y}$, is a functor from *Trans*$(\mathbf{X})$ to *Trans*$(\mathbf{Y})$, where $\mathbf{Y}$ is an N-automaton for a monoid N.

An *abstraction* from $\mathbf{X}$ to $\mathbf{Y}$ is a functor *Trans*$(\mathbf{X})$ to *Trans*$(\mathbf{Y})$ which is surjective on objects and arrows.

A *refinement* of $\mathbf{X}$ in $\mathbf{Y}$ is an inclusion, as a full subcategory, of *Trans*$(\mathbf{X})$ in *Trans*$(\mathbf{Y})$.

In other words, in order to give a refinement of $\mathbf{X}$ one has to specify a bigger system $\mathbf{Y}$ which has a restriction to a system isomorphic to $\mathbf{X}$.

Notice that each arrow in *Trans*$(\mathbf{X})$ is determined by an element $m \in M$ *and* a domain and a codomain $x, y \in X$. Hence many distinct arrows will be labelled with the same element of the monoid.

In what follows, we will be concerned with free monoids on the structured alphabets we discussed. If $M = A^*$ and $N = B^*$, a functor F from

Trans(**X**) to *Trans*(**Y**) is given by a function $F_{state} : X \to Y$ and a function $F_{action} : X \times A \to B^*$ satisfying the condition that if $\alpha \in A$ and $\alpha : x \to x'$ in *Trans*(**X**), then $F_{action}(\alpha) : F_{state}(x) \to F_{state}(y)$ in *Trans*(**Y**) (from now on, we will omit the subscripts when understood). For a refinement there is the further requirement that the function induced by F between $\mathbf{Hom}(x, x')$ and $\mathbf{Hom}(F(x), F(x'))$ is a bijection, and that the function between the state spaces in injective. (Morphisms of distributive automata should be defined by functions $X \to Y$ constructed using the operations of a distributive category, and by functions $A \times X \to B^*$ constructed using the operations of a countably extensive category with products [11], but this requirement is not necessary for the purposes of the present paper.)

Notice that the usual notion of substitution in language theory is a morphism which assigns to a letter a word or a language, but the latter ones are fixed once for all, and not dependent on state. Note also that not all full subcategories of **Y** induce a refinement. We can give also the following, weaker

Definition 3.2 An *expansive mapping* is an inclusion F of *Trans*(**X**) in *Trans*(**Y**) such that whenever $F(x \xrightarrow{\alpha} x') = F(x) \xrightarrow{s} F(x')$, where $\alpha \in A$ and $s \in B^*$, then there are no $x'' \in X$, $s' \in B^*$ such that s' is a proper prefix of s and $F(x) \xrightarrow{s'} F(x'')$.

When an atomic action is refined by an expansive mapping, the set of states spawned by the string it is mapped to lies entirely outside of the image of **X**, except for the initial and final states (which are the image of the domain and of the codomain of the atomic action). We can indeed restate Definition 3.2 as follows:

(i) $Y = X + U$ for some set U;

(ii) if $F(x, a) = b_1 \cdots b_n \in B^*$, then $b_1 \cdots b_k \cdot x \in U$ for $k = 1, 2, \ldots, n-1$.

Expansiveness and fullness are related by the following proposition:

Proposition 3.1 Let **X** and **Y** be A^* and B^* automata, respectively. If a mapping $F : \mathbf{X} \to \mathbf{Y}$ is a refinement, then it is expansive.

Proof. Suppose there are x'' and s' as in Definition 3.2. Then s factors as $s's''$, and $F(x'') \xrightarrow{s''} F(x')$. But because of faithfulness and fullness, there has to exist strings $t', t'' \in A^*$ such that $x \xrightarrow{t'} x''$ and $x'' \xrightarrow{t''} x'$. By composition, we get $t't'' = \alpha$. Thus, either $t' = \alpha$ and $t'' = \epsilon$, or $t' = \epsilon$ and $t'' = \alpha$. In both cases, s' is not a proper prefix of s. □

This proposition cannot be reversed. Take $A = B = \{\alpha, \beta\}$, $X = \{*\}$ and $Y = \{0, 1\}$. Let the action of α be the identity on Y, and the action of β be $n \mapsto 1 - n$. The mapping sending the unique state of X into 0, α to α and β to $\beta\beta$ is expansive, but not full.

There is however a relevant case in which we can reverse Proposition 3.1:

Proposition 3.2 Let **X** and **Y** be A^* and B^* automata, with $A = B = \{\tau\}$. If a mapping $F : \mathbf{X} \to \mathbf{Y}$ is expansive, then it is a refinement.

Proof. If F is not a refinement, consider states $x, y \in X$ and an arrow $F(x) \xrightarrow{\tau^k} F(y)$ which is not image of an arrow from x to y. Assume without loss of generality that k is minimal. Let $F(x) \xrightarrow{\tau^n} F(z)$ be the image through

F of $x \xrightarrow{\tau} z$. If $k > n$, then necessarily $F(z) \xrightarrow{\tau^{k-n}} F(y)$ is not in the image of $\mathbf{X}$, which contradicts the minimality of k. Then $n > k$. But this contradicts expansiveness. □

Example 3.1 When $M = N = \{\tau\}^*$ then refinement takes a particularly simple form. Such an automaton can be analyzed by considering the *orbits*, that is, sequences of states produced by the action of τ starting from a given initial state. A *refinement* of an automaton $\mathbf{X}$ is another automaton $\mathbf{Y}$ with state space of the form $Y = X + U$ such that the orbits of $\mathbf{Y}$, when restricted to $\mathbf{X}$, correspond exactly to orbits of $\mathbf{X}$.

Remark 3.1 It is clear that refinements form a category **Refine**, and that abstractions form a category **Abstract**. However, both refinement and abstraction can be looked at in the opposite direction, i.e., the domain of a refinement can be seen as a system in which space and time have been hidden, while the domain of an abstraction can be seen as a system with finer state space and actions (this is closely related to [12]). Formally, this correspond to the study of the categories $\mathbf{Refine}^{op}$ and $\mathbf{Abstract}^{op}$.

The notion of transition category induces a notion of *behaviour* which is state dependent: for each pair of states x, y we can build the set of arrows between x and y, i.e., the *hom-set* between the objects x and y. Formally,

Definition 3.3 The functor $\mathbf{Behaviour} : \mathbf{Refine} \to \mathbf{Cat/Sets}$ is defined by

$$\mathbf{X} \mapsto \mathbf{Hom} : \mathit{Trans}(\mathbf{X})^{op} \times \mathit{Trans}(\mathbf{X}) \to \mathbf{Sets}$$

on objects, and by $F \mapsto F^{op} \times F$ on morphisms.

Note that $F^{op} \times F$ commutes with $\mathbf{Hom}$ up to isomorphisms exactly because F is a refinement. Note also that $F^{op} \times F$ is a morphism in $\mathbf{Cat/Sets}$; this expresses the fact that the behaviour of $\mathbf{X}$ is a restriction of the behaviour of $\mathbf{Y}$ along the refinement.

4. Examples

4.1. Pseudofunctions

Consider a pseudofunction $\phi : X + U + Y \to X + U + Y$ which calculates the function $f : X \to Y$ by iteration, and suppose that $\phi(x) \in U + Y$ $(x \in X)$. Then from f we may obtain an automaton with a one-letter alphabet and state space $X + Y$ which calculates f in one step. Then the obvious inclusion $X+Y \to X+U+Y$ is a refinement. So, a pseudofunction is just the refinement of a function.

4.2. An IMP(G) Interpreter

The interpreter of **IMP**(G) programs described in [10] is easily seen to be a refinement of each particular **IMP**(G) program. This was in fact the specification of the interpreter.

4.3. Mutual exclusion

Other theories of refinements often require that all the steps in the refinements of two conflicting action (systems) are conflicting. This seems to be reasonable when the word "conflict" means "irrevocable choice", but not when, as usual in applications, conflict comes from access to a common resource (in our setting, this means that two letters use the same part of the state space). Here, we can easily model the situation where the conflict may occur at only one step in the refinement.

4.4. Independent actions are not necessarily parallel

If we consider a fixed machine $\mathbf{Y}$, we may think of refinements of other machines $\mathbf{X}$ in this fixed machine $\mathbf{Y}$ as implementations of abstract machines $\mathbf{X}$ in a system $\mathbf{Y}$. The class of abstract machines has unbounded parallelism—there is no obstruction to considering arbitrary products of abstract machines. However in relation to $\mathbf{Y}$ it is possible to consider questions of resources. We can make the distinction between actions of $\mathbf{X}$ being "independent" and being "parallel". Actions are independent if they are parallel in the abstract machine $\mathbf{X}$. Actions are parallel if they are parallel in the system $\mathbf{Y}$.

The following example can be expressed by saying that independent actions in an abstract machine may not be parallel in the implementation.

Given two automata $\mathbf{X}$, $\mathbf{Y}$, both with alphabet $\{\tau\}$, suppose that there are refinements of $\mathbf{X}$ to $\mathbf{X}'$ and $\mathbf{Y}$ to $\mathbf{Y}'$, where $X' = X + U$ and $Y' = Y + U$, the meaning being that the set U is the state space of some temporarily used (and reset after use) resource like a scratch pad, or printer. Then the synchronous parallel product $\mathbf{X} \times \mathbf{Y}$ of $\mathbf{X}$ and $\mathbf{Y}$ may be refined to an automaton in which there is only one resource U whose use is scheduled between $\mathbf{X}$ and $\mathbf{Y}$. The state space would be $Z = XY + UY + XY + XU$. The two letters α, β would act respectively on the first two and on the last two summands, applying $\langle \tau, \mathbf{1} \rangle$ and $\langle \mathbf{1}, \tau \rangle$, respectively (a trap state would complete the automaton in the obvious way). The injection of XY as first summand of Z would then define a refinement, which would schedule the parallel action $\langle \tau, \tau \rangle$ to $\alpha\beta$.

4.5. Shutdown

Consider a refined description of a system in which a new, destructive action can happen. This is a typical case of a sudden shutdown. We expect that the system can, at any time, be shut down, thus moving into a state which was impossible to reach before. In this case, the refinement space is formed by adding a single element, and a new letter to the alphabet; it sends to the new state any other state. The behaviour of the machine, if we ignore the shutdown state, is unmodified, which is exactly reflected in our definition of refinement.

4.6. Choice

Our refinement being a functor, it assigns to each action of the unrefined system a precise refinement. Hence it is not possible in our model to replace an action by two alternative actions even if two alternative actions may exist in the refined machine (such a thing would correspond to *two* different refinements). This accords with our view that machines, even asynchronous ones, are deterministic; the introduction of a choice in refinement is a non-determinism at the level of morphism. However, different choices can be identified by an abstraction morphism.

5. The Delay-Insensitivity of Distributive Automata

Let us consider a set S of basic functions. We will write $D(S)$ for the set of functions derived from S using the operations of a distributive category (for a detailed definition, see [15]). Consider also a set of functions T such that any function in S admits a refinement to a pseudofunction in $D(T)$.

The Delay-Insensitivity Theorem states that any S-automaton can be refined to a T-automaton. In other words, if each basic function hides the space and time of a complex computation which is expressed in terms of more elementary functions, we can refine an automaton built using the basic functions to another automaton built using the latter, more elementary functions.

The basis for this construction is given by Example 4.1, and by the properties of the **call**[] operator.

Theorem 5.1 Let $\mathbf{X}$ be an automaton on the alphabet A with state space X, and actions taken from $D(S)$. Then there is an automaton $\mathbf{Y}$ on the alphabet A and actions taken from $D(T)$ such that $\mathbf{Y}$ is a refinement of $\mathbf{X}$.

Proof. For each $a \in A$, the function $f_a : X \to X$ admits a refinement into an automaton $\phi_a : X + U_a + X \to X + U_a + X$. We now define

$$Y = I + X + \sum_{a \in A} U_a.$$

The action of $a \neq a'$ on $U_{a'}$ is the unique function $U_{a'} \to I$, while on X and on U_a is defined as ϕ_a. It is then clear that the inclusion $X \to Y$ induces a refinement. □

6. Comparisons

As we remarked in the introduction, our notion of refinement differs markedly from notions currently being considered in Petri nets and process algebra; rather, it is in the spirit of [2, 1, 8]. The definition which is conceptually closest to our approach is the broader definition of Petri net morphism given in [14], where a single Petri net transition can be mapped to an entire computation, possibly composed by many parallel steps. However, due to the freedom with respect to the monoidal product, the mapping is not dependent on the global state of the net.

In contrast to the situation in action refinement ([3],[4]), in our model it is not at all necessary that a refinement of two parallel processors be parallel (§4.4) (and hence we can discuss scheduling of resources), or a refinement of conflicting processors be conflicting in all steps (§4.3) (and hence we can discuss refinements which limit non-parallelism to exactly those points where common resources are needed). In contrast to Petri nets refinement ([16]), we are unable to introduce a choice (§4.6) between actions to refine an action. This limitation simplifies considerably the theory without restricting its expressiveness.

References

[1] M. Abadi and L. Lamport. Composing specifications. In *Stepwise Refinement of Distributed Systems*, number 430 in LNCS, pages 1–41, 1987.

[2] K.M. Chandy and J. Misra. *Parallel Program Design: A Foundation.* Addison-Wesley, 1988.

[3] I. Czaja, R. von Glabbeek, and U. Golz. Interleaving semantics and action refinement with atomic choice. Preprint.

[4] P. Degano, R. Gorrieri, and G. Rosolini. A categorical view of process refinement. In *Semantics: Foundations and Applications*, number 666 in LNCS.

[5] C. Elgot. Monadic computation and iterative algebraic theories. *Studies in Logic and the Foundations of Mathematics*, 80:175–230, 1975.

[6] P. Godefroid, D. Pirottin. Refining dependencies improves partial order verification methods. In C. Courcoubetis, editor, *CAV 93*, number 697 in LNCS, 1993.

[7] A. Heller. An existence theorem for recursion categories. *Journal of Symbolic Logic*, 55(3):1252–1268, 1990.

[8] W. Janssen, M. Poel, J. Zwiers. Action systems and action refinement in the development of parallel systems. In J.C.M. Baeten, J.F. Groote, editors, *CONCUR 91*, number 527 in LNCS, 1991.

[9] D.E. Knuth. *The Art of Computer Programming.* Addison-Wesley, 1973.

[10] W. Khalil and R.F.C. Walters. An imperative language based on distributive categories II. *RAIRO Informatique Théorique et Applications.* To appear.

[11] W. Khalil, E.G. Wagner, and R.F.C. Walters. Fixed-point semantics for programs in distributive categories. In preparation.

[12] N.A. Lynch. Multivalued possibility mappings. In *Stepwise Refinement of Distributed Systems*, number 430 in LNCS, pages 519–543, 1987.

[13] R. Milner. An algebraic definition of simulation between programs. In *Proc. of the 2nd Joint Conference on Artificial Intelligence*, pages 481–489. BCS, 1971.

[14] J. Meseguer and U. Montanari. Petri nets are monoids. *Info. and Co.*, 88:105–155, 1990.

[15] N. Sabadini and R.F.C. Walters. On functions and processors: an automata theoretic approach to concurrency through distributive categories. Mathematics Report 93-7, Sydney University, 1993.

[16] W. Vogler. Modular construction and partial order semantics of Petri nets. Number 625 in LNCS, 1992.

[17] R.F.C. Walters. *Categories and Computer Science.* Carslaw Publications (1991), Cambridge University Press (1992).

The Role of Memory in Object-based and Object-oriented Languages

Eric G. Wagner
Wagner Mathematics, R1 Box 445
Garrison, NY 10524 USA

Abstract

This paper introduces a mathematical memory model appropriate for programming languages with both ground types and objects, and uses the model to explore a number of programming constructs related to an elementary inheritance, overloading, and class specification.

1 Introduction

This paper reports on some the recent theoretical and practical results on programming constructs that came about as part of the continuing project to design, implement, and extend the programming language **LD³** (=Language for Data Directed Design) introduced at the first AMAST conference [7].

The main idea promoted in this paper is that the proper context for talking about many aspects of object-oriented and object-based programming is imperative rather than functional.

In the discussion of objects in Smalltalk-80 at the beginning of [1] they write,

> An object consists of some private memory and a set of operations....
> A *message* is a request for an object to carry out one of its operations....
> The set of messages to which an object can respond is called its *interface* with the rest of the system. The only way to interact with an object is through its interface....

This brief quote suggests several of the properties generally associated with objects:

1. Objects have memory.
2. Objects have an identity – sending a message to an object may change the contents of its memory but it does not change the object itself.
3. Objects are encapsulated, that is, you can only interact with them through a fixed interface and so the details of how the memory is structured and how the operations are implemented can not be exploited.

However, while the quote is suggestive neither it, nor the description of the things it suggests, are very precise. A closer look at the languages Smalltalk [1], Eiffel [3] and C++ [6]. indicates that what is stored in the private memory of an object are references to other objects and that while the references stored in the memory can only be altered through the interface to the memory, it may still be possible to send messages to the referenced objects that will alter their memories. In these languages the "private memory" of an object may consist of a set of *instance variables* or *attributes* whose values are references to objects. It is easy to define objects with the property that the memory of the objects referenced in their instance variables can be altered from outside the object. For example, (forgetting the "untypedness" of Smalltalk) we can define a class **Link** in these languages where an object of type **Link** has two instance variables **next**, and **value** of respective types **Link**, and **Integer**. Consider the situation where we have two objects A and B of class **LINK** and A.**next** $= B$ (i.e., in the content of the instance variable **next** in the object A is a reference to the object B). Sending B a message to change the contents of its **value** instance variable will have the effect of changing the memory of the contents of A's **next** instance variable.

The above example also illustrates the idea that the form of objects can be recursively defined in the sense that a **Link** "has a **Link** in its memory".

Viewing the memory of an object as a tuple of instance variables is essentially equivalent to viewing it as an element of a product. It is not difficult to propose possible objects whose form does not fit this paradigm. An important class of such examples are those where the value of an object is naturally viewed as coming from a sum of products rather than from a single product. A simple example would be a **BinaryTree** where a **BinaryTree** is either an empty tree or a non-empty tree and non-empty trees have instance variables **label**, **leftTree** and **rightTree**. While this kind of structure can be simulated in Smalltalk, see [2], the simulation is awkward. We employ a framework here in which such structure are easily and cleanly definable. While these structures are reminiscent of those in ML [5], the fact that we are employing them in an imperative framework rather than in the functional framework used in ML makes a significant difference – see Section 4.

This paper supplies a mathematical model for such an imperative view of objects – a view that supports objects having an identity, objects being encapsulated, and objects having values that are drawn from a sum of products of sets of objects or ground values. Section 2 provides some mathematical preliminaries. Section 3 defines the notion of a class-basis – essentially an incomplete specification of a set of classes with defined and ground (primitive) types that does not include a specification of the methods. The section presents two equivalent models of states for a class-bases: a categorical model and an equivalent graphical model which provides a precise version of the familiar "pointer diagrams". Section 4 uses the first model of states to provide a mathematical description of the kind of state transformations desired as the semantics of methods and then uses the second model to provide examples of methods with such semantics. Finally, in Section 5, we show how the imperative framework provides a straightforward approach to simple inheritance and illustrate it with a number of examples.

2 Strings and Things

Let ω denote the set of natural numbers, $\omega = \{0, 1, \cdots\}$. For $n \in \omega$ let $[n]$ denote the set $[n] = \{1, \cdots, n\}$, so $[0] = \emptyset$.

For any set K, a *string of length n over K* is a mapping $s : [n] \to K$. Let $\mathbf{Str}_K$ denote the *category of strings over K* with, as objects, all strings over K, and, as morphisms, $\alpha : u \to v$, all triples $\langle u, \overline{\alpha}, v \rangle$ such that $\overline{\alpha} \bullet v = u$. Let K^*

denote the *set of all strings over* K. Given $u \in K^*$ let $|u|$ denote its length, so, $u : [|u|] \to K$. For any $u, v \in K^*$ let $u \cdot v$ denote their *concatenation.*

Let $(K^*)^*$ denote the *set of strings-of-strings* over K, i.e., all mappings $u : [n] \to K^*$ for all $n \in \omega$. We will frequently write $(u_1)(u_2)\cdots(u_n)$for the strings $u : [n] \to K^*$ where $u(i) = u_i \in K^*$, for $i \in K$. We often write $(\ )$for the mapping $[1] \to K^*$ taking 1 to $\lambda : [0] \to K$ (the empty string on K).

Define $\mathbf{SStr}_K$, *the category of strings-of-strings over* K, to have, as objects, all $u \in (K^*)^*$, and, as morphisms $\alpha : u \to v$ for $u : [n] \to K^*$ and $v : [p] \to K^*$, all triples $\langle u, \langle \alpha_0, \alpha_1, \cdots, \alpha_n \rangle, v \rangle$ where α_0 is a mapping $\alpha_0 : [n] \to [p]$, and for $i = 1, \cdots, n$, $\alpha_i : w_{\alpha_0(i)} \to u_i$ in $\mathbf{Str}_K$.

Proposition 2.1 The category $\mathbf{SStr}_K$ has products and coproducts.

If $u =(u_1)(u_2)\cdots(u_n)$and $w =(w_1)(w_2)\cdots(w_p)$then their product object is $u \times w = (u_1 \cdot w_1)(u_1 \cdot w_2)\cdots(u_1 \cdot w_p)(u_2 \cdot w_1)\cdots(u_n \cdot w_p)$, their coproduct object is $u + v = (u_1)\cdots(u_n)(w_1)\cdots(w_p)$, the initial object is the unique mapping $\mathbf{0} : [0] \to K^*$ and the terminal object is $\mathbf{1} =(\ ): [1] \to K^*$, as above.

Proposition 2.2 The category $\mathbf{SStr}_K$ is the free distributive category generated by K. So, in particular, viewing K as a discrete category, any functor $F : K \to \mathbf{Set}$ extends uniquely to a functor $\widehat{F} : \mathbf{SStr}_K \to \mathbf{Set}$ preserving products and coproducts. Furthermore, the construction "$\widehat{\ }$" is functorial in that if $F, G : K \to \mathbf{Set}$ and η is a natural transformation, $\eta : F \to G$, then η extends to a natural transformation $\widehat{\eta} : \widehat{F} \to \widehat{G}$.

Proof For $v \in (K^*)^*$ then $F : K \to \mathbf{Set}$ extends to a functor $\widehat{F}$ where

If $v =(k)$for some $k \in K$, then $\widehat{F}(v) = F(k)$.

If $v =(k_1 \cdots k_n)$then $\widehat{F}(v) = F(k_1) \times \cdots \times F(k_n)$.

If $v =(v_1)\cdots(v_p)$, where $v_i \in K^*$, then $\widehat{F}(v) = \widehat{F}((v_1)) + \cdots + \widehat{F}((v_p))$.

Since the only morphism in K are the identity morphisms the morphism part of $\widehat{F}$ is trivial.

Now given $F, G : K \to \mathbf{Set}$ and a natural transformation $\eta : F \to G$ (i.e., a K-indexed set of mappings $\eta = \langle \eta_k : F(k) \to G(k) \rangle$) we extend η to a natural transformation $\widehat{\eta} : \widehat{F} \to \widehat{G}$ in the obvious inductive manner, i.e., given $v \in (K^*)^*$, define $\widehat{\eta}_v$ as follows:

If $v =(k_1 \cdots k_n)$then $\widehat{\eta}_v = \eta_{k_1} \times \cdots \times \eta_{k_n}$.

If $v =(v_1)\cdots(v_p)$, where $v_i \in K^*$, then $\widehat{\eta}_v = \widehat{\eta}_{(v_1)} + \cdots + \widehat{\eta}_{(v_p)}$.

□

3 Class-bases: states for Object-based Languages

3.1 Class-bases, definition and example

We begin by defining the notion of a class-basis. Informally, a class-basis specifies the names of the classes of primitive and defined objects, the form of the defined objects (i.e., how they are represented), and the actual values and operations for the primitive objects. To get a complete class specification one adds specifications for the methods (operations) for the various classes.

Definition 3.1 A *class-basis* is specified by the following data:

G, a set called the set of names for *ground classes*.

D, a set called the set of names for *defined classes*. Let $K =_{def} G + D$.

$\iota : D \to (K^*)^+$, called the *form function*.

$\mathcal{G}$, a G-sorted algebra, called the *algebra of ground operations* with some signature Γ. We assume that the carriers $\mathcal{G}_g$, are pair-wise disjoint.

□

Example 3.2 Let

$G = \{$`INTeger`, `BOOlean`$\}$

$D = \{$`DOT`, `COLor`, `ColoredDOT`, `PreSTacK`, `STAcK`, `VOID`$\}$

$\iota : D \to (K^*)^*$

`DOT` $\mapsto$ (`INT` $\cdot$ `INT`)

`COL` $\mapsto$ (`INT`)

`CDOT` $\mapsto$ (`DOT` $\cdot$ `COL`)

`PSTK` $\mapsto$ ( )(`PSTK` $\cdot$ `INT`)

`STAK` $\mapsto$ (`PSTK`)

`VOID` $\mapsto$ ( )

$\mathcal{G}$ is the G-sorted algebra with signature Γ where

$\Gamma_{\lambda,\mathtt{BOO}} = \{true,\ false\}$

$\Gamma_{\lambda,\mathtt{INT}} = \{0\}$

$\Gamma_{\mathtt{INT},\mathtt{INT}} = \{su,\ pr\}$

$\Gamma_{\mathtt{INT}\cdot\mathtt{INT},\mathtt{INT}} = \{+, *, -, /\}$

$\Gamma_{\mathtt{INT},\mathtt{BOO}} = \{\leq\}$

where the carriers and operations have "the usual interpretation".

Informally speaking we might think of the value, $\langle x, y\rangle$, of a `DOT` as its x, y-coordinates, the value, c, of a `COLor` as being a color where say we identify the subset $\{1, \ldots, 6\}$ of the integers with the set of colors {*red, orange, yellow, green, blue, purple*}, a `ColoredDOT` is interpreted as a `DOT` which has an additional `COLor` attribute. The class `PreSTacK` will be used to define the class `STAcK` – the reason for it is discussed in section 4, Finally, the class `VOID` is introduced for convenience.

□

3.2 Models of States for Class-bases

We present two equivalent models of states for class-bases. The first is based on categorical constructs, the second is based on graph theoretic constructs. The first model provides a suitable setting for formal semantics while the second model, which is essentially a precise version of "pointer diagrams", provides a convenient starting point for more informal semantics.

3.2.1 A Categorical Model of States

Definition 3.3 Given a class-basis $\mathcal{C} = \langle G, D, \iota, \mathcal{G}\rangle$ a $\mathcal{C}$-*state*, μ, for $\mathcal{C}$ consists of

$I_\mu : K \to \mathbf{Set}$, where each $I_\mu(k)$ is finite set (think of $I_\mu(k)$ the set of instances of class k in state μ).

$V_\mu : K \to \mathbf{Set}$, (think of V_μ the set of possible values for instances of objects of class k in state μ).

$\mu : I_\mu \to V_\mu$, a natural transformation (think of $\mu_k : I_\mu(k) \to V_\mu(k)$ giving the actual value of each instance of class k in state μ).

with this data subject to the restriction that $V_\mu : K \to \mathbf{Set}$ be such that $g \mapsto \mathcal{G}_g$ and $d \mapsto \widehat{O}_\mu(\iota(d))$, where $\widehat{O}_\mu : \mathbf{SStr}_K \to \mathbf{Set}$ is the extension, given by Proposition 2.2, of the functor $O_\mu : K \to \mathbf{Set}$ such that $O_\mu(k) = I_\mu(k) + \mathbf{1}$ for all $k \in K$. Think of $O_\mu(k)$ as the set of objects of class k in state μ, that is, as the instances of class k plus a *nil-object*, Nil_k, of class k.

Given two states μ and μ' we define a morphism $\eta : \mu \to \mu'$ to be a pair of injective natural transformations, $\langle \alpha : I_\mu \to I_{\mu'},\ \beta : V_\mu \to V_{\mu'} \rangle$ such that $\mu' \bullet \alpha = \beta \bullet \mu$, where for each $d \in D$, $\beta_d = \alpha_{\iota(d)}$, and, for each $g \in G$, $\beta_g = 1_{\mathcal{G}_g}$. Here α injective means α_k is injective for every $k \in K$.

Let $\mathbf{ST}_\mathcal{C}$ denote a category of $\mathcal{C}$-states.

□

3.2.2 A Graphical Model for States

Definition 3.4 Given a class-basis $C = \langle G, D, \iota, \mathcal{G} \rangle$ define a *state-graph over* C (a *C-graph*) to be a labeled graph with set of nodes

$$N = \bigcup \langle \mathcal{G}_g \mid g \in G \rangle \cup \bigcup \langle O_k \mid k \in K = G + D \rangle$$

and set of edges $E \subseteq N \times N$ where:

1. We assume, for convenience, that all the carriers $\mathcal{G}_g$ and sets O_k are pairwise disjoint.
2. For each $k \in K$, O_k is a finite set which at least contains a distinguished element, Nil_k, with label $\langle k, 0 \rangle$.
3. If $k = g \in G$ and $x \in O_k$ where $x \neq Nil_k$ then x has label $\langle g, 1 \rangle$ and there is exactly one edge $\langle x, v \rangle$ from x to some $v \in \mathcal{G}_g$.
4. If $k = d \in D$ and $x \in O_k$ where $x \neq Nil_k$ then there exists $i \in [|\iota(d)|]$ such that x is labeled $\langle d, i \rangle$ and, for each $j \in [|\iota(d)_i|]$ there is exactly one edge $\langle x, y_j \rangle$ with label j from x to some $y_i \in N_{\iota(d)_{i,j}}$.

Given $\mathcal{C}$-graphs $G_1 = \langle N_1, E_1 \rangle$ and $G_2 = \langle N_2, E_2 \rangle$, a *$\mathcal{C}$-graph morphism* $h : G_1 \to G_2$ is given by a mapping $h_N : N_1 \to N_2$ such that

1. $h_N(Nil_k) = Nil_k$, for all $k \in K$.
2. $h_N | \mathcal{G}_g = 1_{\mathcal{G}_g}$, for all $g \in G$.
3. $h_N | O_k$ is injective, for all $l \in K$.
4. h_N preserves edges, i.e., if $\langle x, y \rangle$ is an edge in G_1 (with label j) then $\langle h_N(x), h_N(y) \rangle$ is an edge in G_2 (with label j).
5. h_N preserves labels on nodes, i.e., if $n \in O_k$ with label $\langle k, i \rangle$ then $h_N(n)$ has the same label.

□

Proposition 3.5 Let $\mathcal{C} = \langle G, D, \iota, \mathcal{G} \rangle$ be a class-basis. Then the category of $\mathcal{C}$-states and the category of $\mathcal{C}$-graphs are isomorphic.

4 $\mathbf{ST}_\mathcal{C}$-operations

In this section we characterize the possible semantics of methods for a class-bases $\mathcal{C}$ by what we call $\mathbf{ST}_\mathcal{C}$*-operations*. More generally, we capture the notion of a FUNCTion in the computer science sense. That is, an $\mathbf{ST}_\mathcal{C}$-operation, F, of arity $\langle u, v\rangle$ is a possible semantics for FUNCTions with formal parameters specified by the string u and returning results specified by the string v where the execution of a FUNCTion can result in a change of state in addition to the return of a result. The string u specifies the formal parameters in the sense that there are $|u|$ formal parameters and the ith is of class u_i. Similarly, the function returns $|v|$ objects the ith being of class v_i.

In what follows let $\mathcal{C} = \langle G, D, \iota, \mathcal{G}\rangle$ be a given class-basis, and let $K = G+D$.

Definition 4.1 For each $v \in (K^*)^*$ define $U^v : \mathbf{ST}_\mathcal{C} \to \mathbf{Set}$, $\mu \mapsto O_\mu(v)$ and $\langle \alpha, \beta\rangle \mapsto \alpha_v$. to be the functor with the above indicated object- and morphism-parts. □

Definition 4.2 For each $v \in K^*$ we define a category $\mathbf{O}^v_\mathcal{C}$ with, as objects, all pairs $\langle \mu, e\rangle$ where μ is a state and $e \in U^v(\mu) = O_\mu(v)$, and, as morphisms from $\langle \mu, e\rangle$ to $\langle \mu', e'\rangle$, those morphisms $\eta : \mu \to \mu'$ such that $U^v(\eta)(e) = e'$ (so, if $\eta = \langle \alpha, \beta\rangle$ then $\alpha_v(e) = e'$).

For $v \in K^*$, let $\Pi = \Pi^v : \mathbf{O}^v_\mathcal{C} \to \mathbf{ST}_\mathcal{C}$, $\langle \mu, e\rangle \mapsto \mu$ and $\eta \mapsto \eta$. □

Definition 4.3 Given categories $\mathbf{C}$ and $\mathbf{D}$ a *partial functor* F from $\mathbf{C}$ to $\mathbf{D}$ consists of partial maps $|F| : Obj(\mathbf{C}) \to Obj(\mathbf{D})$ and $F : Mor(\mathbf{C}) \to Mor(\mathbf{D})$ such that

1. For $f : A \to B$ in $\mathbf{C}$, $F(f)$ is defined iff both $|F|(A)$ and $|F|(B)$ are defined.
2. If $t(f) = s(g)$ and $F(f)$ and $F(g)$ are defined then $F(g \bullet f)$ is defined and equal to $F(g) \bullet F(f)$.

□

Definition 4.4 Let $F : \mathbf{O}^u \to \mathbf{O}^v$ be a partial functor, then for each $k \in K$ define $\overline{F}_k : \mathbf{O}^v_\mathcal{C} \to \mathbf{Set}$, to be such that if $\langle \mu, e\rangle \in \mathbf{O}^u$ and $F(\langle \mu, e\rangle) = \langle \mu', e'\rangle$ then $\langle \mu, e\rangle \mapsto O_{\mu'}(k)$, and $\langle \alpha, \beta\rangle \mapsto \alpha_k$. Observe that, $\overline{F}_k = U^{(k)} \bullet \Pi^v \bullet F$. □

Definition 4.5 By an $\mathbf{ST}_\mathcal{C}$*-operation* of arity $\langle v, w\rangle \in (K^*)^* \times (K^*)^*$ we mean a partial functor $F : \mathbf{O}^v_\mathcal{C} \to \mathbf{O}^w_\mathcal{C}$ equipped with an injective natural transformation $\iota^{F,k} : \overline{\mathbf{1}}_k \to \overline{F}_k$ for each $k \in K$, where $\mathbf{1}_k$ denotes the identity functor on $\mathbf{O}^{(k)}_\mathcal{C}$. □

The partiality of F is, of course, meant to capture the intuitive idea that the execution of a "function" may not terminate.

The functorality of F captures a somewhat more subtle point, mainly the intuitive idea that if a "function" is defined for a given state μ and input e and μ' is an "extension" of μ then the function is also defined for μ' and e and, indeed, does essentially the same thing then as it did before. The mathematics makes a slightly weaker, but more precise statement.

The requirement that we have an injective natural transformation $\iota^{F,k} : \overline{\mathbf{1}}_k \to \overline{F}_k$ for each $k \in K$ can be interpreted as saying that the execution of F "preserves entities", i.e., that if $F(\langle \mu, e\rangle) = \langle \mu', e'\rangle$ then, roughly speaking,

$I_\mu(k) \subseteq I_{\mu'}(k)$ for every $k \in K$. It might appear that this requirement precludes "garbage collection". However, a more accurate interpretation would be that an implementation with garbage collection must appear, from "the outside", as if it had exactly the above property.

Definition 4.6 Given $\mathbf{ST}_\mathcal{C}$-operations $\langle F, \iota^F\rangle : \mathbf{O}^u_\mathcal{C} \to \mathbf{O}^v_\mathcal{C}$ and $\langle G, \iota^G\rangle : \mathbf{O}^v_\mathcal{C} \to \mathbf{O}^w_\mathcal{C}$, we define their composite, $\langle G, \iota^G\rangle \bullet \langle F, \iota^F\rangle : \mathbf{O}^u_\mathcal{C} \to \mathbf{O}^w$ to be $\langle G \bullet F, \iota^{GF}\rangle$ where, for each $k \in K$, and $\langle \mu, e\rangle \in Obj(\mathbf{O}^u_\mathcal{C})$, $\iota^{GF,k} = \iota^{G,k}_{F(\langle\mu,e\rangle)} \bullet \iota^{F,k}_{\langle\mu,e\rangle}$. □

Proposition 4.7 The $\mathbf{ST}_\mathcal{C}$-operations form a category, $\mathbf{Op}_\mathcal{C}$, with the above defined composition and with the identity morphism, $id_v : \mathbf{O}^u_\mathcal{C} \to \mathbf{O}^u_\mathcal{C}$ being $\langle 1_{\mathbf{O}^u_\mathcal{C}}, \langle 1_{k,\mu} : O_\mu(k) \to O_\mu(k) \mid k \in K, \mu \in \mathbf{ST}_\mathcal{C}\rangle\rangle$.

A *class-system* consists of a class-basis, $\mathcal{C}$, together with a selection of $\mathbf{ST}_\mathcal{C}$-operations for each of the various classes. The operations are specified by *methods.* In this paper a method will consist of a somewhat informal description of a transformation of a $\mathcal{C}$-graph for a class-basis $\mathcal{C}$. See [7] for a more precise, but somewhat different, version of methods. Encapsulation will be achieved here, as in [7], by restricting use of the information concerning the form of objects of a class k (i.e., information concerning $\iota(k)$) to methods for operations that belong to the class k. We will type the parameters of the methods and further require that the first parameter of a method always be of the class which owns it. In what follows we will indicate the typing of an operation α belonging to class k by writing $\alpha : k \cdot u \to k'$ where $u \in K^*$ and $k \in K$ – the semantics of such an operation will be an $\mathbf{ST}_\mathcal{C}$-operation $\mathbf{O}^{(k\cdot u)}_\mathcal{C} \to \mathbf{O}^{(k')}_\mathcal{C}$.

Example 4.8 Here are some methods for the classes PSTK and STAK of Example 3.1.

We will use $\mathcal{C}$-graphs to describe four methods for PSTK and three methods for STAK. In what follows let P be an object of class PSTK (i.e., a node with label ⟨PSTK, i⟩, $i \in \{0,1,2\}$), and let I be an object of class INT (i.e., a node with label ⟨INT, i⟩ $i \in \{0,1\}$), and let S be an object of class STAK (i.e., a node with label ⟨STAK, i⟩, $i \in \{0,1\}$).

Pmake : PSTK → PSTK: The execution of *Pmake*(P) adds a new node to the graph, labels it ⟨PSTK, 1⟩, and returns this new node.

Ppush : PSTK · INT → PSTK: If P has label Nil_{PStk} or I has label Nil_{INT} then the execution of *Ppush*(P, I) returns Nil_{PStk} without changing the graph, but otherwise the execution of *Ppush*(P, I) adds to the graph a new node with label ⟨PSTK, 2⟩, and two edges: one from the new node to P with label 1 and one from the new node to I with label 2, and returns the new node.

Ppop : PSTK → PSTK: The execution of *Ppop*(P) does not change the graph, but if P has label ⟨PSTK, 2⟩, and so has an edge $\langle P, P'\rangle$ with label 1, then it returns P', otherwise it returns P.

Ptop : PSTK → INT: The execution of *Ptop*(P) does not change the graph, but if P has label ⟨PSTK, 2⟩, and so has an edge $\langle P, I'\rangle$ with label 2, then it returns I', otherwise it returns Nil_{INT}.

Empty : STAK → STAK: The execution of *Empty*(S) depends on whether or not $S = Nil_{STAK}$. If $S = Nil_{STAK}$ then the execution adds to the graph a new node with label ⟨STAK, 1⟩, executes the method *Pmake*, and adds an edge labeled 1 from the new node to the object returned by the execution of *Pmake*. If $S \neq Nil_{STAK}$ then there must exist a unique object P of class **PSTK** such that there is an edge $\langle S, P \rangle$, the execution of *Empty*(S) first executes *Pmake*(P) getting a new **PSTK** P' and then replaces edge $\langle S, P \rangle$ with $\langle S, P' \rangle$.

Push : **STAK** × **INT** → **VOID**: Note first that if S is an object of class **STAK** and $S \neq Nil_{STAK}$ then there must exist a unique object P of class **PSTK** such that there is an edge $\langle S, P \rangle$ with label 1. The execution of *Push*(S, I) replaces the edge $\langle S, P \rangle$ with an edge from S to the object returned by the execution of *Ppush*(P, I). The execution returns the value Nil_{VOID}.

Pop : **STAK** → **INT**: Note first that if S is an object of class **STAK** then there must exist a unique object P of class **PSTK** such that there is an edge $\langle S, P \rangle$ with label 1. The execution of *Pop*(S) returns the result of executing *Ptop*(P) and replaces the edge $\langle S, P \rangle$ with an edge from S to the object returned by the execution of *Ppop*(P).

□

Inspection will show that all the above methods yield $\mathbf{ST}_C$-operations that respect encapsulation. There are several significant differences between the **PSTK** and **STAK** classes as regards how well they capture the intuitive notion of a "stack".

- The methods for **PSTK** are essentially functional in the sense that the desired result is the returned value. Even though the *Ppush* operation modifies the state (the graph) the state is not really playing a role as such. This is similar to the approach taken in algebraic specifications or in functional languages.
- The methods for **STAK** might be said to be essentially procedural in that a key part of the executions *Push*(S) and *Pop*(S), for $S \neq Nil_{STAK}$, are in the changes that they make to "the memory of" S. The effect is that the object S "is the stack" – if $S \neq Nil_{STAK}$, then every operation maintains S as the stack. We say that an object of class **STAK** has ***integrity***. Contrast this with the class **PSTK** where each operation changes the object that "is the stack".
- The pop operation for **STAK** is the same as the intuitive *pop* operation – it removes the top element of the stack and returns it.

The peculiar arithmetic of Smalltalk, wherein for an object of class **INT** can be sent a message to "add 1 to itself" is an example of the idea of integrity. This corresponds to an operation *succ* : **INT** → **INT** such that the execution of *succ*(I) changes an edge $\langle I, n \rangle$ ($n \in \mathcal{G}_{INT}$) to the edge $\langle I, su(n) \rangle$ (where *su* is the successor function as in Example 3.1) and returns I. Similarly we can define an operation *pred* : **INT** → **INT** where *pred*(I) changes $\langle I, n \rangle$ to $\langle I, pr(n) \rangle$. We can also define an operation *zero* : **INT** → **INT** which when applied to Nil_{INT} creates a new object, of class **INT** together with an edge from that new object to $0 \in \mathcal{G}_{INT}$ and when applied to a $I \neq Nil_{INT}$ "resets" the value of I to 0. Operations with more than one argument can be handled the same way, for example we can define an operation *add* : **INT** · **INT** → **INT** where the execution of $add(I, I')$ returns Nil_{INT} if either $I = Nil_{INT}$ or $I' = Nil_{INT}$ but otherwise, if there are edges $\langle I, n \rangle$ and $\langle I', p \rangle$ (with $n, p \in \mathcal{G}_{INT}$) then the edge $\langle I, n \rangle$ is replaced by the edge $\langle I, n + p \rangle$. Note that the operation, as we have defined it, makes use of the information on the form of both arguments. This is permissible because the operations are typed and both have the type of the class owning the operation. We can even go further away from the message paradigm and define add^* such that in the execution of $add^*(I, I')$ that $\langle I', p\rangle$ (instead of, or in addition to $\langle I, n\rangle$) is replaced by $\langle I', n+p\rangle$. The claim at the end of the next section suggests why this might be desirable.

5 Inheritance

The study of inheritance brings up many concerns such as reuse, overloading, late binding, coercion, message passing, overriding, and subtyping. Our concerns here are more limited. We look at one way that we can define a new classes from old ones in such a way that encapsulation is not compromised and the new classes inherit the methods of the old classes but we do not consider overriding. We first look at the case where the state is given by instance variables, i.e., $\iota : K \to K^*$, and then generalize to the sums of products case where $\iota : K \to (K^*)^*$.

For simple inheritance in the context where $\iota : K \to K^*$, it is tempting to take "k' is a subclass of k" to require (among other things) that k' "inherits all the instance variables" of k. While this is done in Smalltalk and [4], it is clear that it compromises encapsulation. See [2] and [6] for further discussion on this point. The alternative is require (among other things) k' to have a designated instance variable of class k, for example we could require that $\iota(k) = k \cdot u$ for some $u \in K^*$. An advantage of this approach is that it gives us a canonical coercion from objects of class k' to objects of class k – we coerce the state of the k'-object into the k-object reference by the designated variable.

Example 5.1 Define an operation *move* : `DOT · INT · INT` $\to$ `VOID` such that the execution of *move*$(D, I1, I2)$ in a graph with edges $\langle D, x\rangle$ with label 1 and $\langle D, y\rangle$ with label 2 replaces these edges with edges $\langle D, add(x, I1)\rangle$ and $\langle D, add(y, I2)\rangle$ with respective edges 1 and 2, and returns Nil_{VOID}. We can regard the class `CDOT` as inheriting from the class `DOT`, since ι(`CDOT`) = (`DOT` · `COL`). It is easy to see that applying the *move* operation to an object of class `CDOT` though the above coercion will correctly change the state so as to "move" the `CDOT` while maintaining its color. □

The immediate generalization of these ideas to the more general form function $\iota : K \to (K^*)^*$, by taking $\iota(k') = (k) \times u$, is too restrictive. A better generalization is to exploit isomorphisms of the form $i : \iota(k') \cong ((k) \times u) + v$ of strings-of-strings, to produce coercions and define inheritance with respect to specific such coercions. The precise description of the coercion goes as follows: By Proposition 2.2, if $F : K \to$ **Set**, then F extends to a functor $\widehat{F}$ from the category, $\mathbf{SStr}_K$ of strings-of-strings into the category of sets that preserves products and coproducts. So, in particular, given $k, k' \in K$, $u, v \in (K^*)^*$ and any isomorphism $i : \iota(k') \cong ((k) \times u) + v$ we have a unique mapping

$$\widehat{F}(i) : F(\iota(k')) \to (F(k) \times \widehat{F}(u)) + \widehat{F}(v)$$

Taking $F = O_\mu$ for some state μ and letting $\pi_{k,u} : O_\mu(k) \times \widehat{F}(u) \to O_\mu(k)$ be the indicated projection, letting $t_v : \widehat{F}(v) \to \mathbf{1}$, we get a functor

$$\widehat{i} = [\pi_{k,u},\ nil_k \bullet t_v] \bullet \widehat{F}(i) : \widehat{O}_\mu(\iota(k')) \to O_\mu(k).$$

Combining this with the natural transformation k'-component of $(\mu+1)$ (see definition 3.2.1) we get a coercion

$$i^\sharp = \widehat{\imath} \bullet (\mu+1)_{k'} : O_\mu(k') \to O_\mu(k).$$

To indicate what this can do we sketch how stacks-of-integers can inherit arithmetic operations. We have $\iota(\mathtt{PSTK}) = (\ )(\mathtt{PSTK} \cdot \mathtt{INT}) \cong ((\mathtt{INT}) \times (\mathtt{PSTK})) + (\ ) = (\mathtt{INT} \cdot \mathtt{PSTK})(\ )$. This allows us to coerce a **PSTK** into an **INT**. If we had defined **PSTK** in this manner, as inheriting from **INT** along the isomorphism $\iota(\mathtt{PSTK}) \cong ((\mathtt{INT}) \times (\mathtt{PSTK})) + (\ )$, then **PSTK** would inherit all the operations belonging to **INT**. Inspection of the definition of the coercion $\widehat{\imath}$ will show that applied to an object S of class **PSTK** it returns Nil_{PSTK} if S is Nil_{PSTK} or empty and otherwise it returns the object of class **INT** on the top of the stack. Thus, for example, given two objects S and S' of class **PSTK** execution of $add(S, S')$ would, if both were non-nil and non-empty, result in the top element of S being replaced by the sum of the top elements of S and S', this same sum being returned as the result, and that otherwise there would be no state change and Nil_{INT} would be returned as the result. The intuition here is that while the operation *add* knows nothing about **PSTK** (having been defined for **INT**) it will "send" arguments of any class a message to coerce themselves into **INT**, but then, objects of class **PSTK**, knowing that they can be coerced into **INT** along the isomorphism $i^\sharp$, will do so, these coercions however do not modify the state they just change which objects from the state are being presented to the operation *add*, thus what is presented to *add* is the top elements of the two **PSTK** objects, and the end result of the operation is a new state in which the top element of S now has as value the sum of the values of the top elements of the two stacks at the beginning of the operation.

We can, of course, have **STAK** inherit from **PSTK** and thus, by transitivity, from **INT**. This will give us some probably undesirable operations. However, we claim that (providing arguments are evaluated in a left-to-right order) that: $add^*(pop(S), S)$ will "add the top two elements of the stack and put the result on the stack".

References

[1] Adele Goldberg and David Robson. *Smalltalk-80: The Language and its Implementation.* Addison-Wesley, Reading, MA, 1983.

[2] Wilf R. LaLonde and John R. Pugh. *Inside Smalltalk.* Prentice-Hall, Englewood Clifs, NJ, 1990.

[3] Bertrand Meyer. *Object-Oriented Software Construction. Prentice-Hall International Series in Computer Science,* Prentice-Hall, New York, NY, 1988.

[4] John C. Mitchell. Toward a typed foundation for method specialization and inheritance. In *Proceedings of the 17th POPL,* pages 109–124, ACM, 1990.

[5] Laurence C. Paulson. *ML for the Working Programmer.* Cambridge University Press, Cambridge, 1991.

[6] Bjarne Stroustrup. *The C++ Programming Language. Addison-Wesley Series in Computer Science,* Addison-Wesley, Reading, MA, 2nd edition, 1991.

[7] Eric G Wagner. An algebraically specified language for data directed design. *Theoretical Computer Science,* 77:195–219, 1990.

Abstract and Concrete Objects – An Algebraic Design Method for Object-Based Systems

Ruth Breu
Technische Universität München, Institut für Informatik, D-80290 München
breur@informatik.tu-muenchen.de
Michael Breu
Siemens Nixdorf Informationssysteme AG,
European Methodology and Systems Center, D-81730 München

Abstract

This paper outlines a design method for an object-based system using algebraic specification techniques. A two-tiered approach supports the design of objects. At an abstract level, objects are described by state independent values. The transition to a state based representation of objects is deferred to later stages of the design. Abstraction functions ensure the correctness of the system developed.

1 Introduction

This paper demonstrates the design of an object-based system using algebraic specification techniques. The flexibility of algebraic specifications allows the system to be described at any stage of the design – starting from a descriptive specification and ending at a constructive specification. The latter one is a specification at the level of a program, comprising concrete data representations and machine-executable algorithms.

Since we are developing an object-based system, the algebraic target specification in particular is a specification of *objects*. In our framework objects are entities with a unique identity and an evolving internal state which can be manipulated by the outside through a set of operations (commonly called *methods*). In this paper we are restricting ourselves to environments with exactly one active object at a time. Hence, the resulting specification can be easily translated into a typed sequential object-oriented program such as an Eiffel or C++ program.

In our opinion, the notion of objects is too concrete to be the basis for the whole design. In particular, object states, object sharing and side effects of methods are facilities which are tightly connected with the notion of objects but encounter aspects of abstractness and implementation independence.

Therefore, we suggest a design method which is based on a two-tiered paradigm of object specification. The early stages of the design rely on a notion of *abstract objects*. Abstract objects are stateless values on which a set of functions can be applied yielding other abstract objects. The specification of abstract objects is based on an external view, stating the behaviour of the functions. In particular, abstract objects are independent of data representations and do not have states.

In later stages of the design, abstract objects are implemented by a state based object description. These state dependent objects are called *concrete objects*. Concrete objects exist in *object environments* in which one object may refer to other concrete objects.

During the transition from abstract to concrete objects, a formal notion of implementation has to ensure that the correctness of the system description is preserved. We take the approach of [4] and relate abstract and concrete objects by abstraction functions mapping each state of a concrete object to an abstract object. While in [4] abstraction functions connect algebraic specifications with object-oriented programs in a model based theory, in this paper the axiomatic framework is not left. Following the idea of [3], the abstraction functions are part of the algebraic specification and hence enable reasoning at the level of a formal calculus.

Our approach goes beyond related approaches since it supports the specification of both abstract and concrete objects. In this respect, our framework can be considered as an extension of approaches which pursue the specification of concrete objects ([6], [2]). A similar separation into state dependent and state independent objects together with abstraction functions can be found in [7] and [1]. Unlike these approaches, our framework is based on a uniform logic environment in which both abstract and concrete objects are specified and proofs are performed.

As syntactic and semantic framework, we rely on the algebraic specification language SPECTRUM ([5]). This specification language provides facilities like the specification of partial functions and higher-order functions, admitting formulas of a general predicate logic.

This paper starts with an introduction of the concepts of abstract and concrete objects. Then a transformation of the requirements specification to the implementation is given. It consists of the four steps:

- abstract specification of the implementing functions,
- specification of the abstraction function,
- constructive specification of the implementing functions and
- verification.

We will illustrate our ideas by the common example of binary trees. We do not give complete specifications of the example, but it is quite obvious that this can be done in a purely axiomatic specification language. An extended version of this paper contains a more attractive and complete case study. This case study deals with the implementation of the most general unifier of terms based on an object structure which relies on a shared representation of terms, i.e. a representation by dags. The extended version is available from the authors.

2 The Requirement Specification: Abstract Objects

A primary goal in the first stage of the design of an object-based system is the identification of objects together with the abstract specification of their behaviour.

Since we defer state-oriented aspects to later stages of the design, objects are modelled in this early stage by values of some sort in an algebraic specification. We call these objects *abstract objects* and their associated sort *object sort*. Abstract objects are attached with a family of functions which can be applied to them yielding new abstract objects. The behaviour of abstract objects is specified by a set of axioms which describe the effect and the interaction of the functions.
Abstract objects in our example are binary trees (of object sort *Tree*). Binary trees are as usually attached with two constructors ε: *Tree* and *node: Tree* $\times$ *Nat* $\times$ *Tree* $\rightarrow$ *Tree*. Moreover, *left, right: Tree* $\rightarrow$ *Tree* and *label: Tree* $\rightarrow$ *Nat* denote the projections to the first and second subtree and to the label of the root, respectively. The related specification is straightforward. It can be found for instance in [8].

3 The Target Specification: Concrete Objects

Each concrete object consists of

- a unique identity
- an evolving state which may refer to other concrete objects.

Concrete objects thus do not exist in an isolated setting, but in an object *environment*. Object environments are collections of concrete objects which are connected by a network of references. This includes the facility of references to common subobjects (*object sharing*).
In our example, we implement the abstract tree objects by concrete objects which form a dag structure. Figure 1 depicts an environment of two objects representing the abstract tree *node(node(*ε*, 2,* ε*), 1, node(*ε*, 2,* ε*))*.

Figure 1

In object-oriented languages object environments and object identities are implicitly given. In a framework in which properties are proved formally, an explicit modelling is advantageous in order to keep the logic simple.
We model concrete objects of object sort *s* by an algebraic specification containing the following features.

- A sort Id_s describes the set of object identities.
- A sort $State_s$ describes the set of object states.
- A sort *Env* describes the set of object environments. This set is characterised by associations of object identities with object states.
- Methods are modelled by functions *f:Env* $\rightarrow$ *Env* on object environments. Additional parameters may refer to concrete objects in the environment or to basic values.

It has to be noted that the specification of object identifiers and environments does not necessarily be a specification of a low-level pointer structure. More abstractly, object identifiers can be conceived as identifying keys and object environments as databases relating keys with object states.

4 The Transition from Abstract to Concrete Objects

We relate abstract and concrete objects by abstraction functions. Each abstraction represents a particular state in the lifetime of a concrete object by a stateless value. Formally, the abstraction is a function ***abstr*** mapping environments and object identities to values of the abstract object sort. An application of the abstraction function ***abstr*** in our example of binary trees is sketched in figure 2. Object identities (of sort Id_{Tree}) are indicated by an arrow in the given environment.

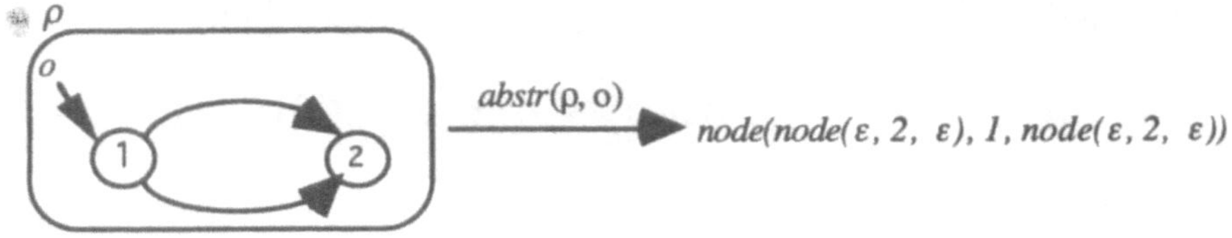

Figure 2

An important property which we require of an abstraction function ***abstr*** is its compatibility with the functional behaviour of objects. This ***homomorphism property*** is characterised in the following diagram.

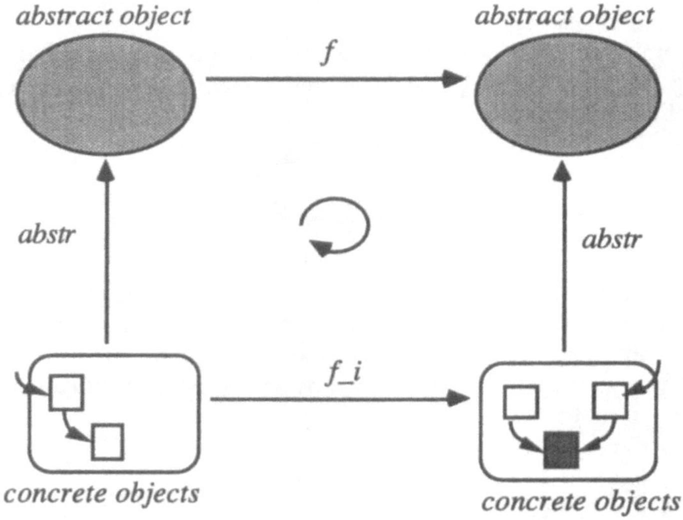

Figure 3

The above diagram commutes for any operation *f* on abstract objects corresponding to a method *f_i* on concrete objects. Thus, abstraction functions between concrete and abstract objects are homomorphisms augmented by a notion of states. These extended homomorphisms have been called *state based homomorphisms* in [4].
More precisely, the implementation of abstract objects of object sort *s* consists of the following four steps. We assume that a specification of object environments (of sort *Env*), object identities (of sort Id_s) and object states (of sort $State_s$) is already given.

I1. Implementation of the functions associated with abstract objects

Each function f in the abstract specification is implemented by a method *f_i* working on environments. Each occurrence of sort s in the arity of f corresponds to the sort Id_s in the arity of *f_i*. In this way, we obtain for instance the arities *node_i*: $Env \times Id_{Tree} \times Nat \times Id_{Tree} \rightarrow Env \times Id_{Tree}$ and *left_i*: $Env \times Id_{Tree} \rightarrow Env \times Id_{Tree}$ in our example of binary trees.
Related axioms describe the behaviour of these functions. In our example, *ε_i* and *node_i* are methods which create new objects, *left_i*, *right_i* and *label_i* do not change the given environment, i.e. are constant on the first argument.

I2. Abstract specification of the abstraction function

In this step we introduce the abstraction function

$abstr: Env \times Id_s \rightarrow s$

together with axioms specifying the homomorphism properties. Since, in general, these properties are too strong to be valid in the set of all object environments, we introduce a constraint on environments

$I: Env \rightarrow \text{Bool}.$

For each function $f: s \rightarrow s$ on abstract objects we introduce the axiom

-- *ABSTR_AX* --

$\forall \rho: Env; x: Id_s$ **in** $I(\rho) \rightarrow abstr(f\_i(\rho, x)) = f(abstr(\rho, x)).$

Axioms related with functions with general arity $f: s_1 \times ... \times s_n \rightarrow s_0$ are obtained in an analogous way.
Additional axioms may describe abstractly the side effect of the functions *f_i* on the argument objects based on the abstraction function. Note that at this stage the boolean function I does not have related axioms, i.e. it is totally loose.

I3. Constructive specification of the abstraction function

The axioms in step I2 describe the function *abstr* in a non-constructive way. In step I3, axioms have to be introduced which define this function explicitly based on the structure of object environments and object states. Moreover, the loose specification of the constraint function I on environments has to be concreted. The specification of this function is deferred to this stage since it is tightly connected with the idea of the implementation of the abstraction function.
In our example, the abstract tree object related with a concrete tree object is obtained by collecting the node information along the trace of references in the environment. The constraint $I(\rho)$ holds if the environment ρ forms a dag structure, i.e. does not contain cyclic networks of objects.

I4. Proofs of correctness

In the last step, the soundness of step I3 with respect to the abstract axioms of step I2 has to be proved. This means that the homomorphism axioms *ABSTR_AX* have to be converted into theorems in the theory of the specification of step I3.
After the elimination of the non-constructive axioms of step 2, the developed target specification should contain axioms which describe algorithms related with

- the functions *f_i* on concrete objects and
- the abstraction function *abstr*.

At this stage, the development has reached a level at which the transition to a machine-executable program does not change the level of abstraction.

5 Conclusion

A main advantage of our design method is the gain of abstractness compared to approaches which are based on the specification of state dependent objects. In particular, our approach supports the separated development of algorithms and data representations.

A second main advantage of our approach is the uniform logic framework of the design. Through the explicit specification of object identifiers and object environments, the simple logic calculus of the functional framework can be applied. Nevertheless, it has to be stressed that the explicit modelling of these state based features does neither have effects on the style nor on the expressiveness of object specifications.

References

1. P. America: *Designing an object-oriented programming language with behavioural subtyping*. In: J.W. de Bakker et al. (eds.): Foundations of Object-Oriented Languages, Proc. REX School/Workshop, The Netherlands, May/June 1990. Lecture Notes in Computer Science 489, Springer, 1991, 60-90
2. P. America, F. de Boer: *A Proof System for Process Creation*. In: Proc. IFIP TC 2 Working Conference on Programming Concepts and Methods, April 1990
3. M. Breu: *Development of Implementations*. In: PROgram Development by SPECification and TRAnsformation, Volume I. Esprit Project 390 PROSPECTRA, Report M2.2.S4 - R - 11.0, 1990 (to appear in the series of Springer Lecture Notes in Computer Science)
4. R. Breu: *Algebraic Specification Techniques in Object Oriented Programming Environments*. Lecture Notes in Computer Science 562, Springer, 1991
5. M. Broy, C. Facchi, R. Grosu, R. Hettler, H. Hussmann, D. Nazareth, F. Regensburger, K. Stølen: *The Requirement and Design Specification Language SPECTRUM – An Informal Introduction, Version 0.3*. Report TUM-I9140, Technische Universität München, 1991
6. J.A. Goguen, J. Meseguer: *Unifying Functional, Object-Oriented and Relational Programming with Logical Semantics*. In: B. Shriver, P. Wegner (eds.): Research Directions in Object-Oriented Programming. MIT Press, 1987, 417-477
7. J. M. Wing: *Writing Larch Interface Language Specifications*. ACM Transactions on Programming Languages and Systems 9:1, 1-24 (1987)
8. M. Wirsing: *Algebraic Specification*. In: J. van Leeuwen (ed.): Handbook of Theoretical Computer Science. Elsevier Science Publishers, 1990

Towards an Algebraic Theory of Inheritance in Object Oriented Programming

Xue-Miao Lu and Tharam S Dillon
Expert & Intelligent Systems Lab., Applied Computing Research Institute
and Department of Computer Science and Computer Engineering,
La Trobe University, Bundoora, Victoria, AUSTRALIA 3083
Email: {lu, tharam}@latcs1.lat.oz.au

Abstract
This paper outlines an algebraic framework for objects, object types, and classes in object oriented programming, with an emphasis on the semantics of inheritance in the framework. An integrated theory of algebraic specification is established combining higher-order type structures, object behaviors, implementation, and inheritance. Classes are formally defined following existing object oriented programming languages and both simple classes and complex classes are considered. Two kinds of objects are dealt with: namely, static objects and dynamic objects, for the two forms of classes. Semantics of inheritance is studied on the two forms of classes using the loose semantic approach. An interesting feature of inheritance is the connection between the instance objects of two classes with the inheritance relationship.

1 Introduction

As the object oriented paradigm[5, 9, 15, 20, 23] has become increasingly important, attempts have been made to give a rigorous mathematical foundation for object oriented systems using the algebraic theories[3, 6, 10, 11, 16, 18]. In particular, algebraic models of inheritance have been studied[6, 13, 14] based on the notion of the order-sorted algebra. The existing models, however, cover only part of the features of object oriented programming, and the inheritance studied using order-sorted algebra is basically what is called *subtyping inheritance*. In this paper we propose an algebraic approach to another kind of inheritance, that is, *incremental inheritance*. Due to space limitations, we only discuss some basic issues and leave out the proofs of most properties, and refer the reader to [19] for details and further discussion.

In object oriented programming, the central concept is an *object*. An object has an identity, attributes and methods. An important feature in object oriented programming is *classification*, which organizes objects into *classes*. Attributes and methods of an object are defined in the class to which the object belongs, and are called *instance attribute* and *instance methods*. In addition, a class can contain *meta-methods, class attributes, class methods*, and *shared instance attributes*[9, 15, 17].

In a class specification, there is an interface part which, by providing attributes and methods, designates how to build and manipulate instance objects of the class[15, 20, 23]. This interface is an (abstract) *object type* specification.

For some classes, this part includes all the features of that class. For others, however, it does not fully characterize the class and another part is needed that concerns implementation of the current type[5, 11, 15, 20, 21, 23]. We call this the *implementation part*. These two parts form an *implementation specification* in terms of algebraic data types.

Inheritance is another important feature of object oriented systems, providing a mechanism for defining attributes and methods for a new class from definitions in another class. There are mainly two kinds of inheritance[2, 7, 8]: *incremental inheritance*[24] and *subtyping inheritance*[1]. In object oriented systems, inheritance also allows *renaming, specialization, overriding* and *redefinition*. Inheritance can be *single* or *multiple* depending on the number of classes from which code is reused by the inheriting type. An interesting feature of inheritance is the relationship between the objects of classes with inheritance relationship. We will show that every static object (a constrained dynamic object, resp.) of an inheriting class is a static object (a dynamic object, resp.) of the inherited class. In other words, an object of an inheriting class has all the features in an object of the parent class. This in some sense is a complementary approach to the order-sorted semantics.

In this paper, we focus on incremental inheritance, which supports additional attributes and methods for the inheriting class other than those inherited from the parent class. Five kinds of components: meta-methods, instance attributes, instance methods, class attributes and class methods, are considered in a class. Higher-order types are used for specifications of object types. Inheritance is studied on two levels: on types and on classes. Two kinds of objects are considered: static objects and dynamic objects. We only discuss single inheritance and assume that an inherited component has the same name as in the source. The loose approach is used, which is especially appropriate for the semantics of inheritance. In including meta-methods, we will see that some conventional notions such as *signature morphism* are not wide enough to provide representation of incremental inheritance and thus a generalized version is introduced.

2 Object Types and Inheritance

We assume familiarity with the basic notions from equational algebraic specification. For a function type $w \rightarrow t$, with $w = s_1 \times \ldots \times s_p$, we will call w the arity, s_i the argument types, and t the coarity. We need the *powerset type* $\mathcal{P}(s)$, and the *bag type* $\mathcal{B}(s)$ for a type s. An *object type* $\sigma = \mathcal{O}(k_1 : s_1, \ldots, k_n : s_n)$ consists of pairs $k_i : s_i$, which we call *components* for the object type. A component $k_i : s_i$ has a name k_i and a type s_i. Denote $K^\sigma = \{k_1 : s_1, \ldots, k_n : s_n\}$. K^σ is divided into three disjoint subsets, K^σ_{mt}, K^σ_{cl} and K^σ_{in}, with $K^\sigma_{in} = \{k_m : s_m, \ldots, k_n : s_n\}$, $1 \leq m < n$. Components in K^σ_{mt} are *meta-methods*, those in K^σ_{cl} are *class attributes* and *class methods*, and those in K^σ_{in} are *instance attributes* and *instance methods*. For each method in K^σ_{mt}, its coarity is exactly σ. In particular, there can be a *construction method* **tup** $: w \rightarrow \sigma \in K^\sigma_{mt}$ with $w = s_m \times \ldots \times s_n$ and a constant operation symbol **create**:$\perp \rightarrow \sigma$. A class method is of the form k: $\mathcal{P}(\sigma) \times s_1 \times \ldots \times s_p \times k'_1 \times \ldots \times k'_q \rightarrow t$, with $k'_1, \ldots, k'_q$ being instance attribute names whose types are $t_1, \ldots, t_q$, respectively, and its type is k_M: $s_1 \times \ldots \times s_p \times \mathcal{B}(t_1) \times \ldots \times \mathcal{B}(t_q) \rightarrow t$. For each method in K^{σ}_{in}, at least one of its arguments, or the coarity, is associated with an instance attribute in K^{σ}_{in} of the same type. Semantically, the association will be the following: If an attribute is associated with an argument type, then the method will use its value whenever the method is activated; and if the attribute is associated with the coarity, the value of the attribute is replaced by the new value produced by the method whenever the method is activated. A class method can also be associated with class attributes in this way. This manner of association of a class method with class attributes is different from the association of a class method with instance attributes.

When an object type τ inherits σ, we write $\tau \rightsquigarrow \sigma$, and in this case, for simplicity, we assume that σ is not an attribute type, or an argument type or the coarity of a method for another object type. A *typed signature* Σ is an S-sorted signature $\Sigma = (S, \Sigma)$ that satisfies the following: (1) S has a unique *central object type* σ which is not a source type or an attribute type of another object type, and which is not an argument type or the coarity of a method in another object type; and any other type is a source type, an attribute type, or an argument type or the coarity type of a method within an object type. (2) For each object type σ, every method name k_i in σ is an operation symbol, and for each $k_i \in K^{\sigma}_{in}$, there is a unary *named projection* operation symbol $k_i \in \Sigma_{\sigma, s_i}$; and if $\tau \rightsquigarrow \sigma$ exists, then for each meta-method $\alpha : s_1 \times \ldots \times s_q \rightarrow \sigma$ for σ, there is a meta-method $\beta : s_1 \times \ldots \times s_q \times \ldots \times s_p \rightarrow \tau$ for τ, $p \geq q$, and β is said to be *compatible* with α. A *typed specification* $HTSP=(\Sigma, E)$ *of* σ consists of a typed signature Σ in which σ is the central sort, and a set E of axioms. A typed specification HTSP is also written HTSP$=(S, \Sigma, E)$.

Several points need to be clarified in our framework. There is a different way of invoking methods in some object oriented programming languages such as the Smalltalk series, in comparison with that in algebraic theories. We will adopt the algebraic approach, and thus a component name is a mapping from the value domain of the object type to the value domain of the component. There are two kinds of function types. The first kind includes attribute types and are treated in the usual way for conventional higher-order types. The second kind covers all the methods in object types and are treated as operation symbols. For the latter kind, only a finite set of functions will be assigned to each type in a model and these functions are called *procedural codes.* Instead of introducing an evaluation operation symbol for a method type, we treat each of these method names as an individual operation symbol. There are other reasons to do so. First, the definition of an evaluation operation for a meta-method type for a class would involve a meta-class, which does not exist in our framework, and take the class itself, rather that any object of the class, as an argument. Second, each of the methods concerned is given a name (the label), and each method name will be associated with exactly one element in any real system. Therefore, an instance component name k_i in an object type σ is associated with two or three subtly different meanings. First, it has a type as a component. If $k_i : t$ is an instance component, $k_i : \sigma \rightarrow t$ is a unary projection operation. In addition, if s is a method type of the form $s_1 \times \ldots \times s_n \rightarrow s_{n+1}$, it is an operation symbol of the same type, $op(k_i)$. Both the projection operation symbols for instance components and the operation symbols corresponding to instance methods are interesting. The former characterize static objects, whereas the latter characterize dynamic objects.

Definition 2.1 An *algebra* A for a typed specification HTSP$=(S, \Sigma, E)$, or an

HTSP-algebra, is a specification algebra, with a *carrier* s^A for each sort $s \in S$, such that for each method name k_i of type t, there is a uniquely assigned operation in t^A, denoted by $op(k_i)$; and such that for every pair of sorts σ and τ with $\tau \rightsquigarrow \sigma$: (1) for each component $k : s$ in K^{σ}_{in}, $k^A : \tau^A \rightarrow s^A$ is a projection operation. (2) each class method $k : \mathcal{P}(\sigma) \times s_1 \times \ldots \times s_p \times k'_1 \times \ldots \times k'_q \rightarrow s$ in K^{σ}, k^A is also an operation: $\mathcal{P}(\tau^A) \times s_1^A \times \ldots \times s_p^A \times k'_1 \times \ldots \times k'_q \rightarrow s^A$. In either of the cases we say that k is *inherited*. σ is said to be (weakly) *inherited by* τ. □

We use Alg(HTSP) to denote the category of HTSP-algebras. Let σ be an object type in HTSP with $K^{\sigma}_{in} = \{k_1 : s_1, \ldots, k_p : s_p\}$, and A be an HTSP-algebra. An element $a \in \sigma^A$ is called an *object snapshot* or a *static object* of type σ. We will assume that a is of the form $(k_1 : a_1, \ldots, k_p : a_p, \ldots)$, for $a_i \in s_i^A$. A static object has access to its (instance) methods, and an access to an instance method can cause the object to evolve into another snapshot. Given two object snapshots $a, b \in \sigma^A$, a is said to be *reducible* to b if there are a (possibly empty) series of instance method invocations *within the object* which change a into b. Each invocation of a meta-method creates an object snapshot, called a *start snapshot*. A *dynamic object* of type σ consists of a start snapshot a of type σ and a snapshot b that is reducible from a, denoted by b_a. In some cases, an object type does not necessarily have a meta-method. In some others, every snapshot in σ^A can be a start snapshot. We will consider any snapshot as a start snapshot.

Let $\tau \rightsquigarrow \sigma$ in HTSP. For an HTSP-algebra A and meta-method β compatible with α, α is said to be *inherited to* β in A if for $a_i \in s_i^A$, $1 \leq i \leq p$, $k_i(\beta(a_1, \ldots, a_q, \ldots, a_p)) = k_i(\alpha(a_1, \ldots, a_q))$ for each instance component k_i in σ. In this case α can be *compatibly adapted* to τ along β in A by defining $\alpha(a_1, \ldots, a_q) = \beta(a_1, \ldots, a_q, c_{q+1}, \ldots, c_p)$ for fixed elements $c_j \in s_j^A$, $q < j \leq p$. σ is said to be *strongly inherited* by τ in A if each meta-method k_i in σ is inherited in A.

Theorem 2.2 *Let $\tau \rightsquigarrow \sigma$ in the typed specification HTSP. (1) For any HTSP-algebra A, let B be obtained from A by replacing σ^A by $\sigma^A \cup \tau^A$, then B is an HTSP-algebra. (2) For any HTSP-algebra A in which σ is strongly inherited by τ, let B be obtained from A by replacing σ^A by τ^A and compatibly adapting each meta-method α to τ in A, then B is an HTSP-algebra.* ∎

In both cases, B being an HTSP-algebra means that static objects of type τ are static objects of σ. They also implies that a dynamic object of τ is a dynamic object of σ, if the reduction in the object uses only the instance methods in σ. This is an important feature in the object oriented framework. For separate specifications of σ and τ, we have:

Corollary 2.3 *Let HTSP be a typed specification of σ, and HTSP1 be a typed specification of τ in which $\tau \rightsquigarrow \sigma$. (1) For each HTSP1-algebra A, we have an HTSP-algebra B such that $\sigma^B = \sigma^A \cup \tau^A$, and $t^B = t^A$ for every $t \neq \sigma$ and $t \in$HTSP. (2) For each HTSP1-algebra A, if σ is strongly inherited by τ in A, we have an HTSP-algebra B such that $\sigma^B = \tau^A$, and $t^B = t^A$ for every $t \neq \sigma$ and $t \in$HTSP, by compatibly adapting each meta-method into τ in A.* ∎

In the previous properties, for typed specification HTSP of σ and HTSP1 of τ with $\tau \rightsquigarrow \sigma$, HTSP-algebras B are constructed from HTSP1-algebras A.

Now we consider another way of obtaining an HTSP-algebra from an HTSP1-algebra. Assume that HTSP=(S,Σ,E) and HTSP1=(S1,Σ1,E1). Then HTSP1 is a consistent and complete extension of HTSP in the conventional sense, with the inclusion morphism h: $S \rightarrow S1$ by $h(t) = t$, for each $t \in$S, and $h(\alpha) = \alpha$ for any operation symbol. Thus there is a *forgetful functor* from Alg(HTSP1) to Alg(HTSP). For the signature morphism h above, we have $h(\sigma) = \sigma$ and $h(\alpha) = \alpha$ for each meta-method type α. What we are interested in is a modified mapping h by $h(\sigma) = \tau$ and $h(t) = t$, for each $t \in S$, $t \neq \sigma$ and t is not a meta-method type, and furthermore $h(t)$ a meta-method type for τ compatible with t for any meta-method type t. For each operation $\alpha : t_1 \times \ldots \times t_q \rightarrow t$, $h(\alpha)$ is of type $h(t_1) \times \ldots \times h(t_q) \rightarrow h(t)$, if α is not a meta-method for σ. This new mapping h is not necessarily a signature morphism in the conventional sense, since it does not preserve the meta-methods. We will call it an *inheritance morphism*. This, though, is an interesting mapping for revealing the inheritance relations between Alg(HTSP1) and Alg(HTSP).

Let $K^{\sigma}_{in} = \{k'_1 : s_1, \ldots, k'_q : s_q\}$ and $K^{\tau}_{in} = \{k'_1 : s_1, \ldots, k'_q : s_q, k'_{q+1} : s_{q+1}, \ldots k'_p : s_p\}$, and h be the modified mapping above. Given an HTSP1-algebra A we construct an HTSP-algebra B as follows. For each sort t in HTSP, $t^B = t^A$, if $t \neq \sigma$ and t is not a meta-method sort for σ. For the sort σ, σ^B is obtained from τ^A in the following way: For each $a \in \tau^A$, $a = (k'_1 : b_1, \ldots, k'_q : b_q, \ldots, k'_p : b_p, *, \ldots, *)$, denote $F(a) = (k'_1 : b_1, \ldots, k'_q : b_q, *, \ldots, *)$. Then $\sigma^B = \{F(a) \mid a \in \tau^A\}$. That is, each $F(a)$ is obtained from a by deleting the components $k_{q+1} : b_{q+1}, \ldots, k_p : b_p$. Then

Theorem 2.4 *Let HTSP, HTSP1, and h be defined as above. For any HTSP1-algebra A, if σ is strongly inherited by τ, then there is an HTSP-algebra B such that $\sigma^B = F(\tau^A)$, and for each $t \in S$, $t \neq \sigma$ and t is not a meta-method type for σ, $t^B = t^A$.* ▮

3 Implementation of Object Types

In this section we briefly discuss the notion of implementation. We utilize existing notions of implementation in the literature[4, 12, 22] and integrate the concepts of object orientation.

Let HTSP and SPEC=(S, Σ, E) be the typed specifications of σ and τ, respectively. The basic idea of implementing σ by τ (or HTSP by SPEC) is to use the features in SPEC to describe those in HTSP. In some cases several sorts, $s_1, \ldots, s_p$, in SPEC are used to describe one sort t in HTSP, and we denote the sequence by $< s_1, \ldots, s_p >$ and call it a *joint sort*. This is essentially a product type. Two or more attributes, $k_1, \ldots, k_p$, in SPEC can be used to describe one attribute k in HTSP, and we denote this sequence by $< k_1, \ldots, k_p >$ and call it a *joint attribute*. Moreover, methods are needed for manipulating these joint attributes. We will call these methods *compound methods*. A compound method involves one or more existing methods in SPEC and consists of a sequence of terms $(t_1, t_2, \ldots, t_u)$ of appropriate types from $T_{\Sigma}(X)$. This is an ordered sequence. With the introduction of a joint sort $s =< s_1, \ldots, s_p >$, a method whose argument types include all the types in s can be rewritten by substituting s for the occurrences of $s_1, \ldots, s_p$.

A joint sort or a joint attribute exists only functionally, that is, it is not a component in a class. A joint sort (attribute) means that several existing sorts (attributes) will be involved for a single action by a (compound) method. In contrast, a compound method is a component of the derived object type.

To implement HTSP by SPEC, we follow the three basic stages, namely, *synthesis*, *restriction*, and *identification* in [12], and use an implementation morphism in a similar manner to [22]. We need a way of obtaining a meta-method for τ from a meta-method α in σ at the syntactical level by adding all the additional component types to the argument types. For a meta-method $\alpha : s_1 \times \ldots \times s_q \rightarrow \sigma$ and additional components $k'_j : t_j$, $1 \leq j \leq p$, for EnSP, we get $\beta : s_1 \times \ldots \times s_q \times t_1 \times \ldots \times t_p \rightarrow \tau$ such that for each existing instance component $k_i : s_i$, we have an axiom $k_i(\beta(x_1, \ldots, x_q, y_1, \ldots, y_p)) = u_i$ if $k_i(\alpha(x_1, \ldots, x_q)) = u_i$ is an existing axiom in SPEC. We call β a *compatible extension* of α.

An *enrichment* EnSP of SPEC is obtained in the following steps: First, adding some additional attributes of existing types (other than σ), then, add some compound methods, after that, add the compatible extensions of meta-methods, and finally, add some compound meta-methods. For an enrichment EnSP of SPEC, there is a mapping h which sends σ to τ, a meta-method in σ to its compatible extension, and leaves any other sort unchanged. h is called the *inclusion morphism*.

In the second stage, EnSP is restricted to EnSP_{impl} by deleting the methods which are not used in simulation. Formally, we introduce the notion of implementation morphisms. An *implementation morphism* from HTSP$=(S, \Sigma, E)$ of σ to EnSP$=(S1, \Sigma1, E1)$ of τ is an injective mapping *impl* from Σ to $\Sigma1$ such that $impl(\sigma) = \tau$; and for any operation symbol $\alpha : s_1 \times \ldots \times s_q \rightarrow s$, if α is a meta-method for σ, then $impl(\alpha)$ is of the form $impl(s_1) \times \ldots \times impl(s_q) \times t_1 \times \ldots \times t_p \rightarrow \tau$, otherwise, $impl(\alpha)$ is of type $impl(s_1) \times \ldots \times impl(s_q) \rightarrow impl(s)$. EnSP_{impl} contains all the attributes in EnSP and the methods that are images under *impl*. The implementation morphism *impl* maps a sort of HTSP to a sort or to a joint sort in EnSP, an attribute to an attribute or a joint attribute, and a method to a method or a compound method.

Finally, in the last stage, representatives are selected from a given EnSP_{impl}-algebra A using a congruence, to simulate an HTSP-algebra. To do so we need the notion of a *congruence* on a given EnSP_{impl}-algebra B, which is defined on an equivalence relation on B. There is, however, a specialty here in that the equivalence relation is induced by an implementation morphism *impl* from HTSP to EnSP_{impl}, and so we call it an *implementation equivalence relation*, denoted by $\equiv_{impl}$, or simply $\equiv$. Let τ_1 be the central sort in EnSP_{impl}. An implementation equivalence relation $\equiv$ on B is a partition on each carrier s^B such that: For an operation α in HTSP of type $s_1 \times \ldots \times s_q \rightarrow s$, and $b_i, d_i \in impl(s_i)^B$, $b_i \equiv d_i$, if α is not a meta-method, then $impl(\alpha)(b_1, \ldots, b_q) \equiv impl(\alpha)(d_1, \ldots, d_q)$; and if α is a meta-method with $impl(\alpha)$ being of type $impl(s_1) \times \ldots \times impl(s_q) \times t_1 \times \ldots \times t_p \rightarrow \tau_1$, then $impl(\alpha)(b_1, \ldots, b_q, c_1, \ldots, c_p) \equiv impl(\alpha)(d_1, \ldots, d_q, c'_1, \ldots, c'_p)$ for any $c_j, c'_j \in t_j^B$, $1 \leq j \leq p$. The poset containing an element b will be denoted by $\bar{b}$.

For typed specifications HTSP, HTSP1 and HTSP2, if h:HTSP$\rightarrow$HTSP1 and g:HTSP1$\rightarrow$HTSP2 are implementation morphisms then so is $g \circ h$: HTSP$\rightarrow$ HTSP2. Here, for $h(t) = \langle t_1, \ldots, t_m \rangle$ with $g(t_i) = \langle t_{i,1}, \ldots, t_{i,p_i} \rangle$, $g \circ h(t) = \langle t_{1,1}, \ldots, t_{1,p_1}, \ldots, t_{m,1}, \ldots, t_{m,p_m} \rangle$.

Definition 3.1 An *implementation* of HTSP=(Σ, E) of σ *on* SPEC is given by an enriched specification EnSP of SPEC and an implementation morphism *impl* from HTSP to EnSP, denoted by (HTSP, *impl*, EnSP, SPEC). A *model* M of the implementation (HTSP,*impl*,EnSP,SPEC) is quadruple $(A, impl^M, B, \equiv_{impl})$ consisting of an HTSP-algebra A, an EnSP_{impl}-algebra B and an injective homomorphism $impl^M$ from A to a congruence $B/\equiv_{impl}$ of B. □

The definition of an implementation is a partial one in the sense that we do not require that every HTSP-algebra can be represented by an EnSP_{impl}-algebra. If EnSP=SPEC in (HTSP, *impl*, EnSP, SPEC), we say that HTSP is implemented *by* SPEC, and denote it by (HTSP, *impl*, SPEC). Generally we say that HTSP is implemented *on* SPEC. We will drop the superscript M from $impl^M$ in the discussion below.

It is natural to define a model of the implementation (HTSP, *impl*, EnSP, SPEC) to be $(A, impl, C, \equiv)$ for an EnSP-algebra C. This can be treated in a similar way[19].

Theorem 3.2 (*Composition of Implementations.*) *Let (HTSP1,*$impl_1$*,EnSP, SPEC) be an implementation and EnHT1 be an enrichment of HTSP1, with* σ_1 *being the central sort in HTSP1. There is an enrichment EnEnSP of EnSP and an implementation (EnHT1,*$impl'_1$*,EnEnSP,SPEC) such that the diagram below commutes on* K^{σ_1}*, i.e., for* $k \in K^{\sigma_1}$, $f_1 \circ impl_1(k) = impl'_1 \circ g(k)$*, where, both* g *and* f_1 *are the inclusion morphisms. Furthermore, if (HTSP,impl,EnHT1, HTSP1) is an implementation, then (HTSP,*$impl'_1 \circ impl$*,EnEnSP,SPEC) is an implementation.* ▮

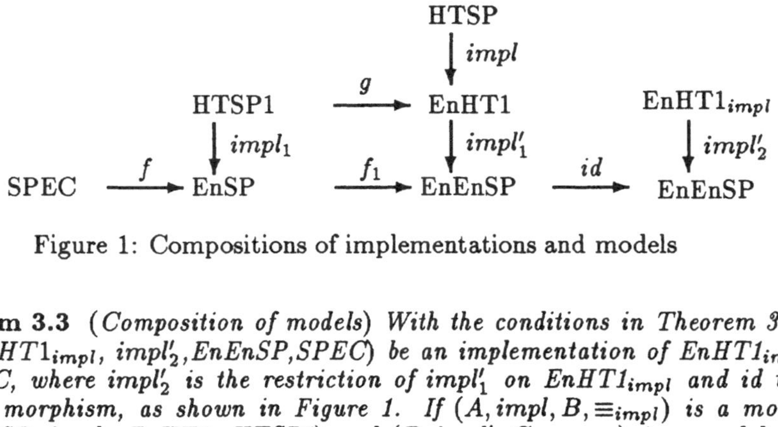

Figure 1: Compositions of implementations and models

Theorem 3.3 (*Composition of models*) *With the conditions in Theorem 3.2. Let (*$EnHT1_{impl}$*,* $impl'_2$*,EnEnSP,SPEC) be an implementation of* $EnHT1_{impl}$ *by SPEC, where* $impl'_2$ *is the restriction of* $impl'_1$ *on* $EnHT1_{impl}$ *and id the identity morphism, as shown in Figure 1. If* $(A, impl, B, \equiv_{impl})$ *is a model for (HTSP, impl, EnHT1, HTSP1) and* $(B, impl'_2, C, \equiv_{impl'_2})$ *is a model for (*$EnHT1_{impl}$*,* $impl'_2$*, SPEC, EnEnSP), then* $(A, impl'_2 \circ impl, C, \equiv_{impl} \circ \equiv_{impl'_2})$ *is a model for (HTSP,* $impl'_2 \circ impl$*, SPEC, EnEnSP), where* $C/(\equiv_{impl} \circ \equiv_{impl'_2}) = (C/\equiv_{impl'_2})/\equiv_{impl}$. ▮

4 Complex Classes and Their Inheritance

In this section we formalize the concept of complex classes based on the framework of implementation.

Definition 4.1 A *complex class* is an implementation CL=(HTSP,*impl*,SPEC) of HTSP by SPEC. A *model* M of a class CL=(HTSP,*impl*,SPEC) is a model (A,*impl*,B,$\equiv_{impl}$) of the implementation. Let σ and ρ be central sorts in HTSP and SPEC_{impl}, respectively. A complex static object of class CL from the model is a triple $(a, impl, b)$ for $a \in \sigma^A$, $b \in \rho^B$ with $impl(a) = \bar{b}$. □

So a (static) complex object $(a, impl, b)$ has an interface object snapshot a, an inner representation object snapshot b, and the implementation morphism *impl*. An interface object snapshot can have many inner representations. These representations form a poset in the congruence. Note that we do not define a (static) object to be $(a, impl, \bar{b})$, since $\bar{b}$ is abstracted from a poset.

Proposition 4.2 *Let CL=(HTSP,impl,SPEC) be a class specification, with σ and ρ being the central sorts of HTSP and SPEC, respectively, M=(A,impl,B,$\equiv$) be a model for the class, and $(a, impl, c)$ be a static object from the model. For any dynamic object b_a of object type σ, there is a dynamic object d_c of ρ, such that $impl(b) = \bar{d}$.* ∎

As a consequence, we call $(b_a, impl, d_c)$ a *dynamic object* of class CL=(HTSP, *impl*,SPEC). b_a is the interface part of the dynamic object and d_c the inner representation. The evolution of the interface part is stepwise associated with that of the inner representation, through the implementation morphism.

Theorem 4.3 (*Compositions of Classes and objects.*) *If (HTSP,impl,HTSP1) and (HTSP1,$impl_1$, SPEC) are two class specifications, then (HTSP,$impl_1 \circ impl$,SPEC) is class specification. For a static object (a,impl,b) of (HTSP,impl, HTSP1) and a static object $(b, impl'_1, b')$ of ($\mathit{HTSP1}_{impl}$, $impl'_1$, SPEC), then $(a,\ impl'_1 \circ impl, b')$ is a static object of (HTSP,$impl_1 \circ impl$,SPEC). Furthermore, if $(c_a, impl, d_b)$ is a dynamic object of class (HTSP,impl,HTSP1) and $(d_b, impl', d'_{b'})$ is a dynamic object of class ($\mathit{HTSP1}_{impl}$,$impl'_1$,SPEC), then $(c_a, impl' \circ impl, d'_{b'})$ is a dynamic object of class (HTSP,$impl_1 \circ impl$,SPEC).* ∎

For typed specification HTSP of σ and HTSP1 of σ_1, with $\sigma_1 \rightsquigarrow \sigma$, implementations of HTSP and HTSP1 can be based on different object types that do not have any connection. The following property motivates a reasonable definition of the inheritance extension of a class.

Theorem 4.4 *Let HTSP and HTSP1 be two typed specifications of σ and σ_1, respectively, with $\sigma_1 \rightsquigarrow \sigma$. If HTSP1 can be implemented on SPEC, then so can HTSP and there are enrichments EnSP and EnSP1 of SPEC, and implementations (HTSP, impl, EnSP) and (HTSP1, $impl_1$, EnSP1), such that the diagram below commutes on K^σ, where h is an inclusion morphism, and g the inheritance morphism.* ∎

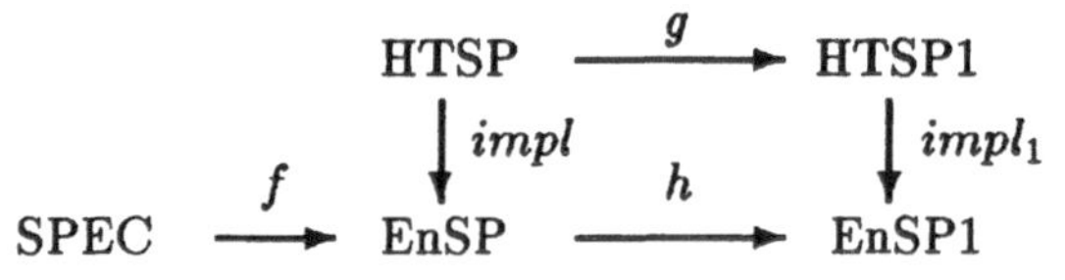

Definition 4.5 Given typed specifications HTSP and HTSP1 of σ and σ_1, with $\sigma_1 \rightsquigarrow \sigma$ and inheritance morphism g, and two classes, CL=(HTSP, *impl*, SPEC) and CL1=(HTSP1, $impl_1$, SPEC1), we say that *CL1 is an inheritance extension of CL* if SPEC1 is an enrichment of SPEC, and if for each component

$k \in K^\sigma$, $h(impl(k)) = impl_1(g(k))$, where h is the inclusion morphism from SPEC to SPEC1. □

This then leads to the interesting correspondence between roles of inheritance and enrichment as shown in the following diagram.

$$\begin{array}{ccc} \text{HTSP} & \xrightarrow{\textit{inheritance extension}} & \text{HTSP1} \\ \downarrow{\scriptstyle impl} & & \downarrow{\scriptstyle impl_1} \\ \text{SPEC} & \xrightarrow{\textit{enrichment}} & \text{SPEC1} \end{array}$$

In what follows we assume that σ and ρ are the central sorts in HTSP and SPEC, respectively, in the class CL=(HTSP, *impl*, SPEC), and σ_1 and ρ_1 are the central sorts in SPEC_{impl} and SPEC1_{impl_1}, respectively, in the class CL1=(HTSP1, $impl_1$, SPEC1).

Proposition 4.6 *Let $(A, impl, B, \equiv)$ be a model of CL1. If ρ_1 strongly inherits ρ in B, with $impl_1(g(\alpha))$ inheriting $impl(\alpha)$ for each meta-method $\alpha \in K^\sigma$, then σ_1 strongly inherits σ in A, with $g(\alpha)$ inheriting α for each meta-method $\alpha \in K^\sigma$.* ▮

Theorem 4.7 *Let the class CL1=(HTSP1,$impl_1$,SPEC1) be an inheritance extension of class CL =(HTSP,impl,SPEC). For a model $M=(A, impl_1, B, \equiv_1)$ of CL1, let $N=(A^*, impl_1^*, B^*, \equiv_1^*)$ be obtained from M by replacing σ^A by $\sigma^A \cup \sigma_1^A$ in A and replacing ρ^B by $\rho^B \cup \rho_1^B$ in B, then N is model of CL1.* ▮

Theorem 4.8 *With the conditions above, let $N=(A^*, impl_1^*, B^*, \equiv_1^*)$ be obtained from M by replacing σ^A by σ_1^A in A and replacing ρ^B by ρ_1^B in B. If ρ is strongly inherited by ρ_1 in B, then N is a model of CL1 by compatibly adapting the meta-methods in A and B, respectively, for σ and ρ.* ▮

These properties are generalizations of those in Theorems 2.2.

5 Concluding Remarks

In this paper an algebraic approach is outlined to the concepts of objects, object types, and classes and inheritance in object oriented programming, with an emphasis on the semantics of incremental inheritance. A more general study of algebraic semantics of inheritance is given in [19], where partial inheritance is allowed and renaming, overriding, and specialization are taken into account, and the notion of compatibility of meta-method is generalized. The study in [19] also considers a syntactical resolution of inheritance and discusses the issue of inheritability of object types.

References

[1] P. America. Designing an object oriented programming language with behavioural subtyping. In *Foundations of Object-Oriented languages*, pages 60–90, 1990. LNCS 489.

[2] P. America. Inheritance and subtyping in a parallel object-oriented language. In *ECOOP'87, European Conference on Object Oriented Programming, Proceedings*, pages 234–242, June 1987. LNCS 276.

[3] E. Astesiano, A. Giovini, G. Reggio, and E. Zucca. An integrated algebraic approach to the specification of data types, processes, and objects. In *Algebraic Methods 1: Theory, Tools and Applications*, pages 91–116, 1989. LNCS 394.

[4] C. Beierle and A. Voß. Implementation specifications. In *Recent Trends in Data Type Specification: 3rd Workshop on Theory and Applications of Abstract Data Types*, pages 39–53, 1985. Informatik-Fachberichte 116.

[5] G. S. Blair. What are object-oriented systems? In G. Blair, et al., *Object-Oriented Languages, Systems and Applications*, chapter 5, pages 108–135, Pitman, London, 1991.

[6] R. Breu. *Algebraic Specification Techniques in Object Oriented Programming Environments*. Springer-Verlag, 1991. LNCS 562.

[7] W. Cook, W. Hill, and P. Canning. Inheritance is not subtyping. In *Proceedings of 17th ACM SIGACT-SIGPLAN Symposium on Principles of Programming Languages(POPL)*, pages 17–19, January 1990.

[8] E. Cusack. Inheritance in object oriented Z. *ECOOP'91, European Conference on Object Oriented Programming, Proceedings*, pages 167–179, 1991. LNCS 512.

[9] T. S. Dillon and P. L. Tan. *Object Oriented Conceptual Modeling*. Prentice-Hall International, 1993.

[10] H. Ehrich, J. A. Goguen, and A. Sernadas. A categorical theory of objects as observed processes. In *Foundations of Object-Oriented Languages*, pages 203–228, 1991. LNCS 489.

[11] H. Ehrich and A. Sernadas. Algebraic implementation of objects over objects. In *Stepwise Refinement of Distributed Systems, Models, Formalism, Correctness*, pages 203–228, 1989. LNCS 430.

[12] H. Ehrig, H. Kreowski, B. Mahr, and P. Padawitz. Algebraic implementation of abstract data types. *TCS*, 20:209–263, 1982.

[13] H. Ganzinger. Order-sorted completion: the many-sorted way. *TCS*, 89(1):3–32, 1991.

[14] J. A. Goguen and J. Meseguer. Order-sorted algebra I: equational deduction for multiple inheritance, overloading, exceptions and partial operations. *TCS*, 105:217–273, 1992.

[15] A. Goldberg and D. Robson. *Smalltalk-80: The Language*. Addison-Wesley, Reading, Mass., 1989.

[16] M. Große-Rhode. Towards object oriented algebraic specifications. In *Recent Trends in Data Type Specification, 7th workshop on specification of ADTs*, pages 98–116, 1991. LNCS 534.

[17] W. Kim. *Introduction to Object Oriented Databases*. MIT Press, Cambridge, Mass., 1990.

[18] X.-M. Lu and T. S. Dillon. An algebraic theory for object oriented systems. 1991. To appear in *IEEE Transactions on Knowledge and Data Engineering*.

[19] X.-M. Lu and T. S. Dillon. An algebraic theory of inheritance in object oriented programming. Technical Report. Dept. of Computer Science and Computer Engineering, La Trobe University.

[20] B. Meyer. *Object Oriented Software Construction*. Prentice-Hall International, 1988.

[21] F. Parisi-Presicce and A. Pierantonio. An algebraic view of inheritance and subtyping in object oriented programming. In *Proceedings of 3rd European Software Engineering Conference, ESEC'91*, pages 364–379, 1991. LNCS 550.

[22] A. Poigné and J. Voss. On the implementation of abstract data types by programming language constructs. *JCSS*, 34:340–376, 1987.

[23] B. Stroustrup. *The C++ Programming Language*. Addison-Wesley, Reading, MA, 1986.

[24] P. Wegner and S. B. Zdonik. Inheritance as an incremental modification mechanism or what like is and isn't like. In *ECOOP'88, European Conference on Object Oriented Programming, Proceedings*, pages 55–77, 1988. LNCS 322.

An Object-Oriented Design for the ACT ONE Environment*

Martin Gogolla
Abt. Datenbanken, TU Braunschweig
D-38023 Braunschweig, Germany

Ingo Claßen
Fachbereich 20, TU Berlin
D-10587 Berlin, Germany

Abstract

The overall aim of this paper is to stabilize and strengthen the algebraic specification method to software engineering and development. We do not introduce new theoretical results, but define a conceptual model, i.e., an information system schema, for the well-established algebraic specification language ACT ONE and its accompanying specification environment.

This paper gives a formal description of suitable database support for an environment supporting the interactive development of ACT ONE specifications. The object-oriented data model of TROLL *light*, a language developed recently within the KorSo project, is used to present the design of such an environment and its dynamic behavior. However, the concepts used are general enough to support other specification and even programming languages as well. Therefore, we feel the design of a conceptual schema for ACT ONE is mainly a case study in employing an object-oriented data model for database support of specification or programming languages. It is therefore a proposal for the consolidation of environments for algebraic specification languages.

1 Introduction

Existing specification systems like ASSPEGIQUE [1], RAP [10], ACT [9, 5], OBJ3 [8] or OBSCURE [13] provide mechanisms to store and retrieve specifications and to operate on them. But in general they employ no systematic approach to information administration. Usually they rely on storage facilities of the underlying programming language and file system. A solution to the information handling problem is the use of information systems or more specific databases. They are already accepted as being important components of software development systems, and, since specification systems can be regarded as parts of general software development systems, the same arguments apply to them.

The use of databases as important parts of specification environments is especially motivated by the following facts: First, the development of algebraic specifications describing software systems of practical relevance usually results in large sets of related specification units. These units arise from the decomposition of complex specifications into smaller pieces by means of the structuring mechanisms provided by specification languages. Additionally algebraic methods and especially specification languages give rise to a bulk of information like proofs, formal transformation steps, formal relations like signature morphisms, etc., which have to be stored to be accessible by various tools. Second, the

*Work reported here has been partially supported by the CEC under Grant No. 6112 (COMPASS) and BMFT under Grant No. 01 IS 203 D (KorSo).

specification task has (or should have) an interactive nature that is characterized by several stages of incompleteness, i.e., stages where certain information is not available. Such stages change during the development process.

These observations lead to the following requirements on the used database technology: The database must be capable to deal with complex (structured) information in a coherent way. This requirement suggests to use object-oriented rather than relational technology. The database must support different degrees of incompleteness and should provide suitable notification mechanisms if the state of incompleteness changes.

This paper gives a formal description of suitable database support for an environment supporting the interactive development of ACT ONE specifications. The object-oriented data model of TROLL *light* [3], a language developed recently within the KorSo project, is used to present the design of such an environment and its dynamic behavior. However, the concepts used are general enough to support other specification and even programming languages as well. Therefore, we feel the design of a conceptual schema for ACT ONE — an overview of the language can be found in [6, 9, 4] — is mainly a case study in employing an object-oriented data model for database support of specification or programming languages. It is therefore a proposal for the consolidation of environments for algebraic specification languages.

2 TROLL *light*

TROLL *light*, a dialect of TROLL [11] and its predecessor OBLOG [14], allows to represent structure and behavior of objects. It is designed to describe the universe of discourse as a system of concurrently existing and interacting objects. Object descriptions are called templates in TROLL *light*. Because of their purely descriptive nature templates may be compared with the notion of class found in object-oriented programming languages. In the context of databases however, classes are also associated with class extensions so that we settled on a fresh designation. Templates show the following structure.

```
TEMPLATE name of the template
  DATA TYPES    data types used in current template
  TEMPLATES     other templates used in current template
  SUBOBJECTS    slots for sub-objects
  ATTRIBUTES    slots for attributes
  EVENTS        event generators
  CONSTRAINTS   restricting conditions on object states
  VALUATION     effect of event occurrences on attributes
  DERIVATION    rules for derived attributes
  INTERACTION   synchronization of events in different objects
  BEHAVIOR      description of object behavior by CSP-like processes
END TEMPLATE
```

We cannot go into the details explaining how TROLL *light* can be translated to the object-oriented database system [12] used in the Braunschweig KorSo project or into the operational semantics of the language [7]. But we will explain the language features of TROLL *light* by means of an example. If we want to specify binary trees then the following template is appropriate for this task.

```
TEMPLATE Node
  DATA TYPES   String, Nat;
  SUBOBJECTS   Children(Name:string):node;
  ATTRIBUTES   Content:nat;
               DERIVED Total:nat;
  EVENTS       BIRTH create;
                     updateContent(Content:nat);
                     createChild(Name:string);
               DEATH destroy;
  CONSTRAINTS CNT(Children)<=2;
  VALUATION    [ updateContent(C) ] Content=C;
  DERIVATION   Total = SUM ( SELECT Total(PRJ2(C))
                             FROM   C IN Children ) + Content;
  INTERACTION SELF.createChild(N) >> Children(N).create;
  BEHAVIOR     PROCESS nodeLife =
                 ( updateContent -> nodeLife |
                   createChild -> nodeLife |
                   { CNT(Children)=0 } destroy -> POSTMORTEM );
               ( create -> updateContent -> nodeLife );
END TEMPLATE
```

The above introduces a template called `Node` and a corresponding object sort `node`. Objects belonging to this template are the nodes of our binary tree.

In the `DATA TYPES` section we have to list which data types are used in the current template. Data types are assumed to be specified in a data specification language.

In the `SUBOBJECTS` section we specify sub-object relationships. A sub-object declaration provides possible sub-object names. Above we have (for each object of sort `node`) an infinite number of such sub-object names, for instance `Children("BlueNode")` and `Children("RedNode")`; however in each state only a finite number of names takes a defined value. Sub-object relationships organize the objects of an object community into a hierarchy. We have decided to use a parameterized sub-object in order to demonstrate this possibility. For the binary tree example a reasonable alternative would be to introduce two non-parameterized sub-objects `left, right:node`.

Observable properties of objects are called attributes and are specified in the `ATTRIBUTES` section. Above we have two non-parameterized, data-valued attributes, namely `Content` and `Total`. But analogously to sub-objects, attributes may have data- and object-valued parameters. We allow attributes to be data- and object-valued and to be multi-valued by means of the predefined type constructors `TUPLE`, `LIST`, `BAG`, `SET`, and `UNION`. Again analogously to sub-objects, only a finite number of attribute names takes a defined value. The difference between sub-objects and attributes is that arbitrary and not only hierarchical relationships may be established by attributes.

Events are specified in the `EVENTS` section of a template. Events represent actions which happen to objects of the current template. In our example nodes can be created and their attribute `Content` can be updated; in nodes children can be created and they can be destroyed. Events can have data- and object-valued parameters.

Integrity constraints restricting the allowed object states, in particular restricting the values which sub-objects and attributes may take, are specified in the CONSTRAINTS section. The above constraint requires that nodes can have at most two children. This is established in the following way. Remember that only a finite number of sub-object names take a defined value. Therefore the term Children can also be viewed as a term of sort SET(TUPLE(string,node)) and in each state this term is evaluated to the finite set of (string,node)-tuples representing the children of the current node. The cardinality of this set is restricted above (CNT stands for count).

The effect of events on (non-derived) attribute is described in the VALUATION section by valuation rules. Such a valuation rule describes that after the occurrence of the event the attribute has the value given by the right-hand side term. Additionally, evaluation rules may have preconditions. The attribute parameters and the right-hand side term as well as the precondition are evaluated in the state before the event occurs. There is a frame rule saying that attributes which are not caught by a suitable valuation rule remain unchanged. Before the birth event, all attributes of an object are assumed to be undefined. Thus if the event in question is a birth event, some attributes may remain undefined.

Derived attributes are marked by the keyword DERIVED in the ATTRIBUTES section of a template. The evaluation of a derived attribute is specified in the DERIVATION section by an equation with the derived attribute as left-hand side and a defining term as the right-hand side. In our example we even have a recursively defined attribute because Total appears on the right-hand side of its defining equation. The inner SELECT term is a (bag-valued) term of our query calculus. In the SELECT expression, Children is used as a term of sort SET(TUPLE(nat,node)). The term describes that we have to sum up the values of the attribute Total of all existing sub-objects of the considered object and have to add the value of the attribute Content.

Communication between objects is specified in the INTERACTION section by event calling. In the general case event calling schemes may have preconditions. Such an event calling scheme expresses the following dependency: Provided the precondition is fulfilled, the occurrence of an event matching the left-hand side causes the simultaneous occurrence of the event on the right-hand side. In our example this means that whenever the event createChild occurs in the super-object the event create occurs in the sub-object. If the object qualifications are missing, we assume that the corresponding event refers to the object for which this interaction is specified. Thus we could have dropped the SELF. part in the interaction rule.

In the BEHAVIOR section admissible life cycles are specified for objects. Life cycles are described by so-called process patterns. Each object has a finite number of possible o-machine states (o for object). For these o-machine states, state transitions caused by event occurrences are specified in the process patterns. Event sequences (for instance create -> updateContent -> nodeLife) as well as event dependent branchings (for instance updateContent -> nodeLife | createChild -> nodeLife) may be described here. Additional preconditions for state transitions allow to forbid event occurrences, i.e., if in a state the precondition for an event is not fulfilled the event is not permitted to occur. Thereby, the admissible life cycles can be restricted further. For example the death event destroy is only allowed to occur if the node in question has no children. Life cycles must start with a birth event and possibly end with a death event. Omitting the BEHAVIOR part allows arbitrary event occurrences after a birth event and before a possible death event.

3 A Design of the ACT ONE Environment

The design of an environment for a specification language like ACT ONE supporting specification development and associated information like specifications, proofs, documentation, etc. in a comprehensive way is a non-trivial task leading to a complex conceptual schema. We focus on some aspects of the design, namely support for the interactive nature of the specification and describe them in TROLL *light*.

To give an indication what is to be modeled let us discuss typical situations of specification development with ACT ONE in an interactive environment. First of all such a development is characterized by the fact that we have certain states of incompleteness. It is, e.g., desirable to simply store the text (provided by some editor) of a type or a parameter without doing any checking. Further steps are to check the context free syntax and the context conditions of the language. A context sensitive check requires, e.g., that all used types are already available.

Second, since a complex specification is a collection of related entities, the modification of one of them may have effects on others. To give an example, if we have a type `NATLIST` which uses types `LIST` and `NAT` and explicitly refers to sort `Nat` and if this name is changed, e.g., to `Number` also the actualization in type `NATLIST` has to be changed. In an batch-oriented environment where the whole specification is checked, this problem is captured by providing appropriate error messages. In an interactive environment a notification mechanism seems to be useful to handle this situation. This means, e.g., that the result of a context sensitive check of a specification unit must be invalidated if imported units have been altered. The following TROLL *light* templates are intended to deal with these situations.

```
TEMPLATE Type
  DATA TYPES   Parser, Analyser;
  TEMPLATES    Schema;
  ATTRIBUTES   Name, Text:string;       UsedList:LIST(string);
               UsingTypes:SET(type);    SyntaxTree:syntree;
               FlatSpec:flatspec;       Super:schema;
               DERIVED IsCfCheckable, UsedTypesAvailable,
                       IsCsCheckable:bool;
  EVENTS       BIRTH create(Name:string,Super:schema,
                            UsingTypes:SET(type));
                     alter(Text:string);
                     cfCheck; mkUsedList; csCheck;
                     invalidate; addUsingType(UsedType:type);
  VALUATION    [ create(N,S,UT) ] Name=N, UsingTypes=UT, Super=S ;
               [ alter(T) ] Text=T, SyntaxTree=BOT, FlatSpec=BOT;
               { DEF(parse(Text)) }
                 [ cfCheck ] SyntaxTree=parse(Text);
               { DEF(SyntaxTree) }
                 [ mkUsedList ] UsedList=getlist(SyntaxTree);
               { DEF(analyse(SyntaxTree)) }
                 [ csCheck ] FlatSpec=analyse(SyntaxTree);
               [ invalidate ] Flatspec=BOT;
               [ addUsingType(T) ] UsingTypes=ADD(UsingTypes,T);
```

```
  DERIVATION  IsCfCheckable = DEF(Text);
              UsedTypesAvailable =
                (LTS(UsedList)=BTS(SELECT PRJ1(T)
                                   FROM   T IN TheTypes(Super)
                                   WHERE  PRJ1(T) IN UsedList));
              IsCsCheckable =
                (UsedTypesAvailable AND DEF(SyntaxTree) AND
                 FORALL N IN LTS(UsedList)
                   DEF(FlatSpec(TheTypes(Super,N))));
  INTERACTION alter(T) >> UsingTypes.invalidate;
              mkUsedList >> Super.triggerUsingType(Name);
  BEHAVIOR    PROCESS typeLife =
                ( alter -> typeLife |
                  { IsCfCheckable } cfCheck ->
                                    mkUsedList -> typeLife |
                  { IsCsCheckable } csCheck -> typeLife |
                  invalidate -> typeLife |
                  addUsingType -> typeLife );
              create -> typeLife;
END TEMPLATE
```

The template **Type** represents structural information of ACT ONE types and introduces the following attributes: **Name**: The name of the type is given by a string. **Text**: Textual representation of the type as provided by some editor. **UsedList**: List of used types represented by a list of names. **UsingTypes**: The types stored in the database that use this type, represented by a set of types. **SyntaxTree**: Syntax tree corresponding to the text of a type as provided by the context free analysis. This is modeled by an appropriate data type **Parser** providing a data sort **syntree** and an operation **parse**. **FlatSpec**: The representation of a type after all structuring mechanisms of the language have been resolved (flattened). This attribute is a result of the context sensitive analysis of a type and modeled by a data type **Analyser** providing a data sort **flatspec** and an operation **analyse**. **Super**: Actually this attribute does not belong to the structural information of an ACT ONE type but is of technical nature as explained below. **IsCfCheckable**: A flag indicating whether the textual representation is available. **UsedTypesAvailable**: A flag indicating whether all used types are actually in the database. **IsCsCheckable**: A flag indicating whether context sensitive analysis is possible.

The possible events and according valuations are (hopefully) more or less self-explanatory. The creation of a new ACT ONE type is triggered by the environment represented in our design by the template **Schema**. Since a type may be used by other types without being available in the database the creation of a new type provides it with a set of using types in the database. How this is realized will be seen when dealing with template **Schema**.

The **DERIVATION** section of template **Type** deals with states of incompleteness. A type is context free checkable if its text is available. All used types are available if for every name in **UsedList** there is an ACT ONE type in the database with this name. Note how this derivation relies on the query calculus provided by TROLL *light*. A type is context sensitive checkable if all used types are in the database and are checked context sensitively and the syntax tree of the type is available.

The `INTERACTION` section deals mainly with the effects of modifications. If the text of a specification is altered, all using types must be notified that their context sensitive check is no longer valid. Note that set-valued events provide a very compact description of this effect. The interaction formula `alter(T) >> UsingTypes.invalidate;` is thereby to be interpreted as follows: If a type performs an `alter` event providing a new text, all using types as given by the set-valued attribute `UsingTypes` must perform an `invalidate` event. The second interaction formula describes the following fact: If the use list of a type is calculated by execution of event `mkUsedList` all types in the database whose name occur in the use list are notified that they are used by this type. The `BEHAVIOR` section finally describes possible sequences of events. After an ACT ONE type has been created it can be altered, checked, etc. Certain events are only possible if appropriate preconditions are satisfied. Now we turn to the template `Schema` providing some kind of frame for interaction in the whole environment.

```
TEMPLATE Schema
  DATA TYPES  String, ...;
  TEMPLATES   Type, ...;
  ...
  SUBOBJECTS  TheTypes(Name:string):type;
  EVENTS      BIRTH createSchema;
                    addType(Name:string);
                    triggerUsingType(Name:string);
  ...
  INTERACTION
    addType(N) >>
      TheTypes(N).create(N,SELF,
                   BTS(SELECT PRJ2(T)
                       FROM   T IN TheTypes
                       WHERE  N IN UsedList(PRJ2(T))));
    triggerUsingType(N) >>
      (SELECT PRJ2(T)
       FROM   T IN TheTypes
       WHERE  Name(PRJ2(T)) IN
              getlist(SyntaxTree(TheTypes(N)))
      ).addUsingType(TheTypes(N));
  ...
END TEMPLATE
```

This template is a result of the *principle of object existence* adopted for TROLL *light* stating that every object can only be discerned as an object by a higher object. In our design this means that we intend only to have one instance of template `Schema`, comprising all ACT ONE types as sub-objects. For this reason the template `Schema` has a parametrized sub-object `TheTypes` where data sort `string` is the type of the parameter. This modeling of sub-objects implies that ACT ONE types must have unique names (according to TROLL *light* conventions).

The template `Schema` is responsible for our notification mechanism by providing appropriate interaction statements. The event `addType` creates a new ACT ONE type by enforcing a `create` event in an object belonging to the template `Type`. The event `triggerUsingType` is forced by the event `mkUsedList` from template `Type` and itself enforces the event `addUsingType`.

4 Conclusion

The main contribution of this paper is a formal description of the dynamic behavior of an environment supporting the interactive development of specifications like this has been done in [2]. Different degrees of incompleteness and an appropriate notification scheme are described. Although the presented TROLL *light* specification captures only some aspects of an envisaged ACT ONE environment, we think that these aspects are quite relevant due to the event driven nature of modern software systems. The description itself exhibits many interesting features of TROLL *light*: Set-valued event calling to model notification, the powerful query calculus to express, e.g., derived attributes, and the interaction section to enforce synchronization between objects. Theses features show the power of TROLL *light* to tackle rather involved situations.

References

[1] M. Bidoit and C. Choppy. ASSPEGIQUE: An Integrated Environment for Algebraic Specifications. In H.Ehrig, C. Floyd, M. Nivat, and J. Thatcher, editors, *Proc. TAPSOFT'85*, pages 246–260. Springer, LNCS 186, 1985.

[2] M. Bidoit, F. Capy, and C. Choppy. The Design and Specification of the ASSPEGIQUE Database. In A. Miola, editor, *Proc. DISCO'90*, pages 205–214. Springer, LNCS 429, 1990.

[3] S. Conrad, M. Gogolla, and R. Herzig. TROLL *light*: A Core Language for Specifying Objects. Informatik-Bericht 92–02, TU Braunschweig, 1992.

[4] I. Claßen. Revised ACT ONE: Categorical constructions for an algebraic specification language. In *Categorical Methods in Computer Science, LNCS 393*, pages 124–141. Springer, 1989.

[5] H. Ehrig, I. Claßen, and D. Wolz. *Algebraic Specification Techniques and Tools for Software Development — The ACT Approach.* AMAST Series in Computing. World Scientific Publishing, 1993.

[6] H. Ehrig, W. Fey, and H. Hansen. ACT ONE: An algebraic specification language with two level of semantics. Technical Report 83/03, TU Berlin, 1983.

[7] M. Gogolla, S. Conrad, and R. Herzig. Sketching Concepts and Computational Model of TROLL *light*. In A. Miola, editor, *DISCO'93*. Springer, Berlin, LNCS, 1993.

[8] J.A. Goguen and T. Winkler. Introducing OBJ3. Research Report SRI-CSL-88-9, SRI International, 1988.

[9] H. Hansen. The ACT-System: Experiences and Future Enhancements. In D.T. Sannella and A. Tarlecki, editors, *Recent Trends in Data Type Specification (WADT'87)*, pages 113–130. Springer, LNCS 332, 1987.

[10] H. Hussmann. Rapid Prototyping for Algebraic Specifications - RAP-System User's Manual. Report MIP 8505, CS Department, Passau University, 1985.

[11] R. Jungclaus, G. Saake, T. Hartmann, and C. Sernadas. Object-Oriented Specification of Information Systems: The TROLL Language. Informatik-Bericht 91–04, Technische Universität Braunschweig, 1991.

[12] C. Lamb, G. Landis, J. Orenstein, and D. Weinreib. The ObjectStore Database System. *Communications of the ACM*, 34(10):50–63, 1991.

[13] J. Loeckx and M. Wolf. The OBSCURE Manual. Technical Report 91/03, Computer Science Department, University of Saabrücken, 1991.

[14] A. Sernadas, C. Sernadas, and H.-D. Ehrich. Object-Oriented Specification of Databases: An Algebraic Approach. In P.M. Stoecker and W. Kent, editors, *Proc. 13th Int. Conf. on Very Large Databases*, pages 107–116. VLDB Endowment Press, Saratoga (CA), 1987.

A Formal Definition of an Abstract Prolog Compiler (Extended Abstract)*

Julio García-Martín   Juan José Moreno-Navarro
Universidad Politécnica de Madrid, LSIIS, Facultad de Informática,
Campus de Montegancedo, Boadilla del Monte, 28660 Madrid, Spain
email: {juliog, jjmoreno}@fi.upm.es.

Abstract
The paper presents an abstract view of the WAM, a Prolog compiler. Optimizations and implementation details are hidden in order to give a description that clearly explains how the WAM implements SLD resolution with a depth search strategy and backtracking. The Abstract WAM is derived by stepwise refinement from SLD resolution. It is formally specified by using abstract data types in an object oriented style.

1 Introduction

In the last few years, the importance of logic programming languages has increased. By logic languages we understand not only Prolog but also several languages that use logical components. The contribution of Warren [13] with the design of an abstract machine points out the possibility of compiling Prolog and getting efficient code. Most current Prolog systems are based on the resulting machine, called the WAM (**W**arren **A**bstract **M**achine).

Even though there are formal descriptions of the WAM ([9, 12] and, specially, [2]) the explanations (e.g. [4, 10], and, best of all [1]) do not seem sufficient to give the reader to a clear view. A new and more clear view must be offered of Prolog compilation, other than a collection of instructions being executed on a memory stack. In this paper we present an abstract view of the WAM using a formal description. By an Abstract WAM we understand a description of the WAM focused on how: a) it implements SLD-resolution with backtracking and b) the main elements of Prolog (unification and backtracking) can be compiled. We are not interested in implementation details and optimizations. The components of the Abstract WAM are described in terms of abstract data types (ADTs) by using an object oriented specification language. This definition forms the middle part of a more ambitious project: the derivation of the Abstract WAM from SLD-resolution by stepwise refinement. Due to the lack of space we do not show the complete formal definition. Likewise, some knowledge about Prolog and the WAM is assumed.

2 Derivation of the WAM

Although it is not the main goal of the paper, the most important points about the derivation of the WAM are given. The derivation is carried out in two ma-

*Work partially supported by the Spanish PRONTIC project TIC93-0737-C02-02

jor stages: the *derivation of the elements of the WAM* and the *optimizations*. The preliminary machine is a stack based description of SLD-resolution solving literals from left to right and using the clauses in textual order. The stack stores resolution steps (called *choice points*) with the current goal, the substitution achieved and the next clause could be used. Now, the program code is used to codify goals, being replaced by argument registers and one program continuation address. Likewise, a program address replaces the next clause.

The next step is the compilation of substitutions. A *heap* allows substitutions to be represented as a set of pairs (variable name, heap address), with the variables bound during the resolution step. Although, the number of variables bound in a step is unknown in advance, it is possible to give names to the local variables of the clause during compilation. The choice point could be responsible for collecting the local variable bindings. Besides this, nonlocal variable bindings are "recorded" in a local trail. Furthermore, if a predicate has only one clause, a full choice point is a waste of memory. It can be simplified in an environment with only local variables and the program continuation label. The and-stack keeps all the environments belonging to a choice point.

We conclude the first stage with the compilation of term representation and unification. Unification is an inherently recursive process, however sequential algorithms are prefered for efficiency. Recursion on unification comes from: i) nested structured term, and ii) the presence of variables that are bound to another term. Source of recursion ii) is hard to handle because it is dynamic, whereas i) is easier to treat because all the information is known at compile time. The (unlimited) chains of nested constructors can be handle by avoiding them and flattening nested terms into simpler ones. A flat term is either a variable, or a constructor applied to variables. Every term can be represented by a set of equations X = *flat term* by using auxiliary variables. Flat terms can be managed by sequential code, so the heap can be traversed sequentially.

Until now, the derivation of the *Abstract WAM* is obtained. The result enhances the abstract behaviour of the WAM without knowing implementation details. As the second major stage, the *optimizations* of the machine are carried out. These operations are performed in the same framework. There are some refinements of the data area, like the use of a global trail, the implementation of the *and-* and the *or-* stacks in a single one and the iterative transformation of the general recursive unification algorithm by using a *push-down list*. The efficient implementation of the data area allows the whole data area to be viewed as a large stack of memory cells with a convenient organization into the memory. The optimization of the compilation and the semantics of the instructions includes: the last call optimization, environment trimming, indexing of clauses, variable classification, initialization "on-the-fly", and the inclussion of specific instructions to handle temporary variables and lists. Finally some others Prolog features, like cuts and built-in predicates are included. As a result of it a formal description of the *real* WAM, as is described in [1], is obtained.

3 Specification of the Abstract WAM

Before more details of the Abstract WAM are given let us discuss the specification language used for the description. At the beginning of the present work, we decided to use an executable language, like OBJ [3]. However, a functional language with ADTs does not seem the most adequate language for the specification of an abstract machine. For these reasons we decided to use an object oriented (O.O.) specification language in the vein of FOOPS [8]. The language allows generic classes to be described and their operations to be specified. Classes are defined either from scratch or from (multiple) inheritance of other class(es) or by instantiation of a generic class. The language uses strong typing, with overloaded mixfix operators. In case of ambiguity, the name of the class is used as a prefix of the operation. The behaviour of the operations is defined by functional axioms. We assume some predefined generic classes: *records* (with automatic field selectors by using the dot notation), *arrays* (with operations to create and modify or consult a given position in the array using the usual notation with square brackets) and, *identifiers* (with operations to create *New_id*, return the *First* identifier and return the *Next* identifier).

We have simplified some O.O. features in order to focus on the specification. Mainly, we use of a very broad notion of visibility: *every object can offer a free view of any of its components.* This facility avoids long chains of selector operations. For instance, we use a generic class *free_record* which provides *records* (as before) but including the operations of every component as operations of the *free_record*. Our language could be easily translated to pure OBJ code.

The following code shows (a part of) the specification of some basic classes used later. Notice the use of the object oriented dot syntax to denote operations. The notation *'object* indicates that it is a self operation of the object. Operations involving at least two objects (as the union of sets) do not use this notation. They correspond to *friend functions* in C++.

```
class set [element] is
   op Insert : 'set * element → 'set
   op Has : 'set * element → bool
   op ∅ : set
   op _∪_ : set * set → set ...
 axioms
   S.Insert(i).Insert(j) = S.Insert(j) if i = j
   S.Insert (i).Has(j) = (i = j) or S.Has(j)
   ¬ ∅.Has (i)
   (S ∪ B).Has(i) = S.Has(i) or B.Has(i)
endclass

class stack [element] is
   op Push : 'stack * element
                              → 'stack
   op Pop : 'stack → 'stack
   op Top : 'stack → element
   op ε : stack
 axioms
   S.Push (e).Pop = S
   S.Push (e).Top = e
endclass
```

Figure 1 shows the complete hierarchical design of the Abstract WAM. In order to describe the formal specification of the WAM we use a top down style of presentation. It helps to understand the decomposition although forces the reader to accept some forward references. Let we start with the WAM state.

```
class wam_state is free_record [da : data_area, wp : wam_prog]
   op Init : Prolog_program → wam_state
   op Failure, Success : 'wam_state → bool
   op semantics : 'wam_state * wam_inst → 'wam_state
   op Transition : 'wam_state → 'wam_state
 axioms
   Init(P).da = New_Rec(Empty, ε, New_Arr(P.#Regs), New_Arr(P.#TRegs))
   Init (P).wp = Compile (P)
   WS.Success = WS.wp.Inst (WS.wp.Consult_P) = stop
   WS.Failure = WS /= Init and WS.da.ost = ε
   WS.Transition = WS                          if WS.Success or WS.Failure
   WS.Transition = WS.semantics(WS.wp.Inst(WS.wp.Consult_P)).Transition
   ...                                         if ¬WS.Success and ¬WS.Failure
endclass
```

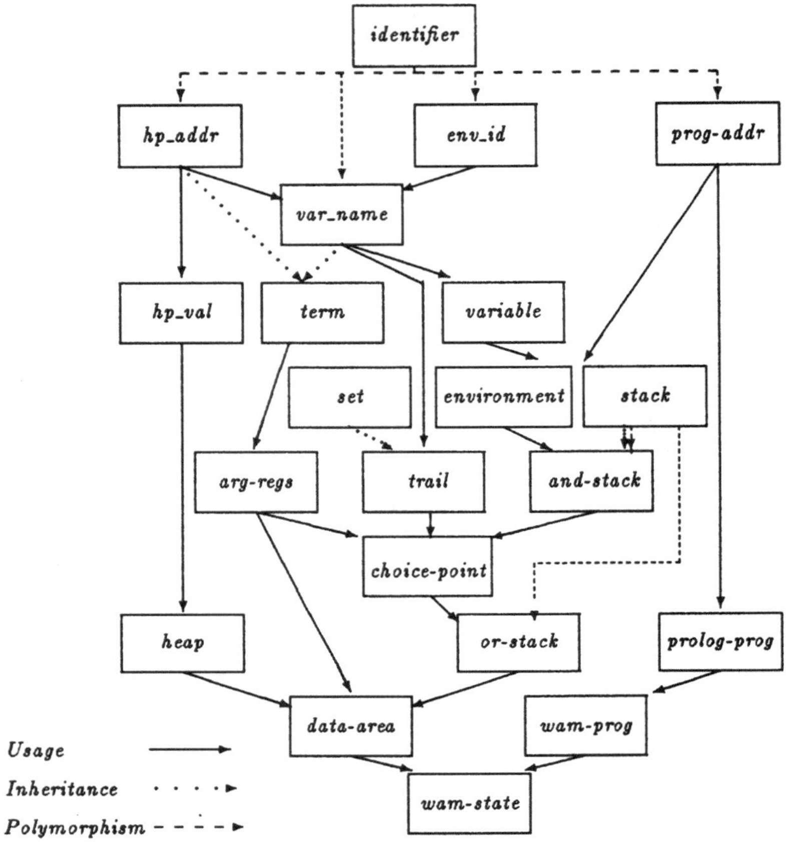

Figure 1: Abstract WAM class structure

A WAM state is formed by the WAM program and the data area. The behaviour of the WAM is directed by the *Transition* operation, which performs the program execution. The instruction pointed by the current program counter is executed (using the semantics function) until a final configuration successful or failing) is reached. *Init.Transition* starts the WAM execution. The semantics function specifies the changes in the data area after executing a given instruction. It is partially defined along sections 5, 6 of this paper.

4 The WAM Program

The WAM program is a collection of label-indexed WAM-instructions. It also contains the program counter, whose value is the label of the current program address (*prog_addr*, an instance of the *identifier* class), and the label of the next alternative. The main operation of the WAM-program is *Compile*. This operation defines the translation function which specifies how Prolog code is compiled into WAM code. The semicolon symbol (;) denotes the composition of programs and it is the obvious concatenation of two programs, relabelling the instructions of the second program. The notation

$$WP = \begin{array}{ll} \text{lb:} & \text{I}_1; \\ \text{lb}_1\text{:} & \text{I}_2 \end{array} \quad \text{is a shorthand for} \quad \begin{array}{l} WP.\text{Inst (First)} = \text{I}_1 \\ WP.\text{Inst (First.Next)} = \text{I}_2 \end{array}$$

with the convention lb = First and lb_1 = First.Next inside I_1, I_2. The specification of the wam_program is shown below.

```
class wam_prog is                                        op Set_P, Set_CP : 'wam_prog
  uses prog_addr, Prolog_prog, wam_inst                        * prog_addr → 'wam_prog
    op Compile : Prolog_prog → wam_prog                  op _;_ : wam_prog * wam_prog
    op Consult_P : 'wam_prog → prog_addr                                    → wam_prog
    op Consult_CP : 'wam_prog → prog_addr                accepts Consult_P      ...
    op Inst : 'wam_prog * prog_addr → wam_inst           endclass
```

The *Compile* operation uses some auxiliary functions. They are typical *private* operations of the wam-program class. *Compile* also assumes a structure in the Prolog program: a Prolog program is a *goal* and a list of *procedures*, one for each predicate in the program; a procedure is a list of *clauses*; a clause is composed of an *atom* (head) and a list of atoms (body) and an atom is a predicate name and a list of *Prolog terms*. The class *const* contains the names of the constructors of a given Prolog program. The class *reg_id* denotes a register, identifying whenever is a temporary or an argument register as well as the number of the corresponding register. Similarly, *Prolog_var* denotes clause or temporary variables. We will use a pattern-like notation to describe auxiliary functions. The first level of the compilation is:

```
Compile(P) =   goaltrans(P.goal) ;
               proctrans(P.proc (p1)) ; ... ; proctrans(P.proc (pn))
```

The compilation of a Prolog program is the compilation of the goal and then the translation of the procedures (clauses for a given predicate). We will present the rest of the compilation of a Prolog program interleaved with the semantic function and the description of the data area.

5 Data Area and Control Components

The data area is a free record containing: the or-stack, argument registers, temporary registers and the heap. The first three components are mainly used for the control of the execution, whereas the last allows term management.

```
class data_area is free_record [hp:heap, ost:or-stack, areg, treg:arg_regs]
  uses term, bool, var_name
    op Occur_Check : 'data_area * var_name * term → bool
    op Unify : 'data_area * term * term → 'data_area * bool
    op Rewind_Trail, Restore_Regs : 'data_area → 'data_area
    op Deref : 'data_area * term → term    ...
endclass
```

The operations of the data area are the operations of each of its fields (notice that it is a free record) plus some auxiliary operations to handle variables (the axioms are not presented). *Unify* is the operation that implements a general unification algorithm using *Occur_Check*. The operation *Deref* accepts a variable as argument and calculates the oldest non-variable term it is bound to. *Rewind_Trail* undoes all the variable bindings recorded into the trail of the last choice-point. *Restore_Regs* restores the argument registers with the values stored into the active choice point.

The argument registers are used for parameter passing during the application of a clause. The temporary registers are used for the new variables needed for the flat representation of terms. Both are simple instances of the class *array* with terms (either a variable name or a heap address) as components.

The or-stack is used to traverse the resolution tree with a depth first strategy. The class *or-stack* is an instance of the class *stack* with choice points as elements, but it accepts operations performed on the top of the stack as own operations. This means, for instance, that the operation *Consult_cp_CP* of the class choice-point (see below) is also an operation of the or-stack. In fact, this feature avoids the explicit definition of the corresponding operation over the or-stack *OS*: *OS.Top.Consult_cp_CP*.

The or-stack contains choice points. Choice points are used to store the information needed for applying any clause to a predicate call. There are several applicable clauses, so this information could be reused several times. The class *choice_point* contains a copy of the argument registers (arguments of the predicate call), the local trail (used to record variable bindings in order to undo them after backtracking), the program address of the next clause (the address of the instruction to be executed in case of failure) and one and-stack into a *free record*. Operations of a choice_point include to set and consult the information of its fields as well as a creation operation.

```
class choice_point is free_record [areg : arg_regs, ast : and-stack,
                                   tr : trail, bp : prog_addr, cp : prog_addr]
   op Create : arg_regs * prog_addr * prog_addr → choice_point
   op Set_Save_Regs : 'choice_point * arg_regs → 'choice_point
   op Consult_Next_Cl, Consult_cp_CP : 'choice_point → prog_addr
   op Set_Next_Cl : 'choice_point * prog_addr → 'choice_point   ...
endclass
```

A trail is a set of variable names. Notice that the implementation of the trail as a stack is, in fact, an optimization detail. We get the and-stack by inheritance from an instantiation of the *stack* with environments as elements. Again, the operations on the Top are accepted as operations of the and-stack. Due to the fact that we have another stack in our specification, the operations of the and-stack are renamed in order to avoid ambiguity. We allow a prefix renaming (with *"andst_"* in this case) of all the operations of a class.

```
class environment is free_record [id : env_id, vars : var_array, cp : prog_addr]
  uses var_name, nat, term
   op Create : nat * prog_addr → 'environment
   op Modify_CP : 'environment * prog_addr → 'environment
   op Mod_Var : 'environment * nat * term → 'environment
   op Consult_Var : 'environment * nat → var_name
   op Consult_env_CP : 'environment → prog_addr   ...
endclass
```

Environments are needed to perform the application of a given clause to a predicate call. For this purpose, an environment contains the program continuation label (beginning of the code of the next predicate call), the variables of the clause, and an identifier (belonging to the class *env_id*, another instance of the *identifier* class), collected into a free-record. Operations of the class *environment* simply consult and store information on its components.

Finally, clause variables are handled in the following way: a *var_array* is a simple array of variables; a *variable* associates a name with its value, which is a term. The class *var_name* is an instance of the class *identifier*. Operations of class variable seem to be clear from the specification. The operation *Older* decides which variable has been created previously. It is needed to make a correct binding in case of the unification of two unbound variables. The newest must point to the old one, because it will be eliminated earlier.

```
class variable is                          op Consult_Value : 'variable → term
  uses var_name, bool, term                op Older : variable * variable → bool
    op Create : var_name → variable        op Set_Value : 'variable * term → 'variable
    op Name : 'variable → var_name         ...
    op Unbound : 'variable → bool        endclass
```

Now we are in the suitable point to define the compilation of clauses and goals, as well as the semantics of instructions related to execution control.

```
goaltrans (G) = clausetrans (:- G) ;          label_{n-1}:     trust_me ;
              . STOP                                          clausetrans (C_n)
proctrans (proc (Pr) = {C}) =                 clausetrans (C = p(t) : - ..., q_i(s_i),...) =
              clausetrans (C)                   allocate (C.#Vars) ;
proctrans (proc (Pr) = {C_1,...,C_n}) =         uniftrans (t) ; ...
              try_me_else (n, label_1) ;        calltrans (s_i, t.var_set ∪ s_1.var_set
              clausetrans (C_1) ;                              ∪ ... ∪ s_i.var_set)) ;
    label_1:  retry_me_else (label_2) ;         call (code_q_i, q_i.arity) ; ...
              clausetrans (C_2) ;  ...          deallocate
```

A procedure with more than one clause needs specific code to handle backtracking: try_me_else, for the first clause, creates a choice point with the address of the next alternative; retry_me_else, for intermediate clauses: the previous choice point is modified with a new alternative address, trust_me, for the last clause: the choice point is no longer needed and is eliminated.

On the other hand, the compilation of a clause needs the following code: an allocate instruction creates a new environment. Some code for unification follows (scheme *uniftrans*). The resultant code for the body is the sum of the code for every atom: First, the actual parameters are stored in the argument registers by the *calltrans* scheme. Then the control is transferred to the code for the predicate atom by using the call instruction. Finally, the environment is eliminated by the deallocate instruction.

```
WS.semantics (call (P)) =                     WS.semantics (try_me_else (L)) =
  WS.Set_CP(WS.Consult_P).Set_P(P)              WS.Push(Create(WS.da.areg,L,
WS.semantics (proceed) =                                        WS.Consult_CP)).Next
  WS.Set_P (WS.Consult_CP).Next               WS.semantics (retry_me_else (L)=
WS.semantics (allocate (n)) =                   WS.Set_CP (WS.Consult_cp_CP).
  WS.andst_Push (Create (n,                       Restore_Regs.andst_MakeEmpty.
    WS.Consult_P)).Next                           Rewind_Trail.Set_Next_Cl (L).Next
WS.semantics (deallocate) =                   WS.semantics (trust_me) =
  WS.Set_CP (WS.Consult_env_CP).                WS.Set_CP (WS.Consult_cp_CP).
    andst_Pop.Next                                Rewind_Trail.Restore_Regs.Pop.Next
```

6 Term Management

The heap is a data structure where flat terms are stored. Basically, a heap is a table which associates a key (a ***heap address***, another instance of the class *identifier*) with (part of) a term: a constant, a constructor or a variable name. A flat term of the form $c(t_1, \ldots, t_n)$ (where t_i is either a variable or a constant) is represented sequentially in the heap, i.e. the constructor name c is stored in a heap-address A, and then the next n heap-addresses contain the representations of $t_1, \ldots, t_n$. Notice that each t_i only needs one heap-address to store its contents. The heap is defined as follows, using heap values as the elements in the table. Both structures are rather complex, but notice that they are responsible for a lot of work.

```
class hp_val is
  uses hp_addr,const,bool,nat,variable
    op Set_Var : hp_addr → hp_val
    op Set_Str : const * nat → hp_val
    op IsConstr : 'hp_val → bool
    op Const : 'hp_val → const * nat
    op IsVar : 'hp_val → bool
    op WhichVar : 'hp_val → variable
  axioms ...
endclass

class heap is
  uses hp_val, hp_addr, variable,
       const, nat, bool, term
    op Empty : 'heap
    op Current_Val : 'heap → hp_val
    op Current_Addr : 'heap → hp_addr
    op Last_Addr : 'heap → hp_addr
    op Next_Term : 'heap → 'heap
    op Read : 'heap → bool
    op Fix_Term : 'heap * hp_addr → 'heap
    op Val : 'heap * hp_addr → 'hp_val
    op Set_New_Var : 'heap → 'heap
    op Set_Cons : 'heap * const * nat → 'heap
    op Set_Ref : 'heap * term → 'heap
    op Mod_Val : 'heap *
                   hp_addr * const → 'heap
    op Bind : 'heap * hp_addr * term → 'heap
  accepts Current_Val
  axioms
    H.Current_Val = H.Val (H.Current_Addr)
    H.Fix_Term (A).Read = true
    H.Set_Cons (c, n).Read = false
    H.Set_Cons (c, n).Last_Addr = New_id
    H.Next_Term.Current_Addr =
                       H.Current_Addr.Next
    H.Set_Cons(c, n).Val(H.Last_Addr) =
                              Set_Str(c, n)
    H.Fix_Term (A).Current_Addr = A    ...
endclass
```

The class ***hp_val*** provides operations to create a heap cell of variable type (*Set_Var*) or of structure type (*Set_Str*), and to consult cell attributes. *Empty* and *Val* are the constructors of the heap. Two pointers are needed: *Last_Addr* is used to add elements to the heap, by means of operations *Set_Cons* and *Set_New_Var*. *Current_Addr* is used to traverse the heap. It is fixed by the *Fix_Term* operation and can be increased by *Next_Term*. *Current_Val*, the heap value located at the current address, simplifies the code for other operations. The *accepts Current_Val* clause allows the operations *IsVar*, *Constr*, etc. to be used freely as operations of the heap. Direct manipulation of a particular heap cell is possible using the instructions *Mod_Val* and *Bind*.

Now, we specify the compilation of the instruction related with the management of terms. We assume that the Prolog program provides flattened terms. A flattened term is represented by a list of equations $A = s$. A is an argument register for the original term or a temporary register for the rest. If $s = c(\bar{t})$, then $\bar{t}$ is represented as a list of variables and constants. A preprocessing step can transform a given term into the corresponding flat representation by adding new temporary variables. For example, the term $c(d(a), b, c(a, Z, d(Z)))$ is replaced by the list $[A = c([X_1, b, X_2]), X_1 = d([a]), X_2 = c([a, Z, X_3]), X_3 = d([Z])]$, where brackets are used to represent lists. For the specification of *calltrans* we have several different cases that are presented in a pattern-rule fashion. Equations $X = s$ are handled by the family of instructions *put*, one for each possible value of *s*. The *put* instructions construct a term into the heap and store the address into the register *A*. The variables and constants inside a structure (i.e. $s = c(\ldots)$) are placed contiguously in the heap by the *set* family of instructions. Notice the difference between *set_variable* for the first appearance of a variable and *set_value* for subsequent appearances. The first needs to create the variable, while the second just consults its value.

```
calltrans ([], V) = % empty code
calltrans ((A = X) :: L, V) =
  put_variable (X, A) ;
  calltrans (L, V.Insert (X))
calltrans ((A = c(t)) :: L, V) =
  put_structure (c, t.arity, A) ;
  settrans (t, V) ;
  calltrans (L, V ∪ t.varset)

settrans (c :: L, V) =
  set_constant (c) ; settrans (L, V)
settrans (X :: L, V) =
  set_variable (X) ;                    if ¬X ∈ V
  settrans (L, V.Insert (X))
settrans (X :: L, V) =
  set_value (X) ; settrans (L, V) if X ∈ V

uniftrans ([], V) = % empty code
uniftrans ((A = X) :: L, V) =
  get_variable (X, A) ;                 if ¬X ∈ V
  uniftrans (L, V.Insert (X))
uniftrans ((A = X) :: L, V) =
  get_value (X, A) ;                    if X ∈ V
  uniftrans (L, V)
uniftrans ((A = c(t)) :: L, V) =
  get_structure (c, t.arity, A) ;
  uniftrans (t, V) ;
  uniftrans (L, V ∪ t.varset)

uniftrans (c :: L, V) =
  unify_constant (c);uniftrans (L, V) ;
uniftrans (X :: L, V) =
  unify_variable (X);                   if ¬X ∈ V
  uniftrans (L, V.Insert (X)) ;
uniftrans (X :: L, V) =
  unify_value(X);uniftrans(L, V)  if X ∈ V
```

The management of the unification part is a bit more complex. Notice that the unification code should behave as a simple check, if the clause and the call have constructors; as a binding of a clause variable, if the clause has an unbound variable, or as a binding to a construction of the clause term into the heap, provided that the variable comes from the call. Warren [13] called the first two situations *read* mode and the last *write* mode. The family of *get* instructions is used to compile equations and the *unify* instruction to compile terms into the equations. As we are using single instructions for each type of term, the operation to distinguish between the *read* mode and the *write* mode must be carried out onto the heap. The heap uses its *Read* mode operation for this purpose. We only present one example of each family of instructions.

```
WS.semantics (put_variable (Y, A)) =
  WS.areg[A.number]
   (WS.Consult_Var (Y.number)).Next
WS.semantics (set_value (Y)) =
  WS.Set_Ref(WS.Consult_Var
   (Y.number)).Next          if Y.InClause
  WS.Set_Ref(WS.treg[Y.number]).Next
                             if Y.Temporary

WS.semantics (get_value (Y, A)) =
  WS.Next
      if WS.Unify (WS.areg[A.number],
           WS.Consult_Var(Y.number))
  WS.Set_P (WS.Consult_Next_Clause)
                          if ¬ WS.Unify (...)
WS.semantics (unify_constant (c)) =
  WS.semantics (set_constant (c))
                          if ¬ WS.Read
  WS.Mod_Val (T, c).Insert (T).Next
                    if WS.Read and T.IsVar
  WS.Set_P (WS.Consult_Next_Clause)
                    if WS.Read and ¬ T.IsVar
                    and WS.Constr(T)/=(c,0)
  WS.Next           if WS.Read and ¬ T.IsVar
                    and WS.Constr(T)/=(c,0)
  where T=WS.Deref(WS.Current_Addr)
```

7 Conclusion

The abstract view of the WAM has been obtained by hiding and postponing implementation details and optimizations. Besides helping in understanding the

WAM, the step by step specification has an additional advantage: the verification of the correctness of the WAM is obtained simply by proving equivalence between every machine and the following. The direct correctness proof presented in [12] is an excellent piece of work but it is rather technical and does not give any hint about why the WAM was designed in the present manner. [2] uses a similar methodology to derive the WAM, including all the optimizations. The authors are more interested in justifying the correctness of the design instead of giving a deduction. [11] completes [9] on the deduction of a Prolog compiler by partial evaluation. It is a very interesting methodology, but they derive a model that differs from the WAM, in which efficient backtracking and data representation lead to some difficulties.

The WAM derivation is also useful to implement new "logic languages" (in a general sense). The WAM has been used as a basis for the implementation of several declarative languages: integration of functional and logic programming, constraint logic programming, logic programming with modules, etc. Now, the designer of a new machine could reuse the design of the WAM, diverging from it in that point of the derivation where the new language differs.

The Abstract WAM is easy to implement and test. Accordingly, we are now employed in the computer visualization of the whole process. Some preliminary prototypes [5, 6] are ready and available from authors on request. In summary, an executable and visualizable formal specification would demonstrate the success of the design decisions taken in the compilation of Prolog and could made them applicable to other logic languages.

References

[1] H. Aït-Kaci: The WAM: A (Real) Tutorial, The MIT Press, 1991

[2] E. Böerger, D. Rosenzweig: The WAM – Definition and Compiler Correctness, Technical Report TR 14/92, Dip. di Informatica, U. di Pisa, Italy, 1992.

[3] K. Futatsugi, J. Goguen, J.P. Jouannaud, J. Meseguer, Principles of OBJ2, Proc. POPL, ACM Press 1985, pp. 52-66.

[4] J. Gabriel, T. Lindholm, E.L. Lusk, R.A. Overbeck: A Tutorial for the WAM for Computational Logic, ANL-64-84, Argonne Nat. Lab., 1985

[5] J. García-Martín, J.J.Moreno-Navarro: Friendly-WAM An Interactive Tool to Understand the Compilation of Prolog, Proc. LPAR 92, LNCS 500, 1992

[6] J. García-Martín, J.J.Moreno-Navarro: Visualization as Debugging: Understanding/Debugging the WAM, AADEBUG'93, LNCS, 1993.

[7] J. García-Martín, J.J.Moreno-Navarro: Formal Specification of an Abstract Prolog Compiler, Technical Report FIM-LSIIS-1993

[8] J. Goguen, J. Meseguer, Extensions and Foundations of Object-Oriented Programming, Sigplan Notices V21, N. 10, October 1986, pp. 153-162.

[9] P. Kursawe: How to Invent a Prolog Machine, New Gen. Comp., 5, 1989.

[10] D. Maier, D.S. Warren: Computing with Logic: Logic Programming with Prolog, Ed. Benjamin Cummings, 1988

[11] U. Nilsson: Towards a Methodology for the Design of Abstract Machines for LP languages, Journal of Logic Programming, vol. 6, n. 1, 1993.

[12] D.M. Russinoff: A Verified Prolog Compiler for the Warren Abstract Machine, J. of Logic Programming, 1992.

[13] D.H.D. Warren: An Abstract Prolog Instruction Set, Tec. Note 309, SRI International, Menlo Park, California, October 1983

Completeness of Equational Definitions over Predefined Algebras

Valentin Antimirov*
Department of Computer Science, University of Copenhagen
DK-2100, Copenhagen, Denmark

Anatoli Degtyarev
Department of Cybernetics, Kiev University
252127, Kiev, Ukraine

Abstract

The notion of equational definitions over predefined algebras (EDPA) was introduced in our previous work in order to provide algebraic semantics for recursive equational definitions of partial functions over given (e.g., built-in) data types. In the present paper we introduce and investigate the safe-completeness and safe-persistency properties of (algebraic presentations of) EDPA. This allow to characterize a class of total equational definitions. We also relate these "safe" properties to the usual ones of many-sorted algebraic specifications and compare EDPA with some other approaches to algebraic specification of partial functions.

1 Introduction and motivation

The notion of *equational definitions over predefined algebras* (EDPA) was introduced in [2] in order to capture two features important for a practical specification framework: predefined structures and partial functions. We concentrated on the following rather typical situation: given a data type D over a signature Σ of predefined functions, a set of new possibly *partial* functions on D is specified by a set R of "recursive equations" of the form

$$f(t_1, \ldots, t_n) = t \tag{1}$$

where $f \in F$ is a name of a new function and $t_1, \ldots, t_n, t$ are terms over the enriched signature $\Sigma + F$.

Despite its simplicity, the construction covers a variety of known particular cases from both computer science and mathematics. To begin with, any partial recursive function can be represented as an equational definition over the algebra of natural numbers on a very restricted signature consisting of the sort **Nat**, the constant zero `0:Nat`, and the successor function `suc_:Nat->Nat`.[1] One can consider first-order functional programs over predefined (built-in or "abstract") data types as a particular class of *functional* EDPA. Algebraic programs in OBJ3 [6] using *built-in sorts*, as well as term-rewriting systems over *built-in algebras* from [3] offer examples of EDPA of a less restrictive form.

For example, consider the following two equational definitions over the algebra **N** of natural numbers with usual operations:

---

*On leave from V.M.Glushkov Institute of Cybernetics, Kiev, Ukraine.

[1] Note that projections are not needed here, for they can easily be *defined* equationally.

```
(a) gcd(0,y) = y;               (b) div(x,x+y+1) = 0 ;
    gcd(x,y) = gcd(y,x);            div(x+y,y) = div(x,y)+1.
    gcd(x+y,y) = gcd(x,y).
```

Here (a) is intended to define the greatest common divisor, a total function on **N**, while (b) is a definition of the partial integer division operation undefined when its second argument is equal to zero.

To give a more substantial example of EDPA, let's mention that it is possible (and actually is not very difficult) to specify an interpretor of a programming language $\mathcal{L}$

```
eval: Prog Data -> Data
```

as an equational definition over the algebra of programs and built-in data types of $\mathcal{L}$. Note that whenever $\mathcal{L}$ is a universal (Turing-complete) language, the function `eval` will be partial; moreover, it can't be extended to a total computable one in this case. Going further, one can specify in the same fashion semantics of a target machine language $\mathcal{L}'$, and a compiler function from $\mathcal{L}$ to $\mathcal{L}'$ and to formulate a question about correctness of the latter. To answer such a question, semantics of EDPA should be equipped with some logic for reasoning about partial functions defined in this way.

In [1, 2] we have started developing *algebraic* semantics of EDPA aimed at the use of equational logic with induction and corresponding term-rewriting techniques for logical reasoning. Our approach is based on the idea to represent an equational definition as a (possibly *non-complete*) enrichment of some algebraic specification SP of the predefined data type D and to extract from the initial model of this enrichment a (possibly partial) interpretation of new function symbols on D. Since different correct specifications of D are possible, the main problem here is to ensure that *any of them determines the same semantics* for a given equational definition over D.[2]

To illustrate the problem, let's consider the following specification of the algebra of natural numbers (we use OBJ-like syntax [6]):

```
spec NAT is
sort Nat
 ops   0  1 : -> Nat .
 op    suc_ : Nat -> Nat .
 ops (_+_) (_-_) : Nat Nat -> Nat .
vars x, y : Nat
eqs
 [e1]  1 = suc 0 .                 [e4]  x - 0 = x .
 [e2]  x + 0 = x .                 [e5]  0 - x = 0 .
 [e3]  x + suc y = suc(x + y).     [e6] (suc x)-(suc y) = x - y .
end
```

One can check that `NAT` is a correct specification of **N** and that the enrichment of `NAT` formed by (b) is *consistent*, i.e. respects the set of ground inequalities valid in **N**. However, as soon as we add one more axiom

```
[e7] (x + y)- y = x
```

to `NAT`, the enrichment becomes inconsistent: it is possible to infer $0 = 1$ using (b) and `[e7]`. The inconsistent enrichment can't provide any reasonable

[2]Otherwise there is no sense to speak about predefined algebras.

interpretation of **div** on $\mathbf{N}$, so the semantics of the EDPA becomes strongly dependent on the choice of axioms for the predefined algebra.

To cope with the problem, we have introduced in [2] a more flexible kind of algebraic presentations with *safe variables* which leads to a so-called *safe* semantics of EDPA . In the present paper we introduce and investigate the *safe-completeness* and *safe-persistency* properties of these algebraic presentations; we also relate these "safe" properties to the corresponding ones of many-sorted algebraic specifications. This in particular will allow us to characterize a class of *total* equational definitions and to demonstrate advantages of our semantics wrt. some other approaches to algebraic specification of partial functions.

In the next section we briefly reproduce the basic definitions and constructions concerning syntax and semantics of EDPA. Then Sect.3 is devoted to the safe/unsafe completeness and persistency, and in Sect.4 we consider related work.

2 Syntax and semantics of EDPA

We use standard notions of algebraic specification [9] and term rewriting theory [4]. In particular, given a set of sorts S, we consider an S-sorted signature Σ, an S-sorted set of variables X, a set of Σ-equations E, algebras of (ground) Σ-terms and their quotients by the least Σ-congruence $=_E$ generated by E (i.e., T_Σ, $T_\Sigma(X)$, $T_\Sigma/_{=_E}$, etc.). Recall that the initial model $I(SP)$ of the algebraic specification $SP = (\Sigma, E)$ is isomorphic to the quotient $T_\Sigma/_{=_E}$.

The S^*-indexed notations for S-indexed sets is used to denote Cartesian products (e.g., $X_w = X_{s1} \times \ldots \times X_{sn}$ where $w = s_1 \ldots s_n$).

2.1 Basic constructions

In what follows, $\mathcal{A}$ denotes a (predefined) Σ_0-algebra over an S-sorted signature Σ_0 and F denotes an S-sorted signature of new function symbols disjoint from Σ_0. Then $\Sigma_0 + F$ is a union of those.

Definition 1 Given an S-sorted signature F and a set R of $\Sigma_0 + F$-rewrite rules (oriented equations) of the form (1) where $f \in F_{w,s}$, $t_1, \ldots, t_n \in T_\Sigma(X)_w$, $t' \in T_\Sigma(X)_s$, the quadruple $(\Sigma_0, \mathcal{A}, F, R)$ (denoted also $(\Sigma_0, F, R)_\mathcal{A}$) is called an *equational definition (of F by R) over $\mathcal{A}$*. This equational definition is called a *functional* one if R is an F-indexed family of rewrite rules of the form (1) where $t_1, \ldots, t_n$ is a list of distinct variables. □

The triple (Σ_0, F, R) forms a syntactic part of the EDPA $(\Sigma_0, F, R)_\mathcal{A}$. To define its semantics means to determine the ***basic interpretation of F on $\mathcal{A}$*** – a set of partial functions

$$F^\mathcal{A} = \{f^\mathcal{A} : \mathcal{A}_w \xrightarrow{\sim} \mathcal{A}_s \mid f \in F_{w,s},\ w \in S^*,\ s \in S\} \tag{2}$$

which should be in a proper logical relation to to the set of equations R.

To do this, we shall use algebraic specifications in a slightly generalized many-sorted language.

2.2 Enrichments with safe variables

Let the set X of all the variables used in axioms contain a distinguished subset X^+ of so-called *safe* variables. Then the variables in $X^- = X \setminus X^+$ are called *unsafe*. We write $E(X^+)$ and $SP(X^+)$ to reflect the fact that some of variables in the set of axioms E of the specification SP belong to X^+.[3]

The presence of safe variables in E does not change the standard algebraic semantics and logic of SP, but it is essential for obtaining a proper semantics of those enrichments of $SP(X^+)$ which are supposed to specify partial functions on the initial model $I(SP)$.

Given such an enrichment $SP'(X^+) = SP(X^+) + (F, R)$, we construct its (standard) model in the following way.

Definition 2 Let $SP'(X^+) = SP(X^+)+(F, R)$ be an enrichment of the equational specification $SP(X^+) = (\Sigma, E(X^+))$. Then

- a $\Sigma + F$-substitution $\theta : X \to T_{\Sigma+F}(X)$ is called *safe* if $\theta(X^+) \subset T_\Sigma(X^+;$
- the *restricted rewrite relation* $\to_{E:R}$ is defined as the following union of two rewrite relations on $T_{\Sigma+F}(X)$

  $$\to_{E:R} \;\rightleftharpoons\; \to_{E:} \cup \to_R$$

  where $\to_R$ is a usual rewrite relation determined by R and $t \to_{E:} t'$ holds if there exists an equation $l = r \in E$, a safe substitution $\theta : X \to T_{\Sigma+F}(X)$ and a position π in t such that $t|_\pi \doteq \theta(l)$ and $t' \doteq t[\theta(r)]_\pi$;
- the *restricted congruence* $=_{E:R}$ on the term algebra $T_{\Sigma+F}(X)$ is the symmetric reflexive transitive closure of the restricted rewrite relation $\to_{E:R}$;
- the quotient $T_{SP'(X^+)} = T_{\Sigma+F}/_{=_{E:R}}$ of the ground term algebra $T_{\Sigma+F}$ is the *standard model* of $SP'(X^+)$.

□

Now the enrichment $SP'(X^+)$ is called

- *safe-consistent* if $t_1 =_{E:R} t_2$ implies $t_1 =_E t_2$ for all ground Σ-terms t_1, t_2;
- *safe-complete* if each congruence class $[t]_{E:R}$ of the quotient $T_{SP'(X^+)}$ contains some Σ-term;
- *safe-persistent* if it is both safe-consistent and safe-complete.

Now we are in a position to describe an appropriate semantics for EDPA.

2.3 Safe semantics of EDPA

Definition 3 Let $SP(X^+) = (\Sigma, E(X^+))$ be an equational specification, called a *base* one, of the algebra $\mathcal{A}$ in the sense that Σ is a finite enrichment of Σ_0 and the Σ_0-reduct of the initial model $I(SP)$ is isomorphic to $\mathcal{A}$. Then the enrichment $SP'(X^+) = SP(X^+) + (F, R)$ is called an *algebraic presentation (with safe variables)* of the EDPA $(\Sigma_0, F, R)_\mathcal{A}$. □

Now the semantics of EDPA is defined in terms of their safe-consistent algebraic presentations.

---

[3]This construction is strongly induced by (and, in fact, is a simplification of) the algebraic specification framework suggested in [5]

Proposition 4 (cf. [2]) If the presentation $SP'(X^+)$ is safe-consistent, then there exists the basic interpretation $F^{I(SP)}$ of F on $I(SP)$ (and so on $\mathcal{A}$) defined as follows for each $f \in F_{w,s}$:

$$f^{I(SP)}(\,[t_1]_E, \dots [t_m]_E) = [\, f(t_1, \dots, t_m)\,]_{E:R} \cap T_\Sigma \tag{3}$$

for all tuples $(t_1, \dots, t_m) \in (T_\Sigma)_w$ provided the right-hand side is not empty, otherwise $f^{I(SP)}$ is undefined on the arguments. The enrichment of $I(SP)$ with $F^{I(SP)}$ forms a partial $(\Sigma + F)$-algebra isomorphic to a subalgebra of $T_{SP'(X^+)}$. □

Since the safe-consistency is an undecidable property in general, the important problem coming from this construction is to characterize a class of base specifications $SP(X^+)$ which provide safe-consistent presentations and algebraic semantics, defined by (3), for any functional EDPA.[4] The following decidable sufficient condition is a generalization of our previous results on this topic (cf. with Theorems 10, 11 in [2]):

Theorem 5 An algebraic presentation $SP(X^+) + (F, R)$ of the functional EDPA $(\Sigma_0, F, R)_\mathcal{A}$ is safe-consistent if each axiom $l = r$ of $SP(X^+)$ satisfies the following *safe non-linearity* condition: any variable occurring non-linear in l or r is safe. □

It is worth noting that presentations of this kind (*with safe non-linearity*) allow to use safely *inductive* equational theorems[5] of SP for reasoning about new functions, because the basic interpretation (3) is consistent with all such equations valid in the predefined algebra $\mathcal{A}$.

Now we turn to the main topic of this paper.

3 Completeness and persistency of EDPA

A *total* equational definition $(\Sigma_0, F, R)_\mathcal{A}$ is supposed to define a total basic interpretation $F^\mathcal{A}$, i.e. one consisting of total functions $f^\mathcal{A}$. Regarding a safe-consistent algebraic presentation $SP'(X^+)$, one can check that the basic interpretation – defined by (3) – is total iff $SP'(X^+)$ is safe-complete (and hence safe-persistent). Combining this with Theorem 5, we obtain the following fact:

Proposition 6 Given a functional EDPA $(\Sigma_0, F, R)_\mathcal{A}$, let $SP(X^+)$ be its base specification satisfying the safe non-linearity condition. Then the presentation $SP'(X^+) = SP(X^+) + (F, R)$ defines the total basic interpretation $F^\mathcal{A}$ iff $SP'(X^+)$ is safe-complete. □

Thus the safe-completeness property is a kind of logical characterization of totalness of functional EDPA.

Note that the possibility to provide a safe-complete presentation for some EDPA strongly depends on the proper usage of unsafe variables in their base specifications. For example, consider the following functional definition over the algebra $\mathbf{N2} = \mathbf{N} \times \mathbf{N}$ of pairs of natural numbers with the pairing and projection functions `<_,_>`, `pr1_`, `pr2_`:

[4] Recall that any functional equational definition can be provided with the well-defined denotational semantics.

[5] Whose non-linear variables are also safe.

```
spec EX1 over N2 is
ops  f,g : Nat -> Nat .
eqs
       f(n) = pr1<n, g(n)> .
       g(n) = pr2<f(n), n> .
end EX1
```

To make this definition total, one needs a base specification of **N2** where the projections are specified as *non-strict* functions by the axioms with unsafe variables:

```
vars x,y : Nat (unsafe)
eqs    pr1<x, y> = x .
       pr2<x, y> = y .
```

If the variable **y** (variable **x**) was declared as safe here, the presentation would fail to define a total basic interpretation for **f** (correspondingly, for **g**).

This is just an illustration of a general fact that the more unsafe variables are used in the base specification $SP(X^+)$, the stronger the restricted congruence $=_{E:R}$ becomes. One can vary the set of safe variables in $SP(X^+)$ to obtain a spectrum of restricted congruences and corresponding basic interpretations $F^{I(SP)}$. Let's consider an extreme case when all the variables become unsafe.

Definition 7 Given a presentation $SP'(X^+) = SP(X^+) + (F, R)$, its ***unsafe version*** is the presentation $SP'(\emptyset) = SP(\emptyset) + (F, R)$ where all the variables $x \in X^+$ are declared as unsafe. □

This unsafe presentation is just a many-sorted enrichment of $SP(\emptyset) = (\Sigma, E)$, so Definition 2 yields for it the usual "unrestricted" or "unsafe" notions of the least congruence $=_{E+R}$, standard initial model, consistency, completeness, and persistency.

We have the following facts relating these safe/unsafe properties.

Theorem 8 For any algebraic presentation $SP'(X^+)$ the following implications hold:

1. If $SP'(X^+)$ is safe-complete, then $SP'(\emptyset)$ is complete.
2. If $SP'(\emptyset)$ is consistent, then $SP'(X^+)$ is safe-consistent.
3. If $SP'(X^+)$ is safe-persistent, then $SP'(\emptyset)$ is persistent and defines the same (total) basic interpretation.

□

For the particular case of functional EDPA this gives the following corollary:

Corollary 9 Let $SP(X^+)$ be a specification with safe non-linearity. Then safe-completeness of an algebraic presentation $SP'(X^+) = SP(X^+) + (F, R)$ of a functional EDPA implies persistency of the unsafe version $SP'(\emptyset)$. □

The converse however is not true:

Proposition 10 There exist a functional EDPA and its safe-consistent presentation $SP'(X^+)$ such that the latter is not safe-complete, but its unsafe version is persistent.

Proof: Consider the base specification **NAT1** obtained as the following enrichment of the specification **NAT** from the introduction:

```
spec NAT1 is NAT +
  eq x - x = 0 .
end NAT1
```

Then the following functional definition

```
op f : Nat -> Nat) .
eq f(y) = f(0) - f(0).
```

is a persistent enrichment of **NAT1**, but becomes not safe-complete when the non-liner variable **x** in **NAT1** is declared as safe. □

This means that sometimes the safe non-linearity requirement is still too strong and gives rise to a partial basic interpretation when it could be total – if some of non-linear variables were made unsafe. However, the following proposition demonstrates the opposite effect:

Proposition 11 There exists a functional EDPA with a safe-consistent and not safe-complete presentation $SP'(X^+)$ such that the unsafe version $SP'(\emptyset)$ is complete and inconsistent (so can't provide any basic interpretation).
Proof: The needed example can be obtained as follows. The base specification is the following enrichment of **NAT** from Sect. 1:

```
spec NAT2 is NAT +
  op h: Nat Nat Nat -> Nat
  eq [e7] (x + y)- y = x .
  eq [e8] h(x, y, 0) = x .
  eq [e9] h(x, y, suc z) = y .
end NAT2
```

Then the equational definition (b) of the function **div** considered in the introduction is a safe-consistent (and not safe-complete) enrichment of **NAT2** with safe variable **y**, but it becomes an inconsistent and complete enrichment of the unsafe version of **NAT2**. (Recall that the equation $0 = 1$ can be inferred using [e7]; then the last two axioms should be used to infer from this the equation **x = y** which obviously implies completeness of the enrichment).□

To put another words, *junk can be the reason of confusion* – if one doesn't protect somehow base axioms from it. The results of this paper show that the safe non-linearity condition is sufficient to provide such a protection for functional EDPA, but is not always necessary and sometimes leads to non-total basic interpretations. The new notions introduced here allow to formulate the "upper bound" of possible weakening of the condition: it should make any presentation $SP'(X^+)$ safe-persistent whenever its unsafe version $SP'(\emptyset)$ is persistent.

4 Related work and discussion

Concerning algebraic specification of partial functions, much work have been done and many different approaches have been proposed (cf. [9] for a survey). Let us consider only two of these which are most relevant to our work.

A simple and elegant idea to relate partial algebras to the total ones was presented in [7]. However, it was implemented within the framework of usual many-sorted enrichments which are in our terms completely unsafe algebraic presentations (with $X^+ = \emptyset$). As we have demonstrated in the introduction and in Prop.11, this may give rise to inconsistency when a base specification includes equational axioms with non-linear variables. The construction we have presented in Prop.4 is an improvement of the approach from [7] through the use of safe variables in such "unsafe" cases.

Stratified specifications were introduced in [8] in order to cope with the inconsistency of non-complete enrichments. In our terms a stratified specification is essentially a "completely protected" algebraic presentation $SP(X^+)$ with $X^- = \emptyset$ (i.e., without unsafe variables). This is just another extreme case which allow to capture only predefined algebras with *strict* operations and gives rise to the problems with completeness pointed out in Prop.10. Note that even the standard conditional function, if-then-else, is normally used as a non-strict one, and so can't be specified within this approach.

Concerning predefined data types, the *algebraic specifications with built-in algebras* [3] are very similar to EDPA. However, their semantics was defined in a different way – using the "completely protected" base specifications consisting of *all* equations valid in the predefined algebra. The absence of unsafe variables here can somehow be compensated due to the use of *conditional* equations defining new functions – thus one doesn't need the non-strict conditionals in the signature. But it is still impossible to incorporate some other non-strict operations into the predefined part (e.g., projections).

Our results suggest the way to improve the last two approaches by relaxing the restrictions on the use of unsafe variables in the known "safe" cases.

References

[1] V. Antimirov and A. Degtyarev. Consistency of equational enrichments. In A. Voronkov, editor, *Logic Programming and Automated Reasoning. International Conference LPAR '92*, volume 624 of *Lecture Notes in Computer Science*. Springer-Verlag, 1992.

[2] V. Antimirov and A. Degtyarev. Semantics and consistency of equational definitions over predefined algebras. In M. Rusinowitch and J.L.Rémy, editors, *Conditional Term Rewriting Systems, Third International Workshop, CTRS-92, Proceedings*, volume 656 of *Lecture Notes in Computer Science*. Springer-Verlag, 1993.

[3] J. Avenhaus and K. Becker. Conditional rewriting modulo a built-in algebra. Technical Report SR-92-11, SEKI, 1992.

[4] N. Dershowitz and J.-P. Jouannaud. Rewrite systems. In J. van Leeuwen, A. Meyer, M. Nivat, M. Paterson, and D. Perrin, editors, *Handbook of Theoretical Computer Science*, volume B. Elsevier Science Publishers, Amsterdam; and MIT Press, 1990.

[5] M. Gogolla, K. Drosten, U. Lipeck, and H.-D. Ehrich. Algebraic and operational semantics of specifications allowing exceptions and errors. *Theoretical Computer Science*, 34:289–313, 1984.

[6] J. A. Goguen and T. Winkler. Introducing OBJ3. Technical Report SRI-CSL-88-9, Computer Science Lab., SRI International, 1988.

[7] H.-J. Kreowski. Partial algebras flow from algebraic specifications. In *ICALP'87, Proc. Int. Coll. on Automata, Languages, and Programming, Karlsruhe*, number 267 in Lecture Notes in Computer Science, pages 521–530. Springer-Verlag, 1987.

[8] G. Smolka, W. Nutt, J. A. Goguen, and J. Meseguer. Order-sorted equational computation. In *Proc. Colloq. on Resolution of Equations in Algebraic Structures, Austin*. Academic Press, 1989.

[9] M. Wirsing. Algebraic specification. In J. van Leeuwen, A. Meyer, M. Nivat, M. Paterson, and D. Perrin, editors, *Handbook of Theoretical Computer Science*, volume B, chapter 13. Elsevier Science Publishers, Amsterdam; and MIT Press, 1990.

An Algebraic Approach to Modeling in Software Engineering

George J. Loegel*
C. V. Ravishankar
Electrical Engineering and Computer Science Department
University of Michigan
Ann Arbor, Michigan USA

1 Universal Algebras, Modeling and Software Engineering

Our work couples the formalism of universal algebras with the engineering techniques of mathematical modeling to develop a new approach to the software engineering process. Our purpose in using this combination is twofold. First, abstract data types and their specification using universal algebras can be considered a common point between the practical requirements of software engineering and the formal specification of software systems[4]. Second, mathematical modeling principles provide us with a means for effectively analyzing real-world systems. We first use modeling techniques to analyze a system and then represent the analysis using universal algebras. The rest of the software engineering process exploits properties of universal algebras that preserve the structure of our original model.

This paper describes our software engineering process and our experience using it on both research and commercial systems.

We need a new approach because current software engineering practices often deliver software that is difficult to develop and maintain. Formal software engineering approaches use universal algebras to describe "computer science" objects like abstract data types, but in practice software errors are often caused because "real-world" objects are improperly modeled. There is a large *semantic gap* between the customer's objects and abstract data types. In contrast, mathematical modeling uses engineering techniques to construct valid models for real-world systems, but these models are often implemented in an *ad hoc* manner. A combination of the best features of both approaches would enable software engineering to formally specify and develop software systems that better model real systems. Software engineering, like mathematical modeling, should concern itself first and foremost with understanding a real system and its behavior under given circumstances, and then with expressing this knowledge in an executable form.

*Current Address: Superconducting Super Collider Laboratory, 2550 Beckleymeade Avenue, Dallas, TX 75237 USA email:loegel@sscvx1.ssc.gov

2 Mathematical Modeling, Formal Models and Software Development

We use the idea of a *model* in both the system modeling sense of Zeigler[12] and Casti[1] and in the foundational sense of Schoenfield[10]. Models in the sense of Zeigler and Casti represent information about the behavior of a system, whereas a formal model demonstrates the existence of a mathematical structure that behaves the same as a formal system. We use equational specifications of universal algebras as the formal notation for our model. Figure 3 shows part of an equational algebraic specification.

Zeigler defines five domains in modeling: the *real system*, the *experimental frame*, the *base model*, the *lumped model*, and the *computer*. The real system represents the product the customer wants, the experimental frame defines the specific behavior the customer wants, the base model contains *all* of the information about the real system, the lumped model represents a simplification of the base model under the constraints of the experimental frame, and the computer provides a means of simulating the system's behavior.

We observe that a successful software engineering project must produce a lumped model that duplicates the behavior of the real system with respect to the customer's experimental frame. One way the mathematical modeler produces valid models is by constructing the model from components similar to those in the real system. Zeigler calls a model that duplicates both the behavior and constituent parts of the real system *structurally valid*.

Not all behaviorally valid models are structurally valid. This is particularly true of models built with software. The real world has physical laws which cannot be violated, whereas the software world is artificially created by the human mind, where only the laws of logic apply. However, software models which respect physical structure and physical laws have several advantages. First, maintaining the structure in the analysis and design of software shortens the semantic gap between the user and the system. Second, incorporating new behavior into the system becomes a matter of identifying the correspondence between components in the real system and the components in the software system. Third, testing the software system can be along the lines of the real system. A software system built using some arcane behavioral model only complicates these activities.

We use equations and domains to specify a structurally valid model of a system. This kind of specification defines an *initial algebra*. Maintaining structural validity between two algebras (models) is equivalent to defining a homomorphism between models. We define the software engineering process as the development of an executable, structurally valid model from an initial algebra that represents an equationally specified model of a system.

3 From Modeling to Algebraic Engineering

We take a pragmatic view of the goal of software engineering as providing a *product* for a *customer*. Software engineering provides methods and techniques to deal with the complexities of software development.

The model building process captures the traditional stages in the software engineering process: analysis, design, implementation, integration, and maintenance. In the *analysis phase*, the user provides an informal description of the system and the software engineer converts the description into a set of formal requirements. Similarly, a modeler starts with an informal description of a real system and identifies the components, observables and interactions present in the experimental frame. This information defines the behavior for the model.

We start our process with the customer's informal description of the product. The informal description is in terms of the behavior and functionality that the customer wants. The software engineer analyzes the customer's description of the components and their behavior in the experimental frame, and generates an *analysis model*. This yields a *signature* for the proposed system, and the behavior of the system in the experimental frame defines a basic set of *axioms* for interpreting the functions. In our approach, the software engineer uses a universal algebra to represent this information in the analysis model. The signature defines the domains used in the algebra, and the axioms define the equivalences between terms. The signature and axioms define an *initial algebra* that formally describes the functional behavior of the system. The software engineer then verifies the analysis model with the customer after describing the components, domains, and functions in the initial algebra. The names used for these entities should be derived from the customer's original description. For example `CreateNewAccount` would be better understood by the customer than `AddRowToDatabase`. Figure 3 shows a signature for a document storage system. Once the customer is satisfied with the analysis model, the design stage begins.

The *design stage* represents the same activity for both a software engineer and a system modeler. In modeling, the design phase identifies the important components of the real-world system and simplifies the behavior of these components without compromising model validity. Similarly, for software engineering, we use techniques that maintain structural validity with respect to the base model. Poor quality software results from simplifications that affect validity. Our method provides a better means of identifying what kinds of simplifications make sense during the design phase. We only permit simplifications that maintain structural validity. Since components and functions embody the structure of a system, we require that the process producing a lumped model define a homomorphism from the original model. That is, all of the objects and functions in our analysis model still exist in the design model, but the design model may contain new components and functions to realize a particular behavior. The design model does not destroy the structural validity of the analysis model. Structural validity encourages both *encapsulation* and *inheritance* during the design stage. New components and functions should be associated with a particular component from the analysis model. New components that appear to be shared by higher-level components need to be further analyzed. They may simply represent multiple instances of the same component or they may indicate an oversimplification. In the latter case, there should be a means of specializing each object from a more general component. There are two parts to the design phase. First, the designer (modelers or software engineer) selects a set of *abstract states*[1] to represent information carried by the system, and then develops a particular representation for the states and components of the lumped model. For an algebraic model, design represents a *refinement* of the initial algebra which introduces *hidden functions*[11] and sorts representing the states and their transition functions. Hidden functions permit finite representations for algebraic models that cannot otherwise be finitely represented.

After selecting abstract states and hidden functions, the design phase further refines the analysis model by selecting the concrete data structures and algorithms. Preserving structural validity requires that the refinement map components into components and functions into functions.

The algebraic model is used indirectly in implementation, integration and maintenance, which are the remaining stages of the software process. The implementation phase translates the data structures and algorithms into statements in a programming language. The number of components and functions in the model converted to software modules can be used to measure progress. After implementation, the product and the model both undergo verification; the algebraic model can be used to isolate discrepancies between program behavior and the desired model behavior. Finally, the maintenance stage must permit the adding of new behaviors to the system. An algebraic model can help here in locating which components are affected by a change.

Our work exploits the methods and techniques of mathematical modeling and the structure of algebraic systems to define a new approach to the software engineering process. The software engineer encodes the desired behavior into a structurally valid model of the system under analysis and then homomorphically transforms the resulting universal algebra into a product. Our use of modeling techniques avoids software engineering methods that can abstract away constraints imposed by the real system. Our powerful human ability to abstract within logical systems like programming languages tempts us to abstract away all details. This tendency is particularly evident when the software engineer is unfamiliar with the customer's domain. The discipline of modeling uses validity to help select the important components and interactions in a system. The refinement of universal initial algebras shows what kind of homomorphisms maintain structural validity.

4 Case Studies

We have used this algebraic approach in several systems. The first, described in the 1984 POPL[7], used an algebraic description of attribute grammars to generate Pcode from Pascal. Our goal in this project was to duplicate the Pascal-to-Pcode compiler from ETH Zurich[8] using an attribute grammar system developed by L. Paulson[9]. In Paulson's system, the components were the productions in the Pascal grammar, and the attribute propagation rules served as axioms. Each attribute belonged to a particular sort, and each constructor function belonged to the signature.

Treating the grammar and propagation rules as a formal specification of a Pascal-to-Pcode translator, we improved on the ETH system in several ways. First, we produced a more compact and understandable description of the Pascal-to-Pcode translation than the corresponding compiler from ETH Zurich. Second, the modular construction made integration easier because we could test a single production for the proper behavior. The modular independence also allowed us to add some local optimizations that were not present in the original compiler. Figure 1 shows a **DOMAIN** definition and a typical production rule. The ↓ and ↑ notation represents inherited and synthesized attributes, respectively.

Our success with the modularization and notation in the Pcode system led

```
DOMAIN
TYPE = scalarType [ SIZE × RANGE × SCALAR-ID]
    + realType [SIZE] + arrayType[SIZE × TYPE × TYPE] + ...
RULE
command ⟨↓ env, ↓ cmdEnv, ↑ cmdEnv2, ↑ pcode⟩ =
    ''case'' expression⟨↓ env, ↓ cmdEnv, ↓ caseVal,
      ↑ model, ↑ cmdEnv1, ↑ pcode⟩ ''of''
   caseList⟨↓ env, ↓ cmdEnv0, ↓ type1, ↓ label, ↓ minmax, ↓ jumpTable,
      ↑ minmax2, ↑ jumpTable2, ↑ cmdEnv2, ↑ pcode2⟩
pcode2 = ''UJP'', arg1
        label1:
       "CHKI", arg3, arg4
       "LDCI", arg3
       "XJMP", arg2
        label2:
```

Figure 1: Pcode Specification

to further use and refinement of our method. A second system, the Capture Storage Element (CSE) of the Optical Digital Image Storage System (ODISS)[1] took further advantage of our approach. In this system, our development of an algebraic model led us to a better implementation which proved valuable during the subsequent phases of the project.

ODISS is a distributed document image storage system consisting of scanners, printers, workstations, optical disks, and intermediate storage subsystems. ODISS was developed by Systems Development Corporation to digitize and store Civil War documents for the National Archives and Records Administration (NARA) of the United States of America. Hooton describes the system from an archivist's point of view in his OIS paper[5].

The original design for ODISS used DeMarco's[2] Data Flow Diagrams (DFDs). The CSE provided intermediate storage for documents before they were written to optical disk. Every other component of ODISS accessed the CSE. After getting the high-level DFDs for the CSE, our team used algebraic modeling for the detailed design. We started by identifying the objects in the system. From the DFDs shown in Figure 2, it appeared that the CSE was a page-oriented device, since the basic unit of data manipulation was a page.

However, when we developed the first algebraic model for the CSE from Figure 2, where each data flow defines a command, we noticed that all the commands had a *document* as an argument.

We decided, based on this analysis, that the algebraic model for the CSE should use *documents* composed of *pages*, as shown in Figure 3. Every other subsystem in ODISS followed the DFDs more closely and simply used *pages*. The different approaches resulted from using a simple, behavioral design based on the DFDs, and a model-based design based on our algebraic description. We justified our model by recognizing that the manual system was *document-based* because all requests were for documents. No one ever requested a single page. Similarly, ODISS workers would work with entire documents throughout the

[1]This work performed under NARA contract NA00A86ASSEB285

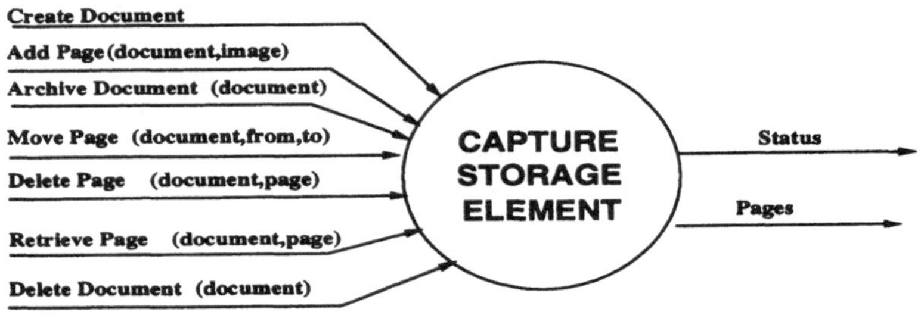

Figure 2: CSE Data Flow Diagram

DOMAIN
DOCUMENT = document-id × num-pages × images
SIGNATURE
`createDocument()` → document-id
`addPageToDocument(number,image)` → document′
`movePageInDocument(from,to)` → document′
`retrievePageFromDocument(number)` → image
`archiveDocument(document-id)` → images
RULE
`addPageToDocument(number,image)` =
  if `number` ≤ numpages+2 then `insertImage()`
    else `return fail`

Figure 3: CSE Model Specification

indexing, quality control and storage process. The basic work unit for both the manual system and ODISS further justified our model choice.

The customer also provided us with an experimental frame that allowed us to make simplifications in the design model. For example, 80% of the documents would be twenty pages or less, so we designed a page descriptor that would fit at least twenty descriptors into a single sector of storage. The mathematical modeler would call this kind of lumping *coarsening* since we do not need a "generalized document storage system", but only a storage system for Civil War personnel documents. Further, since most of the document processing (high-speed scanning, indexing, quality control and archiving) involved sequential access to the pages in a document, our concrete data structures made sequential access easy. In fact, our first implementation of the CSE could handle a maximum of thirty-two pages, but this was sufficient for most of the integration phase.

Our model also allowed us to introduce parallelism into the system, since all documents were independent of each other. Parallelism was also necessary to meet the performance requirements of ODISS.

The algebraic description provided the basis for the programmer interface documentation and the implementation. During the fifteen months of development and integration, only one integration error occurred due to misunderstanding of notation, and only one serious error was found after delivery. The

CSE served as a major debugging tool during the integration phase of the project. Every other subsystem performed single page operations making it difficult to determine the overall system state. Only the CSE maintained the state of documents, making it possible to determine what other components had done. After delivery, one of the first enhancements to ODISS requested by the customer was the ability to query document status, and this capability was easily added.

These systems show various applications of algebraic software engineering, all of which started with a model of the application described using a universal algebra. Each of these systems began the software engineering process by using algebraic specifications to represent the design of the system. Our use of modeling techniques to develop structurally valid specifications made it easier to communicate our design to the customer. Further, our models were invariably better models because they were structurally valid.

The work in subsequent phases depended on these descriptions. In the implementation phase, the algebras provided unambiguous communications between programmers, and a simple measure for progress based on the number of functions coded. The use of algebraic specifications also benefited the integration phase, since the models made it easier to identify complete components for test purposes and what *hidden components* could be "stubbed" or ignored for initial integration work. Further, the abstract states identified in the specification could be used to track system behavior during integration. The specification also simplified maintenance work by again providing unambiguous communication, and simplifying the identification of components involved in changing the system's behavior. The algebraic specification provided not only design information, but also made it easier to track progress, perform integration and maintain these systems.

5 Conclusions

In addition to the benefits described in our case histories, our work leads to several other interesting conclusions. First, by emphasizing models based on "real" system objects we encourage the reuse of software. For example, most organizations build specialized products, so specialized software models provide leverage for future systems with similar components. General purpose libraries, such as NIHCL[3] and the GNU C++ Library[6], provide a wider range of applicability, but the components represent very high-level abstractions.

The basic principles of our approach are (1) that the analysis of a systems benefits from developing structurally valid models consisting of components, observables and their interactions, (2) that algebras not only provide a natural way of representing the results of the analysis phase, but can be useful throughout the software engineering process, and (3) that homomorphic transformations of algebraic specifications provide a valuable paradigm for the software engineering process. Our analysis phase produces a structurally valid model containing static information about the system. The design phase homomorphically transforms the analysis specification, defines the hidden components, and determines the data structures and algorithms. The implementation phase builds and tests each component, and the integration phase combines the components. Our method produces a more reliable, flexible and easily maintained product. Further, a product developed using our algebraic modeling approach to software engineering provides the basis for developing abstract models that foster high levels of software reuse.

From a software engineering viewpoint, our method produces a working system at some level of abstraction early, which also allows system integration to start early in a project. We found that in both large and small projects, the software modules were usually short enough so that bugs could be easily identified even after returning to a particular program module after some time. Our approach works in group projects because most of the problems and idiosyncrasies turn up at integration time, and the ability to quickly "rewire" a software module to adapt to circumstances further speeds up the integration process.

Our case studies show how structurally valid models based on universal algebras benefit a wide variety of systems differing both in kind and size. A model-based algebraic approach provides a sound software engineering approach to the problem of designing software systems.

References

[1] Casti, J. *Alternate Realities: Mathematical Models of Nature and Man*, Wiley-Interscience, 1989

[2] De Marco, T. *Structured Analysis and System Specifications*, Yourdon, Inc., 1978

[3] Gorlen, K. E. Orlow, S. M. and Plexico, P. S. *Data Abstraction and Object-Oriented Programming in C++*, John Wiley & Sons, 1990

[4] Gougen, J. A. Thatcher, J. W. Wagner, E. G. and Wright, J. B. "Initial Algebra Semantics and Continuous Algebras", JACM, v. 24, no. 1, pp. 68-95, 1977

[5] Hooton, W. L. "ODISS-optical digital image storage system – the U.S. National Archives' optical digital image project" in Proceedings of the Sixth Annual Conference on Optical Information Systems (OIS International), pp. 171-173, 1989

[6] Lea, D. *User's Guide to the GNU C++ Library*, Free Software Foundation, 1990

[7] Milos, D. Pleban, U. and Loegel, G. "Direct Implementation of compiler specifications, or: The Pascal P-compiler revisited", Conference Record of the 11th Annual ACM SIGPLAN/SIGACT Symposium on Principles of Programming Languages, 1984, pp. 196-207

[8] Nori, K. V., Ammann, U., Jensen, K., Nageli, H. H., Jacobi, C. *The Pascal ⟨P⟩-Compiler : Implementation Notes* (Revised Edition), ETH Zurich, Institut fur Informatik, 1976

[9] Paulson, L. *A Compiler Generator for Semantic Grammars*, Ph.D. dissertation, Stanford University, 1982

[10] Schoenfield, J. R. *Mathematical Logic*, Addison-Wesley, 1967

[11] Thatcher, J. W., Wagner, E. G. and Wright, J. B. "Data Type Specification: Parameterization and the Power of Specification Techniques", ACM TOPLAS, v. 4, no. 4, pp. 711-732, 1982

[12] Zeigler, B. P. *Theory of Modelling and Simulation*, Wiley-Interscience, 1976

Automated Proof of the Correctness of a Compiling Specification

E.A. Scott
Department of Mathematical and Computing Sciences
University of Surrey, England

Since the early work of Cohn [4] in the LCF system, compiler proofs have attracted a lot of attention as test cases for automated theorem provers, see for example [14, 15]. Recently Broy [2] has used the Larch theorem prover (LP) to verify a code generator for a functional language. In our study the source language for the compiler is PL_0 [9], a subset of **OCCAM2**, and the target language, ML_0, is based on the machine language for the transputer [6]. Both languages were developed as part of the ESPRIT ProCos project [1]. Our work differs from earlier studies in that we start with a hand proof of compiler correctness [7] and attempt to use a theorem prover to verify the proof.

The system in which the proof is carried out is an extension, PL_0^+, of PL_0. Properties of the semantics of the source and target languages are defined within this system, as is the formal meaning of compiler correctness. In [7] a compiling specification is given and it is proved that a compiler satisfying this specification must satisfy a formal definition of correctness. In other words, the compiling specification is proved correct. We show that it is possible to give an automated proof of the correctness, and we describe mistakes in the hand proof which have been uncovered by the automation.

As discussed in [12], when automating an existing hand proof the system in which the result is expressed must first be specified in the logic of the theorem prover. We are given some form of specification of the system which we have to translate into an equivalent *theorem prover specification* in the logic of the theorem prover. We can then use the proof techniques that the theorem prover has available to try to prove the result. Thus there are two issues:

(i) Can the system in which the proofs are to be carried out be specified in the logic of the theorem prover?

(ii) Are the proof techniques of the theorem prover able to prove the results?

Here (i) is equivalent to 'can we specify PL_0^+ in the logic of LP?', which itself turned out to be a major project, [12]. In this paper we concentrate on (ii).

In our experience with LP we have found that if a system can be specified in the logic of LP but an original hand proof cannot be reproduced using LP then this is because the original proof contained mistakes. A mistake is *correctable* if there exists a correct proof of the result and *uncorrectable* if the result can not be proved. In the case of correctable mistakes we have been able to find a correct proof using LP. Uncorrectable mistakes can arise in two ways: either a misunderstanding of an implicit assumption led to the mistaken belief that a result should be true, or the original specification does not have the properties that were intended. In the first case once the misunderstanding is identified we have been able to produce revised, provable versions of the results. In the second case the specification is modified to allow the proof of the result. Such modifications usually involve 'tightening up' implicit assumptions.

As a result of this study we found both types of mistake in the original hand proofs. In the case of correctable mistakes the proofs were easily modified. The discovery of uncorrectable mistakes lead to the need to modify both the specification of PL_0^+ and the formal definition of compiler correctness in order for the results to be proved.

This paper is based on a study which is reported in full in [13]. A full description of the LP specifications and the complete LP input required to prove the correctness theorems discussed here can be found there.

Note: Since this study began there have been two revisions of [7], see [8]. As the revisions do not address the issues that we raise, we have chosen to limit this study to the original aim of automating the system given in [7]. We also note that in [11] there is an automated proof of the correctness of a compiling specification for assignment in a smaller PL_0-like language using OBJ3.

1 Introduction

Intuitively, we expect to call a compiler correct if for all programs p, p and its compiled version have the same meaning. However, to give a formal proof we must first formally define the semantics of the source and target languages. In this section we shall give an overview of our approach to language specification and compiler correctness, and a brief introduction to LP.

1.1 The languages PL_0 and ML_0

We use the approach that was developed in [10] and [7]. The basic idea is to begin by defining an extension PL_0^+ of PL_0. A refinement relation, $\sqsubseteq$, is defined on PL_0^+ which captures enough of the semantics of the language to prove the results. The semantics of PL_0 are inherited directly from PL_0^+. A key aspect of this approach is that the necessary properties of the semantics of ML_0 are also *defined* in terms of PL_0^+. There is given a function I from ML_0 to PL_0^+, and the meaning of process m in ML_0 is defined to be the meaning of $I(m)$ in PL_0^+. This allows a direct comparison of the meanings of elements of PL_0 and ML_0. The function I is the composition of the functions *mtrans* and *Interp*.

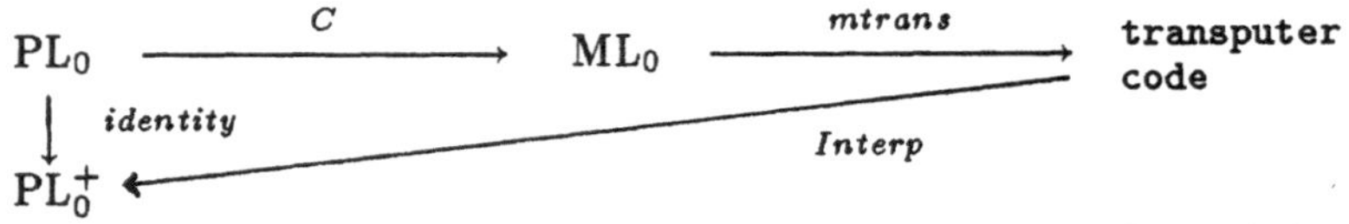

An advantage of the refinement relation approach is that proofs carried out are valid for any language which has the properties described by $\sqsubseteq$. Thus if PL_0, and hence PL_0^+, are later extended to richer languages the proofs discussed in this work will remain valid provided the properties required for the proofs still hold. Thus it is important that all the properties used in the proofs are explicitly stated so that it is clear what must be preserved in future extensions.

The objection to this approach is that the semantics of a machine language cannot be *defined* in this way because there will be a natural semantics given by the induced machine behaviour. In [7] this issue is not addressed, it is assumed that the semantics are defined by PL_0^+. If we were to begin with prescribed semantics for ML_0 it would be necessary to prove the properties which in this work are defined by I, i.e. we would have to prove the correctness of I. This should be possible if the prescribed semantics are sufficiently explicit, for the properties assumed here are all explicitly stated in the LP specification of PL_0^+. An alternative approach is to consider the function I as providing a specification for the target language. Then we have (partial) source language, target language and compiler specifications together with a proof that the compiling specification is correct for all languages satisfying the specifications. As our aim is to automate the proofs given in [7], we take this view.

1.2 Compiler correctness

For a given compiler C we cannot expect to prove that p and $I(C(p))$ are equal. The compiled version of a program will contain identifiers, corresponding to things such as the program pointer and error flag, for which there will be no analogous identifiers in the original program. Thus we consider a PL_0^+ process Q_p that renames the identifiers in $I(C(p))$ and ends the scope of identifiers introduced for machine purposes (see Section 3.1). It is reasonable to assert that $SEQ(Q_p, p)$ has the same meaning as p, where SEQ is process concatenation. We allow that $C(p)$ may be a 'more reliable version' (refinement) of p. Thus we define a compiler C to be correct if, for all PL_0 processes p,

$$SEQ(Q_p, p) \sqsubseteq SEQ(I(C(p)), Q_p).$$

In other words, after renaming certain identifiers and ending the scopes of others the compiled version of p must be a refinement of p.

In [7] there are given sets of conditions $\mathcal{C}_p$ on ML_0 programs, and theorems of the form:

$$\text{If } m \text{ satisfies } \mathcal{C}_p \text{ then } SEQ(Q_p, p) \sqsubseteq SEQ(I(m), Q_p).$$

The theorems show that for a correct compiler C it is sufficient to take $C(p)$ be any sequence of code m which satisfies $\mathcal{C}_p$. Thus the set of all the $\mathcal{C}_p$ forms a compiling specification and the theorems prove that this specification is correct.

1.3 The Larch theorem prover

The Larch Prover is an equational reasoning theorem prover developed at MIT [5]. It is intended primarily as an interactive proof assistant or debugger, and it is in this capacity that we have used it. LP is a theorem prover for a subset of multisorted first-order logic with equality. Equations are asserted by the user then ordered by LP into a rewrite system which can be used to prove other equations. The logic also contains *deduction rules*, statements of the form

When [(FORALL $x_1, \ldots, x_n$)] ⟨hypotheses⟩ Yield ⟨conclusions⟩

where x_i are variables, and where ⟨hypotheses⟩ and ⟨conclusions⟩ are sequences of equations. A specification in the LP logic can be axiomatized with induction rules. The statement

assert *sort* generated by *operators*

ensures that the only elements of *sort* are those that can be constructed using the specified *operators*. While results are ultimately proved by term rewriting, LP supports proofs by induction, cases, and contradiction, and equations can be proved by performing critical pair calculations.

2 The specification of PL_0^+ and ML_0

In this section we give a brief discussion of the specification of the languages PL_0^+ and ML_0. Full details can be found in [12] and [13].

2.1 The specification of PL_0^+

We give the syntax, in BNF fashion, of the part of PL_0^+ which we use:

$$\begin{aligned}
\mathrm{p} &::= \langle x_1, \ldots, x_m \rangle := \langle e_1, \ldots, e_m \rangle \mid \mathrm{SKIP} \mid \mathrm{STOP} \mid \mathrm{ABORT} \mid \mathrm{WHILE(b,p)} \\
&\quad \mid \mathrm{SEQ}(p_1, \ldots, p_m) \mid \mathrm{IF}(b_1 \rightarrow p_1, \ldots, b_m \rightarrow p_m) \mid \mathrm{end}(x_1, \ldots, x_m) \\
\mathrm{e} &::= \mathrm{x} \mid \mathrm{n} \mid e_1 + e_2 \mid e_1 - e_2 \mid e_1 \times e_2 \mid e_1 \div e_2 \\
\mathrm{b} &::= \mathrm{T} \mid F \mid b_1 \wedge b_2 \mid b_1 \vee b_2 \mid \neg b \mid e_1 < e_2 \mid e_1 \leq e_2 \mid e_1 \neq e_2 \mid e_1 = e_2
\end{aligned}$$

Here n is an integer and x is an identifier, a string of letters.

SKIP is the empty process, STOP is a terminated process, and ABORT is thought of as a broken or totally unpredictable process. $\mathrm{SEQ}(p_1, \ldots, p_m)$ is the concatenation of $p_1, \ldots, p_m$, which are carried out in order, and $\mathrm{WHILE}(b, p)$ repeatedly carries out p until b is false, when it becomes SKIP. The intended meaning of an IF construct $\mathrm{IF}(b_1 \rightarrow p_1, \ldots, b_m \rightarrow p_m)$ is that it should behave like p_i, where b_i is true and all b_j to the left are false.

PL_0 is obtained by removing the processes ABORT and $\mathrm{end}(x_1, \ldots, x_m)$ and including only single assignment statements rather than multiple assignments.

A transitive ordering, $\sqsubseteq$, is defined on PL_0^+ which captures enough of the semantics of the language to prove the results. For example we have $\mathrm{ABORT} \sqsubseteq p$ and $\mathrm{SEQ(SKIP}, p) = p$, for all processes p. (Here $p = q$ abbreviates $(p \sqsubseteq q)\&(q \sqsubseteq p)$.) The full list of equations which form the definition of $\sqsubseteq$ can be found in [7], [12] or [13].

2.2 The specification of ML_0

The semantics of ML_0 are given via **transputer code** [6], which consists of lists of address names and contents. Three addresses, A, B, and C, are used as a stack, one, P, is used as a program pointer and one, E, as an error flag. There is a data space, *Dspace*, which contains addresses that can be used to correspond to PL_0 identifiers and can be used by the machine as a work space. We use *IntW* to denote the (finite) set of integers that lie within the scope of the machine. The error flag is activated when processes contain numbers beyond the bounds of the machine, or try to use inaccessible memory locations (those outside *Dspace*). The work space and the storage space for PL_0 identifiers must be kept disjoint from each other. Thus we consider subsets, *Wspace*, of *Dspace* that are used for internal machine calculations. There is a special address, *value*, that is used to store the result of a machine evaluation of a PL_0 expression. For technical reasons involved in the definition of the correctness of expression evaluation we need to have *value* separated from the rest of *Wspace*.

The language ML_0 consists of a set of instructions, some of which take an integer argument from *IntW*. There is a function *mtrans* that take an ML_0 instruction and returns the corresponding transputer code, (see [3] for a full definition and discussion of *mtrans*). The function *Interp* takes a list of addresses (transputer code) and returns a PL_0^+ processes. The images of *Interp* involve a subprocess *mstep* which is thought of as a conditional statement

$\mathrm{IF}(b_1 \rightarrow p_1, \ldots, b_n \rightarrow p_n)$. In order to be able to formally prove the correctness theorems from the specification of PL_0^+ it was necessary to introduce an additional equation specifying the way *mstep* 'absorbs' preceding assignments to the pointer and error flag. This property is not given in [7] but can, with a certain amount of hand waving, be deduced from the specification of *mstep* in [7] as an IF construct.

3 Compiler correctness

3.1 Formal definition of compiler correctness

Associated with any compiler is a family of symbol tables, Ψ say, that associate identifiers in the programming language with addresses in the machine language. We view Ψ as a family of maps, ψ_p, one for each PL_0 process p. Part of the compiling specification is to specify the ψ_p. In fact the only requirement that we have is that the ranges of these functions, $\mathrm{ran}\psi_p$, are disjoint from the workspace *Wspace* and the special addresses A, B, C, P, E and *value* described above.

Let (C, Ψ) be a compiler and associated set of symbol tables. For each PL_0 process p we define a PL_0^+ process restoreψ_p that assigns to each identifier x, in p, the final value held in the address corresponding x once the compiled version of p has been executed. Thus restoreψ_p is a multiple assignment process

$$\langle x_1, \ldots, x_n \rangle := \langle \psi_p(x_1), \ldots, \psi_p(x_n) \rangle,$$

where $x_1, \ldots, x_n$ are the identifiers appearing in p.

The PL_0^+ process end$V$ ends the scope of all identifiers in the set V. For sets U, U' of machine addresses we define

$$\mathrm{MI}(U, U') = U \cup U' \cup \{A, B, C, P, E\}.$$

We shall write $\mathrm{MI}(\psi_p)$ for $\mathrm{MI}(\mathrm{ran}\psi_p,\ \mathit{Wspace})$. Then we have:

Definition of Compiler Correctness (C, Ψ) is said to be *correct* if for all PL_0 processes p, $\mathrm{ran}\psi_p$ is disjoint from $\mathit{Wspace} \cup \{A, B, C, P, E, \mathit{value}\}$ and

$$\begin{array}{l} \mathrm{SEQ}(\mathrm{restore}\psi_p,\ \mathrm{end\ MI}(\psi_p),\ \mathrm{end}(\mathit{value}),\ p) \\ \qquad \sqsubseteq\ \ \mathrm{SEQ}(I(C(p)),\ \mathrm{restore}\psi_p,\ \mathrm{end\ MI}(\psi_p),\ \mathrm{end}(\mathit{value})), \end{array}$$

here $I(C(p)) = \mathit{Interp}(\mathit{srt}(as), \mathit{fsh}(as), as)$, $as = \mathit{mtrans}(C(p))$, and $\mathit{srt}(as)$ and $\mathit{fsh}(as)$ denote the start and finish address, respectively, of the list as.

3.2 The structure of the correctness proof

The proof of correctness is carried out by proving a sequence of theorems. The theorems are actually the base and inductive steps of a proof by structural induction on PL_0 processes. The hypotheses of each theorem are conditions on lists of transputer code. The conclusion of each theorem is that the specification of some program construct is correct. Thus the hypotheses can be seen as a compiling specification and the proofs of the theorems prove that any compiler that satisfies the hypotheses is correct according to the above definition of correctness. As discussed in Section 1.1, in this paper we take the view that

Interp is part of a specification for the target language. Thus we are not concerned with the 'correctness' of *Interp* here.

For the inductive step in the proof we need a stronger form of the induction hypotheses than is provided by the assumption that the compiled version of p is correct with respect to the symbol table ψ_p. We require that the compiled version of p is correct with respect to ψ_q where q is any process that has p as a subprocess. We also need the more general situation in which the compiled code *as* contains the compiled version of p, not just that case when *as* is exactly the code corresponding to p. Thus we define a function *dom* that returns the set of identifiers involved in a process p, and prove that under certain hypotheses on the code *as*,

$$\begin{aligned}&\mathrm{SEQ}(\mathrm{restore}\psi_q,\ \mathrm{end}\ \mathrm{MI}(\psi_q),\ \mathrm{end}(value), p)\\ &\qquad \sqsubseteq\quad \mathrm{SEQ}(Interp(l,k,as),\ \mathrm{restore}\psi_q,\ \mathrm{end}\ \mathrm{MI}(\psi_q,),\ \mathrm{end}(value)),\end{aligned}$$

for all processes q such that $dom(p) \subseteq dom(q)$, (l, k are addresses in *as* with $l \leq k$.) The need for this more general situation does not seem to have been addressed in [7].

Let $\mathrm{Res}(\psi_q) \;=\; (\mathrm{restore}\psi_q, \mathrm{end}(\mathrm{MI}(\psi_q)), \mathrm{end}(value))$.
It will also be useful to denote by $\mathrm{ResEx}(\psi_p)$ the list of processes:

$$\mathrm{ResEx}(\psi_q) \;=\; (value := A,\ \mathrm{restore}\psi_q,\ \mathrm{end}(\mathrm{MI}(\psi_q)).$$

As discussed above, we need to be able to hypothesize that a subprocess of a process has been correctly compiled thus we consider the following predicate

$$CM(p,l,k,as,\psi_q) = \begin{cases}\mathrm{SEQ}(\mathrm{Res}(\psi_q),\ p) \sqsubseteq \mathrm{SEQ}(Interp(l,k,as),\ \mathrm{Res}(\psi_q)), & \\ \qquad\qquad \text{if } l \leq k \text{ and } dom(p) \subseteq dom(q), & \\ true & \text{otherwise.}\end{cases}$$

The correctness theorems each have hypotheses, C_p, which are conditions on the code lying between l and k in *as*, and a conclusion of the form $CM(p,l,k,as,\psi_q) = true$, for all PL_0 processes q. As an example we give the correctness theorem for STOP:

when $\mathrm{inseg}(mtrans(\mathtt{stopp}),m(a,as)) = T,\quad l < k,\quad size(\mathtt{stopp}) = k - l$
yield $CM(\mathrm{STOP},l,k,as,\psi_q) = true.$

It is also necessary to ensure that the evaluation of expressions is carried out correctly in the compiled process. This is part of the conditions C_p for some processes p such as $x := e$, and hence must be proved as part of the overall structural induction argument. The value obtained for an expression is constrained to be stored in the special address *value* and the evaluation must be carried out correctly with respect to any PL_0 process q that contains e. Thus we define the predicate $CE(e,l,k,as,\psi_q)$ to be the result of replacing p by e and *Res* by *ResEx* in the definition of $CM(p,l,k,as,\psi_q)$ above.

We have automated proofs of the correctness theorems for SKIP, STOP, assignment and the operator SEQ, together with the correctness of expression compilation for identifiers, integers and sums of expressions. See [13] for full details. We have not proved all the correctness theorems, they are not all proved in [7], however we have proved a sufficiently wide range to show that all the theorems could be proved by LP if the effort were considered to be worthwhile.

The automated proofs for SKIP, STOP and SEQ are short and involved very little user direction. However, the proofs of the correctness of expression compilation and assignment require a great deal of user interaction and direction. This reflects the fact that there were many implicit assumptions in the original hand proofs which needed to be detailed in the automated versions. The more complicated proofs give rise to more user interaction in the automated version, and more 'handwaving' in the hand version.

4 Summary And Conclusions

As a consequence of the attempt to automate the proofs we discovered both correctable and uncorrectable mistakes. The discovery of uncorrectable mistakes lead to the need to modify both the specification of PL_0^+ and the formal definition of compiler correctness. Modifications to the original specification of PL_0^+ were necessary because there were not enough laws given to prove the theorems. In particular we have had to add extra properties to the specification of identifiers and assignment, and we have had to give a more precise definition of the function *mstep*. This is not a serious problem because the original specification was never intended to be complete. Rather it was just meant to be detailed enough to allow the proofs of the theorems, see [7]. So we merely added the necessary extra laws to the specification. The problems with the definition of *mstep* were correctable errors in the sense defined at the beginning of this paper. Essentially all that was involved was the addition of some assignments which ensured that the proofs followed from the specific laws stated and did not rely on any implicit assumptions.

A more serious problem was that the induction proof given in [7] required predicate $CE(e, l, k, as, \psi_q)$ to be true in case where *Wspace* contained the element *value*. This can never be true for any compiler, and so we needed to specify that *value* lies outside *Wspace* and modify the definitions of correctness. See [13] for further details. This is an example of a mistake where the incorrectness of the result was unnoticed because some assumptions about the original specification were only made implicitly. Once these assumptions were identified we were able to reformulate the definition of correctness so that the result could be proved.

We also found that the theorems in [7] were not sufficient to prove that $C(p)$ would be correct for all p. For example, $C(\mathrm{SEQ}(p,q))$ is proved correct under the assumption that $C(p)$ and $C(q)$ are known to be correct. Thus, when $r = \mathrm{SEQ}(p,q)$, we need

$$\mathrm{SEQ}(Q_r, p) \sqsubseteq \mathrm{SEQ}(I(m), Q_r)$$

to prove that $C(r) = m$ is correct. So we needed to prove stronger theorems:

$$\text{If } m \text{ satisfies } C_p \text{ then } CM(p, l, k, I(m), \psi_q) = true,$$

whereas in [7] the conclusion was just $CM(p, l, k, I(m), \psi_p) = true$. After correcting these and other minor errors, we were able to use LP to produce automated proofs of the specification theorems.

The pragmatic conclusions that can be drawn from this work are that the (modified) compiler specification is correct, and that there already exist automated theorem provers capable of showing this. Furthermore, the compiling specification was developed independently of the automation, so this is a good test of the capabilities of the theorem prover used. However, perhaps the most powerful conclusion to be drawn from this study is the importance of automated theorem provers in the detection of mistakes in implicit aspects of a hand proof. It is in the implicit assumptions of a hand proof that errors most often occur and remain undetected (by human checkers). Automated proofs require implicit aspects to be made explicit thus exposing such errors.

References

[1] D. Bjørner, C.A.R Hoare, J.P Bowen, et. al., A ProCos project description – ESPRIT BRA 3014, Bulletin of EATCS, **39**, pages 60–73, 1989.

[2] M.Broy, Experiences with machine supported software and system specifications and verification using LP, the Larch proof assistant, preprint, 1992.

[3] J.P Bowen, Formal specification of the PROCOS/safemos instruction set, Microprocessors and Microsystems, **14** 10, pages 631–643, 1990.

[4] A.Cohn, Machine assisted proofs of recursion implementation, Ph.D. Thesis, Dept. of Comp. Sci., University of Edinburgh, 1979.

[5] S.J.Garland, J.V.Guttag, An overview of LP, the Larch Prover, Proc. 3rd International Conf. Rewriting Techniques and Applications, ed N. Dershowitz, LNCS **355** pages 137–151, Springer–Verlag, 1989.

[6] INMOS Ltd, Transputer instruction set: a compiler writers guide, Prentice-Hall, 1988.

[7] He Jifeng, P. Pandya, J. Bowen, Compiling specification for ProCos level 0 language, 1990. Procos Technical Report [OU HJF 4].

[8] He Jifeng, J. Bowen, Compiling specification for ProCos language PL_0^R, 1991. Procos Technical Report [OU HJF 6].

[9] H.H. Løvengreen, K.M. Jensen, Definition of the ProCoS programming language level 0, 1989. Procos Technical Report [ID/DTH HHl 2].

[10] A.W. Roscoe, C.A.R. Hoare, The laws of occam programming, Theoretical Computer Science **60**, pages 177–229, 1988

[11] A. Sampaio, A comparative study of theorem provers: proving correctness of compiling specifications, Oxford University PRG Tech. Report PRG–TR–20–90, 1990.

[12] E.A. Scott, K.J.Norrie, A study of PL_0^+ using the Larch Prover, First International Workshop on Larch, Dedham 1992, eds U.Martin, J.Wing, Springer-Verlag Workshops in Computing Series, 1993, 227–245.

[13] E.A. Scott, An automated proof of the correctness of a compiling specification, University of Surrey Technical Report CS–93–01, 1993.

[14] D. Weber–Wulff, Proof movie, Proving the Add–Assign Compiler with the Boyer–Moore Prover, to appear in Formal Aspects Of Computing.

[15] W.D.Young, A mechanically verified code generator, Journal of Automated Reasoning, **5**, 1989

System Demonstrations

RELVIEW – A Computer System for the Manipulation of Relations

Rudolf Berghammer, Gunther Schmidt
Fakultät für Informatik, Universität der Bundeswehr München
Werner–Heisenberg–Weg 39, D–85577 Neubiberg, Germany

People working with relations very often use a greater or smaller example and manipulate it with pencil and paper in order to prove or disprove some property. For supporting such a task by machine, the RELVIEW system ([3]) has been constructed at the Bundeswehr-University Munich.

RELVIEW is a totally interactive and completely video-oriented computer system for the manipulation of concrete relations which are considered as Boolean matrices. Its screen is divided into two parts. The left part is the drawing-window; here matrices can be drawn and manipulated using a mouse. The right part contains the command buttons and the scrollbars. The scrollbars can be used for showing a part of a relation the size of which exceeds the maximal window size. Also textual input and output is requested and shown, respectively, in this part.

One relation, the so-called working copy, is displayed on the screen for editing. A whole collection of relations can be kept in the working memory during a working session. Such a collection may also be saved on permanent memory, e.g., on a hard disk. If a stored relation from the memory is displayed into the drawing-window for editing, a duplicate working copy is created. Editing with the mouse does only affect the working copy and thus does not change the original. To overwrite the original by the working copy, a specific RELVIEW command has to be used.

Execution of system commands is possible by clicking on command buttons. If a command requires arguments, then execution starts not before the last argument is given. Thus, if the user inadvertently has chosen a wrong button, undo consists in choosing the correct button – provided the argument input has not been finished. Besides some management commands, first, the system provides commands implementing the basic operations on relations. Furthermore, we have commands for residuals, quotients, and closures, for certain tests on relations, and commands which implement the operations important in relation-algebraic domain description (compare [4, 6]). And, finally, RELVIEW allows the user to define and apply its own functionals on relations, where in the case of a unary functional with identical domain and range also repeated application is possible. A useful fact in applications is that the latter command can be used to compute fixpoints of monotone functionals.

A detailed description of how to draw on the drawing-window, how to use the scrollbars, and how to execute a command is given in [1, 2]. The first report also presents some implementation details, e.g., the internal representation of relations, and outlines fast algorithms for computing products, symmetric quotients, and residuals of relations. In the second report, also an example for prototyping using RELVIEW is presented, viz. the computation of the cut completion of a partially ordered set.

In the meantime, a lot of other studies have been performed with the RELVIEW system including further graph- and order-theoretic questions resp. algorithms, DAG-languages, domain constructions, relational specifications, and relational semantics. Of course, computation with RELVIEW is limited in space and time. The limit, however, depends heavily on the type of problem handled.

Let us close with a few remarks on further developments of RELVIEW. It turns out that the system is a good tool for the interactive manipulation of relations. However, experience has shown that for some tasks certain additional features will be very helpful. A main improvement is possible in the layout. The present Boolean matrix visualization of relations is well-suited for many tasks, in particular, if the intention is to get insight into an "abstract" relational problem. However, if the system is used to solve concrete problems on graphs or related structures by relational methods, then it seems better to visualize homogeneous relations as directed graphs. Therefore, for the future we plan the incorporation of commands realizing a transition between Boolean matrices and graphs. Especially, it should be possible to edit a relation as a graph. For a visualization of results, furthermore, the user should be given the option to display a relation on the screen as a directed graph and to emphasize a specific subset of the nodes described by a vector.

Besides this main extension, we plan also some minor extensions of the system. E.g., we are concerned with interfaces to other systems. The ability for producing scientific papers on relations which mix text and drawings of Boolean matrices and graphs, respectively, can be obtained by interfacing the RELVIEW system with some typesetting systems. Furthermore, an interface to the relational formula manipulation system and proof checker RALF (also developed at Bundeswehr-University Munich [5]) is planned.

References

[1] Abold-Thalmann H., Berghammer R., Schmidt G.: Manipulation of concrete relations: The RELVIEW-system. Report Nr. 8905, Fakultät für Informatik, Universität der Bundeswehr München (1989)

[2] Berghammer R.: Computing the cut completion of a partially ordered set – An example for the use of the RELVIEW-system. Report Nr. 9205, Fakultät für Informatik, Universität der Bundeswehr München (1992)

[3] Berghammer, R., Schmidt, G.: The RELVIEW-system. In: Choffrut C., Jantzen M. (eds.): Proc. STACS '91, LNCS 480, Springer, 535–536 (1991)

[4] Berghammer R., Schmidt G., Zierer H.: Symmetric quotients and domain constructions. Inform. Proc. Letters 33, 3, 163–168 (1989/90)

[5] Brethauer R.: Ein Formelmanipulationssystem zur computergestützten Beweisführung in der Relationenalgebra. Diplomarbeit, Fakultät für Informatik, Universität der Bundeswehr München (1991)

[6] Zierer H.: Relation algebraic domain constructions. Theoret. Comput. Sci. 87, 163–188 (1991)

RALF – A Relation-Algebraic Formula Manipulation System and Proof Checker

Claudia Hattensperger, Rudolf Berghammer, Gunther Schmidt
Fakultät für Informatik, Universität der Bundeswehr München
Werner–Heisenberg–Weg 39, D–85577 Neubiberg, Germany

In the last years, relational calculus of Tarski and his co-workers has widely been used by computer scientists who view it as a convenient formalism for describing fundamental concepts of programming languages. Among other things, this was motivated by the simple component-free and "linear" nature of the relational formulae and terms which allows formal and often very concise manipulations. As has been demonstrated in a lot of articles, this makes programs and their properties more handy for theoretical investigations e.g., concerning proofs of transformation rules or verification rules.

Relation algebra is based on a small set of axioms, see [3] for example. Hence, a supporting (of course not an automatic) computer system can easily be implemented and manipulations can even be checked with computer assistance.

During the last years, such a relation-algebraic formula manipulation system and proof checker, called RALF, has been developed at our group; compare [2]. The RALF system is a multi-user system, written in the C programming language, and its graphical interface has been developed under OpenWindows 3.0. RALF is a completely video-oriented system. Its screen is divided into three parts. The top panel contains the command buttons and the theorem the user wants to prove together with its name. Below at the right side, RALF writes down the proof steps. The main part of the window is a canvas in which the theorem will be depicted as a tree.

The syntax of theorems being entered is "hypotheses => assertion". Here, the hypotheses are a list of formulae and the assertion is a singleton formula. Formulae are built up over the usual language of relations enriched by some additional (predefined resp. user-defined) functions and predicates using the propositional connectives and quantifiers. An example for a simple theorem is (cf. [3])

```
det(R)  =>  Q.(R&S)=Q.R&Q.S,
```

where the predicate "`det`" tests a relation for being deterministic, "`&`" is the meet operation, and "." is the composition operation. The necessary definition of the predicate "`det`" should have been entered after clicking the button `DEFINITION` as

```
det(R) :<-> R^T.R<I,
```

where `R^T` means the converse relation of `R` and "<" is the relation inclusion. You can get a detailed description of the RALF syntax if you select the buttons `Syntax` or `Grammar` from the menu `ADMINISTRATION`.

In RALF, formulae and theorems are presented in tree form, so complex expressions are easy to read. To transform a subtree, you mark it by clicking the left mouse button over its root. The selected part will be inverted. Upon clicking the right mouse button, RALF shows you all the transformations of this expression RALF could perform according to the present state of rules in the catalog. RALF can apply all the theorems the superuser entered as such and the proven theorems of the user currently working with RALF which have no hypotheses (see below). You can choose one of them by selecting it and clicking **`Transform`**. After each transformation, RALF examines whether the proof is finished, i.e., whether RALF recognizes the expression as true or false.

Also, the user has the possibility to introduce so-called metarules like the modus ponens or the chain rule. One main application of metarules is to split a proof. In the example above, you can divide the proof into two parts:

```
(1) det(R) => Q.(R&S)<Q.R&S.R
(2) det(R) => Q.(R&S)>Q.R&S.R.
```

After having proved the first part, RALF will ask the user to continue with the second. In particular, metarules are helpful in coping with large trees.

The theorem and its proof can be saved, regardless of whether the proof is finished or not. Thus, you are able to load a theorem with unfinished proof and continue proving it. Theorem and proof are saved as potentially human-readable ASCII files.

As already noted above, RALF is a multiuser system. Users are authorized by a password mechanism and there is a superuser having special rights, like defining theorems, metarules and definitions that may be used by everyone. So all users have common theorems and definitions in addition to their own ones to work with. A detailed description of RALF (including a user's manual and some implementation details) can be found in [2].

Finally, some remarks on further developments of RALF: At the moment it is capable of full propositional calculus but only parts of predicate calculus on the metalevel of handling relational calculus. For the future we plan extensions towards full predicate calculus. In addition, we envisage RALF being able to examine the application of a theorem with hypotheses. Then, it will be the task of the user to prove, whether the hypotheses of the theorem are satisfied. Besides, the possibility of printing proofs in typical mathematical manner is planned. And, finally, we are concerned with an interface to RELVIEW, a computer system for the manipulation of relations and also developed at Bundeswehr-University Munich (cf. [1]).

References

[1] Berghammer, R., Schmidt, G.: The RELVIEW-system. In: Choffrut C., Jantzen M. (eds.): Proc. STACS '91, LNCS 480, Springer, 535–536 (1991)

[2] Brethauer R.: Ein Formelmanipulationssystem zur computergestützten Beweisführung in der Relationenalgebra. Diplomarbeit, Fakultät für Informatik, Universität der Bundeswehr München (1991)

[3] Schmidt G., Ströhlein T.: Relationen und Graphen. Reihe Mathematik für Informatiker, Springer (1989); English version: Relations and graphs. Discrete Mathematics for Computer Scientists, EATCS Monographs on Theoret. Comput. Sci., Springer (1993)

Towards an Integrated Environment for Concurrent programs Development

Naïma BROWN
Dominique Méry
CRIN-CNRS & INRIA-Lorraine, BP239
54506 Vandœuvre-lès-Nancy, France email: brown@loria.fr, mery@loria.fr

The methodology underlying formal methods is first to specify precisely the behaviour of a piece of software, then to write this software and finally to prove whether or not that actual implementation meets its specification. *Unity* [5, 7] is a formal method that attempts to decouple a program from its implementation. For that propose, *Unity* separates logical behaviour from implementation, provides predicates for specifications, and proof rules to derive specifications directly from the program text. This type of proof strategy is often clearer and more succinct than arguing about a program's operational behaviour. Our research fits into *Unity*'s methodology. Its aim is to develop a proof environment suitable for mechanical proof of concurrent programs [1]. This proof is based on *Unity* [5], and may be used to specify and verify both safety and liveness properties.
Our verification method is based on theorem proving, so that an axiomatization of the operational semantics is needed. We use Dijkstra's *wp*-calculus to formalise the *Unity* logic, so we can always derive a sound relationship between the operational semantics of a given *Unity* specification and the axiomatic one from which theorems in our logic will be derived. In a mechanically verified proof, all proof steps are validated by a computer program called a *theorem prover*. Hence, whether a mechanically verified proof is correct is really a question of whether the theorem prover is sound. The theorem prover used in our research is *B-Tool* [4, 3, 2]. *B* provides a platform for solving the problem specification and correct construction of software systems. It is a flexible inference engine which forms the basis of a computer-aided system for the formal construction of provably correct software. Using a mechanized theorem prover to validate a proof presents an additional burden for the user, since machine validated proofs are longer and more difficult to produce. However, if one trusts the theorem prover, one may then focus attention on the specification that was proved. This analysis may be facilitated by consulting the mechanized proof script.

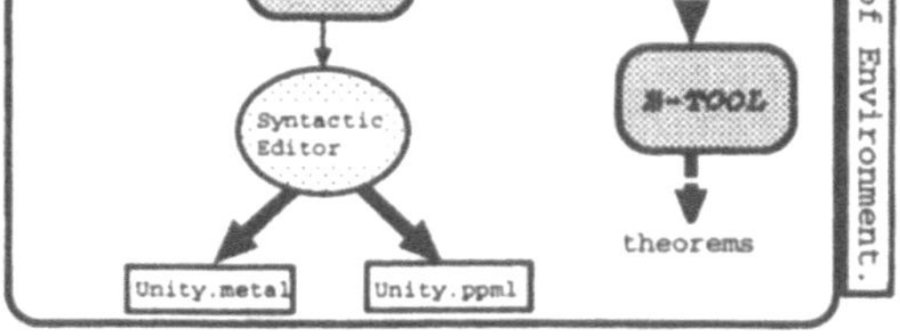

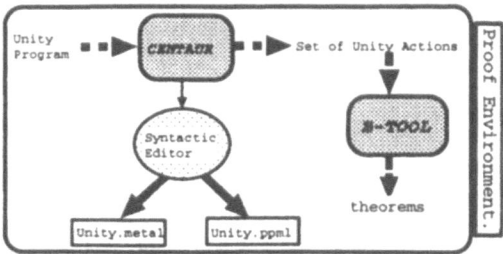

Figure 1: The Proof Environment

The design of the programming environment consists in several steps that are either automatic, or semi-automatic (Fig.1). The first step consists in writing a METAL specification of the *Unity* language using *Centaur*. This specification defines the concrete syntax, the abstract syntax and the rules of trees formation that express the correspondence between abstract and concrete syntax. The METAL-PPML generates tables and programs used to generate a parser from this specification. The generation of a parser is not completely automatic and the user has to supply some files names along with those generated by METAL-PPML. The semantics of the language is handled by the TYPOL environment. The second step writes the PPML specification of the rules of textual representation (or unparsing) for the *Unity* formalism from its abstract syntax. The unparser for the *Unity* formalism is generated using the *compile* command of the METAL-PPML environment. The *Unity* environment comprises two kinds of editors: textual and structural. The user can easily write a *Unity* program in a textual form. A parser checks it. If the program is syntactically correct, the parser generates the internal representation. The user can run an interface to the prover that allows him to prove the correctness of the *Unity* program using the set of its actions (statements). The prover is designed according to the *enrichment principle.* A basic layer represents the Dijkstra's *wp*-calculus [6]. This is successively enriched with other theories for reasoning on *Unity* programs. To *wp-theory,* we have supplied another layer for deriving *safety* properties which we denote by *unless-thy. Ensures-thy* and *leads-to-thy* define the most interesting progress properties.

More information on:

◇ *C entaur* :
Centaur Distribution
c\o Sophie Honnorat
INRIA - Sophia Antipolis
BP 93
06902 Sophia Antipolis CEDEX
FRANCE

◇*B – Tool* :
The Distribution Manager,
Edinburgh Portable Compilers Ltd,
17 Alva Street,
Edinburgh, EH2 4PH.
Email: support@epc.ed.ac.uk

Keywords: *Automated theorem proving, concurrency, program verification, formal specifications, Unity, B-Tool.*

References

[1] N. Brown and D. Mery. A Proof Environment for Concurrent Programs . In J. C. P Woodcock and P. G. Larsen, editors, *FME'93: Industrial-Strength Formal Methods.* Springer Verlag, 1993. Lecture Notes in Computer Science 670.

[2] BP Innovation Centre and Edinburgh Portable Compilers Ltd. *B-Tool Version1.1, Reference Manual,* 1991.

[3] BP Innovation Centre and Edinburgh Portable Compilers Ltd. *B-Tool Version1.1, Tutorial,* 1991.

[4] BP Innovation Centre and Edinburgh Portable Compilers Ltd. *B-Tool Version1.1, User Manual,* 1991.

[5] K.M. Chandy and J. Misra. *Parallel Program Design A Foundation.* Addison-Wesley Publishing Company, 1988. ISBN 0-201-05866-9.

[6] E.W. Dijkstra. *A Discipline of Programming.* Prentice-Hall, 1976.

[7] E. Knapp. An exercise in the formal derivation of parallel programs: Maximum flows in graphs. *Transactions On Programming Languages and Systems,* 12(2):203–223, 1990.

The LOTOS Toolbox

Thony van der Vloedt
Information Technology Architecture B.V.
Institutenweg 1, 7521 PH Enschede, The Netherlands
Phone: +31 53 309682, Fax: +31 53 309669, email: tools@ita.nl

The LOTOS toolbox is a coherent set of tools in support of the ISO standard Formal Description Technique LOTOS [3]. This language is theoretically based on process algebra. For data typing the ADT ACT-ONE is used. LOTOS finds it main application in the area of distributed systems and data communications [6].

One of the initial goals of the language was to be able to specify in a precise, yet implementation free way, the OSI data communication standard services and protocols. Currently, for many OSI standards related Working Papers exist in which the protocol or service is formally specified in LOTOS.

LOTOS can also be utilized to aid in the design of distributed systems [5]. The advantages of usage of LOTOS in design include increased precision in the communication between designers mutually, and between designers and future users of the system, improved quality of the system through tool supported validation and testing, and animation and prototyping which allows early assessment of the system to be built.

The LOTOS toolbox contains a number of cooperating tools supporting the specification and implementation of LOTOS specifications. The tools cover:

- the TOPO front-end syntax checking and static semantic checking,
  This tools produces a LOTOS specification in Common Representation (CR) format which is used as input by other tools,

- the structure editor CRIE
  The structure editor guides the user in the correct use of LOTOS and provides syntax and static semantic checking on the fly. It also produces CR format specifications.

- the system validator SMILE,
  provides symbolic execution of LOTOS [1, 2]. SMILE allows the user to dynamically analyse the behaviour of his specification (CR format) by stepping through allowable events,

- the graphical browser GLOW,
  transforms a textual LOTOS specification (CR format) in a graphical representation according to the graphical LOTOS standard,

- the TOPO back-end C-code generator,
  "compiles" an implementation oriented LOTOS specification into a prototype which can be used for early evaluation of the designed system [4].

Available platforms:
Sun 3,Sun 4, SunOS 16Mb memory, 35 Mb disk
HP, HP Unix, 16Mb memory, 35Mb disk
The tools are commercially available.

References

[1] H. Eertink, D. Woltz, Symbolic execution of LOTOS specifications, Memoranda Informatica 91-47, University of Twente, Enschede, 1991.

[2] P. van Eijk, H. Eertink, Design of the LotosPhere symbolic LOTOS simulator, Formal Description Techniques, III - Proceedings of the FORTE 90 Conference, North-Holland, Amsterdam, 1991.

[3] ISO, Information processing systems - Open Systems Interconnection - LOTOS - A formal description technique based on the temporal ordering of observational behaviour, IS 8807, Geneva 1992.

[4] J.A. Manas, T. de Miguel, From LOTOS to C, Formal Description Techniques, I - Proceedings of the Forte 88 Conference, North-Holland, Amsterdam, 1988.

[5] L.F. Pires, C.A. Vissers, Overview of the Lotosphere Design Methodology, ESPRIT Conf. 1990, pp. 371-387, Kluwer Academic Publishers, Dordrecht, 1990.

[6] K.J. Turner (Ed.), Using Formal Description Techniques, An Introduction to Estelle, LOTOS and SDL, John Wiley & Sons, Chinchester, 1993.

The ASF+SDF Meta-environment

A. van Deursen, T.B. Dinesh, and E.A. van der Meulen
Department of Software Technology, CWI
P.O Box 94079, 1090 GB Amsterdam, The Netherlands

Introduction Algebraic specifications facilitate formal reasoning about software, in addition to providing means for rapid prototyping [2]. In particular, specifying various aspects of a programming language provides tools which can be part of a programming environment for the language. In Amsterdam, at CWI and UvA, the GIPE[1] group has been investigating tool generation from algebraic specifications. Thus far, this has resulted in:

- An algebraic specification formalism, ASF+SDF, especially designed for defining the syntax and semantics of programming languages [2, 6];
- The ASF+SDF tool generator, deriving parsers and term rewriting machines from algebraic specifications [7];
- The ASF+SDF Meta-environment, giving support when developing ASF+SDF specifications [7].

The ASF+SDF system is built on top of Centaur [1] and distributed as part of it. The ASF+SDF formalism and system are especially designed to support easy specification of all relevant properties of programming languages: syntax, static semantics, dynamic semantics, transformations, and so on.

The ASF+SDF Formalism The ASF+SDF formalism is the result of the marriage of ASF [2] with SDF [6]. ASF is an Algebraic Specification Formalism, supporting many-sorted first-order signatures, (conditional) equations, and modularization. SDF is a Syntax Definition Formalism, defining lexical, concrete, and abstract syntax all at once. Each SDF rule corresponds both to a context-free grammar production, and a function declaration in a signature. The combination of ASF and SDF features user-definable syntax for the representation of terms.

The ASF+SDF Meta-environment From an SDF definition, a parser can be derived, which in turn can be used to derive a syntax-directed editor. The equations of an ASF+SDF module can be executed as term rewriting systems. Both the parsers and the term rewriting systems are generated incrementally, so small updates in the specifications lead to adaptations rather than regeneration from scratch.

The ASF+SDF system and formalism have been used successfully for the derivation of environments for (subsets of) λ-calculus,Eiffel, Action Semantics, modelling of financial products, Pascal, Lotos and so on. Another typical use of ASF+SDF is teaching of term rewriting, algebraic specifications or abstract

[1]Partial support has been received from the European Communities under ESPRIT project 2177 (Generation of Interactive Programming Environments II - GIPE II) and from the Netherlands Organization for Scientific Research – NWO, project *Incremental Program Generators*

data types. Moreover, language designers can benefit from the incrementality of the system and the executability of their specifications.

Current Research Current research activities include incremental rewriting (small changes in the initial term cause adaptations of the normal form rather than recomputation from scratch) [10]; origin tracking (automatically maintaining relations between initial term and normal form, with applications to the generation of error handlers and run-time animators from specifications of static or dynamic semantics of programming languages) [5]; generation of C-code from algebraic specifications [9]; customizable user-interface for generated environments [8]; experiments with the use of an abstract-interpretation style for specification and generation of type checkers [4]; generation of adaptable pretty printers from the syntax-definition of languages [3].

More Information More information on the ASF+SDF system can be obtained by anonymous ftp: get file abstracts.ps.Z from ftp.cwi.nl in directory pub/gipe. A mailing list is reachable by contacting asf+sdf-list-request@cwi.nl.

References

[1] P. Borras, D. Clément, Th. Despeyroux, J. Incerpi, B. Lang, and V. Pascual. CENTAUR: the system. In *Proceedings of the ACM SIGSOFT/SIGPLAN Software Engineering Symposium on Practical Software Development Environments*, pages 14–24, 1989. Appeared as *SIGPLAN Notices* 14(2).

[2] J.A. Bergstra, J. Heering, and P. Klint, editors. *Algebraic Specification*. ACM Press Frontier Series. The ACM Press in co-operation with Addison-Wesley, 1989.

[3] M.G.J. van den Brand. Prettyprinting without losing comments. Report P9315, University of Amsterdam, 1993. Available by *ftp* from ftp.cwi.nl:/pub/gipe as Bra93.ps.Z.

[4] T. Dinesh. Type checking revisited: Modular error handling. In *International Workshop on Semantics of Specification Languages*, 1993. Full version available by *ftp* from ftp.cwi.nl:/pub/gipe as Din93.ps.Z.

[5] A. van Deursen, P. Klint, and F. Tip. Origin tracking. *Journal of Symbolic Computation*, 15:523–545, 1993. Special Issue on Automatic Programming.

[6] J. Heering, P.R.H. Hendriks, P. Klint, and J. Rekers. The syntax definition formalism SDF - reference manual. *SIGPLAN Notices*, 24(11):43–75, 1989.

[7] P. Klint. A meta-environment for generating programming environments. *ACM Transactions on Software Engineering Methodology*, 2(2):176–201, 1993.

[8] J.W.C. Koorn. Connecting semantic tools to a syntax-directed user-interface. Report P9222, Programming Research Group, University of Amsterdam, 1992. Available by *ftp* from ftp.cwi.nl:/pub/gipe as Koo92a.ps.Z.

[9] J. F. Th. Kamperman and H.R. Walters. ARM, abstract rewriting machine. Technical Report CS-9330, Centrum voor Wiskunde en Informatica, 1993. Available by *ftp* from ftp.cwi.nl:/pub/gipe as KW93.ps.Z.

[10] E.A. van der Meulen. Deriving incremental implementations from algebraic specifications. In *Proceedings of the Second International Conference on Algebraic Methodology and Software Technology*, Workshops in Computing, pages 277–286. Springer-Verlag, 1992. Full version available by *ftp* from ftp.cwi.nl:/pub/gipe as Meu90.ps.Z.

Executing Action Semantic Descriptions using ASF+SDF

Arie van Deursen
Department of Software Technology, CWI
P.O Box 4079, 1009 AB Amsterdam, The Netherlands

Peter D. Mosses
Computer Science Department, Aarhus University
DK-8000 Aarhus C, Denmark

Introduction *Action Semantics* is a framework for describing the semantics of programming languages [3]. It is based on:

- *Action Notation*, used for expressing so-called *actions*, which represent the semantics of programming constructs; and
- *Unified Algebras*, used for specifying the data processed by actions, as well as for defining the abstract syntax and semantic functions for particular programming languages, and the symbols used in Action Notation.

Currently, only little tool support for action semantics exists. Tool support, however, is becoming more and more important, now that an increasing number of researchers and practitioners are starting to use action semantics. Having simple tools that perform parsing, editing, checking or interpretation of action semantic descriptions is essential when writing large specifications.[1]

In the ASF+SDF approach to tool generation [1, 2], the syntax of a language is described using the Syntax Definition Formalism SDF, which defines context-free syntax and signature at the same time. Functions operating on terms over such a signature are defined using (conditional) equations in the algebraic specification formalism ASF. Typical functions describe type checking, interpreting, compiling, etc., of programs. These functions are executed by interpreting the algebraic specifications as term rewriting systems. Moreover, from SDF definitions, parsers can be generated, which in turn are used for the generation of syntax-directed editors.

The MetaNotation Unified Algebra definitions are written in a particular *MetaNotation*. A syntax of this MetaNotation has been given in [3, Appendix F], which we have transformed into an SDF definition. Although the MetaNotation supports a great deal of syntactic freedom, in that 'mixfix' operations may be introduced, a context-free grammar could be given by choosing a liberal syntax for symbols and terms. This automatically resulted in a generated syntax-directed editor for the MetaNotation.

Checking MetaNotation Modules In the MetaNotation, symbols can be introduced and given functionalities, and then be used in formulae (equations).

---

[1] One of the main advantages of Action Semantics over other frameworks is that it scales up smoothly to the description of larger practical languages, such as Standard Pascal [4].

With the ASF+SDF parser generator at hand, an easy way to check consistency between definition and use is to derive SDF rules from functionality declarations, and to use these rules to try to parse the formulae. Thus we have written, in ASF+SDF, a translator taking a MetaNotation module as input and producing SDF rules from each functionality declaration in that module.

Executing MetaNotation Modules Though the formulae allowed in the MetaNotation can be very general, a substantial number of equations in it (in particular, the equations defining semantic functions) can be interpreted as rewrite rules. Thus, we have written a translation function in the ASF+SDF formalism, taking a MetaNotation module as input and producing ASF equations.

Tool Summary In summary, we have given algebraic specifications of (1) the abstract syntax of the MetaNotation, (2) a function translating MetaNotation function declarations to many-sorted signatures, and (3) a function mapping MetaNotation equations to rewrite rules. Using the ASF+SDF Meta-environment to execute these specifications has resulted in the following tools:

- Parsing and syntax-directed editing of MetaNotation descriptions;
- Checks on use of sorts for functions introduced in MetaNotation descriptions;
- Translation of MetaNotation modules to corresponding ASF+SDF modules, allowing, e.g., execution of MetaNotation descriptions as term rewriting systems, as well as generation of parsers from grammar definitions given in MetaNotation.

These tools are intended primarily for use with action semantic descriptions, but may also be applied to arbitrary MetaNotation modules.

In the demonstration, we illustrate the use of these tools by showing the action semantic description of a small imperative language called *Pico*. We see syntax-directed editing of this definition, incremental generation of ASF+SDF modules from it, syntax-directed editing of Pico programs based on the generated SDF definition, and translation of Pico programs to ActionNotation by interpreting the semantic equations as rewrite rules.

References

[1] J.A. Bergstra, J. Heering, and P. Klint, editors. *Algebraic Specification.* ACM Press Frontier Series. The ACM Press in co-operation with Addison-Wesley, 1989.

[2] P. Klint. A meta-environment for generating programming environments. *ACM Transactions on Software Engineering Methodology*, 2(2):176–201, 1993.

[3] P.D. Mosses. *Action Semantics*, volume 26 of *Cambridge Tracts in Theoretical Computer Science*. Cambridge University Press, 1992.

[4] Peter D. Mosses and David A. Watt. Pascal action semantics. Version 0.6. Available by FTP from ftp.daimi.aau.dk in pub/action/pascal, March 1993.

Author Index

Published in 1990–92

AI and Cognitive Science '89, Dublin City University, Eire, 14–15 September 1989
A. F. Smeaton and G. McDermott (Eds.)

Specification and Verification of Concurrent Systems, University of Stirling, Scotland, 6–8 July 1988
C. Rattray (Ed.)

Semantics for Concurrency, Proceedings of the International BCS-FACS Workshop, Sponsored by Logic for IT (S.E.R.C.), University of Leicester, UK, 23–25 July 1990
M. Z. Kwiatkowska, M. W. Shields and R. M. Thomas (Eds.)

Functional Programming, Glasgow 1989
Proceedings of the 1989 Glasgow Workshop, Fraserburgh, Scotland, 21–23 August 1989
K. Davis and J. Hughes (Eds.)

Persistent Object Systems, Proceedings of the Third International Workshop, Newcastle, Australia, 10–13 January 1989
J. Rosenberg and D. Koch (Eds.)

Z User Workshop, Oxford 1989, Proceedings of the Fourth Annual Z User Meeting, Oxford, 15 December 1989
J. E. Nicholls (Ed.)

Formal Methods for Trustworthy Computer Systems (FM89), Halifax, Canada, 23–27 July 1989
Dan Craigen (Editor) and Karen Summerskill (Assistant Editor)

Security and Persistence, Proceedings of the International Workshop on Computer Architecture to Support Security and Persistence of Information, Bremen, West Germany, 8–11 May 1990
John Rosenberg and J. Leslie Keedy (Eds.)

Women into Computing: Selected Papers 1988–1990
Gillian Lovegrove and Barbara Segal (Eds.)

3rd Refinement Workshop (organised by BCS-FACS, and sponsored by IBM UK Laboratories, Hursley Park and the Programming Research Group, University of Oxford), Hursley Park, 9–11 January 1990
Carroll Morgan and J. C. P. Woodcock (Eds.)

Designing Correct Circuits, Workshop jointly organised by the Universities of Oxford and Glasgow, Oxford, 26–28 September 1990
Geraint Jones and Mary Sheeran (Eds.)

Functional Programming, Glasgow 1990
Proceedings of the 1990 Glasgow Workshop on Functional Programming, Ullapool, Scotland, 13–15 August 1990
Simon L. Peyton Jones, Graham Hutton and Carsten Kehler Holst (Eds.)

4th Refinement Workshop, Proceedings of the 4th Refinement Workshop, organised by BCS-FACS, Cambridge, 9–11 January 1991
Joseph M. Morris and Roger C. Shaw (Eds.)

AI and Cognitive Science '90, University of Ulster at Jordanstown, 20–21 September 1990
Michael F. McTear and Norman Creaney (Eds.)

Software Re-use, Utrecht 1989, Proceedings of the Software Re-use Workshop, Utrecht, The Netherlands, 23–24 November 1989
Liesbeth Dusink and Patrick Hall (Eds.)

Z User Workshop, 1990, Proceedings of the Fifth Annual Z User Meeting, Oxford, 17–18 December 1990
J.E. Nicholls (Ed.)

IV Higher Order Workshop, Banff 1990
Proceedings of the IV Higher Order Workshop, Banff, Alberta, Canada, 10–14 September 1990
Graham Birtwistle (Ed.)

ALPUK91, Proceedings of the 3rd UK Annual Conference on Logic Programming, Edinburgh, 10–12 April 1991
Geraint A.Wiggins, Chris Mellish and Tim Duncan (Eds.)

Specifications of Database Systems
International Workshop on Specifications of Database Systems, Glasgow, 3–5 July 1991
David J. Harper and Moira C. Norrie (Eds.)

7th UK Computer and Telecommunications Performance Engineering Workshop
Edinburgh, 22–23 July 1991
J. Hillston, P.J.B. King and R.J. Pooley (Eds.)

Logic Program Synthesis and Transformation
Proceedings of the LOPSTR 91, International Workshop on Logic Program Synthesis and Transformation, University of Manchester, 4–5 July 1991
T.P. Clement and K.-K. Lau (Eds.)

Declarative Programming, Sasbachealden 1991
PHOENIX Seminar and Workshop on Declarative Programming, Sasbachwalden, Black Forest, Germany, 18–22 November 1991
John Darlington and Roland Dietrich (Eds.)

Building Interactive Systems: Architectures and Tools
Philip Gray and Roger Took (Eds.)

Functional Programming, Glasgow 1991
Proceedings of the 1991 Glasgow Workshop on Functional Programming, Portree, Isle of Skye, 12–14 August 1991
Rogardt Heldal, Carsten Kehler Holst and Philip Wadler (Eds.)